World Tennis Magazine's
Guide to
The Best Tennis Resorts

# WORLD TENNIS MAGAZINE'S GUIDE TO THE BEST TENNIS RESORTS

## PETER M. COAN
### WITH BARRY STAMBLER

A CITADEL PRESS BOOK
PUBLISHED BY CAROL PUBLISHING GROUP

A Citadel Press Book
Published by Carol Publishing Group

Citadel Press is a registered trademark of Carol Communications, Inc.
Editorial Offices: 600 Madison Avenue, New York, N.Y. 10022
Sales & Distribution Offices: 120 Enterprise Avenue, Secaucus, N.J. 07094
In Canada: Musson Book Company, a division of General Publishing
    Company, Ltd., Don Mills, Ontario M3B 2T6

Queries regarding rights and permission should be addressed to
Carol Publishing Group, 600 Madison Avenue, New York, N.Y. 10022

Carol Publishing Group books are available at special discounts for bulk
purchases, for sales promotions, fund raising, or educational purposes.
Special editions can be created to specifications. For details, contact:
Special Sales Department, Carol Publishing Group, 120 Enterprise Avenue,
Secaucus, N.J. 07094

Manufactured in the United States of America
10  9  8  7  6  5  4  3  2  1

**Library of Congress Cataloging-in-Publication Data**

Coan, Peter M.
    World tennis magazine's guide to the best tennis resorts / by
Peter M. Coan with Barry Stambler.
      p.  cm.
    "A Citadel Press Book."
    ISBN 0-8065-1272-5
    1. Tennis resorts—North America—Directories.  2. Tennis resorts—
Caribbean Area—Directories.  I. Stambler, Barry.  II. World
tennis.  III. Title.
GV1002.95.N7C63  1992                                    91-33230
796.34′20680257—dc20                                     CIP

This book is dedicated to
my wife, Nazli, and my daughter,
Melissa.

# CONTENTS

Acknowledgments                                                        xi
Introduction                                                            1
How to Choose a Tennis Resort                                           5
Family Tennis Resorts                                                  13
Overseas Travel                                                        15
1.  The Caribbean                                                      16
Caneel Bay   17
Casa De Campo   18
Curtain Bluff   19
Four Seasons Nevis   20
Half Moon Golf, Tennis & Beach Club   21
Hyatt Cerromar Beach   22
Hyatt Dorado Beach   23
Hyatt Regency St. John   24
Jumby Bay   25
Little Dix Bay   26
Mullet Bay Resort & Casino   27
Ocean Club   28
Peter Island Resort   29
St. James's Club   30
Stouffer Grand Beach Resort   31
Swept Away   32
Tryall Golf, Tennis & Beach Club   33

2.  Florida                                                            34
Amelia Island Plantation   35
Bluewater Bay   36

Boca Raton Resort & Club 37
The Breakers 38
Cheeca Lodge 39
The Colony Beach & Tennis Resort 40
Doral Resort & Country Club 41
Fisher Island 42
Grenelefe Resort & Conference Center 43
Hawk's Cay Resort & Marina 44
Hyatt Regency Grand Cypress Resort 45
Indian River Plantation 46
Innisbrook 47
Longboat Key Club 48
Marriott's Bay Point Resort 49
Marriott's Orlando World Center 50
Naples Bath & Tennis Club 51
Ocean Reef Club & Resort 52
Palm-Aire Spa Resort 53
PGA National 54
Ponte Vedra Inn & Club 55
The Registry 56
The Ritz-Carlton Naples 57
Saddlebrook Golf & Tennis Resort 58
Sandestin Beach Resort 59
Sheraton Bonaventure Resort & Spa 60
Sheraton Palm Coast 61
Sonesta Sanibel Harbour Resort 62
South Seas Plantation 63
Tops'l 64
Turnberry Yacht & Country Club 65

3.  The Southeast                                    66
Boar's Head Inn 67
Callaway Gardens 68
The Cloister 69
The Greenbrier 70
The Homestead 71
Kiawah Island 72
Palmetto Dunes 73

Pinehurst Resort & Country Club   74
Sea Palms Golf & Tennis   75
Sea Pines Plantation   76
Wild Dunes   77
Wintergreen Resort   78

**4. Bermuda**                                                    **79**
Elbow Beach Hotel   80
Grotto Bay Hotel   81
Sonesta Beach Hotel & Spa   82
Southampton Princess   83

**5. New England and New York**                                  **84**
Concord Resort Hotel   85
Mount Washington Hotel & Resort   86
New Seabury   87
Ocean Edge Resort & Conference Center   88
The Omni Sagamore   89
Stratton Mountain Inn   90
Sugarbush Resort   91
Tennis Village   92
Topnotch at Stowe   93
The Villages at Killington   94
The Woodstock Inn & Resort   95

**6. Canada**                                                    **96**
Gray Rocks Inn   97
The Inn at Manitou   98
Jasper Park Lodge   99

**7. The Northwest**                                             **100**
Elkhorn Resort   101
Sun Valley Lodge   102
Sunriver Lodge & Resort   103

**8. The Southwest**                                             **104**
Arizona Biltmore   105
The Broadmoor   106

Cheyenne Mountain   107
Marriott's Camelback Inn   108
The Phoenician   109
Rancho Encantado   110
The Registry Resort   111
Scottsdale Princess   112


**9.  California**                                          **113**
Carmel Valley Ranch Resort   114
Hyatt Grand Champions   115
Hyatt Newporter   116
John Gardiner's Rancho Valencia   117
La Costa Hotel & Spa   118
La Quinta   119
Marriott's Desert Springs Resort   120
Meadowood   121
Ojai Valley Inn & Country Club   122
The Racquet Club   123
Rancho Bernardo Inn   124
Rancho Las Palmas Resort   125
The Ritz-Carlton Rancho Mirage   126
Silverado   127


**10.  Hawaii**                                             **128**
Coco Palms Resort   129
Hyatt Regency Waikoloa   130
Kahala Hilton   131
Kapalua Bay Hotel & Villas   132
Kiahuna Plantation Resort   133
Maui Inter-Continental Wailea   134
Mauna Kea Beach Resort   135
Mauna Lani Bay Hotel & Bungalows   136
The Ritz-Carlton Mauna Lani   137
Westin Kauai   138


**11.  Mexico**                                             **139**
Acapulco Princess   140
Camino Real Ixtapa   141

El Cid Mega Resort   142
Fiesta Americana Plaza Vallarta   143
Las Brisas   144
Las Hadas   145
Villa Vera Hotel & Racquet Club   146

**Top 10 Lists**                                              **147**
Top 10 Pet Peeves About All Types of Resorts   147
Top 10 Pet Peeves About Tennis Resorts   147
Top 10 European Tennis Resorts   148
Top 10 Off-the-Beaten-Path Tennis Resorts   150
Top 10 Potpourri for 1991   151
Top 10 Family Tennis Resorts   153
Top 10 Romantic Island Getaways   155
Top 10 Best Tennis Resorts   156

**Tennis Camp Directory**                                     **158**

**Helpful Information**                                       **206**
U.S. Tourist Boards   206
Caribbean Tourist Boards   207
Airlines   208
Rental Car Companies   208
Major Hotel Chains   209

# ACKNOWLEDGMENTS

I would like to thank the following people without whose efforts this demanding project could not have been completed: Neil Amdur, the former editor of *World Tennis*, who gave me the go-ahead to create a travel editorial; Barry Stambler, former *World Tennis* travel editor, who expertly fact-checked all of the resort reviews; and former *World Tennis* senior editor Susan Festa Fiske, who meticulously edited all of the copy herein. I would also like to thank the travel writers—our connoisseurs—whose superlative knowledge of resorts, sports, and travel contributed immensely to this book: Bill and Cheryl Alters Jamison, Samantha Stevenson, Kimberly Grant, Christine Davidson, Marilyn McFarlane, and former *World Tennis* staff members Dan Rosenbaum, David Sparrow, and Kara Segreto. And, as always, I thank my representatives: attorney Harry Weinberg, for his guidance and friendship; and my agent, Carol Mann, who did such a wonderful job representing me on my first book, *Taxi: The Harry Chapin Story*.

# INTRODUCTION

The purpose of this book is to help you decide where to take your next tennis vacation and to give you the best tennis resorts from which to choose.

Every resort reviewed in this book received an on-site inspection by one of *World Tennis* Magazine's reviewers, and in some cases, the resort was visited more than once. Except in unavoidable instances, our reviewers traveled incognito—the resort never knew the reviewer was there. In this way, we could make an objective appraisal, without the bias that occurs when one receives the red-carpet treatment.

The *World Tennis* Travel Guide was created as a regular monthly feature of the magazine in 1988. Until that time, our readers would call our offices asking us to recommend a tennis resort. When they called us, they said our travel editorial—published sporadically throughout the year—was not genuinely helpful. Every resort sounded wonderful—you know, "balmy beaches, swaying palms," etc., with glossy feature spreads and greeting-card prose, typical of most travel articles. Because our articles didn't distinguish one resort from another, they didn't help our readers decide where to take their vacations.

So we went to the drawing board.

We decided that instead of writing about resorts, we would rate them across five areas: 1. tennis facilities and programs, 2. accommodations, 3. food, 4. service, and 5. special features—qualities that give a resort its unique personality.

In addition, we gave our readers essential information about the criteria, with comments as to why we rated each individual area

1

as we did. We used a 1–5 rating system: 1 = poor; 2 = fair; 3 = good; 4 = very good; 5 = excellent. So if a resort were to receive a "5" or "excellent" in all five areas its cumulative score would be 25—the highest possible mark.

Of course, we were taking a big risk. No other consumer travel magazine had ever rated resorts for fear that low ratings would offend potential or existing advertisers. If we were going to stick out our necks, we had to make sure our assessments were fair and accurate—be they negative or positive, the resort large or small, prominent or not.

We considered numerous factors when judging a resort in any one area. Quantity was rarely the determining factor. In the tennis category, for instance, a resort did not receive a 5 just because it had a large number of courts. Other factors were considered: Did the resort have multiple court surfaces? What was the ratio of rooms to courts? What percentage of the courts were lit for night play? How well were they maintained? Did the resort have a stadium court for tournament play? How good of an instructor was the head pro? Was he available to all guests, regardless of their level of play? Was the pro shop well-stocked?

In terms of accommodations, a large number of the rooms alone did not merit a favorable rating. Instead, we looked for the intangibles that separate one hotel room from another, such as layout and interior design. Was there a motif? Did most of the rooms have a water view? Or better yet, were they situated on a beach or lake? Did they have a dressing area in the bathroom? Did the bathroom have a Jacuzzi? Did the room have a balcony or terrace? A minibar and/or refrigerator? Full kitchen? Cable television and VCR? Room service? Were non-smoking rooms available?

In the food and service categories, the yardsticks were more subjective, but once again the emphasis was on overall excellence. Were personal requests handled promptly and efficiently? Was the food well-presented and well-prepared? Was attention personal or canned? Did the resort sacrifice individual attention for a "get 'em-in and get 'em-out" approach? Our reviewers discovered that there's a big difference between a restaurant that's truly gourmet and one that's merely overpriced.

Finally, when looking for special features, we sought out those things that made a resort distinct. Did the resort, for instance, have cascading waterfalls in its pools, a private airstrip, or a five-mile stretch of private beach? Did it have a baby-sitting service, a children's program, or a children's zoo? Were there off-beat features like a nude beach, a doll museum, or a coral reef for snorkeling and scuba diving?

In the final analysis, price was not a dominant factor in whether a resort was selected for review, except when we reviewed resorts for family travel. Reader response has told us that you want the best—a resort that rates well in all five areas—and are willing to pay for it. All of the resorts we reviewed were pre-selected with the notion of trying to give you a complete vacation experience.

Of the more than 350 resorts reviewed since 1988, only 120 are included in this book. These are resorts that had a cumulative score of at least 20 out of a possible 25, meaning that all of them are equivalent to very good or excellent in our rating system.

Because only the best tennis resorts have been selected for inclusion in this book, and all of them have superior service, we decided to replace the service category, and therefore redundant service comments, with practical information on "Nearby Tourist Attractions." Is a tennis resort, for instance, near a nature preserve, theme park, historic landmark, or natural wonder for sightseeing? In addition, we decided not to include the ratings for each resort, since all of them would look similar. The rating system used by *World Tennis* Magazine is only important so far that you understand how tennis resorts were judged and that the ones that made it into this book are the cream of the crop. As a result, it is unavoidable that many of the comments are favorable.

Only eight resorts ever received a cumulative score of 25, a "5" or "excellent" in all areas. Those resorts can be found in the Top 10 section of this book.

Note: Since the information—particularly the prices—included in this book were compiled at the beginning of 1991, it is subject to change. Please check with the resort before booking your vacation. Also, for optimal benefits, this book should be used as a starting reference point in identifying the tennis resort or resorts you want to visit. Then consult your travel agent or the resort itself for more specific information.

Finally, with the September 1991 issue, *World Tennis* Magazine, after nearly forty years, officially changed its name to *Tennis Illustrated* for marketing reasons. But just prior to that issues release, Family Media, Inc., the parent company that owned Tennis Illustrated plus six other titles, officially declared bankruptcy, or Chapter 7. It was a sudden and inglorious end to America's first and oldest tennis publication. This book, then, may represent the final chapter of World Tennis and a revered past that dates back to 1952. It is sad. It is unfortunate. But it is life.

# HOW TO CHOOSE A TENNIS RESORT

Anyone who plays tennis and wants to take a vacation that involves the game must decide how much tennis they want to play and where creature comforts rank on their list of priorities.

Tennis vacations come in three forms. First, there are vacations for the casual or social player, someone who ranks food, service, and accommodations above everything else but still wants to take a lesson or two, or simply hit a few balls. For this holiday seeker, tennis is not a primary focus. Such players will find a plentiful supply of resorts that offer tennis as well as other sports like golf and windsurfing. Most highly rated hotels have at least two or three courts to sate the hacker. But these are not *tennis resorts,* just resorts that have tennis.

Next, there are vacations for active players. These people seek the luxurious resort craved by the casual player, but demand great tennis as well. They want it all and are willing to pay for it.

The active player is generally an experienced competitor who plays at least once or twice a week and belongs to a tennis club or league. Though he is not above taking a lesson or two to improve certain facets of his game, it is competition he craves, so the chosen resort must (even if not officially) guarantee him a partner. This player's skill level is usually B or C, occasionally A, but even casual players harboring inflated estimates of their skills are known to frequent top tennis meccas.

No matter what his skill level, the active player looks good at courtside, decked out in fashion's finest, sporting the latest high-priced, high-tech tennis gear, from widebody rackets and Nike Air or Reebok Pump shoes to the newest shock dampeners to ward off tennis elbow.

Resorts that cater to such clients know what these players expect: tennis with all the trimmings, including top-flight instructors to straighten their strokes, ball machines to encourage perfection, and video analysis to review it all. Also expected are multiple court surfaces and courts lit for night play.

Not surprisingly, the field of premier resorts dramatically narrows when we enter the realm of the bona fide tennis resort— places that have achieved cult status with pro players, coaches, and people in the know. These resorts have received a cumulative 20 rating or better for their tennis facilities, programs, and creature comforts. These resorts offer a complete tennis vacation.

Finally, we come to vacations for the serious player, who may not be any more serious about tennis than the active player, or any more skilled than the casual player. Still, this tennis enthusiast insists on total tennis during the vacation; never mind the creature comforts. This player's grand design is to improve—and if that means hitting the ball from morning till night, all the better. Nothing would please him more.

Ultimately, this player will find the most satisfaction at a tennis camp. There are more than three hundred such camps worldwide, but the majority are in the United States (see the Tennis Camp Directory at the end of this book). With few exceptions, tennis camps do not deliver the kind of food, service, or accommodations found at a resort that's received a cumulative rating of 20 or better.

Since camps vary so much in quality and program emphasis, choosing the right one is tricky. For instance, some camps offer adult, junior, specialty, or tournament level programs. Others offer them all—jacks-of-all-trades, masters of none. There are camps with superior accommodations and there are those that offer bunks in the woods. It all depends on how "campy" you want to get.

Your best bet is to get firsthand advice from a friend who has attended a camp. If this is impossible, contact the camp director. Key questions to ask include:

- What are the qualifications of the teaching staff?
- If the head pro is famous, is he actually on site or is he merely lending his name to the camp?
- How much of the instruction is individual? How much is with a group?
- If group instruction is the order of the day (it usually is), what is the ratio of students to instructors? (It should not be more than 6 to 1.)
- Finally, how much of the camp is truly devoted to tennis? (Some camps merely bill themselves as tennis camps as a ploy to augment business.)

This book is primarily dedicated to the active player who seeks a bona fide tennis resort—one with the luxury of a fine hotel but also the superior tennis facilities normally found only at a tennis camp. In general, Florida, Southern California, Arizona, and New England have the greatest number of these tennis resorts, with Florida being number one.

Here's a checklist to help you evaluate whether a tennis resort is bona fide. Keep in mind that no resort is perfect—some will exceed many of the following criteria and fall short in others.

☐ 1. **The resorts should have courts lit for night play.** This is essential because most desirable resort destinations are just too hot during the day, and unless you're a masochist, or are in incredibly good shape, you cannot bear this heat-on-the-court fare. Resorts that don't have courts lit for night play don't take their tennis seriously. This is especially true of casino hotels, which would rather have you playing roulette than out on the court improving your backhand.

☐ 2. **The resort should guarantee you a game.** In other words, they should get you a partner if you need one. This should be done at no charge. Remember, while the dimensions of every golf course are different, and therefore the challenges, the dimensions of every tennis court are identical. The only challenge for the tennis player is the person on the other side of the net.

☐ 3. **The resort's ratio of rooms to courts should not exceed 16 to 1.** If it does, you may have trouble getting court time. As an example, if a resort has 200 rooms, it should have at least 12 courts. On the other hand, if a resort has 40 rooms and 4 courts, then it rates equally high with one caveat. Such small resorts tend to be very exclusive and very expensive, so what you gain in privacy and pampering you lose in services like ball machines, video analysis, and a fully stocked pro shop. But then such resorts are usually reserved for the rich and famous only, e.g. Antigua's **Jumby Bay** (38 rooms, 3 courts) and **Curtain Bluff** (61 rooms, 4 courts).

Of course, the ideal ratio is 1 room to 1 court and there are only two resorts that can boast this: **John Gardiner's Tennis Ranch** in Carmel Valley, California (14 rooms, 14 courts) and **Tennis Village** in West Dover, Vermont (10 homes, 10 courts).

☐ 4. **The resort should offer multiple court surfaces to accommodate different styles of play.** There are numerous types of surfaces: Deco-Turf, Laykold, grass, Cal-Grass, clay, cement, all-weather, Har-Tru, etc. Call them what you will, but all surfaces are either slow or fast, and the resort should have at least one of each.

However, most resorts offer fast, hard courts because tennis has dramatically moved away from slow surfaces such as clay (the French Open is the only Grand Slam tournament played on clay). Tennis has become a power game played on hard courts. Still, here is a glossary of court surfaces and how they differ:

**Deco-Turf:** A brand name for a cushion system that is applied in layers to an asphalt court surface. It plays slow-to-medium depending on the size and amount of rubber used.

**Plexicushion:** Similiar to Deco-Turf, but manufactured by a different company.

**Laykold:** A brand name for hard courts that have an acrylic court surface. It plays fast.

**Plexipave:** A brand name for a hard court with an acrylic coating similar to Laykold. It plays fast.

**Hard Court:** A generic term for asphalt and concrete (cement) courts. It plays fast. Surfaces grouped under hard courts include: Plexipave, Plexicushion, Deco-Turf, Laykold, and all-weather.

**Natural Grass:** It is what it is. It plays slow.

**Cal-Grass:** A brand name for a synthetic grass court that is similar to Astro-Turf.

**Omni:** An Astro-Turf type surface that contains sand so that you're able to slide on it like a clay court.

**Fast-Dry:** A generic term for a composition court composed of stone chips. It plays slow-to-medium.

**Har-Tru:** A brand name for a composite court, very similar to Fast-Dry. It plays slow-to-medium.

**All-Weather:** A generic term for hard courts. It plays fast.

**Clay:** It is what it is. It plays slow.

Resorts that offer a superb surface mix include **La Quinta** in La Quinta, California (21 Plexipave, 6 grass, 3 Har-Tru); **La Costa Hotel & Spa** in Carlsbad, California (17 Plexipave, 4 clay, 2 grass); **Maui Inter-Continental Wailea,** dubbed "Wimbledon West", in Wailea, Hawaii (11 hard, 3 grass); and **Turnberry Yacht & Country Club** in North Miami, Florida (15 hard, 9 Har-Tru).

☐ 5. **The resort's tennis operation should be concession-run, and the instructors should not be hotel employees.** Generally, concessions offer better instruction because they are an independent business within the resort. Instruction is how they make their living. Resort employees tend to be less qualified and earn a straight salary, so they don't care a sack of beans whether you improve your serve or not.

☐ 6. **Check to see if the resort has a stadium or center court.** If it does, it's a good bet that the resort hosts professional tournaments. Although you have no need for these courts, they are a good sign that the resort takes tennis seriously.

☐ 7. **Check to see if the resort is affiliated with a tennis**

**school.** If it is you'll enjoy the best of both worlds: the luxury of a resort that's received a cumulative rating of 20 or better, coupled with a vigorous tennis environment usually found (as vacations go) only at tennis camps. Good examples are **Saddlebrook Golf & Tennis Resort** and its Harry Hopman School in Wesley Chapel, Florida; **The Villages at Killington** and its Killington School for Tennis in Killington, Vermont; and **Sugarbush Resort** and its Sugarbush Sports Center in Warren, Vermont.

☐ 8. **Check to see if the resort has ball machines and video analysis.** You may not use these services and you will pay extra for them, but it's nice to know they're there. Serious players who are looking to improve one facet of their game will use them—guaranteed.

☐ 9. **The resort should offer tennis packages.** If they do, take advantage of them. The typical package is 4 days/3 nights and includes deluxe accommodations (such as a junior suite), free court time, limited free individual instruction (one hour per day is standard), and unlimited group clinics. Some resorts will also include unlimited use of their ball machines. The price range for such a package is $225–275 per person double occupancy, without meals. These rates will increase considerably during high season (Christmas through Easter for southern and tropical resorts, summertime for northern resorts). Beware of resorts that skimp on court time and instruction, but clutter their packages with nonsensicalities like a free T-shirt, complimentary can of tennis balls, continental breakfast, or that nebulous surprise "tennis gift."

☐ 10. **The resort should have a well-stocked pro shop.** This is an automatic. All of the resorts reviewed in this book rent rackets to guests at the pro shop, but if you have a particular favorite don't forget to pack it. The selection of rackets at pro shops is often limited to one or two manufacturers and models, usually from the companies who sponsor the head pro, who then obscenely marks up the goods. The same is true of the clothing. Such items are available to you out of convenience, not practicality. Few people go to a resort to buy their rackets and clothing. The real value of a pro shop is in its services: a stringing machine should one of your strings break, a ball machine for practice, a matching service to help you find a partner at your skill level, plus the usual need for fresh tennis balls, and grips and overwraps should the old ones on your racket handle become worn. In short, a well-stocked pro shop tends to be a full-service pro shop, and that's the kind of service you're looking for.

☐ 11.  **The resort should offer group clinic instruction (for beginners and children especially) as well as private instruction (for more advanced players).** Another automatic.

☐ 12.  **Tennis "ambience."** This refers to the social part of tennis, the intangibles such as staff friendliness and the ability to accommodate special requests, and the tangibles such as staff-organized round-robin tournaments for singles, doubles, and mixed doubles.

How do you gauge such criteria? Brochures won't help. A friend's recommendation is always the best way. But if you're on the blind, call the pro shop and ask questions. The response you get will probably tell you all you need to know.

☐ 13.  **Watch out for resorts with famous head pros.** Such pros usually lend their name only; they are on the property but a few weeks a year. Just because these pros know how to play, doesn't mean they know how to teach. The best tennis instruction is basic instruction—stroke production, footwork, concentration, and mental toughness—things that former pro players know by instinct but can't necessarily teach to others. And worse, their private lessons are fabulously expensive, usually double or triple the average rate of $50 per hour.

Frequently, the best resort instructors are no-names, failed pros who know how to teach and who can turn an errant forehand into a straight one in less than an hour. Of course, there is no way to know in advance how good a pro is—both as a person and as an instructor—but if the resort meets all of the criteria we've discussed, you can be sure it puts a premium on tennis, including its pros.

If you insist on playing with a famous head pro, make a reservation to do so before you arrive at the resort.

☐ 14. **Your safest bet are resorts that call themselves "golf and tennis resorts."** Though most of these cater to the affluent golfer and not the tennis player, the resort's tennis facilities will still be better than most. And you are guaranteed superior food, service, and accommodations.

☐ 15. **Finally, look to book your tennis vacation during the "shoulder period" just before or just after "high season."** The weather is usually the same as during the high season, and you can enjoy a five-star resort at three-star rates and play without the crowds.

# FAMILY TENNIS RESORTS

If you're looking for a bona fide tennis resort that is also geared to families, the field of choices narrows sharply. You'll want to add the following to the previous checklist: a babysitting service; a refrigerator in your room to chill your infant's milk and juice; a hot plate to warm the milk; a daytime supervised children's program so that you can sneak in a set without feeling guilty; other children your children's age; and tennis clinics specifically designed for children.

The best family tennis resorts tend to be condominium properties, places where you can rent a house, villa, or two-bedroom, two-bath suite. The East Coast has the most family-oriented tennis resorts, particularly in New England, South Carolina, and Florida.

The family travel market has exploded because of the dramatic increase in working parents who have to coordinate their vacation time with their children's school breaks. Knowing that families are traveling together, Hyatt Resorts recently created Kamp Hyatt at eighty hotels and thirteen resorts worldwide, which provides supervised day and evening recreation programs for children so that parents can spend time together alone.

Parents want to spend time with their kids, but still have enough left over for themselves. Add to that the desire for a tennis-oriented vacation and planning can become a logistical nightmare. Also, adults vacation differently when they're with their kids than when they're alone. The priorities are different.

See the Top Ten Lists chapter for the Top 10 Family Tennis

Resorts. The resorts were chosen because they cater to families, are reasonably priced, and have superior tennis facilities and programs.

# OVERSEAS TRAVEL

If you're thinking of taking a vacation at a European tennis resort, think again. They are expensive—in part because there are not that many of them. In fact, the typical four-star European hotel is not likely to have even a single tennis court.

It's simply a questions of priorities. Americans take their sports seriously. So do Europeans, but at private clubs and camps, not hotels. You will not find many European hotels, or many resorts outside the Continental U.S. for that matter, with tennis facilities. The few European resorts that offer tennis as a primary focus are listed in the Top 10 Lists chapter under the heading Top 10 European Tennis Resorts.

Here's an interesting note: Although there are no Club Meds reviewed in this book (because their accommodations, food, and service do not meet our minimum rating of 4, or "very good"), Club Meds overseas have better tennis facilities and programs than most foreign resorts and hotels. Also, by international standards, their accommodations, food, and service tend to be better than the average foreign resort.

# 1

# THE CARIBBEAN

The weather in the Caribbean (heat, heat, and more heat) has a great influence on when tennis can be played. Because of the extreme heat, most guests don't use the courts between 10:00 A.M. and 4:00 P.M. As a result, Caribbean resorts keep the number of courts to a minimum (the average is four).

Yet, according to a 1990 *World Tennis* Magazine Reader Poll, the Caribbean remains the most desirable resort destination for tennis vacationers because of its exotic environs, small hotels, and personalized service.

And because the Caribbean is so large—fifty major islands plus hundreds of smaller ones—you won't have much trouble finding a bona fide tennis resort.

# CANEEL BAY, P.O. Box 720, St. John, V.I. 00830. (809) 776-6111

## *Tennis*

**Courts:** 11
**Court Surfaces:** Deco-Turf
**Courts Lit For Night Play:** None
**Director of Tennis:** Bruce Haase **Head Pro:** Bruce Haase
**Instruction Rates:** $50 per hour/individual; group rates vary
**Court Time:** No charge
**Video Analysis:** None
**Ball Machines:** 1; No charge
**Tournaments:** None
**Tennis Packages:** Tennis Plan starts from $350 per person, double occupancy for 4 days/3 nights, including two hours of individual instruction, snorkeling trip and cocktail cruise.
**Comments:** "A top-notch tennis facility in an attractive garden setting."

## *Accommodations*

**Rooms:** 171
**Rooms With Water View:** 135
**Rates:** Start from $190 per room, per night, double occupancy; children 8 and under not permitted
**Type of Crowd:** Couples
**Nearest Airport:** 90 minutes from St. Thomas Airport; taxis available to Caneel ferry
**Comments:** "Rooms are spread throughout property, so choose the location near tennis courts and beaches; while spacious and genteel, most accommodations are ordinary."

## *Food*

**Restaurants:** Turtle Bay (French), Caneel Beach Terrace (West Indian), Sugar Mill (buffet)
**Comments:** "Local seafood and regional specialties complement classic cuisine; bountiful buffets at lunch; gracious dining experiences."

## *Special Features*

170-acre peninsula encircled by seven beaches. Water sports included in rates.
**Nightlife:** Live entertainment in Caneel Bay Lounge.

## *Nearby Tourist Attractions*

Trunk Bay; Reef Bay Trail; Virgin Gorda; St. Thomas shopping.

# CASA DE CAMPO, P.O. Box 140, Laromana, Dominican Republic. (800) 336–5520, (809) 523–3333, (305) 856–5405

## *Tennis*

**Courts:** 13
**Court Surfaces:** Har-Tru
**Courts Lit For Night Play:** 10
**Director of Tennis:** Paco Hernandez          **Head Pro:** Paco Hernandez
**Instruction Rates:** $40 per hour/individual; group rates vary
**Court Time:** $16 per hour/day; $19 per hour/night
**Video Analysis:** None
**Ball Machines:** 4; No cnarge
**Tournaments:** None
**Tennis Packages:** The Weekender starts from $352 for 4 days/3 nights, including eight hours of coaching on your own level of play and unlimited court time.
**Comments:** "Beautifully landscaped; each court has its own scoreboard; ball boys will tend to your match for a small fee, and if you're looking for a partner, they're very good players too."

## *Accommodations*

**Rooms:** 950
**Rooms With Water View:** 300
**Rates:** Start from $90 per room, per night, double occupancy; no charge for children 12 and under with parents
**Type of Crowd:** Conventions, couples, families
**Nearest Airport:** 80 minutes from Las Americas Airport; no shuttle service
**Comments:** "All rooms are air-conditioned; villas have their own kitchen, dining room and private bath."

## *Food*

**Restaurants:** Casa del Rio (French), La Terraza (continental), El Sombrero (Mexican), La Piazetta (Italian), Cafe del Sol (continental), Tropicana (seafood), El Patio (cafe), Lago Grill (American), 19th Hole (American), El Pescador (seafood, salads)
**Comments:** "Guests never go hungry; seafood is particularly well-prepared."

## *Special Features*

Private landing strip; two 18-hole golf courses; polo; uninhabited Catalina Island for snorkeling, 5,000-seat amphitheater, fourteen swimming pools, equestrian center; trap and skeet shooting facilities, fitness center.
**Nightlife:** Dancing in Genesis disco.

## *Nearby Tourist Attractions*

Altos de Chavon; Regional Museum of Archeology.

# CURTAIN BLUFF, Old Road P.O. Box 288, St. John's, Antigua, B.W.I. (212) 289-8888, (809) 462-8400

## *Tennis*

**Courts:** 4
**Court Surfaces:** Laykold
**Courts Lit For Night Play:** 2
**Director of Tennis:** Kent Lewis        **Head Pro:** Kent Lewis
**Instruction Rates:** $55 per hour/individual; group rates vary
**Court Time:** No charge
**Video Analysis:** None
**Ball Machines:** None
**Tournaments:** None
**Tennis Packages:** None
**Comments:** "Courts are well-maintained within a tropical backdrop; good instruction in relaxed atmosphere."

## *Accommodations*

**Rooms:** 61
**Rooms With Water View:** All
**Rates:** $395 per room, per night, double occupancy. Includes breakfast, lunch and dinner daily; $65 per night for children 5 and under staying with parents
**Type of Crowd:** Couples, families
**Nearest Airport:** 30 minutes from V.C. Bird International Airport; no shuttle service
**Comments:** "Wonderful Caribbean sea breezes eliminate the need for air-conditioning; terraces look out onto the water."

## *Food*

**Restaurants:** The Main Dining Room (international)
**Comments:** "Amazing seafood offerings and desserts; 25,000-bottle wine cellar."

## *Special Features*

Scuba diving; deep-sea fishing; island excursions.
**Nightlife:** Band plays nightly outside The Main Dining Room.

## *Nearby Tourist Attractions*

English Harbor; Shirley Heights; St. John's for shopping.

# FOUR SEASONS NEVIS, P. O. Box 565, Nevis, West Indies. (800) 332-3442, (809) 469-1111

### Tennis

**Courts:** 10
**Court Surfaces:** 6 All-weather, 4 clay
**Courts Lit For Night Play:** All
**Director of Tennis:** Peter Burwash International    **Head Pro:** Greg Smith
**Instruction Rates:** $50 per hour/individual; group rates vary
**Court Time:** $15 per hour
**Video Analysis:** $60 per hour
**Ball Machines:** 2; $15 per hour
**Tournaments:** None
**Tennis Packages:** Triple Getaway starts from $975 double occupancy for 4 days/3 nights, including unlimited court time, one hour of instruction, three cans of balls, evening strategy sessions, instructional videos and breakfast and dinner daily.
**Comments:** "This new program leaps to the forefront of Caribbean offerings; a fine tennis package."

### Accommodations

**Rooms:** 196
**Rooms With Water View:** 160
**Rates:** Starts from $200 per room, per night, double occupancy. No charge for children 18 and under with parents.
**Type of Crowd:** Business groups, couples, independent travelers
**Nearest Airport:** 30 minutes from St. Kitts Airport; hotel's luxury sea launch $25 per couple, each way.
**Comments:** "Rooms are more contemporary corporate than tropical, but very comfortable and classy."

### Food

**Restaurants:** Dining Room (continental), Grill Room (grill)
**Comments:** "Kitchen still learning, but the the Four Seasons chain is devoted to excellence; fresh lobster from the hotel's grotto."

### Special Features

Cosmopolitan hideaway on pristine island; beach; water sports; fitness center.
**Nightlife:** Music in Tap Room.

### Nearby Tourist Attractions

Driving and hiking through Nevis; town of Baserterre on St. Kitts.

# HALF MOON GOLF, TENNIS & BEACH CLUB, Montego Bay, Jamaica. (800) 237-3237, (809) 953-2211

### Tennis

**Courts:** 13
**Court Surfaces:** Laykold
**Courts Lit For Night Play:** 7
**Director of Tennis:** Richard Russell        **Head Pro:** Richard Russell
**Instruction Rates:** $25 per hour/individual; group rates vary
**Court Time:** No charge
**Video Analysis:** $75 per hour
**Ball Machines:** None
**Tournaments:** None
**Tennis Packages:** Tennis, Squash and Fitness Plan starts from $1,020 double occupancy, for 4 days/3 nights, including unlimited court time, one-hour tennis or squash clinic daily, three meals daily and airport transfers.
**Comments:** "A sports resort; Half Moon is great for players who like to play tennis, and golf."

### Accommodations

**Rooms:** 208
**Rooms With Water View:** 190
**Rates:** Start from $150 per room, per night, double occupancy; no charge for children 12 and under with parents
**Type of Crowd:** Business groups, couples, families
**Nearest Airport:** 10 minutes from Donald Sangster International Airport; no shuttle service
**Comments:** "Rooms vary substantially in size, features and location; the moderately-priced deluxe rooms and superior suites are the best values."

### Food

**Restaurants:** Seagrape Terrace (international), Sugar Mill (grill)
**Comments:** "Half Moon deserves plaudits for serving more local specialties than most Caribbean resorts."

### Special Features

18-hole golf course; one mile-long beach; water sports; fitness center; horseback riding.
**Nightlife:** Music nightly in Cedar Bar.

### Nearby Tourist Attractions

Shopping in Montego Bay; nature excursions to the Jamaican interior.

# HYATT CERROMAR BEACH, Dorado, Puerto Rico 00646. (800) 233-1234, (809) 796-1234

## Tennis

**Courts:** 14; 7 at nearby Dorado Beach
**Court Surfaces:** Hard
**Courts Lit For Night Play:** 2
**Director of Tennis:** Robert Smith     **Head Pro:** Rafael Amor
**Instruction Rates:** $65 per hour/individual; group rates vary
**Court Time:** $15 per hour
**Video Analysis:** Included in individual instruction rate
**Ball Machines:** 1; $25 per hour
**Tournaments:** Puerto Rico Open
**Tennis Packages:** Tennis Advantage starts from $305 per person, double occupancy for 4 days/3 nights, including unlimited court time, two tennis clinics, one can of balls, tennis bag and round-trip airport transfers.
**Comments:** "Pros are excellent with juniors; you're guaranteed to leave here with an improved game."

## Accommodations

**Rooms:** 504
**Rooms With Water View:** All
**Rates:** Start from $175 per room, per night, double occupancy; no charge for children 15 and under with parents
**Type of Crowd:** Conventions, couples, families
**Nearest Airport:** 40 minutes from San Juan International Airport; shuttle service $13 per person, each way
**Comments:** "Rooms, while not distinctive, are contemporary, pleasant and well-maintained."

## Food

**Restaurants:** Medici's (Italian), Casa de Oro (steakhouse), The Swan Cafe (continental)
**Comments:** "Medici's is an excellent choice for Italian food lovers."

## Special Features

1,776-foot river pool; health club; children's program, two 18-hole golf courses.
**Nightlife:** Entertainment in El Coqui Sports Bar.

## Nearby Tourist Attractions

Old San Juan; Las Fortaleza, the governor's residence; San Jose Church; Museum of Colonial Architecture; El Morro.

# HYATT DORADO BEACH, Route 693, Dorado Beach, Puerto Rico 00643. (800) 233-1234, (809) 796-1234

## *Tennis*

**Courts:** 7
**Court Surfaces:** Hard
**Courts Lit For Night Play:** 2
**Director of Tennis:** Robert Smith     **Head Pro:** Gilbert Sanchez
**Instruction Rates:** $60 per hour/individual; group rates vary
**Court Time:** $15 per hour
**Video Analysis:** None
**Ball Machines:** 1; $20 per hour
**Tournaments:** None
**Tennis Packages:** None
**Comments:** "Smith runs a terrific program that features thematic clinics; round-robin tournaments and match-up games are arranged weekly."

## *Accommodations*

**Rooms:** 300
**Rooms With Water View:** 204
**Rates:** Start from $205 per room, per night, double occupancy; no charge for children 15 and under with parents
**Type of Crowd:** Couples
**Nearest Airport:** 35 minutes from San Juan International Airport; shuttle service $12 per person, each way
**Comments:** "Ocean view houses with sliding glass panels and private balconies are your best bet. The standard rooms are just that—standard."

## *Food*

**Restaurants:** Su Casa (Spanish), The Surf Room (seafood), The Ocean Terrace (continental)
**Comments:** "Su Casa, renowned for its traditional Spanish and Caribbean cuisine, is a must."

## *Special Features*

Two 18-hole golf courses, private beach; free shuttle service to Hyatt Cerromar Beach Resort.
**Nightlife:** Casino

## *Nearby Tourist Attractions*

Old San Juan; riverboat cruise tours; Bacardi Rum factory; El Yunque Rainforest.

# HYATT REGENCY ST. JOHN, Great Cruise Bay, St. John, V.I. 00830. (800) 233-1234, (809) 776-7171

## *Tennis*

**Courts:** 6
**Court Surfaces:** Omni
**Courts Lit For Night Play:** All
**Director of Tennis:** George Lewis     **Head Pro:** George Lewis
**Instruction Rates:** $45 per hour/individual; group rates vary
**Court Time:** No charge
**Video Analysis:** None
**Ball Machines:** 1; complimentary
**Tournaments:** None
**Tennis Packages:** None
**Comments:** "Lewis is a player and instructor; courts here, like many in the Caribbean, have sand on them."

## *Accommodations*

**Rooms:** 285
**Rooms With Water View:** 225
**Rates:** Start from $205 per room, per night, double occupancy; no charge for children 15 and under with parents
**Type of Crowd:** Couples, families
**Nearest Airport:** 60 minutes from St. Thomas Airport; free shuttle service by van to private boat to hotel
**Comments:** "Rooms with little touches like a coffee pot compensate for nice, unspectacular accommodations."

## *Food*

**Restaurants:** Chow Bella (Italian, Chinese), Cafe Grand (continental), Splash Bar (snacks)
**Comments:** "Chow Bella is the gourmet dining room; Splash Bar is great for afternoon or evening noshes."

## *Special Features*

Children's program; water sports; private beach.
**Nightlife:** Live entertainment in Cafe Grand and Chow Bella.

## *Nearby Tourist Attractions*

Snorkeling at Trunk Bay; St. Thomas shopping; Coral World in St. Thomas.

# JUMBY BAY, P.O. Box 243, St. John's, Antigua B.W.I. (800) 421-9016, (809) 462-9016

## *Tennis*

**Courts:** 3
**Court Surfaces:** Hard
**Courts Lit For Night Play:** 2
**Director of Tennis:** John Maginley    **Head Pro:** John Maginley
**Instruction Rates:** $50 per hour/individual; group rates vary
**Court Time:** No charge
**Video Analysis:** None
**Ball Machines:** 1; no charge
**Tournaments:** None
**Tennis Packages:** None
**Comments:** "Clinics during the week are well supervised; good instruction in a very comfortable atmosphere."

## *Accommodations*

**Rooms:** 38
**Rooms With Water View:** All
**Rates:** Start from $695 per room, per night, double occupancy. Includes breakfast, lunch and dinner daily; children 8 and under not permitted
**Type of Crowd:** Couples, hideaway for the rich and famous
**Nearest Airport:** 15 minutes from V.C. Bird International Airport; free shuttle service to boat that takes you to resort
**Comments:** "Rooms are simple yet elegant; everything you need is at your fingertips; guests are pampered."

## *Food*

**Restaurants:** The Estate House (international), The Beach Pavillion (continental)
**Comments:** "Food is terrific, especially the seafood."

## *Special Features*

All-inclusive resort; twenty-four-hour security; the ultimate in privacy; located on a pristine, exclusive island.
**Nightlife:** None

## *Nearby Tourist Attractions*

Downtown St. John's; Nelson's Dockyard; Shirley Heights.

# LITTLE DIX BAY, Box 70, Virgin Gorda, B.V.I. (800) 223-7673, (809) 495-5555

## *Tennis*

**Courts:** 7
**Court Surfaces:** Hard
**Courts Lit For Night Play:** None
**Director of Tennis:** Jarcenchal Jaikan      **Head Pro:** Fabio Vasconcellos
**Instruction Rates:** $40 per hour/individual; group rates vary
**Court Time:** No charge
**Video Analysis:** None
**Ball Machines:** 1; no charge
**Tournaments:** None
**Tennis Packages:** None
**Comments:** "A solid Peter Burwash program; free use of courts and ball machine makes room rates reasonable."

## *Accommodations*

**Rooms:** 102
**Rooms With Water View:** All
**Rates:** Start from $440 per room, per night, double occupancy. Includes breakfast, lunch and dinner daily; children 8 and under not permitted
**Type of Crowd:** Couples
**Nearest Airport:** 10 minutes from Virgin Gorda Airport; free shuttle service
**Comments:** "Rooms refurbished in recent years; unpretentious refinement in the Rockresort tradition."

## *Food*

**Restaurants:** Pavillion (American), Sugar Mill and Bar (grill) Beach House (light lunches)
**Comments:** "Conventional preparations of good but often frozen ingredients; abundant lunch buffets; dine alfresco in the evening."

## *Special Features*

One of the original Rockresorts; grand 500-acre estate; horseback riding; water sports; day sailing.
**Nightlife:** Music in the Pavillion.

## *Nearby Tourist Attractions*

Road Town on Tortola; day sails to the North Sound of Virgin Gorda; the Baths on Virgin Gorda.

# MULLET BAY RESORT & CASINO, Netherlands, Antilles, Sint Maarten. (800) 468-5538

### *Tennis*

**Courts:** 14
**Court Surfaces:** Laykold
**Courts Lit For Night Play:** 2
**Director of Tennis:** Jose Orteza        **Head Pro:** Jose Orteza
**Instruction Rates:** $40 per hour/individual; group rates vary
**Court Time:** $8 per hour/singles; $16 per hour/doubles
**Video Analysis:** None
**Ball Machines:** None
**Tournaments:** None
**Tennis Packages:** None
**Comments:** "Orteza is an adequate instructor, and you will have no problem getting court time."

### *Accommodations*

**Rooms:** 600
**Rooms With Water View:** 21
**Rates:** Start from $140 per room, per night, double occupancy; no charge for children 12 and under with parents
**Type of Crowd:** Couples, families, groups
**Nearest Airport:** 5 minutes from Juliana International Airport; no shuttle service
**Comments:** "Resort recently underwent $15 million renovation; modern, comfortable suites have kitchen facilities; but rent a car, otherwise you'll rely on a mini-bus to get around."

### *Food*

**Restaurants:** Bamboo Garden (Chinese), Little Italy (Italian), The Frigate (steaks), The Deli (American), Caneel Coffee Shop (American), The Ship Wreck (American), Ocean Reef (seafood).
**Comments:** "Cuisine, for the most part, is well-prepared; large number of restaurants ensures satisfaction for the discriminating palate."

### *Special Features*

Casino; 16,000-square-foot conference center; 18-hole golf course; beach.
**Nightlife:** Dancing in Le Club.

### *Nearby Tourist Attractions*

Phillipsburg; Orient Beach; Marigot Shopping Center.

# OCEAN CLUB, P.O. Box N4777, Paradise Island, Bahamas. (800) 321-3000, (809) 363-2501

## Tennis

**Courts:** 9
**Court Surfaces:** Har-Tru
**Courts Lit For Night Play:** 4
**Director of Tennis:** John Farrington	**Head Pro:** John Farrington
**Instruction Rates:** $42 per hour/individual; group rates vary
**Court Time:** No charge
**Video Analysis:** Included in tennis clinics
**Ball Machines:** Included in tennis clinics
**Tournaments:** Merv Griffin Celebrity Tournament
**Tennis Packages:** None
**Comments:** "Farrington is always available when guests want to hit; gardens surrounding courts make playing a pleasure."

## Accommodations

**Rooms:** 71
**Rooms With Water View:** 28
**Rates:** Start from $145 per room, per night, double occupancy; no charge for children 12 and under with parents
**Type of Crowd:** Couples
**Nearest Airport:** 25 minutes from Nassau International Airport; no shuttle service
**Comments:** "Private villas with patios and Jacuzzi are your best bet."

## Food

**Restaurants:** Courtyard Terrace (continental)
**Comments:** "The seafood specialities at the elegant Courtyard Terrace are your best bet."

## Special Features

Complimentary use of all Paradise Island Resort and Casino facilities; private beach; free shuttle to casino.
**Nightlife:** Casino at nearby Paradise Island Resort and Casino.

## Nearby Tourist Attractions

Coral World; Stra Market in Nassau; Bay Street; Fincastle overlooking Nassau Harbor; Fort Montagu; Ardastra Gardens.

# PETER ISLAND RESORT, P.O. Box 212, Road Town Tortola, Peter Island, B.V.I. (800) 346–4451, (809) 494–2561

## Tennis

**Courts:** 4
**Court Surfaces:** Laykold
**Courts Lit For Night Play:** 2
**Director of Tennis:** Dick Myers        **Head Pro:** Dick Myers
**Instruction Rates:** $50 per hour/individual; group rates vary
**Court Time:** No charge
**Video Analysis:** None
**Ball Machines:** 1; no charge
**Tournaments:** None
**Tennis Packages:** None
**Comments:** "Courts are new and located near the beach; pros take care of you if you're serious about playing."

## Accommodations

**Rooms:** 50
**Rooms With Water View:** All
**Rates:** Start from $325 per couple, per night, double occupancy. Includes breakfast, lunch and dinner daily; add $75 for extra person in room
**Type of Crowd:** Couples, families
**Nearest Airport:** 40 minutes from Tortola International Airport; $15 per person round-trip taxi to complimentary ferry
**Comments:** "Refurbished rooms are bright and airy with colorful decor; all the basic necessities are present."

## Food

**Restaurants:** Tradewinds (American), Deadman's Beach Bar & Grill (American)
**Comments:** "Several years of honing chef's skills is paying off; expect fine cooking at the Tradewinds."

## Special Features

1,800 acres of beautiful hills; three beaches; seven miles of biking trails; most of the island is undeveloped; water sports included in rates.
**Nightlife:** Steel drum band plays nightly by the pool.

## Nearby Tourist Attractions

Wreck of the Rhone for diving; Tortola; Norman Island; Deadman's Chest; The Baths.

# ST. JAMES'S CLUB, P.O. Box 63, St. John's, Antigua, B.W.I. (800) 274-0008, (809) 460-5000

### *Tennis*

**Courts:** 7
**Court Surfaces:** Hard
**Courts Lit For Night Play:** 5
**Director of Tennis:** Debbie Davis          **Head Pro:** Debbie Davis
**Instruction Rates:** $50 per hour/individual; group rates vary
**Court Time:** No charge
**Video Analysis:** Included in tennis clinics
**Ball Machines:** $1; $20 per hour
**Tournaments:** None
**Tennis Packages:** The Ace Package starts from $300 per person, double occupancy for 4 days/3 nights, including four one-hour lessons, video analysis, unlimited use of ball machine and one can of balls.
**Comments:** "Davis is a fine instructor; some courts need resurfacing; well-stocked pro shop."

### *Accommodations*

**Rooms:** 85; plus 20 suites, 72 villas
**Rooms With Water View:** All
**Rates:** Start from $240 per room, per night, double occupancy, $20 charge for extra person staying in room
**Type of Crowd:** Couples, groups
**Nearest Airport:** 25 minutes from V.C. Bird International Airport; shuttle service for 1-4 people $21, each way
**Comments:** "Suites and villas are your best bet; elegant, truly first-rate; no wonder it's the playground of Whitney Houston and Jean-Paul Belmondo."

### *Food*

**Restaurants:** The Rainbow Garden (continental), The Dockside Cafe (seafood), Piccolo Mondo (Italian)
**Comments:** "Piccolo Mondo is ordinary for Italian fare; try the seafood at The Dockside Cafe."

### *Special Features*

Casino; scuba diving; yacht club; marina; horseback riding; babysitting; twenty-four-hour room service.
**Nightlife:** Entertainment in Jacaranda Club.

### *Nearby Tourist Attractions*

The Devil's Bridge tour; Nelson's Dockyard; Shirley Heights; sightseeing tour of Antigua.

# STOUFFER GRAND BEACH RESORT, P.O. Box 8267, St. Thomas, V.I. (800) 233-1935, (809) 775-1510

## Tennis

**Courts:** 6
**Court Surfaces:** 4 Deco-Turf, 2 Omni
**Courts Lit For Night Play:** All
**Director of Tennis:** Al Richards   **Head Pro:** Al Richards
**Instruction Rates:** $50 per hour/individual; group rates vary
**Court Time:** No charge
**Video Analysis:** None
**Ball Machines:** 1; $18 per hour
**Tournaments:** None
**Tennis Packages:** None
**Comments:** "Richards is available day and night for instruction; he's great with adults and fantastic with children."

## Accommodations

**Rooms:** 297
**Rooms With Water View:** 204
**Rates:** Start from $240 per room, per night, double occupancy; no charge for children 18 and under
**Type of Crowd:** Couples, families
**Nearest Airport:** 20 minutes from St. Thomas' Cyril E. King Airport; no shuttle service
**Comments:** "Nicely decorated with spectacular views; very spacious; balconies off of every room."

## Food

**Restaurants:** Baywinds (Caribbean), Smugglers (grill)
**Comments:** "Smugglers has an exhibition kitchen that allows diners to watch as food is prepared."

## Special Features

Two swimming pools, health club, water sports center, diving center, children's program.
**Nightlife:** Live entertainment at Baywinds.

## Nearby Tourist Attractions

Coral World; Atlantics Submarine; island of St. John.

# SWEPT AWAY, P.O. Box 77, Negril, Jamaica. (800) 545-7937, (809) 957-4061

## *Tennis*

**Courts:** 8
**Court Surfaces:** 4 clay, 4 hard
**Courts Lit For Night Play:** All
**Director of Tennis:** Noel Rutherford       **Head Pro:** Noel Rutherford
**Instruction Rates:** No charge
**Court Time:** No charge
**Video Analysis:** None
**Ball Machines:** 3; no charge
**Tournaments:** None
**Tennis Packages:** None
**Comments:** "With three of Jamaica's top five players as pros, instruction is unrivaled; five hundred-seat stadium court will be completed in late 1991."

## *Accommodations*

**Rooms:** 130 veranda suites
**Rooms With Water View:** All
**Rates:** Start from $315 per room, per night, double occupancy. Includes breakfast, lunch and dinner daily; children not permitted
**Type of Crowd:** Couples only
**Nearest Airport:** 90 minutes from Donald Sangster International Airport; free shuttle service
**Comments:** "An ocean view from every window—even the shower; you can't help relaxing in these somewhat spartan rooms."

## *Food*

**Restaurants:** The Main Dining Room (continental), Feathers (Italian)
**Comments:** "The fresh pasta, gourmet pizza and fruit/vegetable bar are winners; emphasis on healthy foods."

## *Special Features*

All-inclusive resort; private beach, weight room; two pools, squash and racquetball courts; twenty-four-hour security.
**Nightlife:** Live entertainment nightly in The Main Dining Room.

## *Nearby Tourist Attractions*

Rick's Cafe (for sunsets).

# TRYALL GOLF, TENNIS & BEACH CLUB, Montego Bay, Jamaica. (800) 336–4571, (809) 952–5110

### Tennis

**Courts:** 9
**Court Surfaces:** Laykold
**Courts Lit For Night Play:** 5
**Director of Tennis:** Harold Phillips    **Head Pro:** Harold Phillips
**Instruction Rates:** $34 per hour/individual; group rates vary
**Court Time:** $6 per person per hour
**Video Analysis:** $40 per hour
**Ball Machines:** 1; $15 per hour
**Tournaments:** Tryall Tennis Classic
**Tennis Packages:** Details not available at press time
**Comments:** "Hotel manager is former pro Bob Raedisch, he has made an excellent program even better."

### Accommodations

**Rooms:** 52; plus 42 staffed villas
**Rooms With Water View:** 44
**Rates:** Start from $150 per room, per night, double occupancy; no charge for children 12 and under with parents
**Type of Crowd:** Couples
**Nearest Airport:** 25 minutes from Donald Sangster International Airport; no shuttle service
**Comments:** "Spacious, modern hotel rooms attached to historic Great House are near the ocean; stylish one-to-five-bedroom villas come with private pools and a full staff for cooking and pampering."

### Food

**Restaurants:** Great House Verandah (continental), Beach Cafe and Bar (American, Jamaican), Tennis Bar (light meals)
**Comments:** "Delightful atmosphere and competent cooking."

### Special Features

Scenic 2,200-acre former plantation featuring stately 150-year-old Great House; one of the Caribbean's best golf courses; water sports.
**Nightlife:** Music nightly at the Great House.

### Nearby Tourist Attractions

Town of Negril; shopping in Montego Bay.

# 2

# FLORIDA

There are more tennis (and golf) resorts in Florida than in any other state in the U.S. Two big reasons are Florida's warm climate and its proximity to major population centers along the eastern seaboard,

While Florida's east coast was developed first (with beach resorts), there are now more tennis resorts on the West or Gulf Coast. There are few tennis resorts in central Florida, where the main attractions are Disney World and EPCOT Center, or in the Keys, where the only two tennis resorts of note are **Cheeca Lodge** and **Hawk's Cay.**

The premier Florida tennis resorts are marketed as "golf and tennis resorts." You'll find that these resorts offer every conceivable style and price of accommodation, from two-bedroom, two-bath suites with kitchen (most typical) to condominiums to standard rooms in luxury, high-rise hotels.  And because hoteliers tend to pursue the more affluent golfer, you'll find that the best accomodations at these golf and tennis resorts are invariably near the golf course. Still, you will enjoy the best when it comes to tennis facilities and programs. Is it any wonder that Florida is both training ground and home to the likes of Monica Seles, Steffi Graf, and Jennifer Capriati?

# AMELIA ISLAND PLANTATION, Highway A1A South, Amelia Island, Florida 32034. (800) 874-6878, (904) 261-6161

## Tennis

**Courts:** 25
**Court Surfaces:** 19 clay, 4 Omni, 2 Deco-Turf
**Courts Lit For Night Play:** 3
**Director of Tennis:** John Morris    **Head Pro:** John Morris
**Instruction Rates:** $42 per hour/individual; group rates vary
**Court Time:** $7 per person per hour/singles; $4.50 per person per hour/doubles
**Video Analysis:** None
**Ball Machines:** 1; $14 per hour
**Tournaments:** Bausch & Lomb Championships, DuPont All-American Championships
**Tennis Packages:** Tennis Instruction Package starts from $133 per person, per night, double occupancy, including two hours of instruction, unlimited court time, use of ball machine, round-robin tournaments and use of fitness center.
**Comments:** "For the beginner or advanced player, this is a superb tennis facility; tennis packages are definitely worth the investment."

## Accommodations

**Rooms:** 900
**Rooms With Water View:** 342
**Rates:** Start from $133 per room, per night, double occupancy; no charge for children 12 and under with parents
**Type of Crowd:** Conventions, couples, families
**Nearest Airport:** 35 minutes from Jacksonville International Airport; shuttle service $39 per person, each way
**Comments:** "Tremendous variety, from standard hotel rooms to oceanfront villas and rooms which are a crowd favorite."

## Food

**Restaurants:** The Dune Side Club (gourmet), The Beach Club (American), The Verandah (seafood), Golf Shop Restaurant (American), Putter Club (continental), The Coop (continental)
**Comments:** "The Dune Side Club, with a stunning view of the Atlantic, mixes the mystery and romance of the sea with a menu of local and international cuisine to create an unforgettable dining experience."

## Special Features

Children's program; fitness center; sport fishing charters; 45 holes of golf; horseback riding; bicycle trails.
**Nightlife:** Live entertainment in Admiral's Lounge and The Beach Club.

## Nearby Tourist Attractions

Jacksonville Landing shopping area; Little Talbott State Park; St. Augustine; Kingsley Plantation; Fernandina Beach.

## BLUEWATER BAY, P.O. Box 247, Niceville, Florida 32578. (800) 874–2128, (904) 897–3613

### Tennis

**Courts:** 21
**Court Surfaces:** 10 clay, 9 hard, 2 grass
**Courts Lit For Night Play:** 12
**Director of Tennis:** Skip Singleton      **Head Pro:** Skip Singleton
**Instruction Rates:** $45 per hour/individual; group rates vary
**Court Time:** $3 per person per hour
**Video Analysis:** Add $8 to instruction rate
**Ball Machines:** 2; $8 per hour
**Tournaments:** USPTA Grand Prix
**Tennis Packages:** Tennis Tune-up starts from $64 per person, per night, double occupancy for 3 days/2 nights, including unlimited court time, half-hour daily lesson, unlimited use of ball machine and full breakfast each morning.
**Comments:** "Activities and matches for all levels and ages; pros provide positive, practical instruction; excellent junior program."

### Accommodations

**Rooms:** 220
**Rooms With Water View:** 74
**Rates:** Start from $80 per room, per night, double occupancy; no charge for extra person staying in room
**Type of Crowd:** Families
**Nearest Airport:** 15 minutes from Fort Walton/Eglin Airport; no shuttle service
**Comments:** "Vacation villas with fully-equipped kitchens ideal for a family."

### Food

**Restaurants:** Greenhouse (continental), Flags (continental)
**Comments:** "The Greenhouse, overlooking the fairways, serves breakfast and lunch in a cozy, casual atmosphere."

### Special Features

Three 9-hole golf courses; full-service marina with 120 slips; three swimming pools.
**Nightlife:** Not a focus here.

### Nearby Tourist Attractions

Sea World; The Zoo; Air Force Museum; Raceway Park; Island Golf Center; The Track Recreation Center.

# BOCA RATON RESORT & CLUB, 501 East Camino Real, Boca Raton, Florida 33432. (800) 327-0101, (407) 395-3000

*Tennis*

**Courts:** 29
**Court Surfaces:** Clay
**Courts Lit For Night Play:** 9
**Director of Tennis:** Chuck Gill     **Head Pro:** Chuck Gill
**Instruction Rates:** $60 per hour/individual; group rates vary
**Court Time:** $15 per person per day
**Video Analysis:** Included in instruction rate
**Ball Machines:** 1; no charge
**Tournaments:** Prudential-Bache Grand Champions
**Tennis Packages:** Starts from $340 per person, double occupancy for 4 days/3 nights, including unlimited court time, one hour pro tennis clinic daily, can of balls and manager's cocktail reception.
**Comments:** "Excellent facilities and instruction in a most picturesque setting; few resorts offer a head pro of Gill's caliber."

*Accommodations*

**Rooms:** 963
**Rooms With Water View:** 333
**Rates:** Start from $185 per room, per night, double occupancy; no charge for children 16 and under with parents
**Type of Crowd:** Conventions, couples, families
**Nearest Airport:** 45 minutes from Fort Lauderdale International Airport; limousine service $32.50 per person, each way
**Comments:** "Elegant and classy, the Gold Coast doesn't get any better."

*Food*

**Restaurants:** Patio Grill (continental), The Cabana (American), The Terrace (American), Nick's Fishmarket (continental, seafood), Chauncey's Court (continental), Spanish Terrace (Spanish), Top of the Tower (Mediterranean)
**Comments:** "The discriminating palate will not be disappointed; quality matches the quantity; steak lovers shouldn't miss the Patio Grill."

*Special Features*

Private beach; fitness center; five swimming pools; jogging trail; water sports; full marina; movies; shopping on property.
**Nightlife:** Live entertainment in El Largo Lounge.

*Nearby Tourist Attractions*

Palm Beach sightseeing cruise; Palm Beach shopping center; Mizner Park; Boca Raton Children's Museum at Singing Pines; Ocean World; Lion Country Safari; Whitehall Museum.

# THE BREAKERS, 1 South Country Road, Palm Beach, Florida 33480. (800) 883-3141, (407) 655-6611

## *Tennis*

**Courts:** 20
**Court Surfaces:** Har-Tru
**Courts Lit For Night Play:** 11
**Director of Tennis:** Bob Hein     **Head Pro:** Joe Santisi (at Breakers West)
**Instruction Rates:** $60 per hour/individual; group rates vary
**Court Time:** $10 per person per hour
**Video Analysis:** $75 per hour
**Ball Machines:** None
**Tournaments:** None
**Tennis Packages:** Mini-Vacation starts from $250 per person, double occupancy for 3 days/2 nights, including unlimited tennis and golf (excluding cart), two-hour use of bicycles, two full-American breakfasts and one dinner.
**Comments:** "With programs, tournaments and clinics designed for children and adults, Hein and Santisi keep the action moving all day long."

## *Accommodations*

**Rooms:** 528
**Rooms With Water View:** 396
**Rates:** Start from $180 per room, per night, double occupancy; no charge for children 17 and under with parents
**Type of Crowd:** Conventions, families
**Nearest Airport:** 10 minutes from Palm Beach International Airport; limousine service $20 per couple, each way
**Comments:** "All guest rooms have been upgraded recently; the rooms overlooking the water and golf course are a favorite of repeat guests."

## *Food*

**Restaurants:** The Florentine Room (continental), The Circle Dining Room (American), Beach Club (buffet), Fairways Cafe (continental), Beach Club Patio (grill and snacks).
**Comments:** "Decor and cuisine of Florentine and Circle Dining Rooms are not to be missed; impressive wine lists."

## *Special Features*

Two 18-hole golf courses; dance studio; fitness center; croquet; water sports; Gulf stream charters; children's program; beach.
**Nightlife:** Dancing and live entertainment in Alcazar Lounge.

## *Nearby Tourist Attractions*

Jai alai; The Kennel Club; Palm Beach polo; Norton Gallery of Art; Flagler Museum.

# CHEECA LODGE, 82 Mile Marker Oceanside, Islamorada, Florida 33036. (800) 327-2888, (305) 664-4651

## Tennis

**Courts:** 6
**Court Surfaces:** Laykold
**Courts Lit For Night Play:** All
**Director of Tennis:** Tim Adams        **Head Pro:** Tim Adams
**Instruction Rates:** $30 per hour/individual; group rates vary
**Court Time:** $10 per hour
**Video Analysis:** None
**Ball Machines:** None
**Tournaments:** None
**Tennis Packages:** Sportsmen Package starts from $265 per room, per night, double occupancy, including unlimited tennis and golf
**Comments:** "Atmosphere is laid-back; fun, recreational tennis for both the beginner and advanced player."

## Accommodations

**Rooms:** 203
**Rooms With Water View:** 56
**Rates:** Start from $175 per room, per night, double occupancy; no charge for children 16 and under with parents
**Type of Crowd:** Couples, families
**Nearest Airport:** 75 minutes from Miami International Airport; shuttle service $20 per person, each way
**Comments:** "Unpretentious luxury; in the middle of the Keys; a favorite bonefishing spot for President Bush."

## Food

**Restaurants:** The Atlantic Edge (continental, seafood), Ocean Terrace Grill (casual), Raw Bar (seafood)
**Comments:** "Atlantic Edge chef is outstanding; seafood is especially good."

## Special Features

Natural saltwater lagoon; water sports; fishing from private pier; conference center.
**Nightlife:** None

## Nearby Tourist Attractions

Theater of the Sea; Swim With the Dolphins; Everglades airboat rides.

# THE COLONY BEACH & TENNIS RESORT, 1620 Gulf of Mexico Drive, Longboat Key, Florida 34228. (800) 237-9443, (813) 383-6464

### *Tennis*

**Courts:** 21
**Court Surfaces:** 11 hard, 10 clay
**Courts Lit For Night Play:** 2
**Director of Tennis:** Scott Brogan　　**Head Pro:** Scott Brogan
**Instruction Rates:** $45 per hour/individual; group rates vary
**Court Time:** No charge
**Video Analysis:** Add $15 to instruction rate
**Ball Machines:** None
**Tournaments:** Bud Collins Hacker's Open
**Tennis Packages:** Not available at press time
**Comments:** "Courts are well-maintained; excellent facility throughout; The Colony guarantees you a partner for a game."

### *Accommodations*

**Rooms:** 235
**Rooms With Water View:** 19
**Rates:** Start from $205 per room, per night, double occupancy; no charge for children 5 and under with parents
**Type of Crowd:** Couples, families
**Nearest Airport:** 20 minutes from Sarasota-Bradenton Airport; shuttle service $15 for first person, $2 for the second, each way
**Comments:** "All accommodations are luxuriously appointed and landscaped."

### *Food*

**Restaurants:** The Colony (gourmet), Windows (American), Bamboos (grill)
**Comments:** "Superior culinary offerings; impressive wine list."

### *Special Features*

Fitness center; miles of beachfront along the Gulf of Mexico; sailing school; children's program; water sports.
**Nightlife:** Live entertainment in the Colony Lounge.

### *Nearby Tourist Attractions*

Botanical Gardens; St. Armon Circle; specialty boutiques; Ringling Brothers Museum.

# DORAL RESORT & COUNTRY CLUB, 4400 NW 87th Ave., Miami, Florida 33178. (800) 327–6334, (305) 592–2000

## Tennis

**Courts:** 15
**Court Surfaces:** 8 hard, 7 Har-Tru
**Courts Lit For Night Play:** 4
**Director of Tennis:** David Bailey  **Head Pro:** Sadiq Abdullahi
**Instruction Rates:** $50 per hour/individual; group rates vary
**Court Time:** $15 per hour
**Video Analysis:** $65 per hour
**Ball Machines:** 2; $15 per hour
**Tournaments:** Junior Easter Bowl
**Tennis Packages:** Doral Rally starts from $259 per person, double occupancy for 3 days/2 nights, including welcome reception, unlimited court time, one-hour tennis clinic, one-hour use of ball machine, half-hour private lesson, cocktail party and two full-American breakfasts.
**Court Surfaces:** "Bailey covers all the bases from daily clinics to intensive tennis instruction for players of all levels; guests can also play beachside at Doral Beach Club."

## Accommodations

**Rooms:** 650
**Rooms With Water View:** 100
**Rates:** Start from $105 per room, per night, double occupancy; no charge for children 16 and under with parents
**Type of Crowd:** Conventions, families
**Nearest Airport:** 10 minutes from Miami International Airport; no shuttle service
**Comments:** "Plush; rooms with lake views are a favorite of Doral clientele."

## Food

**Restaurants:** Sandpiper (American), Provare (Italian), Champions (coffee shop)
**Comments:** "The steak and seafood at the Sandpiper can't be beat; Italian food at Provare is ordinary."

## Special Features

Equestrian center; 99 holes of golf; Doral Corporate lodge for conferences; health spa; complimentary shuttle to Doral Beach Club.
**Nightlife:** Live entertainment and dancing in Rousseau's Lounge; Staggerbush Sports Bar; piano player in Champions Atrium.

## Nearby Tourist Attractions

Art deco district of Miami Beach; Calder Race Track; Everglades boat rides.

# FISHER ISLAND, 7 Fisher Island Drive, Fisher Island, Florida 33109. (800) 624-3251, (305) 535-6071

## Tennis

**Courts:** 17
**Court Surfaces:** 14 Har-Tru, 3 grass
**Courts Lit For Night Play:** All
**Director of Tennis:** Gardnar Mulloy      **Head Pro:** Gardnar Mulloy
**Instruction Rates:** $50 per hour/individual; group rates vary
**Court Time:** No charge
**Video Analysis:** Included in instruction rate
**Ball Machines:** 2; no charge
**Tournaments:** Fisher Island Pro Celebrity Tennis Classic
**Tennis Packages:** None
**Comments:** "First-rate, head pro 'Silver Fox' Mulloy won a Wimbledon doubles title."

## Accommodations

**Rooms:** 49
**Rooms With Water View:** 25
**Rates:** Start from $300 per room, per night, double occupancy; no charge for extra person in room (maximum of two extra people per room)
**Type of Crowd:** Couples, families
**Nearest Airport:** 20 minutes from Miami International Airport; no shuttle service
**Comments:** "Exemplary; Spanish-style buildings are patterned after original Vanderbilt mansion that now serves as Fisher Island Clubhouse."

## Food

**Restaurants:** Vanderbilt Mansion (gourmet), Porto Cervo (Mediterranean), Beach Club (continental), Golf Club (continental), Pasta Trattoria (Italian), Spa Cafe (spa cuisine), Tennis Center (American)
**Comments:** "Excellent food and service; try Vanderbilt Mansion for gourmet at its finest; pasta lovers shouldn't miss Pasta Trattoria."

## Special Features

One mile-long beach; paddle tennis; six swimming pools (one of which was built by the Vanderbilt family in the 1920s).
**Nightlife:** Dancing and entertainment in Cafe Tangier.

## Nearby Tourist Attractions

Bayside Market; downtown Miami; Coconut Grove; Aviary with rare and exotic collection of birds.

# GRENELEFE RESORT & CONFERENCE CENTER,
3200 State Road 546, Grenelefe, Florida 33844-9732. (800) 237-9549, (813) 422-7511

### Tennis

**Courts:** 19
**Court Surfaces:** 9 Har-Tru, 8 Laykold, 2 grass
**Courts Lit For Night Play:** 11
**Director of Tennis:** Rick Macci    **Head Pro:** Rick Macci
**Instruction Rates:** $45 per hour/individual; group rates vary
**Court Time:** $8 per person per hour; $5 surcharge for grass courts
**Video Analysis:** Included in instruction rates
**Ball Machines:** 1; $10 per half-hour
**Tournaments:** USTA adult and junior tournaments
**Tennis Packages:** The Grand Slam starts from $234.95 per person 3 days/2 nights, including two-hour intensive tennis instruction with video analysis, unlimited court time and use of ball machine, one T-shirt, two cans of balls, a "welcome" wine, cheese and fruit basket, two full-American breakfasts and two picnic lunches.
**Comments:** "Macci is unusually attentive to player's needs; the video analysis instruction program is a must for those who want to improve their game; 1,700-seat stadium and two grass courts are special."

### Accommodations

**Rooms:** 960
**Rooms With Water View:** None
**Rates:** Start from $115 per room, per night, double occupancy; no charge for children 18 and under with parents
**Type of Crowd:** Conventions, families
**Nearest Airport:** 45 minutes from Orlando International Airport; shuttle service $22 per person, each way
**Comments:** "Rooms are spacious with housing clusters in wooded areas; great place for those who like privacy; the suites are spacious and comfortable for large groups or families."

### Food

**Restaurants:** Camelot (American), Green Heron (gourmet), Forest Pub (sandwiches)
**Comments:** "For succulent prime rib of beef, filet mignon and rack of lamb, the Green Heron can't be beat; for more leisurely meals the Camelot pleases the palate with tasty American dishes."

### Special Features

Three 18-hole golf courses; five swimming pools; nature trails; airboat rides; fishing, sailing and water sports on 6,400-acre Lake Marion; children's program.
**Nightlife:** Live music and dancing in Lancelot Lounge.

### Nearby Tourist Attractions

Walt Disney World; Universal Studios; EPCOT Center; Cypress Gardens.

# HAWK'S CAY RESORT & MARINA, 61 Mile Marker, Dock Key, Florida 33050. (800) 432-2242, (305) 743-7000

## *Tennis*

**Courts:** 8
**Court Surfaces:** 6 hard, 2 clay
**Courts Lit For Night Play:** 2
**Director of Tennis:** Tim Farwell        **Head Pro:** Tim Farwell
**Instruction Rates:** $40 per hour/individual; group rates vary
**Court Time:** $3 per person per hour/hard; $5 per person per hour/clay
**Video Analysis:** included in tennis clinics
**Ball Machines:** 1; included in tennis clinics
**Tournaments:** None
**Tennis Packages:** Tennis in Paradise starts from $190 per person, double occupancy for 3 days/2 nights, including two free group lessons and unlimited court time.
**Comments:** "Farwell is first-rate—he cares about his guests (he's also head of PR); well-maintained courts; well-stocked pro shop; the best tennis in the Florida Keys."

## *Accommodations*

**Rooms:** 177; plus 22 marina villas
**Rooms With Water View:** 125
**Rates:** Start from $130 per room, per night, double occupancy; no charge for children 15 and under with parents
**Type of Crowd:** Couples, families
**Nearest Airport:** 10 minutes from Marathon Airport; free shuttle service
**Comments:** "Not the Ritz by any stretch of the imagination; good solid accommodations even if they are a little ordinary; great resort to take the kids to because everything is within eye view."

## *Food*

**Restaurants:** The Ship's Pub & Galley (seafood), The Cantina (continental), The Caribbean Room (Caribbean)
**Comments:** "Solid fare; locally caught bonefish or pompano is best bet; Ship's Pub & Galley on marina is the most charming."

## *Special Features*

Daily dolphin and sea lion training exhibitions; kids can swim with dolphins; deep-sea fishing.
**Nightlife:** Live music in Ship's Pub & Galley.

## *Nearby Tourist Attractions*

Ernest Hemingway's House in Key West.

# HYATT REGENCY GRAND CYPRESS RESORT, 1
Grand Cypress Blvd., Orlando, Florida 32819. (800) 228–9000, (407) 239–1234

## Tennis

**Courts:** 12
**Court Surfaces:** 8 Har-Tru, 4 Deco-Turf
**Courts Lit For Night Play:** 5
**Director of Tennis:** Jeff Crowne      **Head Pro:** Thad Hawkes
**Instruction Rates:** $50 per hour/individual; group rates vary
**Court Time:** $8 per person per hour
**Video Analysis:** $50 per hour
**Ball Machines:** 1; $10 per half-hour
**Tournaments:** USTA adult and junior tournaments
**Tennis Packages:** Tennis in Grand Style starts from $956 per couple, for 4 days/3 nights, including unlimited court time, use of ball machine, three hours of semi-private instruction, one half-hour lesson per person, video analysis, written evaluation of your game and use of health club and recreational facilities.
**Comments:** "Courts are manicured, top-flight individual instruction; unique tennis clinic for children three to eight years of age; excellent, intensive instruction at the Grand Cypress Tennis Academy for the more serious player."

## Accommodations

**Rooms:** 900
**Rooms With Water View:** 300
**Rates:** $185 per room per night, double occupancy; no charge for children with parents (maximum of five can stay in one room)
**Type of Crowd:** Conventions, couples, families, singles
**Nearest Airport:** 25 minutes from Orlando International Airport; shuttle service $12 per person, each way
**Comments:** "From the lakeview rooms to the private Regency Club, there is good variety here; rooms are bright and airy with all the modern amenities; try the executive suite for luxurious comfort; monster-size resort."

## Food

**Restaurants:** Hemingway (seafood), La Coquina (French), Cascade (continental), White Horse (western), Palm Cafe (buffet)
**Comments:** "Wide variety of offerings; you can't leave without trying La Coquina for the finest French cuisine."

## Special Features

Half-acre swimming pool; twelve waterfalls; 21-acre lake; 45 holes of golf; health club; hiking; jogging trails; children's program; horseback riding.
**Nightlife:** Country-western music in White Horse Saloon; live entertainment including piano player in Trelis's.

## Nearby Tourist Attractions

Walt Disney World; EPCOT Center; Sea World; Cypress Gardens; Universal Theme Park Studios.

# INDIAN RIVER PLANTATION, 555 Northeast Ocean Blvd., Hutchinson Island, Stuart, Florida 34996. (800) 444-1432, (407) 225-1155

## *Tennis*

**Courts:** 13
**Court Surfaces:** Omni
**Courts Lit For Night Play:** 7
**Director of Tennis:** Gary Gallian     **Head Pro:** Gary Gallian
**Instruction Rates:** 40 per hour/individual; group rates vary
**Court Time:** $14 per hour
**Video Analysis:** None
**Ball Machines:** 1; $8 per hour
**Tournaments:** None
**Tennis Packages:** Island Funaway starts from $54.50 per person, per night, double occupancy (two-night minimum), including one hour of court time daily.
**Comments:** "Meticulous courts; daily round robins and clinics; pros make an extra effort to find the right match for each guest."

## *Accommodations*

**Rooms:** 323
**Rooms With Water View:** 124
**Rates:** Start from $100 per room, per night, double occupancy; no charge for children 17 and under with parents
**Type of Crowd:** Families, couples, conventions
**Nearest Airport:** 45 minutes from Palm Beach International Airport; limousine service $28 per couple, each way
**Comments:** "Great variety of rooms, suites and villas; decor in older villas not as modern and luxurious as new hotel rooms."

## *Food*

**Restaurants:** Scalawags (seafood), Inlet (gourmet), Porch Steak House (continental), Emporium (continental), 19th Hole (light snacks)
**Comments:** "Scalawags has eclectic, sophisticated decor and a gourmet menu to match; try The Porch for lunch."

## *Special Features*

River cruises; golf course, including an aqua driving range; children's program.
**Nightlife:** Live entertainment in Gilbert's Lounge.

## *Nearby Tourist Attractions*

Lion Country Safari; Worth Ave.

## INNISBROOK, P.O. Drawer 1088, Tarpon Springs, Florida 34688-1088. (800) 456-2000, (813) 942-2000

### Tennis

**Courts:** 15
**Court Surfaces:** 11 clay, 4 hard
**Courts Lit For Night Play:** 7
**Director of Tennis:** Terry Addison     **Head Pro:** Phil Green
**Instruction Rates:** $70 per hour/individual; group rates vary
**Court Time:** $20 per hour
**Video Analysis:** Available with certain clinics
**Ball Machines:** 2; $20 per court per hour
**Tournaments:** None
**Tennis Packages:** Preferred Tennis starts from $99 per person, per night (three-night minimum), including two hours court time daily; tennis clinics and half-hour use of ball machine daily.
**Comments:** "Terry Addison is a no-nonsense instructor who gets results."

### Accommodations

**Rooms:** 1,000
**Rooms With Water View:** 49
**Rates:** Start from $167 per room, per night, double occupancy; no charge for children 17 and under with parents
**Type of Crowd:** Conventions, couples, families
**Nearest Airport:** 45 minutes from Tampa International Airport; shuttle service $15 per person, each way
**Comments:** "All rooms are spacious and comfortable; one-bedroom suite overlooking golf course is your best bet."

### Food

**Comments:** Copperhead Coral (western), The Sandpiper (Caribbean), The Island Vintage Tea Room (gourmet)
**Comments:** "The Island Vintage Tea Room lives up to its billing as 'one of West Florida's finest.' "

### Special Features

Sixty-three holes of golf; four indoor racquetball courts; bass fishing at Lake Tarpon.
**Nightlife:** Live entertainment in Sandpiper Lounge.

### Nearby Tourist Attractions

Busch Gardens; Walt Disney World; Tarpon Spring Sponge Docks; Gulf beaches.

**LONGBOAT KEY CLUB,** 301 Gulf of Mexico Drive, Longboat Key, Florida 34228. (800) 237-8821, (813) 383-8821

*Tennis*

**Courts:** 18
**Court Surfaces:** Har-Tru
**Courts Lit For Night Play:** 6
**Director of Tennis:** John Woods     **Head Pro:** John Woods
**Instruction Rates:** $40 per hour/individual; group rates vary
**Court Time:** $10 per day
**Video Analysis:** Available during clinics
**Ball Machines:** 1; included in court time rate
**Tournaments:** None
**Tennis Packages:** None
**Comments:** "Relaxed and professional; Woods and staff do an excellent job of matching players with club members and other guests."

*Accommodations*

**Rooms:** 221
**Rooms With Water View:** 165
**Rates:** Start from $120 per room, per night, double occupancy; no charge for extra person in club suite
**Type of Crowd:** Conventions, families, social groups
**Nearest Airport:** 15 minutes from Sarasota-Bradenton Airport; no shuttle service
**Comments:** "The club suites featuring king-sized beds and well-designed kitchens are a guest favorite."

*Food*

**Restaurants:** Orchids (seafood), Island House (continental), Spike (grill)
**Comments:** "Orchids, the club's gourmet restaurant, should not be missed."

*Special Features*

Club surrounded by Sarasota Bay and Gulf of Mexico; wildlife sanctuary; championship golf course.
**Nightlife:** Live entertainment in the Island House.

*Nearby Tourist Attractions*

St. Armand's Circle; Ringling Brothers Museum; Selby Botanical Gardens.

# MARRIOTT'S BAY POINT RESORT 100 Delwood Beach Road, Panama City, Florida 32411-7207. (800) 874-7105, (904) 234-3307

## *Tennis*

**Courts:** 12
**Court Surfaces:** Har-Tru
**Courts Lit For Night Play:** 4
**Director of Tennis:** Robert Fisher     **Head Pro:** Butch Mitchell
**Instruction Rates:** $55 per hour/individual; group rates vary
**Court Time:** $14 per court per hour
**Video Analysis:** $20 per hour
**Ball Machines:** None
**Tournaments:** DuPont National Intercollegiate Clay Court Championships
**Tennis Packages:** The tennis package starts from $89 per person, per night, double occupancy (two night minimum), including four hours of court time and breakfast for two at Fiddler's Green daily.
**Comments:** "Lots of personal attention from pros in friendly club atmosphere; 1,400 club membership provides resort guests with playing partners."

## *Accommodations*

**Rooms:** 355
**Rooms With Water View:** 95
**Rates:** Start from $114 per room, per night, double occupancy; no charge for children 18 and under with parents
**Type of Crowd:** Conventions, couples, families
**Nearest Airport:** 15 minutes from Panama City Airport; shuttle service $7.50 per person, each way
**Comments:** "Standard rooms are spacious; private terraces overlook bay or golf course."

## *Food*

**Restaurants:** Fiddler's Green (seafood), Stormy's (grill), Teddy Tuckers (continental), 19th Hole (American), Green House (Cajun), Sunset Grill (seafood), Terrace Court (gourmet)
**Comments:** "Fiddler's Green has seafood specialties like oak-grilled prawns and fresh native grouper; Green House and Terrace Court at country club offer romantic settings and gourmet fare."

## *Special Features*

Natural lagoon; two golf courses; 145-slip marina; water sports.
**Nightlife:** Live entertainment in Circles Lounge and Teddy Tuckers.

## *Nearby Tourist Attractions*

Bay Point Sports Park; The Miracle Strip; Barnacle Bay.

# MARRIOTT'S ORLANDO WORLD CENTER, World
Center Drive, Orlando, Florida 32821.  (407) 239–4200

## *Tennis*

**Courts:**  12
**Court Surfaces:**  Hard
**Courts Lit For Night Play:**  All
**Director of Tennis:**  Jim Herzberger          **Head Pro:**  Jim Herzberger
**Instruction Rates:**  $40 per hour/individual; group rates vary
**Court Time:**  $12 per court per hour
**Video Analysis:**  Add $10 to instruction rate
**Ball Machines:**  2; $20 per hour
**Tournaments:**  Marriott's Orlando Junior Classic
**Tennis Packages:**  The tennis package starts from $199 per person, per night, double occupancy, including unlimited court time, one hour use of ball machine, one can of balls and unlimited use of fitness center
**Comments:**  "Good teaching staff puts a heavy emphasis on developing your strengths."

## *Accommodations*

**Rooms:**  1,503
**Rooms With Water View:**  328
**Rates:**  Start from $189 per room, per night, double occupancy; no charge for extra person staying in room
**Type of Crowd:**  Conventions, couples, families
**Nearest Airport:**  20 minutes from Orlando International Airport; shuttle service $12 per person, each way
**Comments:**  "Rooms are well-designed for families; all have balconies with views of lush grounds and Lake Buena Vista; so big you can get lost there."

## *Food*

**Restaurants:**  Mikados (Japanese), Garden Terrace (American), The Golf Grill (American), Stachios (American), The Regent Court (gourmet)
**Comments:**  "Exciting variety; seafood lovers should try The Regent Court."

## *Special Features*

18-hole golf course; children's program; four heated swimming pools; fitness center.
**Nightlife:**  Live entertainment in Overtures.

## *Nearby Tourist Attractions*

Disney World; Universal Studios; Church Street Station; Sea World; Pleasure Island.

# NAPLES BATH & TENNIS CLUB, 4995 Airport Road North, Naples, Florida 33942. (800) 225-9692, (813) 649-2034

## Tennis

**Courts:** 38
**Court Surfaces:** 37 Har-Tru, 1 Laykold
**Courts Lit For Night Play:** 14
**Director of Tennis:** Michael Kopp **Head Pro:** Michael Kopp
**Instruction Rates:** $40 per hour/individual; group rates vary
**Court Time:** Free
**Video Analysis:** Included in instruction rate
**Ball Machines:** 2; $6 per hour
**Tournaments:** Grand Masters Tennis Tournament
**Tennis Packages:** Start from $325 per person (not including room), for 4 days/3 nights including thirteen hours of tennis instruction and unlimited court time.
**Comments:** "Huge complex with plenty of tennis to go around; Kopp does a great job of matching up players for singles and doubles."

## Accommodations

**Rooms:** 62 (1- 2- and 3-bedroom condominiums)
**Rooms With Water View:** All
**Rates:** Start from $130 per room, per night, double occupancy
**Type of Crowd:** Couples, families
**Nearest Airport:** 30 minutes from Fort Myers Southwest Regional Airport; no shuttle service
**Comments:** "This club is also a resort; it's not necessary to be recommended by a member to stay here; condos are spacious for groups and families of all sizes."

## Food

**Restaurants:** The Grand Masters Pub (American), main dining room (American)
**Comments:** "Food aspires to gourmet standards, but is really just mediocre."

## Special Features

Privacy and serenity of 160 tropical acres; seven lakes where alligators doze and peacocks drink; junior Olympic-size pool; fitness center.
**Nightlife:** Live entertainment and dancing in the lounge.

## Nearby Tourist Attractions

Naples Philharmonic; The Everglades; Jungle Larry's Zoo; Tin City shopping area; Naples beaches.

## OCEAN REEF CLUB & RESORT, Key Largo, Florida 33037, (800) 741–REEF

### *Tennis*

**Courts:**  11
**Court Surfaces:**  6 clay, 5 hard
**Courts Lit For Night Play:**  6
**Director of Tennis:**  Bob Ecuyer          **Head Pro:**  Bob Ecuyer
**Instruction Rates:**  $65 per hour/individual; group rates $20 per person, per hour (4 person maximum)
**Court Time:**  $10 per day, per person
**Video Analysis:**  $65 per hour
**Ball Machines:**  2; $10 per hour
**Tournaments:**  None
**Tennis Packages:**  Starts from $99 per room, per day with unlimited tennis plus a free golf cart (which you'll need to get around the property)
**Comments:**  "Ecuyer has been the head pro here since 1971; video analysis used regularly as part of instruction; numerous other clubs on property affords Ecuyer the ability to guarantee you a game."

### *Accommodations*

**Rooms:**  143, plus 1–3 bedroom villas
**Rooms With Water View:**  Most
**Rates:**  Start from $230 per room, per night, double occupancy; no charge for children 16 and under with parents
**Type of Crowd:**  Very upscale, families, V.I.P.
**Nearest Airport:**  60 minutes from Miami International Airport (however the resort has its own private airstrip for V.I.P.'s; no shuttle service
**Comments:**  "One of the most exclusive resorts in America; air-tight security; favorite of President Richard Nixon; so exclusive guests can only visit twice in their lifetime unless they become club members or buy property; bring lots of insect repellent because mosquitoes thrive here."

### *Food*

**Restaurants:**  The Gazebo Bar (American), Buccaneer Island Patio (snacks), The Caribbean Cafe (seafood), The Pelican Oyster Bar (seafood), The Ocean Room (continental). The Carysfort Grille (continental), The Galley Restaurant and Burgee Bar (casual), The Raw Bar and Fish Market (seafood)
**Comments:**  "The Carysfort Grille is unpretentious gourmet dining at its best; The Caribbean Cafe has a delightful Florida Keys feel—try the blackened swordfish."

### *Special Features*

Offshore/reef fishing; private marina; two 18-hole golf courses; children's programs; fitness center; private shopping village.
**Nightlife:**  Music, dancing, live entertainment in The Reef Lounge.

### *Nearby Tourist Attractions*

John Pennekamp Coral Reef State Park; town of Key Largo.

# PALM-AIRE SPA RESORT, 2501 Palm-Aire Drive North, Pompano Beach, Florida 33069. (800) 327–4960, (305) 972-3300

## *Tennis*

**Courts:** 37
**Court Surfaces:** 31 Har-Tru, 6 hard
**Courts Lit For Night Play:** 6
**Director of Tennis:** Jeff Cohen        **Head Pro:** Jeff Cohen
**Instruction Rates:** $45 per hour/individual; group rates vary
**Court Time:** $8 per person per hour/singles; $6 per person per/hour/doubles
**Video Analysis:** None
**Ball Machines:** 1; $10 per hour
**Tournaments:** None
**Tennis Packages:** Unlimited Tennis starts from $139.90 per person, double occupancy for 3 days/2 nights, including unlimited court time, two forty-five-minute group lessons and breakfast daily.
**Comments:** "Lots of choice and service here; pro and staff meet each guest's needs; good children's program."

## *Accommodations*

**Rooms:** 191
**Rooms With Water View:** None
**Rates:** Start from $174.40 per room, per night, double occupancy; no charge for children 12 and under with parents
**Type of Crowd:** Conventions, families
**Nearest Airport:** 20 minutes from Fort Lauderdale International Airport; shuttle service $24 per couple, each way
**Comments:** "The 1-bedroom suites, with terraces overlooking the golf course, are your best bet."

## *Food*

**Restaurants:** Spa Dining Room (spa cuisine), Peninsula Dining Room (continental), Oaks Country Club (American), Palms (American)
**Comments:** "Cuisine well-prepared and presented; the Spa Dining Room is a must for those on calorie control alert."

## *Special Features*

Five 18-hole golf courses; fitness trail; squash; racquetball; health spa.
**Nightlife:** Live entertainment in the hotel Bar and Lounge.

## *Nearby Tourist Attractions*

Ocean World; Pompano Harness Track; Pompano Beach; The Everglades.

# PGA NATIONAL, 400 Ave. of the Champions, Palm Beach Gardens, Florida 33418. (800) 633-9150, (407) 627-2000

## *Tennis*

**Courts:** 19
**Court Surfaces:** Clay
**Courts Lit For Night Play:** 12
**Director of Tennis:** Ruth Barnett        **Head Pro:** Chuck Williams
**Instruction Rates:** $50 per hour/individual; group rates vary
**Court Time:** $5 per person per day
**Video Analysis:** $25 per hour
**Ball Machines:** None
**Tournaments:** PGA National Summer Championships
**Tennis Packages:** "Just Tennis" starts from $164 per person, double occupancy for 3 days/2 nights, including one day of resort's full tennis program.
**Comments:** "Emphasis is on having fun; good junior clinics, with children 4 and over participating."

## *Accommodations*

**Rooms:** 335
**Rooms With Water View:** 78
**Rates:** Start from $185 per room, per night, double occupancy; no charge for children 17 and under with parents
**Type of Crowd:** Conventions, families
**Nearest Airport:** 15 minutes from West Palm Beach International Airport; no shuttle service
**Comments:** "Spacious; private balconies overlook pool, lake or golf course."

## *Food*

**Restaurants:** The Citrus Tree (continental), Colonel Bogey's (steak and seafood), The Explorers (gourmet)
**Comments:** "Delicious mesquite-grilled steaks and chops at Colonel Bogey's; the Spanish paella at The Explorers is very popular."

## *Special Features*

Five croquet courts; 26-acre lake with man-made beach; five championship golf courses; Captain Max children's camp; health spa.
**Nightlife:** Live entertainment in Legend's lounge.

## *Nearby Tourist Attractions*

Flagler Museum; The Harbour; Gardens Mall; Worth Ave.

# PONTE VEDRA INN & CLUB, 200 Ponte Vedra Blvd., Ponte Vedra Beach, Florida 32082. (800) 234-7842, (904) 285-1111

## *Tennis*

**Courts:** 15
**Court Surfaces:** Har-Tru
**Courts Lit For Night Play:** 7
**Director of Tennis:** Z. Mincek   **Head Pro:** Diane Farrell
**Instruction Rates:** $40 per hour/individual; group rates vary
**Court Time:** $10 per person per day
**Video Analysis:** Included in instruction rate
**Ball Machines:** 3; $16 per hour
**Tournaments:** Ponte Vedra Adult Championship
**Tennis Packages:** The tennis package starts from $178 per room, per night, double occupancy for 3 days/2 nights, including unlimited tennis, one hour of tennis instruction daily, and T-shirt.
**Comments:** "Courts in excellent condition; a complete tennis facility, but only one court surface."

## *Accommodations*

**Rooms:** 200
**Rooms With Water View:** All
**Rates:** Start from $129 per room, per night, double occupancy; no charge for children 16 and under with parents
**Type of Crowd:** Conventions, couples, families
**Nearest Airport:** 45 minutes from Jacksonville International Airport; shuttle service $40 per couple, each way
**Comments:** "One of Florida's oldest resorts; on 200-plus acres with beach; most people have been coming here for years."

## *Food*

**Restaurants:** The Inn Gourmet Room (gourmet), Seafoam (gourmet), Florida Room (continental)
**Comments:** "Seafood is the main fare; for ocean side dining try the Seafoam."

## *Special Features*

Two 18-hole golf courses; sailing; croquet; fitness center; spa; water sports.
**Nightlife:** Live entertainment in Audubon Lounge and Sea Horse Lounge.

## *Nearby Tourist Attractions*

St. Augustine; Jacksonville Landing; Marineland; Cummer Art Gallery; Alexander Brest Planetarium.

# THE REGISTRY, 475 Sea Gate Drive, Naples, Florida 33940. (800) 247-9810, (813) 597-3232

## Tennis

**Courts:** 15
**Court Surfaces:** Har-Tru
**Courts Lit For Night Play:** 5
**Director of Tennis:** Bill Bowden    **Head Pro:** ~~Ronnie Hilburn~~
**Instruction Rates:** $50 per hour/individual; group rates vary
**Court Time:** $15 per court per hour
**Video Analysis:** Included in individual instruction
**Ball Machines:** 1; $10 per hour
**Tournaments:** None
**Tennis Packages:** "Resort Courts" start from $205 per person, double occupancy for 3 days/2 nights, including unlimited court time, two and one-half hours of lessons, video analysis, one can of balls, welcome cocktail beach cabana, use of health club and supervised children's activities.
**Comments:** "Beautiful new courts; pro staff are outgoing and friendly; first-rate instruction."

## Accommodations

**Rooms:** 320
**Rooms With Water View:** All
**Rates:** Start from $180 per room, per night, double occupancy; no charge for children 18 and under with parents
**Type of Crowd:** Conventions, families
**Nearest Airport:** 30 minutes from Fort Myers' Southwest Regional Airport; shuttle service $18 per person, each way
**Comments:** "Interior designers did stupendous job in all accommodations; tennis villas clustered around Tennis Center have separate bedrooms and pretty patios."

## Food

**Restaurants:** Cafe Chablis (American), Brass Pelican (seafood and steak), Lafite (gourmet)
**Comments:** "From veal medallions to the Maine lobster, Lafite is gourmet at its best; seafood lovers shouldn't miss the Brass Pelican."

## Special Features

Lagoon-like swimming pool and grotto; health club with tanning beds; adjacent golf course.
**Nightlife:** Dancing in Garrett's nightclub.

## Nearby Tourist Attractions

Automobile museum; Thomas Edison's winter home; Old Naples shopping district; Naples Pier; Naples Center for Performing Arts; Sanibel and Captiva islands.

## THE RITZ-CARLTON NAPLES, 280 Vanderbilt Beach Road, Naples, Florida 33963. (800) 241–3333, (813) 598–3300

### Tennis

**Courts:** 6
**Court Surfaces:** 3 Har-Tru, 3 hard
**Courts Lit For Night Play:** All
**Director of Tennis:** Jim Biddle     **Head Pro:** Jim Biddle
**Instruction Rates:** $50 per hour/individual; group rates vary
**Court Time:** $20 per court per hour
**Video Analysis:** $25 per hour
**Ball Machines:** None
**Tournaments:** None
**Tennis Packages:** None
**Comments:** "Biddle provides expert instruction; tennis pavillion and courts are very basic; not for die-hard players."

### Accommodations

**Rooms:** 463
**Rooms With Water View:** All
**Rates:** Start from $220 per room, per night, double occupancy; no charge for children 16 and under with parents
**Type of Crowd:** Couples, families
**Nearest Airport:** 30 minutes from Fort Myers' Southwest Regional Airport; shuttle service $34 per person, each way
**Comments:** "Rooms are beautifully appointed; all overlook Gulf of Mexico."

### Food

**Restaurants:** The Dining Room (Mediterranean), The Grill (seafood), The Cafe (spa cuisine, Italian), The Bean Pavillion (American)
**Comments:** "Excellent cuisine in settings of exquisite taste; service can be a bit slow; don't leave without trying the seafood at The Grill."

### Special Features

Fitness center; adjacent golf course; sailing; water sports.
**Nightlife:** Dancing and live entertainment in The Club.

### Nearby Tourist Attractions

Nature preserves; The Collier Museum; Naples Center for Performing Arts; Everglades boat rides; Sanibel and Captiva islands.

# SADDLEBROOK GOLF & TENNIS RESORT, 100 Saddlebrook Way, Wesley Chapel, Florida 33543. (800) 729-8383, (813) 973-1111

## *Tennis*

**Courts:** 46
**Court Surfaces:** 32 clay, 10 hard, 2 red clay, 2 grass
**Courts Lit For Night Play:** 8
**Director of Tennis:** Howard Moore     **Head Pro:** Tommy Thompson
**Instruction Rates:** $40 per hour/individual; group rates vary
**Court Time:** $12 per hour
**Video Analysis:** Included in Hopman Tennis Package
**Ball Machines:** 2; $10 per hour
**Tournaments:** None
**Tennis Packages:** Hopman Tennis Package starts from $720 per person, double occupancy for 6 nights/5 days, including five hours of tennis instruction daily.
**Comments:** "Solid tennis menu that rarely deviates and never disappoints; home of the renowned Harry Hopman International Tennis Academy."

## *Accommodations*

**Rooms:** 500
**Rooms With Water View:** None
**Rates:** Start from $130 per room, per night, double occupancy, no charge for children 12 and under with parents
**Type of Crowd:** Families, couples
**Nearest Airport:** 45 minutes from Tampa International Airport; shuttle service $15 per person, each way
**Comments:** " 'Walking Village' concept of scattered condos is pleasant, providing you are not far from the main pool."

## *Food*

**Restaurants:** Cypress (surf and turf), Little Club (surf and turf), Little Club Patio (casual)
**Comments:** "The Little Club menu is your best bet; Cypress is for formal dining; be prepared to wait at Little Club Patio."

## *Special Features*

Two 18-hole golf courses; 270-foot-long swimming pool; nature trails, bass fishing on-site; health club and spa; children's program.
**Nightlife:** Live entertainment and dancing in Polo Lounge.

## *Nearby Tourist Attractions*

Busch Gardens; Sea World; Walt Disney World.

## SANDESTIN BEACH RESORT, 5500 Highway 98 East, Destin, Florida 32541. (800) 277-0800, (904) 267-8000

### Tennis

**Courts:** 14
**Court Surfaces:** 6 hard, 5 clay, 3 grass
**Courts Lit For Night Play:** None
**Director of Tennis:** Dennis Fortenberry      **Head Pro:** Dennis Fortenberry
**Instruction Rates:** $38 per hour/individual; group rates vary
**Court Time:** $24 per hour/grass; $14 per hour/clay; $12 per hour/hard
**Video Analysis:** Add $20 to instruction rate
**Ball Machines:** 1; $12 per hour
**Tournaments:** Sandestin Professional Grass Court Championships
**Tennis Packages:** Not available at press time
**Comments:** "First-rate instruction; worth it for grass courts alone; the Tennis Masters Academy is here; perhaps the best tennis resort in Northwest Florida."

### Accommodations

**Rooms:** 575
**Rooms With Water View:** 275
**Rates:** Start from $77 per room, per night, double occupancy; no charge for extra person staying in room
**Type of Crowd:** Conventions, couples, families
**Nearest Airport:** 30 minutes from Okaloosa Walden Airport; shuttle service $22 per person, each way
**Comments:** "Modern, luxurious rooms; one-bedroom villas beachfront are your best bet."

### Food

**Restaurants:** Elephant Walk (French country), Babes (seafood), Chan's Deli (American), Sandcastles (American), Harry T's (continental), Marina Cafe (continental)
**Comments:** "Cuisine at Elephant Walk is wonderfully prepared and presented."

### Special Features

Twenty-two hundred acres of breathtaking natural scenery; 36 holes of golf; babysitting; children's program; marina and sportfishing; Sports Science lab; spa and fitness center.
**Nightlife:** Live entertainment in Elephant Walk Lounge.

### Nearby Tourist Attractions

Air Force Museum; Eden State Park; seaside community.

# SHERATON BONAVENTURE RESORT & SPA, 250 Racquet Club Road, Fort Lauderdale, Florida 33326. (800) 327-8090, (305) 389-3300

## *Tennis*

**Courts:** 24
**Court Surfaces:** 17 Har-Tru, 7 asphalt
**Courts Lit For Night Play:** 14
**Director of Tennis:** Dan Flietstra    **Head Pro:** Tom Parkes
**Instruction Rates:** $45 per hour/individual; group rates vary
**Court Time:** $15 per person per day
**Video Analysis:** Included in instruction rate
**Ball Machines:** 2; $10 per hour
**Tournaments:** Haagen Dazs Junior Tennis Classic; 35-and-over Men's Clay Court Nationals
**Tennis Packages:** The Bonaventure Escape starts from $362.50 per person, for 3 days/2 nights, including all meals, unlimited court time, three and one-half hours of private lessons and three one-hour clinics.
**Comments:** "Flietstra and staff cover all the bases with organized group clinics, private instruction and tournament play; excellent junior program."

## *Accommodations*

**Rooms:** 500
**Rooms With Water View:** 308
**Rates:** Start from $155 per room, per night, double occupancy; no charge for children 17 and under with parents
**Type of Crowd:** Families, conventions, couples
**Nearest Airport:** 20 minutes from Fort Lauderdale International Airport; limousine service $60 per couple, each way
**Comments:** "One-bedroom suites overlooking golf course are your best bet."

## *Food*

**Restaurants:** Renaissance (California cuisine), The Garden (continental), Spa Restaurant (health-oriented), The Falls Cafe (American)
**Comments:** "For romantic dining in a rain-forest setting, nothing beats the Renaissance."

## *Special Features*

Two 18-hole golf courses; health spa; equestrian center; racquetball; squash; bowling alley.
**Nightlife:** Dancing and live entertainment in The Terrace Lounge.

## *Nearby Tourist Attractions*

Butterfly World; Discovery Center; Museum of Art (one of the country's leading children's museums); Fort Lauderdale Beach; Seminole Native Village; The Everglades.

# SHERATON PALM COAST, 300 Clubhouse Drive, Palm Coast, Florida 32137. (800) 325-3535, (904) 445-3000

*Tennis*

**Courts:** 18
**Court Surfaces:** 12 clay, 4 hard, 2 grass
**Courts Lit For Night Play:** 10
**Director of Tennis:** Jim Vidamour      **Head Pro:** Tom Warneke
**Instruction Rates:** $40 per hour/individual; group rates vary
**Court Time:** $16 per court per hour (hard); $20 (clay); $28 (grass)
**Video Analysis:** Add $10 to instruction rate
**Ball Machines:** 1; $25 per hour
**Tournaments:** None
**Tennis Packages:** The tennis package starts from $80 per person, per night, double occupancy, including unlimited tennis (surcharge for use of grass courts).
**Comments:** "Vidamour keeps the action moving on the courts with clinics, round-robin tournaments and intensive instruction programs for players of all skill levels."

*Accommodations*

**Rooms:** 156; plus 68 villas
**Rooms With Water View:** 156
**Rates:** Start from $105 per room, per night, double occupancy; no charge for children 17 and under with parents
**Type of Crowd:** Conventions, couples, families
**Nearest Airport:** 30 minutes from Daytona Airport; no shuttle service
**Comments:** "Rooms are spacious and clean and chain hotelish; villas are a crowd favorite."

*Food*

**Restaurants:** Flaglers (continental)
**Comments:** "Breakfast, lunch and dinners are good not great; but you can't leave without trying the Sunday brunch."

*Special Features*

Three swimming pools; five golf courses; miniature golf; fitness center; children's program.
**Nightlife:** Live entertainment in Henry's.

*Nearby Tourist Attractions*

St. Augustine; Daytona Beach; Marineland.

# SONESTA SANIBEL HARBOUR RESORT, 17260 Harbour Point Drive, Fort Myers, Florida 33908. (800) SONESTA, (813) 466–4000

## Tennis

**Courts:** 13
**Court Surfaces:** 8 clay, 5 hard
**Courts Lit For Night Play:** All
**Director of Tennis:** Jerry Walters        **Head Pro:** Jerry Walters
**Instruction Rates:** $50 per hour/individual; group rates vary
**Court Time:** $12
**Video Analysis:** $50 per person per hour
**Ball Machines:** 1: $15 per hour
**Tournaments:** None
**Tennis Packages:** Tennis Getaway starts from $170 per person, double occupancy for 3 days/2 nights, including four hours of court time daily, two half-hour lessons, one stroke-of-the-day clinic, one-hour use of ball machine, round robins and matchmaking play.
**Comments:** "Walters runs a phenomenal facility; matchmaking operation creates a game for everyone; formerly home to Jimmy Connors."

## Accommodations

**Rooms:** 240, 100 condominiums
**Rooms With Water View:** 306
**Rates:** Start from $125 per room, per night, double occupancy; no charge for children 18 and under with parents
**Type of Crowd:** Couples, families
**Nearest Airport:** 20 minutes from Fort Myers' Southwest Regional Airport; shuttle service $9 per person, each way
**Comments:** "Resembles old-Florida resort; rooms overlook San Carlos Bay."

## Food

**Restaurants:** The Promenade Cafe (continental), Courtside Bar & Grill (American), The Toucan Room (continental)
**Comments:** "Best bets are faultless Sunday brunch at Promenade Cafe and seafood at Courtside Bar & Grill."

## Special Features

**Just Us Kids** program; water taxis to Sanibel Island; 1,000-foot-long beach; health spa; four racquetball courts; 25-slip marina; charter fishing guides; three swimming pools.
**Nightlife:** Live entertainment in Courtside Bar & Grill and Islevista Lounge.

## Nearby Tourist Attractions

Thomas Edison's winter home; beaches of Sanibel and Captiva islands; Old Napels shopping district.

# SOUTH SEAS PLANTATION, Captiva Island, Florida 33924. (800) 282-3402, (800) 237-3102

## Tennis

**Courts:** 22
**Court Surfaces:** Laykold
**Courts Lit For Night Play:** 7
**Director of Tennis:** John Williams     **Head Pro:** John Williams
**Instruction Rates:** $50 per hour/individual; group rates vary
**Court Time:** $9 per court per hour
**Video Analysis:** Included in individual instruction rate
**Ball Machines:** None
**Tournaments:** None
**Tennis Packages:** "High-Impact Tennis Island Style" starts from $293 per person, double occupancy for 4 days/3 nights, including tennis instruction, round-robin tournaments and video analysis.
**Comments:** "Well-rounded staff; strong instructional focus on player's reaction time as well as mechanics."

## Accommodations

**Rooms:** 600
**Rooms With Water View:** 500
**Rates:** Start from $145 per room, per night, double occupancy; no charge for children 12 and under with parents
**Type of Crowd:** Families
**Nearest Airport:** 45 minutes from Fort Myers' Southwest Regional Airport; shuttle service $16 per person, each way
**Comments:** "Tremendous variety; one- and two-bedroom villas are best bet for tennis buffs, but even the standard rooms are spacious enough for a family."

## Food

**Restaurants:** Chadwick's (seafood), Cap'n Al's (American), The King's Crown (continental), Mama Roses (Italian)
**Comments:** "Something for everyone here; Chadwick's is especially nice for families."

## Special Features

Marina and yacht harbor; two and a half miles of private beach; children's program; island excursions; eighteen swimming pools; conference centers.
**Nightlife:** Live entertainment in King's Crown lounge.

## Nearby Tourist Attractions

Ding Darling's wildlife; Thomas Edison's winter home; The Everglades; Sanibel Island; Naples Performing Arts Center; Naples Pier.

# TOPS'L, 5550 Highway 98 East, Destin, Florida 32541. (800) 476-9222, (904) 267-9222

## Tennis

**Courts:** 12
**Court Surfaces:** 10 Rubico, 2 Plexipave
**Courts Lit For Night Play:** 10
**Director of Tennis:** Steve Pennington       **Head Pro:** Steve Pennington
**Instruction Rates:** $35 per hour/individual; group rates vary
**Court Time:** No charge
**Video Analysis:** Included in tennis package
**Ball Machines:** 2; $5 per hour
**Tournaments:** Clarence Chaffee Memorial
**Tennis Packages:** Tops'l Tennis Weekend starts from $109 per person, for 3 days/2 nights (four people in two-bedroom condominium), including unlimited court time, round-robin tournament, two-hour clinic, video tape clinic and brunch.
**Comments:** "The entire style and feel of the resort is geared for tennis."

## Accommodations

**Rooms:** 150
**Rooms With Water View:** 86
**Rates:** Start from $120 per two-bedroom condominium per night; no charge for extra person in room
**Type of Crowd:** Couples, families
**Nearest Airport:** 60 minutes from Pensacola Regional Airport; no shuttle service
**Comments:** "Well-appointed rooms and suites; most with invigorating view of Gulf of Mexico; comparatively small size of resort creates a more intimate environment."

## Food

**Restaurants:** Center Court Dining Room (regional American), Ocean Club (Creole Caribbean), The Pavillion (sandwiches)
**Comments:** "Not much selection, but the food is excellent; the Center Court offers fine dining."

## Special Features

Fitness center; babysitting; child day-care in summer; fireplaces in villas; hot tubs; beauty salon.
**Nightlife:** None

## Nearby Tourist Attractions

Destin Fishing Village; seaside community; Sandestin Market Place.

# TURNBERRY YACHT & COUNTRY CLUB, 19999 West Country Club Drive, Aventura, Florida 33180. (800) 327-7028, (305) 932-6200

## Tennis

**Courts:** 24
**Court Surfaces:** 15 hard, 9 Har-Tru
**Courts Lit For Night Play:** 18
**Director of Tennis:** John Lehmann    **Head Pro:** Ricardo Martinez
**Instruction Rates:** $55 per hour/individual; group rates vary
**Court Time:** $10 per court per hour
**Video Analysis:** $75 per hour
**Ball Machines:** 4; $25 per hour
**Tournaments:** None
**Tennis Packages:** Turnberry's Hit starts from $680 per person, double occupancy for 5 days/4 nights, including five one-hour lessons, video analysis, unlimited court time, one can of balls, a "welcome" cocktail, fruit basket, sun visor and free shuttle service to ocean club.
**Comments:** "Pros stress fundamentals for both the serious and social player yet maintain balance between fun and competitiveness."

## Accommodations

**Rooms:** 345
**Rooms With Water View:** 78
**Rates:** Start from $175 per room, per night, double occupancy; no charge for children 14 and under with parents
**Type of Crowd:** Conventions, couples, VIPs
**Nearest Airport:** 15 minutes from Fort Lauderdale International Airport; limousine service for $70 per couple, each way
**Comments:** "Very luxurious; choose from the exclusive Yacht Club Hotel or the newly refurbished country club; the latter has some of the most beautiful bathrooms of any resort found in this book."

## Food

**Restaurants:** The Monaco (American), The Veranda (continental), The Grill (continental), Sunset Cafe (continental), Ocean Club Deli (American)
**Comments:** "Good seafood, grilled meats and regional specialties; above average."

## Special Features

Two championship golf courses; luxurious spa; full-service marina; private ocean club; babysitting service.
**Nightlife:** Dancing in The Disco and live entertainment in The Monaco Lounge.

## Nearby Tourist Attractions

Art-deco district; Coconut Grove; Sea Aquarium; Metro Zoo.

# 3

# THE SOUTHEAST

In the Southeast, or the "Old South," you'll discover an unusual vacation environment; one where a canvas of grand settings, laid-back splendor, and old-world style peacefully co-exist beneath the bold strokes of new-world modernism. You'll experience sprawling plantations, hospitable service, and simple "down-home" cuisine while indulging in some of the best suites, spas, and tennis facilities in the United States.

The only drawback with these resorts is that they tend to be so vast that you need to rent a car just to get around the property so that you can enjoy what they have to offer. An excellent example is **Sea Pines Plantation**, Hilton Head Island, South Carolina, which is situated on 5,200 gorgeous acres. But if you want to play tennis, go to the beach, or even just buy a newspaper, you're going to need an automobile. In addition, most of the tennis resorts in this chapter, because of their size, are not near major urban centers, so if nothing else you will need a car just to get to and from the airport. If you pay for a taxi, you will pay through the nose.

# BOAR'S HEAD INN, Box 5307, Charlottesville, Virginia 22905. (800) 476–1988, (804) 296–2181

*Tennis*

**Courts:**   17; 3 indoor
**Court Surfaces:**   10 clay, 7 Grass-Tex
**Courts Lit For Night Play:**   3
**Director of Tennis:**   Buddy Weiner        **Head Pro:**   Leo Evans
**Instruction Rates:**   $36 per hour/individual; group rates vary
**Court Time:**   $14 per hour/outdoors, $18 per hour/indoors
**Video Analysis:**   Included in tennis clinics
**Ball Machines:**   1; $12 per hour
**Tournaments:**   None
**Tennis Packages:**   None
**Comments:**   "Well-organized programs and superb court maintenance."

*Accommodations*

**Rooms:**   174
**Rooms With Water View:**   60
**Rates:**   Start from $105 per room, per night, double occupancy; no charge for children 18 and under with parents
**Type of Crowd:**   Couples, families, singles
**Nearest Airport:**   15 minutes from Charlottesville Airport; free shuttle service
**Comments:**   "King-size beds in rooms, with balconies that overlook lake and scenic hills."

*Food*

**Restaurants:**   The Old Mill Dining Room (fine dining), The Tavern (continental), The Sports Club (continental)
**Comments:**   "For an elegant experience, try the Old Mill Dining Room; for a more casual atmosphere, check out The Tavern."

*Special Features*

Scenic Blue Ridge Mountains; local vineyards; shops on premises; hot air ballooning; skydiving; antique prints throughout hotel; adjacent to University of Virginia; historic Colonial sites.
**Nightlife:**   Entertainment in The Tavern Lounge.

*Nearby Tourist Attractions*

Monticello, home of Thomas Jefferson; University of Virginia; Skyline Drive.

# CALLAWAY GARDENS, U.S. Highway 27, P.O. Box 2000, Pine Mountain, Georgia 31822. (800) 282-8182, (404) 663-5032

### Tennis

**Courts:** 17
**Court Surfaces:** 9 Plexipave, 8 Rubico
**Courts Lit For Night Play:** All
**Director of Tennis:** Bill Champion          **Head Pro:** Steve DiFeliciantonio
**Instruction Rates:** $38 per hour/individual; group rates vary
**Court Time:** $14 per hour/clay; $12 per hour/hard
**Video Analysis:** $60 per hour
**Ball Machines:** 2; $20 per hour
**Tournaments:** None
**Tennis Packages:** The Deluxe Tennis Package starts from $103.25 per person, per night, double occupancy for 3 days/2 nights, including two hours of court time daily and breakfast and dinner buffet daily.
**Comments:** "Champion is a long-time pro; solid, if unspectacular, tennis facility."

### Accommodations

**Rooms:** 800
**Rooms With Water View:** None
**Rates:** $120 per room, per night, double occupancy; no charge for children 17 and under with parents
**Type of Crowd:** Couples, families
**Nearest Airport:** 80 minutes from Atlanta's Hartsfield Airport; shuttle service $25 per person, each way
**Comments:** "Homey; you can stay in the inn or in country cottages scattered throughout a woodland area that covers 12,000 acres."

### Food

**Restaurants:** Plantation Room (buffet), Georgia Room (fine cuisine), Flower Mill (pizza), Country Kitchen (continental), The Gardens (steak and seafood), The Veranda (Italian)
**Comments:** "The Georgia Room is the top spot; simple southern cooking."

### Special Features

On Robin Lake with world's largest man-made beach; butterfly center; horticulture center; 63 holes of golf; garden paths.
**Nightlife:** Entertainment in the Vineyard Green Lounge.

### Nearby Tourist Attractions

The Little White House; downtown Warm Springs; Columbus historic district; Military Museum at Fort Benning; West Point Lake at LaGrange.

# THE CLOISTER, Sea Island, Georgia 31561. (800) 732–4752, (912) 638–3611

## *Tennis*

**Courts:** 18
**Court Surfaces:** 17 Har-Tru, 1 hard
**Courts Lit For Night Play:** None
**Director of Tennis:** David McLean          **Head Pro:** Dickie Anderson
**Instruction Rates:** $40 per hour/individual; group rates vary
**Court Time:** $18 per hour
**Video Analysis:** $50 per hour
**Ball Machines:** 1; $24 per hour
**Tournaments:** None
**Tennis Packages:** The tennis package starts from $133 per person, per night, double occupancy for 4 days/3 nights, including unlimited court time, can of balls and breakfast, lunch and dinner daily.
**Comments:** "Pros are good teachers and motivators; quick-dry courts are a plus."

## *Accommodations*

**Rooms:** 264
**Rooms With Water View:** 132
**Rates:** Start from $248 per room, per night, double occupancy; no charge for children 18 and under with parents
**Type of Crowd:** Couples, families
**Nearest Airport:** 20 minutes from Brunswick Airport; shuttle service $10 per person, each way
**Comments:** "Spanish Mediterranean architecture, rooms with porches overlooking the Atlantic are a real treat."

## *Food*

**Restaurants:** The Main Dining Room (gourmet), The Georgian Dining Room (continental), The Beach Club (American), Sea Island Golf Club (American), The Island Club (continental)
**Comments:** "The Main Dining room fare is quite good; beach clubs offer seafood and lots of it."

## *Special Features*

Oceanfront sports; trapshooting; livery stables with bridle paths; 10,000-acre resort; five miles of private beach.
**Nightlife:** Entertainment in the Cloister Club Room.

## *Nearby Tourist Attractions*

Art colonies on Fort Frederica; Christ Church.

# THE GREENBRIER, White Sulphur Springs, West Virginia 24986. (800) 624-6070, (304) 536-1110

## *Tennis*

**Courts:** 20; 5 indoor
**Court Surfaces:** 15 Har-Tru, 5 Dyna-Turf
**Courts Lit For Night Play:** 5
**Director of Tennis:** Ron Bohrnstedt     **Head Pro:** Ron Bohrnstedt
**Instruction Rates:** $60 per hour/individual; group rates vary
**Court Time:** $20 per hour/outdoor; $30 per hour/indoor
**Video Analysis:** None
**Ball Machines:** 1; add $10 to court time rate
**Tournaments:** None
**Tennis Packages:** Deluxe Tennis Package starts from $399 per person, double occupancy for 3 days/2 nights, including two hours of court time daily, one-hour clinic daily, can of balls and breakfast and dinner daily.
**Comments:** "Excellent year-round facility, elegant surroundings for play."

## *Accommodations*

**Rooms:** 700
**Rooms With Water View:** None
**Rates:** Start from $152 per person, per night, double occupancy, including breakfast and dinner daily; no charge for children 1 and under
**Type of Crowd:** Couples, families, groups
**Nearest Airport:** 15 minutes from Greenbrier Valley Airport; no shuttle service
**Comments:** "From traditional hotel rooms and suites to cottages and condominiums, no two lodgings are alike, but all have an old-world elegance."

## *Food*

**Restaurants:** The Main Dining Room (continental), Draper's Cafe (American), The Tavern Room (continental), The Grille Room (continental), The Golf Club Dining Room (American)
**Comments:** "Regional cuisine is best bet; The Main Dining Room's six-course dinner and lavish luncheon buffet are legendary."

## *Special Features*

Health spa; carriage rides; lawn bowling; Civil War landmarks.
**Nightlife:** Entertainment in Old White Club and dancing in The Tavern Lounge.

## *Nearby Tourist Attractions*

Greenbrier River; The National Fish Hatchery; town of Lewisburg.

# THE HOMESTEAD, Hot Springs, Virginia 24445. (800) 336–5771, (703) 839–5500

*Tennis*

**Courts:** 19
**Court Surfaces:** 15 Har-Tru, 4 hard
**Courts Lit For Night Play:** None
**Director of Tennis:** Tom Morgan          **Head Pro:** Tom Morgan
**Instruction Rates:** $40 per hour/individual; group rates vary
**Court Time:** $15 per hour/singles; $25 per hour/doubles
**Video Analysis:** None
**Ball Machines:** 1; $20 per hour
**Tournaments:** None
**Tennis Packages:** Start from $247 per person, double occupancy for 3 days/2 nights, including two hours of court time daily, one-hour group lesson and a can of balls.
**Comments:** "Facilities and treatment of players befit Homestead elegance."

*Accommodations*

**Rooms:** 600
**Rooms With Water View:** None
**Rates:** Start from $215 per room, per night, double occupancy; no charge for children 12 and under with parents
**Type of Crowd:** Couples, families
**Nearest Airport:** 90 minutes from Roanoke Regional Airport; no shuttle service
**Comments:** "Old-world elegance extends from the main lobby to each room."

*Food*

**Restaurants:** Cafe Albert (continental), Cascade Club (continental), The Casino (American), The Dining Room (continental), The Grille (continental), Lower Cascade Lounge (continental), Sam Snead's Tavern (American), Homestead Club (American), Ski Lodge (American)
**Comments:** "Each restaurant is so good they released their own cookbook; some of the most delicious dining the South has to offer."

*Special Features*

One of the oldest family resorts in America; owned by a private family since the 1890s; carriage rides; trap-and-skeet shooting; thermal baths; archery; clock tower; children's program.
**Nightlife:** Entertainment in the Homestead Club.

*Nearby Tourist Attractions*

Lexington; Gathright Dam; historical Bath County.

# KIAWAH ISLAND, P.O. Box 12910, Charleston, South Carolina 29142. (800) 6–KIAWAH

## Tennis

**Courts:** 28
**Court Surfaces:** 23 Har-Tru, 5 hard
**Courts Lit For Night Play:** 2
**Director of Tennis:** Roy Barth          **Head Pro:** Henri Lents
**Instruction Rates:** $12 per hour/individual; group rates vary
**Court Time:** $15 per hour
**Video Analysis:** Included in instruction rate
**Ball Machines:** 2; $9 per half-hour
**Tournaments:** U.S. Men's Clay Court Championships
**Tennis Packages:** Start from $59 per person, per night for 3 days/2 nights, including unlimited court time, one "Stroke-a-Day Clinic," use of ball machine, round robins and demo-racket use.
**Comments:** "Excellent facilities; fabulous setting for peaceful and unique tennis playing; packages are worth looking into."

## Accommodations

**Rooms:** 150 rooms, 300 1–4 bedroom villas
**Rooms With Water View:** All rooms at Inn have water view
**Rates:** Start from $100 per night; no charge for children 12 and under with parents
**Type of Crowd:** Couples, families
**Nearest Airport:** 45 minutes from Charleston International Airport, shuttle service $22 per person, each way
**Comments:** "The Inn offers a resort-like setting while the villas offer a private setting."

## Food

**Restaurants:** Sundancer's Grill (casual), Indigo House (casual), Jonah's (seafood), Jasmine Porch (seafood), Jilich's (continental)
**Comments:** "Sample the authentic low country cooking at Jasmine Porch—the seafood is very fresh; all the herbs and spices are grown on nearby John's Island."

## Special Features

Kiawah Kollege; an interpretive nature tour of the island; supervised children's recreation; ten miles of beach; ten pools.
**Nightlife:** Entertainment in Topsider Lounge.

## Nearby Tourist Attractions

Historic Charleston; Barrier Island beaches; area plantations.

# PALMETTO DUNES, P.O. Box 5606, Hilton Head, South Carolina 29938. (800) 845–6130, (803) 785–7300

## Tennis

**Courts:** 25
**Court Surfaces:** 19 clay, 4 Supergrasse, 2 hard
**Courts Lit For Night Play:** 6
**Director of Tennis:** John Kerr    **Head Pro:** John Kerr
**Instruction Rates:** $40 per hour/individual; group rates vary
**Court Time:** No charge
**Video Analysis:** Add $24 to individual instruction rate
**Ball Machines:** 2; $20 per hour
**Tournaments:** Hilton Head Junior Clay Court Championships
**Tennis Packages:** None
**Comments:** "Clinics emphasize the Australian method, upon which so many great players were nurtured."

## Accommodations

**Rooms:** 527 villas
**Rooms With Water View:** 160
**Rates:** Start from $105 per villa, per night; no charge for extra person in room
**Type of Crowd:** Couples, families, groups
**Nearest Airport:** 60 minutes from Savannah International Airport; shuttle service $18 per person, each way
**Comments:** "Villas are spacious; great for families; but choose one near the resort center or you'll hike—often."

## Food

**Restaurants:** Austin's (steak), Alexander's (seafood), The Commodore (seafood), Jones, Fazio & Hills Course Grills (grill), Little Venice (Italian), Patti Arbuckle's Restaurant & Bar (continental), Pisces (seafood), P.J.'s Incredible Edibles (deli), Pralines (seafood), Scott's (continental)
**Comments:** "Great choice of restaurants, but none are outstanding."

## Special Features

Bicycle paths that cross lagoons; twelve miles of beach; four golf courses; exercise room.
**Nightlife:** Entertainment in Club Indigo and Scarlett's Lounge.

## Nearby Tourist Attractions

Mall at Shelter Cove; historical ruins and old forts at Hilton Head Plantation.

# PINEHURST RESORT & COUNTRY CLUB, P.O. Box 4000, Pinehurst, North Carolina 28374. (800) 334–9560, (919) 295–6811

## Tennis

**Courts:** 24
**Court Surfaces:** 18 Har-Tru, 6 Laykold
**Courts Lit For Night Play:** 4
**Director of Tennis:** Larry Wolf          **Head Pro:** Larry Wolf
**Instruction Rates:** $40 per hour/individual; group rates vary
**Court Time:** $10 per person per hour/singles; $8 per person per hour/doubles
**Video Analysis:** $60 per hour including individual instruction
**Ball Machines:** 1; $7.50 per hour
**Tournaments:** USTA State League Championships
**Tennis Packages:** None
**Comments:** "Big Bill Tilden won first North and South Open here in 1919."

## Accommodations

**Rooms:** 310; 140 1–3 bedroom condominiums; 47 rooms at the Manor Inn
**Rooms With Water View:** None
**Rates:** Start from $112 per person, per night, double occupancy, including breakfast and dinner daily; no charge for children 5 and under with parents
**Type of Crowd:** Couples, families, groups
**Nearest Airport:** 75 minutes from Raleigh/Durham Airport; shuttle service $30 per couple, each way
**Comments:** "The rooms are all decorated in grand, southern fashion."

## Food

**Restaurants:** The Carolina Dining Room (gourmet), Italian Restaurant (Italian)
**Comments:** "Breakfasts are outrageously good; dinners feature native North Carolina dishes such as smoked pork chops with apple cider sauce."

## Special Features

Seven golf courses; gun club; 200-acre lake; five swimming pools; children's program; riding trails are a favorite of Jacqueline Kennedy Onassis.
**Nightlife:** Entertainment in Ryder Cup Lounge.

## Nearby Tourist Attractions

North Carolina Zoological Park; PGA World Golf Hall of Fame; Seagrove Pottery.

# SEA PALMS GOLF & TENNIS, 5445 Frederica Road, St. Simons Island, Georgia 31522.  (800) 841–6268

## *Tennis*

**Courts:**  12
**Court Surfaces:**  Clay
**Courts Lit For Night Play:**  3
**Director of Tennis:**  Vishnu Maharaj      **Head Pro:**  Vishnu Maharaj
**Instruction Rates:**  $40 per hour/individual; group rates vary
**Court Time:**  $4 per half-hour
**Video Analysis:**  None
**Ball Machines:**  1; $6 per hour
**Tournaments:**  USTA-sanctioned tournaments
**Tennis Packages:**  "Set Point" starts from $113 per room, per night, double occupancy for 3 days/2 nights, including unlimited tennis, one hour of instruction daily, thirty-minute use of ball machine and use of health club daily.
**Comments:**  "Smooth operation; never a problem finding a game; Maharaj has been here for sixteen years and treats guests as if they were visiting his home."

## *Accommodations*

**Rooms:**  300
**Rooms With Water View:**  250
**Rates:**  Start from $109 per room, per night, double occupancy; no charge for children 14 and under with parents
**Type of Crowd:**  Couples, families
**Nearest Airport:**  30 minutes from Brunswick Airport, shuttle service $15 per person, each way
**Comments:**  "Spacious and comfortable; most units available with kitchen facilities; comparable to luxury apartments."

## *Food*

**Restaurants:**  Cafe Oglethorpe (continental)
**Comments:**  "Cafe Oglethorpe must be tried to be believed—everything is cooked the way you want it."

## *Special Features*

Conference facilities; 27 holes of golf; health club; indoor/outdoor pool; horseback riding.
**Nightlife:**  None.

## *Nearby Tourist Attractions*

Fort Frederica; Christ Church; Old Lighthouse on St. Simons Island; Jeckyll Island.

# SEA PINES PLANTATION, P.O. Box 7000, Hilton Head Island, South Carolina 29938. (800) 845-6131, (803) 785-3333

## Tennis

**Courts:** 29
**Court Surfaces:** 24 Har-Tru, 5 hard
**Courts Lit For Night Play:** 5
**Director of Tennis:** Kurt Kamperman     **Head Pro:** Job de Boer
**Instruction Rates:** $40 per hour/individual; group rates vary
**Court Time:** No charge
**Video Analysis:** $50 per hour
**Ball Machines:** 6; $8 per hour
**Tournaments:** Family Circle Magazine Cup
**Tennis Packages:** The "Long Weekender" starts from $377 per couple, double occupancy for 4 days/3 nights, including four hours of instruction, court time and a welcome gift.
**Comments:** "Stan Smith Tennis Academy is popular with juniors; well-organized clinics and lovely center court; be sure to check out the Prince Performance Corner."

## Accommodations

**Rooms:** 500 villas and condominiums
**Rooms With Water View:** 300
**Rates:** Start from $80 per 1-bedroom villa per night, double occupancy; no charge for extra person in room
**Type of Crowd:** Conventions, couples, families
**Nearest Airport:** 75 minutes from Savannah International Airport; no shuttle service
**Comments:** "Resort community highlighted by clusters of beautifully appointed homes and villas; lovely views but so spread out you can get lost."

## Food

**Restaurants:** Twelve on the grounds of Sea Pines Plantation
**Comments:** "Fresh-from-the-dock seafood; best dining choice is Harbour Town Grill."

## Special Features

Three 18-hole golf courses; fantastic sunsets; harbor front location; horseback riding; children's program.
**Nightlife:** Entertainment in the Quarterdeck.

## Nearby Tourist Attractions

Hilton Head Museum; Pinckney Island Wildlife Sanctuary; historic Savannah and Beaufort.

# WILD DUNES, P.O. Box 1410, Charleston, South Carolina 29402. (800) 845-8880

*Tennis*

**Courts:** 15
**Court Surfaces:** Har-Tru
**Courts Lit For Night Play:** 6
**Director of Tennis:** Randy Chamberlain        **Head Pro:** Randy Chamberlain
**Instruction Rates:** $38 per hour/individual; group rates vary
**Court Time:** $16 per hour
**Video Analysis:** None
**Ball Machines:** 2; $10 per hour
**Tournaments:** None
**Tennis Packages:** Start from $135.50 per room, per night, double occupancy for 3 days/2 nights, including unlimited court time and group instruction daily.
**Comments:** "Staff tries hard to accommodate each player's needs."

*Accommodations*

**Rooms:** 200 villas
**Rooms With Water View:** 125
**Rates:** Start from $95 per room, per night, double occupancy; no charge for extra person staying in room
**Type of Crowd:** Couples, families, groups
**Nearest Airport:** 30 minutes from Charleston International Airport; no shuttle service
**Comments:** "Located 15 miles outside of Charleston on the Isle of Palms; the scenery can't be beat."

*Food*

**Restaurants:** The Links (continental), The Beach Pavillion (continental)
**Comments:** "Can't go wrong dining at The Links, which is open year-round."

*Special Features*

Two and a half miles of private beach; two 18-hole golf courses; children's program; convention facilities.
**Nightlife:** None.

*Nearby Tourist Attractions*

Historic Charleston, Middleton Place Gardens; Fort Sumter; Boone Hall Plantation.

# WINTERGREEN RESORT, P.O. Box 706, Wintergreen, Virginia 22958. (800) 325-2200, (804) 325-2200

### Tennis

**Courts:** 25
**Court Surfaces:** 20 clay, 5 hard
**Courts Lit For Night Play:** None
**Director of Tennis:** Clay Robinson     **Head Pro:** Clay Robinson
**Instruction Rates:** $35 per hour/individual; group rates vary
**Court Time:** $20 per hour/mountain top clay; $18 per hour/hard; $12 per hour/valley clay
**Video Analysis:** Included in tennis clinics and individual instruction
**Ball Machines:** 2; $18 per hour
**Tournaments:** None
**Tennis Packages:** None
**Comments:** "Beautiful setting, with some courts in valley and some mountainside."

### Accommodations

**Rooms:** 400 condominiums
**Rooms With Water View:** None
**Rates:** Start from $110 per room, per night, double occupancy; no charge for extra person staying in room
**Type of Crowd:** Couples, families, groups
**Nearest Airport:** 45 minutes from Charlottesville Airport; no shuttle service
**Comments:** "Mountain setting was built with skiers in mind, but it satisfies the needs of all."

### Food

**Restaurants:** Cooper's Vantage (casual), The Garden Terrace (continental), The Copper Mine (continental)
**Comments:** "Casual to formal, featuring Virginia specialties and seafood; ordinary."

### Special Features

Guests can play tennis, golf and ski all in same day; two golf courses; equestrian center; Wintergarden Spa; children's program; six swimming pools; 20-acre lake; 25 miles of hiking trails; babysitting service.
**Nightlife:** Entertainment in Cooper's Vantage.

### Nearby Tourist Attractions

Monticello, home of Thomas Jefferson; Luray Caverns; Charlottesville shopping area.

# 4

# BERMUDA

Bermuda has earned a reputation as an island for honeymooners. It also boasts the most golf courses per square mile of any country or island in the world. While tennis can be found at many of the resorts throughout this subtropical island, it is primarily offered only as a guest amenity—not as the main attraction. The only Bermuda resorts reviewed in this book are those that take their tennis seriously.

Because most Bermuda hotels are small—many of them cottage colonies with only one or two courts—you will not have trouble securing court time, although you will do without the frills of a major tennis resort, like ball machines, a pro shop, and video analysis. (It's a good idea to bring your own racket and balls.) But nowhere else will you find resorts more quaint and charming than the ones here, particularly **Ariel Sands, Pink Beach Club,** and **Stonington Beach.**

Don't forget to explore the island. Bermuda is unique and beautiful, and very British. The "empire" still proudly rules here. Nowhere else in the world will you find an island culture without poverty or unemployment. Here you can tour the island on a moped or bicycle—a Bermuda tradition. Go back to another century by walking the narrow cobblestone streets of St. George. Stroll through Hamilton and its modern, if pricey, shops. Speaking of money, bring your credit cards, because Bermuda is prohibitively expensive—the kind of place where you can spend $15 for a can of tennis balls!

# ELBOW BEACH HOTEL, P.O. Box 455 HMBX, Hamilton, Bermuda. (800) 223–7434, (809) 236–3535

*Tennis*

**Courts:** 5
**Court Surfaces:** Hard
**Courts Lit For Night Play:** 2
**Director of Tennis:** Eugene Woods          **Head Pro:** Eugene Woods
**Instruction Rates:** $36 per hour/individual; group rates vary
**Court Time:** $5 per hour/day; $8 per hour/night
**Video Analysis:** None
**Ball Machines:** 1; included in tennis clinics
**Tournaments:** None
**Tennis Packages:** The tennis package starts from $625 per couple, for 6 days/ 5 nights, including unlimited court time, one hour of night court time, round-robin tournaments, one-hour use of ball machine, one can of balls, use of health club and breakfast and dinner daily.
**Comments:** "Avid tennis players can always find a game here; Woods runs a serious program for players of all levels."

*Accommodations*

**Rooms:** 300
**Rooms With Water View:** 230
**Rates:** Start from $92 per person, per night, double occupancy, including breakfast and dinner; no charge for children 2 and under with parents
**Type of Crowd:** Couples, families
**Nearest Airport:** 30 minutes from Bermuda Civil Air Terminal; no shuttle service
**Comments:** "Lots of variety here; junior beachfront suites are a crowd favorite."

*Food*

**Restaurants:** Terrace Dining Room (American), Sea Horse Grill (continental), Surf Club (seafood)
**Comments:** "You can't go wrong at any of the dining facilities; terrific seafood at the Surf Club."

*Special Features*

Half-mile private beach; two miles from downtown Hamilton; health club; children's summer program; climate-controlled swimming pool; shopping mall in main hotel.
**Nightlife:** Live entertainment in the Peacock Lounge.

*Nearby Tourist Attractions*

Hamilton shopping; Horseshoe Beach; St. George; The Botanical Garden.

# GROTTO BAY HOTEL, No. 11 Blue Hole Hill, Hamilton Parish, Bermuda. (800) 223-0888, (809) 293-8333

### Tennis

**Courts:** 4
**Court Surfaces:** Plexipave
**Courts Lit For Night Play:** 2
**Director of Tennis:** John Sinclair      **Head Pro:** John Sinclair
**Instruction Rates:** $45 per hour/individual; group rates vary
**Court Time:** $5 per hour/day; $7 per hour/night
**Video Analysis:** Included in individual instruction rate
**Ball Machines:** 1; $15 per hour
**Tournaments:** None
**Tennis Packages:** Bermuda Tennis Academy starts from $390 per person, double occupancy for 6 days/5 nights, including unlimited court time, five hours of private instruction, three hours of group instruction daily, two-hour use of ball machine and round-robin tournaments.
**Comments:** "Sinclair is one of the few pros in Bermuda who puts his heart and soul into a tennis program; the junior program is especially good."

### Accommodations

**Rooms:** 201
**Rooms With Water View:** All
**Rates:** Start from $92 per person, per night, double occupancy, including breakfast and dinner daily; no charge for children 6 and under with parents
**Type of Crowd:** Couples, families
**Nearest Airport:** 5 minutes from Bermuda Civil Air Terminal; no shuttle service
**Comments:** "Even the least expensive rooms have ocean views and balconies, cable TV, coffeemakers, and air-conditioning—nothing fancy."

### Food

**Restaurants:** The Hibiscus Room (American), Supper Club (American)
**Comments:** "The cuisine and dining services are good, the better of the two is The Hibiscus Room."

### Special Features

Proximity to airport makes it a perfect place to start or finish a vacation; water sports center.
**Nightlife:** Entertainment in Prosperous Cave Disco.

### Nearby Tourist Attractions

The Glass Blowing Studio; Bermuda Perfumery; Crystal Cave; Lemington Cave.

# SONESTA BEACH HOTEL & SPA, Southampton, Bermuda. (800) 766-3782, (809) 238-8122

## *Tennis*

**Courts:** 6
**Court Surfaces:** Hard
**Courts Lit For Night Play:** 2
**Director of Tennis:** Cal Simmons        **Head Pro:** Cal Simmons
**Instruction Rates:** $35 per hour/individual; group rates vary
**Court Time:** $8 per hour
**Video Analysis:** None
**Ball Machines:** 1; included in tennis clinics
**Tournaments:** None
**Tennis Packages:** The tennis package starts from $2,258 per couple for 7 days/6 nights, including three half-hour tennis lessons, three tennis clinics, one can of balls, use of health club and breakfast and dinner daily.
**Comments:** "From general instruction to round-robin tournaments, there's always some activity in progress; courts adjacent to Atlantic Ocean."

## *Accommodations*

**Rooms:** 300
**Rooms With Water View:** 125
**Rates:** Start from $190 per room, per night, double occupancy; no charge for children 3 and under with parents
**Type of Crowd:** Conventions, couples, families
**Nearest Airport:** 40 minutes from Bermuda Civil Air Terminal; no shuttle service
**Comments:** "Hotel sprawls over fifty acres of Bermuda's south shore; suites have balconies, wet bars, cable TV and king-size beds."

## *Food*

**Restaurants:** Port Royal (American), Lillian's (gourmet), The Boat Bay Club (casual)
**Comments:** "Good variety of restaurants, plus beach cafe for drinks and light fare; buffet breakfast is worth getting up for."

## *Special Features*

Health club; croquet; snorkeling; windsurfing; scuba diving.
**Nightlife:** Live entertainment in Boat Bay Lounge.

## *Nearby Tourist Attractions*

Gibb's Lighthouse; Henry VII restaurant; Port Royal Golf Course; Horseshoe Beach.

# SOUTHAMPTON PRINCESS, Box 1379, Hamilton, Bermuda. (800) 223-1818, (809) 238-8000

## *Tennis*

**Courts:** 11
**Court Surfaces:** Hard
**Courts Lit For Night Play:** 3
**Director of Tennis:** Bruce Sims        **Head Pro:** Debbie Harper
**Instruction Rates:** $50 per hour/individual; group rates vary
**Court Time:** $10 per hour
**Video Analysis:** None
**Ball Machines:** None
**Tournaments:** None
**Tennis Packages:** None
**Comments:** "Harper teaches all levels and will match players for games; it has the most courts of any Bermuda resort; beach courts have breathtaking views."

## *Accommodations*

**Rooms:** 600
**Rooms With Water View:** All
**Rates:** Start from $305 per room, per night, double occupancy, including breakfast and dinner daily; no charge for children 16 and under with parents
**Type of Crowd:** Conventions, couples, families
**Nearest Airport:** 40 minutes from Bermuda Civil Air Terminal; no shuttle service
**Comments:** "The only difference in room quality is the view, which is better the higher up you go."

## *Food*

**Restaurants:** Newport Room (gourmet), Waterlot Inn (gourmet), The Whaler Inn (seafood), Windows on the Sound (continental), The Rib Room (steaks), Wickets (American)
**Comments:** "Don't leave without trying the Waterlot Inn; dance and dine at Windows on the Sound; very expensive, all."

## *Special Features*

Children's summer program; horseback riding; free shuttle service throughout grounds; health club; cycle shop.
**Nightlife:** Dancing in "The Touch".

## *Nearby Tourist Attractions*

Dockyard; Hamilton shopping; Bermuda Perfumery; St. George.

# 5

# NEW ENGLAND AND NEW YORK

New England's spring, summer, and fall climate makes the area well-suited for tennis. You can play against a backdrop of rustic woodlands, rugged mountains, lush verdant valleys, and spring-fed lakes. Cool winds and low humidity permit play during hot summer days.

The most popular places to play are at resorts in the Green Mountains of Vermont, colonial tourist towns such as Lenox, Massachusetts, and, of course, Cape Cod. Resorts in the Green Mountains—**Sugarbush Resort, The Villages at Killington** and **Topnotch at Stowe**—are sprawling properties best-suited for those who want a two- or three-bedroom condominium or chalet. In Lenox and on Cape Cod you'll find smaller, more exclusive resorts with fewer courts, but with services and amenities typical of the standard hotel. In New York, the Catskill Mountains attracts the most tennis enthusiasts, with **The Concord Hotel** and its forty courts make it the main tennis mecca.

# CONCORD RESORT HOTEL, Kiamesha Lake, New York 12751. (914) 794–4000

### Tennis

**Courts:** 40; 16 indoor
**Court Surfaces:** Hard
**Courts Lit For Night Play:** 16
**Director of Tennis:** Steve White          **Head Pro:** Steve White
**Instruction Rates:** $40 per hour/individual; group rates vary
**Court Time:** $15 per hour/day; $10 per hour/night
**Video Analysis:** None
**Ball Machines:** 2; $12 per half-hour
**Tournaments:** Concord Jr. Men's and Women's Invitational
**Tennis Packages:** Details not available at press time
**Comments:** "White keeps his players busy with lessons and tournament competition; Billie Jean King and Ilie Nastase give annual clinics and exhibitions."

### Accommodations

**Rooms:** 1,220
**Rooms With Water View:** 250
**Rates:** Not available at press time
**Type of Crowd:** Conventions, couples, families, singles, everyone
**Nearest Airport:** 90 minutes from LaGuardia International Airport; no shuttle service
**Comments:** "Lots of variety; Tower rooms are your best bet."

### Food

**Restaurants:** Main Dining Room (continental)
**Comments:** "Menus are varied but food is nothing special; get 'em in, get 'em out."

### Special Features

Two 18-hole golf courses; one 9-hole course; ice skating rink; basketball court; health club; horseback riding; miniature golf; indoor/outdoor pool; paddleboats.
**Nightlife:** Live entertainment in the Night Owl Lounge; attracts the best live shows and talent of any resort in the Catskills.

### Nearby Tourist Attractions

Apollo Mall; Sullivan County.

# MOUNT WASHINGTON HOTEL & RESORT, Route 302, Bretton Woods, New Hampshire 03575. (800) 258-0330, (603) 278-1000

### *Tennis*

**Courts:** 12
**Court Surfaces:** Clay
**Courts Lit For Night Play:** 1
**Director of Tennis:** Tom Over        **Head Pro:** Tom Over
**Instruction Rates:** $10 per hour/individual; group rates vary
**Court Time:** No charge
**Video Analysis:** None
**Ball Machines:** None
**Tournaments:** None
**Tennis Packages:** Details not available at press time
**Comments:** "Over has worked with the best, including Rod Laver, Marty Riessen and Tom Okker."

### *Accommodations*

**Rooms:** 200
**Rooms With Water View:** None
**Rates:** Start from $85 per person, per night, double occupancy; no charge for children 5 and under with parents
**Type of Crowd:** Couples, families
**Nearest Airport:** 2 1/2 hours from Boston's Logan International Airport; no shuttle service
**Comments:** "Vast array of room choices, from Victorian inn to town houses."

### *Food*

**Restaurants:** Stickneys (continental), The Main Dining Room (continental), The Bretton Arms (American), Darby's (continental), Fabian's (continental)
**Comments:** "The Main Dining Room has gorgeous views and good food to go with them."

### *Special Features*

Dancing to orchestra in grand ballroom; 18-hole golf course; national historic landmark.
**Nightlife:** Entertainment in The Cave.

### *Nearby Tourist Attractions*

The Cog Railroad; shopping in North Conway.

# NEW SEABURY, Box A, New Seabury, Massachusetts 02649. (800) 752-9700, (508) 477-9400

*Tennis*

**Courts:** 16
**Court Surfaces:** All-weather
**Courts Lit For Night Play:** None
**Director of Tennis:** Buzz Friend    **Head Pro:** Buzz Friend
**Instruction Rates:** $35 per hour/individual; group rates vary
**Court Time:** $12 per hour
**Video Analysis:** None
**Ball Machines:** 1; included in court time rate
**Tournaments:** None
**Tennis Packages:** Tennis Anyone starts from $75 per person, per night, double occupancy for 3 days/2 nights, including one hour of daily court time.
**Comments:** "Cape Cod's largest tennis facility; courts are shielded from ocean breezes and terraced on both sides of club."

*Accommodations*

**Rooms:** 100 villas at Maushop; 30 suites at Tidewatch; 40 patio villas at The Mews
**Rooms With Water View:** 45
**Rates:** Start from $80 per room, per night, double occupancy; no charge for extra person in room
**Type of Crowd:** Couples, families
**Nearest Airport:** 30 minutes from Hyannis' Barnstable Municipal Airport; free shuttle service
**Comments:** "Huge complex on 2,200-acre peninsula; villas set up to look like Nantucket fishing village."

*Food*

**Restaurants:** The Player's Club (continental), The Popponesset Inn (continental), The Marketplace Cafe (continental), The Raw Bar (seafood)
**Comments:** "Romantic beachfront dining at Popponesset Inn; raw bar and cafe in The Marketplace Cafe."

*Special Features*

Two 18-hole golf courses; country club.
**Nightlife:** Entertainment in The Player's Club.

*Nearby Tourist Attractions*

Sandwich Plantation; Martha's Vineyard; scenic Route 6A; The Woodstable.

# OCEAN EDGE RESORT & CONFERENCE CENTER,
Route 6A, Brewster, Massachusetts 02631. (800) 321–1837, (508) 896–2781

### *Tennis*

**Courts:** 11
**Court Surfaces:** 6 Plexipave, 5 Har-Tru
**Courts Lit For Night Play:** None
**Director of Tennis:** Scott Stetler    **Head Pro:** Steve Kajander
**Instruction Rates:** $32 per hour/individual; group rates vary
**Court Time:** $12 per hour
**Video Analysis:** None
**Ball Machines:** 2; $5 per hour
**Tournaments:** None
**Tennis Packages:** None
**Comments:** "If you want to learn the game, this is the place to play; pros are strongly committed to instruction."

### *Accommodations*

**Rooms:** 250
**Rooms With Water View:** None
**Rates:** Start from $105 per room, per night, double occupancy; no charge for children 18 and under
**Type of Crowd:** Couples, families, groups
**Nearest Airport:** 20 minutes from Hyannis' Barnstable Municipal Airport; shuttle service $10 per person, each way
**Comments:** "Pristine environment; condos scattered around golf course."

### *Food*

**Restaurants:** Villages (family), Mulligan's (grill), Ocean Grill (gourmet)
**Comments:** "Award-winning executive chef oversees dining facilities and it shows."

### *Special Features*

18-hole golf course; conference facilities; Olympic-sized outdoor pool; new swim center; deep-sea fishing.
**Nightlife:** Entertainment in Bayzo's Lounge.

### *Nearby Tourist Attractions*

Whale watching; Provincetown; Cape Cod National Seashore; Cape Cod Art Museum.

# THE OMNI SAGAMORE, 110 Sagamore Road, Bolton Landing, New York 12814. (800) 358-3585, (518) 644-9400

## *Tennis*

**Courts:** 6; 2 indoor
**Court Surfaces:** 2 Har-Tru, 2 hard (outdoor), 2 hard (indoor)
**Courts Lit For Night Play:** All
**Director of Tennis:** Bud York          **Head Pro:** Bud York
**Instruction Rates:** $40 per hour/individual; group rates vary
**Court Time:** $15 per hour
**Video Analysis:** Available in tennis clinics
**Ball Machines:** 1; $25 per hour
**Tournaments:** None
**Tennis Packages:** None
**Comments:** "Expanded pro shop; round-robin tournaments are a favorite with the guests."

## *Accommodations*

**Rooms:** 350; 100 at hotel, 240 at lodge, 10 at executive retreat
**Rooms With Water View:** 175
**Rates:** Start from $156 per room, per night, double occupancy; no charge for children 2 and under with parents
**Type of Crowd:** Conventions, couples, families
**Nearest Airport:** 75 minutes from Albany County Airport; shuttle service $55 per couple, each way
**Comments:** "The Victorian-style lakeview suites at the hotel are your best bet."

## *Food*

**Restaurants:** The Trillium (gourmet), The Club Grill (continental), The Sagamore Dining Room (continental), Dr. Brown's (American)
**Comments:** "You can't go wrong at any of the dining facilities, but don't leave without trying The Trillium; first rate, all."

## *Special Features*

70-acre island resort on Lake George in the heart of the Adirondack Mountains; 18-hole golf course; children's program.
**Nightlife:** Entertainment in The Verandah.

## *Nearby Tourist Attractions*

Lake George shopping; town of Bolton Landing; Adirondack Mountains.

# STRATTON MOUNTAIN INN, Stratton, Vermont 05155. (800) 843–6867, (802) 297–2200

## *Tennis*

**Courts:** 19
**Court Surfaces:** 9 Deco-Turf, 8 Har-Tru, 2 hard
**Courts Lit For Night Play:** 2
**Director of Tennis:** Kelly Gunterman    **Head Pro:** Kelly Gunterman
**Instruction Rates:** $45 per hour/individual; group rates vary
**Court Time:** $15 per hour
**Video Analysis:** Included in individual instruction
**Ball Machines:** 1; $10 per hour
**Tournaments:** None
**Tennis Packages:** The Weekend Stratton Tennis School starts from $295 per person, double occupancy for 3 days/2 nights, including ten hours of instruction, use of sports center and lunch daily.
**Comments:** "Spectacular mountain setting; great deal on tennis package."

## *Accommodations*

**Rooms:** 125
**Rooms With Water View:** None
**Rates:** Start from $69 per room, per night, double occupancy; no charge for children 18 and under with parents
**Type of Crowd:** Couples, families
**Nearest Airport:** 90 minutes from Albany Airport; no shuttle service
**Comments:** "Nicely decorated; good views; very reasonably priced."

## *Food*

**Restaurants:** Cafe Applause (continental)
**Comments:** "Fun atmosphere and good food—what else can you ask for?"

## *Special Features*

Self-contained village resort; sports center; 27 holes of golf designed by Geoffrey Cornish.
**Nightlife:** Entertainment in Cafe Applause.

## *Nearby Tourist Attractions*

Hildene; Manchester shopping village; town of Westin.

# SUGARBUSH RESORT, Warren, Vermont 05674. (800) 451–4320, (802) 583–2301

## *Tennis*

**Courts:**  35; 5 indoor
**Court Surfaces:**  19 Har-Tru, 11 hard, 5 red clay
**Courts Lit For Night Play:**  None
**Director of Tennis:**  Larry Abrams          **Head Pro:**  Larry Abrams
**Instruction Rates:**  $44 per hour/individual; group rates vary
**Court Time:**  $12 per hour/indoor; $10 per hour/outdoor
**Video Analysis:**  Included in individual instruction rate
**Ball Machines:**  6; $4 per hour
**Tournaments:**  None
**Tennis Packages:**  Details not available at press time
**Comments:**  "Abrams is on the ball with various programs designed to please players of all levels; huge complex allows for plenty of court time; weekly packages for seniors, juniors and children are worth looking into."

## *Accommodations*

**Rooms:**  108
**Rooms With Water View:**  None
**Rates:**  Start from $90 per night, per room; no charge for children 12 years old and under with parents.
**Type of Crowd:**  Couples, families
**Nearest Airport:**  50 minutes from Burlington International Airport, no shuttle service
**Comments:**  "Some deluxe rooms in the gate house with sitting rooms; condos are private, with sun decks."

## *Food*

**Restaurants:**  Onion Patch (burgers), The Colonial Dining Room (continental), The Terrace Room (continental)
**Comments:**  "The Onion Patch is cute and cozy; service can be as formal as you wish; competent chef."

## *Special Features*

18-hole golf course; outdoor/indoor swimming pool; sports center; children's program.
**Nightlife:**  Entertainment in the Onion Patch.

## *Nearby Tourist Attractions*

Ben & Jerry's Plant; Shelburne Museum; Lake Champlain.

# TENNIS VILLAGE, P.O. Box 623, West Dover, Vermont 05356. (802) 464-5773

### Tennis

**Courts:** 10
**Court Surfaces:** 9 clay, 1 Mateflex
**Courts Lit For Night Play:** 1
**Director of Tennis:** Tom Doshna    **Head Pro:** Tom Doshna
**Instruction Rates:** $20 per hour/individual; group rates vary
**Court Time:** No charge
**Video Analysis:** $10 per hour
**Ball Machines:** 1; no charge
**Tournaments:** None
**Tennis Packages:** None
**Comments:** "Each home comes with its own court; there's a pro on hand from mid-June through Labor Day."

### Accommodations

**Rooms:** 10 custom luxury homes
**Rooms With Water View:** None
**Rates:** Start from $475 per home for 3 nights (1–8 people)
**Type of Crowd:** Couples, families, groups
**Nearest Airport:** 75 minutes from Keene (New Hampshire) Airport; no shuttle service
**Comments:** "Houses have five to ten bedrooms each; some have saunas, an indoor pool and a solarium; condos share two courts, but court time is never a problem."

### Food

**Restaurants:** None; all units have completely equipped kitchens

### Special Features

Units set up in woods offer up to 7,000 square feet of living space; lots of privacy; fishing; boating; three 18-hole golf courses nearby.
**Nightlife:** Local clubs at nearby Mount Snow village.

### Nearby Tourist Attractions

Mount Snow skiing; town of West Dover.

## TOPNOTCH AT STOWE, Box 1458, Stowe, Vermont 05672. (800) 451-8686, (802) 253-8585

### Tennis

**Courts:** 14; 4 indoor
**Court Surfaces:** 8 Deco-Turf, 4 Deco-Turf II, 2 clay
**Courts Lit For Night Play:** 4
**Director of Tennis:** Lori Zacharius-Verdi
**Head Pro:** Lori Zacharius-Verdi
**Instruction Rates:** $44 per hour/individual; group rates vary
**Court Time:** $15 per hour/indoor; $10 per hour/outdoor
**Video Analysis:** Included in tennis package
**Ball Machines:** 2; $22 per hour
**Tournaments:** None
**Tennis Packages:** The Tennis Camp starts from $110 per person, per night, double occupancy for 4 days/3 nights, including two hours of daily clinics, unlimited court time and use of ball machine.
**Comments:** "First-rate instruction; can't go wrong here if you want to improve your game, and not just hit."

### Accommodations

**Rooms:** 107
**Rooms With Water View:** None
**Rates:** Start from $87 per person, per night, double occupancy, including breakfast and dinner daily; no charge for children 12 and under with parents
**Type of Crowd:** Couples, families
**Nearest Airport:** 40 minutes from Burlington International Airport; no shuttle service
**Comments:** "Every detail attended to, from private stock of books to imported toiletries; more elegant than most of its competitors."

### Food

**Restaurants:** The Dining Room (continental), Evergreens (spa cuisine), The Buttertub (bar menu)
**Comments:** "For those watching their calories, try Evergreens."

### Special Features

Hydromassage; art studio; health spa.
**Nightlife:** Entertainment in Buttertub Lounge.

### Nearby Tourist Attractions

Ben & Jerry's Plant; The Alpine Slide; Cold Hollow Cider Mill; Stowe village.

# THE VILLAGES AT KILLINGTON, P.O. Box 05751, Killington, Vermont 05751. (800) 343–0762, (802) 422–3101

## *Tennis*

**Courts:**  8
**Court Surfaces:**  4 clay, 4 Har-Tru
**Courts Lit For Night Play:**  5
**Director of Tennis:**  Barry Stout        **Head Pro:**  Barry Stout
**Instruction Rates:**  $35 per hour/individual; group rates vary
**Court Time:**  $30 per hour/individual; group rates vary
**Video Analysis:**  Included in tennis clinics
**Ball Machines:**  8; $20 per hour
**Tournaments:**  None
**Tennis Packages:**  The Killington School for Tennis starts from $349 per person, double occupancy for 2 days/2 nights, including use of ball machine, video analysis and breakfast and dinner daily.
**Comments:**  "Well-respected tennis school; courts are carefully groomed; the school is separate from the resort and they make a big deal about this."

## *Accommodations*

**Rooms:**  700 condominiums
**Rooms With Water View:**  None
**Rates:**  Start from $64 per room, per night, double occupancy; no charge for extra person staying in room
**Type of Crowd:**  Couples, families, groups
**Nearest Airport:**  30 minutes from Rutland Airport; no shuttle service
**Comments:**  "There are more attractive places to stay in the area, but the tennis program here is terrific."

## *Food*

**Restaurants:**  Pogonips (American)
**Comments:**  "Pogonips in base lodge is delightful; it better be since there's not much else."

## *Special Features*

Live summer theater; biggest ski area in Northeast.
**Nightlife:**  Surprisingly none.

## *Nearby Tourist Attractions*

Norman Rockwell Museum; Simon Pearce Glass Blowers; Hilden Estate in Manchester.

# THE WOODSTOCK INN & RESORT, 14 The Green, Woodstock, Vermont 05091. (800) 448-7900, (802) 457-1100

### Tennis

**Courts:** 12; 2 indoor
**Court Surfaces:** 6 clay, 6 Deco-Turf
**Courts Lit For Night Play:** None
**Director of Tennis:** Rob Purdy        **Head Pro:** Rob Purdy
**Instruction Rates:** $42 per hour/individual; group rates vary
**Court Time:** $11.50 per person per hour
**Video Analysis:** Included in individual instruction rate
**Ball Machines:** 2; add $6 to court time rate
**Tournaments:** None
**Tennis Packages:** The Sportscenter Tennis Plan starts from $153 per person, double occupancy for 3 days/2 nights, including unlimited court time, use of ball machine, half-hour private lesson and use of sports center.
**Comments:** "Private lessons are highly recommended if you want to learn the game while getting a great workout."

### Accommodations

**Rooms:** 143; 3 town houses
**Rooms With Water View:** None
**Rates:** Start from $125 per room, per night, double occupancy; no charge for children 14 and under with parents
**Type of Crowd:** Couples, families
**Nearest Airport:** 20 minutes from Lebanon (New Hampshire) Airport; no shuttle service
**Comments:** "Beds covered with handmade quilts; large guest rooms."

### Food

**Restaurants:** The Main Dining Room (American), The Eagle Cafe (continental), Fireside Lounge (continental), Courtside Lounge (continental)
**Comments:** "Elegant Main Dining Room offers quality New England cuisine; elaborate luncheon buffet shouldn't be missed; extensive wine list; most popular spot in town."

### Special Features

Colonial New England town; eighteenth-century tavern; horseback riding; croquet.
**Nightlife:** Music in The Main Dining Room.

### Nearby Tourist Attractions

Billings Farm and Museum; Simon Pearce Glass Blowers; Woodstock shopping village.

# 6

# CANADA

Canada's cold climate confines most tennis resort activity to the summers (indoor courts are rare). So it is no surprise that Canadian resorts have steered clear of tennis. After all, this is hockey and ski country, aye!

Although there are not a large number of Canadian tennis resorts, the best ones do have excellent tennis facilities. And only three such resorts made it into this book: **Gray Rocks Inn** in Quebec, **The Inn at Manitou** in Ontario, and **Jasper Park Lodge** in Alberta. Sorry, that's all she wrote.

# GRAY ROCKS INN, CP 1000, St. Jovite, Quebec, Canada JOT 280. (800) 567-6767, (819) 425-2771

## *Tennis*

**Courts:** 22
**Court Surfaces:** Har-Tru
**Courts Lit For Night Play:** None
**Director of Tennis:** Stan Gendron          **Head Pro:** Stan Gendron
**Instruction Rates:** $27 per hour/individual; group rates vary
**Court Time:** $7 per hour
**Video Analysis:** No charge
**Ball Machines:** 6; $17 per hour
**Tournaments:** None
**Tennis Packages:** The Tennis Week starts from $580 per person, double occupancy for 6 days/5 nights, including twenty hours of instruction, use of health club and three meals daily.
**Comments:** "A staff of 28 pros boasts an extensive junior program."

## *Accommodations*

**Rooms:** 300
**Rooms With Water View:** 125
**Rates:** Start from $90 per room, per night, double occupancy; no charge for children 2 and under with parents
**Type of Crowd:** Couples, families
**Nearest Airport:** 90 minutes from Montreal's Dorval International Airport; no shuttle service
**Comments:** "A well-established family resort that caters to kids, yet you can go there as a couple alone and not feel like you are stepping over them."

## *Food*

**Restaurants:** The Main Dining Room (American); Ladoeceur (French)
**Comments:** "Generous portions of average resort fare."

## *Special Features*

Snow Eagle Ski School; 18-hole golf course; horseback riding; white-water rafting; indoor pool; all boating activities; health club.
**Nightlife:** Piano playing in the Sunset Room.

## *Nearby Tourist Attractions*

Monttremblant Village; Ottawa; Montreal.

## THE INN AT MANITOU, 251 Davenport Road, Toronto, Ontario, Canada M54 1J9. (416) 967-3466, (212) 772-0594

### Tennis

**Courts:** 13; 1 indoor
**Court Surfaces:** Plexipave
**Courts Lit For Night Play:** 1
**Director of Tennis:** Ed Bakker    **Head Pro:** Ed Bakker
**Instruction Rates:** $44 per hour/individual; group rates vary
**Court Time:** No charge
**Video Analysis:** No charge
**Ball Machines:** 2; no charge
**Tournaments:** None
**Tennis Packages:** Start from $560 per person, double occupancy for 4 days/3 nights, including three hours of clinics daily, individual instruction, tournaments, nightly exhibition matches and use of health club.
**Comments:** "Daily clinics as well as unlimited individual instruction; staff of fourteen pros play exhibition matches every evening."

### Accommodations

**Rooms:** 32 chalets
**Rooms With Water View:** 22
**Rates:** Start from $120 per person, per night, double occupancy. Includes breakfast and lunch; no charge for children 6 and under with parents
**Type of Crowd:** Conventions, couples, families
**Nearest Airport:** 2 1/2 hours from Toronto International Airport; limousine service $250 per car, each way
**Comments:** "Has all the comforts of home; ideal for families or a group of friends who want to get away; a tad on the costly side."

### Food

**Restaurants:** The Main Dining Room (French)
**Comments:** "Expensive gourmet cuisine with an extensive wine list."

### Special Features

Jacuzzis; sauna; masseuse; sailing; water skiing; canoeing; conference center.
**Nightlife:** Dancing in The Lounge.

### Nearby Tourist Attractions

Ontario Science Museum; "30,000 Island" cruise; Stratford Shakespeare Festival.

# JASPER PARK LODGE, Box 80, Jasper, Alberta, Canada POE 1EO. (800) 268-9411, (403) 852-3301

## *Tennis*

**Courts:** 4
**Court Surfaces:** Plexipave
**Courts Lit For Night Play:** None
**Director of Tennis:** Frank James    **Head Pro:** Frank James
**Instruction Rates:** $15 per hour/individual; group rates vary
**Court Time:** No charge
**Video Analysis:** Included in tennis clinics
**Ball Machines:** None
**Tournaments:** None
**Tennis Packages:** None
**Comments:** "Not a serious tennis resort by any stretch, but who cares—the surroundings more than compensate, and there's nothing else for literally hundreds of miles."

## *Accommodations*

**Rooms:** 400
**Rooms With Water View:** 390
**Rates:** Start from $125 per room, per night, double occupancy; no charge for children 17 and under with parents
**Type of Crowd:** Couples, families
**Nearest Airport:** 4 hours from Edmonton International Airport; no shuttle service
**Comments:** "A sprawling, rustic lodge in 900-acre Jasper National Park; gorgeous mountain views; scenery is heavenly."

## *Food*

**Restaurants:** Edith Cavell Room (French), The Beauvert (continental), The Moose's Nook (continental), The Meadows Cafe (continental)
**Comments:** "Connoisseurs of fine French cuisine should not miss the new Edith Cavell Room."

## *Special Features*

Hiking; seven lakes; 18-hole golf course; horseback riding; lakeside swimming pool; croquet.
**Nightlife:** Live entertainment in Tent City.

## *Nearby Tourist Attractions*

Maligne Canyon; Pyramid Lake; Maligne Lake.

# 7

# THE NORTHWEST

The Northwest, known for its national parks, big-game hunting, fishing, and white-water rafting, will appeal to the adventurous traveler who isn't interested in a tennis-only vacation. There are few resorts to choose from, much less bona fide tennis resorts. But we did find three gems, places that rival any in this book: **Elkhorn Resort** and **Sun Valley Lodge** in Sun Valley, Idaho, and **Sunriver Lodge & Resort** in Sunriver, Oregon.

## ELKHORN RESORT, P.O. Box 6009, Sun Valley, Idaho 83354. (800) 632–4101, (800) 635–4356, (208) 622–4511

### *Tennis*

**Courts:** 18
**Court Surfaces:** Laykold
**Courts Lit For Night Play:** None
**Director of Tennis:** Bill Van Dyne       **Head Pro:** Bill Van Dyne
**Instruction Rates:** $35 per hour/individual; group rates vary
**Court Time:** No charge
**Video Analysis:** Included in tennis clinics
**Ball Machines:** 1; No charge
**Tournaments:** None
**Tennis Packages:** None
**Comments:** "Tennis clinics include adult programs, men's and women's leagues, round-robin tournaments and junior and tiny-tot programs."

### *Accommodations*

**Rooms:** 220
**Rooms With Water View:** None
**Rates:** Start from $68 per room, per night, double occupancy; no charge for children 12 and under with parents
**Type of Crowd:** Couples, families
**Nearest Airport:** 25 minutes from Hailey's Sun Valley Airport; free shuttle service
**Comments:** "Major re-modeling has added a touch of class to this top-notch resort."

### *Food*

**Restaurants:** The Clubhouse (American), Dino's (Italian), Tequilla Joe's (Mexican), Jesse's (steak and seafood)
**Comments:** "Jesse's is a must for all seafood lovers; for good Mexican food, try Tequilla Joe's."

### *Special Features*

Children's day camp; jazz and classical concerts; ballet; five swimming pools; rock climbing; 18-hole golf course.
**Nightlife:** Live entertainment in The Lobby Lounge. (and you know how hip those lobby lounges can be—especially in Idaho).

### *Nearby Tourist Attractions*

River rafting; Ore Wagon Museum; Sun Valley skiing; Silver Creek Preserve.

# SUN VALLEY LODGE, Sun Valley Road, Sun Valley, Idaho 83353. (800) 786-8259, (800) 632-4104

## *Tennis*

**Courts:** 18
**Court Surfaces:** Hard
**Courts Lit For Night Play:** None
**Director of Tennis:** Jack Crawford    **Head Pro:** Jack Crawford
**Instruction Rates:** $34 per hour/individual; group rates vary
**Court Time:** $6 per person per hour/singles; $3 per person per hour/doubles
**Video Analysis:** $10 per hour
**Ball Machines:** 2; $20 per hour
**Tournaments:** None
**Tennis Packages:** None
**Comments:** "Tennis club has gorgeous view of mountains; Crawford provides good instruction for all players."

## *Accommodations*

**Rooms:** 600
**Rooms With Water View:** None
**Rates:** Start from $55 per room, per night, double occupancy; no charge for children 17 and under with parents
**Type of Crowd:** Couples, families
**Nearest Airport:** 20 minutes from Hailey's Sun Valley Airport; free shuttle service
**Comments:** "Luxurious and affordable lodging in a casual atmosphere."

## *Food*

**Restaurants:** The Lodge Dining Room (elegant), Gretchens (continental), Konditorei (American), Ore House (steakhouse), The Ram Restaurant (American), Continental Cafe (continental)
**Comments:** "Try The Lodge Dining Room—marble stairs, crystal chandeliers, white linens and candles, all overlooking the Bald Mountains."

## *Special Features*

Children's ice-skating program; golf course; horseback riding; babysitting service.
**Nightlife:** Live entertainment in The Ram Bar.

## *Nearby Tourist Attractions*

River rafting; hiking; Sawtooth National Recreation Area.

# SUNRIVER LODGE & RESORT, P.O. Box 3609, Sunriver, Oregon 97707. (800) 962-1770, (503) 593-1221

*Tennis*

**Courts:** 31; 3 indoor
**Court Surfaces:** Plexipave
**Courts Lit For Night Play:** 3
**Director of Tennis:** Larry Hunter **Head Pro:** Gary Jones
**Instruction Rates:** $35 per hour/individual; group rates vary
**Court Time:** No charge
**Video Analysis:** Included in tennis clinics
**Ball Machines:** 1; $9 per hour
**Tournaments:** None
**Tennis Packages:** None
**Comments:** "Tennis pros run complete programs for juniors and adults."

*Accommodations*

**Rooms:** 320
**Rooms With Water View:** None
**Rates:** Start from $85 per room, per night, double occupancy; no charge for extra person staying in room
**Type of Crowd:** Conventions, couples, families
**Nearest Airport:** 40 minutes from Redmond/Bend Airport; no shuttle service
**Comments:** "All lodge-operated rooms have fireplaces and private decks; suites accommodate up to six people and have full kitchens."

*Food*

**Restaurants:** Meadows Dining Room (high desert cuisine), Provisions Company (family style)
**Comments:** "Try the Provisions Company for a cozy, family style atmosphere."

*Special Features*

Dry desert country with ponderosa pines; Cascade Mountain Range; horseback riding; bicycle paths; two 18-hole golf courses; children's program.
**Nightlife:** Live entertainment in Owl's Lounge.

*Nearby Tourist Attractions*

Mount Bachelor for skiing; High Desert Museum.

# 8

# THE SOUTHWEST

When you speak of tennis resorts in the Southwest, you are really talking about Arizona, and in particular Tucson, Phoenix, Scottsdale, and Sedona. Except for the odd resort in Santa Fe, New Mexico, or St. George, Utah—Arizona is where the action is.

Like the Southwest's southern counterparts, Florida to the east, and Palm Springs to the west, tennis is a major focus here. The sport excels not so much in the quantity as in the quality of tennis resorts, of which there are only perhaps ten or twelve. But these are all superior in terms of our five-criteria rating system, and a handful are world-class by any standard, such as the **Scottsdale Princess** and **The Phoenician.** And Arizona's sunsets alone are worth the trip.

Note: In this chapter, we included resorts that are farther north than what would technically be considered the Southwest.

## ARIZONA BILTMORE, 24th St. and Missouri Ave., Phoenix, Arizona 85016. (800) 528-3696, (602) 955-6600

### Tennis

**Courts:** 17
**Court Surfaces:** 14 asphalt, 3 Astro-Turf
**Courts Lit For Night Play:** 16
**Director of Tennis:** Lucky Cotten        **Head Pro:** Lucky Cotten
**Instruction Rates:** $45 per hour/individual; group rates vary
**Court Time:** $14 per hour
**Video Analysis:** $50 per half-hour
**Ball Machines:** 1; $15 per hour
**Tournaments:** None
**Tennis Packages:** Start from $318 per couple, per night, including one clinic and one hour of daily court time.
**Comments:** "Cotten knows how to manage a top tennis resort so that everyone is involved at all times."

### Accommodations

**Rooms:** 502
**Rooms With Water View:** None
**Rates:** Start from $210 per room, per night, double occupancy; no charge for children 18 and under with parents
**Type of Crowd:** Couples, families
**Nearest Airport:** 15 minutes from Phoenix Sky Harbor International Airport; no shuttle service
**Comments:** "Frank Lloyd Wright-inspired architecture is refreshing, with furnishings in rooms to match; bathrooms are oversized and unique."

### Food

**Restaurants:** Cafe Sonora (coffee shop), Orangeria (gourmet), The Gold Room (continental), Cabana Club (American)
**Comments:** "Cafe Sonora, with its casual home cooking, is wonderful for families."

### Special Features

Two 18-hole golf courses; three swimming pools; croquet; lawn chess.
**Nightlife:** Live entertainment in The Gold Room.

### Nearby Tourist Attractions

Biltmore Fashion Park; Phoenix Art Museum; Heard Museum; red rocks of Sedona; Grand Canyon.

# THE BROADMOOR, 1 Lake Ave., Colorado Springs, Colorado 80906. (800) 634-7711, (719) 634-7711

## Tennis

**Courts:** 16; 4 indoor
**Court Surfaces:** 13 Plexipave, 3 Master-Turf
**Courts Lit For Night Play:** 4
**Director of Tennis:** Bob Scott        **Head Pro:** Bob Scott
**Instruction Rates:** $35 per 45 minutes/individual; group rates vary
**Court Time:** $16 per hour
**Video Analysis:** None
**Ball Machines:** 1; $10 per hour
**Tournaments:** None
**Tennis Packages:** The Sporting Chance starts from $452 per couple, per night, including unlimited court time, use of ball machine, no green fees and use of golf cart.
**Comments:** "Scott is a solid, knowledgeable teacher who provides well-run clinics and junior/adult programs."

## Accommodations

**Rooms:** 550
**Rooms With Water View:** 250
**Rates:** Start from $210 per room, per night, double occupancy; no charge for children 12 and under with parents
**Type of Crowd:** Conventions, couples, families
**Nearest Airport:** 15 minutes from Colorado Springs Municipal Airport; shuttle service $15 per person, round trip
**Comments:** "Broadmoor rooms are old-world elegant, spacious and functional."

## Food

**Restaurants:** The Tavern (steak and seafood), The Penrose (continental), Charles Court (southwestern), Golf Club (American), Golden Bee (steak and seafood), Julie's (American), Lake Terrace Dining Room (American)
**Comments:** "Charles Court by the lake offers excellent service and food; others pale in comparison."

## Special Features

Children's program; 18-hole golf course; three squash courts; three swimming pools; paddleboats; Olympic ice-skating rink.
**Nightlife:** Nightly entertainment in the Golden Bee.

## Nearby Tourist Attractions

Pikes Peak; Air Force Academy.

# CHEYENNE MOUNTAIN, 3225 Broadmoor Valley Road, Colorado Springs, Colorado 80906. (800) 648–5717, (719) 576–4600

### Tennis

**Courts:** 18; 6 indoor
**Court Surfaces:** 16 Plexipave, 2 clay
**Courts Lit For Night Play:** 10
**Director of Tennis:** Richard Hillway          **Head Pro:** Richard Hillway
**Instruction Rates:** $36 per hour/individual; group rates vary
**Court Time:** $36 per 90 minutes/indoor; $24 per 90 minutes/outdoor
**Video Analysis:** None
**Ball Machines:** 2; $36 per hour including court fee
**Tournaments:** None
**Tennis Packages:** The Recreation Package starts from $85 per person, per night, double occupancy, including unlimited court time, breakfast daily, and use of country club.
**Comments:** "Hillway is the tennis historian of Colorado; he works well with children."

### Accommodations

**Rooms:** 268
**Rooms With Water View:** 156
**Rates:** Start from $170 per room, per night, double occupancy; no charge for children 12 and under with parents
**Type of Crowd:** Conventions, couples, families
**Nearest Airport:** 10 minutes from Colorado Springs Municipal Airport; shuttle service $8.50 per person, each way
**Comments:** "Rooms are clustered in lodge setting; clean and airy."

### Food

**Restaurants:** Remingtons (elegant), The Mountain View (American), The Pine View (American)
**Comments:** "Main dining room serves bountiful breakfast and lunch buffets; Remingtons is a five-star restaurant worth the hefty expense."

### Special Features

18-hole golf course; four swimming pools; squash and racquetball courts; fitness center; water sports on 35-acre lake.
**Nightlife:** Live entertainment in Remingtons Lounge.

### Nearby Tourist Attractions

Air Force Academy; Pikes Peak; Cog Railway; Olympic Training Center.

# MARRIOTT'S CAMELBACK INN, 5402 E. Lincoln Drive, Scottsdale, Arizona 85253. (800) 242-2635, (602) 948-1700

## Tennis

**Courts:** 10
**Court Surfaces:** 6 Plexipave, 4 Omni
**Courts Lit For Night Play:** 5
**Director of Tennis:** Brian Thorfinnson    **Head Pro:** Brian Thorfinnson
**Instruction Rates:** $45 per hour/individual; group rates vary
**Court Time:** $10 per hour
**Video Analysis:** Included in tennis clinics
**Ball Machines:** 1; $25 per hour
**Tournaments:** None
**Tennis Packages:** None
**Comments:** "Daily clinics and weekly guest tournaments; there's a serene feeling at Thorfinnson's tennis complex."

## Accommodations

**Rooms:** 423
**Rooms With Water View:** None
**Rates:** Start from $185 per room, per night, double occupancy; no charge for children 12 and under with parents
**Type of Crowd:** Couples, families
**Nearest Airport:** 20 minutes from Phoenix Sky Harbor International Airport; no shuttle service
**Comments:** "Luxurious rooms in a casual setting; private patios; kitchenettes."

## Food

**Restaurants:** The Chaparral (gourmet), Navajo Room (casual), Sprouts (spa cuisine), Golf Club (American)
**Comments:** "The art of home cooking has not been forgotten here; price is right; the Navajo Room has to be the best family dining experience in the Southwest."

## Special Features

Health spa; two 18-hole golf courses; children's program; two swimming pools.
**Nightlife:** Live entertainment in Chaparral Lounge.

## Nearby Tourist Attractions

Heard Museum; Frank Lloyd Wright School of Architecture and Engineering; Rawhide; downtown Scottsdale.

## THE PHOENICIAN, 6000 East Camelback Road, Scottsdale, Arizona 85251. (602) 941-8200

### Tennis

**Courts:** 11
**Court Surfaces:** Plexicushion
**Courts Lit For Night Play:** All
**Director of Tennis:** Yazdegerd "Yaz" Tavatl
**Head Pro:** Yazdegerd "Yaz" Tavatl
**Instruction Rates:** $60 per hour/individual; group rates vary
**Court Time:** $16 per hour/singles; $24 per hour/doubles
**Video Analysis:** $100 per hour
**Ball Machines:** 1; $20 per hour
**Tournaments:** None
**Tennis Packages:** Start from $1,070 per couple, for 4 days/3 nights, including unlimited court time, daily clinic, one can of balls, half-hour evaluation of game, half-hour video analysis, half-hour private lesson, one hour use of ball machine, unlimited use of health and beauty spa and three full breakfasts.
**Comments:** "Yaz is an international teacher who has brought state-of-the-art tennis to the desert."

### Accommodations

**Rooms:** 580
**Rooms With Water View:** 177
**Rates:** Start from $270 per room, per night, double occupancy; no charge for children 12 and under with parents
**Type of Crowd:** Couples, families
**Nearest Airport:** 15 minutes from Phoenix Sky Harbor International Airport; no shuttle service
**Comments:** "Nothing is spared in luxury; rooms feature McGuire Rattan furniture."

### Food

**Restaurants:** Mary Elaines (gourmet), Terrace Dining Room (continental), Windows on the Green (southwestern), Oasis (American), Cafe (snack shop)
**Comments:** "From gourmet French to hamburgers at the golf course, the Phoenician is a delightful place to dine; pricey, but wonderful."

### Special Features

$25-million art collection; 18-hole golf course; health club; tiered swimming pool tiled in mother-of-pearl; water slide.
**Nightlife:** Live entertainment in The Thirsty Camel.

### Nearby Tourist Attractions

Grand Canyon; Heard Museum; Desert Botanical Garden.

# RANCHO ENCANTADO, Route 4, Box 57C, Santa Fe, New Mexico 87501. (505) 982–3537

## Tennis

**Courts:** 2
**Court Surfaces:** Plexipave
**Courts Lit For Night Play:** None
**Director of Tennis:** Sonny Martinez    **Head Pro:** Sonny Martinez
**Instruction Rates:** $30 per hour/individual; group rates vary
**Court Time:** $10 per hour/singles; $16 per hour/doubles
**Video Analysis:** None
**Ball Machines:** 1; $5 per hour
**Tournaments:** None
**Tennis Packages:** None
**Comments:** "Martinez grew up in Santa Fe and takes pride in his teaching; good private instruction."

## Accommodations

**Rooms:** 72
**Rooms With Water View:** None
**Rates:** Start from $175 per room, per night, double occupancy; no charge for children 2 and under with parents
**Type of Crowd:** Families; couples
**Nearest Airport:** 90 minutes from Albuquerque International Airport; no shuttle service
**Comments:** "Robert Redford calls the Ranch home, and it's easy to see why: casitas are charming and come complete with kiva fireplaces and tiled bathrooms."

## Food

**Restaurants:** Rancho Encantado (continental)
**Comments:** "Absolutely delicious; popular with the locals (that's how you know its good)."

## Special Features

Horse ranch; fishing; cantina with big screen cable TV; game room; hiking trails; children's program.
**Nightlife:** Entertainment nightly in Rancho Encantado.

## Nearby Tourist Attractions

Santa Fe; downtown Plaza; Bandalier National Monument; Taos Pueblo.

# THE REGISTRY RESORT, 7171 N. Scottsdale Road, Scottsdale, Arizona 85253. (800) 247–9810, (602) 991–3800

## *Tennis*

**Courts:** 21
**Court Surfaces:** 20 Plexipave, 1 western red clay
**Courts Lit For Night Play:** All
**Director of Tennis:** Chris Cummings    **Head Pro:** Chris Cummings
**Instruction Rates:** $40 per hour/individual; group rates vary
**Court Time:** $15 per hour
**Video Analysis:** Add $10 to instruction rate
**Ball Machines:** 3; $20 per hour
**Tournaments:** Junior Fiesta Bowl Championships
**Tennis Packages:** Deluxe tennis package starts from $210 per person, double occupancy for 3 days/2 nights, including unlimited court time, three-hour daily clinic and breakfast daily.
**Comments:** "Great staff provides thorough instruction for all ages."

## *Accommodations*

**Rooms:** 318
**Rooms With Water View:** None
**Rates:** Start from $170 per room, per night, double occupancy; no charge for children 12 and under with parents
**Type of Crowd:** Conventions, couples, families
**Nearest Airport:** 5 minutes from Scottsdale Airport; free shuttle service
**Comments:** "Small rooms but luxurious; 2-story town houses are best bet for families; located right in downtown Scottsdale."

## *Food*

**Restaurants:** La Champagne (southwestern), Cafe Brioche (continental)
**Comments:** "La Champagne caters to the discerning palate; chef willingly makes dietary adjustments."

## *Special Features*

Victorian lobby; three swimming pools; two 18-hole golf courses; health club; high tea.
**Nightlife:** Piano playing in the Fountain Lounge.

## *Nearby Tourist Attractions*

Scottsdale Fashion Square; jeep tours; Heard Museum.

# SCOTTSDALE PRINCESS, 7575 East Princess Drive, Scottsdale, Arizona 85255. (800) 244–4758, (602) 585–4848

## *Tennis*

**Courts:** 9; including 10,000-seat stadium court
**Court Surfaces:** Hard
**Courts Lit For Night Play:** 6
**Director of Tennis:** Andrew Pattison          **Head Pro:** Andrew Pattison
**Instruction Rates:** $65 per hour/individual; group rates vary
**Court Time:** $15 per hour
**Video Analysis:** $50 per hour
**Ball Machines:** 1; $18 per hour
**Tournaments:** Eagle Classic of Scottsdale
**Tennis Packages:** Royal Escapade tennis package starts from $352 per person, for 3 days/2 nights, including unlimited court time, two hours of instruction, one hour use of ball machine, video analysis and use of health club.
**Comments:** "Pattison, a former world Top Twenty player, has all the bases covered at this fabulous tennis spot."

## *Accommodations*

**Rooms:** 600
**Rooms With Water View:** None
**Rates:** Start from $190 per room, per night, double occupancy; no charge for children 12 and under with parents
**Type of Crowd:** Couples, families, older crowd
**Nearest Airport:** 30 minutes from Phoenix Sky Harbor International Airport; no shuttle service
**Comments:** "The casitas embody luxury and elegance combined with warmth and comfort; get a casita near the main lobby."

## *Food*

**Restaurants:** La Hacienda (Mexican), Marquesa (gourmet), The Grill (American), Las Ventanas (coffee shop)
**Comments:** "The food and presentation are spectacular; you can't get any better than La Hacienda for Mexican food and the tequila–shot waitress."

## *Special Features*

Two 18-hole golf courses; health club; racquetball courts; hot-air balloon rides; three swimming pools.
**Nightlife:** None.

## *Nearby Tourist Attractions*

Cave Creek; Crefree; Frank Lloyd Wright School; Fleischer Museum.

# 9

# CALIFORNIA

Like Arizona, when you speak of tennis resorts in California, you are back in the desert again. Yes, the wine country of Northern California, such as Sonoma Valley and Napa Valley, has a few jewels—mainly small, exclusive bed and breakfasts. And there are a couple of gems between Carmel and Los Angeles. San Diego is represented well with **Rancho Bernardo Inn** and the elite **Hotel Del Coronado**, where President George Bush and his sons play tennis.

But for many travelers and most Californians—celebrities included—the quest for year-long tennis begins and ends in Palm Springs. Once a lone shimmering jewel in the vast desert, Palm Springs and Mayor Sonny Bono now have some company: **Rancho Mirage, Indian Wells, Palm Desert**, and **La Quinta**. All of these desert resort communities are in thick competition for your vacation dollar, because in this part of the country, tennis is a way of life.

# CARMEL VALLEY RANCH RESORT, 1 Old Ranch Road, Carmel, California 93923. (800) 4–CARMEL, (408) 625–9500

## *Tennis*

**Courts:** 12
**Court Surfaces:** Har-Tru
**Courts Lit For Night Play:** None
**Director of Tennis:** Bobby McGomery          **Head Pro:** Bobby McGomery
**Instruction Rates:** $36 per day/individual; group rates vary
**Court Time:** $10 per day
**Video Analysis:** None
**Ball Machines:** None
**Tournaments:** None
**Tennis Packages:** None
**Comments:** "Remodeled Spanish-style clubhouse dates back to 1895; pleasant atmosphere for a tennis game."

## *Accommodations*

**Rooms:** 100
**Rooms With Water View:** None
**Rates:** Start from $225 per room, per night, double occupancy; no charge for children 16 and under with parents
**Type of Crowd:** Families, groups
**Nearest Airport:** 15 minutes from Monterey Peninsula Airport; free shuttle service
**Comments:** "Suites are luxurious; all have woodburning fireplaces, authentic Amish bed quilts and oversized private decks."

## *Food*

**Restaurants:** The Dining Room (gourmet), Golf Dining Room (American), Tennis Dining Room (American)
**Comments:** "Sumptuous fare in The Dining Room; wine list of award-winning stature."

## *Special Features*

1,700-acre resort; 18-hole golf course; two swimming pools.
**Nightlife:** Entertainment nightly in The Lounge.

## *Nearby Tourist Attractions*

Carmel-by-the-Sea; Monterey Bay Aquarium; Cannery Row; Big Sur; downtown Carmel.

# HYATT GRAND CHAMPIONS, 44-600 Indian Wells Lane, Indian Wells, California 92210. (800) 228-9000, (619) 341-1000

## *Tennis*

**Courts:** 12
**Court Surfaces:** 8 hard, 6 grass, 6 clay
**Courts Lit For Night Play:** 8
**Director of Tennis:** Ray Moore     **Head Pro:** Greg Felich
**Instruction Rates:** $50 per hour/individual; group rates vary
**Court Time:** $30 per court per hour (grass and clay), $15 per hour per court (hard)
**Video Analysis:** Included academy program
**Ball Machines:** 2; $12 per hour
**Tournaments:** Newsweek Champions Cup; ATP Senior Tournament; ATP Challenger Series; Adidas Invitational
**Tennis Packages:** Tennis Stay and Play starts from $170 per room, per night, double occupancy, including unlimited tennis on all court surfaces and use of health and fitness center.
**Comments:** "The Hyatt Grand Champions Tennis Academy is a must for those who want to improve their game; Moore and staff provide students with a variety of programs including daily clinics, lectures, video analysis and programmable ball machines."

## *Accommodations*

**Rooms:** 336
**Rooms With Water View:** 105
**Rates:** Start from $180 per room, per night, double occupancy; no charge for children 18 and under with parents
**Type of Crowd:** Couples, families
**Nearest Airport:** 20 minutes from Palm Springs Airport; no shuttle service
**Comments:** "Not quite up to five-star standards; regency club rooms are your best bet."

## *Food*

**Restaurants:** Trattoria (Italian), Charlie's (southwest grill), Jasmine (Oriental)
**Comments:** "Charlie's, serving innovative California cuisine, is by far your best choice."

## *Special Features*

Children's program; health and fitness center; 36 holes of golf; two spas.
**Nightlife:** Live entertainment at Pianissimo Lounge.

## *Nearby Tourist Attractions*

Palm Springs Museum; McCallum Theater; Living Desert Reserve; hot-air ballooning.

# HYATT NEWPORTER, 1107 Gamborce Road, Newport Beach, California. (800) 422-4240, (800) 341-1474, (714) 729-1234

## Tennis

**Courts:** 16
**Court Surfaces:** Hard
**Courts Lit For Night Play:** All
**Director of Tennis:** Phil Dent          **Head Pro:** John Fullerton
**Instruction Rates:** $45 per hour/individual; group rates vary
**Court Time:** $10 per person per day
**Video Analysis:** None
**Ball Machines:** 2; $5 per half-hour
**Tournaments:** None
**Tennis Packages:** None
**Comments:** "John Wayne Tennis Club is privately owned but shares property with Newporter; full facility and pro shop; excellent instruction by former pro, Dent."

## Accommodations

**Rooms:** 410
**Rooms With Water View:** 50
**Rates:** Start from $149 per room, per night, double occupancy; no charge for children 18 and under with parents
**Type of Crowd:** Conventions, couples, families
**Nearest Airport:** 5 minutes from John Wayne Orange County Airport
**Comments:** "Above-average hotel rooms; comfortable beds; impeccable maid service."

## Food

**Restaurants:** The Jamboree Cafe (California cuisine), Ristorante Cantori (Italian), The Wine Cellar (French)
**Comments:** "Good food in all dining facilities; The Wine Cellar is a local favorite."

## Special Features

Three outdoor swimming pools; 9-hole golf course; downtown Newport Beach.
**Nightlife:** Live entertainment in Dukes Nightclub.

## Nearby Tourist Attractions

Balboa Island; Newport Harbor; Newport Dunes; Fashion Island; Southcoast Plaza; Disneyland.

# JOHN GARDINER'S RANCHO VALENCIA, P.O. Box 9126, Rancho Santa Fe, California 92067. (800) 548-3664, (619) 756-1123

## *Tennis*

**Courts:** 17
**Court Surfaces:** Hard
**Courts Lit For Night Play:** None
**Director of Tennis:** Sam Nunez        **Head Pro:** Sam Nunez
**Instruction Rates:** $45 per hour/individual; group rates vary
**Court Time:** $10 per person per day
**Video Analysis:** Add $30 to individual instruction rate
**Ball Machines:** 3; $15 per hour
**Tournaments:** None
**Tennis Packages:** Weekend Tiebreaker starts from $650 per person, double occupancy for 3 days/2 nights, including unlimited court time, two tennis clinics, three meals daily and cocktail reception.
**Comments:** "Tennis instruction is a happening; try the host lessons."

## *Accommodations*

**Rooms:** 43 suites
**Rooms With Water View:** None
**Rates:** Start from $295 per room, per night, double occupancy; no charge for children 12 and under with parents
**Type of Crowd:** Couples
**Nearest Airport:** 35 minutes from San Diego Lindbergh Field International Airport; shuttle service $45 per van, each way
**Comments:** "All the splendor of a California hideaway, and you pay for it, but you can't beat the ratio of rooms to courts."

## *Food*

**Restaurants:** La Tapenade (French)
**Comments:** "The local clientele love La Tapenade; chefs add a special touch to each dish."

## *Special Features*

18-hole golf course; two swimming pools; croquet court; hydrotherapy pools; spa; Olympic-size pool.
**Nightlife:** Live entertainment at La Sala.

## *Nearby Tourist Attractions*

Hot-air ballooning; polo; Del Mar Beach; La Jolla Beach; Rancho Santa Fe.

118      CALIFORNIA

# LA COSTA HOTEL & SPA, Costa del Mar Road, Carlsbad, California 92009. (800) 854-5000, (619) 438-9111

*Tennis*

**Courts:** 23
**Court Surfaces:** 17 hard, 4 clay, 2 grass
**Courts Lit For Night Play:** 5
**Director of Tennis:** Nels Peterson      **Head Pro:** Pancho Segura
**Instruction Rates:** $50 per hour/individual; group rates vary
**Court Time:** $15 per hour
**Video Analysis:** None
**Ball Machines:** 6; $12 per hour
**Tournaments:** Mazda Tennis Classic
**Tennis Packages:** La Costa Tennis Challenge starts from $230 per room, per night, double occupancy, including two hours of court time and one half-hour lesson.
**Comments:** "Tremendous tennis complex; a lesson with Segura is a must; clubhouse and pro shop are spectacular."

*Accommodations*

**Rooms:** 478
**Rooms With Water View:** None
**Rates:** Start from $215 per room, per night, double occupancy; no charge for children 18 and under with parents
**Type of Crowd:** Couples, families
**Nearest Airport:** 45 minutes from San Diego Lindbergh Field International Airport; shuttle service $35 per person, each way
**Comments:** "Attractive, but rooms can be musty from previous smokers; La Costa suites are your best bet."

*Food*

**Restaurants:** Champagne Room (gourmet), Gaucho Steak House (Argentine), Ristorante Figaro (Italian), Pisces (gourmet seafood), Jose Wong's (oriental), Brasserie La Costa (casual), Spa Dining Room (spa cuisine), Center Court (casual)
**Comments:** "Every choice is a good one; the spa restaurant is wonderful."

*Special Features*

Camp La Costa for Kids; health spa; Tony Ray's Beauty Salon; two 18-hole golf courses.
**Nightlife:** Live entertainment in Tournament of Champions Lounge.

*Nearby Tourist Attractions*

San Diego Zoo; Sea World; Wild Animal Park; Old Town San Diego; La Jolla shopping; Horton Plaza.

## LA QUINTA, 49–499 Eisenhower Drive, P.O. Box 69, La Quinta, California 92253. (800) 472–4316, (800) 854–1271

### *Tennis*

**Courts:** 30
**Court Surfaces:** 21 Plexipave, 6 grass, 3 Har-Tru
**Courts Lit For Night Play:** 11
**Director of Tennis:** Jackie Cooper   **Head Pro:** Jackie Cooper
**Instruction Rates:** $50 per hour/individual; group rates vary
**Court Time:** No charge
**Video Analysis:** $70 per hour
**Ball Machines:** 3; $10 per hour
**Tournaments:** Nabisco Junior Grand Prix
**Tennis Packages:** None
**Comments:** "Jackie Cooper was a great player before the Open era; courts are a favorite of Ivan Lendl, John McEnroe and Jimmy Connors; the class tennis operation of the desert."

### *Accommodations*

**Rooms:** 640
**Rooms With Water View:** None
**Rates:** Start from $195 per room, per night, double occupancy; no charge for extra person in room
**Type of Crowd:** Couples, families
**Nearest Airport:** 25 minutes from Palm Springs International Airport; shuttle service $15 per person, each way
**Comments:** "Deluxe king room is best deal; 1920s decor takes you back in time."

### *Food*

**Restaurants:** La Mirage (gourmet), Morgans (American), Adobe Grill (Mexican), Golf Dining Room (continental), Tennis Dining Room (continental)
**Comments:** "Every restaurant is simply wonderful."

### *Special Features*

Manicured grounds once home to Clark Gable and Greta Garbo; twenty-three pools; three 18-hole golf courses.
**Nightlife:** Live entertainment in La Cantina.

### *Nearby Tourist Attractions*

Living Desert Reserve; hot-air ballooning; McCallum Theater; Palm Springs Desert Museum; El Paseo shopping.

# MARRIOTT'S DESERT SPRINGS RESORT, 74855 Country Club Drive, Palm Desert, California 92260. (800) 228-9290, (619) 341-2211

## *Tennis*

**Courts:** 20
**Court Surfaces:** 15 hard, 3 clay, 2 grass
**Courts Lit For Night Play:** 8
**Director of Tennis:** Dan Aubuchon    **Head Pro:** Jim Leupold
**Instruction Rates:** $50 per hour/individual; group rates vary
**Court Time:** $16 per hour/hard; $20 per hour/clay; $35 per hour/grass
**Video Analysis:** $60 per hour
**Ball Machines:** 1; $10 per half-hour
**Tournaments:** None
**Tennis Packages:** None
**Comments:** "You get more than your money's worth with Aubuchon's instruction; and let's not forget those (rare) grass courts."

## *Accommodations*

**Rooms:** 891
**Rooms With Water View:** 400
**Rates:** Start from $180 per room, per night, double occupancy; no charge for children 12 and under with parents
**Type of Crowd:** Conventions, couples, families
**Nearest Airport:** 15 minutes from Palm Springs Municipal Airport; free shuttle service
**Comments:** "Rooms are top-notch; gorgeous views of golf course; room service menu for kids is marvelous."

## *Food*

**Restaurants:** Mikado (Japanese), Sea Grill (seafood), Tuscany (Italian), Lakeview (California cuisine), Club Room (continental)
**Comments:** "These's something for everyone at all five dining facilities; food is cooked in front of you at Mikado."

## *Special Features*

18-hole putting course; health spa; gondola rides to restaurants; children's program; 36 holes of golf.
**Nightlife:** Live entertainment in Costas.

## *Nearby Tourist Attractions*

Palm Springs Tramway; Living Desert Reserve; El Paseo shopping; Oasis Water Park; hot-air ballooning.

# MEADOWOOD, 900 Meadowood Lane, St. Helena, California 94574. (800) 458-8080, (707) 963-3646

## *Tennis*

**Courts:**  6
**Court Surfaces:**  Hard
**Courts Lit For Night Play:**  None
**Director of Tennis:**  Doug King        **Head Pro:**  Doug King
**Instruction Rates:**  $42 per hour/individual; group rates vary
**Court Time:**  $10 per hour
**Video Analysis:**  Included in tennis clinics
**Ball Machines:**  1; $15 per hour
**Tournaments:**  Vitner's Cup
**Tennis Packages:**  None
**Comments:**  "Apart from resort guests, there are 400 local club members anxious to set up a game."

## *Accommodations*

**Rooms:**  70
**Rooms With Water View:**  None
**Rates:**  Start from $200 per room, per night, double occupancy; no charge for children 12 and under with parents
**Type of Crowd:**  Couples
**Nearest Airport:**  90 minutes from Oakland Airport; no shuttle service
**Comments:**  "Rooms have sylvan settings and are stylish, tasteful and understated."

## *Food*

**Restaurants:**  Starmont (continental), Fairway Grill (casual)
**Comments:**  "Gourmet cuisine combining the best of French and California preparations."

## *Special Features*

Wine classes; two croquet lawns; 9-hole executive golf course.
**Nightlife:**  None.

## *Nearby Tourist Attractions*

Napa Valley wineries; Mount St. Helena; Conestaga Hot Springs.

# OJAI VALLEY INN & COUNTRY CLUB, P.O. Box 1886, Ojai, California 93023. (800) 422-6524, (805) 646-5511

## *Tennis*

**Courts:** 8
**Court Surfaces:** Foam-cushioned
**Courts Lit For Night Play:** 4
**Director of Tennis:** Tim Howell    **Head Pro:** Tim Howell
**Instruction Rates:** $40 per hour/individual; group rates vary
**Court Time:** $12 per hour
**Video Analysis:** $40 per hour
**Ball Machines:** 1; $15 per hour
**Tournaments:** None
**Tennis Packages:** Start from $298 per room, per night, double occupancy for 3 days/2 nights, including unlimited court time, unlimited use of ball machine, one can of balls and two breakfasts and two dinners.
**Comments:** "Ask a junior who came up in the ranks about Ojai—they love it here; favored by local tennis junkies."

## *Accommodations*

**Rooms:** 216
**Rooms With Water View:** None
**Rates:** Start from $180 per room, per night, double occupancy; no charge for extra person in room
**Type of Crowd:** Couples, families
**Nearest Airport:** 60 minutes from Santa Barbara Airport; no shuttle service
**Comments:** "Artistic works displayed in rooms; colorful interiors."

## *Food*

**Restaurants:** Vista Dining Room (gourmet), Oak Grill (Italian)
**Comments:** "Good food along with fresh mountain air makes for a winning combination."

## *Special Features*

18-hole golf course; bicycle paths; hiking trails; Spanish architecture; children's program; babysitting service.
**Nightlife:** Live entertainment in the Club Bar.

## *Nearby Tourist Attractions*

Whale watching; National Forest.

# THE RACQUET CLUB, 2743 N. Indian Avenue, Box 1747, Palm Springs, California 92263. (800) 423-6588, (800) 367-0946, (619) 325-1281

## *Tennis*

**Courts:** 12
**Court Surfaces:** Laykold
**Courts Lit For Night Play:** 10
**Director of Tennis:** Leoncio Collas    **Head Pro:** Leoncio Collas
**Instruction Rates:** $50 per hour/individual; group rates vary
**Court Time:** $10 per hour
**Video Analysis:** $60 per hour
**Ball Machines:** 2; $15 per hour
**Tournaments:** None
**Tennis Packages:** None
**Comments:** "Collas trying to restore tennis program to heyday of the 1940s."

## *Accommodations*

**Rooms:** 120
**Rooms With Water View:** None
**Rates:** Start from $99 per room, per night, double occupancy; no charge for children 12 and under with parents
**Type of Crowd:** Groups
**Nearest Airport:** 10 minutes from Palm Springs Municipal Airport; free shuttle service
**Comments:** "The rooms are bland, though clean and spacious."

## *Food*

**Restaurants:** Lawrence's (continental)
**Comments:** "Best kept secret in the desert; food is tops."

## *Special Features*

Charlie Farrell House; Clark Gable Bridge; four swimming pools; four Jacuzzis; health club.
**Nightlife:** Live entertainment in Bamboo Bar.

## *Nearby Tourist Attractions*

Palm Springs Tramway; Palm Springs Desert Museum.

# RANCHO BERNARDO INN, 17550 Bernardo Oaks Drive, San Diego, California 93023. (800) 542-6096, (800) 854-1065

## Tennis

**Courts:** 12
**Court Surfaces:** Hard
**Courts Lit For Night Play:** 4
**Director of Tennis:** Paul Navratil     **Head Pro:** Paul Navratil
**Instruction Rates:** $40 per hour/individual; group rates vary
**Court Time:** $12 per hour
**Video Analysis:** No charge
**Ball Machines:** 4; $12 per hour
**Tournaments:** Rancho Bernardo Senior Grand Prix Masters
**Tennis Packages:** Start from $266 per person, double occupancy for 3 days/2 nights, including unlimited court time, breakfast and dinner daily and transfers to/from airport.
**Comments:** "Navratil oversees four teaching pros, all of whom give solid instruction to players of all levels; excellent program for juniors."

## Accommodations

**Rooms:** 287
**Rooms With Water View:** None
**Rates:** Start from $165 per room, per night, double occupancy; no charge for children 3 and under with parents
**Type of Crowd:** Conventions, couples, families
**Nearest Airport:** 30 minutes from San Diego Lindbergh Field International Airport; shuttle service $20 per person, each way
**Comments:** "Rooms are cozy; great place to get away for rest and relaxation."

## Food

**Restaurants:** El Biccocho (French), Veranda (casual)
**Comments:** "El Biccocho is extravagant and romantic and expensive."

## Special Features

Health and fitness center; two swimming pools; children's camp; high tea; 45 holes of golf.
**Nightlife:** Nightly entertainment in La Bodega and La Taberna.

## Nearby Tourist Attractions

San Diego Zoo; Wild Animal Park; Seaworld; Tijuana.

# MARRIOTT'S RANCHO LAS PALMAS RESORT,
41000 Bob Hope Drive, Rancho Mirage, California 92270.
(800) 288-9290, (619) 568-2727

## Tennis

**Courts:** 25
**Court Surfaces:** 22 hard, 3 red European clay
**Courts Lit For Night Play:** 8
**Director of Tennis:** Bill Ray      **Head Pro:** Scott Hull
**Instruction Rates:** $40 per hour/individual; group rates vary
**Court Time:** $16 per hour/hard; $20 per hour/clay
**Video Analysis:** None
**Ball Machines:** 2; $8 per half-hour
**Tournaments:** USPTA National Championships
**Tennis Packages:** Rancho tennis package starts from $420 per room, per night, double occupancy for 3 days/2 nights, including unlimited tennis, welcome tennis gift and breakfast daily.
**Comments:** "Courts well-maintained; pros take time to teach the game; don't leave without playing on the red clay."

## Accommodations

**Rooms:** 450
**Rooms With Water View:** None
**Rates:** Start from $185 per room, per night, double occupancy; no charge for children 18 and under with parents
**Type of Crowd:** Conventions, couples, families
**Nearest Airport:** 15 minutes from Palm Springs International Airport; shuttle service $15 per person, each way
**Comments:** "Rooms are spacious and comfortable; suites are special and worth the investment."

## Food

**Restaurants:** Fountain Court (family), Cabrillo Room (gourmet), Sunrise Terrace (breakfast buffet)
**Comments:** "The Fountain Court spreads out to the swimming pool for casual dining day and night; try the Cabrillo Room for a more formal atmosphere."

## Special Features

Old-fashioned barber shop; 27-hole golf course; home to the Secret Service and staff during former President Ronald Reagan's New Year's visits.
**Nightlife:** Live entertainment in Miguel's Lounge.

## Nearby Tourist Attractions

Palm Springs Tramway; jeep tours; hot-air ballooning.

# THE RITZ-CARLTON RANCHO MIRAGE, 68-900
Frank Sinatra Drive, Rancho Mirage, California 92270. (800) 241-3333, (619) 321-8282

## Tennis

**Courts:** 10
**Court Surfaces:** 9 hard, 1 Har-Tru
**Courts Lit For Night Play:** All
**Director of Tennis:** Tom Gorman
**Head Pros:** Alan Forster and Doug Towler
**Instruction Rates:** $40 per hour/individual; group rates vary
**Court Time:** $10 per person per day
**Video Analysis:** None
**Ball Machines:** 1; $10 per half-hour
**Tournaments:** None
**Tennis Packages:** None
**Comments:** "The mountain scenery invigorates your game; it doesn't get any better than (Davis Cup coach) Tom Gorman at the Ritz."

## Accommodations

**Rooms:** 240
**Rooms With Water View:** None
**Rates:** Start from $200 per room, per night, double occupancy; no charge for children 18 and under with parents
**Type of Crowd:** Families, conventions
**Nearest Airport:** 20 minutes from Palm Springs Municipal Airport; no shuttle service
**Comments:** "Each Ritz room has its own unique charm."

## Food

**Restaurants:** Dining Room (modern French), The Cafe (casual), The Grill (continental)
**Comments:** "The Dining Room and The Cafe serve wonderful treats; room service has a fun children's menu."

## Special Features

Fitness center; Marcy Lacy's sports massage treatment; $2 million art exhibit; children's program.
**Nightlife:** Live entertainment in The Lounge.

## Nearby Tourist Attractions

Big Horn Sheep Reserve; Restaurant Row; Desert Off-Road Jeep Adventures; hot-air ballooning; Polo Grounds; Desert Museum; Living Desert Reserve; Oasis Water Park.

# SILVERADO, 1600 Atlas Peak Road, Napa Valley, California 94558. (800) 532-0500, (707) 257-0200

### *Tennis*

**Courts:** 23
**Court Surfaces:** Plexipave
**Courts Lit For Night Play:** 3
**Director of Tennis:** Giuseppe Cammaroto
**Head Pro:** Giuseppe Cammaroto
**Instruction Rates:** $50 per hour/individual; group rates vary
**Court Time:** $12 per day
**Video Analysis:** Included in individual instruction rate
**Ball Machines:** 3; $20 per hour
**Tournaments:** None
**Tennis Packages:** The Refresher Program starts from $200 per person, double occupancy, for 3 days/2 nights, including one-hour clinic daily and unlimited court time.
**Comments:** "Courts designed in units of 2; excellent pro shop."

### *Accommodations*

**Rooms:** 280
**Rooms With Water View:** None
**Rates:** Start from $175 per room, per night, double occupancy; no charge for children 14 and under with parents
**Type of Crowd:** Couples, families
**Nearest Airport:** 75 minutes from San Francisco International Airport; shuttle service $20 per person, each way
**Comments:** "Condos have beautiful views of the mountains and vineyards."

### *Food*

**Restaurants:** Vintner's Court (continental), Royal Oak (steakhouse), Silverado Bar & Grill (American)
**Comments:** "Vintner's Court is for formal dining with an excellent wine list; the Silverado Bar & Grill is casual and nothing to write home about."

### *Special Features*

Eight swimming pools; two 18-hole golf courses; bicycle and jogging trails; colonial-style mansion.
**Nightlife:** Live entertainment at Patio Lounge.

### *Nearby Tourist Attractions*

Over two hundred wineries; Napa Valley; Wine Train; Calistoga Spas; hot-air ballooning.

# 10

# HAWAII

Airfare to Hawaii is costly, and once you arrive the prices remain high. Be prepared to spend a small fortune vacationing at Hawaiian hotels, many of which are now owned by the Japanese.

But the expenses just may be justified. Hawaii has some of the best and most beautiful tennis resorts in the world. Playing a set at **Kapalua Bay Hotel & Villas'** "Tennis Garden" with the Pacific surf thrashing in the background is pretty close to paradise.

The only problem is that Hawaiian resorts tend to be enormous (350-room hotels are standard), and not enough tennis courts are built to commensurate with that number of rooms. This makes for a poor room-to-court ratio. In fact, very few Hawaiian resorts meet our standard 16-to-1 ratio. All of which means it will be difficult to secure court time or individual instruction when you want it. The high demand and low supply also means you're going to pay dearly for the privilege. Rare is the Hawaiian resort that offers court time at no charge, and individual instruction costs top dollar. But once you have your court reservation, you're going to love it, because the scenery is fantastic and Hawaii attracts some of the world's best teaching pros.

# COCO PALMS RESORT, P.O. Box 631, Lihue, Kauai, Hawaii 96766. (808) 822–4921

## *Tennis*

**Courts:** 9
**Court Surfaces:** 6 Laykold, 3 clay
**Courts Lit For Night Play:** 2
**Director of Tennis:** Koko Chang        **Head Pro:** Koko Chang
**Instruction Rates:** $35 per hour/individual; group rates vary
**Court Time:** $7 per person per day/hard; $9 per person per day/clay
**Video Analysis:** None
**Ball Machines:** 1; $12 per hour
**Tournaments:** Clay Court State Championships
**Tennis Packages:** The Sports Package starts from $175 per couple, per night, double occupancy, including one-hour clinic and two hours of court time daily.
**Comments:** "The clay courts are the facility's best attraction; staff is friendly and competent."

## *Accommodations*

**Rooms:** 390
**Rooms With Water View:** 195
**Rates:** Start from $110 per room, per night, double occupancy; no charge for children 17 and under with parents
**Type of Crowd:** Couples, families
**Nearest Airport:** 15 minutes from Lihue Airport; no shuttle service
**Comments:** "In keeping with Hawaiian tradition, none of the buildings are taller than a coconut tree."

## *Food*

**Restaurants:** Lagoon Dining Room (American), The Seashell (seafood)
**Comments:** "Lagoon Dining Room is best for nighttime torchlighting ceremony."

## *Special Features*

Set on oldest coconut grove in Hawaii; wedding chapel built in 1954 for Rita Hayworth; Elvis Presley got married in it during the filming of *Blue Hawaii*; mini-zoo; lagoon pole-fishing.
**Nightlife:** Entertainment in The Lagoon Terrace Lounge.

## *Nearby Tourist Attractions*

The Fern Grotto; Hikina Heiau (stone temple) in Lydgate State Park.

# HYATT REGENCY WAIKOLOA, One Waikoloa Beach Resort, Kohala Coast, Hawaii 96743. (800) 228-9000, (808) 885-1234

## Tennis

**Courts:** 8
**Court Surfaces:** 6 Plexicushion, 2 clay
**Courts Lit For Night Play:** None
**Director of Tennis:** Joel Root          **Head Pro:** Craig Pautler
**Instruction Rates:** $40 per hour/individual; group rates vary
**Court Time:** $20 per hour
**Video Analysis:** None
**Ball Machines:** 1; included in court time rate
**Tournaments:** None
**Tennis Packages:** None
**Comments:** "Pautler is great with players of all levels; clay courts are recommended."

## Accommodations

**Rooms:** 1,241
**Rooms With Water View:** 329
**Rates:** Start from $235 per room, per night, double occupancy; no charge for children 12 and under with parents
**Type of Crowd:** Couples, families
**Nearest Airport:** 20 minutes from Keahole/Kona Airport; shuttle service $17 per person, each way
**Comments:** "Resort has used its funds for unique features, not accommodations."

## Food

**Restaurants:** Cascades (continental), Donatoni's (Italian), Imari (Japanese), The Water's Edge (continental), Orchid Cafe (Californian cuisine), Kona Provision Company (seafood), King Kamehameha Court (Polynesian)
**Comments:** "Cascades serves one of the finest buffets in Hawaii; dining showplace is The Water's Edge."

## Special Features

Children's program; two swimming pools; four-acre beach-rimmed lagoon; 62 acres of shoreline.
**Nightlife:** Entertainment in Spats Disco.

## Nearby Tourist Attractions

Mauna Kea; Kona; Hapuna Beach; Hulihe Palace.

**KAHALA HILTON,** 5000 Kahala Avenue, Honolulu, Hawaii 96816. (808) 734-2211

*Tennis*

**Courts:** 6
**Court Surfaces:** Plexipave
**Courts Lit For Night Play:** All
**Director of Tennis:** Charlie Panui     **Head Pro:** None
**Instruction Rates:** $53 per hour/individual; group rates vary
**Court Time:** $20 per hour
**Video Analysis:** $65 per hour
**Ball Machines:** 1; $26 per hour
**Tournaments:** None
**Tennis Packages:** None
**Comments:** "Well-run daily clinics combined with beautifully maintained courts create a comfortable tennis atmosphere."

*Accommodations*

**Rooms:** 369
**Rooms With Water View:** 166
**Rates:** $210 per room, per night, double occupancy; no charge for children 16 and under with parents
**Type of Crowd:** Couples, families
**Nearest Airport:** 20 minutes from Honolulu International Airport; no shuttle service
**Comments:** "Suntan lotion, a sewing kit and orchids on pillow nightly; every amenity you need is here."

*Food*

**Restaurants:** Hala Terrace (American), Plumeria Cafe (American), Maile (gourmet)
**Comments:** "Lush food presentation at Maile; Plumeria Cafe is fun for snacks, lunch and simple dinner."

*Special Features*

Dolphin lagoon on grounds; Kamp Kahala for kids; catamaran picnic/snorkel trips.
**Nightlife:** Renowned for great nightly stage shows; Danny Kaleikini Hawaiian Review in the Hala Terrace.

*Nearby Tourist Attractions*

Hanauma Bay; Iolani Palace; Pearl Harbor Memorial; Sea Life Park; Polynesian Cultural Center.

# KAPALUA BAY HOTEL & VILLAS, 500 Bay Drive, Lahaina, Hawaii 96761. (800) 367–8000, (800) 545–0018, (808) 669–5656

## Tennis

**Courts:** 10
**Court Surfaces:** Plexipave
**Courts Lit For Night Play:** 4
**Director of Tennis:** Steve Miller       **Head Pro:** Steve Miller
**Instruction Rates:** $45 per hour/individual; group rates vary
**Court Time:** $10 per person per day
**Video Analysis:** Add $10 to instruction rate
**Ball Machines:** 1; $15 per hour
**Tournaments:** None
**Tennis Packages:** Start from $345 per room, per night, double occupancy for 4 days/3 nights, including unlimited court time, use of ball machine, one-hour private lesson and one can of balls.
**Comments:** "Beautiful tropical gardens surround courts; daily round-robin pairing service."

## Accommodations

**Rooms:** 195; 125 villas at Kapalua Bay Hotel, 70 vacation rentals at The Kapalua Villas
**Rooms With Water View:** 118
**Rates:** Start from $215 per room, per night, double occupancy; no charge for children 14 and under with parents
**Type of Crowd:** Couples, families
**Nearest Airport:** 40 minutes from Kahalui Airport; no shuttle service
**Comments:** "Intimate; low-key Hawaiian; rooms have spectacular views; getaway for celebrities; villas at the Kapalua Bay Hotel are your best bet."

## Food

**Restaurants:** Champions (gourmet), The Bay Club (seafood), The Plantation Veranda (Hawaiian), The Garden Restaurant (regional), The Pool Terrace (casual), The Grill and Bar (American), The Market Cafe (deli), The Village Cafe (casual), Pineapple Hill (steaks)
**Comments:** "The Plantation Veranda is known for its Caesar salad; The Bay Club is famous for its fresh fish."

## Special Features

Horseback riding; helicopter rides; two 18-hole golf courses; promenade with more than 20 boutiques and galleries.
**Nightlife:** Entertainment in the Garden Lounge.

## Nearby Tourist Attractions

Lahaina town; The Baldwin Home; Hard Rock Cafe.

# KIAHUNA PLANTATION RESORT, 2253 Popipu Road, Koloa, Kauai, Hawaii 96756. (800) 367–7052, (808) 742–6411

## *Tennis*

**Courts:** 10
**Court Surfaces:** Plexipave
**Courts Lit For Night Play:** None
**Director of Tennis:** Wayne Barnes          **Head Pro:** Wayne Barnes
**Instruction Rates:** $40 per hour/individual; group rates vary
**Court Time:** $9 per person per hour
**Video Analysis:** None
**Ball Machines:** 1; $12 per hour
**Tournaments:** None
**Tennis Packages:** Start from $706.56 per couple, double occupancy for 4 days/3 nights, including unlimited court time, three clinics, round-robin tournaments, one can of balls and free rental car for entire stay.
**Comments:** "Daily round-robin tournaments for juniors and adults; stroke-of-the-day clinics are special."

## *Accommodations*

**Rooms:** 333
**Rooms With Water View:** 75
**Rates:** Start from $145 per room, per night, double occupancy (four people per unit)
**Type of Crowd:** Couples, families
**Nearest Airport:** 25 minutes from Lihue Airport; no shuttle service
**Comments:** "Beautiful suites facing ocean or lush gardens have full kitchens and microwave ovens; geared for family vacationers; nearby grocery, pizza parlor and bakery, plus on-site barbecue pits; for the budget-conscious."

## *Food*

**Restaurants:** Plantation Gardens (continental)
**Comments:** "Plantation Gardens is romantic, basic and moderately priced."

## *Special Features*

Tropical gardens; waterfalls; six beaches; snorkeling and surfing.
**Nightlife:** Entertainment in Plantation Gardens.

## *Nearby Tourist Attractions*

Kiahuna shopping center; Old Koloa town; The Fern Grotto; Waimea Canyon.

# MAUI INTER-CONTINENTAL WAILEA, P.O. Box 779, Wailea, Hawaii 96753. (800) 367-2960, (808) 879-1922

## *Tennis*

**Courts:** 14
**Court Surfaces:** 11 hard, 3 grass
**Courts Lit For Night Play:** 3
**Director of Tennis:** Tim Fitzgerald    **Head Pro:** Tim Fitzgerald
**Instruction Rates:** $48 per hour/individual; group rates vary
**Court Time:** $10 per person per day
**Video Analysis:** Included in tennis academy program
**Ball Machines:** 2; $20 per hour
**Tournaments:** None
**Tennis Packages:** None
**Comments:** "One of Maui's best tennis clubs; on-site tennis academy is worth the investment and includes detailed video analysis."

## *Accommodations*

**Rooms:** 550
**Rooms With Water View:** 500
**Rates:** Start from $145 per room, per night, double occupancy; no charge for children 14 and under with parents
**Type of Crowd:** Couples, families
**Nearest Airport:** 25 minutes from Kahuli Airport; no shuttle service
**Comments:** "$10 million renovation shows; casual atmosphere makes this a great place to unwind and relax."

## *Food*

**Restaurants:** The Lanai Terrace (continental), La Perouse (elegant), Hula Moons (seafood)
**Comments:** "From poolside dining to gourmet cuisine, palates are sated."

## *Special Features*

Three swimming pools; weekly luaus; children's program; hiking; water sports.
**Nightlife:** Live entertainment in Inu Inu Lounge.

## *Nearby Tourist Attractions*

Wailea Beach; Ulua Beach; whale watching; Haleakala Crater.

# MAUNA KEA BEACH RESORT, 1 Mauna Kea Beach Drive, Kohola Coast, Hawaii 967743–9706. (800) 882–6060, (808) 882–7222

## Tennis

**Courts:** 13
**Court Surfaces:** Plexipave
**Courts Lit For Night Play:** None
**Director of Tennis:** Jay Paulson    **Head Pro:** Jay Paulson
**Instruction Rates:** $60 per hour/individual; group rates vary
**Court Time:** $18 per hour
**Video Analysis:** None
**Ball Machines:** 1; add $4 to court time rate
**Tournaments:** None
**Tennis Packages:** Start from $720 per couple, for 4 days/3 nights, including unlimited court time, round-robin tournaments and fifty-dollar gift certificates to spend in pro shop.
**Comments:** "See and hear sounds of ocean while playing; no guest goes without a match; beautiful facilities."

## Accommodations

**Rooms:** 310
**Rooms With Water View:** 206
**Rates:** Start from $250 per room, per night, double occupancy; $25 charge for extra person in room
**Type of Crowd:** Couples, families
**Nearest Airport:** 30 minutes from Kona Airport; shuttle service $18 per person, each way
**Comments:** "Ocean view brings the sea into your room; the resort was once the Shangri-la of Lawrence Rockefeller."

## Food

**Restaurants:** The Batik (gourmet), The Garden (continental), The Pavillion (continental), Teppanyaki (Japanese)
**Comments:** "Everything is fresh; menus are pricey; if you like Japanese food, try Teppanyaki."

## Special Features

One of the most exquisite beaches in the Hawaiian Islands, 18-hole golf course.
**Nightlife:** Consists of luaus held weekly.

## Nearby Tourist Attractions

Atlantis submarine; Waipio Valley; whale watching; Waimea shopping area.

# MAUNA LANI BAY HOTEL & BUNGALOWS, P.O. Box 4000, Kohala Coast, Hawaii 96743. (800) 367-2323, (808) 885-6622

### Tennis

**Courts:** 10
**Court Surfaces:** Plexipave
**Courts Lit For Night Play:** All
**Director of Tennis:** Craig Pautler    **Head Pro:** Craig Pautler
**Instruction Rates:** $45 per hour/individual; group rates vary
**Court Time:** $7 per person per hour
**Video Analysis:** Add $5 to instruction rate
**Ball Machines:** 2; $18 per hour
**Tournaments:** None
**Tennis Packages:** Start from $810 per room, for 4 days/3 nights, including unlimited court time, one hour use of ball machine, daily round-robin tournament and one can of balls.
**Comments:** "Courts are newly resurfaced and offer varying speeds; since many guests come for golf or the beach, there is seldom heavy competition for the courts."

### Accommodations

**Rooms:** 354
**Rooms With Water View:** 325
**Rates:** Start from $260 per night, double occupancy; no charge for children 12 and under with parents
**Type of Crowd:** Couples, independent travelers
**Nearest Airport:** 30 minutes from Kona Airport; shuttle service $16.25 per person, each way
**Comments:** "Rooms recently refurbished in a classy tropical style; new 4,000-square-foot bungalows with private pools and a twenty-four-hour staff are the most opulent suites in Hawaii."

### Food

**Restaurants:** Canoehouse (Pacific Rim cuisine), Le Soleil (French), Bay Terrace (American), Ocean Grill (light meals)
**Comments:** "With Alan Wong in the kitchen at the Canoehouse and Daniel Delbrel at Le Soleil, the Mauna Lani Bay is a food lover's paradise."

### Special Features

Two 18-hole golf courses; two beaches; water sports; ancient Hawaiian fishponds surround the hotel.
**Nightlife:** Hawaiian music and hula dancing nightly.

### Nearby Tourist Attractions

Parker Ranch Country in North Kohala; jeep and wagon trips to Waipio Valley; submarine tours of the coral reefs; Volcanoes National Park.

## THE RITZ-CARLTON MAUNA LANI, 1 North Kaniku Drive, Kohala Coast, Hawaii 96743. (800) 241-3333, (808) 885-2000

### Tennis

**Courts:** 11
**Court Surfaces:** Plexipave
**Courts Lit For Night Play:** 9
**Director of Tennis:** Nancy Hunter          **Head Pro:** Nancy Hunter
**Instruction Rates:** $50 per hour/individual; group rates vary
**Court Time:** $6 per hour per person
**Video Analysis:** $10 per hour
**Ball Machines:** 2; $20 per hour
**Tournaments:** None
**Tennis Packages:** Tennis Time starts from $1,320 per couple, for 4 days/3 nights, including unlimited court time, two hours of private lessons and one hour use of ball machine daily.
**Comments:** "This tennis facility is as fresh and classy as the new hotel; less competition for playing time than court/room ratio suggests because many guests are attending business meetings."

### Accommodations

**Rooms:** 542
**Rooms With Water View:** 400
**Rates:** Start from $250 per room, per night, double occupancy; no charge for children 18 and under with parents
**Type of Crowd:** Business groups, independent travelers
**Nearest Airport:** 30 minutes from Kona Airport; no shuttle service
**Comments:** "Rooms are elegantly European in style rather than tropical; sumptuous bathrooms."

### Food

**Restaurants:** The Dining Room (French), The Grill (steak and seafood), The Cafe (Asian and spa cuisine), Ocean Bar and Grill (light meals)
**Comments:** "Chef Philippe Padovani is the best classical chef in Hawaii; The Dining Room may be the finest French restaurant in the tropics."

### Special Features

Two 18-hole golf courses; three beaches; full range of water sports; historic park in walking distance.
**Nightlife:** Hawaiian music in the early evening at the Ocean Bar and Grill.

### Nearby Tourist Attractions

Parker Ranch Country in North Kohala; Waipio Valley; town of Kailua-Kona for shopping and submarine tours of coral reefs; Volcanoes National Park.

# WESTIN KAUAI, Kalapaki Beach, Lihue, Hawaii 96766.
## (800) 245-5050, (808) 228-3000

### *Tennis*

**Courts:** 8
**Court Surfaces:** Plexipave
**Courts Lit For Night Play:** 1
**Director of Tennis:** Ron Romano          **Head Pro:** Ron Romano
**Instruction Rates:** $45 per hour/individual; group rates vary
**Court Time:** $20 per hour including use of health spa (7 A.M.–11 A.M.); $10 per hour including use of health spa (11 A.M.–3 P.M..)
**Video Analysis:** Included in individual instruction rate
**Ball Machines:** 1; $25 per hour including use of health spa
**Tournaments:** None
**Tennis Packages:** The Get Fit tennis package starts from $357.50 per person, double occupancy for 4 days/3 nights, including unlimited court time, one-hour tennis lesson, one can of balls and daily admission to spa.
**Comments:** "Kauai Lagoons Tennis Academy on premises; Romano knows his tennis and is great with kids."

### *Accommodations*

**Rooms:** 846
**Rooms With Water View:** 315
**Rates:** Start from $95 per person, per night, double occupancy; no charge for children 18 and under with parents
**Type of Crowd:** Couples, families
**Nearest Airport:** 5 minutes from Lihue Airport; free shuttle service
**Comments:** "Rooms with pool and ocean view are like a picture—comfortable and spacious with sitting areas."

### *Food*

**Restaurants:** Prince Bill's (steak and seafood), The Terrace (spa cuisine), Inn on the Cliffs (seafood), Tempura Garden (Japanese), Cook's at the Beach (continental), Duke's Canoe Club (Hawaiian), Sharky's (seafood), The Colonade (breakfast), Kalapaki Grill (burgers)
**Comments:** "Cuisine brings Hawaii to you; very commercial; The Terrace is the best bet for lunch."

### *Special Features*

Camp Kalapaki for kids; 26,000-square-foot pool; 47 horse-drawn carriages; animals wander throughout the property; $2.5-million art collection.
**Nightlife:** Dancing in The Paddling Club.

### *Nearby Tourist Attractions*

Waimea Canyon; Napali Cliffs; Kukui Grove; Kalapaki Beach.

# 11

# MEXICO

It used to be that Mexican tennis was not much better than Mexican drinking water, but that situation has changed. The best tennis resorts in Mexico are on the Pacific coast, from Puerto Vallarta to Acapulco. Most of these resorts are part of large hotel chains where the food, service, and accommodations are standardized. They're good, not great. But they do have water purification plants, which can't be said of the average Mexican resort. For more upscale experiences, you can choose among a handful of private chichi operations like **La Brisas** or **Las Hadas** where you will pay dearly but get to mingle with the rich and famous, many of them Hollywood celebrities.

The Caribbean coast of Mexico is almost exclusively comprised of beach resorts, and that means Cancun—Mexico's "party capital" for the American tourist. You will be hard-pressed to find even a single decent tennis resort there, much less one that meets the high standards of those included in this book. You don't go to Cancun to play tennis, but should you visit there, consider a short plane or ferry ride to the island of Cozumel where the **Stouffer Presidente Cozumel** and the **Fiesta Americana Sol Caribe** have decent tennis operations—and some of the best snorkeling and scuba diving in the world.

# ACAPULCO PRINCESS, P.O. Box 1351, Acapulco, Mexico. (800) 223-1818

## Tennis

**Courts:** 11; 2 indoor
**Court Surfaces:** 9 Laykold, 2 Sportface
**Courts Lit For Night Play:** All
**Director of Tennis:** Tomas Flores          **Head Pro:** Tomas Flores
**Instruction Rates:** $24 per hour/individual/outdoors; $30 per hour/individual/indoors
**Court Time:** $14 per hour/day; $20 per hour/night; $23 per hour/indoors
**Video Analysis:** None
**Ball Machines:** Add $3 to court time rate
**Tournaments:** None
**Tennis Packages:** None
**Comments:** "Tennis is a pleasure here with ball boys retrieving balls and comfortable indoor courts, if the weather is inclement; pros try hard to improve your game."

## Accommodations

**Rooms:** 1,020
**Rooms With Water View:** 500
**Rates:** Start from $130 per room per night double occupancy; no charge for children 12 and under with parents
**Type of Crowd:** Families, groups, honeymooners
**Nearest Airport:** 10 minutes from Acapulco International Airport; no shuttle service
**Comments:** "Nice variety of rooms; bright and colorful decor; one-bedroom oceanfront suites are your best bet."

## Food

**Restaurants:** Veranda (international), Chula Vista (Spanish), La Posadita (international), La Princesa (continental), El Jardin (continental), Le Gourmet (French), La Hacienda (Mexican)
**Comments:** "You can't get much better than La Hacienda for terrific Mexican cuisine; Chula Vista and La Posadita are a must for fabulous international buffets."

## Special Features

18-hole golf course; four swimming pools; children's wading pool; babysitting; complimentary shuttle service to Pierre Marques.
**Nightlife:** Dancing in the Tiffany disco.

## Nearby Tourist Attractions

La Quebrada cliff divers; downtown Acapulco shopping.

# CAMINO REAL IXTAPA, Playa Vista Hermosa, Ixtapa, Mexico. (800) 228-3000, (011) 52-743-32121

## Tennis

**Courts:** 4
**Court Surfaces:** Hard
**Courts Lit For Night Play:** All
**Director of Tennis:** None    **Head Pro:** Armando Arredondo
**Instruction Rates:** $20 per hour/individual; group rates vary
**Court Time:** $7 per hour
**Video Analysis:** None
**Ball Machines:** None
**Tournaments:** None
**Tennis Packages:** None
**Comments:** "Arredondo is a solid pro and one of the best in Mexico."

## Accommodations

**Rooms:** 428
**Rooms With Water View:** All
**Rates:** Start from $110 per room, per night, double occupancy; no charge for children 18 and under with parents
**Type of Crowd:** Business groups, couples, families
**Nearest Airport:** 20 minutes from Zihuatanejo Airport; no shuttle service
**Comments:** "Every room has a terrace with a hammock and a grand view of the sun setting over the Pacific; suites come with a Jacuzzi or private pool on the balcony."

## Food

**Restaurants:** Portofino (Italian), El Mexicana (refined Mexican cuisine), Azulejos (international), La Cueva (beachfront grill)
**Comments:** "The restaurants offer ample variety and occasionally excel; the seafood dishes are usually the best."

## Special Features

Extraordinary "Mexican minimalist" architecture by Ricardo Legoretta; private beach; four swimming pools.
**Nightlife:** Mariachi music in the Lobby Bar.

## Nearby Tourist Attractions

Zihatanejo fishing village; Isle Ixtapa; secluded Las Gatas Beach; Playa La Ropa.

# EL CID MEGA RESORT, P.O. Box 813, Mazatlan, Mexico. (800) 525-1925, (011) 52-678-33333

### Tennis

**Courts:**  17
**Court Surfaces:**  13 hard, 4 clay
**Courts Lit For Night Play:**  6
**Director of Tennis:**  Pablo Sergio Franco          **Head Pro:**  Jose Cruz
**Instruction Rates:**  $20 per hour/individual; group rates vary
**Court Time:**  $5 per hour/day; $8 per hour/night
**Video Analysis:**  None
**Ball Machines:**  1; included in instruction rate
**Tournaments:**  None
**Tennis Packages:**  None
**Comments:**  "Mexico's most extensive tennis resort center."

### Accommodations

**Rooms:**  1,100
**Rooms With Water View:**  980
**Rates:**  Start from $45 per room, per night, double occupancy; no charge for children 12 and under with parents
**Type of Crowd:**  Business groups, couples, families
**Nearest Airport:**  25 minutes from Mazaltan Airport; no shuttle service
**Comments:**  "Room size, decor, price and views vary substantially; rooms with view of pools on lower floors of the residential towers are a good value."

### Food

**Restaurants:**  Twelve in Mazaltan Resort area
**Comments:**  "The quality is uneven, but if you pick carefully you can eat moderately well."

### Special Features

Beach; six swimming pools; 18-hole golf course; squash; racquetball; fitness center; water sports; more shops than some small cities.
**Nightlife:**  Music in the Lobby Bar and dancing in El Caracol Tango Palace disco.

### Nearby Tourist Attractions

Mazatlan has many shops, restaurants, and clubs, but no compelling sights or other attractions.

## FIESTA AMERICANA PLAZA VALLARTA, Avenida de las Garzas, Puerto Vallarta, Mexico. (800) 223-2332, (011) 52-322-24448

### Tennis

**Courts:** 8
**Court Surfaces:** 4 Laykold, 4 clay
**Courts Lit For Night Play:** All
**Director of Tennis:** Miguel Angel Reyesvarela     **Head Pro:** Martin Parra
**Instruction Rates:** $30 per hour/individual; group rates vary
**Court Time:** $8 per hour
**Video Analysis:** $40 per hour
**Ball Machines:** None
**Tournaments:** None
**Tennis Packages:** Start from $780 per room, double occupancy for 8 days/7 nights, including one-hour clinic, four hours of court time, breakfast daily and one dinner.
**Comments:** "The hotel's John Newcombe Tennis Club is the top facility in Puerto Vallarta and one of the most complete in Mexico."

### Accommodations

**Rooms:** 438
**Rooms With Water View:** 250
**Rates:** Start from $75 per room, per night, double occupancy; no charge for children 12 and under with parents
**Type of Crowd:** Couples, singles
**Nearest Airport:** 15 minutes from Puerto Vallarta Airport; no shuttle service
**Comments:** "Rooms are standard in most respects, but a superb value for conventional comfort."

### Food

**Restaurants:** Los Cantaros (international), Los Peces (seafood), Place Vendome (Cajun and Creole)
**Comments:** "The food is moderately priced and moderately good; avoid the 'Louisiana specialties' which are more trendy than tasty."

### Special Features

One of the few modern low-rise hotels in the city; swimming pool; garden courtyard; beach.
**Nightlife:** Music in the Lobby Bar.

### Nearby Tourist Attractions

Downtown Puerto Vallarta; village of Yelapa.

# LAS BRISAS, P.O. Box 281, Acapulco, Mexico. (800) 228-3000, (011) 52-748-42269

## *Tennis*

**Courts:** 5
**Court Surfaces:** Laykold
**Courts Lit For Night Play:** All
**Director of Tennis:** None        **Head Pro:** Felix Campos
**Instruction Rates:** $23 per hour/individual; group rates vary
**Court Time:** $10 per hour/day; $15 per hour/night
**Video Analysis:** None
**Ball Machines:** None
**Tournaments:** None
**Tennis Packages:** None
**Comments:** "Courts are spectacularly located, at the top of the hillside hotel; Campos knows his game even though he can't offer the frills."

## *Accommodations*

**Rooms:** 265
**Rooms With Water View:** All
**Rates:** Start from $125 per room, per night, double occupancy; no charge for children 18 and under with parents
**Type of Crowd:** Couples, honeymooners
**Nearest Airport:** 15 minutes from Acapulco International Airport; no shuttle service
**Comments:** "The patios are the highlight, featuring a private or semi-private pool overlooking Acapulco Bay; the casitas on levels three through five offer one of the grandest panoramas in the world."

## *Food*

**Restaurants:** Bellavista (continental), El Mexicana (nouvelle Mexican), La Concha (international)
**Comments:** "The cooking is inconsistent, but occassionally rivals the superb ocean views from the restaurants."

## *Special Features*

Frequently called the most romantic hotel on earth; beach club; water sports.
**Nightlife:** Dancing nightly in El Tulipan.

## *Nearby Tourist Attractions*

La Quebrada cliff divers; town of Taxco; downtown Acapulco.

# LAS HADAS, Manzanillo, Mexico. (800) 228-3000, (011) 52-333-30000

## Tennis

**Courts:** 10
**Court Surfaces:** 8 hard, 2 clay
**Courts Lit For Night Play:** 8
**Director of Tennis:** None     **Head Pro:** Mario Correa
**Instruction Rates:** $30 per hour/individual; group rates vary
**Court Time:** $12 per hour
**Video Analysis:** None
**Ball Machines:** 2; $30 per hour including court time
**Tournaments:** None
**Tennis Packages:** Start from $1,050 per room, double occupancy for 8 days/7 nights, including three hours of tennis, ball boy services, breakfast daily and free admission to disco.
**Comments:** "One of the most progressive programs in Mexico, if not comparable to the better tennis resorts in the U.S."

## Accommodations

**Rooms:** 220
**Rooms With Water View:** All
**Rates:** Start at $125 per room, per night, double occupancy; no charge for children 12 and under with parents
**Type of Crowd:** Business groups, couples, families
**Nearest Airport:** 25 minutes from Manzanillo Airport; no shuttle service
**Comments:** "Rooms are designed to be opulent, but aren't always well maintained; ocean views can be very limited."

## Food

**Restaurants:** Legazpi (continental), El Terral (Mexican), Los Delfines (seafood), El Palmar (international)
**Comments:** "Food varies from average to good, but is seldom a value."

## Special Features

Fanciful Moorish architecture helped make Las Hadas famous in the 1970s; 18-hole golf course; water sports; major marina somewhat polluted water and fair beach.
**Nightlife:** Music nightly in Lobby Lounge.

## Nearby Tourist Attractions

Town of Manzanillo; Costa de Careyes.

# VILLA VERA HOTEL & RAQUET CLUB, Lomas del Mar 35, Acapulco, Mexico. (800) 223-6510, (011) 52-748-40333

## *Tennis*

**Courts:** 3
**Court Surfaces:** Clay
**Courts Lit For Night Play:** All
**Director of Tennis:** Baltazar Mojica          **Head Pro:** Baltazar Mojica
**Instruction Rates:** $25 per hour/individual; group rates vary
**Court Time:** $18 per hour
**Video Analysis:** None
**Ball Machines:** None
**Tournaments:** None
**Tennis Packages:** Start from $400 per room, double occupancy for 4 days/3 nights, including unlimited court time.
**Comments:** "Despite lack of services, Villa Vera is as dedicated to tennis as any resort in Mexico; the courts—the first constructed at any hotel in the country—remain among the best."

## *Accommodations*

**Rooms:** 80
**Rooms With Water View:** 23
**Rates:** Start from $120 per room, per night, double occupancy; children 16 and under not permitted
**Type of Crowd:** Couples, singles
**Nearest Airport:** 25 minutes from Acapulco International Airport; no shuttle service
**Comments:** "The least expensive rooms are standard quarters, and are comfortable but not compelling; the suites with semi-private pools are far more desirable and a good value; the villas, with a staff of three each, are magnificent."

## *Food*

**Restaurants:** Villa Vera Restaurant (international)
**Comments:** "The restaurant sits by the main pool; the cooking is only slightly above average."

## *Special Features*

A main Hollywood hangout in Acapulco's glory days, Villa Vera retains the feel of the jet-set; beach services provided by a nearby hotel.
**Nightlife:** Watching the lights of Acapulco from the alfresco bar.

## *Nearby Tourist Attractions*

La Quebrada cliff divers; downtown Acapulco.

# TOP 10 LISTS

*In the best spirit of David Letterman, but with a lot more seriousness, these Top 10 Lists were composed using information gathered over the last four years from* World Tennis *readers and reviewers, as well as players and coaches.*

## Top 10 Pet Peeves About All Types of Resorts

10. Stale-smelling rooms.
 9. Brusque, incompetent front desk personnel.
 8. Late or missed wake-up calls.
 7. Poor water pressure.
 6. Unfriendly service.
 5. Inability to get an outside telephone line.
 4. Room keys that don't work.
 3. Hard pillows.
 2. Having to wait interminably to check in and check out.
 1. Thin, cheap bath towels.

## Top 10 Pet Peeves About Tennis Resorts

10. Tennis balls without ample air pressure.

9. Rackets with poor string tension.

8. Pro shops that do not string rackets.

7. Pro shops that only rent aluminum rackets.

6. Instructors who put too many pupils in group clinics, forcing those pupils to spend an inordinate amount of time "standing around."

5. Instructors who watch the clock.

4. Instructors who don't finish a lesson at the appointed time, leaving the next pupil or pupils waiting.

3. Nets that slouch.

2. No towels, soft drinks, or water at courtside, or in the pro shop.

1. No matching service to find you an opponent or partner to play with—at your skill level.

## Top 10 European Tennis Resorts

10. Hanbury Manor, Thundridge, Hertfordshire, England, tel. (092) 048-7722. A new hotel 45 minutes northwest of London, but built in the old-fashioned Victorian style. Gorgeous antique decor. 3 hard courts.

9. Club Med Kamarina, Sicily, Italy, tel. 800-Club-Med. Set in a small village on southwest Sicilian coast with beautiful beaches and numerous historic sites. 21 clay, 7 hard courts.

8. Crieff Hydro Hotel, Crieff, Perthshire, Scotland, tel. (44)764-2401-9. Luxury hotel in verdant Scottish countryside near Perthshire. Offers, among other things, horseback riding, golf, and croquet. 3 clay, 2 all-weather courts.

7. Hotel Montechero, Albufeira, Algarve, Portugal, tel. (089) 526-5113. Luxury 362-room resort with beautiful ocean views, disco, water sports, and pools. 8 all-weather courts (2 lit).

6. Club Med Pompadour, Pompadour, France, tel. 800–Club–Med. In southwest France near Limoges (Renoir's birthplace), this Club Med has a ball machine and video analysis, with 1-, 2- and 3- bedroom suites. 19 clay courts.

5. Puente Romano, Marbella, Spain, tel. (52) 770100 or (800) 223–6800. Situated on one of Marbella's best beaches. Private cottages with pools, lush garden, and paths. Bjorn Borg was the touring pro in the early 1980s. Located near jet-set fishing village/marina of Puerto Banos. Other hotels nearby with superior tennis include Los Monteros, Marbella Club, and Hotel Don Pepe. 12 hard courts.

4. Hotel Stanglwirt, Going/Tyrol, Austria, tel. 0043/5358–2000. Nestled in the Austrian Alps near Strousburg, this luxurious hotel has magnificent scenery and a superb tennis program run by Peter Burwash. 11 clay courts (3 indoor).

3. Lew Hoad's Campo de Tennis, Mijas, Costa del Sol, Spain, tel. 0103/452474858. One of Europe's most popular tennis facilities. Conveniently located near Malaga Airport. 1- and 2-bedroom apartments. 8 hard courts.

2. Pierre Barthes at Cap d'Agole, Languedoc, France, tel. (011) 3367260006. 62 courts (including 16 lit, 6 indoors) In the south of France, known for years as the largest tennis center in the world. Within walking distance to beaches. A bed and breakfast. 62 courts (including 16 lit, 6 indoor).

1. The Palace, Gstaad, Switzerland, tel. 831–31. Plush, family-owned, 150-room hotel set in the Swiss Alps. 7 hard courts (3 indoor).

# Top 10 Off-the-Beaten-Path Tennis Resorts

10. Walley's Hot Springs, Genoa, Nevada, (702) 782–8155
    This bed and breakfast, originally established as a bath
    house in 1862, is situated in Nevada's first settled town.
    There are 5 cottages at the foothills of the Sierra Nevada
    Mountains and 6 natural mineral springs to restore mind
    and body. 2 hard courts.

9. 'Tween Waters Inn, Captiva Island, Florida, (813) 472–
   5161 Modern 2-story lodge encircles Olympic-size pool
   and tennis complex and is adjacent to a bird sanctuary. 3
   hard courts (all lit).

8. Hotel du Village, New Hope, Pennsylvania, (215) 862–
   9911 Quaint bed and breakfast with 20 rooms and superb
   French country cuisine, and all reasonably priced. 2 all-
   weather courts.

7. Christopher Inn, Excelsior, Minnesota, (612) 474–6816
   Posh bed and breakfast in an 8-room Victorian mansion
   with antiques and fireplaces galore. The inn's claim to fame
   is that it has the only grass court in the state and is ideally
   situated on Lake Minnetonka. Ironically, the inn is run by a
   man named Howard Johnson. 1 grass court.

6. Clevelands House, Minett, Ontario, Canada, (705) 765–
   3171 Tennis is the principal attraction at this 175-room
   lakeside lodge some 150 miles north of Toronto. Accommodations are scattered among 5 lodge buildings and individual bungalows. There is a 9-hole golf course and the
   tennis program is geared for children as well as adults. 16
   Plexipave courts.

5. Sangra de Cristo Racquet Club, Santa Fe, New Mexico,
   (505) 983–7978 Has only 1 hotel suite available to rent at
   $70 per night; understandably it's nearly impossible to

book.  7 hard courts (1 indoor).

4.  Mendocino Tennis Club, Mendocino, California, (707)
    937–0007 Lush woodlands surround this 3-bedroom bed
    and breakfast 2 miles from the Pacific Ocean, with a hot
    tub and swimming pool. Run by a husband (a USPTA
    instructor) and wife.  3 hard courts.

3.  The American Club, Kohler, Wisconsin (414) 457–8000
    162-room resort with old Alpine look, whose main lodge is
    on National Register of Historic Places and is adjacent to
    an 800-acre wildlife preserve. 6 hard courts (3 indoor).

2.  Lakeway Resort & Conference Center, Austin, Texas,
    (800) LAKEWAY A sprawling assemblage of town homes
    sprinkled among golf fairways and a man-made lake.  A
    sort of Saddlebrook of Texas and the best that Texas has to
    offer. 32 hard courts (26 lit, 2 indoor).

1.  Lodge of the Four Seasons & Racquet Club, Lake Ozark,
    Missouri, (800) THE–LAKE The Midwest headquarters of
    Dennis Van der Meer is nestled among forests and lakes
    and has total privacy. 23 hard, 4 clay courts.

# Top 10 Potpourri for 1991

10. **Best New Caribbean Resort:** Swept Away, Negril,
    Jamaica.  An impressive sports and fitness complex that
    includes 8 courts (4 hard, 4 clay) plus a 500-seat stadium
    court.  The Caribbean isn't known for its tennis facilities,
    so this resort really stands out.

9.  **Resort With the Most Potential:** The Westin Mission
    Hills Resort, Rancho Mirage, California.  This totally
    renovated 512-room resort opened in September 1991 and
    offers a complete health and fitness center featuring 7 hard

courts (all lit for night play) and a 500-seat stadium court.

8. **Most Exclusive Resort:** Jumby Bay, Antigua, British West Indies. On its own island, Superb food. Only 38 rooms. Simple elegance. No telephone, radio, TV, air conditioner, mini-bar—nothing. It's called "reverse marketing." And you pay for it, baby!

7. **Best New Canadian Resort:** King Ranch Resort & Spa, King City, Ontario, Canada. For its 6 new Poly-Court 500 tennis courts and a 70,000-square-foot health spa.

6. **Best Service at a Resort:** The Omni Sagamore, Bolton Landing, New York. Sparkling thoroughness, from the maitre d' to the bellhop.

5. **Most Overwritten About Resort:** La Costa, Carlsbad, California. The public relations director deserves a raise.

4. **Most Underrated Resort:** Gray Rocks Inn, St. Jovite, Quebec, Canada. Well-managed, well-fed, with 25 tennis pros serving 22 courts. C'est magnifique!

3. **Most Commercial Resort Destination:** Cancun, Mexico. For the teenager or college student looking to spend his or her vacation in Margaritaville. Cancun was built from scratch for the American tourist; it is a Mexican version of Miami Beach, overbuilt, overrated and pretty darn expensive when you consider what things cost in Mexico. Worse, the once-tantalizing turquoise water now has, at times, an offensive aroma, toilet paper has been seen bobbing in the water.

2. **Most Charming Resort Destination:** Bermuda. Nowhere else can you find such small, quaint cottage resorts. Each resort may only have one or two courts, but that's all you need. The town of St. George is right out of another

century with its cobblestone streets and tiny shops. Very British. Very expensive. But unlike the Caribbean, there's no poverty here. One of the few vestiges of the British Empire that still retains its charm.

1. **Nightmare Airport of the Year:** Donald Sangster International Airport, Montego Bay, Jamaica. For its shoddy appearance and the unsavory characters who populate it. There is no telling who or what you'll find lurking in the men's room. There is always a scam going on, be it counterfeit jewelry or drugs. And whatever you do, keep an eye on your wallet. Credit card fraud is a major industry here. And because the tour buses also carry locals to and from the hotels, say good-bye to anything you accidentally leave behind.

## Top Ten Family Tennis Resorts

10. Bolongo Bay Beach & Tennis Club, St. Thomas, Virgin Islands, (800) 524–4746. For people watching their budget. Kids' Korner for ages 3–12. Two-bedroom suites or villas come with full kitchens. Tennis program run by the dean of tennis on St. Thomas, 65-year-old Vic Everson. 4 hard courts.

9. Sundial Beach & Tennis Resort, Sanibel Island, Florida, (800) 237–4184. Children ages 14 and under stay free with parents. "Pelican Pete's" supervised program for ages 5–12. 13 Har-Tru courts.

8. Hyatt Cerromar Beach, Dorado, Puerto Rico, (800) 233–1234. Children ages 12 and under stay free with parents. Unlimited court time. The Dorado and its sister resort, the Hyatt Regency Dorado Beach, share the same tennis facilities as well as a children's camp—Kamp Hyatt. 21 hard courts.

7. Longboat Key Club, Longboat Key, Florida, (800) 237–8821. This Gulf Coast resort offers its courts and stroke and strategy clinics for adults and children at no charge. There are also supervised children's programs, from Olympic-style competitions and off-property excursions to pizza and movie parties. 18 Har-Tru courts.

6. Boscobel Beach, Ocho Rios, Jamaica, (800) 858–8009. This resort is totally geared to kids, from popcorn machines and game rooms to kiddie pools and a fabulous petting zoo near the courts so parents can play a set while the kids pet away within eye contact. "Super Nannies" look after your children 12 hours per day. 4 hard courts.

5. Hawk's Cay Resort & Marina, Duck Key, Florida, (800) 327–7775. Children ages 11 and under stay free with parents. Kid's Club provides 7 hours of daily supervision. The Hawk's Cay Tennis School offers instruction to children and adults. There are daily dolphin shows and, for an extra $40, your child can actually swim with the dolphins. If you're going to take the kids to the Florida Keys, this is it. 6 hard, 2 Har-Tru courts.

4. Sea Pines Plantation, Hilton Head, South Carolina, (800) 845–6131. Sprawling property. Great place for a family to rent a private house or condo on the beach or bay. You're given a key and left alone. You need a car to get practically everywhere. Racquet Club is majestic; site of Family Circle Magazine Cup and touring pro Stan Smith. 24 clay, 5 hard courts.

3. Club Med's Baby Club, at The Sandpiper, Port St. Lucie, Florida, (800) Club-Med. The Baby Club is designed for ages 2 and under. Professionally staffed nursery from 8 A.M. to 6 P.M.. 19 Plexipave courts.

2. Franklin D. Resort, St. Ann, Jamaica, (800) 654–1FDR.

Compact sea-side property. Children are always within eye-view. Sixty-seven beautifully appointed suites, and the best part: You get your own "Girl Friday" to look after your children from morning till night. An improvement on the Boslobel "Super Nanny" concept. 1 hard court (with 2 more planned).

1. The Colony Beach & Tennis Resort, Longboat Key, Florida, (800) 237-9443 Children ages 18 and under stay free with parents. Complimentary program for children ages 4-12 from 9 A.M. to 4 P.M. daily. 15 hard, 6 soft courts.

## Top 10 Romantic Island Getaways

10. San Souci, Ocho Rios, Jamaica, (800) 237-3237. Spa resort with mineral pools. Situated on mountain hillside above the Caribbean Sea. 3 hard courts.

9. Southampton Princess, Southampton, Bermuda, (800) 223-1818. Play tennis overlooking subtropical turquoise waters. 11 hard courts.

8. Ocean Club Golf & Tennis Resort, Paradise Island, Bahamas, (800) 321-3000. Secluded, simple elegance. There are only 71 rooms. Great room to court ratio. 9 Har-Tru courts.

7. Enchanted Garden, Ocho Rios, Jamaica, (800) 654-1337. Spanking new hillside retreat for adults amidst 20 acres of lush gardens with waterfalls. And its priced all-inclusive. 2 hard courts.

6. Hyatt Regency St. John, St. John, U.S. Virgin Islands, (809) 776-7171. Formerly the Virgin Grand. Set on a private bay. 6 Omni courts.

5. Caneel Bay Plantation, St. John, U.S. Virgin Islands, (800) 223-7637. Besides the Hyatt, this is the island's other upscale playground. Unspoiled water and beach. Luxurious accommodations, and very expensive. 11 hard courts.

4. Stouffer Presidente Cozumel, Cozumel, Mexico, (800) HOTELS-1. Situated along unspoiled tropical reef. Courts are brand-new but rarely used so you can play when you want. Book one of the "reef suites." 2 hard courts.

3. Curtain Bluff, Antigua, British West Indies, (809) 462-8400. Small, exclusive, and private. A special place for special people. Some of the best tennis in the Caribbean. 5 Laykold courts.

2. Kapalua Bay Hotel & Villas, Kapalua, Maui, Hawaii, (800) 367-8000. Gorgeous tennis garden and unbelievable ocean views. 10 Plexipave courts.

1. Hotel La Samanna, St. Martin, (800) 372-1323. Glorious! Forty-six suites, and villas on 50 acres of private beachfront. The cuisine is as good as it gets—anywhere. 3 hard courts.

## Top 10 Best Tennis Resorts

Unfortunately there are only eight of them, eight resorts that have scored all 5's in our five areas for judging: tennis, food, service, accommodations, and special features. These eight tennis resorts tie for first. More information on these resorts can be found in the book under the appropriate geographical locations.

Boca Raton Resort & Club, Boca Raton, Florida

Fisher Island, Fisher Island, Florida

The Phoenician, Scottsdale, Arizona

La Quinta Hotel, La Quinta, California (the only resort to receive a 5+ rating for tennis).

Ritz-Carlton, Rancho Mirage, California

St. James's Club, Antigua, British West Indies

Topnotch at Stowe, Stowe, Vermont

Scottsdale Princess, Scottsdale, Arizona

# TENNIS CAMP DIRECTORY

This complete international tennis camp directory lists camps alphabetically, first state-by-state within the U.S. and then in Canada, Europe and Australia, New Zealand and Fiji. Entries include the camp's name, location, type of accommodations, number and type of courts, student/instructor ratio and whether the camp is co-ed. Camps are coded to indicate adult and/or junior programs ("A" for adult, "J" for junior, "AJ" for both). Addresses and business telephone numbers are also included for obtaining additional information. Where appropriate, tournament-level sessions, age ranges for juniors, and specialized group programs (for singles, seniors, teams, etc.) are also included. Special distinguishing features have been noted, where appropriate, in descriptions provided by camp directors. Things to consider when choosing a camp that's right for you:

**Accommodations**: Camps in college settings often house their guests in college dormitories. If you would prefer living in a hotel, choose a camp in a resort setting.

**Food**: Not all camps serve low-calorie or health-conscious meals. If this is important to you, find out about the camp's food plan before making your decision.

**Instructors**: The experience and reputation of a camp's instruction staff will be a major consideration. Try to speak to a former guest or someone who knows the instructors before deciding on a camp.

**Instructor/Student Ratio**: Individual attention is essential to learning in camp, as well as in school. The best situations to look for are low student/instructor ratios (about four-to-one), and groups with one instructor who stays with you throughout your visit.

**Level of Play**: Most camps are designed to teach at all levels, but make sure your skill level is appropriate for the camp you are considering.

Whichever camp you choose, don't expect instant, dramatic improvement. What you learn at camp will pay off, but not right away. Incorporating what you learn into your game is a matter of time and practice. Tennis camp will help you improve your weaknesses and sharpen your strategy, but remember: Ivan Lendl wasn't built in a day!

# United States

## ALABAMA

J   Alabama Tennis Academy, Marion Military Institute, Marion, Ala. Dormitory. 9 courts. 5:1. Co-ed (ages 7–17). Contact: John H. McWilliams III, 530 Ravenwood Dr., Selma, Ala. 36701. (205) 875–7505.

J   Crimson Tide Tennis Camp, University of Alabama, Tuscaloosa, Ala. Dormitory. 30 lit hard courts; 4 indoor. 5:1. Co-ed (ages 9–18). Contact: John Kreis, 821 Ashland Dr., Tuscaloosa, Ala. 35406. (205) 348–3686 or 348–6161.

J   Jim Moortgat Tennis Academy, Birmingham, Ala. Dormitory. 11 courts (10 outdoor; 1 indoor), all lit. 4:1. Co-ed (ages 10–18). Contact: Jim Moortgat, 1232 Krin Ave., Birmingham, Ala. 35213. (205) 956–5245 (home) or (205) 870–2592 (work).

## ARIZONA

A J   Arizona Biltmore Resort Camp, Phoenix, Ariz. Resort hotel. 14 hard, 3 artificial grass courts. 5:1. Co-ed (ages 8–14). Contact: Lucky Cotten, Director of Tennis, Arizona Biltmore, 24th Street & Missouri, Phoenix, Ariz. 85016. (602) 954–2508.

A J Elite Tennis Program, Scottsdale, Ariz. Hotel. 21 courts. 4:1. Contact: Registry Resort, 7171 N. Scottsdale Rd., Scottsdale, Ariz. 85253. (602) 991-3800.

A John Gardiner's Tennis Ranch on Camelback, Scottsdale, Ariz. Resort hotel. 24 courts. 4:1. Co-ed. Contact: John Gardiner's Tennis Ranch on Camelback, 5700 E. McDonald Dr., Scottsdale, Ariz. 85253. (800) 245-2051.

A The Pointe at Tapatio Cliffs, Phoenix, Ariz. Resort hotel. 6 courts. 6:1. Weekdays: 6-hour, 9-hour, and 15-hour year-round clinics. Contact: Mike Popescue, The Pointe at Tapatio Cliffs Racquet Club, 11111 N. 7th St., Phoenix, Ariz. 85020. (602) 866-7500 ext. 7170 (club), (602) 977-7777 (reservations), or (800) 528-0428.

A Westward Look Resort, Tuscon, Ariz. Deluxe resort. 8 courts, 5 lit. 4:1. Sessions run 4 days, 3 hours/day. Contact: John Davis, USPTA (Director of Recreation), Westward Cook Resort, 245 East Ina Rd., Tuscon, Ariz. 85704. (602) 297-4758.

A Wickenburg Inn Tennis and Guest Ranch, Wickenburg, Ariz. Resort hotel. 11 outdoor courts. 4:1. Co-ed. Contact: Chuck Fowler, Director of Tennis, P.O. Box P, Wickenburg, Ariz. 85358. (602) 684-7811.

## CALIFORNIA

J Adidas/Irvine Tennis Camp, University of California at Irvine, Irvine, Calif. Dormitory. 12 outdoor courts. 5:1. Co-ed (ages 9–18). Contact: U.S. Sports Development, 919 Sir Francis Drake Blvd., Kentfield, Calif. 94904. (800) 433-6060 or (415) 490-0459.

J  Adidas/Santa Cruz Tennis Camp, University of California at Santa Cruz, Calif. Dormitory. 10 outdoor courts. 5:1 Co-ed (ages 9–18). Contact: U.S. Sports Development, 919 Sir Francis Drake Blvd., Kentfield, Calif. 94904. (800) 433–6060 or (415) 459–0459.

J  Adidas/Stanford Tennis Camp, Stanford University, Palo Alto, Calif. Dormitory. 18 outdoor courts. 5:1. Co-ed (ages 10–17). Contact: U.S. Sports Development, 919 Sir Francis Drake Blvd., Kentfield, Calif. 94904. (800) 433–6060 or (415) 459–0459.

J  Adidas/Tahoe Tennis Camp, Granlibalcken Resort, Lake Tahoe, Calif. Condominium. 8 outdoor courts. 5:1. Co-ed (ages 9–18). Contact: U.S. Sports Development, 919 Sir Francis Drake Blvd., Kentfield, Calif. 94904. (800) 433–6060 or (415) 459–0459.

A  Reed Anderson Tennis School, Palm Springs, Calif. Hotel (suites). 6 outdoor courts. 5:1. Contact: Reed Anderson, Gene Autrey Hotel, 4200 E. Palm Canyon Dr., Palm Springs, Calif. 92264. (800) 288–1171.

J  The Bassett–Martin Tennis Camp, Ojai Valley, Calif. Dormitory, hotel. 10 outdoor courts. 5:1. Co-ed (ages 9–18). Contact: Billy Martin, The Bassett–Martin Tennis Camp, P.O. Box 27446, Rancho Bernardo, Calif. 92198–1446. (213) 473–6660 or (619) 485–9030.

A J  Bear Valley Tennis Club, Bear Valley, Calif. Condominium, dormitory, hotel. 6 outdoor hard courts. 5:1. Co-ed (ages 12–18). Contact: Felix P. Barbera, P.O. Box 794, Twain Harte, Calif. 95383. (209) 753–6440 or (209) 586–2464.

A   Rancho Bernardo Inn Tennis College, San Diego, Calif. Hotel/resort. 12 hard courts. 5:1. Year-round 2-, 4- and 5-day sessions. Contact: Paul Navratil, Rancho Bernardo Inn Tennis College, 17550 Bernardo Oaks Dr., San Diego, Calif. 92128. (619) 487–2413 or (800) 854–1065 or (800) 542–6096 in California.


A J   Chuck Boyle Tennis Academy at Ramona Canton Racquet Club, San Diego, Calif. Condominium. 20 outdoor courts. 6:1. Co-ed (ages 10–18). Contact: Chuck Boyle, 24554 Tesoro Way, Ramona, Calif. 92065. (619) 788–0253.


A J   Vic Braden Tennis College, Coto de Caza, Calif. Tennis village. 16 courts. 6:1. Co-ed (ages 10 and over). Year-round. Contact: Vic Braden Tennis College, 23335 Avenida La Caza, Coto de Caza, Calif. 92679. (800) CALL-VIC in state, or (800) 42–COURT out of California.


J   Frank Brennan Tennis Academy, Stanford University, Palo Alto, Calif. Dormitory. 18 outdoor courts; 1 indoor court. 1:5. Co-ed (ages 9–17). Contact: Frank Brennan, Dept. of Athletics, Stanford University, Palo Alto, Calif. 94305. (415) 948–8781 or (415) 723–9540.


J   California State University, Hayward Junior Tennis Camp, Hayward, Calif. Dormitory. 9 hard courts. 5:1. Co-ed (ages 10–18). Contact: Kris or Kevin Milligan, 2992 Sombrero Circle, San Ramon, Calif. 94583. (415) 867–1696, outside California: (800) 346–0163.


J   Carmel Valley Tennis Camp, Carmel, Calif. Dormitory-style. 8 hard courts; additional practice areas. 3:1. Co-ed (ages 8–18). Contact: Susan Reeder, 27300 Rancho San Carlos Rd., Carmel, Calif. 93923. (800) 234–7117.

J   The Carmel Valley Inn Junior Tennis Camp, Carmel Valley, Calif. Lodge. 7 hard courts. 5:1. Co-ed (ages 10–18). Contact: Kris Milligan, 2992 Sombrero Circle, San Ramon, Calif. 94583. (415) 867–1696, outside California: (800) 346–0163.

A J   Ed Collins USD Tennis Camp, San Diego, Calif. Dormitory. 8 outdoor courts. 6:1. Co-ed (ages 10–17). Contact: Deb Pint, Ed Collins USD Tennis Camp, University of San Diego, Alcala Park, San Diego, Calif. 92110. (619) 260–4593.

J   Allen Fox/Adidas Tennis Camp at Malibu, Pepperdine University, Malibu, Calif. Dormitory. 11 outdoor courts. 5:1. Co-ed (ages 9–18). Contact: U.S. Sports Development, 919 Sir Francis Drake Blvd., Kentfield, Calif. 94904. (800) 433–6060 or (415) 459–0459.

J   John Gardiner Tennis Camp, Carmel Valley, Calif. Dormitory. 17 courts. 3:1. Co-ed (ages 9–16). Contact: Jeff Stewart, John Gardiner Tennis Camp, P.O. Box 227, Carmel Valley, Calif. 93924.

J   Bob Johns Tennis Camp at University of California at Santa Barbara, University of California, Santa Barbara, Calif. Dormitory. 24 outdoor courts. 6:1. Co-ed (ages 8–18). Contact: Bob Johns, Ph.D., Dept. of Physical Activities, University of California, Santa Barbara, Santa Barbara, Calif. 93106. (805) 968–8443.

J   Prince Tennis Camp, University of California at San Diego, San Diego, Calif. Dormitory. 8 outdoor courts. 5:1. Co-ed (ages 10–18). Contact: Bill Scott, 1381 Camino Lujan, San Diego, Calif. 92111. (619) 560–8870 or (800) 628–5391.

J   Shadow Mountain Resort—The Desert Tennis Academy. Palm Desert, Calif. Hotel and condominium. 16 hard courts (5 lit). 5:1. Co-ed (ages 6–16). Contact: Owen Gillen, Shadow Mt. Resort and Racquet Club, 45–750 San Luis Rey, Palm Desert, Calif. 92260. (619) 346–6123.

J   Stanford National Junior Training Camp, Stanford University, Palo Alto, Calif. Dormitory. 18 outdoor courts. 5:1. Co-ed (ages 10–17). Contact: U.S. Sports Development, 919 Sir Francis Drake Blvd., Kentfield, Calif. 94904. (800) 433–6060 or (415) 459–0459.

## COLORADO

J   Aspen Club Junior Tennis Program, Aspen, Colo. Condominium and house. 9 courts (7 outdoor; 2 indoor). 4–6:1. Co-ed (ages 7–18). Contact: Mike White, Aspen Club, 1450 Crystal Lake Rd., Aspen, Colo. 81611. (303) 925–8900.

J   Benson's Tennis Camp of Colorado. University of Colorado, Boulder, Colo. Dormitory. 14 outdoor courts. 5:1. Co-ed (ages 8–18). Contact: Bill Benson, 5090 S. Franklin St., Englewood, Colo. 80110. (303) 781–7036.

A   Copper Mountain Resort Weekend Clinic, Copper Mountain, Colo. Hotel or condominium. 8 courts (6 outdoor; 2 indoor). 4:1. Contact: Dave Turrin, Copper Mountain Resort, P.O. Box 3001, Copper Mountain, Colo. 80443. (303) 968–2882.

J   Keystone Tennis Center, Keystone, Colo. Hotel and condominium. 14 courts (12 outdoor; 2 indoor). 4:1. Co-ed (ages 6–12). Contact: John O'Connor, Keystone Tennis Center, P.O. Box 38, Keystone, Colo. 80435. (303) 468–4220.

A   Vail Racquet Club Tennis Camp. Vail, Colo. Condominium and townhouse. 4:1. Contact: Simon Robinson, Vail Racquet Club, P.O. Box 1088, Vail, Colo. 81658. (303) 476-3267.

A J   Bill Wright's Tennis Camps, Vail, Colo. Hotel accommodations for juniors only. 23 courts. Juniors: 4:1, adults: 5:1. Co-ed (ages 10-17). Contact: Kathy Payne, P.O. Box 1462, Vail, Colo. 81658. (303) 476-5823. Off-season: Vail Metro Recreational District, 292 West Meadow Dr., Vail, Colo. 81658. (303) 479-2280.

## CONNECTICUT

J   Ken-Mont and Ken-Wood Camps, Kent, Conn. Cabin. 20 outdoor courts (4 lit). 5:1. Brother/sister camp (ages 6-16). Contact: Lloyd Albin. Winter: 2 Spencer Pl., Scarsdale, N.Y. 10583. (914) 725-4333. Summer: North Spectacle Lake, Kent, Conn. 06755. (203) 927-3042.

J   University of Connecticut/Bishop-Kirtland Tennis Camp, Storrs, Conn. Dormitory. 23 courts (20 outdoor; 3 indoor). 4-5:1 on-court; 8:1 off-court. Co-ed (ages 6-17). Contact: Ben Kirtland, 33 Dubcaster Lane, Vernon, Conn. 06066. (203) 486-3863.

## DELAWARE

A J   Sea Colony Tennis Camps. Sea Colony Tennis Resort, Bethany Beach, Del. Condominium. 21 courts (18 outdoor; 3 indoor). 4-5:1. Co-ed (ages 5-17). Contact: Dave Marshall, Director of Tennis, Sea Colony Tennis Resort, Bethany Beach, Del. 19930. (302) 539-4488.

# FLORIDA

A   Terry Addison's Australian Tennis Institute. Innisbrook Resort and Golf Club, Tarpon Springs, Fla. Condominium. 18 courts. 4:1. Contact: Terry Addison, Innisbrook Resort and Golf Club, P.O. Drawer 1088, Tarpon Springs, Fla. 34688-1088. (813) 942-2000.

A J   Patricio Apey's Tennis Academy. Sheraton/Royal Biscayne Resort, Key Biscayne, Fla. Hotel. 10 courts. 4-6:1. Co-ed (ages 4-18). Contact: Patricio Apey, Sheraton/Royal Biscayne Pro Shop, 555 Ocean Dr., Key Biscayne, Fla. 33149. (305) 361-3030.

A J   Nick Bollettieri Tennis Summer Camp, Nick Bollettieri Tennis Academy, Bradenton, Fla. Apartments, with two bedrooms and bathrooms, living and dining area. 54 courts (35 outdoor hard; 15 outdoor soft clay; 4 indoor hard). 4:1. Co-ed. Contact: Londa Franjola, NBTA, 5500 34th Street West, Bradenton, Fla. 34210. (813) 755-1000 or (800) USA-NICK.

A   Peter Burwash International "Tennis for Life Camps," Miami, Fla. Hotel (Doral Resort). 15 courts (8 hard with lights; 7 Har-Tru). 4:1. Contact: Dave Bailey, Peter Burwash International Doral Resort and Country Club, 4400 NW 87th Ave., Miami, Fla. 33178-2192. (800) 327-6334 outside Florida or (800) FOR-A-TAN in Florida.

A J   The Eve Ellis School of Tennis, Orange Lake Country Club, Kissimmee, Fla. Suite and villa accommodations. 16 hard courts. 4-6:1. Co-ed (4-years-old minimum). Year-round. Contact: Eve Ellis, P.O. Box 367, New York, N.Y. 10024-0367. (800) 877-6522 or (407) 239-0000.

J   Gulf Coast Tennis Academy, University of Florida, Pensacola, Fla. Townhouse and dormitory. 12 outdoor hard courts. Co-ed (ages 10–17). Contact: John McWilliams, Gulf Coast Tennis Academy, 530 Ravenwood Dr., Selma, Ala. 36701. (205) 875–7507.

A J   Tom Gullikson Tennis Clinics, Palm Coast Players Club, Palm Coast, Fla. Hotel. 18 courts (12 clay; 4 hard; 2 grass). 4:1. Co-ed (ages 13 and up with parents). Contact: Jim Vidamour, 1 Palm Harbor Parkway, Palm Coast, Fla. 32151. (904) 446–6360.

A J   Bill Hennessy's Tennis Camp, World Tennis Center, Naples, Fla. 2 bedroom/2 bath condominium. 16 courts (11 clay; 5 hard) Co-ed (ages 4–16 with adults). Contact: Bill Hennessy World Tennis Center, 4800 Airport Road, Naples, Florida 33942. (813) 263–7411.

A J   Harry Hopman/Saddlebrook International Tennis, Wesley Chapel, Fla. Condominium suites. 37 courts (27 clay; 10 hard). 4:1. Year-round. Contact: Sales Office, Harry Hopman/Saddlebrook International Tennis, 100 Saddlebrook Way, Wesley Chapel, Fla. 33543. (813) 973–1111 ext. 4215 or (800) 729–8383.

J   Intelligent Junior Tennis Camp, Bluewater Bay, Fla. No accommodations. 21 outdoor courts (10 clay; 9 hard; 2 synthetic grass). 4:1. Co-ed (ages 9–18). Contact: Skip Singleton, Bluewater Bay, P.O. Box 247, Niceville, Fla. 32578. (904) 897–3679.

A J   International Academy of Tennis, Palm Harbor, Fla. Juniors are housed with families; adults in condominiums. 19 courts (16 clay; 3 hard). 4:1. Co-ed (ages 9–19 with adults). Contact: Jeanne Morrison, 301 East Lake Woodlands Pkwy., Palm Harbor, Fla. 34682–0860. (813) 786–5525.

A J  International Tennis Center, Delray Beach, Fla. No accommodations. 44 outdoor courts (24 Har-Tru; 20 hard). 4:1. Co-ed (ages 8–18 with adults). Contact: Jayne Bernard, 2350 Jaeger Dr., Delray Beach, Fla. 33444. (407) 278-1602.

J  Gary Kesl Tennis Academy, Deer Creek Racquet Club, Deerfield Beach, Fla. Condominium. 17 courts (14 clay; 3 hard). 4–5:1. Co-ed (ages 8–18). Contact: Dr. Gary Kesl, Gary Kesl Tennis Academy, 2950 Deer Creek Country Club Blvd., Deerfield Beach, Fla. 33442. (305) 421-7890.

A J  Rick Macci International Tennis Academy, Grenelefe Resort, Grenelefe, Fla. Condominium. 20 courts (9 hard; 8 clay; 3 grass). 5:1. Co-ed (ages 5–18). Contact: Joy Macci, RMITA, 3200 SR546, Grenelefe Resort, Grenelefe, Fla. 33844. (813) 421-5012.

A J  Doug Maynard Tennis Academy. Tennis Club of Palm Beach, West Palm Beach, Fla. Condominium. 25 courts. 5:1. Co-ed. Year-round sessions. Contact: Doug Maynard, Tennis Club of Palm Beach, 2800 Haverhill Rd., West Palm Beach, Fla. 33417. (407) 683-5603.

A J  Francisco Montana Tennis Academy, Miami, Fla. Off-campus apartments. 13 outdoor courts (9 hard and lit; 4 clay). 7:1 beginners, 4:1 for national level. Co-ed (ages 6–18). Contact: Francisco Montana, 10700 SW 97 Avenue, Miami, Fla. 33176 (305) 595-4929.

A J  Craig Petra's Tennis Academy, Fort Lauderdale, Fla. Hotel (Marriott Marina Racquet Club). 8 outdoor courts. 6:1. Co-ed (ages 8–16) Contact: Craig Petra, 1881 SE 17th Causeway, Fort Lauderdale, Fla. 33316. (305) 527-6745.

A J　Ponte Vedra Tennis Clinics, Ponte Vedra Beach, Fla. Hotel (Ponte Vedra Inn and Club). 15 Har-Tru courts. 6:1 juniors; 4:1 adults. Co-ed (ages 8–18). Contact: Z. Mincek, P.O. Box 1264, Ponte Vedra Beach, Fla. 32004. (904) 285-3856.

J　Carey Powell Tournament Camp, West Palm Beach, Fla. Condominium. 24 courts (20 clay; 2 grass; 2 hard). 4:1. Co-ed (ages 10–17). Contact: Carey Powell, 13198 Forest Hill Blvd., West Palm Beach, Fla. 33414. (407) 798-7207.

J　Sabin-Mulloy-Garrison Tennis Camp, Clermont, Fla. 5 rooms. 5 courts (4 clay; 1 hard). 4:1. Co-ed (ages 8–16). Contact: Dickey Garrison, 11550 Lastchance Rd., Clermont, Fla. 34711. (904) 394-3543.

A J　Top Seed, Sonesta Sanibel Harbour Resort and Spa, Fort Myers, Fla. 13 courts (8 Har-Tru; 5 hard). 4:1. Co-ed (Munchkins ages 12 and under; Juniors ages 13–17). Contact: Jerry Walters, Sonesta Sanibel Harbour Resort and Spa, 17260 Harbor Pointe Drive, Fort Myers, Fla. 33908. (813) 466-2159 or 466-4000.

J　Tournament Tough Training, Bonaventure Resort, Fort Lauderdale, Fla. Four-Star Hotel—Sheraton Bonaventure. 24 courts (17 clay; 7 hard). 4:1. Co-ed (ages 11–18). Contact: Carlos Gioffi, 1013 Marsh Point, John's Island, S.C. 29445. (803) 768-9797.

J　University of Florida Tennis Camp, Gainesville, Fla. Dormitory. 24 outdoor hard courts. 5:1. Co-ed (ages 9–17). Contact:

M.B. Chafin, Director, 214 Florida Gym, University of Florida, Gainesville, Fla. 32611. (904) 392–0581 or 376–8030.

A J  Welby Van Horn Tennis Camp, Boca Raton Hotel & Club, Boca Raton, Fla. Hotel, villas. 34 courts. 3–4:1. Co-ed (ages 8–18). Contact: Welby Van Horn Tennis Camp, P.O. Box 259, Gracie Station, New York, N.Y. 10028. (212) 734–1037.

A J  Villarroel Tennis Camp/Mission Inn Golf and Tennis Resort, Howey in the Hills, Fla. Hotel. 6 courts. 5:1. Co-ed (ages 9–17). Contact: Cesar Villarroel, P.O. Box 441, Howey-in-the-Hills, Fla. 32737. (904) 324–3101 ext. 7145.

## GEORGIA

J  Adidas/Emory Tennis Camp, Emory University, Atlanta, Ga. Dormitory. 17 outdoor courts. 5:1. Co-ed (ages 9–18). Contact: Pat Gustafsson, U.S. Sports Development, 919 Sir Francis Drake Blvd., Kentfield, Calif. 94904. (415) 459–0459 or (800) 433–6060.

J  Jekyll Island Tennis Center Summer Camps for Juniors, Jekyll Island, Ga. Hotel accommodations. 13 outdoor clay courts (7 lit). 6:1. Co-ed (ages 6–18). Contact: Pete Poole, Director, Jekyll Island Tennis Center, 400 Captain Wylly Road, Jekyll Island, Ga. 31520. (912) 635–3154.

J  Southern Tennis Academy, Berry College, Rome, Ga. Dormitory. 14 hard courts (6 lit). 6:1. Co-ed (ages 9–17). Contact; M.B. Chafin, Director, P.O. Box 14401, Gainesville, Fla. 32064. (904) 392–0581 or 376–8030.

## HAWAII

A J   Nick Bollettieri Tennis Camp, Kuilima Resort, Kahuku, Hawaii. Hotel cabana (Turtle Bay Hilton). 10 outdoor Plexipave courts. Co-ed (ages 8–18). Contact: Jim Haugh, Turtle Bay Hilton, Kuilima Resort, P.O. Box 187, Kahuku, Hawaii 96731 (808) 293–8811.

J   Elite Tennis Academy, Laie, Hawaii. Hotel (Turtle Bay Hilton). 10 outdoor courts. 4:1. Co-ed (ages 10–18). Contact: John Lee or Allen Bornstein, P.O. Box 1358, Union, N.J. 07083. (201) 575–1611 or 686–6635.

A   Kapalua Tennis Camp, Maui, Hawaii. Luxury hotels and villas. 10 outdoor courts. 5:1. Contact: Steve Miller and Kaz Yamanoha, 100 Kapalua Dr., Kapalua, Maui, Hawaii 96761. (808) 669–5677.

J   Tennis: Europe's California-Hawaii. A tennis tournament circuit of 5–6 sanctioned hard-court events, with USTPA professional coaching. For serious junior players who are at least of high school varsity caliber, or have a USTA district, state, sectional or national ranking in San Diego, Los Angeles, Honolulu, Kauai, Maui. Contact: Dr. Martin Vinokur, 146 Cold Spring Road, No. 13, Stamford, Conn. 06905. (203) 964–1939. Fax: (203) 967–9499.

## ILLINOIS

J   Barry Nixon Tennis Camp, Illinois Western University, Bloomington, Ill. Dormitory. 8:1. Co-ed (ages 10–18). Contact: Barry Nixon, 1509 Fort Jesse Road, No. 18, Normal, Ill. 61761. (309) 454–3639.

# INDIANA

J Adidas/Notre Dame, Notre Dame University, South Bend, Ind. Dormitory. 18 outdoor courts. 5:1. Co-ed (ages 9–18). Contact: Pat Gustafsson, U.S. Sports Development, 919 Sir Francis Drake Blvd., Kentfield, Calif. 94904. (415) 459–0459 or (800) 433–6060.

J Culver Summer Camps, Culver Academies Campus, Culver, Ind. Dormitory and cabin. 17 courts (15 outdoor; 2 indoor), 1:5. Co-ed (ages 9–17). Contact: Frederick D. Lane, Box 138, CEF, Culver, Ind. 46511. (219) 842–3311.

J Loring–Hydinger Indiana University Tennis Camp, Bloomington, Ind. Sorority house. 18 courts (10 outdoor; 8 indoor). 4:1. Co-ed (ages 10–17). Contact: Lin Loring, Tennis Coach, Assembly Hall, Indiana University, Bloomington, Ind. 47405. (812) 855–4791.

J Purdue Tennis Camp, West Lafayette, Ind. Dormitory. 18 courts (15 outdoor; 3 indoor). 4:1. Co-ed (ages 8–18). Contact: Ed Dickson, Tennis Coach, Purdue University, Room 60, Mackey Arena, West Lafayette, Ind. 47907. (317) 494–4600.

# KANSAS

J Bethany College Tennis Camp, Lindsborg, Kan. Dormitory. 10:1. Co-ed (ages 8–18). Contact: Becky Johnson, Summer Programs, 421 North First, Lindsborg, Kan. 67456. (913) 822–3311 ext. 132.

J Emporia State Tennis Camp, Emporia, Kan. Dormitory. 7 courts (4 outdoor; 3 indoor). 8:1. Co-ed (ages 10–17). Contact:

Dr. George Milton, 1200 Commercial Rd., Emporia, Kan. 66801. (316) 343–5948 (work), (316) 342–8806 (home).


A J   Scott Perelman's Jayhawk Tennis College, University of Kansas, Lawrence, Kan. Dormitory. 18 courts (14 outdoor; 4 indoor). 6:1. Co-ed (ages 8–18). Contact: Andrea Perelman, 411 Country Club Court, Lawrence, Kan. 66044. (913) 841–7240.


## KENTUCKY

J   Dennis Emery's Wildcat Tennis Camp, University of Kentucky, Lexington, Ky. Dormitory. 28 courts (24 outdoor; 4 indoor). 4–5:1. Co-ed (ages 9–17). Contact: Dennis Emery, Tennis Coach, University of Kentucky, Lexington, Ky. 40506. (606) 257–3283 or 223–8315.


J   Bennie Purcell's Mid-South Tennis Camp, Murray State University, Murray, Ky. Dormitory. 20 courts (4 indoor; 16 outdoor). 1:5. Co-ed (ages 10–18). Contact: Bennie Purcell, Athletic Dept., Murray State University, Murray, Ky. 42071. (502) 762–6124/2187; 753–6441 (home).


A J   Ramey Tennis Schools, Inc. Owensboro, Ky. Dormitory, cottage; hotel for adults only. 7 courts (4 outdoor; 3 indoor). 4:1. Co-ed (ages 9–18). Contact: Mrs. Joan Ramey-Ford, Ramey Tennis Schools, Inc., 5931 Kentucky No. 56, Owensboro, Ky. 42301. (502) 771–4723 or 771–5590.


## LOUISIANA

A J   Tiger Tennis, LSU Campus, Baton Rouge, La. Dormitory. 4:1. 22 outdoor courts. Co-ed (ages 9–17). Contact: Steve Carter, 1563 Audubon Ave., Baton Rouge, La. 70806. (504) 924–0735.

# MISSISSIPPI

J Mississippi State Tennis Camp, Starkville, Miss. Dormitory. 12 courts. 5:1. Co-ed (ages 9–17). Contact: Andy Jackson, P.O. Drawer 5327, Starkville, Miss. 39762. (601) 323–9124.

J Mississippi University for Women Tennis Camp, Columbus, Miss. Dormitory. 10 courts (8 outdoor; 2 indoor). 6:1. Co-ed (ages 8–17). Contact: Terrie Gooch, P.O. Box W-1636, Columbus, Miss. 39701. (601) 329–7225.

J Moortgat/Eklund Tennis Academy, Louis, Miss. Villas. 8 clay courts. 4:1. Co-ed (ages 10–18). Contact: Jim Moortgat or Magnus Eklund, 1232 Kirin Ave., Birmingham, Ala. 35213. (205) 956–5245 (Jim) or (601) 255–2525 (Magnus).

# MAINE

J Androscoggin, Wayne, Maine. Bunks w/facilities. 12 courts. 1:3. Boys only (ages 8–15). Contact: Stan or Peter Hirsch, 733 West Street, Harrison, N.Y. 10528. (914) 835–5800 or (207) 685–4441.

J Kippewa for Girls, Winthrop, Maine. Cabins with bathrooms. 6 outdoor courts (4 lit). 4:1. Girls (ages 7–15). Contact: Marty or Paul Silverman, 60 Mill Street, P.O. Box 307, Westwood, Maine 02090. (207) 933–2993.

J Camp Laurel, Echo Lake, Readfield, Maine. Cabins. 3:1. 11 outdoor courts. Co-ed (ages 7–15). Contact: Ron Scott, Camp Laurel, P.O. Box 4378, Boca Raton, Fla. 33429. (407) 391–1579.

J    Camp Walden, Denmark, Maine. Bunks. 7 courts. 4:1. Co-ed (ages 10–18). Contact: Wendy Cohen, P.O. Box 3427, Charlottesville, Va. 22903. (207) 452-2901.

J    Camp Wekeela for Boys and Girls, Canton, Maine. Cabins. 6 outdoor courts. 3:1. Co-ed (ages 6–16). Contact: Eric Scoblionko, RFD 1, Box 275, Canton, Maine 04221. (207) 224-7878. Fax: (207) 224-7999. Off-season: 130 S. Merkle Road, Columbus, Ohio 43209. (614) 235-3619. Fax: (614) 235-3619.

A    World Tennis Clinics in Bar Harbor, Bar Harbor, Maine. Bed and breakfast inns. 4 courts. 4:1. Contact: Everett Sherman, 4821 Arlington Ave., Bronx, N.Y. 10471. (212) 549-0100.

A J    Camp Wyonegonic Family Camp, Denmark, Maine. Rustic cabins. 6 clay courts. Co-ed; no age limits; any family combination welcome. Contact: George and Carol Sudduth, RRI Box 186, Denmark, Maine 04022. (207) 452-2051.

## MARYLAND

A J    Blue Ridge Tennis Camp, Inc., Mount St. Mary's College, Emmitsburg, Md. Dormitory and/or apartment. 12 courts (8 outdoor w/lights; 4 indoor). 4:1. Co-ed (ages 9–18). Contact: Alicia von Lossberg, 5044 Schalk Rd., No. 1, P.O. Box 114, Lineboro, Md. 21088. (301) 239-7225 or 447-5383.

A    Campbell Tennis Camps, Hood College, Frederick, Md. and Western Maryland College, Westminster, Md. Dormitory or apartment. 6 outdoor courts (indoor courts nearby at both locations). 6:1. Contact: Ray Campbell, 7130 Deer Valley Rd., Highland, Md. 20777. (301) 663-3131.

A J  The Steve Krulevitz Tennis Program, St. Paul's School, Brooklandville, Md. 8 outdoor courts (access to 8 indoor). 5:1. Co-ed (ages 8–18). Contact: Steve or Ann Krulevitz, P.O. Box 371, Brooklandville, Md. 21022. (301) 486–8140.

A J  Leroy Levi Mid-Atlantic Junior Tennis Academy, St. Timothy School, Stevenson, Md. Dormitory. 23 courts (14 indoor). 5:1 with senior roving pro. Co-ed (ages 5–18). Contact: Leroy Levi, P.O. Box 953, Brooklandville, Md. 21153. (301) 484–LEVI or 486–1142.

J  Salisbury State University Tennis Camp, Salisbury, Md. Dormitory. 17 courts (5 indoor). 6:1. Co-ed (ages 11–17). Contact: Dean Burroughs, Salisbury State University Tennis Camp, Salisbury, Md. 21801. (301) 543–6344.

## MASSACHUSETTS

J  Adidas/Williams, Williams College, Mass. Dormitory. 26 courts (18 outdoor; 8 indoor). 5:1. Co-ed (ages 9–18). Contact: Pat Gustafsson, U.S. Sports Development, 919 Sir Francis Drake Blvd., Kentfield, Calif. 94904. (415) 459–0459 or (800) 433–6060.

J  Nick Bollettieri Tennis Summer Camp, Mt. Holyoke, Mass. Dormitory. 22 courts (16 outdoor; 6 indoor). 5:1. Co-ed (ages 8–18). Contact: N.B.T.A. Reservation Dept., 5500 34th St., W. Bradenton, Fla. 43210. (813) 755–1000 or (800) USA–NICK.

A J  Bollettieri/Chang Tennis Center, Boston, Mass. No accommodations. 11 courts (6 outdoor clay; 5 indoor Tru-Flex). 6:1. Co-ed (ages 8–18). Contact: Tony Zanoni, Bollettieri/Chang Tennis Center, 123 River St., Middleton, Mass. 01940. (508) 777–0880 or (800) USA–NICK.

J   Arthur  Carrington  Tennis  Academy,  Hampshire  College,
Amherst, Mass. Dormitory. 14 courts (10 outdoor; 4 indoor). 6:1.
Co-ed (ages 8–18). Contact: Arthur Carrington, Jr., 1025 Main
St., Holyoke, Mass. 01040. (413) 549–4600, ext. 300.


J   Crane Lake Camp, West Stockbridge, Mass. Cabins. 10 courts
(6 outdoor; 4 indoor). 3:1. Co-ed (ages 10–15). Contact: Ed
Ulanoff, 10 West 66th St., New York, N.Y. 10023. (212) 549–
8930 or 362–1462.


J   Camp Emerson, Hinsdale, Mass. Cabins. 6 courts. 3:1. Co-ed
(ages 7–15). Contact: Marvin Lein, 5 Brassie Rd., Eastchester,
N.Y. 10707. (914) 779–9406.


J   Greylock/Romaca, Beckett, Mass. (Berkshires). Cabins. 3:1.
Brother/sister  (ages  9–16).  Contact:  Bert  Margolis,  Camp
Greylock/Romaca, Suite 307, 200 West 57th St., New York, N.Y.
10019. (212) 582–1042 or (413) 623–8921.


J   Camp Mah-Kee-Nac, Lenox, Mass. Cabins. 18 outdoor clay
courts. 3:1. Boys only (ages 7–15). Contact: Dan Metzger, Camp
Mah-Kee-Nac, Lenox, Mass. 01240. (413) 637–0781 (summer) or
Camp Mah-Kee-Nac, 190 Linden Ave., Glen Ridge, N.J. 07028.
(201) 429–8522 (winter).


J   Offense-Defense Tennis Camp, Curry College, Milton, Mass.
Dormitory. 46 courts (34 outdoor; 12 indoor). 4:1. Co-ed (ages
10–18). Contact: Offense-Defense Tennis Camp, P.O. Box 295,
Trumbull, Conn. 06611. (203) 374–7171.


A   Total Tennis, Williston–Northampton School, Easthampton,
Mass. Dormitory. 38 courts (15 outdoor; 10 red clay; 5 hard; 8

hard indoor). 4:1. Contact: Ed Fondiller, Director, P.O. Box 1106, Wall Street Station, New York, N.Y. 10268. (718) 636-6141 or (800) 221-6496 outside N.Y. state.

A World Tennis Clinics on Martha's Vineyard. Martha's Vineyard, Mass. Townhouse and vacation home. 5 courts. 4:1. Contact: Everett Sherman, 4821 Arlington Ave., Bronx, N.Y. 10471. (212) 549-0100.

## MICHIGAN

J Brian Eisner Tennis Camps, University of Michigan, Ann Arbor. Dormitory. 9 outdoor; 6 indoor. 4:1. Co-ed (ages 10-18). Contact: Brian Eisner, 3000 Parkridge Dr., Ann Arbor, Mich. 48103. (313) 665-7114 or 665-3738.

J Kalamazoo College Tennis Camp, Kalamazoo, Mich. Dormitory. 15 courts (11 outdoor, 5 lit; 4 indoor). 4:1. Co-ed (ages 10-17). Contact: George H. Acker, Director, Kalamazoo College Tennis Camp, Kalamazoo College, 1200 Academy St., Kalamazoo, Mich. 49007. (616) 383-8422 or 372-2194.

J Spartan Tennis School, Michigan State University, East Lansing, Mich. Dormitory. 20 outdoor courts; 8 indoor courts. 6:1. Co-ed (ages 12-17). Contact: Robert A. Stehlin, MSU Summer Sports School, 222 Jenison Fieldhouse, East Lansing, Mich. 48824-1025. (517) 355-5264.

A Techniques in Tennis by Bob Hartwick, Trout Creek Condominium Resort, Harbor Springs, Mich. Condominium. 8 outdoor hard courts. 4:1. Co-ed. Contact: Bob Hartwick, 4749 Pleasantview Rd., Harbor Springs, Mich. 49740. (800) 748-0245.

## MINNESOTA

J    Adidas/Minnesota Tennis Camp, Carleton College, Northfield, Minn. Dormitory. 12 outdoor courts. 5:1. Co-ed (ages 9–18). Contact: Pat Gustafsson, U.S. Sports Development, 919 Sir Francis Drake Blvd., Kentfield, Calif. 94904. (415) 459–0459 or (800) 433–6060.

J    Blazer Tennis Camps, College of St. Benedict, St. Joseph, Minn. Dormitory. 6 hard courts. 4–5:1. Co-ed (ages 11–18). Contact: Jerry Sales, Blazer Tennis Camps, College of St. Benedict, St. Joseph, Minn. 56374. (612) 363–5878 (summer), or 1509 13th Ave. S., St. Cloud, Minn. 56301. (612) 251–3629 (winter).

J    Lake Hubert Tennis Camp, Lake Hubert, Minn. (near Brainerd). Cabins. 12 outdoor; indoor available. 4:1. Co-ed (ages 8–16). Contact: Sam Cote, Camp Lincoln/Camp Lake Hubert, 5201 Eden Circle, Minneapolis, Minn. 55436. (612) 922–2545 or (800) 328–4827 ext. 1985.

J    Camp Lincoln/Camp Lake Hubert, Lake Hubert, Minn. Log cabins. 10 outdoor courts. 4:1. Brother/sister camp (ages 8–17). Contact: Sam Cote or Bill Jones, 5201 Eden Circle, Minneapolis, Minn. 55436. (612) 922–2545 or (800) 328–4827 ext. 1985.

A J    Tennis and Life Camps, Gustavus Adolphus College, St. Peter, Minn. Dormitory. 30 courts (10 indoor and 20 outdoor). 4:1. Co-ed (ages 10–18). Contact: Steve Wilkinson, Tennis and Life Camps, Gustavus Adolphus College, St. Peter, Minn. 56082. (507) 931–1614.

# MISSOURI

J   Bearcat Tennis, Bolivar, Mo. Dormitory. 9 lit outdoor courts. 4:1. Co-ed (ages 10-18). Contact: John Bryant, Southwest Baptist University, Bolivar, Mo. 65613. (417) 326-1747.

A J   Northwest Missouri State Tennis Camp, Maryville, Mo. Dormitory. 10 outdoor; 2 indoor. 6:1. Co-ed (ages 8-18). Contact: Coach Mark Rosewell, Lankin Gym-Tennis, Northwest Missouri State University, Maryville, Mo. 64468. (816) 562-1306 (office) or 562-2751 (home).

A J   Van Der Meer Tennis University Midwest, The Lodge of Four Seasons Racquet Club, Lake Ozark, Mo. Lodge or condominium. 16 hard courts; 4 indoor; 3 clay. 6:1. Co-ed (no age limits). Contact: Mike Young, Four Seasons Racquet Club, P.O. Box 397, Lake Ozark, Mo. 65049. (314) 365-3000 or (800) THE-LAKE.

## NEBRASKA

A J   Cornhusker Tennis Camps, Lincoln, Neb. Dormitory. 17 courts (14 outdoor; 3 indoor). 4:1. Co-ed (ages 9-18). Contact: Scott Jacobson, Men's Tennis, Devaney Sports Center, Lincoln, Neb. 68588. (402) 472-2271.

## NEVADA

A   Bill Fallon Tennis Clinic, Hyatt Regency, Lake Tahoe, Nev. Resort hotel. 2 outdoor courts. 4:1. Contact: Bill Fallon, Bill Fallon Tennis Clinic, P.O. Box AJ, Incline Village, Nev. 89450. (702) 831-1111.

## NEW HAMPSHIRE

J Adidas/Dartmouth, Dartmouth College, Hanover, N.H. Dormitory. 12 courts (8 outdoor; 4 indoor). 5:1. Co-ed (ages 9–18). Contact: Pat Gustafsson, U.S. Sports Development, 919 Sir Francis Drake Blvd., Kentfield, Calif. 94904. (415) 459–0459 or (800) 433–6060.

J Chase Golf and Tennis Camp, Bethlehem, N.H. New England Inn. 15 outdoor clay courts. 5:1. Co-ed (ages 12–17). Contact: Neil or Linda Chase, Chase Camp, P.O. Box 1446, Manchester, Mass. 01944. (800) 242–7348.

J Camp Cody for Boys, Freedom, N.H. Cabins and lodges. 6 courts, all lit. 3:1. Boys only (ages 7–16). Contact: Alan J. Stolz, 5 Lockwood Circle, Westport, Conn. 06880. (203) 226–4389 or 226–3932 or (603) 539–4997.

J Exeter Tennis School, Phillips Exeter Academy, Exeter, N.H. Dormitory. 5:1. 26 courts (23 outdoor; 3 indoor). Co-ed (ages 10–17). Contact: Elaine White, Summer Sports Schools, Phillips Exeter Academy, Exeter, N.H. 03833. (603) 772–4311 ext. 423.

J New Hampshire Tennis Camp, Concord, N.H. Cabins. 10 courts (6 indoor Har-Tru; 4 outdoor). 3:1. Co-ed (ages 6–16). Contact: Werner Rothschild, 14 Joyce Lane, Woodbury, N.Y. 11797. (516) 364–8099 (winter); Rt. 2, Contoocook, N.H. (603) 746–3195 (summer).

A J Tamarack Tennis Camp, Franconia, N.H. Cabins. 12 outdoor clay courts. 4:1. Co-ed (ages 10–16). Contact: Peg Kenney, Tamarack Tennis Camp Franconia, N.H. 03580. (603) 823–5656 (camp).

J   The Tennis Camp at Dartmouth College, Hanover, N.H. Dormitory. 9 outdoor hard courts; 4 indoor. Co-ed (ages 10–17). Contact: Chuck Kinyon, Head Tennis Coach, Alumni Gym, Dartmouth College, Hanover, N.H. 03755. (603) 646–3819.

J   WI-CO-SU-TA, Bristol, N.H. Dormitory. 10 outdoor courts. 3:1. Brother/sister (ages 7–16). Contact: Irwin Boagart, (603) 744–3301 (winter), or (914) 761–5496 (summer).

## NEW JERSEY

J   Adidas/Frank Brennan Tennis Academy, The Peddie School, Hightown, N.J. Dormitory. 19 courts (14 outdoor; 5 indoor). 5:1. Co-ed (ages 9–18). Contact: U.S. Sports, 919 Sir Francis Drake Blvd., Kentfield, Calif. 94904. (800) 433–6060 or (415) 459–0459.

J   Elite Tennis Academy, West Caldwell, N.J. No accommodations (day camp). 6 indoor hard courts. 4:1. Co-ed (ages 5–18). Contact: John Lee or Allen Bornstein, P.O. Box 1358, Union, N.J. 07083. (908) 686–6635 or (201) 575–1611.

J   Lawrenceville Tennis Camp, Lawrenceville, N.J. Dormitory. 19 courts (16 outdoor; 3 indoor). 5:1. Co-ed (ages 9–18). Contact: Jim Poling, P.O. Box 6037, Lawrenceville, N.J. 08648. (609) 896–0054.

J   Project Excel Tennis Program. No accommodations (day camp). West Orange Tennis Club, West Orange, N.J. 23 courts (11 indoor). Co-ed (ages 6–17) Contact: Bob Staffutti, West Orange Tennis Club, 1448 Pleasant Valley Way, West Orange, N.J. 07052. (201) 731–1740.

## NEW MEXICO

J   Adidas/Lobo Tennis Camp. Albuquerque, N.M. Dormitory. 5:1. 18 hard courts. Co-ed (ages 9–18). Camp is limited to 72 students. Contact: Pat Gustafsson, U.S. Sports Development, 919 Sir Francis Drake Blvd., Kentfield, Calif. 94904. (800) 433–6060.

## NEW YORK

J   Binghamton Tennis Center–Summer Camp, Binghamton, N.Y. Day camp, with housing available. 12 courts (6 outdoor clay, 4 indoor hard, and 2 outdoor hard). 4:1. Co-ed (ages 5–18). Contact: Michael Starke, P.O. Box 117, Binghampton Tennis Center, Mill Street, Binghamton, N.Y. 13903. (607) 722–3491.

A J   Eve Ellis School of Tennis, Central Park, N.Y. No accommodations. 30 courts on premises; 4 teaching courts. 4–6:1. Co-ed (ages 8–18), plus the "Bean Sprouts" program (ages 4–7). Contact: Eve Ellis, P.O. Box 376, New York, N.Y. 10024–0367. (212) 362–7901.

A J   Future Stars Tennis Camp at Hampton Athletic Club, East Quogue, N.Y. Day camp. 22 Har-Tru courts. 4:1. Co-ed (ages 3–18). Contact: Bob Jenkins, 302 East Shore Rd., Great Neck, N.Y. 11023. (516) 466–3716.

J   Future Stars Tennis Camp at Manhattanville College, Purchase, N.Y. Day camp. 6 courts. 4:1. Co-ed (ages 5–17). Contact: Bob Jenkins, 302 East Shore Rd., Great Neck, N.Y. 11023. (516) 466–3716.

J   Future Stars Tennis Camp at SUNY-Purchase, Purchase, N.Y. Day camp. 10 courts. 4:1. Co-ed (ages 12–18). Contact: Bob Jenkins, 302 East Shore Rd., Great Neck, N.Y. 11023. (516) 466-3716.

J   Kutsher's Sports Academy, Monticello, N.Y. Cabin and dormitory. 17 courts (14 outdoor w/lights; 3 indoor). 4:1. Co-ed (ages 7–17). Contact: Bob Trupin, 3 Snowflake Lane, Westport, Conn. 06880. (914) 794-5400.

A J   Bill Martire's Tennis Camp, Montauk Yacht Club, Star Island, Montauk, N.Y. Hotel. 9 courts. 4:1. Co-ed (ages 10–18). Contact: Bill or Christina Martire, 41 Tally Dr., Freehold, N.J. 07728. (908) 308-1547.

J   Jeff Miller Tennis Camp, SUNY-Stony Brook, Stony Brook, N.Y. Dormitory. 26 courts (20 outdoor; 6 indoor). 4:1. Co-ed (ages 8–18). Contact: Jeff Miller, 421 Woodland Ave., Westfield, N.J. 07090. (908) 654-1008 or (516) 632-6079.

J   Point O'Pines Camp for Girls, Brant Lake, N.Y. Cabins. 12 courts (8 clay; 4 hard). 4:1. Co-ed (ages 7–15). Contact: Sue and Jim Himmoff, 40 East 78th St., New York, N.Y. 10021. (212) 288-0246 or (518) 494-3213.

A J   Pat Panzarella's, St. Bonaventure Tennis Camp, St. Bonaventure, N.Y. Dormitory. 10 courts (6 outdoor; 4 indoor). 5:1. Co-ed (ages 8–17). Contact: Dr. Pat Panzarella, P.O. Box 14, St. Bonaventure University, St. Bonaventure, N.Y. 14778. (716) 373-2429.

J   Camp Redwood, Walden, N.Y. Cabins. 9 courts (3 indoor). Young children, 2–3:1 ratio, children age 10 and up, 4–5:1 ratio. Co-ed (ages 5–18). Contact: Irma and Buddy Estis, 500 Rock Cut

Rd., Walden, N.Y. 12586. (914) 564-1180 or 564-1128 (April through October 15), 9600 NW 13th St., Plantation, Fla. 33322. (305) 475-7246 (winter).

J   Camp Scatico, Elizaville, N.Y. Cabins. 11 courts (10 lit). 4:1. Co-ed (ages 7-16). Contact: Camp Scatico, 25 Fennimore Rd., New Rochelle, N.Y. 10804. (914) 632-7791.

A J   The Tennis Camp West, C.W. Post, Stony Brook, N.Y. Dormitory. 14 courts (9 outdoor; 5 indoor). 4:1. Co-ed (ages 7-16). Contact: Spencer P. Edelbaum, P.O. Box 616, Stony Brook, N.Y. 11790. (516) 584-9150.

A J   Roger Wootton Tennis Academy, Pittsford, N.Y. 18 courts (4 indoor). 4:1. Adults: mini-week and weekends. Juniors (ages 8-18): day and overnight camps, 1-to-10-week sessions. Contact: Roger Wootton Tennis Academy, 834 Pittsford Mendon Center Road, Pittsford, N.Y. 14534. (716) 582-1320.

## NORTH CAROLINA

J   All-Star Tennis Camp, High Point College, High Point, N.C. Dormitory. 12 courts (10 outdoor; 2 indoor off-campus). 5:1. Co-ed (ages 8-17). Contact: Ray S. Alley, P.O. Box 19445, Greensboro, N.C. 27419. (919) 292-7015.

J   Belmont Abbey College Tennis Camp, Belmont, N.C. Dormitory. 6 courts. 5:1. Co-ed (ages 7-17). Contact: Dr. Mike Reidy, Belmont Abbey College Tennis Camp, Belmont, N.C. 28012. (704) 825-6801 or 867-1711.

A J  Davidson College Wildcat Tennis Camp, Davidson College, Davidson, N.C. Dormitory. 21 courts (12 hard; 5 clay; 4 indoor). 4:1. Co-ed (ages 9–17). Contact: Jeff Frank, P.O. Box 1612, Davidson, N.C. 28036. (704) 892-2377.

J  Duke Tennis Camp, Durham, N.C. Dormitory. 41 outdoor courts; 2 indoor. 4:1. Co-ed (ages 8–18). Contact: Barbara Strome, 5319 Stephens Lane, Durham, N.C. 27712. (919) 477-3849.

J  Elon College Tennis Camp, Elon College, N.C. Dormitory. 12 hard courts with lights. 6:1. Co-ed (ages 10–17). Contact: Tom Parham, Athletics Elon College, Elon College, N.C. 27244. (919) 584-2420 or 228-1564.

A J  Gardner-Webb College Tennis Camp, Boiling Springs, N.C. Dormitory. 8 outdoor courts. 4:1 or 3:1. Co-ed (ages 9–17). Contact: Bill Naylor, Tennis Coach, Gardner-Webb College, P.O. Box 877, Boiling Springs, N.C. 28017. (704) 434-2361.

A J  Mary Lou Jones Tennis Camp, St. Mary's College, Raleigh, N.C. Dormitory. 4:1. 12 outdoor courts. Co-ed (ages 6–18). Contact: Mary Lou Jones, St. Mary's College, 900 Hillsborough St., Raleigh, N.C. 27603. (919) 839-4056.

J  Wake Forest University Tennis Camp, Winston-Salem, N.C. Air-conditioned dormitory. 17 courts (13 outdoor; 4 indoor). 5:1. Co-ed (ages 10–18). Contact: Ian Crookenden, Tennis Director, Wake Forest University, P.O. Box 7548, Reynolda Station, Winston-Salem, N.C. 27109. (919) 759-5634.

# OHIO

A J   Adidas/Oberlin Tennis Camp, Oberlin College, Oberlin, Ohio. Dormitory. 16 courts (7 indoor). 5:1. Co-ed (ages 9–17). Contact: Bob Peiron, U.S. Sports, 919 Sir Francis Drake Blvd., Kentfield, Calif. 94904. (800) 433–6060.

J   The Axe Factory, Youngstown, Ohio. Private residence. 1 indoor; 1 outdoor court. 3:1. Co-ed (ages 10–16) Contact: John Wendle, 1245 Cherokee Drive, Youngstown, Ohio 44511. (216) 793–0328.

J   Bearcat Tennis Camp, University of Cincinnati, Cincinnati, Ohio. No accommodations (hotel nearby). 10 courts (9 outdoor; 1 indoor). 6:1. Co-ed (ages 9–17). Contact: Paul Klaczak, Bearcat Sports Camps, University of Cincinnati, Athletic Dept., ML No. 21, Cincinnati, Ohio 45221. (513) 556–5601.

J   Wooster Tennis Camp, College of Wooster, Wooster, Ohio. Dormitory. 13 outdoor courts (access to 4 indoor courts). 4:1. Co-ed (ages 11–18). Contact: Hayden Schilling, Director, College of Wooster, Wooster, Ohio 44961. (216) 263–2500.

# OREGON

A J   Oregon Tennis School, University of Oregon, Eugene, Oreg. and Inn of 7th Mountain, Bend, Oreg. Dormitory/mountain resort. 15 courts (9 indoor, 6 outdoor—Univ. of Oregon; 7 outdoor courts—Inn of 7th Mountain). 5:1. Co-ed (ages 9–19). Contact: Buzz Summers, 290 W. 37th Ave., Eugene, Oreg. 97405. (503) 346–5476.

A J   Steve Vaughan's Old West Tennis Camp, Mt. Bachelor Tennis Village, Bend, Oreg. Condominium. 6 outdoor courts. 5:1.

Co-ed (ages 8–18). Contact: Steve Vaughan, Steve Vaughan's Old West Tennis Camp, 19717 Mt. Bachelor Dr., Bend, Oreg. 97702. (503) 389–5900 or 665–4142.

## PENNSYLVANIA

J Camp Akiba, Reeders, Pa. Cabins. 21 outdoor courts. Ratio varies 1:1–6:1. Brother/sister camp (ages 7–16). Contact: Joel Glickman (general info.), or Brian Thomas (tennis info.), Camp Akiba, P.O. Box 400, Bala Cynwyd, Pa. 19004. (215) 649–7877 (winter) or (717) 629–1671 (summer).

J Bloomsburg University Junior Tennis Camp, Bloomsburg University, Bloomsburg, Pa. Dormitory. 20 courts (18 outdoor; 2 indoor). 1:6. Co-ed (ages 11–17). Contact: Burt Reese, Nelson Field House, Bloomsburg Univ., Bloomsburg, Pa. 17815. (717) 389–4555.

A J Bollettieri/Nigro Tennis Center, Philadelphia, Pa. Dormitory. 16 courts. 5:1. Co-ed (ages 8–18). Contact: Eric Cormouls, Bollettieri/Nigro Tennis Center, 46 East Church Rd., Elkins Park, Pa. 19117. (215) 379–5425 or (800) USA–NICK.

J Camp Canadensis, Canadensis, Pa. (Pocono Mountains). Cabins with individual bathrooms. 3:1. 16 tennis courts, 12 lit. Co-ed (ages 6–16). Contact: Steven Saltzman, P.O. Box 182, Wyncote, Pa. 19095. (215) 572–8222 or (717) 595–7461. Fax: (215) 572–8298.

J Camp Conrad Weiser, Wernersville, Pa. (near Reading). Cabins and tents. 3 outdoor courts. 5:1. Co-ed (ages 13–16). Contact: South Mountain YMCA–Camp Conrad Weiser, P.O. Box 147, Wernersville, Pa. 19565. (215) 670–2267.

A J Central Penn Tennis Camp, Elizabethtown College, Elizabethtown, Pa. Air-conditioned dormitory. 18 hard courts (10 outdoor; 8 indoor). 4:1. Co-ed (ages 10–18). Contact: Tom Sweitzer, Central Penn Tennis Service, 988 Briarcrest Drive, Hershey, Pa. 17033. (800) 525–2759 or (717) 534–2724. Fax: (717) 533–0361.

J Central Penn Tennis Camp, Shippensburg University, Shippensburg, Pa. Dormitory. 27 hard courts (24 outdoor; 3 indoor). 4:1. Co-ed (ages 10–18). Contact: Tom Sweitzer, Central Penn Tennis Service, 988 Briarcrest Drive, Hershey, Pa. 17033. (800) 525–2759 or (717) 534–2724. Fax: (717) 533–0361.

J Greyhound Tennis Camp, Moravian College, Bethlehem, Pa. Dormitory. 24 courts (20 outdoor; 4 indoor). 6:1. Co-ed (ages 8–18). Contact: Jim Walker, Moravian College, Bethlehem, Pa. 18018. (215) 861–1531.

J Julian Krinsky School of Tennis, Haverford College, Wayne, Pa. Dormitory. 66 courts (44 outdoor, 8 clay; 22 indoor). 4–5:1. Co-ed (ages 9–18). Contact: Julian Krinsky, 696 Raven Road, Wayne, Pa. 19087. (215) 664–2696.

A J Lake Bryn Mawr Camp, Honesdale, Pa. Cabins. 18 outdoor courts; 8 lit. 3:1. Girls only (ages 6–15). Contact: Herb Kutzen, P.O. Box 612, 81 Falmouth St., Short Hills, N.J. 07078. (201) 467–3518.

A J Jim Overbaugh's Tennis Academy, Millersville University, Millersville, Pa. Dormitory. 23 courts (17 outdoor, 3 lit; 6 indoor) 5:1. Co-ed (ages 8–18). Contact: Jim Overbaugh, 501 Gatehouse Lane, West York, Pa. 17402. (717) 757–5909.

J Peak Performance and Developmental Tennis Camp, Frog
Hollow Tennis Club, Worcester, Pa. Day camp. 8 courts (5 Har-
Tru; 3 Grass-Tex indoor). 6:1. Co-ed (ages 8–18). Contact: Sam
Chrome, Frog Hollow Tennis Club, P.O. Box 44, Worcester, Pa.
19490. (215) 584–5502.

J Penn State Tennis Camps, University Park, Pa. Dormitory. 12
courts (8 outdoor; 4 indoor). 5:1. Co-ed (grades 7–12). Contact:
William R. Sterner, 410 Neller Conference Center, University
Park, Pa. 16802. (814) 865–9173.

J Pine Forest Camps, Greeley, Pa. Bunks with bathrooms. 24
outdoor hard courts. 3:1 average. Co-ed (ages 7–16). Contact:
Marvin or Mickey Black, Pine Forest Camps, Super Star Tennis,
407 Benson East, Jenkintown, Pa. 19046. (215) 887–9700
(winter) or (717) 685–7141 (summer).

A J Fritz Schunck Tennis Camps, Seven Springs Mountain
Resort, Champion, Pa. Chalet for juniors; hotel and condo for
adults. 3–5:1. 12 outdoor courts (6 lit); 12-court indoor facility
nearby. Co-ed (ages 9–17). Contact: Fritz Schunck, 418 Concord
Ave., Greensburg, Pa. 15601. (412) 832–0277.

J Tennis Camps Ltd. at Swarthmore College, Swarthmore, Pa.
Dormitory. 18 courts (12 outdoor; 6 indoor). Maximum ratio 5:1.
Co-ed (ages 9–17). Contact: Lois Broderick (800) 223–2442, Bob
Feller (215) 328–8589, or Lisa Brighenti (215) 328–8339.

J Camp Wayne Girls & Boys, Preston Park, Pa. Cabins. 14 outdoor courts. 4:1. Co-ed (ages 6–16). Contact: Noel Corpuel, 12
Allevard Street, Lido Beach, N.Y. 11561 (winter); Camp Wayne,

Preston Park, Pa. 18455 (summer). (717) 798–2511 (boys) or (717) 798–2591 (girls).

## RHODE ISLAND

J  Elite Tennis Academy, Kingston, R.I. Dormitory (University of Rhode Island). 12 outdoor courts. 4:1. Contact: John Lee or Allen Bornstein, P.O. Box 1358, Union, N.J. 07083. (201) 686–6635 or 575–1611.

## SOUTH CAROLINA

A J  Roy Barth Mini Camp, East Beach Tennis Center, Charleston, S.C. Hotels and villas available. East Beach Tennis: 12 outdoor courts; West Beach Tennis: 16 outdoor courts, 2 with lights. 4:1. Co-ed (ages 8–18). Contact: Roy Barth, P.O. Box 12357, Charleston, S. C. 29422. (803) 768–2121 ext. 4010.

A  Grand Slam Camp, Rod Laver Tennis Center, Palmetto Dunes, Hilton Head Island, S.C. Hotels (Hyatt Regency, Mariner's Inn, Palmetto Dunes Resort Villas). 25 outdoor courts. 5:1. Contact: Lori Proto/John Kerr, Rod Laver Tennis Center, Palmetto Dunes, P.O. Box 4798, Hilton Head Island, S.C. 29938. (803) 785–1152.

J  Chuck Kriese's Clemson Total Tennis Training Camp, Clemson, S.C. Dormitory. 25 courts (21 outdoor; 4 indoor). 4:1. Co-ed (ages 9–17). Contact: Peggy Johnston, P.O. Box 965, Clemson, S.C. 29633. (803) 654–5784.

A J  Port Royal Racquet Club, Hilton Head Island, S.C. Hotels, motels, and villas available; there are no accommodations at the club. 16 available courts (10 clay; 4 hard; 2 grass). 6:1. Co-ed. Contact: Tanda A. Witherspoon, Activities Director, Port Royal Racquet Club, 1 Grasslawn Ave., Hilton Head Island, S.C. 29928. (803) 681-3322.

A J Paul Scarpa's 22nd Annual Furman University Tennis Camp, Greenville, S.C. Dormitory. 21 courts (15 hard-courts; 6 Har-Tru). Co-ed (ages 9-16). Contact: Paul Scarpa, Furman University Athletic Department, Greenville, S.C. 29613. (803) 294-2039.

A J Stan Smith Tennis Academy, Sea Pines Racquet Club, Hilton Head Island, S.C. Villa, home. 24 clay courts; 5 lit hard courts. 4:1 (juniors); 6:1 (adults). Co-ed (ages 9-14). Contact: Lynn Welch, Head Professional, Sea Pines Racquet Club, Hilton Head Island, S.C. 29928. (803) 671-2494.

A J Joey Towe Adult and Junior Mini Camps, Fripp Island Racket Club, Fripp Island, S.C. Villa, townhouse, suite and hotel units. 10 courts (8 clay; 2 hard). 4:1. Co-ed (ages 8-16). Adult sessions. Contact: Joey Towe, 301 Tarpon Blvd., Fripp Island, S.C. 29920. (803) 838-2500.

A J Wild Dunes Tennis Camp, Charleston, S.C. Luxury villas. 18 courts. 4:1. Co-ed (ages 12 and up). Contact: Randy Chamberlin, Wild Dunes, P.O. Box 1410, Charleston, S.C. 29402. (800) 845-8880.

## TENNESSEE

J Freed-Hardeman University Tennis Camp, Henderson, Tenn. Dormitory. 6 courts (outdoor). 7:1. Co-ed (ages 10-18). Contact:

Charlie Smith, Freed-Hardeman University, Henderson, Tenn. 38340. (901) 989-6046.

## TEXAS

A J Champions Tennis Camp at T Bar M Tennis Ranch and Conference Center, New Braunfels, Texas. Dormitory, hotel, and condo. 14 courts (12 outdoor; 2 indoor). 5:1. Co-ed (ages 8–18). Contact: John Benson, P.O. Box 310714, New Braunfels, Texas 78130. (512) 625–7738 or (800) 753–8227.

A J The John Newcombe Tennis Ranch, New Braunfels, Tex. Juniors: cottages and cabins; Adults: two-bedroom condominium and motel. 28 hard courts (4 covered; 8 lit) Juniors: 5:1; Adults: 4:1. Co-ed (ages 8–18). Contact: Patti Corrigan/Cheryl Barnard, Highway 46 West, New Braunfels, Tex. 78130. (512) 625–9105 or (800) 444–6204. P.O. Box 310469, New Braunfels, Tex. 78131–0469 (mailing address).

J Longhorn Tennis Camp, The University of Texas at Austin, Austin, Tex. Dormitory. 12 outdoor courts with 40 additional available. 5:1. Co-ed (ages 8–17). Contact: Dave Snyder or Bob Hangen, Longhorn Tennis Camp, 718 Belmont Hall, University of Texas, Austin, Tex. 87871. (512) 471–4404.

J Texas A&M "Wilson" Tennis Camp, Texas A&M University, College Station, Tex. Dormitory. 42 outdoor courts. 6:1. Co-ed (ages 9–17). Contact: David Kent/Bobby Kleinecke, 2619 Rustling Oaks, Bryan, Tex. 77802. (409) 845–2816 (office), 774–7221 (home), or 845–4627 (dorm).

J Trinity University "Home of Champions" Tennis Camp, San Antonio, Tex. Dormitory. 16 outdoor courts (4 lit). 6:1. Co-ed (ages 8–17). Contact: Butch Newman, Trinity University, 715 Stadium Drive, San Antonio, Tex. 78212. (512) 736–7011.

J   Tyler Junior College Tennis Camp, Tyler, Tex. Dormitory. 10 courts (8 outdoor; 2 indoor). 4–6:1. Co-ed (ages 8–18). Contact: Paul N. Soliz, Tyler Junior College, P.O. Box 9020, Tyler, Tex. 75711. (903) 510–2473 (work) or (214) 581–5181 (home).

## UTAH

A J   The Vic Braden Tennis College, St. George, Utah. Condominium. 19 courts (15 outdoor; 4 indoor). 4:1. Co-ed (ages 10–18). Contact: Dave Nostrant, 1515 W. Canyon View Dr., St. George, Utah 84770. (800) 237–1068 or in Utah (801) 628–8060.

## VERMONT

A J   Ian Fletcher Tennis School, Bolton Valley Resort, Bolton, Vt. Hotel, condominium. 10 courts (8 outdoor; 2 indoor). 5:1. Co-ed (ages 8–17). Contact: Reservations Office, Bolton Valley Resort, Bolton, Vt. 05477. (800) 451–5025, in Vt. (802) 434–2769.

A   The Killington School for Tennis, Killington, Vt. Motor inn or condominium. 8 courts (4 lit), plus 8 ball lanes. 4:1. Contact: Barry Stout or John Rohan, Killington School for Tennis, 881 Killington Rd., Killington, Vt. 05751. (802) 422–3101 or (800) 343–0762.

A J   Topnotch at Stowe Resort and Spa, Stowe, Vt. 90 hotel rooms/suites plus 17 luxury town homes, 12 courts (8 outdoor; 4 indoor). Contact: Topnotch at Stowe, Mountain Rd., Stowe, Vt. 05672. (800) 451–8686 (U.S. and Canada), (802) 253–8585 (worldwide).

J  Windridge Tennis Camp at Craftsbury Common, Craftsbury Common, Vt. Cabins. 17 clay courts. 4:1. Co-ed (ages 10–15). Contact: Anne Jenkins, P.O. Box 463, Richmond, Vt. 05477. (802) 434–2505.

A J  Windridge Tennis Camp at Teela-Wooket, Roxbury, Vt. Cabins. 13 clay; 8 Har-Tru. 4:1. Co-ed (ages 9–15). Contact: Anne Jenkins, P.O. Box 463, Richmond, Vt. 05477. (802) 434–2199.

## VIRGINIA

A J  4 Star Tennis Academy, University of Virginia, Charlottes-ville, Va. Dormitory and hotel for adults. 13 courts. 4:1. Co-ed (ages 10–18). Contact: Marietta Naramore, P.O. Box 790, McLean, Va. 22101. (703) 893–4428.

A J  First-Serve Tennis Camps, Richmond, Va. Dormitory and hotel. 10 hard courts. 5:1. Co-ed (ages 9–18). Contact: Eric O'Neill, 8610 Trable Rd., Richmond, Va. 23235. (804) 272–9574.

A  The Homestead Tennis Package, The Homestead, Hot Springs, Va. Resort hotel. 19 courts (15 Har-Tru; 4 hard). 6:1. Co-ed. Contact: Tom Morgan, Director of Tennis, The Home-stead, Hot Springs, Va. 24445. (703) 839–5500.

J  William & Mary–Ray Reppert Tennis Camp, Williamsburg, Va. Dormitory. 14 hard courts. 4–5:1. Co-ed (up to age 18). Contact: Ray or Kriss Reppert, 108 Druid Drive, Williamsburg, Va. 23185. (804) 220–0631.

## WASHINGTON

J Adidas/Northwest, Pacific Lutheran University, Tacoma, Wash. Dormitory. 10 outdoor courts. 5:1. Co-ed (ages 9–18). Contact: Pat Gustafsson, U.S. Sports Development, 919 Sir Francis Drake Blvd., Kentfield, Calif. 94904. (415) 459–0459 or (800) 433–6060.

J Janet Adkinson's Tennis Adventures, Crystal Mountain Resorts, Wash. Chalets (Alpine Inn). 4 courts. 5:1 (juniors); 4:1 (competitive camp). Co-ed (ages 10–18). Contact: Janet Adkinson, 3320 122nd Pl. NE, Bellevue, Wash. 98005. (206) 885–5620.

A Janet Adkinson's Tennis Adventures, Roche Harbor Resort, San Juan Island, Wash. Condominium and cabins. 2 courts. 4:1. Contact: Janet Adkinson, 3320 122nd Pl. NE., Bellevue, Wash. 98005. (206) 378–2155.

A Adult Progressive Camp at Sudden Valley. Resort hotel. 5 outdoor courts; 3 lit. 4:1. Contact: JoAnn Andrews, Sudden Valley Resort, 2145 Lake Whitcom Blvd., Bellingham, Wash. 98226. (206) 734–6434 or (206) 733–5050.

A J Progressive Tennis Day Camps, Fairhaven Health and Racquet Club, Bellingham, Wash. 2 outdoor and 2 indoor courts. 6:1 for juniors and 4:1 for adults. Co-ed (ages 8–18). Contact: JoAnn Andrews, 800 McKenzie Rd., Bellingham, Wash. 98225. (206) 733–5050.

J Progressive Tennis Camp at Western Washington University, Bellingham, Wash. Dormitory. 8 outdoor courts. Indoor access if necessary. 4:1. Co-ed (ages 12 and up). Contact: JoAnn Andrews, Carver Gym, Western Washington University, Bellingham, Wash. 98226. (206) 676-3109 or 733-5050.

## WISCONSIN

J  Birch Knoll, Eagle River, Wis. Cabins. 5 hard courts. 4:1. Co-ed (ages 8-16). Contact: Gary Baier, 5589 Treehaven Circle, Fort Myers, Fla. 33907. (800) 843-2904.

J  Nick Bollettieri Tennis Summer Camp, Wayland Academy, Beaver Dam, Wis. Dormitory, with community bath, lounge with television, linens and towels provided. 15 courts (11 outdoor; 4 indoor). 5:1. Co-ed (ages 8-18). Contact: NBTA Reservations, 5500 34th Street West, Bradenton, Fla. 34210. (813) 755-1000 or (800) USA-NICK.

J  Camp Nicolet for Girls. Eagle River, Wis. Cabins. 4 hard courts. 4:1. (ages 8-15). Contact: Georgianna S. Starz, P.O. Box 1359, Eagle River, Wis. 54521. (715) 545-2522.

J  Stap Schroeder National Tennis Camp at Carthage College, Kenosha, Wis. Dormitory. 24 courts (20 outdoor; 4 indoor). 5:1. Co-ed (ages 9-18). Contact: Rob and Myrnna Schroeder, 4920 Olde Orchid Road, Skokie, Ill. 60077. (708) 673-6401 or 967-1400 or (414) 551-6517.

J  Towering Pines, Eagle River, Wis. Cabins. 5 outdoor courts. 3:1. Boys (ages 7-16). Contact: John M. Jordan, 242 Bristol St., Northfield, Ill. 60093. (708) 446-7311.

A J  Warhawk Tennis Camps, University of Wisconsin, Whitewater, Wis. Dormitory. 24 outdoor courts (19 lit). 5:1. Co-ed (ages 11–17). Contact: Mrs. Lou Zahn, Continuing Education Office, 2005 Roseman Bldg., UW-Whitewater, Whitewater, Wis. 53190 (414) 472–5165.

J  Camp Woodland, Eagle River, Wis. Cabins. 3 outdoor courts. 3:1. Girls (ages 7–16). Contact: John M. Jordan, 242 Bristol St., Northfield, Ill. 60093. (708) 446–7311.

## WYOMING

A J  Teton Pines, Jackson, Wyo. Country club suites. 10 courts (7 outdoor; 3 indoor). Adults: 4:1; juniors: 5:1. Co-ed (ages 8–16). Contact: Dave Luebbe, 3450 North Clubhouse Dr., Jackson, Wyo. 83001. (307) 733–9248.

# Canada

A J   Bishop's University Tennis Camp, Lennoxville, Quebec, Canada. University residence. 9 courts. 6:1. Co-ed (ages 10–17). Contact: Rick Pellerin, Bishop's University Tennis Camp, Lennoxville, Quebec, Canada J1M 1Z7. (819) 822–9672.

A J   Gray Rocks Tennis School, Saint-Jovite, Quebec, Canada. Hotel rooms and resort condominium. 22 outdoor Har-Tru courts. 4–6:1. Co-ed (ages 11–17). Contact: Luce Meilleur, P.O. Box 1000, Saint-Jovite, Quebec, Canada J0T 2H0. (819) 425–2771 or (800) 567–6767.

J   Manitou-Wabing Tennis Camp, Parry Sound, Ontario, Canada. Cabins. 16 hard courts. 4:1. Co-ed (ages 9–17). Contact: Jordana Wise, Manitou-Wabing Sports: Arts Centre, 251 Davenport Rd., Toronto, Ontario, Canada M5R 1J9.

A J   Matchpoint: Gray Rocks, Saint-Jovite, Quebec, Canada. Hotel rooms (3 per room, maximum). 22 outdoor Har-Tru. 4–6:1. Co-ed (ages 11–17). Contact: Luce Meilleur, P.O. Box 1000, Saint-Jovite, Quebec, Canada J0T 2H0. (819) 425–2771 or (800) 567–6767.

AJ Richard Thomson International Tennis School, Collingwood, Ontario, Canada. Hotel and chalet. 12 courts (9 hard; 3 soft). 4:1. Co-ed (ages 9–17). Contact: Richard Thomson, P.O. Box 56, Station S, Toronto, Ontario, Canada M5M 4L6. (416) 638–1596.

AJ University of British Columbia Tennis Centre, Vancouver, B.C., Canada. Accommodations through conference center. 6:1/ juniors; 4:1/adults; 3:1/academy juniors. 14 outdoor courts (6 lit); 8 indoor courts. Co-ed (ages 5–18). Contact: Patricio Gonzales, Director, or Brett Hobdon, Head Professional, University of British Columbia Tennis Centre, 6184 Thunderbird Blvd., Osborne Building Unit No. 2, Vancouver, B.C., Canada V6T 1W5.

# Europe

A J   Peter Burwash International Tennis Camp, Park Hotels Waldhaus, CH-7018 Flims-Waldhaus, Waldhaus, Switzerland. 5-star hotel. 11 courts (9 outdoor clay; 2 indoor carpet). 4:1. Co-ed (ages 13 and up). Contact: Roger Darrohn, Peter Burwash International, Postfach 21 A-6353, Going/Tyrol, Austria. Tel. 05358–3310 or (Fax) 05358–200031.

A J   Peter Burwash International Tennis Camp, Hotel Stanglwirt, Tirol, Austria. Hotel. 14 clay courts (8 outdoor; 6 indoor). 4:1. Co-ed (ages 13 and older). Contact: Roger Darrohn, Peter Burwash International, Postfach 21 A-6353, Going/Tyrol. Austria. Tel. 05358–3310 or (Fax) 05358–200031.

A   Steve Furgal's International Tennis. Italy & France. Hotel. Contact: Steve Furgal or Anne O'Neill, Steve Furgal's International Tennis, 11828 Rancho Bernardo Rd., Suite 123305, San Diego, Calif. 92128. (619) 487-7777.

J   Steve Furgal's International Tennis. Spain, Portugal & Italy. Hotel & host families. 6:1. Co-ed (ages 10–19). Contact: Steve Furgal or Anne O'Neill, Steve Furgal International Tennis, 11828 Rancho Bernardo Rd., Suite 123305, San Diego, Calif. 92128. (619) 487-7777.

A J   The Jonathan Markson Oxford Tennis Camp, Hertford College, Oxford University, Oxford, England. Private room in Hertford College. 4–6:1. 25 courts (12 grass; 12 hard; 1 indoor).
Co-ed. Juniors must be 14 if they wish to reside in the college;
otherwise the youngest campers are 8 years old. 4:1 for advanced
players. Contact: Michael Mahony, Jonathan Markson Oxford
Tennis Camp, 245 Mitchan Rd., London SW17 9JQ, England.
Tel. 081–767–8710.

J   Ramey-Ford Tennis School's European Tour. Accommodations
vary from private home stays to hotels to clubs. Court facilities
and surfaces vary. Co-ed (ages 15–20). Need 4.5 USTA ranking.
Contact: Joan Ramey-Ford, Ramey Tennis Schools, 5931 Highway 56, Owensboro, Ky. 42301. (502) 771–4723.

J   Ramey Tennis School's International Exchange. Private home
stay. Court facilities and surfaces vary depending on club. Co-ed
(ages 14–18). Contact: Joan Ramey-Ford, Ramey Tennis Schools,
5931 Highway 56, Owensboro, Ky. 42301. (502) 771–4723.

A J   Sporting Isola Bella NBTA Italia, Bianchi, Italy. Dormitory,
hotel. 6 indoor lit courts. 5:1. Co-ed (ages 8–18). Contact: Lino
Ballardini, 20075 Lodi Via Mose, Bianchi, Italy. Tel. 39–371–
426745 or 39–371–423360 or (800) USA–NICK.

J   Students Abroad, Summer Ski and Tennis Camp I. Hotel and
condominium. One week each in France, Switzerland, Italy and
Austria. Court facilities and surfaces vary depending on location.
5:1. Co-ed (ages 14–18). Contact: Edward Finn, 42-D Edgewood
Ave., Mt. Vernon, N.Y. 10552. (914) 699–8335.

J   Students Abroad, Summer and Ski Camp II. Hotel and condominium. Three weeks in France and two weeks in Austria.

Court facilities and surfaces vary depending on location. 5:1. Co-ed (ages 14–18). Contact: Edward Finn, 42-D Edgewood Ave., Mt. Vernon, N.Y. 10552. (914) 699–8335.


J  Students Abroad, Summer and Ski Camp III. Hotel and condominium. Three weeks in France or Switzerland. Court facilities and surfaces vary depending on location. 5:1. Co-ed (ages 14–18). Contact: Edward Finn, 42-D Edgewood Ave., Mt. Vernon, N.Y. 10552. (914) 699–8335.


A J  Tennis Camp Reino, Jyllinge, Denmark, at the Roskilde Fjord. Co-ed. Contact: Reino and Ingrid Nyyssonen, Postgarden, Nordmarksvej 14 A-B-C, DK-4040 Jyllinge 46–78–97–20 or, from September–April, Ingrid Nyyssonen, Kink St. 1, A-9020 Klagenfurt, Austria 463–51–18–28.


J  Tennis: Europe. Hotels or home stays with tennis families. From 3–50 courts, depending on tournament location. 5:1. Co-ed. (junior teams: ages 14–18; college teams: ages 18–22). Contact: Dr. Martin Vinokur, Director, 146 Cold Spring Road, No. 13, Stamford, Conn. 06905. (203) 964–1939. Fax: (203) 967–9499.

# Australia, New Zealand, Fiji

A   Steve Furgal's International Tennis Australian Open tennis tour. Hotel. Contact: Steve Furgal or Anne O'Neill, Steve Furgal's International Tennis, 11828 Rancho Bernardo Rd., Suite 123305, San Diego, Calif. 92128. (619) 487-7777.

J   Steve Furgal's International Tennis, Australia, New Zealand, Fiji. Hotel and host families. 6:1. Co-ed (ages 10–19). Contact: Steve Furgal or Anne O'Neill, Steve Furgal's International Tennis, 11828 Rancho Bernardo Rd., Suite 123305, San Diego, Calif. 92128. (619) 487-7777.

J   Tennis: Europe's Down Under-Hawaii Team. Two sanctioned junior tournaments in Australia, plus a week of friendly matches in Honolulu with USTPA professional analysis, coaching and intensive practice sessions: Melbourne, Sydney, Adelaide and Honolulu. Contact: Dr. Martin Vinokur, 146 Cold Spring Road, No. 13, Stamford, Conn. 06905. (203) 964-1939. Fax: (203) 967-9499.

# HELPFUL INFORMATION

Since a vacation is not comprised of tennis alone, we are providing you with the telephone numbers of tourist boards, airlines, rental car companies, and hotel chains. Keep this information handy when planning your next vacation.

## U.S. Tourist Boards

| | | | |
|---|---|---|---|
| Alabama | (800) 252-2262 | Missouri | (314) 751-4133 |
| Alaska | (907) 465-2010 | Montana | (800) 541-1447 |
| Arizona | (602) 542-8687 | Nebraska | (800) 228-4307 |
| Arkansas | (800) 643-8383 | Nevada | (800) 638-2328 |
| California | (800) 862-2543 | New Hampshire | (603) 271-2666 |
| Colorado | (800) 433-2656 | New Jersey | (800) 537-7397 |
| Connecticut | (800) 243-1685 | New Mexico | (800) 545-2040 |
| Delaware | (800) 441-8846 | New York | (800) 225-5697 |
| D.C. | (202) 789-7000 | North Carolina | (800) 847-4862 |
| Florida | (904) 487-1462 | North Dakota | (800) 437-2077 |
| Georgia | (800) 847-4842 | Ohio | (800) 282-5393 |
| Hawaii | (808) 923-1811 | Oklahoma | (800) 652-6552 |
| Idaho | (800) 635-7820 | Oregon | (800) 547-7842 |
| Illinois | (800) 223-0121 | Pennsylvania | (800) 847-4872 |
| Indiana | (800) 292-6337 | Rhode Island | (401) 277-2601 |
| Iowa | (800) 345-4692 | South Carolina | (803) 734-0122 |
| Kansas | (913) 296-2009 | South Dakota | (800) 843-1930 |
| Kentucky | (800) 252-6727 | Tennessee | (615) 741-2158 |
| Louisiana | (800) 334-8626 | Texas | (800) 888-8839 |
| Maine | (800) 533-9595 | Utah | (801) 538-1030 |
| Maryland | (800) 543-1036 | Vermont | (802) 828-3236 |
| Massachusetts | (800) 447-6277 | Virginia | (804) 786-4484 |
| Michigan | (800) 543-2937 | Washington | (206) 753-5600 |
| Minnesota | (800) 657-3700 | West Virginia | (800) 225-5982 |
| Mississippi | (800) 647-2290 | Wisconsin | (800) 432-8747 |
| Wyoming | (800) 225-5996 | | |

# Caribbean Tourist Boards

Anguilla Tourist
Information Office
271 Main Street
Northport, N.Y. 11768
(800) 553-4939

Antigua & Barbuda
Tourist Board
610 Fifth Avenue
New York, N.Y. 10017
(212) 541-4117

Aruba Tourism Authority
521 Fifth Avenue
New York, N.Y. 10017
(212) 246-3030

Bahamas Tourist Office
150 East 52nd Street
New York, N.Y. 10023
(212) 758-2777

Barbados Board of Tourism
800 Second Avenue
New York, N.Y. 10017
(212) 986-6516

Bonaire Tourist Office
275 Seventh Avenue
New York, N.Y. 10001
(212) 242-7707

British Virgin Islands
Tourist Board
370 Lexington Avenue
New York, N.Y. 10017
(212) 696-0400

Cayman Islands Department
of Tourism
420 Lexington Avenue
New York, N.Y. 10170
(212) 682-5582

Curacao Tourist Board
400 Madison Avenue
New York, N.Y. 10017
(212) 751-8266

French West Indies
Tourist Board
610 Fifth Avenue
New York, N.Y. 10020
(212) 757-1125

Grenada Tourist Board
141 East 44th Street
New York, N.Y. 10017
(212) 687-9554

Jamaica Tourist Board
866 Second Avenue
New York, N.Y. 10017
(212) 688-7650

Puerto Rico Tourism Company
575 Fifth Avenue
New York, N.Y. 10017
(212) 599-6262

St. Kitts & Nevis Tourist Board
414 East 75th Street
New York, N.Y. 10001
(212) 535-1234

St. Lucia Tourist Board
820 Second Avenue
New York, N.Y. 10017
(212) 867-2950

St. Vincent & The Grenadines
801 Second Avenue
New York, N.Y. 10017
(212) 687-4981

U.S. Virgin Islands Tourism
1270 Avenue of the Americas
New York, N.Y. 10020
(212) 582-4520

Trinidad & Tobago Tourist Board
118-35 Queens Boulevard
Forest Hills, N.Y. 11375
(718) 575-3909

Turks & Caicos Tourist Office
271 Main Street
Northport, N.Y. 11768
(516) 261-9600

# Airlines

| Aero Mexico | (800) 237-6639 | Hawaiian | (800) 367-5320 |
|---|---|---|---|
| Aloha | (800) 367-5250 | Iberia | (800) 772-4642 |
| Air Canada | (800) 422-6232 | KLM | (800) 777-5553 |
| Air France | (800) 237-2747 | Lufthansa | (800) 645-3880 |
| Air Jamaica | (800) 523-5585 | Mexicana | (800) 531-7923 |
| Alitalia | (800) 223-5730 | Midway | (800) 866-9000 |
| America West | (800) 247-5692 | Northwest | (800) 225-2525 |
| American | (800) 433-7300 | Pan Am | (800) 221-1111 |
| Bahamas Air | (800) 222-4262 | Southwest | (800) 531-5601 |
| British Airways | (800) 247-9297 | Swissair | (800) 221-4750 |
| BWIA | (800) 327-7401 | TWA | (800) 221-2000 |
| Continental | (800) 231-0856 | United | (800) 241-6522 |
| Delta | (800) 221-1212 | U.S. Air | (800) 428-4322 |
| Virgin Atlantic | (800) 862-8261 | | |

# Rental Car Companies

| Alamo | (800) 327-9633 | National | (800) 227-7368 |
|---|---|---|---|
| Avis | (800) 331-1212 | Snappy | (800) 669-5252 |
| Budget | (800) 527-0700 | Thrifty | (800) 331-9111 |
| Dollar | (800) 421-6868 | Tropical | (800) 367-5140 |
| General | (800) 327-7607 | USA | (800) USA-CARS |
| Hertz | (800) 654-3131 | Value | (800) 327-2501 |

# Major Hotel Chains

| | |
|---|---|
| Best Western | (800) 334-7234 |
| Canadian Pacific | (800) 828-7447 |
| Ciga Hotels (Italy) | (800) 221-2340 |
| Clarion Hotels | (800) CLARION |
| Colony Hotels | (800) 367-6046 |
| Cunard Hotels | (800) 222-0939 |
| Days Inn | (800) 633-1414 |
| Divi Resorts | (800) 367-3484 |
| Four Seasons Hotels | (800) 332-3442 |
| Hilton Hotels | (800) HILTONS |
| Holiday Inn | (800) HOLIDAY |
| Hyatt Hotels | (800) 233-1234 |
| InterContinental Hotels | (800) 33-AGAIN |
| Leading Hotels of the World | (800) 223-6800 |
| Marriott Hotels | (800) 228-9290 |
| Meridien Hotels | (800) 543-4300 |
| Omni Hotels | (800) THE OMNI |
| Preferred Hotels | (800) 323-7500 |
| Premier Hotels | (800) 223-6620 |
| Princess Hotels | (800) 223-1818 |
| Quality Inn | (800) 228-5151 |
| Radisson Hotels | (800) 333-3333 |
| Ramada | (800) 2-RAMADA |
| Relaix & Chateaux | (800) 372-1323 |
| Ritz-Carlton | (800) 241-3333 |
| Rock Resorts | (800) 223-7637 |
| Royce Resorts | (800) 237-6923 |
| Sheraton | (800) 334-8484 |
| Sofitel | (800) 221-4542 |
| Sonesta | (800) 343-8484 |
| Stouffer | (800) HOTELS-1 |
| Trusthouse Forte Hotels | (800) 225-5843 |
| Westin | (800) 228-3000 |
| Wyndham Hotels | (800) 822-4200 |

# ABOUT THE AUTHORS

**PETER M. COAN** was the Executive Editor of *World Tennis* Magazine (recently renamed *Tennis Illustrated*) and is the author of the controversial and critically acclaimed biography *Taxi: The Harry Chapin Story*. Mr. Coan resides in Forest Hills, New York, with his wife, Nazli and their daughter, Melissa Kimberly.

**BARRY STAMBLER** was Travel Editor of *World Tennis* Magazine. Previously he was associated with CBS Sports and Sportschannel in various capacities after his graduation from SUNY at Albany with a degree in communications.

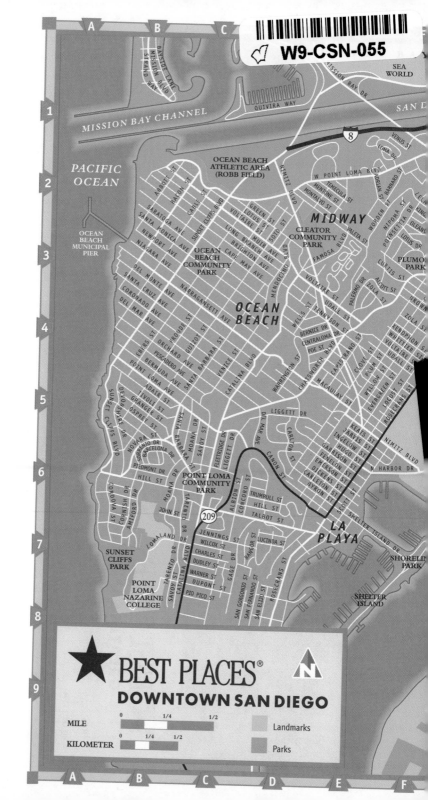

MM  NN  OO  PP  QQ  RR

Sweetwater
Reservoir

Second San Diego Aqueduct

905

USA
MEXICO

Tijuana

1

2

Lemon
Grove

National
City

Chula
Vista

OTAY VALLEY RD

OTAY MESA RD

CANYON RD

TELEGRAPH

805

MAIN ST

Otay River

PALM AVE

Tijuana River

HOLLISTER ST

3

94

East
San
Diego

15

EUCLID AVE

4TH AVE

L ST

5

BEACH BLVD

San
Diego

SAN DIEGO ZOO

75

SAN DIEGO-CORONADO TOLL BRIDGE

San
Diego
Bay

75

SILVER
STRAND
STATE
BEACH

Imperial
Beach

TIJUANA RIVER
NATIONAL
ESTUARINE
SANCTUARY

4

282

NORTH
ISLAND
NAVAL AIR
STATION

Coronado

US NAVAL
AMPHIBIOUS
BASE

5

6

209

PACIFIC
OCEAN

Point
Loma

7

★ BEST PLACES®
GREATER SAN DIEGO

N

Landmarks

Parks

8

MILES       0 1/2 1    2    3    4    5

KILOMETERS  0 1/2 1    2    3    4    5

9

MM  NN  OO  PP  QQ  RR

# Praise for Best Places® Guidebooks

"Best Places *are the best regional restaurant and guide books in America.*"
—THE SEATTLE TIMES

"Best Places *covers must-see portions of the West Coast with style and authority. In-the-know locals offer thorough info on restaurants, lodgings, and the sights.*"
—NATIONAL GEOGRAPHIC TRAVELER

"*. . . travelers swear by the recommendations in the* Best Places *guidebooks . . .*"
—SUNSET MAGAZINE

"*For travel collections covering the Northwest, the* Best Places *series takes precedence over all similar guides.*"
—BOOKLIST

"Best Places Northwest *is the bible of discriminating travellers to BC, Washington and Oregon. It promises, and delivers, the best of everything in the region.*"
—THE VANCOUVER SUN

"*Not only the best travel guide in the region, but maybe one of the most definitive guides in the country, which many look forward to with the anticipation usually sparked by a best-selling novel. A browser's delight,* Best Places Northwest *should be chained to dashboards throughout the Northwest.*"
—THE OREGONIAN

"*Still the region's undisputed heavyweight champ of guidebooks.*"
—SEATTLE POST-INTELLIGENCER

"*Trusting the natives is usually good advice, so visitors to Washington, Oregon, and British Columbia would do well to pick up* Best Places Northwest *for an exhaustive review of food and lodging in the region. . . . An indispensable glove-compartment companion.*"
—TRAVEL AND LEISURE

"Best Places Southern California *is just about all the inspiration you need to start planning your next road trip or summer vacation with the kids.*"
—THE FRESNO BEE

"Best Places Alaska *is the one guide to recommend to anyone visiting Alaska for the first or one-hundredth time.*"
—KETCHIKAN DAILY NEWS

"Best Places Northern California *is great fun to read even if you're not going anywhere.*"
—SAN FRANCISCO CHRONICLE

# TRUST THE LOCALS

The original insider's guides, written by local experts

## COMPLETELY INDEPENDENT
- No advertisers
- No sponsors
- No favors

## EVERY PLACE STAR-RATED & RECOMMENDED

★★★★ The very best in the region

★★★ Distinguished; many outstanding features

★★ Excellent; some wonderful qualities

★ A good place

## MONEY-BACK GUARANTEE
We're so sure you'll be satisfied, we guarantee it!

## HELPFUL ICONS
Watch for these quick-reference symbols throughout the book:

 FAMILY FUN

 GOOD VALUE

 ROMANTIC

 EDITORS' CHOICE

# BEST PLACES®

## SAN DIEGO

The Best Restaurants, Lodgings,
and a Complete Guide to the City

Edited by
MARIBETH MELLIN

EDITION

SASQUATCH BOOKS
SEATTLE

Printed in the United States of America
Distributed by Publishers Group West

2nd edition
09 08 07 06 05 04 03     5 4 3 2 1

ISBN: 1-57061-348-6
ISSN: 1524-9247

Series editor: Kate Rogers
Cover and interior design: Nancy Gellos
Cover photograph: David G. Houser/CORBIS
Fold-out and interior maps: GreenEye Design

**SPECIAL SALES**
Best Places guidebooks are available at special discounts on bulk purchases for
corporate, club, or organization sales promotions, premiums, and gifts. Special
editions, including personalized covers, excerpts of existing guides, and corporate
imprints, can be created in large quantities for specific needs. For more information, contact your local bookseller or Special Sales, Best Places Guidebooks, 615
Second Avenue, Suite 260, Seattle, Washington 98104, 800/775-0817.

Sasquatch Books
615 Second Avenue
Seattle, WA 98104
206/467-4300
bestplaces@SasquatchBooks.com
www.SasquatchBooks.com

# CONTENTS

Introduction and Acknowledgments   ix
Contributors   xi
About Best Places® Guidebooks   xii
How to Use This Book   xiii
   *Best Places® Star Ratings*   *xv*

**PLANNING A TRIP   1**
How to Get Here   2
When to Visit   4
Tips for Special Travelers   7
   *Freeway Frenzy*   *4*
   *In the Beginning*   *8*

**LAY OF THE CITY   11**
Orientation   12
Visitor Information   14
Getting Around   15
Essentials   17
Local Resources   20
   *How to Pass for a Local*   *13*
   *Places of Worship*   *18*
   *Holes in the Ground*   *22*

**TOP 150 RESTAURANTS   27**
Restaurants by Star Rating   28
Restaurants by Neighborhood   30
Restaurants by Food and Other Features   32
Restaurant Reviews   37
   *Doggie Dining*   *40*
   *Fresh from the Sea*   *89*

**LODGINGS   97**
Downtown   98
Airport Area   101
Coronado   102
Point Loma/Shelter Island   103
Old Town and Mission Valley   104
Mission Bay   105
Pacific Beach   106
La Jolla   107
Del Mar   111
Rancho Santa Fe   112
Cardiff-by-the-Sea   113

Carlsbad 113
Oceanside 115
Rancho Bernardo 115
Julian 116
Borrego Springs 116
*Sleeping on a Shoestring 101*
*Spas and Salons 108*

## EXPLORING 117
Top 25 Attractions 118
Neighborhoods 138
Museums 149
Art in Public Places 154
Galleries 156
Gardens 159
Beaches and Parks 160
Organized Tours 167
*Top 25 Attractions 119*
*A Maze of Neighborhoods 141*
*Tide Pool Tango 162*

## SHOPPING 171
Neighborhoods and Malls 172
Shops from A to Z 173
*Designer Shopping 176*
*Growth and Dreams 195*

## PERFORMING ARTS 201
Theater 202
Fringe Theaters 208
Classical Music and Opera 208
Dance 211
Film 214
Literature 215
*Ticket Alert 203*
*Clowning Around 210*
*Airport Art 213*

## NIGHTLIFE 217
Nightlife by Features 218
Nightlife by Neighborhood 220
Music and Clubs 221

Bars, Pubs, and Taverns   227
Desserts, Coffees, and Teas   233
   *Alternative Venues   223*
   *Love, San Diego Style   228*

## ITINERARIES   235
Three-Day Tour   236
La Jolla Day   239
A Day at the Beach   239
   *Kids' Play   237*
   *Mister Horton Builds a City   238*

## DAY TRIPS   241
Carlsbad and Environs   242
Escondido and Environs   244
Palomar Mountain and Julian   246
Anza-Borrego Desert and Borrego Springs   248
Temecula   250
Disneyland   252
   *Beautiful View   243*
   *Gambling Goes Native   249*

## BAJA   255
Baja, California, Mexico   257
Tijuana   257
Rosarito   262
Puerto Nuevo (Newport)   264
Ensenada   265
   *Border Sense   260*
   *The Whole Enchilada   266*

## RECREATION   271
Outdoor Activities   272
Spectator Sports   293
   *Weird Sports   279*
   *Above It All   286*
   *Contamination Blues   291*

Index   297
Money-Back Guarantee   313
Best Places® Report Form   315

# Introduction and Acknowledgments

This book is a lot like my garden. Both claim enormous energy, effort, and persistence; both seem like hopeless muddles at times. Then, after hours, days, and months of digging, weeding, cultivating, and pruning, they're ready to go public. I'm never sure what the end result will be. This year, my garden has a small field of sunflowers and corn to tempt the wild green parrots flying around the beach. Scarlet-throated hummingbirds hover above pink foxgloves and violet delphiniums. Skunks burrow under Mexican sage. And the scent of night-blooming jasmine and orange blossoms drifts through my consciousness even when I spend the better part of my days at the computer.

Amazingly enough, this patch of paradise exists in the middle of the nation's seventh-largest city. My neighborhood is far from rural. The sounds of sirens, airplanes, amateur bands, and barking dogs are ever present. But the beach is just five blocks from home, and the climate nurtures an astonishing array of wildlife. Living here is like being dropped into a movie. The people are friendly. The streets are clean. The sky is persistently blue. Bad things happen here, for sure. But somehow, San Diego retains the air of a perfect community.

Perfection has its drawbacks, however. It's easily confused with superficiality and complacence. That's where *Best Places San Diego* comes in handy. Uncovering the finest sides of this seemingly idyllic city and county is a slippery matter. In trendy Southern California, restaurants, shops, and activities are easily discarded when something new comes along. It takes a seasoned eye to find the stars that endure whimsical trends and are worthy of inclusion in this second edition. The contributors to this book have been around long enough to have faith in their favorites, and are both perceptive and flexible. They know which new businesses are likely to succeed with San Diegans, and which deserve recognition for their staying power. It takes a healthy dose of bravado to assume one has found all the best places in San Diego. I'm sure some readers will disagree with our choices; others will be thrilled to find their favorites included (or overlooked, if secrecy is desired).

I'm fortunate to work with a small cadre of friends who helped create the first edition of this book and have refined their work the second time around. Some of the best insights came from those who joined my excursions throughout the region. Patrick Mellin approached downtown, Ocean Beach, and Tijuana with infectious enthusiasm. As always, Gary Grimaud provided consistency and an amazing knowledge of geography and obscure trivia. Others who deserve acknowledgment include the Humphrey, Onstott, and Grimaud families. I am most fortunate to be working with Sasquatch Books, and thank Kate Rogers and project editor Laura Gronewold for their patience, guidance, commitment, and kindness.

Finally, I dedicate this book to my mother, who passed away as I began working on the first edition of *Best Places San Diego*. I will forever cherish her sense of curiosity, the source of my own creativity.

—*Maribeth Mellin, Editor*

# Contributors

Editor **MARIBETH MELLIN** has authored and contributed to over 20 travel books including guides to Mexico, Costa Rica, Peru, Hawaii, and Argentina. She keeps returning to San Diego and has written countless articles for *San Diego Magazine* and the *San Diego Union Tribune*. Her articles and photographs have appeared in many publications from the *Baltimore Sun* to *China Skies*.

**SUSAN HUMPHREY** carted her three kids around the county to cover San Diego's beaches, parks, and "kid-friendly" attractions. She has contributed to all the chapters in both editions of this book as a writer, editor, and organizational whiz. Her assistance is invaluable.

Writer and artist **JANE ONSTOTT** is the author of the several guidebooks and is a diehard explorer. An expert on south of the border experiences, she authored the Baja chapter and contributed to several other chapters, including Exploring, Recreation, Restaurants, and Shopping. She lives in the countryside with her chickens, dog, and cat—but always threatens to move back to Mexico.

Native San Diegan **ROBIN KLEVEN DISHON** has overseen the restaurant chapter since this book's inception. A gifted writer with a discerning attitude toward dining, wine, and world travel, she manages to sort through San Diego's trendy dining spots to find the lasting gems. After 12 years as a reporter and editor at the *San Diego Union-Tribune*, she left to launch Microsoft's sidewalk.com, an arts and entertainment guide. She currently freelances for a variety of online and print publications.

A fortunate encounter with **WILL K. SHILLING** at the San Diego Computer Museum led to the inside tips for our nightlife chapter. A freelance writer and associate editor at *SLAMM-San Diego's Music Magazine,* he moved from the South Bay of Los Angeles to San Diego in 1992 and was so impressed with the local music scene he immediately began writing music reviews. His work has appeared in *The San Diego Reader, The Boston Globe* and *KPBS On Air* magazine. He lives in Ocean Beach, where they keep driving him to the city limits, but he always finds his way back.

A San Diego resident since first grade, **LESLIE VENOLIA** has worked as the "Events" editor at *The San Diego Reader* for ten years, so she knows there are always great things to do in this town.

Several writers contributed to the first edition of *Best Places San Diego*—their imprint remains.

**ALISON ASHTON** wrote about San Diego's mountains, deserts, and neighborhoods and offered her insights on hotels and restaurants throughout the county. She is a freelance travel writer and author of a weekly travel column syndicated by Copley News Service.

Freelance writer **PETER JENSEN** covered his neighborhood of Del Mar, along with restaurants, design shops, and San Diego history. Jensen contributes regularly to *Sunset, This Old House, Coastal Living, San Diego Home/Garden* and other periodicals. He is the author of several books regarding travel destinations in the West.

**MARAEL JOHNSON** is an award-winning freelance travel writer whose interests range from fine restaurants and North County neighborhoods to the amusements at Disneyland. She has authored or contributed to many travel guidebooks.

# About Best Places® Guidebooks

People trust us. Best Places guidebooks, which have been published continuously since 1975, represent one of the most respected regional travel series in the country. Each guide is written completely independently: no advertisers, no sponsors, no favors. Our reviewers know their territory, work incognito, and seek out the very best a city or region has to offer. Because we accept no free meals, accommodations, or other complimentary services, we are able to provide tough, candid reports about places that have rested too long on their laurels, and to delight in new places that deserve recognition. We describe the true strengths, foibles, and unique characteristics of each establishment listed.

*Best Places San Diego* is written by and for locals, and is therefore coveted by travelers. It's written for people who live here and who enjoy exploring the city's bounty and its out-of-the-way places of high character and individualism. It is these very characteristics that make *Best Places San Diego* ideal for tourists, too. The best places in and around the city are the ones that denizens favor: independently owned establishments of good value, touched with local history, run by lively individuals, and graced with natural beauty. With this second edition of *Best Places San Diego*, travelers will find the information they need: where to go and when, what to order, which rooms to request (and which to avoid), where the best music, art, nightlife, shopping, and other attractions are, and how to find the city's hidden secrets.

We're so sure you'll be satisfied with our guide, we guarantee it.

**NOTE:** *The reviews in this edition are based on information available at press time and are subject to change. Readers are advised that places listed in previous editions may have closed or changed management, and may no longer be recommended by this series. The editors welcome information conveyed by users of this book. A report form is provided at the end of the book, and feedback is also welcome via email: bestplaces@ SasquatchBooks.com.*

# How to Use This Book

This book is divided into twelve chapters covering a wide range of establishments, destinations, and activities in and around San Diego. All evaluations are based on numerous reports from local and traveling inspectors. Best Places reporters do not identify themselves when they review an establishment, and they accept no free meals, accommodations, or any other services. Final judgments are made by the editors. Every place featured in this book is recommended.

**STAR RATINGS** *(for Top 150 Restaurants and Lodgings only)* Restaurants and lodgings are rated on a scale of one to four stars (with half stars in between), based on uniqueness, loyalty of local clientele, performance measured against the establishment's goals, excellence of cooking, cleanliness, value, and professionalism of service. Reviews are listed alphabetically, and every place is recommended.

| | |
|---|---|
| ★★★★ | The very best in the city |
| ★★★ | Distinguished; many outstanding features |
| ★★ | Excellent; some wonderful qualities |
| ★ | A good place |
| [unrated] | New or undergoing major changes |

(For more on how we rate places, see the Best Places Star Ratings box, below.)

**PRICE RANGE** *(for Top 150 Restaurants and Lodgings only)* Prices for lodgings are based on peak season rates for one night's lodging for two people (i.e., double occupancy). Off-season rates vary but can sometimes be significantly less. Prices for restaurants are based primarily on dinner for two, including dessert, tax, and tip. When prices range between two categories (for example, moderate to expensive), the lower one is given. Call ahead to verify, as all prices are subject to change.

| | |
|---|---|
| $$$$ | Most Expensive (more than $125 for dinner for two; more than $250 for one night's lodgings for two) |
| $$$ | Expensive (between $85 and $125 for dinner for two; between $150 and $250 for one night's lodgings for two) |
| $$ | Moderate (between $35 and $85 for dinner for two; between $85 and $150 for one night's lodgings for two) |
| $ | Inexpensive (less than $35 for dinner for two; less than $85 for one night's lodgings for two) |

**RESERVATIONS** We used one of the following terms for our reservations policy: reservations required, reservations recommended, no reservations, or reservations accepted. "No reservations" means either that they're not necessary or not accepted.

**ADDRESSES AND PHONE NUMBERS** Every attempt has been made to provide accurate information on an establishment's location and phone number. But it's always a good idea to call ahead and confirm. For establishments with two or more locations, we try to provide information on the original or most recommended branches.

**CHECKS AND CREDIT CARDS** Most establishments that accept checks also require a major credit card for identification. Note that some places accept only local checks. Credit cards are abbreviated in this book as follows: American Express (AE); Carte Blanche (CB); Diners Club (DC); Discover (DIS); Japanese credit card (JCB); MasterCard (MC); Visa (V).

**EMAIL AND WEB SITE ADDRESSES** Email and web site addresses for establishments have been included where available. Please note that the web is a fluid and evolving medium, and that web pages are often "under construction" or, as with all time-sensitive information, may no longer be valid.

**MAP INDICATORS** The letter-and-number codes appearing at the end of most listings refer to coordinates on the fold-out map included in the front of the book. Single letters (for example, F7) refer to the downtown San Diego map; double letters (FF7) refer to the Greater San Diego map on the flip side. If an establishment does not have a map code listed, its location falls beyond the boundaries of these maps.

**HELPFUL ICONS** Watch for these quick-reference symbols throughout the book:

**FAMILY FUN** Family-oriented places that are great for kids—fun, easy, not too expensive, and accustomed to dealing with young ones.

**GOOD VALUE** While not necessarily cheap, these places offer you the best value for your dollars—a good deal within the context of the city.

**ROMANTIC** These spots offer candlelight, atmosphere, intimacy, or other romantic qualities—kisses and proposals are encouraged!

**EDITORS' CHOICE** These are places that are unique and special to the city, such as a restaurant owned by a beloved local chef or a tourist attraction recognized around the globe.

&. Appears after listings for establishments that have wheelchair-accessible facilities.

**INDEXES** In addition to a general index at the back of the book, there are five specialized indexes: restaurants are indexed by star-rating, features, and location at the beginning of the Restaurants chapter, and nightspots are indexed by features and location at the beginning of the Nightlife chapter.

**READER REPORTS** At the end of the book is a report form. We receive hundreds of reports from readers suggesting new places or agreeing or disagreeing with our assessments. They greatly help in our evaluations, and we encourage you to respond.

**MONEY-BACK GUARANTEE** See "We Stand by Our Reviews" at the end of this book.

## BEST PLACES® STAR RATINGS

Any travel guide that rates establishments is inherently subjective—and Best Places is no exception. We rely on our professional experience, yes, but also on a gut feeling. And, occasionally, we even give in to a soft spot for a favorite neighborhood hangout. Our star-rating system is not simply a AAA-checklist; it's judgmental, critical, sometimes fickle, and highly personal. And unlike most other travel guides, we pay our own way and accept no freebies: no free meals or accommodations, no advertisers, no sponsors, no favors.

For each new edition, we send local food and travel experts out to review restaurants and lodgings anonymously, and then to rate them on a scale of one to four, based on uniqueness, loyalty of local clientele, performance measured against the establishment's goals, excellence of cooking, cleanliness, value, and professionalism of service. That doesn't mean a one-star establishment isn't worth dining or sleeping at—far from it. When we say that *all* the places listed in our books are recommended, we mean it. That one-star pizza joint may be just the ticket for the end of a whirlwind day of shopping with the kids. But if you're planning something more special, the star ratings can help you choose an eatery or hotel that will wow your new clients or be a stunning, romantic place to celebrate an anniversary or impress a first date.

We award four-star ratings sparingly, reserving them for what we consider truly the best. And once an establishment has earned our highest rating, everyone's expectations seem to rise. Readers often write us letters specifically to point out the faults in four-star establishments. With changes in chefs, management, styles, and trends, it's always easier to get knocked off the pedestal than to ascend it. Three-star establishments, on the other hand, seem to generate healthy praise. They exhibit outstanding qualities, and we get lots of love letters about them. The difference between two and three stars can sometimes be a very fine line. Two-star establishments are doing a good, solid job and gaining attention, while one-star places are often dependable spots that have been around forever.

The restaurants and lodgings described in *Best Places San Diego* have earned their stars from hard work and good service (and good food). They're proud to be included in this book—look for our Best Places sticker in their windows. And we're proud to honor them in this, the second edition of *Best Places San Diego*.

# PLANNING A TRIP

# PLANNING A TRIP

## How to Get Here

### BY AIRPLANE

**SAN DIEGO INTERNATIONAL AIRPORT AT LINDBERGH FIELD** (3707 N Harbor Dr, downtown; 619/231-2100; www.portofsandiego.org; map:I5) is smack in the middle of the city, 3 miles northwest of downtown, paralleling San Diego Bay. The airport includes Terminal 1, Terminal 2, and a Commuter Terminal. Large road signs on Harbor Drive list the different airlines served by each terminal. The **RED BUS SHUTTLE** travels between terminals, and though it is possible to walk between Terminals 1 and 2, the Commuter Terminal is in a separate complex with no pedestrian access. If you're flying on a small regional airline or one of the large airlines' commuter carriers, ask the airlines for the terminal and gate info in advance; many passengers get to the airport only to find their flight is departing quite a ways down the road.

**TRAVELERS AID** stations in Terminals 1 and 2 are open daily from 8am to 11pm, providing services for disabled or elderly passengers and children traveling alone as well as free information and referrals for getting around town. The **LOST AND FOUND** office is at Terminal 2 (619/686-8002). Both terminals have shops and eating establishments; the eateries Rubio's Mexican in Terminal 1 and La Salsa in Terminal 2 are especially good.

When the airport was remodeled and expanded in 1998, local travelers were appalled at some of the changes and found the airport to be less user-friendly in some ways. Passengers must hike long distances to get to baggage claim; then, to reach cabs, shuttles, and parking lots, they must retrace their steps and use escalators and elevators to return to the second floor, walk across a skybridge, descend again, and cross one or more streets (depending on the terminal). Airport officials responded to complaints by creating a couple of ground-level crosswalks to the taxi, shuttle, and parking areas; the skybridge is a good way to avoid traffic congestion and bad weather, however. Drivers may park outside the terminal only to drop off or pick up passengers or luggage, but taxis dropping off passengers cannot pick up passengers here. For comprehensive information on flight arrivals and departures, and parking, car rental, and paging services, call the airport information line (619/231-2100).

**PARKING** at the airport can be challenging, so allow enough time to cruise for one of the 3,000 spots. Rates are per hour; 1 hour costs $1, 6 to 7 hours $16, 7 to 24 hours $18, and anything into the next 24-hour period is $24, for up to 30 days. For example, leaving your car for four days would cost $90. Major credit cards are accepted. The parking lots are fenced except for a few crosswalks; a skybridge provides terminal access. For questions regarding parking at the airport, call 619/291-2087.

### AIRPORT TRANSPORTATION

A convenient way to get to and from San Diego's Lindbergh Field is by shuttle, accessible from the airport at the transportation plazas across from Terminals 1 and 2 (by way of the skybridge) and curbside at the Commuter Terminal. Airport personnel there can assist you. **SHUTTLE SERVICE** to and from the airport is available through Cloud 9 Shuttle (858/974-8885 or 800/974-8885), Coastline Shuttle (619/234-4770), Access Shuttle (619/299-8287), or Supreme Shuttle (619/295-1863). San Diego is a big county, and the price will vary considerably depending on where you are coming from.

**TAXIS** from the airport to downtown (or vice versa) run $10 to $12.

## BY CHARTER OR PRIVATE AIRPLANE

Most charter airplane and helicopter companies are based at the smaller airports in San Diego County: McClellan-Palomar Airport (760/431-4646; map:CC8), Montgomery Field (858/573-1440; map:KK4), and Gillespie Field (619/956-4800; map:JJ1). Services include aircraft rentals and flying lessons. Call the San Diego flight service station (800/992-7433) for up-to-date weather reports and flight-related information.

## BY BUS

**GREYHOUND BUS LINES** (120 W Broadway, downtown; 619/239-3266, 800/231-2222; www.greyhound.com; map:N7) offers low-cost transportation to San Diego from all over the country. The terminal, open 24 hours a day, is located in downtown San Diego, just up the street from the Santa Fe train depot and conveniently close to trolley stops. Many bus companies offer charter services to local and long-distance points of interest. Gray Line San Diego (619/491-0011 or 800/331-5077) is a good bet.

## BY TRAIN

**AMTRAK**'s Santa Fe depot (1050 Kettner Blvd, downtown; 619/239-9021 or 800/872-7245; www.amtrak.com; map:M7) near the harbor is a beautiful Spanish colonial–style building, with high ceilings and walls decorated with lovely old tiles. Train service up the coast to Los Angeles and on to Santa Barbara is offered several times daily. Local train service is also available via the Coaster (619/685-4900 or 800/262-7837), a commuter train with a stop in Old Town and six stops in North County. Fares vary depending on the distance traveled; most are between 50 cents and $4.75. Parking is free at all stations except Santa Fe and Sorrento Valley.

## BY CAR

Our first advice: get a good map. Until you become accustomed to it, the freeway system in San Diego is a quagmire of looping roads and intimidating on- and off-ramps. Interstate 8 is San Diego's main artery, moving people and their vehicles east and west from its starting point in Ocean Beach, through Mission Valley and El Cajon, over the mountains and down into the California desert, culminating in Arizona. Connecting points north and south is Interstate 5, commencing at the border with Mexico and carving through San Diego County to Los Angeles (120 miles away) and on to Oregon and Washington. The beach communities of Imperial Beach, Mission Beach, Pacific Beach, La Jolla, and Del Mar are all accessed from Interstate 5; it is also your connection to the Coronado Bay Bridge. Interstate 805 is another main drag through the county—and a drag it is to those hapless commuters caught during rush hour. Like salmon fighting their way upstream, morning and late-afternoon drivers struggle mightily on 805 to reach their desti-

## FREEWAY FRENZY

San Diego runs on wheels. You must have a car, unless you're a first-time visitor content with packaged tours. Convertibles are nice; so are Range Rovers and Jeeps. Maps are an absolute necessity. San Diegans are ruthless drivers. They act as if mellowness is best left at the beach. Forget slowing down for merging traffic; locals love to speed up and challenge anyone with utter temerity. Study your entrances and exits before hitting the freeways, especially during rush hour. In fact, stay off major byways when workers and students are hell-bent on following their daily schedules. If you're a tourist, take the surface streets. San Diegans also have a blind spot when it comes to using turn signals to change lanes; cutting off traffic is part of the game. Keep your defenses finely tuned, but don't express outrage. The tangle of freeways is a confounding source of frustration even for locals—everyone has a story of driving in circles on three or four interchanges before reaching their destination. Directions sound like this: "Take the 8 to the 5 to the 163 to the 15 and go north." Take our advice and get detailed directions before hitting the road. If you do get lost, ask for help immediately unless you want an extended high-speed tour of San Diego's baffling freeways.

—Maribeth Mellin

nations. From its southern end near the Mexican border to its connection with Interstate 5 in Sorrento Valley, this freeway gets more congested every year. The merge of Interstates 5 and 805 is particularly horrid; stay away during rush hour. Interstate 15 is another north-to-south route, farther inland than I-5, running up to Escondido and the Wild Animal Park and on to Temecula. Highway 163 is a small but important stretch of road, with an especially pretty section called the Cabrillo Freeway, which runs through Balboa Park. Highway 52, going east and west with connections to 5, 805, 163, and 15, has relieved some of the congestion on Interstate 8.

During the peak hours of 7am to 9am and 4pm to 6pm, do your best to avoid the freeways altogether, especially Interstate 8 heading east through Mission Valley, Interstate 805 from the Interstate 8 connector going north, and I-15 from Mira Mesa to Escondido.

# When to Visit

There is no bad season to visit San Diego. The weather is pleasant and balmy most of the year, and interesting events are held year-round. Keep in mind when you look at the temperature chart below that these averages were derived from the weather at the coast; some parts of northern and eastern San Diego County positively sizzle during the summer. Visitors to the Wild Animal Park in Escondido will find the heat fairly blistering during August and September. Call the local weather service's recorded forecast (619/289-1212) before venturing out, and dress appropriately.

## WEATHER

Tired of sunshine? Head to the coast, where sea breezes and low-lying clouds can cast a gray chill until noon. Tired of gloom? Head 5 miles east toward blue skies. Though San Diego's climate is temperate, there's enough variety to please everyone. While surfers in wet suits are riding the waves in January, kids are sledding down snow-covered hills just 50 miles east in the Laguna Mountains. As beach dwellers shiver in the chill winter dampness, desert rats run about in shades and shorts. The ocean is rarely as warm as the air, and only surfers in wet suits and pale out-of-towners venture into the water in winter. The best months for swimming are August and September, when the water nears 70 degrees. Rain, a great cause of celebration for farmers and gardeners, seems to baffle drivers, whose windshield wipers have cracked and dried in the sunshine. Commonsense warnings to drive slowly are utterly ignored; thus, disabled vehicles from all sorts of fender benders litter the streets. High winds can also wreak havoc with traffic in the mountains and deserts.

### Average temperature and precipitation by month

| Month | Daily Maximum Temp. (DEGREES F) | Daily Minimum Temp. (DEGREES F) | Monthly Precipitation (INCHES) |
|---|---|---|---|
| JANUARY | 66 | 49 | 1.80 |
| FEBRUARY | 67 | 51 | 1.53 |
| MARCH | 66 | 53 | 1.77 |
| APRIL | 68 | 56 | .79 |
| MAY | 69 | 59 | .19 |
| JUNE | 72 | 62 | .07 |
| JULY | 76 | 66 | .02 |
| AUGUST | 78 | 67 | .10 |
| SEPTEMBER | 77 | 66 | .24 |
| OCTOBER | 75 | 61 | .37 |
| NOVEMBER | 70 | 51 | 1.45 |
| DECEMBER | 66 | 49 | 1.57 |

*Source: National Weather Service*

## TIME

San Diego is on Pacific Standard Time (PST)—three hours behind New York, two hours behind Chicago, one hour behind Denver, one hour ahead of Alaska, and two hours ahead of Hawaii (three hours during Daylight Saving Time). Daylight Saving Time is observed, beginning in early April and ending in late October.

## WHAT TO BRING

Sunscreen and sunglasses are essential accoutrements year-round in sunny San Diego, as are comfortable walking/running shoes and flip-flops. Everything else is up for grabs in this anything-goes clime. Shorts are worn everywhere—but please don't wear them with calf-high socks. Stockings are also verboten, unless you must work in some staid office. Think a summer afternoon in your backyard (minus mosquitoes) and you'll have your wardrobe nailed. A light jacket or sweater comes in handy even in summer, when night winds can be chilly (especially when wafting across sunburned skin). Only a few restaurants have dress codes beyond "no shirt, no shoes, no service"; for men, sport jackets with jeans or khakis serve most special occasions nicely. Women will do well with sundresses of any length (some think shorter is better), paired with sexy sandals. Kids need clothes that withstand rough play (bring plenty of premoistened towelettes and Band-Aids).

## GENERAL COSTS

San Diego's economy rarely falters. It seems the natural climate encourages good luck for businesses. San Diego's "real" Gross Regional Product (GRP) was $110.2 billion in 2000. Forecasters predict continued growth as the region continues to adapt to changing economic forces. San Diego's prosperity originated with the presence of the military and an abundance of defense industries. Base closures haven't harmed the economy; San Diego is still home to United States Navy and Marine bases stationing more than 100,000 military personnel, and manufacturing has diversified to include everything from golf clubs to supercomputers. Carlsbad, in north San Diego County, is home to three big-name golf equipment manufacturers: Callaway, Taylor Made, and Cobra. Gateway Computers secured San Diego's place in high technology by moving its headquarters here in 1999. An educated workforce (almost 33 percent of San Diego's residents over 25 have graduated from college) and an abundance of research centers, including the Salk Institute, fuel the scientific community. Health-care manufacturers abound, and more than 200 local companies specialize in biotechnology. San Diego County has become one of the largest telecommunications centers in the world, dominated by Qualcomm (the stadium now bears the company's name), and four Fortune 500 companies—Qualcomm, SAIC, Sempra Energy, and Gateway—help lead the way for the region.

Though manufacturing and high-tech industries attract the most attention, tourism is San Diego's largest employer and greatest economic indicator. And thanks to the service industries, the unemployment rate hovers around 3.4 percent, far lower than California's 5.8 percent. The San Diego Convention and Visitors Bureau reported that in 2000, 15.2 million overnight visitors stayed in the county, breaking all previous records. Many of those visitors return to stay, forming the base of an ongoing real estate boom. New communities multiply like rabbits in the few undeveloped regions of the county, and housing prices continue to rise. In the first quarter of 2001, the median price of all homes sold in San Diego County was a staggering $265,000. As a result, housing is affordable to only 24 percent of San Diego's householders (with a median household income of $56,900), compared to a national rate of 63.4 percent. Affordable housing is one of the largest drawbacks for companies looking to relocate in San Diego. But that doesn't seem to discourage newcomers from moving to the region: the 2000 U.S. Census put the population of San Diego County at 2,813,933.

## Average costs for lodging and food

Double room:

| | |
|---|---|
| **INEXPENSIVE** | **$60–$90** |
| **MODERATE** | **$90–$175** |
| **EXPENSIVE** | **$175–$300** |
| **VERY EXPENSIVE** | **$300 AND UP** |

Lunch for one:

| | |
|---|---|
| **INEXPENSIVE** | **$8–$12** |
| **MODERATE** | **$12–$19** |
| **EXPENSIVE** | **$19 AND UP** |

Beverages in a restaurant:

| | |
|---|---|
| **GLASS OF WINE** | **$5–$20** |
| **PINT OF BEER** | **$4–$8** |
| **COCA-COLA** | **$2** |
| **DOUBLE TALL ICED MOCHA** | **$3** |

Other common items:

| | |
|---|---|
| **MOVIE TICKET** | **$8.75** |
| **ROLL OF FILM** | **$5.50** |
| **TAXI PER MILE** | **$2** |
| **RAY-BANS** | **$50–$200** |
| **SAN DIEGO SOUVENIR T-SHIRT** | **$10–$15** |

# Tips for Special Travelers

## FAMILIES WITH CHILDREN

In an emergency, dial 911, day or night. If you fear that your child has swallowed a toxic substance, call the San Diego division of the California Poison Control System, located at UCSD Medical Center (800/876-4766). To find appropriate health-care services for your child, call Children's Healthcare Referral Service (800/788-9029). Several local publications offer information on events for families, as well as articles geared to parents. *San Diego Parent Magazine* (www.parenthood. com) is distributed free at many stores, libraries, schools, and attractions around town. The *San Diego Weekly Reader* (www.sdreader.com) is another good source for info on family activities.

Families are as important as conventioneers to local hoteliers, even downtown. Though the hotels closest to the Convention Center are packed with business travelers, they still have kids' pools and game rooms. Hotels in Mission Bay and the beaches seem completely geared to families; many have in-room refrigerators and joysticks for video games (for an additional fee that can add up quickly) along with water- and land-toy rentals. Some of the larger chains have supervised children's programs, freeing parents for adult pleasures. Most restaurants have children's menus.

Watch for this icon throughout the book; it indicates places and activities that are great for families.

## IN THE BEGINNING

**JUAN RODRÍGUEZ CABRILLO,** a Portuguese explorer in the employ of Spain, discovered San Diego Bay in 1542. Cabrillo sailed on north, leaving the indigenous **LA JOLLA AND KUMEYAAY INDIANS** alone in their warm, food-rich home. The La Jolla peoples stuck close to the coast in small settlements. Discarded shells and fish bones, some still visible today as white layers in the crumbling cliff edges of Point Loma, Pacific Beach, La Jolla, and Del Mar, attest to these early residents' bountiful harvests from the sea and coastal marshes. The Kumeyaay, who began forcing the La Jollans out as the dominant populace around 1000 B.C., arrived from the Colorado River region to hunt deer, harvest acorns, and spend summers at cooler elevations in the mountain ranges 50 miles from the coast. Their grinding rocks can still be found beside most shady San Diego County streams wherever oak trees spread their limbs in neighboring groves.

Everything changed when the Spaniards settled in with great determination after 1769, giving San Diego its own equivalent of Plymouth Rock, now lying beneath earthen mounds on Presidio Hill above Mission Valley. The ruins of the first European garrison and settlement in California sit atop grassy hills beside the Junipero Serra Museum (2727 Presidio Dr, Old Town; 619/297-3258). Father Junipero Serra established the first California mission, **BASILICA SAN DIEGO DE ALCALÁ,** on the hill in 1769. The soldiers and missionaries brought new agricultural methods and beliefs to the region, as well as deadly European diseases that killed many of the Indians. The padres moved the mission away from the coast in 1774 to place it closer to the freshwater rivers in Mission Valley, where the **MISSION BASILICA SAN DIEGO DE ALCALÁ** (10818 San Diego Mission Rd, Mission Valley; 619/281-8449) now stands.

## SENIORS

Aging and Independent Services, a County of San Diego department (858/505-6399 or 800/510-2020), offers information for seniors on health and welfare resources, as well as transportation and leisure opportunities. San Diego public transportation is offered to senior citizens 60 years and older at a reduced rate ($1) with a transit ID card, available for $2.50 at the Transit Store (102 Broadway, downtown; 619/234-1060; map:N7).

## PEOPLE WITH DISABILITIES

Accessible San Diego (858/279-0704) is a nonprofit information center for people with disabilities traveling or living in San Diego. This group makes available a wealth of information, from restaurants that provide menus in Braille to which tour operators can accommodate a wheelchair. It also provides a calendar of events. Check out their web site at www.accessandiego.com. For information on public transportation, call the Metro Info line at 619/233-3004 or 800/COMMUTE (TTY-TDD 619/234-5005).

The original, presidio-protected settlement gradually expanded down the hill into what today is called **OLD TOWN**. San Diego was still considered a part of Mexico, and when Mexico won its independence from Spain in 1821, the Spanish influence began to dwindle. The Mexican flag rose over the Presidio, and a new system of enormous, 10,000-acre-plus ranchos took hold to encourage colonization. The ranch owners were called the Silver Dons (for their silver-decorated saddles), and a Mexican-European Californio culture took hold. The Dons lived lavishly and raised large, extended families in grand sprawling houses made of sun-hardened adobe walls roofed with tile. The Californios' forte was cattle ranching, and the sweet grasses of San Diego's valleys and nearby mountains became some of the most productive lands for raising beef cattle in the world. A hide trade flourished, with Yankee trading ships arriving regularly from around Cape Horn, a journey immortalized in Richard Henry Dana's sensational account of an 1834 voyage, *Two Years Before the Mast*.

During the Mexican-American War in 1846, Californio forces—mounted vaqueros armed with lances—easily trapped the 300-strong "American Army of the West," led by General Stephen Kearny, at a site in the San Pasqual Valley. Kearny's forces had left Fort Leavenworth, Kansas, only six months before on foot and horseback and were now exhausted. With many unable to fire their guns because of damp gunpowder, 18 of the weary Yankees died on the ends of long lances. But victory was brief for the Californios. In San Diego, American warships held the harbor. A new Yankee fort was erected above Old Town. Other settlements up north were also besieged, and California fell from Mexican hands in 1847.                                                          *—Peter Jensen*

## WOMEN
San Diego is safer than most cities its size, though of course women should use the same precautions they would anywhere. For health and reproductive services call Planned Parenthood at 619/683-7526. The Rape Crisis Hotline is at 858/272-1767.

## PET OWNERS
Dogs are pampered nearly as much as kids in this outdoor-oriented community. Dog owners have become far more responsible about cleaning up after their pets; plastic bags and pooper-scoopers are essential items to carry when walking your pet along neighborhood sidewalks. Here are San Diego's off-leash areas:
**DOG BEACH** at Ocean Beach, next to the jetty.
**FIESTA ISLAND** at Mission Bay.
The westernmost section of the **CITY BEACH** in Coronado.
**DEL MAR** (Camino del Mar at 29th St), but only September through June.
**GRAPE STREET PARK,** at Balboa Park, at Grape Street and Granada Avenue.

## GAYS AND LESBIANS

San Diego's gay community has evolved into a visible part of the civic scene; San Diegans even voted a lesbian member to the State Assembly in 2000. The gay scene is centered around Hillcrest, with a plethora of gay-focused bars, clubs, bookshops, and cafes. The *Gay and Lesbian Times,* a weekly newspaper, is distributed on Fridays and available free at most coffee shops and bookstores. The Greater San Diego Business Association (3737 5th Ave, Ste 207, downtown; 619/296-4543; www. gsdba.org; map:N3) provides a business directory and a calendar of events that include gay-oriented establishments and activities. The Lesbian and Gay Men's Community Center (3909 Centre St, North Park; 619/692-2077; map:P2) sponsors nightly activities as well as discussion and support groups. One of the largest selections of gay and lesbian books and magazines can be found at Obelisk Books (1029 University Ave, Hillcrest; 619/297-4171; map:O2).

## FOREIGN VISITORS

Since few international flights land in San Diego—only a few from Mexico and one daily flight from London—most foreign visitors arrive in Southern California via Los Angeles. For foreign currency exchange, try Travelex America at the airport (Terminal 1, lower level; 619/295-1501) or the Thomas Cook Foreign Exchange office downtown in Horton Plaza (800/287-7362; map:N7). The International Visitors Center (11 Horton Plaza at 1st Ave and F St, downtown; 619/236-1212; map:N7) is well staffed with bilingual clerks and can contact translators for most languages. Most foreign consulates are located in Los Angeles; the only full consulate in San Diego is the Consulate General de Mexico (1549 India St, downtown; 619/231-8414; map:M7).

## WEB INFORMATION

San Diego is well connected and represented on the Internet, with web sites for many local businesses and attractions. The City of San Diego's site is **WWW.SANNET.GOV.** The San Diego Convention and Visitors Bureau maintains a site at **WWW.SAN DIEGO.ORG.** Other helpful sites:

| | |
|---|---|
| **WWW.SIGNONSANDIEGO.COM** | (Union-Tribune Publishing) |
| **WWW.SDREADER.COM** | (*The Reader*) |
| **WWW.SANDIEGO-ONLINE.COM** | (*San Diego* magazine) |
| **WWW.UCSD.EDU/** | (University of California at San Diego) |
| **WWW.SDSU.EDU/** | (San Diego State University) |

# LAY OF THE CITY

# LAY OF THE CITY

## Orientation

Desert, mountains, canyons, and mesas shape San Diego's landscape and character. Don't be fooled by tropical palms and birds-of-paradise; this place is dry, dry, dry, and a major drain on the distant Colorado River and Northern California. Fresh water is sometimes so precious that people are cautioned against irrigating gardens or flushing toilets, and rainstorms bring transplanted residents outdoors to celebrate moist air and damp earth. Most times, the wind is scented with salt and suntan oil. Transplants bemoan the lack of seasons in this idyllic and idiosyncratic climate. It takes years to catch on to the subtle changes. Summer begins with the dreaded June Gloom, gray low-lying clouds that block out the sun till noon. The ocean doesn't get tolerably warm until August—at least for those who won't dabble a toe in the water until it hits 68 degrees. In fact, beach devotees are fond of September, when the water reaches its warmest and the summer hordes have left the sand to its natural beauty. Fall is heralded by mystical Santa Ana winds, so hot and dry and swift they topple power lines and crack sensitive lips.

Locals are always surprised when they have to ignite gas pilots on their wall heaters in November and are horrified when the thermometer dips into the 50s around January. We actually do have a winter, marked by days of chilly rain, fog, and floods. February brings snow to the **LAGUNA MOUNTAINS** 50 miles east of downtown, while wildflowers and cacti burst into bloom in the desert in March. Then comes spring, full of blue skies and the fragrance of orange blossoms and night-blooming jasmine. Yes, we do have seasons, though our median temperature is a steady 72 degrees.

San Diegans live in clusters of microclimates (a favorite term among bored weather announcers). **SAN DIEGO BAY** casts a coastal coolness over downtown, where the **EMBARCADERO** (Harbor Dr and Grape St, downtown; map:M6) serves as host to massive cruise ships, navy freighters, and all manner of watercraft. The waterfront sidewalk runs south from the tall-sailed *Star of India* to the Cruise Ship Pier and Seaport Village, a treasure trove for tourists and entrepreneurs. Next, after a series of high-rise hotels, is the San Diego Convention Center, topped with white sails. Built with considerable expense and heated debate, the Convention Center shifted the focus of downtown to the waterfront. Its success and recent expansion have changed downtown forever.

The financial, legal, and civic center of downtown lies along Broadway, where a series of 1980s office towers and hotels lead to **HORTON PLAZA,** a phantasmagoric (some say garish) shopping mall. East of the plaza, the historic **GASLAMP QUARTER** runs along Fourth and Fifth Avenues back toward the waterfront. Much of San Diego's history lies in this once-derelict neighborhood, where 19th-century Victorian mansions and erstwhile clapboard brothels now house offices, cafes, and hotels.

## HOW TO PASS FOR A LOCAL

A San Diego native is a rare gem indeed; it seems everyone has moved here from somewhere else. The U.S. Navy and Marines have done their part to swell the population, as have émigrés from Portugal, France, Vietnam, Laos, Cambodia, Mexico, Brazil, and Guatemala. On the surface, the city looks pure WASP. But its food, music, and culture are so much of a melting pot, locals hardly notice outside influence. It's easy to blend in if you use the right mix of style and flexibility.

**THE LOOK:** Casual and trendy, with lots of bare skin. No cutoff jeans or button-down shirts (collared shirts with muted fish themes are fine). Thongs (a.k.a. flip-flops) or running shoes. No socks. Polarized sunglasses in every imaginable shape (keep the cartoon characters on the kids). Baseball caps and hats with enormous straw brims.

**THE LINGO:** Many San Diegans speak Spanglish, a mix of Spanish and English that comes naturally after you've been here a few years. *Gracias* (thank you), *hasta luego* (see you later), *adiós* (good-bye), and *cerveza* (beer) are all part of the local tongue. Surf slang sprinkles beach and all other talk. Waves are gnarly and form tubes at their crest; on a nice day everybody "shines on" all practical tasks.

**THE ATTITUDE:** Yes, we're a laid-back, fun-loving lot, but we're also quite driven in a roundabout way. Scholars, scientists, researchers, writers, and actors all behave as if they're in a mini L.A., striving for great achievements while jogging at Mission Bay. Conservatives reign on talk radio; salutes are common in many parts of town. The flag is treated with respect. And despite San Diego's mellow image, many locals are ruthless drivers. Study your maps.

**THE SNACKS:** Ketchup ranks second to salsa on most kitchen tables, and guacamole and corn chips are far more common than potato chips and dip. Sushi and fish tacos are served at the ballpark. Everyone carries a water bottle nearly everywhere.

**THE WHEELS:** Skateboards are ubiquitous on beach city streets; unfortunately, they also rumble along sidewalks and occasionally lash out at pedestrians. Beach cruiser bikes with fat tires have surfboard clamps on their frames; bike helmets are the law. The resurgence of convertibles makes sun lovers crave new cars, though you'll see plenty of old VW buses with custom paint jobs. "Suburban Assault Vehicles" (or SUVs to those of you who drive them) are as common as Mercedes coupes. Blessed are those who live in pedestrian-friendly neighborhoods.

*—Maribeth Mellin*

The **SAN DIEGO–CORONADO BRIDGE** spans the bay, connecting the south side of downtown to the picture-perfect city of Coronado. Steep hills climb east to Mission Hills and Hillcrest, both chic and trendy neighborhoods. Train and trolley tracks, freeways, and side streets head north to Old Town, where Spanish soldiers and missionaries were once garrisoned in the late 1700s on Presidio Hill overlooking the San Diego River and Mission Valley.

Beach towns line the coast north of downtown, starting with the promontory at **POINT LOMA** through **OCEAN BEACH, MISSION BEACH,** and **PACIFIC BEACH:** three funky communities with individual quirks. **LA JOLLA** goes the opposite direction attitudinally, with the class and cultured air of a Mediterranean coastal city. **DEL MAR** marks the beginning of the North Coast, a lineup of small towns and burgeoning cities that runs into Camp Pendleton Marine Base, a natural greenbelt between San Diego and Orange Counties.

Though it seems coastal San Diego could easily tip into the ocean under the weight of its popularity (a few natural earthquake-inclined faults in the area make this possibility not so far-fetched), plenty of San Diegans are lured inland by clean, dry air, a bit of a break on real estate, and a topography laced with boulder-strewn mountains and fishing lakes. All locals take pride in the proximity of the piney Cuyamaca and Laguna Mountains and seemingly endless desert; many of them head east to witness meteor showers and snow.

San Diego's southern border is its most controversial. An invisible line stretches east from the ocean to the desert, separating what once was called Alta (higher) California from Baja (lower) California in Mexico. Said to be the busiest border crossing in the world, the line between San Diego and **TIJUANA** is blurred in many ways. Commuters pass back and forth, families visit relatives, shoppers search for bargains on both sides of the border, and San Diegans think nothing of driving down Baja to Tijuana, Rosarito, and Ensenada on day and overnight escapes.

# Visitor Information

San Diego can be downright confusing if you wander off the beaten track—which you undoubtedly will, since exploring is what a visit to this city is all about. If you're staying downtown, visit the **SAN DIEGO CONVENTION AND VISITORS BUREAU** (401 B St, Ste 1400, downtown; 619/232-3101; www.sandiego.org; map:N7) for tickets to local attractions, reservations, and referral services. Call ahead for bilingual assistance. It's open Monday through Saturday from 8:30am to 5pm. More information can be garnered at the **INTERNATIONAL INFORMATION CENTER** (11 Horton Plaza at 1st and F Sts, downtown; 619/236-1212; map:N7) open Monday through Saturday 8:30am to 5pm (and Sunday 11am to 5pm during the summer). The center has an impressive array of multilingual personnel, though how multi depends on who's on duty that day. If you're wandering the beach areas, stop by the **SAN DIEGO VISITOR INFORMATION CENTER** (2688 East Mission Bay Dr, Mission Bay; 619/276-8200; map:KK6); open 9am to dusk daily. The center sits on a slight hill by the Interstate 5 Mission Bay exit; plenty of parking is usually available (even for RVs), and the playground and picnic tables are perfect spots for reviewing your brochures.

# Getting Around

## BY BUS

San Diego has an adequate bus system running through the city and county. Granted, it can take hours to get where you're going, but at least you're not dodging freeway traffic. The **SAN DIEGO TRANSIT COMPANY** (619/233-3004 or www.sd commute.com for bus route information) operates the **TRANSIT STORE** (102 Broadway, downtown; 619/234-1060; map:N7), open 8:30am to 5pm Monday through Friday and 10am to 4pm Saturday and Sunday. Here you'll find a wealth of information on any and all public transportation from the border through North and East Counties. Also available are discounted frequent-rider coupons, bus passes, and route maps. Bus fare varies between $1.50 and $3.50, depending on which route you take. The rate for seniors and disabled is $1; children 5 years and younger ride free. A one-day pass for all buses and trolleys is $5; two-day is $8; three-day is $10; four-day is $12. All San Diego buses are wheelchair accessible and most can accommodate bicycles (call the information number to confirm). Bus stops are marked with a blue-and-white sign designating which routes they serve. For bus tours, see Guided Tours in the Exploring chapter.

## BY TROLLEY

The bright red electric **SAN DIEGO TROLLEY** (619/233-3004 or 619/595-4949; fares and schedule information also available at the Transit Store, see By Bus, above) has become a model for transit systems worldwide. The first route ran from downtown San Diego to the border with Mexico. Additional routes now run to various points in downtown, Old Town, Mission Valley, Qualcomm Stadium, and East County; fares range from $1.25 to $2.50 and bicycles are allowed. Unlimited trolley passes for one month cost between $54 and $82, depending on the route. Ticket machines for trolley tickets are available at all stops. On board, trolley cops check for tickets; a passenger sans ticket will pay a hefty fine.

## BY CAR

California and cars are synonymous; without wheels you're not really taking in the whole experience. You needn't have a car for your whole stay, but will likely wish you had one for at least a couple of days. Most of the major **RENTAL CAR COMPANIES** have offices at the airports or courtesy shuttle buses that will take you to their locations. Alamo (800/327-9633), Avis (800/230-4898), Budget (800/527-0700), Hertz (800/654-3131), and National (800/227-7368) all have offices throughout the city. **AAA SOUTHERN CALIFORNIA** (815 Date St, downtown; 619/233-1000, 800/400-4222 for roadside assistance, 800/222-5000 for travel services; map:O6) has excellent **ROAD MAPS** available to members and can help you plan your routes to outlying areas. Locals rely on Thomas Brothers Maps (800/899-6277; www.thomas.com) to find beach streets and the new communities that sprout up in the county like crabgrass.

    **PARKING** is relatively easy downtown except during special events. Public lots charge $5 to $10 a day, depending on location; those closest to Horton Plaza, Seaport Village, the Gaslamp Quarter, and the Embarcadero tend to be expensive (though some honor validation). Side streets are cheaper—try Ash and B Streets and J through L Streets. Parking meters cost 25 cents per 15 minutes, with a two-hour limit. You must move your car after two hours or risk getting a ticket.

Beach parking is another story. There are free parking lots along W Mission Bay Drive and at Belmont Park, but lucky is the fellow who grabs a spot after 10am on a sunny summer Sunday. All the main beaches have free lots—cruising around for a space will afford you the time to check out the surfers and families. Neighborhood side streets are a good bet, as long as you arrive early. If you're unlucky enough to return and find no car, call the **SAN DIEGO POLICE DEPARTMENT** (619/531-2000) to see if it has been impounded or towed. If not, then report it as stolen. Car theft, alas, is relatively common in San Diego, as are car break-ins. Take your valuables with you.

## BY TAXI

Here's the deal: cab drivers have to cover significant distance to get you from downtown to the beach. The fare from the airport to downtown is $10 to $12; from downtown to Ocean Beach, $15 to $20; and $30 to $40 from downtown to La Jolla. Cabs are metered; rates are usually around $2 per mile. Local companies include Yellow Cab (619/234-6161), San Diego Cab (619/226-8294), and Orange Cab (619/291-3333).

## BY BICYCLE

Bikes are the perfect touring vehicle within parts of San Diego, including Coronado, Mission Bay, Shelter and Harbor Islands, and the beaches. Bike rentals are available at all these locations. For suggestions on scenic bike circuits, see the Recreation chapter. Biking downtown is not enjoyable on weekdays (though bike commuters have their routes down), but can be great fun on a Sunday morning. A map of bike routes in San Diego County, as well as information on bike lockers, is available from **RIDELINK** (619/237-7665). **BIKE TOURS OF SAN DIEGO** (509 5th Ave, downtown; 619/238-2444; www.bike-tours.com; map:N8) delivers rental bikes; daily rates are $20; open 8am to 7pm daily. Bike racks are available at tourist attractions, the Convention Center, and in beach parking lots. Use a good lock. To rent a bike try **MISSION BEACH CLUB** (704 Ventura Pl; 858/488-5050; map:LL7) near the boardwalk in Mission Beach, **BIKES AND BEYOND** (1201 First St; 619/435-7180; map:M9) at the Ferry Landing in Coronado, or **PLAY IT AGAIN SPORTS** (1401 Garnet Ave; 858/490-0222; map:KK7) in Pacific Beach. For descriptions and pointers on particularly pleasant trails, see the Recreation chapter.

## BY FERRY

Until the San Diego–Coronado Bridge opened in 1969, ferries were the only transport between the island (actually it's an isthmus) and downtown. Ferry service was suspended for nearly two decades until the bridge debt was paid off. Service was reinstated in the late 1980s, much to the delight of islanders and sightseers. The **SAN DIEGO–CORONADO BAY FERRY** (San Diego Harbor Excursions; 619/234-4111) departs from the Broadway Pier downtown daily on the hour from 9am to 9pm Sunday through Thursday, and 9am to 10pm on Friday and Saturday. The ferry departs Ferry Landing on First Street in Coronado on the half hour from 9:30am to

9:30pm Sunday through Thursday, and 9:30am to 10:30pm Friday and Saturday. The fare is $2 each way; bicycles are an additional 50 cents. Bike rentals are available at the Coronado Ferry Landing, as are public buses.

# Essentials

## PUBLIC REST ROOMS
Public rest rooms are available downtown at Horton Plaza, Seaport Village, and the Embarcadero. Government buildings and libraries are a good choice as well. In many park and beach facilities, the doors have been removed from the stalls and the toilets are chilly metal contraptions. The rest rooms are usually clean, except for the sand, grass, and dirt tracked on the floors; some, such as those at La Jolla Cove, have showers and dressing areas.

## MAJOR BANKS
ATMs are as abundant as parking meters throughout San Diego, though many neighborhood banks still have friendly tellers who know their customers. Currency exchange is not available at all branches; a Thomas Cook office (800/287-7362, in San Diego call 619/235-0901) downtown in Horton Plaza is open Monday through Saturday from 10am to 6pm, Sunday from 11am to 4pm. For information on bank services and branches, call the downtown offices of Bank of America (450 B St; 619/515-7574; map:N7), Union Bank (1201 5th Ave; 619/230-4666; map:N7), Washington Mutual (101 W Broadway; 619/702-9208; map:N7), or Wells Fargo (401 B St; 619/699-3070; map:N7).

## POLICE AND SAFETY
In serious, life-threatening emergencies, call 911. In nonemergency situations call the San Diego Police Department at 619/531-2000. San Diego is far safer than other cities of its size; with 1.25 million people (the county has nearly 2.9 million residents), it's the seventh largest in the nation. But pickpockets, auto thieves, and threatening elements do exist, particularly downtown and in seedier parts of beach towns. Keep hold of your possessions when wandering about, and keep an eye on them at the beach. Don't put everything in your trunk at your parking space—that's way too enticing for petty thieves.

## HOSPITAL AND MEDICAL/DENTAL SERVICES
World-class science and research centers have inspired renowned surgeons and physicians to settle in San Diego; as a result, San Diegans have an abundance of excellent medical facilities from which to choose. UCSD Medical Center (200 W Arbor Dr, Hillcrest; 619/543-6222 or 800/926-8273; map:N1), a Level I Trauma Center, is the teaching and research hospital for the University of California at San Diego. Clinics in every imaginable specialty are available. Most area hospitals are part of a conglomerate, with branch hospitals and clinics around the county. The major chains are Sharp (Sharp Memorial Hospital, 7901 Frost St, Kearny Mesa; 858/541-3400; map:KK5) and Scripps (Scripps Memorial Hospital, 9888 Genesee Ave, La Jolla; 858-457-4123; map:II6). In nonemergency situations, call ahead to find out if your insurance is accepted. Kaiser (4647 Zion Ave, Mission Gorge;

## PLACES OF WORSHIP

Though it often seems that San Diego's main place of worship is the beach, those in search of more conventional religious environs can find everything under the sun. Padre Junipero Serra's first mission, **MISSION BASILICA SAN DIEGO DE ALCALÁ** (10818 San Diego Mission Rd, Mission Valley; 619/283-7319; map:KK2), established in 1769, continues to hold mass each day in the simple wooden chapel. **MARY STAR OF THE SEA** (7727 Girard Ave, La Jolla; 858/454-2631; map:JJ6) offers more elegant surroundings and is convenient to après-prayer shopping. Be sure to note the beautiful mural over the altar, painted in 1956 by Polish-born artist Jan Henryk de Rosen. The Jewish community gathers at the conservative **CONGREGATION BETH EL** (8660 Gilman Dr, La Jolla; 858/587-1967; map:II5) and the reform temple **CONGREGA-TION BETH ISRAEL** (9001 Towne Centre Dr, University City; 858/657-0200; map:II5). The **CATHEDRAL CHURCH OF SAINT PAUL** (2728 6th Ave, downtown; 619/298-7261; map:O6) is an exquisite edifice for Episcopalians, with an exceptionally fine chorus. Methodists need look no further than the **UNITED METHODIST CHURCH** (6063 La Jolla Blvd, La Jolla; 858/454-7108; map:KK6), a Mission-style conglomeration of buildings that also includes a former trolley depot, Mexican restaurant, and bar. The **1890 GRAHAM MEMORIAL PRESBYTERIAN CHURCH** (959 C Ave, Coronado; 619/435-6860; map:NN4) was designed by architect James Reid, of Hotel del Coronado fame. The 10-foot gold-leaf statue of the angel Moroni and 10 alabaster spires rising from the blindingly white temple of the **CHURCH OF JESUS CHRIST OF LATTER-DAY SAINTS** (9527 La Jolla Farms Rd, La Jolla; 858/452-7256; map:II7) are enough to hypnotize anyone off the freeway and into the Mormon religion. The **SELF-REALIZATION FELLOWSHIP** (939 2nd St, Encinitas; 760/436-7220; map:EE8), combining Eastern and Western teachings with enough meditation and Indian inferences to please any New Ager, shelters an ashram, hermitage, koi ponds, and ethereal gardens within a white-walled compound with golden lotus-flower spires.

—*Marael Johnson*

619/528-5000; map:KK3) serves members from its nationwide program. Scripps Health (800/727-4777) can help you find a specialist in your area. For a dental emergency, call 800/917-6453 to be referred to a local dentist.

## POST OFFICE
San Diego's main U.S. Post Office (11251 Rancho Carmel Dr, Miramar; general information 800/275-8777 for all branches; map:GG3) is inconveniently located far from downtown. The neighborhood offices are much more accessible; some are open Saturdays. Send your postcards from any box on the street or the downtown branch (815 E St; map:O7), the large Midway office near Point Loma (2535 Midway Dr; map:H2), or Pacific Beach (4640 Cass St; map:KK7).

## GROCERY STORES
The major chains in San Diego are Vons, Ralph's, and Albertson's, with branches all over the county. Downtown, the only large-scale supermarket is Ralph's (101 G St; 619/595-1581; map:N8) near Horton Plaza, open 24 hours.

## PHARMACIES
Several of the major chains in the area have toll-free numbers to help you locate the branch nearest you or one that's open 24 hours. Try Rite Aid (800/748-3243), Sav-On (888/746-7252), or Longs (800/865-6647). Longs has a branch downtown in Horton Plaza (619/231-9135). Park Boulevard Pharmacy (3904 Park Blvd, Hillcrest; 619/295-3109; map:P2) has delivery service for most of the central San Diego area.

## DRY CLEANERS AND LAUNDROMATS
Many of the local hotels either offer room-service dry cleaning at a reasonable premium or will recommend a cleaner. Clean Touch (945 Market St, downtown; 619/234-4200; map:O8) has pickup and delivery within the downtown and neighboring areas and a one-day turnaround; they can also help with alterations or repairs. In the Mission Valley area, try Royal Touch Cleaners (4242 Camino del Rio N; 619/624-0989; map:LL3) for pickup service or alterations. Most laundromats are located within strip malls so you can run other errands while your laundry finishes. Take lots of quarters. Some have full-time attendants and offer a fluff-and-fold service. At the One Stop Laundry in Pacific Beach (4617 Cass St; 858/483-1344; map:KK7), you can have them do your laundry while you head across the street to the Cass Street Bar & Grill for a bite and a beer.

## LEGAL SERVICES
The San Diego County Bar Association (800/464-1529) and the Lawyer Referral & Information Service (619/231-8585) offer an attorney referral service with a free initial consultation of up to 30 minutes.

## BUSINESS, COPY, AND MESSENGER SERVICES
Kinko's, that wonder of a 24-hour instant office, has 15 branches in neighborhoods and downtown. Three convenient locations are downtown (532 C St; 619/645-3300; map:N7), Pacific Beach (1834 Garnet Ave; 858/483-1852; map:KK7), and Mission Valley (7510 Hazard Center Dr; 619/294-3877; map:LL4). Storefronts offering mailing services are nearly as common as gas stations. Mail Boxes Etc. (501 W Broadway, downtown; 619/232-0332 or 800/789-4623; map:O7) has an automated locator to help find your nearest location. Postal Annex has roughly 25 outlets in the greater San Diego area. Convenient locations include Pacific Beach (1666 Garnet Ave; 858/483-6001; map:KK7) and Mission Valley (7710 Hazard Center Dr; 619/295-8810; map:LL4). There are several messenger services available, including CMX (619/758-0555), Hesco (858/571-7395), and Messenger Express (858/550-1400).

## PHOTOGRAPHY EQUIPMENT AND SERVICES
The best all-around shop for photographic supplies and high-level service is Nelson Photo Supplies (1909 India St, downtown; 619/234-6621; map:L4). They've been open since 1950, yet keep current on the latest equipment and also sell used equipment on consignment. The pros take their slide film to Chrome Photo Labs & Digital (2345 Kettner Blvd, downtown; 619/233-3456; map:M5). Gaslamp Photo (422

Market St, downtown; 619/696-8733; map:N8) is a favorite for one-hour film processing of color and black-and-white prints; camera repairs are available at Professional Photographic Repair (7910 Raytheon Rd, Kearny Mesa; 858/277-3700; map:JJ5). And although it's out of the way, the competent staff of Kurt's Camera Repair (7811 Mission Gorge Rd, Ste P, San Diego; 619/286-1810; map:KK3) can usually find the fix when your camera refuses to operate—and they're patient with novices, a real bonus.

## COMPUTER REPAIRS AND RENTAL
Radio Shack advertises that it can fix anything no matter where you bought it. To find the location nearest you, call 1-800/THE-SHACK. Same-day, on-site service is offered at many locations; try the one in Pacific Beach (1603 Garnet Ave; 858/274-3631; map:KK8). Computer Care (3769 32nd St, Normal Heights; 619/281-5551; map:MM4) is near downtown and has some loaners available. Computer Clinic (9340 Carmel Mountain Rd, Penasquitos; 858/484-7314; map:GG5) provides free pickup and delivery. According to the Convention and Visitors Bureau, San Diego has upward of 1,000 conventions, trade shows, and the like each year. If you need to rent equipment, there are several companies that can help: try Bit by Bit Computer Rentals (858/278-9666), Mac Rentals (858/454-8535 or 800/756-6227), or Electro Rent (858/622-0065 or 800/688-1111). If you can't resist checking out nifty computer shops, try Datel (4611 Mercury St, Kearny Mesa; 619/571-3100; map:JJ5).

## PETS AND STRAY ANIMALS
Call San Diego Animal Control (619/236-4250) to report a lost pet or stray animal. The San Diego Humane Society (887 Sherman St, Bay Park; 619/299-7012; map:LL5) also gets a fair share of lost pets and has plenty of abandoned animals available for adoption. The VCA Emergency Animal Hospital and Referral Service (2317 Hotel Circle S, Mission Valley; 619/299-2400; map:K1) is centrally located in Mission Valley and has 24-hour service.

## SPAS AND SALONS
Day spas and full-service salons abound in image-conscious San Diego. Some of the finest in convenient locations include Primo (500 Hotel Circle N; 619/220-0014; map:M1) in the Town & Country Hotel in Mission Valley; Gaia Day Spa (1299 Prospect St; 858/456-8797; map:JJ7) in La Jolla; Beauty Kliniek (3268 Governor Dr; 858/457-0191; map:JJ6) in the Golden Triangle; Walden Ashe (930 W Washington St; 619/295-7302; map:M2) in Mission Hills; and Details (4993 Niagara St; 619/222-6777; map:B3) in Ocean Beach.

# Local Resources

## NEWSPAPERS
San Diego has an appalling lack of local newspapers. **THE SAN DIEGO UNION-TRIBUNE** (350 Camino de la Reina, Mission Valley; 619/299-3131; map:LL5) once published two papers with separate editors and reporters—the *Union* in the morning, and the *Tribune* in the afternoon. Now the two have merged into one paper, with San Diego, North County, and East County editions. The *Union*'s

Thursday Night & Day section is packed with reviews and up-to-date event listings. The **LOS ANGELES TIMES,** which has more international coverage, can be subscribed to by calling 800/252-9141. The free weekly **READER** (1703 India St, Middletown; 619/235-3000; map:M6) offers some investigative reporting and full coverage of the arts, entertainment, and restaurants, along with listings of local events. The **SAN DIEGO DAILY TRANSCRIPT** (2131 3rd Ave, downtown; 619/232-4381; map:N5) covers business and legal affairs. Local business issues get more in-depth coverage in the **SAN DIEGO BUSINESS JOURNAL** (4909 Murphy Canyon Rd, Kearny Mesa; 858/277-6359; map:JJ4). Most neighborhoods have weeklies of varying journalistic quality; check out the **SAN DIEGO METROPOLITAN UPTOWN EXAMINER** (1250 6th Ave, downtown; 619/233-4060; map:N7) for downtown news and events, and the **LA JOLLA LIGHT** (565 Pearl St, La Jolla; 858/459-4201; map:JJ7) for a view of society soirees. **NORTH COUNTY TIMES** has offices in Escondido (760/745-6611) and Vista (760/631-6600).

## PUBLIC LIBRARIES

The San Diego main library (820 E St, downtown; 619/236-5800; map:O7) boasts 2.1 million volumes and is open Monday to Thursday 10am to 9pm, Friday and Saturday 9:30am to 5:30pm, and Sunday 1pm to 5pm. It also has current subscriptions to papers in more than 50 cities across the United States, in case you want to catch up on the home front while you are away, along with international papers covering news from London, Vancouver, the Philippines, Russia, and Mexico. If you need to do research on local or statewide issues, use the California Room. Internet access is free at the library; you can sign up for time up to seven days in advance. Free movies are shown every Monday night at 6pm and the first and third Sunday of the month at 2pm. At the branch libraries, you might want to check out the children's storytelling programs. Hours vary at the branch libraries but most are open Monday and Wednesday noon to 8pm, and Tuesday, Thursday, Friday, and Saturday 9:30am to 5:30pm. Some are open Sunday. The County of San Diego public library system (858/694-2414) has 31 branches and two bookmobiles. Each branch offers different programs and hours.

## MAJOR DOWNTOWN BOOKSTORES

Most booksellers have shunned downtown, opting instead for Mission Valley and other urban neighborhoods. There is, however, a B. Dalton (619/615-5373; map:N7) at Horton Plaza. Also at Horton Plaza is the Rand McNally Map & Travel Store (619/234-3341), a good source for guidebooks and maps. Everyone interested in travel info stops by Le Travel (745 4th Ave, downtown; 619/544-0005; map:O8). The Upstart Crow Bookstore & Coffeehouse (835 West Harbor Dr, Seaport Village, downtown; 619/232-4855; map:M8) is your best choice for children's books, local history, and vacation novels. For more bookstores, see the Shopping chapter.

## RADIO AND TV

San Diego's radio scene changes frequently as large conglomerates gobble up local stations. The best stations for news, weather, and traffic reports are KSDO and KPBS, the local PBS station.

## HOLES IN THE GROUND

If you've ever tried navigating a city under construction, you'll feel right at home in San Diego. At times, it seems that all of downtown is a construction site, and cranes are an integral part of the city skyline.

The revitalization of downtown began in the late 1980s with the construction of the **SAN DIEGO CONVENTION CENTER** and **HORTON PLAZA** and the gentrification of the **GASLAMP QUARTER.** The Convention Center has already been enlarged during a construction project that tied up traffic on Harbor Drive for two years. High-rise hotels and condo buildings have risen on the waterfront; now, construction of a second tower for the sleek, skinny **MANCHESTER GRAND HYATT** is under way, with completion expected in the summer of 2003. The hotel is promoted as the tallest and largest hotel on the West Coast—not necessarily a plus for the vocal protesters who'd like to keep the waterfront views open to the public.

The focus of redevelopment has now turned to the **EAST VILLAGE,** a 26-block parcel that has long been home to warehouses, small businesses, and residential hotels. Many of the buildings in the neighborhood have been razed to make way for a 46,000-seat **BALLPARK,** scheduled to open in time for the 2004 baseball season. Thus far, the ballpark doesn't have an official name or corporate sponsor, and lawsuits and political controversies have delayed construction. But the enormous swath of dirt at Harbor Drive and Eighth Avenue will soon hold stands for fans who can gaze toward San Diego Bay as they watch high-flying home runs. Several ultra-expansive high-rise residential buildings are also slated for construction in the East Village, along with several hotels.

Not all the land in downtown will be consumed by trophy buildings containing million-dollar condos. The city is also creating a **PARK TO BAY LINK** between Balboa Park and the waterfront along 12th Avenue, beautifying the street and constructing pedestrian walkways with landscaping. The street will be renamed Park Boulevard, reflecting the link to the boulevard at Balboa Park. Citizens who have vociferously protested the construction of the ballpark may be somewhat appeased by the possibility of gaining a new main **PUBLIC LIBRARY** in the East Village. The City Council voted in July 2001 to pay architects $1 million to prepare detailed designs for the library, and land near Broadway and the San Diego Depot was set aside for the building. But a dismaying lack of funding and political infighting have delayed construction. Now a plot of land bounded by 10th, J, and 12th Streets and the new Park Boulevard has been reserved for architect Rob Quigley's much-lauded library of the future—though no construction date has yet been set.

Bulldozers and cranes are also part of the landscape in the **MARINA DISTRICT,** another major redevelopment area along Market and Island Streets south of Horton

Plaza. **CORTEZ HILL** at Eighth Avenue and Date Street has become one of downtown's most exclusive residential enclaves. A linear park called **TWEET STREET** is in the works for the edge of the hill, with pathways lined with birdhouses to attract human and avian nature lovers.

The transformation of **LITTLE ITALY** from a run-down neighborhood of pizza parlors, Italian restaurants, and small houses into an upscale, artsy downtown neighborhood is nearly completed. Artists have moved into new loft spaces, and several interesting interior-design shops and cafes have opened along India Street just a half-dozen blocks from downtown's business district.

If you're interested in the evolution of downtown, stop by the **DOWNTOWN INFORMATION CENTER** (225 Broadway; 619/235-2222; map:N7) and check out the large model that shows the areas of current and future developments. The center offers guided tours of the redevelopment districts on the first and third Saturdays of each month; reservations are required.

You can expect clouds of dust, a proliferation of holes in the ground, the constant presence of earthmovers and cranes, and as many blocked-off streets as it will take to make it all happen. Driving through these areas can be frustrating—you're much better off parking your car and using foot power or the trolley to get around.

*—Maribeth Mellin*

Several cable operators rule TV land in San Diego, making channel-surfing confusing. Channels are mostly consistent for the major networks, but everything else is up for grabs. Check the extensive chart in the front pages of the *Union*'s TV listings for the right numbers in your area.

## Radio Stations

| | | |
|---|---|---|
| ALTERNATIVE ROCK | 91.1 | XTRA FM |
| ALTERNATIVE ROCK | 92.1 | KFSD FM |
| CLASSIC ROCK | 101.5 | KGB FM |
| CLASSICAL | 540 | XBACH AM |
| CONTEMPORARY | 96.5 | KYXY FM |
| CONTEMPORARY | 100.7 | KFMB FM |
| COUNTRY | 97.3 | KSON FM |
| JAZZ | 98.1 | KIFM |
| NEWS, TALK | 600 | KOGO AM |
| NEWS, TALK | 760 | KFMB AM |
| NEWS, TALK | 1130 | KSDO AM |
| NEWS, TALK | 1170 | KCBQ AM |
| OLDIES | 103.7 | KPLN FM |
| PUBLIC BROADCASTING | 89.5 | KPBS FM |

| THE '80S | 94.9 | KBZT FM |
|---|---|---|
| ROCK | 102.1 | KPRI FM |
| SPANISH CONTEMPORARY | 104.5 | XLTN FM |
| SPANISH POP | 97.7 | XTIJ FM |
| TIJUANA PUBLIC RADIO | 88.7 | XITC |

## TV Stations

| ABC | 10 | KGTV |
|---|---|---|
| NBC | 7/39 | KNSD |
| CBS | 8 | KFMB |
| FOX | 6 | XETV |
| PBS | 15 | KPBS |

## INTERNET ACCESS

At **CYBER CAFÉ** (800 Broadway, downtown; 619/702-2233; map:O8) you can get a pastry and coffee with your Internet access. It costs $8 an hour to log on; cafe hours are 10am to midnight. **KINKO'S** offers Internet access (see Business, Copy, and Messenger Services, above) on Macs and PCs. The **SAN DIEGO MAIN PUBLIC LIBRARY** and most branches have free Internet access; see Public Libraries, above, for hours.

## UNIVERSITIES

San Diego is said to have more Nobel laureates than any other city in the United States; many are affiliated with the University of California at San Diego (9500 Gilman Dr, La Jolla; 858/534-2230; map:JJ7). San Diego State University (5500 Campanile Dr, College area; 619/594-5200; map:LL3) has an active local alumni association and a popular football team, the Aztecs. Both schools have extension classes and other learning programs for non-students. Lovingly designed in the Spanish revival style, the University of San Diego (5998 Alcala Park, Normal Heights; 619/260-4600; map:LL6) is a private Catholic college with an excellent law school. Career development classes are available at the University of Phoenix (3890 Murphy Canyon Rd, Kearny Mesa; 800/473-4346; map:JJ4) and National University (4141 Camino del Rio S, Mission Valley; 619/563-7100; map:LL3).

### Important Telephone Numbers

| AAA SAN DIEGO (TRAVEL SERVICES) | 800/222-5000 |
|---|---|
| AAA EMERGENCY ROAD SERVICE (24 HOURS) | 800/400-4222 |
| AARP | 619/641-7020 |
| AIDS HOTLINE | 800/342-2437 |
| ALCOHOLICS ANONYMOUS | 619/265-8762 |
| AMBULANCE | 858/974-9792 |
| AMTRAK | 800/872-7245 |
| ANIMAL CONTROL | 619/236-4250 |
| AUTO IMPOUND | 619/531-2000 |
| BALBOA PARK INFORMATION | 619/239-0512 |
| BETTER BUSINESS BUREAU | 858/496-2131 |
| BIRTH AND DEATH RECORDS | 619/237-0502 |
| BLOOD BANK | 619/296-6393 |

| | |
|---|---|
| CALIFORNIA HIGHWAY PATROL | 619/220-5492 |
| CHAMBER OF COMMERCE | 619/544-1300 |
| CHILD ABUSE HOT LINE | 800/344-6000 |
| CHILD CARE REFERRALS | 800/481-2151 |
| CITY OF SAN DIEGO INFORMATION | 619/236-5555 |
| CITY PARKS VISITOR INFORMATION | 619/221-8901 |
| COAST GUARD | 619/683-6300 |
| COAST GUARD EMERGENCY | 619/295-3121 |
| CUSTOMS (U.S.) | 619/557-5360 |
| DIRECTORY ASSISTANCE | 411 OR 619/555-1212 |
| DOMESTIC VIOLENCE HOT LINE | 800/272-1767 |
| FBI | 858/565-1255 |
| FIRE DEPARTMENT | 858/974-9706 |
| GASLAMP HISTORICAL FOUNDATION | 619/233-4692 |
| GREYHOUND BUS SAN DIEGO TERMINAL | 619/239-3266 |
| IMMIGRATION AND NATURALIZATION SERVICE | 800/375-5283 |
| LOST PETS | 619/236-4250 |
| MARRIAGE LICENSES | 619/237-0502 |
| MISSING PERSONS | 619/531-2000 |
| PLANNED PARENTHOOD | 619/683-7526 |
| POISON CONTROL HOT LINE | 800/876-4766 |
| POST OFFICE INFORMATION | 800/275-8777 |
| PUBLIC TRANSPORTATION | 800/266-6883 |
| RAPE CRISIS HOT LINE | 888/272-1767 |
| RED CROSS | 619/542-7400 |
| SAN DIEGO CONVENTION AND VISITORS BUREAU | 619/232-3101 |
| SAN DIEGO DEPARTMENT OF PUBLIC HEALTH | 619/515-6770 |
| SENIOR SOCIAL SERVICES | 619/236-6905 |
| SURF REPORT | 619/221-8824 |
| SUICIDE HOT LINE | 800/479-3339 |
| TICKETMASTER | 619/220-8497 |
| TRAVELERS AID SOCIETY | 619/295-8393 |
| WEATHER | 619/289-1212 |
| ZIP CODE INFORMATION | 800/275-8777 |

# TOP 150
# RESTAURANTS

# Restaurants by Star Rating

★★★★
Mille Fleurs

★★★½
The Marine Room
The Sky Room

★★★
Azzura Point
Bertrand at Mr. A's
Cafe W
Delicias
Dobson's Bar &
   Restaurant
El Agave
El Bizcocho
Indigo Grill
Laurel Restaurant & Bar
Le Fontainebleau
150 Grand Cafe
Rancho Valencia
   Restaurant
Star of the Sea
The 3rd Corner
Top o' the Cove
Vivace
When in Rome

★★★½
Americana
Azul La Jolla
Bully's
Cafe Pacifica
Chez Loma
George's at the Cove
The Grant Grill
Hash House a Go Go
Hob Nob Hill
Jasmine
Kemo Sabe
King's Fish House
Korea House
Market Cafe

MiXX
Morton's of Chicago
Nine Ten
Pamplemousse Grille
The Prince of Wales
Roy's
Saffron Noodles & Saté
Spices Thai Cafe
Taste of Thai
Thee Bungalow
Trattoria Acqua
Tutto Mare Ristorante
Via Italia Trattoria
The Whaling Bar
WineSellar & Brasserie

★★
Adam's Steak & Eggs
Aladdin Mediterranean
   Cafe
Athens Market Taverna
Bai Yook Thai Cuisine
Bayou Bar and Grill
Bella Luna
Bellefleur Winery &
   Restaurant
Bombay
The Brigantine
Cafe 222
Cafe Japengo
Cafe Zinc
California Cuisine
Candelas
Cass Street Bar & Grill
Chilango's Mexico City
   Grill
Dave & Buster's
Del Mar Pizza
Epazote
Fio's Cucina Italiana
Fish Market Restaurant
French Pastry Shop
Gulf Coast Grill

Ichiban
Joe's Crab Shack
Kaiserhof
Karl Strauss Brewery &
   Grill
Kensington Grill
Mission Hills Cafe
Montanas
Nick's at the Beach
Old Town Mexican Cafe
Ono Sushi
Ortega's
Pacifica Del Mar
Pacific Coast Grill
Panda Inn Chinese
   Restaurant
Parallel 33
Pizza Nova
The Prado Restaurant at
   Balboa Park
Royale Brasserie
Sally's
Sammy's California
   Woodfired Pizza
Sante Ristorante
Sevilla
Tori Tori New Japanese
   Cuisine
The Venetian
Yoshino

★★½
Blue Point Coastal Cuisine
Cafe Zucchero
Cecil's Cafe & Fish
   Market
Downtown Johnny
   Brown's
D. Z. Akin's
El Indio Shop
Greek Islands Cafe
Hodad's
Il Fornaio

Jimmy Carter's Cafe
Jyoti Bihanga
La Fresqueria
La Taverna
Mimmo's Italian Village
Olé Madrid
Piatti
Pizza Port
Point Loma Seafoods
Qwiigs Bar & Grill
Red Sails Inn
Roppongi Restaurant, Bar, and Cafe
Rubio's
Sushi on the Rock
Tip Top Meats
Tony's Jacal
T's Cafe
The Vegetarian Zone
Vigilucci's

★
Alfonso's
Bellefleur Winery & Restaurant
The Big Kitchen
Blumberg's at Samson's La Jolla
Cafe Athena
Chart House
The Cheese Shop
Crest Cafe
Fairouz Restaurant & Gallery
Fidel's
Filippi's Pizza Grotto
Hamburger Mary's
Jake's Del Mar
Ki's
Kono's Cafe

Mission Cafe & Coffee Shop
Old Venice Italian Restaurant Caffe & Bar
Porkyland
Ruby's Diner
Shakespeare Pub and Grille
Souplantation
Sushi Deli
Trophy's
Turf Supper Club
The Waterfront
World Curry

# Restaurants by Neighborhood

**CARDIFF-BY-THE-SEA**
Ki's

**CARLSBAD**
Bellefleur Winery &
    Restaurant
Fidel's
Pizza Port
Sevilla
Tip Top Meats
Vivace

**CLAIREMONT**
Aladdin Mediterranean
    Cafe
Via Italia Trattoria

**CORONADO**
Azzura Point
Chez Loma
Il Fornaio
Market Cafe
The Prince of Wales

**DEL MAR**
Americana
Bully's
Del Mar Pizza
Epazote
Il Fornaio
Jake's Del Mar
Pacifica Del Mar
Taste of Thai

**DOWNTOWN**
Athens Market Taverna
Bayou Bar and Grill
Bella Luna
Bertrand at Mr. A's
Blue Point Coastal Cuisine
Cafe 222
Cafe Zucchero
Candelas
Chart House
The Cheese Shop

Dobson's Bar & Restaurant
Downtown Johnny
    Brown's
Filippi's Pizza Grotto
Fio's Cucina Italiana
Fish Market Restaurant
The Grant Grill
Greek Islands Cafe
Hob Nob Hill
La Fresqueria
Laurel Restaurant & Bar
Le Fontainebleau
Mimmo's Italian Village
Morton's of Chicago
Olé Madrid
Panda Inn Chinese
    Restaurant
The Prado Restaurant at
    Balboa Park
Royale Brasserie
Sally's
Sevilla
Star of the Sea
Sushi Deli
The Waterfront

**ENCINITAS**
Vigilucci's
When in Rome

**ESCONDIDO**
150 Grand Cafe

**GOLDEN HILL**
The Big Kitchen
Turf Supper Club

**HILLCREST**
Bai Yook Thai Cuisine
Bombay
California Cuisine
Cafe W
Chilango's Mexico City
    Grill

Crest Cafe
Hamburger Mary's
Hash House a Go Go
Ichiban
Jimmy Carter's Cafe
Kemo Sabe
MiXX
Montanas
Ono Sushi
Parallel 33
Taste of Thai
The Vegetarian Zone

**KEARNY MESA**
Jasmine
Korea House

**KENSINGTON**
Kensington Grill

**LA JOLLA**
Alfonso's
Azul La Jolla
Blumberg's at Samson's La
    Jolla
Cafe Japengo
The Cheese Shop
French Pastry Shop
George's at the Cove
La Taverna
The Marine Room
Nine Ten
Piatti
Porkyland
Roppongi Restaurant, Bar,
    and Cafe
Roy's
Sammy's California
    Woodfired Pizza
Santé Ristorante
The Sky Room
Sushi on the Rock
Top o' the Cove

Trattoria Acqua
Tutto Mare Ristorante
The Whaling Bar

**LA MESA**
D. Z. Akin's
Little Italy
Indigo Grill

**LOGAN HEIGHTS**
Porkyland

**MIDDLETOWN**
El Indio Shop
Saffron Noodles & Saté
Shakespeare Pub and
  Grille
Yoshino

**MIDWAY**
Fairouz Restaurant &
  Gallery
Souplantation

**MISSION BEACH**
Mission Cafe & Coffee
  Shop

**MISSION HILLS**
Mission Hills Cafe

**MISSION VALLEY**
Adam's Steak & Eggs
Bully's
Dave & Buster's
Joe's Crab Shack

King's Fish House
Ruby's Diner
Trophy's

**NORMAL HEIGHTS**
Jyoti Bihanga

**OCEAN BEACH**
The 3rd Corner
Cecil's Cafe & Fish
  Market
Hodad's
Kaiserhof
Ortega's
Qwiigs Bar & Grill
Thee Bungalow

**OLD TOWN**
Cafe Pacifica
El Agave
Old Town Mexican Cafe

**PACIFIC BEACH**
Cafe Athena
Cass Street Bar & Grill
Ichiban PB
Joe's Crab Shack
Kono's Cafe
Nick's at the Beach
Rubio's
World Curry

**POINT LOMA**
Old Venice Italian
  Restaurant Caffe & Bar

Pizza Nova
Point Loma Seafoods
The Venetian

**RANCHO BERNARDO**
El Bizcocho

**RANCHO SANTA FE**
Delicias
Mille Fleurs
Rancho Valencia
  Restaurant
Shelter Island
The Brigantine
Red Sails Inn

**SOLANA BEACH**
Cafe Zinc
Fidel's
Pacific Coast Grill
Pamplemousse Grille
Pizza Port
Tony's Jacal
T's Cafe

**SORRENTO VALLEY**
Karl Strauss Brewery &
  Grill
Spices Thai Cafe
WineSellar & Brasserie

**UNIVERSITY HEIGHTS**
Gulf Coast Grill
Tori Tori New Japanese
  Cuisine

# Restaurants by Food and Other Features

## BAKERY
Il Fornaio
D. Z. Akin's

## BREAKFAST
Adam's Steak & Eggs
Americana
Cafe 222
Cafe Zinc
Cecil's Cafe & Fish
    Market
Don's Country Kitchen
French Pastry Shop
Hash House a Go Go
Jimmy Carter's Cafe
Kono's Cafe
Market Cafe
Mission Hills Cafe

## BREAKFAST ALL DAY
The Big Kitchen

## BRUNCH
Chez Loma
Epazote
Il Fornaio
Jake's Del Mar
Le Fontainebleau
The Marine Room
The Market Cafe
Pacifica Del Mar
Qwiigs Bar & Grill
Trattoria Acqua

## BURGERS
The Brigantine
Bully's
Cass Street Bar & Grill
Crest Cafe
Downtown Johnny
    Brown's
Hamburger Mary's
Hodad's

Karl Strauss Brewery &
    Grill
Kensington Grill
Trophy's
The Waterfront

## CAJUN/CREOLE
Blue Point Coastal Cuisine
Bayou Bar and Grill
Gulf Coast Grill

## CALIFORNIA CUISINE
California Cuisine
Bertrand at Mr. A's
Cecil's Cafe & Fish
    Market
Delicias
Dobson's Bar &
    Restaurant
El Bizcocho
George's at the Cove
Kemo Sabe
Mille Fleurs
Montanas
The Prado Restaurant at
    Balboa Park
Rancho Valencia
    Restaurant
Sally's
The Sky Room
Star of the Sea
Thee Bungalow

## CHINESE
Panda Inn Chinese
    Restaurant
Jasmine

## CONTINENTAL
Azzura Point
The Grant Grill
The Marine Room
Santé Ristorante
The Sky Room

Thee Bungalow
The Whaling Bar

## DESSERTS (EXCELLENT)
Cafe Pacifica
Cafe Zucchero
French Pastry Shop
George's Ocean Terrace
Morton's of Chicago
Pamplemousse Grille
The Sky Room
When in Rome

## DINER
Hob Nob Hill
Ruby's Diner

## EDITORS' CHOICE
Azzura Point
The Brigantine
California Cuisine
Cass Street Bar & Grill
Cecil's Cafe & Fish
    Market
El Indio Shop
Epazote
George's at the Cove
Hodad's
Ki's
Kono's Cafe
The Marine Room
MiXX
Point Loma Seafoods
Qwiigs Bar & Grill
Red Sails Inn
Rubio's
Tony's Jacal

## FAMILY
Adam's Steak & Eggs
The Big Kitchen
Blumberg's at Samson's La
    Jolla
D. Z. Akin's

El Indio Shop
Filippi's Pizza Grotto
Fish Market Restaurant
Greek Islands Cafe
Ichiban PB
Jasmine
King's Fish House
Korea House
Market Cafe
Mimmo's Italian Village
Ruby's Diner
Souplantation
Tony's Jacal
The Venetian

**FIREPLACE**
Brigantine Point Loma
Delicias
Epazote
150 Grand Cafe
Rancho Valencia
    Restaurant
Red Sails Inn
Santé Ristorante
T's Cafe
The 3rd Corner
The Whaling Bar
Tony's Jacal
When in Rome

**FRENCH**
Azzura Point
Bertrand at Mr. A's
Chez Loma
Delicias
El Bizcocho
French Pastry Shop
Laurel Restaurant & Bar
Le Fontainebleau
Mille Fleurs
Pamplemousse Grille
Rancho Valencia
    Restaurant
Royale Brasserie
The Sky Room
The 3rd Corner

Thee Bungalow
Top o' the Cove

**GERMAN**
Kaiserhof
Karl Strauss Brewery &
    Grill

**GOOD VALUE**
Adam's Steak & Eggs
The Brigantine
Bully's
Cafe Athena
Cass Street Bar & Grill
Cecil's Cafe & Fish
    Market
The Cheese Shop
Fairouz Restaurant &
    Gallery
Hob Nob Hill
Ichiban PB
Jake's Del Mar
Jimmy Carter's Cafe
Joe's Crab Shack
Ki's
Kono's Cafe
Mimmo's Italian Village
Mission Hills Cafe
Pizza Nova
Porkyland
Rubio's
Sammy's California
    Woodfired Pizza
Souplantation
Spices Thai Cafe
Sushi Deli
Tip Top Meats
Tori Tori New Japanese
    Cuisine
T's Cafe
Vigilucci's
The Waterfront
Yoshino

**GOURMET TAKEOUT**
D. Z. Akin's
French Pastry Shop

Il Fornaio
Sushi on the Rock

**GREEK**
Aladdin Mediterranean
    Cafe
Athens Market Taverna
Cafe Athena
Fairouz Restaurant &
    Gallery
Greek Islands Cafe

**GRILL**
Bayou Bar and Grill
Cass Street Bar & Grill
Kensington Grill
Montanas
Qwiigs Bar & Grill

**HEALTH CONSCIOUS**
Jyoti Bihanga
Ki's
La Fresqueria
Souplantation
Sushi on the Rock

**INDIAN**
Bombay

**INVENTIVE ETHNIC**
Cafe Pacifica
California Cuisine
Indigo Grill
Kemo Sabe
MiXX
Parallel 33
Roppongi Restaurant, Bar,
    and Cafe

**ITALIAN**
Bella Luna
Del Mar Pizza
Fio's Cucina Italiana
Il Fornaio
La Taverna
Mimmo's Italian Village
Old Venice Italian
    Restaurant Caffe & Bar

Piatti
Pizza Nova
Pizza Port
Trattoria Acqua
Via Italia Trattoria
The Venetian
Vigilucci's
When in Rome

**JAPANESE**
Ichiban PB
Ono Sushi
Sushi Deli
Sushi on the Rock
Tori Tori New Japanese
    Cuisine
Yoshino

**KITSCH**
Cafe 222
Hodad's
Turf Supper Club

**KOREAN**
Korea House

**LATE NIGHT**
Crest Cafe
Nick's at the Beach

**MEDITERRANEAN**
Azul La Jolla
Azzura Point
Cafe Pacifica
Laurel Restaurant & Bar
150 Grand Cafe
Rancho Valencia
    Restaurant
Sally's
Star of the Sea
Thee Bungalow
Top o' the Cove
Trattoria Acqua

**MEXICAN**
Alfonso's
Candelas

Chilango's Mexico City
    Grill
El Agave
El Indio Shop
Fidel's
La Fresqueria
La Salsa
Old Town Mexican Cafe
Ortega's
Porkyland
The Prado Restaurant at
    Balboa Park
Rubio's
Tony's Jacal

**MIDDLE EASTERN**
Aladdin Mediterranean
    Cafe
Fairouz Restaurant &
    Gallery

**OUTDOOR DINING**
Adam's Steak & Eggs
Alfonso's
Azul
Bayou Bar and Grill
Bombay
The Brigantine
Cafe W
Cafe Zinc
Cafe Zucchero
California Cuisine
Downtown Johnny
    Brown's
Greek Islands Cafe
Fish Market Restaurant
Hash House a Go Go
Indigo Grill
La Taverna
MiXX
Nick's at the Beach
Nine Ten
Old Town Mexican Cafe
150 Grand Cafe
Pacific Coast Grill

The Prado Restaurant at
    Balboa Park
Red Sails Inn
Sally's
Shakespeare Pub and
    Grille
Market Cafe
Tony's Jacal
Trattoria Acqua
The Vegetarian Zone

**PAN ASIAN /
PACIFIC RIM**
Cafe Japengo
Kemo Sabe
150 Grand Cafe
Pacifica Del Mar
Roppongi Restaurant, Bar,
    and Cafe
Roy's
Top o' the Cove

**PIZZA**
Aladdin Mediterranean
    Cafe
Del Mar Pizza
Embers Grille
Filippi's Pizza Grotto
Old Venice Italian
    Restaurant Caffe & Bar
Pizza Nova
Pizza Port
Sammy's California
    Woodfired Pizza
Trattoria Acqua
The Venetian

**PRIVATE ROOMS**
Bellefleur
Bertrand at Mr. A's
Candelas
Dave & Buster's
Laurel Restaurant & Bar
Montanas
Morton's of Chicago
Roppongi Restaurant, Bar,
    and Cafe

Royale Brasserie
T's Cafe
When In Rome

**ROMANTIC**
Athens Market Taverna
Azzura Point
Cafe Pacifica
California Cuisine
Chez Loma
Delicias
El Bizcocho
Fish Market Restaurant
George's at the Cove
Il Fornaio
Le Fontainebleau
The Marine Room
Market Cafe
Mille Fleurs
Old Venice Italian
    Restaurant Caffe & Bar
150 Grand Cafe
The Prince of Wales
Rancho Valencia
    Restaurant
Santé Ristorante
The Sky Room
Star of the Sea
Thee Bungalow
Top o' the Cove
Trattoria Acqua
Vigilucci's
The Whaling Bar

**SEAFOOD**
Azul La Jolla
Azzura Point
Blue Point Coastal Cuisine
The Brigantine
Cafe Pacifica
Candelas
Chart House
Delicias
Fish Market Restaurant
George's at the Cove
The Grant Grill

Jake's Del Mar
Joe's Crab Shack
King's Fish House
Mille Fleurs
Nine Ten
Pacifica Del Mar
Point Loma Seafoods
Qwiigs Bar & Grill
Red Sails Inn
Sally's
Star of the Sea
The 3rd Corner
Top o' the Cove
Tutto Mare Ristorante

**SPANISH**
Olé Madrid
Sevilla

**SOUP/SALAD/
    SANDWICH**
Blumberg's at Samson's
    La Jolla
Cafe Zinc
Cass Street Bar & Grill
The Cheese Shop
Crest Cafe
Downtown Johnny
    Brown's
D. Z. Akin's
Hamburger Mary's
Souplantation
Tip Top Meats

**SOUTHWEST**
Bellefleur Winery &
    Restaurant
Blue Point Coastal Cuisine
Epazote
Kemo Sabe
Montanas

**STEAK**
The Brigantine
Bully's
Chart House
The Grant Grill

Morton's of Chicago
Turf Supper Club

**SUSHI**
Ichiban PB
Ono Sushi
Sushi Deli
Sushi on the Rock
Tori Tori New Japanese
    Cuisine

**TAPAS**
Epazote
Olé Madrid
Roppongi Restaurant, Bar,
    and Cafe
Sevilla

**TAKEOUT**
Blumberg's at Samson's
    La Jolla
Chilango's Mexico City
    Grill
Downtown Johnny
    Brown's
Del Mar Pizza
El Indio Shop
Filippi's Pizza Grotto
Ichiban PB
La Salsa
Mimmo's Italian Village
Pizza Nova
Pizza Port
Point Loma Seafoods
Porkyland
Rubio's
Saffron Noodles & Saté
Tip Top Meats
Tori Tori New Japanese
    Cuisine
The Vegetarian Zone
World Curry

**THAI**
Bai Yook Thai Cuisine
Blue Point Coastal Cuisine
Saffron Noodles & Saté

Taste of Thai
Spices Thai Cafe

**VEGETARIAN**
Bombay
Jyoti Bihanga
Cafe Zinc
The Vegetarian Zone

**VIEW**
Azul
Bertrand at Mr. A's

Cecil's Cafe & Fish
   Market
Epazote
George's at the Cove
Jake's Del Mar
The Marine Room
Market Cafe
Nick's at the Beach
Pacifica Del Mar
Pizza Nova
Point Loma Seafoods

Qwiigs Bar & Grill
Sally's
The Sky Room
Star of the Sea
Top o' the Cove

# RESTAURANTS

## Adam's Steak & Eggs / ★★

**1201 HOTEL CIRCLE S, MISSION VALLEY; 619/291-1103** Go on a weekday at 10am and you might not have to wait for a table at what may be the best breakfast hangout in town. Yes, you can get a plump, perfect steak and eggs here, with fresh, crispy fried potatoes, but regulars who stop by for a quick meal or full family celebration have more discerning tastes. They order the down-home corn fritters with honey butter, the homemade sausage patty, the enormous Spanish omelet smothered in spicy sauce and sour cream, or the meal-size cinnamon bun. Kids love the fruit smoothies and pancakes. Check out the daily specials, including the Philly steak and eggs covered with sautéed onions—order it with melted cheese on top. The wood tables are tightly packed, and strangers end up sharing sugar, cream, and local tidbits. Adam's is only open till 11:30am (1pm on Saturday and Sunday), but some of the breakfast items are served throughout the day at Albie's, the adjacent steak house. *$; AE, DC, DIS, MC, V; no checks; breakfast every day; full bar; no reservations; self parking; map:L1* &

## Aladdin Mediterranean Cafe / ★★

**5420 CLAIREMONT MESA BLVD, CLAIREMONT; 619/573-0000 / 1220 CLEVELAND AVE, HILLCREST; 619/574-1111** Despite its suburban strip-mall location in Clairemont, this delightful restaurant provides a great escape for anyone craving Middle Eastern fare. The menu is extensive, ranging from the usual hummus, tabbouleh, and gyros to wood-fired pizzas with deliciously puffy crusts. Standout dishes are the stuffed grape leaves, lamb kebabs, generous Greek salads, succulent chicken shawerma, and fat pita sandwiches. And don't pass up those pizzas: they're worth a visit all by themselves. Sample one of these pies topped with juicy bites of chicken shawerma or smoky grilled veggies and lots of fresh herbs, and you may never settle for plain pepperoni again. The place has a casual, comfy feel, with a shaded front patio (facing the parking lot, but still pleasant) and lots of indoor seating. It's equally popular with local workers and families (kids, especially, love all these finger foods). At the Clairemont location, a market area inside the restaurant sells imported olive oil, Middle Eastern spices, and assorted groceries. The Hillcrest restaurant is adjacent to Uptown Center; if you can't find street parking, there's a large lot behind the Trader Joe's store. *$; MC, V; no checks; lunch, dinner every day; beer and wine; reservations required for large parties; self parking; map:JJ5 and P2* &

## Alfonso's / ★

**1251 PROSPECT ST, LA JOLLA; 858/454-2232** Margaritas by the pitcher, chips, hot bean dip, carne asada burritos, and guacamole are the perfect ingredients for an afternoon gossip session at this prime people-watching cafe. La Jollans have been hanging out at the sidewalk tables since 1971, and many a family celebration has graced the overcrowded, dark dining rooms. The cooks firmly resist trends, relying on basic enchiladas, burritos, and tacos to please the crowds. Don't spend the big bucks on fancy entrees; stick with the old standards, appetizers, and drinks for a rewarding shopping break. *$; AE, DC, DIS, MC, V; no checks; lunch, dinner every day; full bar; reservations recommended for parties of 6 or more; self parking; map:JJ7*

## Americana / ★★☆

**1454 CAMINO DEL MAR, DEL MAR; 858/794-6838** Chef owner Randy Gruber has a hit on his hands with this versatile dining room, which serves breakfast, lunch, and dinner. During the morning hours, the place feels like a bright and cozy coffee shop, complete with just-baked muffins, challah French toast, omelets, and pancakes with your choice of adds like granola or chocolate chips. Lunch brings an equally homey lineup: egg salad sandwiches, a classic BLT, turkey burgers, and lots of attractive salads. At dinnertime, however, Americana takes on a much more sophisticated aura, with candlelight, white tablecloths, and artful gourmet cuisine at quite reasonable prices. Don't miss the quickly seared scallops with red lentils, the silken sliced duck breast paired with perfect green beans and pearly couscous, or the salmon perched on a clever succotash of beans and vegetables. For dessert, there's lemon tart brûlée or an unusual banana tarte Tatin. The wine list, while short on by-the-glass selections, offers a decent lineup of food-friendly varietals. Service can seem a bit reserved unless you're a regular, but is otherwise adequate. In addition to the small dining room and bar area, there's seating on the front patio, a prime place for breakfast, lunch, and people-watching. *$$; AE, DC, DIS, MC, V; no checks; breakfast, lunch every day, dinner Tues–Sat; beer and wine; reservations recommended; street parking; map: GG7* &

## Athens Market Taverna / ★★

**109 WEST F ST, DOWNTOWN; 619/234-1955** This Greek restaurant is a favorite with lawyers and other downtown professionals for lunch, dinner, and after-work cocktails; their well-heeled, well-dressed demeanor goes nicely with the understated, elegant white linen tablecloths and napkins, tiny candles, and dried flowers gracing each table. Owner Mary Pappas has been cooking up sublime Greek food downtown since 1974, and her devoted clientele followed her from her first location at Fourth Avenue and E Street to the current digs just south of Horton Plaza. Among the most succulent dishes is the fall-off-the-bone baked lemon chicken, served with rice pilaf, roasted potato wedge, vegetable, and soup or salad. The lentil soup is zesty, though the egg-lemon soup is almost too subtle. Still, there's something so chic yet comfortable about Athens Market Taverna that a less-than-inspired batch of soup is instantly forgiven. *$$; AE, DC, DIS, MC, V; no checks; lunch, dinner Mon–Fri, dinner Sat; full bar; reservations recommended; street parking; map:N8* &

## Azul La Jolla / ★★☆

**1250 PROSPECT ST, LA JOLLA; 858/454-9616** Since opening in 1999, this striking eatery owned by the Brigantine Restaurant Corporation has become a destination for both tourists and locals lured by the wide-ranging menu and the terrific locale. Azul (Spanish for blue) is anchored on the hill above La Jolla Cove with a see-forever view of the Pacific. An extensive renovation turned this site of many a failed restaurant into a gorgeous grotto-like room, dramatically lit and decorated. The best tables are along the windows, of course, but the two-level dining room assures an ocean view from many of the booths farther back. The menu, which changes often, is heavy on Mediterranean-influenced dishes, including seafood paella, a marinated calamari salad, and assorted tapas served as a buffet. As befits the seaside locale, fish is a specialty—do try the salmon on a bed of ratatouille and the John Dory offered as a nightly special. Service is unfailingly pleasant, and there's a special menu just for kids. Along with the dining room, there's seating in a more intimate bar area and a patio warmed by a fire. *$$; AE, DC, MC, V; no checks; lunch Tues–Sat, dinner every day, brunch Sun; full bar; reservations recommended; street parking; www.azul-la jolla.com; map:JJ7* &

## Azzura Point / ★★★

**4000 CORONADO BAY RD (LOEWS CORONADO BAY RESORT), CORO-NADO; 619/424-4477** A perennial contender for most scenic restaurant in San Diego, this dining room at the Loews Coronado Bay Resort is a star. A multimillion-dollar renovation turned the harbor-view restaurant into a vision of safari chic that perfectly reflects the resort atmosphere. Service is polished and knowledgeable, the wine list extensive (and expensive). Despite a few chef changes over recent years, the kitchen still turns out fantastic dishes incorporating Pacific Rim, classic French, and Mediterranean flavors. Pristinely fresh fish and shellfish imported from around the world always sparkle; particular standouts are the oysters splashed with sake vinaigrette, the lobster risotto, and France's rare loup de mer. Hearty red meat dishes like beef tenderloin complemented with a heavenly blue cheese tart are also nicely done. Nightly prix fixe dinners offer multicourse tasting menus that are a signature of this dining room and a fine way to sample the cuisine. A lighter menu of small plates and appetizers is available in the adjacent bar. *$$$–$$$$; AE, MC, V; no checks; dinner Tues–Sun; full bar; reservations recommended; valet and self parking; www.loewshotels.com; map:NN5* &

## Bai Yook Thai Cuisine / ★★

**1260 UNIVERSITY AVE, HILLCREST; 619/296-2700** Typical of many a local restaurant, this stellar Thai kitchen is tucked into a nondescript mall. But don't miss it: the green papaya salad redolent of garlic and fish sauce just might be the best version in town. After that, chow down on one of the curry or noodle dishes, all of which come with meats, seafood, or vegetables. Don't have a favorite dish? Try the red curry with green beans (pad prik khing); the panang curry flavored with basil, green peppers, and coconut; or the familiar pad thai sprinkled with peanuts and bean sprouts. The small dining room is very casual and doesn't offer much privacy, but the soft blue walls and Asian art add a touch of serenity that's all too rare on the informal dining scene. *$; AE, DC, DIS, MC, V; no checks; lunch Mon–Sat, dinner every day; beer and wine; reservations recommended; self parking; map:O2*

## Bayou Bar and Grill / ★★

**329 MARKET ST, DOWNTOWN; 619/696-8747** Bringing a little bit of Bourbon Street to Market Street—that's what San Diego's best Cajun restaurant is about. Between the Dixieland jazz (including live performances for New Year's Eve and Mardi Gras), the Big Easy posters, and the huge selection of chile sauces for sale, it's easy to imagine yourself in the French Quarter. The Southern cooking delivers authentic punch as well, generating lots of requests for the jambalaya, shrimp po' boy, fiery

## DOGGIE DINING

When it comes to pets and restaurants, San Diego isn't as progressive as Paris, where the bearded guest sitting next to you might be an Airedale. La belle France understands that well-behaved dogs, much like well-mannered children, deserve to go out for a good meal. (Of course, one never encounters a poorly behaved French dog or child in Paris.) While the San Diego health department prohibits canines (except for service dogs) in restaurant interiors, a number of enlightened eateries offer pup-friendly patios. Many places, including Bread & Cie, Greek Islands Cafe, and Sammy's, even keep a water bowl filled for their four-legged guests. Although it's mostly casual places that welcome dogs, several upscale places with outdoor dining areas also permit them. Both Mille Fleurs and the Market Cafe at Loews Coronado Bay Resort, each known for top-notch atmosphere and fine cuisine, offer terraces where mannerly mutts and polite purebreds are welcome. A word to the wise: help keep local restaurants pet-friendly by making sure your dog is quiet and under control. And remember to bring some cleanup supplies, just in case.

—Robin Kleven

blackened fish, and soft-shell crab. Save a little room for dessert because the place is famous for a chilled peanut butter mousse pie and a bourbon-spiked bread pudding. In addition to the bar area and dining rooms, there's patio seating on the sidewalk fronting Market Street, a favorite vantage point on busy weekend nights. If you're in town during Mardi Gras season, this is the place to be for hearty partying and Hurricanes that go down smooth and cold. *$$; AE, CB, DC, DIS, MC, V; no checks; dinner every day; full bar; reservations recommended; street parking; bayoubar@ aol.com; map:N8* &

### Bella Luna / ★★

**748 5TH AVE, DOWNTOWN; 619/239-3222** Downtown's Gaslamp Quarter offers a staggering number of trattorias, but those in the know keep going back to this eye-catching Italian restaurant whose name means "beautiful moon." The dining room is one of the Gaslamp's most striking; the ceiling evokes blue sky and clouds and has dozens of artworks celebrating the moon. There's also seating at the bar and on the sidewalk patio, a prime vantage point for Fifth Avenue people-watching. The tempting menu is strong on appetizers, with assorted carpaccios (we especially like the salmon version) and a particularly nice starter of tiny grilled eggplant wrapped in pine nuts and raisins. Main courses of note include the veal saltimbocca, bow-tie pasta with fresh salmon and spinach, spicy penne with eggplant, and risottos that change with the season. Along with a decent wine selection, the restaurant serves six varieties of grappa and a number of fine aged tequilas. Service is skilled (though it can lag when there's a crowd), and the restaurant has a distinctively European cachet that sets it apart from the crowd. *$$; AE, DC, MC, V; no checks; lunch, dinner every day; full bar; reservations recommended; valet and street parking; map:O7*

## Bellefleur Winery & Restaurant / ★★

**5610 PASEO DEL NORTE, CARLSBAD; 760/603-1919** Looking somewhat like a beautiful fish out of water, this upscale restaurant/bar anchors one end of an outlet store mall (the Carlsbad Company Stores) just off Interstate 5. It's a welcome presence among the fast-food joints, the discount shoe stores, and the displays of last year's fashions. Inside the villa-esque building, soaring ceilings and graceful architecture provide a chic showcase for an international lineup of foods. The restaurant has recently undergone restructuring, with new management creating an ambitious menu influenced by Pacific Rim, Italian, French, and classic American styles. Fancy wood-fired pizzas and Tuscan white bean soup rub elbows with cheeseburgers, grilled lamb loin, and steamed local mussels in a yellow curry sauce; on the bar menu, you'll find smoked salmon, sushi-style, alongside French onion soup. At lunch, the place has a casual feeling; a dressier, older crowd shows up at night. Some customers may enjoy the wines sold under the Bellefleur label, but discerning drinkers will want to shell out some extra dough for the better-known California brands on the extensive list. *$$$; AE, DC, DIS, MC, V; no checks; lunch, dinner every day; full bar; reservations recommended; self parking; map:CC7* &

## Bertrand at Mr. A's / ★★★

**2550 5TH AVE, DOWNTOWN; 619/239-1377** Generations of San Diegans have counted on this 12th-floor restaurant to deliver sweeping views, formal service, and "special occasion" atmosphere. Now, the fare is equally notable. Mr. A's, as the place used to be known, was purchased by local restaurateur Bertrand Hug (of Mille Fleurs fame) in spring 2000 and completely refurbished. Gone are the red velvet wallpaper and heavy draperies, as well as the old-fashioned menu. These days, the rooms are dressed in sleek, self-assured neutrals and the kitchen staff turns out modern French and California cuisine. Dishes change often, but be on the lookout for standout versions of cassoulet, duck confit, roasted veal, and Maine lobster (the lobster salad with a truffle strudel is to swoon for). The book-size wine list is heavy on fine Bordeaux and Burgundy, as well as California's top reds, and the skilled bartenders make a darn good Cosmopolitan. Although the restrictive dress code of days past is no more (jacketless men and women in pants were once frowned upon), this is definitely the place to dress for success. Most tables offer wonderful views of downtown, the harbor, or Balboa Park, making this a can't-miss choice for out-of-town guests, business associates—or a special date. Valet parking is available underneath the building, with an entrance on Fourth Avenue. *$$$$; AE, DC, DIS, MC, V; no checks; lunch Mon–Fri, dinner every day; full bar; reservations recommended; valet and street parking; asrestaurant@aol.com; www.bertrandatmister as.com; map: N5* &

## The Big Kitchen / ★

**3003 GRAPE ST, GOLDEN HILL; 619/234-5789** Judy the Beauty on Duty, the irrepressible owner of this neighborhood icon, has rules for her patrons printed on the first page of the menu. Rule number two is "Do not deliver your baby in my cafe."

Other than that, Judy's darn accommodating, and she's garnered a colorful following over several decades. Whoopi Goldberg used to eat here when she was in town, and her favorite breakfast now bears her name. (If you must know, it's eggs, potatoes, and a large OJ.) Other meals honor lesser-known, quirky patrons. Check out Lily's Special—a bowl of rice with cheese, spinach, and roasted garlic, a small fruit plate, and a homemade muffin. Most people come for the enormous, fluffy omelets or spinach and eggs, both served with golden-brown home fries and toast. Regulars slide onto their favorite seats at the three-sided bar, holding forth on liberal politics while holding out their mugs for a refill. Daily lunch specials are straight out of *American Graffiti:* there's chicken with biscuits and gravy on Tuesdays and turkey 'n' fixin's on Wednesdays. A plant-filled, kid-friendly back patio and a second dining room (filled with original art) are packed on weekend mornings. Breakfast may not be the cheapest in town, but they're friendly enough to keep 'em coming back. *$; no credit cards; checks OK; breakfast, lunch every day; no alcohol; no reservations; street parking; map:MM4* &

## Blue Point Coastal Cuisine / ★★

**565 5TH AVE, DOWNTOWN; 619/233-6623** Chalk up this Gaslamp Quarter restaurant's success to a number of factors. Prime among them is the dynamite location on busy Fifth Avenue, where the comings and goings of the after-dark crowd provide constant entertainment. Blue Point is also one of the rare seafood houses in the area offering an oyster bar along with a multicultural menu that leans heavily on fish. This is one spot in the Gaslamp where pasta doesn't rule; instead, in-the-know diners choose Baja-style clam chowder, ahi sashimi, juicy pan-seared scallops, or grilled swordfish in an orangy glaze. The setting is both flashy and attractive, offering big, cushy booths, bold flower arrangements, and some of the best-looking bartenders around. These guys know their stuff, whipping up smooth, shaken-not-stirred martinis that would make Dean Martin purr. The food isn't always as consistent as the drinks, but Blue Point's still a fun place to drop anchor. *$$$; AE, DC, DIS, MC, V; no checks; dinner every day; full bar; reservations recommended; street parking; www.cohnrestaurants.com; map:O8* &

## Blumberg's at Samson's La Jolla / ★

**8861 VILLA LA JOLLA DR, LA JOLLA; 858/455-1461** Samson's has always been one of San Diego's legends when it comes to bounteous portions of classic deli fare. The name's been changed to Blumberg's, but the familiar menu remains the same. You're guaranteed to roll out feeling satisfied, most likely carrying a box of leftovers for the next day. This is the place to find platters of lox, smoked whitefish, and chopped liver (call ahead to ask about catering and local delivery). All the standard deli sandwiches are here, including piled-high versions served with your choice of potato pancakes, coleslaw, french fries, or potato salad. The bowl of chicken soup complete with oversize matzo ball is Jewish comfort food at its best, as is beef brisket served with a side of noodle kugel. An on-site bakery prepares German chocolate cake, rugelach, and cheesecakes, as well as traditional challah and bagels. The informal atmosphere, spacious dining room, and reasonable prices attract lots of families as well as patrons from the nearby movie theaters. Just remember: bring a hearty appetite. *$; AE, DC, DIS, MC, V; checks OK; breakfast, lunch, dinner every day; beer and wine; reservations recommended; self parking; map:JJ7* &

## Bombay / ★★

**3975 5TH AVE, HILLCREST; 619/298-3155** This Indian restaurant is a pleasing place to pass the time over lunch or dinner, especially if you sit near the trickling indoor fountain or on the sheltered outdoor patio. It's a peaceful refuge from bustling Fifth Avenue, with unobtrusive service and calming earth-toned decor. The wide-ranging menu is designed to please just about everyone. Top selections for carnivores are the excellent lamb stews (the red-hot vindaloo with ginger is a standout) and the moist tandoori-style chicken prepared in a real tandoor oven. Vegetarians will be delighted with a choice of more than 20 meat-free dishes, especially the curries and the delicious purée of fresh spinach. And everyone should love the breads, especially a garlicky naan that's just right for sopping up any last bits of sauce. Prices have gone up in the past year or so, but the best deal here is still a luncheon buffet for around $9; it's all-you-can-eat and includes basmati rice, various stews and curries, condiments, soups, and that terrific tandoori chicken. *$$; AE, DIS, MC, V; no checks; lunch, dinner every day; beer and wine, reservations recommended; self parking; www. bombayrestaurant.com; map:N2* &

## The Brigantine / ★★

 **2725 SHELTER ISLAND DR, SHELTER ISLAND (AND BRANCHES); 619/224-2871** San Diego's nicest restaurant chain offers multiple locations and a crowd-pleasing menu heavy on fresh seafood. Decor might be called Nautical Fern Bar, with dark wood, a fireplace, America's Cup memorabilia, and friendly fresh-faced servers. Young singles, early-bird retirees, and entire families gather in Brig bars, dining rooms, and patios from Old Town to Del Mar. Steaks, pastas, and the chicken tequila are best bets if you don't care for fish. Otherwise, take advantage of the fresh swordfish, salmon, mahi mahi, and ono grilled or broiled. Both the shrimp cocktail and the deep-fried coconut-crusted shrimp are first rate. Dinners include a choice of soup or salad (the Italian/blue cheese house dressing is outstanding) and rice pilaf or baked potato. Fish tacos, offered on the bar menu, are some of the best in town. The wine list is extensive and well priced, the hand-shaken margaritas frosty and potent. *$$; AE, CB, DC, MC, V; checks OK; lunch, dinner every day; full bar; reservations recommended; self parking; info@ brigantine.com; www.brigantine.com; map:E7*

## Bully's / ★★★

**1404 CAMINO DEL MAR, DEL MAR; 858/755-1660 / 4401 CAMINO DEL RIO S, MISSION VALLEY; 619/291-2665** Though the atmosphere is not quite the same since California's no-smoking law went into effect (some places are just meant to have clouds), Bully's still exudes plenty of character (and characters). At the Del Mar location, locals and the summer racetrack crowd have been patronizing the dark and clubby restaurant with its deep red booths since the 1960s—making it their preferred haunt for a meat fix. In Mission Valley, the crowd has a definite fondness for sports. The restaurant is near Qualcomm Stadium, and local heroes have been known to fuel up here after games. Another nice touch here is the table for singles at the end of the bar; you needn't eat alone if you don't want to. The full- or half-cut prime rib, filet mignon, New York, porterhouse, and prime top sirloin steaks are renowned among local meat lovers (the prime rib is hand-selected USDA Choice, prime-grade Midwestern, corn-fed aged beef). Both top sirloin and prime rib can be ordered as a combo plate with lobster, crab leg, or shrimp, and every meal comes with soup or salad and baked potato, french fries, rice pilaf, or Spanish rice. Other favorites include the steadfast Bully Burger, French dip, New York steak sandwich, and baby back ribs. Non-bovine eaters can select from various seafood or chicken dishes, or daily specials that might feature fresh sea bass or halibut. The bars are local institutions, particularly during summer. *$$; AE, DC, MC, V; local checks only (Mission Valley); breakfast, lunch, dinner every day (Del Mar); lunch, dinner every day, breakfast Sat–Sun (Mission Valley); full bar; no reservations; self parking; map:GG7* &

## Cafe Athena / ★

**1846 GARNET AVE, PACIFIC BEACH; 858/274-1140** Service has always been the Achilles heel of this comfy, casual Greek eatery in one of Pacific Beach's wood-shingled strip malls, but the food makes up for it. Locals in casual clothes amble in to eat and converse, not to see and be seen. The restaurant's interior, although architecturally uninspired, is gladdened by oil paintings of the Greek isles crowding the walls. In addition to satisfying dishes such as lemon chicken soup (a bit chunky with lots of rice) and cinnamon-laced moussaka with a side of rice pilaf, there are some memorable house specialties. Try the Shrimp Scorpio: shrimp grilled and then baked in a spicy sauce of garlic, olive oil, parsley, and tomatoes. Spinach pastitsio is another house specialty; it's a creamy casserole of penne pasta, spinach, and béchamel sauce. For an appetizer, split an order of four delicately flavored bourekia, fried rolls of phyllo stuffed with flavorful ground lamb, onion, and pine nuts. The hummus, tzatziki, and taramasalata are all inspired. There's a brisk business in takeout and catering service too. *$; AE, CB, DC, DIS, MC, V; no checks; lunch, dinner every day; beer and wine; reservations recommended for 6 or more; self parking; map:KK7* &

## Cafe Japengo / ★★

**8960 UNIVERSITY CENTER LN, LA JOLLA; 858/450-3355** Owned by the adjacent Hyatt Regency La Jolla, Cafe Japengo is one of the most stylish and sophisticated restaurants in San Diego County, catering to the unabashedly trendy who relish attitude along with their order. (On weekend nights in particular, the young professional crowd pours in for drinks, sushi, and a serious singles scene.) The decor is a marvelous combination of industrial chic, Asian design, and California cliché—exposed-duct ceilings, Japanese-pebble flooring, Chinese paper lanterns, bamboo, birds-of-paradise, an exhibition kitchen, and showpiece sushi bar. The menu is well coordinated with the environment—an eclectic blend of Asian inspiration and North and South American influences. Dinners include an excellent green-tea-smoked salmon paired with pearly Israeli couscous, slow-roasted duck served moo-shu style with plum sauce and tortillas, glistening pot stickers to be dipped in cilantro pesto, and 10-ingredient wok-fried rice. For dessert, exotic gelatos in flavors like red bean or green tea make refreshing palate cleansers. *$$$; AE, DC, DIS, MC, V; no checks; lunch Mon–Fri, dinner every day; full bar; reservations recommended; valet and self parking; www.cafejapengo.com; map:II6 W*

## Cafe Pacifica / ★★½

**2414 SAN DIEGO AVE, OLD TOWN; 619/291-6666** When it opened in 1980, Cafe Pacifica was one of the first places in town to offer exotic dishes like New Zealand green-lipped mussels. Today, this culinary pioneer continues to present fresh, carefully prepared versions of everything from catfish to seafood-studded pastas. The clam chowder makes a fine starter, as does a portobello mushroom stuffed with crab. Signature dishes include lobster bouillabaisse, seared ahi (often served with a ginger butter), and crab-stuffed sole. And don't miss the crème brûlée for dessert; it's one of the best in the area. Best seating is in the upper dining room, which has an airy, patiolike ambiance, though the see-and-be-seen crowd prefers to be seated by the front door. Although the place has a sophisticated menu with wine prices to match, there's no need to dress up; service and ambiance are pretty low-key. Take advantage of the valet service, as parking is notoriously tight in this tourist-heavy neighborhood. *$$; AE, DC, DIS, MC, V; no checks; dinner every day; full bar; reservations recommended; valet and street parking; www.cafepacifica.com; map:J2*

## Cafe 222 / ★★

**222 ISLAND AVE, DOWNTOWN; 619/236-9902** "The man who gets breakfast in bed is probably in the hospital," reads the menu at this irreverent egg-and-waffle eatery, run by the imaginative Terry Gavre. The cafe is tiny—a corner storefront with a half dozen tables and whimsical chandeliers made of teacups and spoons. The menu is hearty: "big, thick, golden brown waffles" are irresistible—we're especially fond of the five-grain and pumpkin versions. The kids' pancake is "supposed to look like Mickey Mouse, but often looks like a pig or small dog." Despite the lighthearted prose and the rubber chickens hanging on the wall, the food is great and attracts a waiting line of hungry downtowners. For breakfast, order Joe's special—"a frittata-ish thing with toast." For lunch, choose grilled turkey, goat cheese, and pesto on rosemary focaccia or one of 222's other trendy sandwiches. A smaller breakfast menu is served until closing time. Gavre writes restaurant reviews and is always hip to the local dining scene. *$; cash only; breakfast, lunch every day; no alcohol; no reservations; street parking; www.cafe222.com; map:N8*

## Cafe W / ★★★

**3680 6TH AVE, HILLCREST; 619/291-0200** This snazzy new restaurant is a dream come true, both for foodies and for chef/owner Chris Walsh. Walsh, who spent more than a decade as the executive chef at California Cuisine, opened Cafe W in late 2001 to immediate acclaim. Created as a reflection of the way he himself likes to dine—grazing on a variety of little items—Walsh's dining room features about 40 "small plates," or appetizer servings. Just about everything on the menu is appealing, but our current faves are the rare, marinated steak served over citrus-dressed greens; grilled sweetbreads accompanied by mushroom duxelles and truffle oil; crab cakes (blended with scallops) served with a curry-garlic coleslaw; and mussels steamed in coconut milk. Most of the beautifully presented dishes are priced well under $10. The setting oozes style, from the well-spaced tables and shiny steel fireplace to the servers dressed in fitted T-shirts and camouflage pants. The wine list is short, but long on unusual choices such as New Zealand Pinot Noir and Rueda, a Spanish white; for beer drinkers, there's Guinness on tap. In addition to the main dining room, front and back patios offer alfresco dining. *$$; AE, MC, V, no checks; dinner Wed–Mon; beer and wine; reservations recommended; street parking; map: N3* &

## Cafe Zinc / ★★

**132 S CEDROS AVE, SOLANA BEACH; 858/793-5436** The first eatery to set up shop in the Cedros Design District was destined to be a hit just by virtue of location. The fact that the food is terrific is a happy bonus. Though several tables are positioned indoors, dining is mainly alfresco on the people-watching front patio, in the sunny side area, or in the reclusive rear yard (where tables teeter precariously atop gravel). Feel free to bring well-mannered dogs; there's almost always a laid-back Lab or bright-eyed terrier accompanying a doting owner here. Breakfast items run from simple bagels and muffins to oatmeal with sour cherry and nut topping to frittata with cucumber salsa; ever-comforting fruit crisp or bread pudding is available on weekends. Lunch entrees, salad samplers, and specialty soups change daily, and all creations are meatless. Good bets are the vegetarian Zinc burger and the colorful mixed vegetable sandwich (pain rustique filled with thinly sliced fennel, aioli, red and green bell peppers, radish, celery, arugula, hard-boiled egg, olive tapenade, and vinaigrette). Personal pizzas are nouvelle hard-liners with pesto, Mexican, or Southwestern toppings. *$; no credit cards; checks OK; breakfast, lunch every day; no alcohol; no reservations; self parking; map:FF7* &

## Cafe Zucchero / ★★½

**1731 INDIA ST, DOWNTOWN; 619/531-1731** Arguably the best Italian restaurant in Little Italy, Cafe Zucchero gets the nod for stylish decor, pleasant service, and some outstanding dishes. The place is small but inviting, with marble tables and floors inside, a few tables on the sidewalk, and a charming patio out back. Lunch is this cafe's strong point, and diners in the know order the panini (sandwiches) filled with grilled vegetables and Gorgonzola or chicken and feta cheese. On the lighter side, the kitchen also turns out appealing salads and a nice assortment of antipasti. At night, go for pastas: either the veggie-packed primavera or the salmon-stuffed shells nestled in a creamy sauce. And save room for dessert: they make marvelous cannoli here, and the cafe is famous throughout town for its expertly made gelati. The smooth, intense Italian ice cream comes in classic flavors including hazelnut, chocolate, vanilla, and mascarpone. Sit out on the patio on a sunny day, and you might as well be in Siena. *$; AE, DIS, MC, V; no checks; breakfast, lunch, dinner every day; beer and wine; no reservations; street parking; map:M6* &

## California Cuisine / ★★

**1027 UNIVERSITY AVE, HILLCREST; 619/543-0790** As the name implies, this chic little Hillcrest dining room was one of the first in town to showcase the signature flavors of California-style cuisine. Although longtime chef Chris Walsh has moved on (opening his own Cafe W in 2001), the restaurant still serves up an ever-changing menu based on local seasonal produce, fresh fish, and imaginative com-

*Cafe Sevilla · 555 4th Ave 92101*
*La Tapas Bar*

binations of flavor and texture. Stalwarts of the menu include a warm chicken salad prepared with pleasingly bitter greens and a creamy seafood pasta usually made with mussels and rock shrimp. The dining room is sleek and stylish, accented with contemporary art, floral arrangements, and a great-looking clientele. Out back, a multilevel patio decorated with greenery and fountains offers one of the coziest retreats in town for a leisurely lunch or dinner. *$$$; AE, DC, DIS, MC, V; no checks; lunch Tues–Fri, dinner Tues–Sun; beer and wine, reservations recommended; street parking; map: N2* &

## ✓ Candelas / ★★

**416 3RD AVE, DOWNTOWN; 619/702-4455** This lovely Mexican restaurant is plenty pricey, but worth a visit for gourmets in search of something out of the ordinary. Candelas (Spanish for candles, which decorate the dining rooms and bar) features the distinctive haute cuisine of Mexico City, former home of chef Eduardo Baeza as well as the restaurant's owners. The food often feels more French than Latin American, but the telltale flavors of various chiles, mole sauces, and Mexican cheeses remind diners that this is still authentic south-of-the-border cooking. Baeza has a special flair for seafood, and to miss his signature stuffed lobster tail flavored with jalapeños and aged tequila would be a shame. Other highlights of the menu are the superb mahi mahi (topped with an intriguingly nutty cheese and garnished with white wine cream) and a beautiful dessert combo of chocolate-coffee torte and raspberry sorbet. Decor is sophisticated hacienda, with soft lighting, lots of framed mirrors, rustic furniture, and folk art. Along with the main dining room, Candelas offers a spacious private room and separate bar that attracts a lively late-night crowd on the weekends. There's a fine selection of wines by the bottle, but by-the-glass selections are few and overpriced. Service is attentive but not pushy, and guests are welcome to linger over dessert and espresso until they request their check. *$$$; AE, DC, DIS, MC, V; no checks; lunch Mon–Fri, dinner every day; full bar; reservations recommended; self parking; map: N8* &

## Cass Street Bar & Grill / ★★

**4612 CASS ST, PACIFIC BEACH; 858/270-1320** No fussy yuppie bar this. Cass Street Bar and Grill caters to locals, who drop by for the camaraderie, the pool tables, the connoisseur's beer selection, and the best bar fare at the beach. Burgers are a customer favorite, and those in the know choose a topping of sautéed onions and melted cheese. The chicken sandwich decorated with avocado and served on a baguette is pretty impressive, and there's a reason that huge marlin is hanging on the wall: the fish is great. Get a fish taco platter with grilled or fried fish, or the fresh fish of the day served with two side dishes, and you'll have plenty to cheer about besides the low prices, microbrews, and congenial crowd. Lose the tie and the high heels before you drop by; this is a shorts and T-shirt kind of a place. *$; cash only; breakfast, lunch, dinner every day; beer and wine; no reservations; street parking; map:KK7* &

## Cecil's Cafe & Fish Market / ★★☆

**5083 SANTA MONICA AVE, OCEAN BEACH; 619/222-0501** Even if this ultracasual cafe with the weathered, lived-in look weren't right across from the beach, we'd come here often. (Of course, the unobstructed views of surfers, seagulls, and the Ocean Beach Pier are a nice touch, as is the westerly sea breeze you get at the outside tables.) Diners of all ages jam the place during weekend breakfasts—arguably the best meal of the day here—to feast on good old-timey oatmeal, spicy Mexican egg scrambles, substantial pancakes, and Belgian waffles. The coffee refills are timely, the short-order cooks fast, and the wait staff friendly. At dinner, choose the lobster bisque, the excellent chili, or one of the simply prepared seafood dishes or sandwiches. Parking can be difficult, so be prepared to park on a side street and walk at least a block or two. Watch for no-parking signs that mention specific street-cleaning days; you don't want a ticket to ruin such a laid-back, beachy experience. *$; AE, CB, DC, DIS, MC, V; no checks; breakfast, dinner every day; full bar; reservations recommended; street parking; map:B2* &

## Chart House / ★

**525 HARBOR DR, DOWNTOWN (AND BRANCHES); 619/233-7391** Weary conventioneers rely on soothing breaks at this dependable steak and seafood restaurant perched atop 30 wood pilings above San Diego Bay. The peaked-roof white building was dedicated as headquarters for the San Diego Rowing Club in 1900; club members held firm to their home until 1974, when they moved to Mission Bay. The Chart House chain then renovated the sagging building into a charming restaurant filled with nautical memorabilia. The prime rib, grilled fish, seared ahi, salad bar, and warm chocolate lava cake are the menu's best offerings. Though the quality of the cooking doesn't match that of other downtown steak houses, the views of the bay and nostalgic setting are worth a visit and a sunset drink. *$$$; AE, CB, DC, DIS, MC, V; no checks; dinner every day; full bar; reservations recommended; self parking; map:N9* &

## The Cheese Shop / ★

**627 4TH AVE, DOWNTOWN; 619/232-2303 / 2165 AVENIDA DE LA PLAYA, LA JOLLA; 858/459-3921** Can a downtown restaurant thrive on the simple premise of putting thinly sliced meats between two slices of bread? The Cheese Shop can because it makes every sandwich into a teetering tower of Dagwoodian generosity. Heaps of roasted-on-the-premises turkey breast or rare beef aren't enough: the sandwich makers here love adding at least another inch of fresh avocado, plus plenty of tomato, onion, and lettuce. In short, the slippery, fresh, gooey "works." Imported and domestic cheeses allow you to customize sandwiches to a higher gourmet standard. Ask owner Dave for his thoughts on peanut butter sandwiches (he likes 'em with Dijon mustard!). Lunchtime here is a scene: suited executives next to blue-jeaned artists. Each knows this is the best value in the Gaslamp. The La Jolla location is a great place to pick up a quick lunch for a beach picnic. *$; AE, MC, V; local checks only; breakfast, lunch every day; beer and wine; no reservations; street parking; map: N8 and JJ7* &

## Chez Loma / ★★★

**1132 LOMA AVE, CORONADO; 619/435-0661** Before you even enter this restaurant, you'll be charmed by the handsome Victorian house and old-money elegance of the Coronado neighborhood. Inside, chef Ken Irvine's graceful mix of classic and updated French cuisine is sure to impress. The small menu emphasizes seasonal seafood and usually includes stellar preparations of duck, salmon, and filet mignon (including a signature steak in a heady blue cheese sauce). The servers here are particularly well trained—always available when needed, but never intrusive. Add a carefully chosen wine list, romantic enclosed patio, and very fair prices for the quality, and you've got one of Coronado's most delightful eateries. It's an especially good choice for couples celebrating anniversaries. Although children are welcome, this is one of the more grown-up-feeling establishments in town. *$$–$$$; AE, DC, DIS, MC, V; no checks; dinner every day, brunch Sun; full bar; reservations recommended; street parking; www.chezloma.com; map:NN5*

## Chilango's Mexico City Grill / ★★

**142 UNIVERSITY AVE, HILLCREST; 619/294-8646** Some of the most interesting and authentic Mexican fare in San Diego is served here in the heart of Hillcrest. The restaurant is small and so are the prices, but the flavors are big, bold, and irresistible. Bring an asbestos palate for the super-spicy chicken-tortilla soup, a particular favorite here (for something milder, choose the black bean porridge). Move on to entrees such as roasted chicken, distinctively flavored with citrus juice and achiote paste; huaraches (thick corn tortillas topped with pork, salsa, and Mexican cheese); and chilaquiles, the comfort-food casserole fashioned from tortillas, chicken, onion, and cilantro. Need a palate quencher? Sample the fresh fruit salad laced with lime juice and cilantro, and you'll never touch fruit cocktail again. *$; DIS, MC, V; lunch, dinner Tues–Sun; no alcohol; no reservations; street parking; map:N2*

## Crest Cafe / ★

**425 ROBINSON AVE, HILLCREST; 619/295-2510** Although prices have been creeping up over the years, the funky Crest Cafe remains a favorite destination for upscale but reasonable diner fare in enormous portions. The lengthy menu is best known for its burger selection: juicy, jumbo-size patties with imaginative toppings and excellent french fries on the side. Other specialties include the grilled vegetable sandwich, spicy Mexican machaca, and the notorious onion loaf (think of thin, lightly battered onion rings baked in a meatloaf pan). Bonus: the cafe is open until midnight, a plus in this town that tends to close down early, and the energetic staff is always cheerful. Tables are close together and eavesdropping is unavoidable, but with this collection of young and old, gay and straight, liberal and conservative, the listening is just as good as the food. *$; AE, DIS, MC, V; no checks; breakfast, lunch, dinner every day; beer and wine; reservations recommended; street parking; www.crestcafe.com; map:N2*

## Dave & Buster's / ★★

**2931 CAMINO DEL RIO N, MISSION VALLEY; 619/280-7115** Fun's the name of the game at this popular restaurant–bar–game arcade, part of a large nationwide chain. Although the dozens of video games, sports simulators, and classic pastimes like Skee-ball attract lots of families, D&B's actually caters to the over-21 crowd. The food and service both tend to be excellent, with a welcoming, hardworking staff and an ambitious menu that runs from nibbles to full-scale noshes. A few of our favorite plates: crisp bacon-topped potato skins, a shiitake-avocado quesadilla, falling-off-the-bone pork ribs, halibut-stuffed fish tacos, and a generous cut of rib-eye steak. Other excellent choices: the unusual Cobb salad topped with spicy, batter-fried chicken fingers; the Philly cheesesteak sandwich; and the moist grilled mahi mahi. For dessert, both the Key lime pie and the chilled bananas Foster dessert are worthwhile. In addition to a small wine list, D&B's has several dozen beers and scores of fancy cocktails. Food service is available in the spacious main dining room as well as at the booths and tables scattered throughout the game room. Minors (anyone under 21) must be accompanied by an adult at all times, and the entire place is off limits to minors after 10pm nightly (11pm during the summer). *$–$$; AE, DC, DIS, MC, V; no checks; lunch, dinner every day; full bar; no reservations; valet and self parking; www.daveandbusters.com; map: LL4* &

## Delicias / ★★★

**6106 PASEO DELICIAS, RANCHO SANTA FE; 858/756-8000** Named for the tony street that runs through Rancho Santa Fe's chic village center, Delicias is definitely a celebrity on the San Diego County dining scene. For one thing, it's drop-dead gorgeous, and not a single designer touch has been neglected. Spectacular flower arrangements punctuate the bar and adjacent dining room, which is bedecked with intricate tapestries. The place even has miniature footstools for ladies' purses, so that Vuitton bag never has to be slung over a chair. The visibly affluent, well-groomed clientele comes as much for the scene as for the cuisine, and you'd better not walk in unless you're dressed to impress and ready to turn heads. The cuisine defies easy description, but tends to be a well-balanced mix of new California and classic French. The kitchen has a winning way with fish, and regulars here have learned that you can never go wrong with any of the seafood specials. Swordfish, salmon, escolar, and ahi make regular appearances, generally grilled and served with anything from tropical fruit salsa to polenta to garlic- or truffle-mashed potatoes. Hearty risottos are another specialty, and if they're serving the oversize veal chop, go for it. Desserts are simpler than the rest of the menu, with homey selections like apple bread pudding or "chocolate baby cakes." Prime seating is at the bar near the entrance, at the edges of the grand dining room, or on the flower-filled patio near the wood-burning fireplace. Definitely a place for those with Dom Perignon tastes and titanium credit cards, this gorgeous restaurant is a delicious find indeed. *$$$; AE, CB, DC, DIS, MC, V; no checks; dinner every day; full bar; reservations recommended; self parking; map:EE5* &

## Del Mar Pizza / ★★

**211 15TH ST, DEL MAR; 858/481-8088** A neon sign posted in the window of this simple storefront operation proclaims Tony the proprietor "King of the Crust." New Yorkers homesick for real pizza pies, as well as anyone just wondering what all the fuss is about, make a beeline for this Del Mar hideaway, with its dozen or so little tables covered in red-and-white-checkered cloths. Even the most critical aficionados agree the pizza tastes like the real thing as they munch away on that fabulous crisp crust, served with classic ingredients including sausage, pepperoni, and baby anchovies called alici. The pizzas come in small or large, and cheese or pepperoni pies are available by the slice. Other menu items include straightforward stuffed eggplant parmigiana, lasagne, pastas, hot sandwiches, and Italian subs. Tony used to have a sign reading, "I'm open when I'm ready. I'm closed when I'm tired." But too many customers would rather starve than go elsewhere, so his hours are as steady as his pizzas are dependably delicious. *$; cash only; lunch, dinner every day; beer and wine; no reservations; street parking; map:GG7*

## Dobson's Bar & Restaurant / ★★★

**956 BROADWAY CIRCLE, DOWNTOWN; 619/231-6771** One of San Diego's classiest watering holes, Dobson's has a big-city ambiance and a clientele to match. Downstairs, the local mover-and-shaker crowd congregates at the polished bar for well-made martinis and smart conversation. Upstairs, a smallish dining room offers marvelous American and French cuisine. Specialties of the house include a rich-as-sin mussel bisque flavored with lobster stock and crowned with puff pastry, sautéed sweetbreads with a texture "like buttah," fresh fish specials, and rack of lamb. For lunch, try the Greek salad or the soup du jour, along with several refills of the warm house sourdough. This is a popular place for pre-theater dining and a good destination for a business lunch or dinner. The favored tables are upstairs overlooking the ever-bustling bar (where you can also dine). For a romantic evening, request the tiny upstairs alcove that's perfect for two. *$$; AE, CB, DC, MC, V; no checks; lunch Mon–Fri, dinner Mon–Sat; full bar; reservations recommended; self parking; map:N7*

## Downtown Johnny Brown's / ★★☆

**1220 3RD AVE, DOWNTOWN; 619/232-8414** Comfortable, casual, and cool, Johnny's is a roll-up-your-shirtsleeves, shoot-some-pool-over-lunch kind of place. The perennially popular bar and grill overlooks the plaza of the busy community concourse, a center for activities ranging from purebred cat shows to opera premieres. Lots of local office folks come by for lunch or happy hour as well. That leads to a pretty eclectic crowd at Johnny's, and everybody knows the drill: line up, place your order at the counter, then snag a table inside or on the patio. When your meal's ready, they'll call you. Good-size burgers are hot sellers here, and come with a mountain of french fries so tasty it's worth trying to eat them all. Grilled chicken and taco salads are a sure bet too, and if they're serving grilled ahi, go for it—it's awesome. The setting is nothing fancy, but there's a rockin' loud jukebox and plenty of great beer on tap and by the bottle. *$; AE, DIS, MC, V; no checks; lunch, dinner every day; full bar; no reservations; street parking; downtownjohnnybrowns@hotmail. com; map:N7*

## D. Z. Akin's / ★★☆

**6930 ALVARADO RD, LA MESA; 619/265-0218** When it comes to delicatessens, San Diego is no New York or Los Angeles. Luckily, there's D. Z.
Akin's, which legions of fans consider the best deli in town. Owners Debbie
and Zvika Akin have created a deli faithful to the classic model: leatherette booths,
a crock of dill pickles on every table, hardworking waitresses, and a dizzying lineup
of sandwiches, smoked fish, entrees, and desserts. The piled-high triple-decker sandwiches here have been known to make first-time visitors gasp, and even the regular-
size sandwiches can stupefy those with smaller appetites. Sharing the spotlight with
pastrami on rye are matzo ball soup, excellent knishes, and chopped liver. The
casual, bustling atmosphere attracts lots of families, and it's not uncommon to see
three or four generations seated at the Formica tables. On your way out, check out
the bakery and counter area for sliced meats and cheeses, salads, side dishes, and
freshly baked breads and pastries to go. *$$; AE, MC, V; no checks; breakfast, lunch,
dinner every day; beer and wine; reservations recommended for 6 or more; self
parking; map:LL2* ㅎ

## El Agave / ★★★

**2304 SAN DIEGO AVE, OLD TOWN; 619/220-0692** Notorious for its incredible
selection of fine tequilas, El Agave is also considered the city's top destination for
regional Mexican cuisine. It's a welcome change from most of the other eateries in
Old Town, where gringo-style chimichangas and gooey enchiladas reign. This is the
place to savor real mole sauce ladled over chicken or pork (the dark, smoky mole
poblano here is a standout), rarely seen Mexican soups (the squash soup shouldn't
be missed), and other artful dishes, including quesadillas stuffed with vegetables,
Mexican cheeses, or shredded seasoned poultry. Force us to choose a favorite and it
would be the marinated shrimp tossed with beans, cactus strips, and orange. For
dessert, authentic versions of flan, a custardlike dish, showcase the sweeter side of
Latin cuisine. Now, about that tequila: the restaurant offers more than 100 varieties
by the shot, ranging in price from around $4 for familiar brands to well over $100
for rare aged tequilas smoother than old sippin' whiskey. *$$; AE, MC, V; no checks;
lunch, dinner every day; full bar; reservations recommended; self parking; www.el
agaverestaurant.com; map:J2*

## El Bizcocho / ★★★

**17550 BERNARDO OAKS DR (RANCHO BERNARDO INN), RANCHO BERNARDO;
858/675-8500** One of the most consistent dining rooms in the county, El Bizcocho
charms diners with artful service, gifted chefs, and understated elegance. The spacious room evokes an upmarket country inn, with a fireplace, well-spaced tables,
and a view of the carefully groomed golf course. Updated French cuisine has always
been a signature here, with classics like escargot topped with puff pastry and quickly
seared foie gras sharing billing with more innovative creations. Depending on the
season, these inventions could be fingertip-size scallops arranged on ravioli and driz-
zled with vanilla, or a napoleon of lobster and caviar amid layers of phyllo. Fresh
fish is treated with special reverence, so don't miss the roasted monkfish (garnished
with black truffles and wild mushrooms) or sautéed John Dory paired with fennel

and tiny potatoes. Roasted free-range chicken and braised duckling paired with fresh fruit are other standouts. Order the dessert soufflés at the beginning of a meal, and they'll arrive airy and perfect, right on schedule, just as you're ready for espresso. Waiters are personable yet professional and the wine list is superb, with several hundred top-notch brands from California and France from which to choose. An adjoining bar often features live piano music, providing an extra touch of class to this stately hacienda. Sunday brunch is an elegant affair, worth an extra night's stay at the hotel so you can take a proper siesta afterward. *$$$; AE, CB, DC, DIS, MC, V; checks OK; dinner every day, brunch Sun; full bar; reservations recommended; self parking; www.ranchobernardoinn.com; map: FF3* &

## El Indio Shop / ★★

**3695 INDIA ST, MIDDLETOWN; 619/299-0333** In San Diego, the name El Indio is pretty much synonymous with Mexican food. Just about everyone in town knows this little shop, which has built a reputation on tortilla chips, fresh salsa, beef taquitos, and combo plates. The chile-dusted tortilla chips and freshly prepared corn or flour tortillas are favorite souvenirs—locals regularly mail these as care packages to less-fortunate East Coast dwellers. In a nod to the times, a vegetarian menu was added a few years ago, offering surprisingly tasty items such as mashed potato tacos and vegetarian tamales. Dine inside or across the street on a patio in the shadow of Interstate 5. To order, head for the counter, then wait until your number is called. Be prepared at lunch: some days it seems as though everyone in town is lined up and ready to place their order. Catering is available too—many a local wedding reception has featured El Indio selections—and many items on the menu are available refrigerated or frozen for bulk orders. *$; MC, V; checks OK; breakfast, lunch, dinner every day; beer and wine; no reservations; street parking; www.elindio.net; map:L3* &

## Epazote / ★★

**1555 CAMINO DEL MAR, DEL MAR; 858/259-9966** An enduring favorite of the North County see-and-be-seen crowd, Epazote features Southwestern decor and cuisine with an ocean view. The dining room is bright, light, and chic, though most diners clamor for seats on the patio-with-a-view. The vast assortment of tapas grabs top honors, and the wait staff doesn't sniff at those who make a meal out of green corn tamales with lime cream, Dungeness crab corn cakes with chipotle aioli and tropical fruit salsa, shrimp pot stickers, or Navajo flatbread pizza. Favorite entrees include enchiladas suizas topped with tomatillo sauce, an unusual shrimp and scallop enchilada, and the soft taco platter starring your choice of grilled fish, smoked or grilled chicken, or carne asada. Frosty margaritas are the beverage of choice, followed closely by so-called Power Cocktails made with Red Bull and vodka. Service can be leisurely to a fault, but the bar is a happening spot at sunset, and live jazz is featured every Wednesday night. *$$; AE, DC, MC, V; no checks; lunch, dinner every day, brunch Sun; full bar; reservations recommended; valet and self parking; www.epazote.com; map:GG7* &

## Fairouz Restaurant & Gallery / ★

**3166 MIDWAY DR #102, MIDWAY; 619/225-0308** Fairouz is an oasis of fine Greek and Lebanese cuisine and contemporary art in the wasteland of car washes and strip joints that line Midway Drive. Dark blue carpet and wood-grain Formica tables provide a simple backdrop for owner Ibrahim Al Nashashibi's stylized acrylic paintings, which completely fill two dining rooms. Al Nashashibi runs the restaurant with his Moroccan wife; his sister does the cooking. Lovers of Greek food will recognize their favorites, including a very lemony avgolemono (chicken and rice soup), admirable tabbouleh, hummus, tzatziki, and gyros. It's hard to resist the daily lunch and dinner buffets: both are excellent values for carnivores or vegetarians, and a big hit with kids. The problem is, even if you try just half of the offerings in small portions, you come away significantly stuffed. Buffets consist of lots of salad ingredients, hot and cold potatoes, saffron rice, moussaka, lamb meatballs, and much more—in addition to the foods already mentioned. If humanly possible, save room for a dessert of rice pudding with rose water. Fairouz also caters. *$; AE, MC, V; no checks; lunch, dinner every day; beer and wine; no reservations; self parking; map:H2* &

## Fidel's / ★

**607 VALLEY AVE, SOLANA BEACH; 858/755-5292 / 3003 CARLSBAD BLVD, CARLSBAD; 760/729-0903** Unlike the more stalwart Tony's Jacal nearby, Fidel's has a touristy feel and real appeal to anyone who wants Mexican-party ambiance without crossing the border. The sprawl of dining rooms, bars, and patios, combined with Mexican tile, dangling piñatas, and norteño music, all contribute to the atmosphere. Accordingly, the place is a frenzied mélange of first dates, celebratory groups, families, and fair and racetrack goers, not counting the buoyant students and surfers who show up for happy hour and the cheap taco bar. Standard Mexican favorites top the menu and nachos remain the appetizer of choice. Specialties include various renditions of chiles rellenos, carne and chicken asada, tortas, and tostadas. For something different, try nopales (nopal cactus in a spicy tomato and chile serrano sauce, topped with Monterey Jack cheese), or pescado ranchero (grilled dorado, topped with semispicy ranchero sauce). Burgers and fries are at the ready for kids, and logo T-shirts and baseball caps are for sale. At the newer Fidel's Norte in Carlsbad, prime dining is on the sunny patio. *$–$$; MC, V; no checks; breakfast, lunch, dinner every day; full bar; reservations recommended for 8 or more; self parking; map:FF7 and CC8*

## Filippi's Pizza Grotto / ★

**1747 INDIA ST, DOWNTOWN (AND BRANCHES); 619/232-5094** Mom and Pop are long gone, but seven sisters and brothers run this string of dependable Italian restaurants, situated all over San Diego. The original is in Little Italy and is the only one with a store. (That's how Filippi's began.) To enter, customers file past cases of cheese, sliced meats, a barrel of salted and filleted cod, breads from three bakeries, oils, vinegars, and every kind of pasta imaginable. The fragrance is overwhelmingly Parmesan. The restaurant itself is large, with an open kitchen and pizza oven, grotto-dark and busy-noisy. Tables are covered with red-checked cloths; Chianti bottles (hundreds, maybe thousands) hang from the rafters. The same theme prevails in other Filippi's locations in Pacific Beach and outlying neighborhoods. Specialties are lasagne, pizza, ravioli, spaghetti, hot sausage (made on the premises), and a variety of sandwiches on freshly crisp buns. Servings are ample; most diners leave with leftovers. Customers are clearly regulars, addressed by name by waitresses who seem to have been there forever. *$; AE, DC, DIS, MC, V; no checks; lunch, dinner every day; beer and wine; no reservations; self parking (downtown); map:M6* &

## Fio's Cucina Italiana / ★★

**801 5TH AVE, DOWNTOWN; 619/234-3467** Fio's is both culinary landmark and downtown pioneer. It opened on a lonely corner in the Gaslamp Quarter more than a decade ago, long before the run-down neighborhood blossomed into a popular nighttime destination. While its upscale Italianate menu has been much copied by surrounding restaurants, Fio's still draws a faithful crowd that includes the occasional celebrity. Pastas rule the roost; both the wild mushroom ravioli and ravioli stuffed with pumpkin and squash are consistently good. There's a reliable chicken pesto dish too, and the kitchen is adept with seared salmon and peppery rare-cooked ahi. (Skip the lamb chops and the tiramisu, however.) The back dining rooms tend to be crowded and a bit noisy; ask to sit near the windows or out on the sidewalk patio for a more enjoyable evening. Along with a full bar, Fio's offers a fair wine selection, including some gorgeous Tuscan reds like Sassicaia. *$$; AE, CB, DC, DIS, MC, V; no checks; dinner every day; full bar; reservations recommended; valet and street parking; fiosfios@aol.com; www.fiositalian.com; map:O7* &

## Fish Market Restaurant / ★★
## Top of the Market / ★★

**750 N HARBOR DR, DOWNTOWN; 619/232-3474** The panoramic views of San Diego Bay are as much an attraction as the huge menu of fresh catches at the Fish Market Restaurant and its upstairs, upscale sister, Top of the Market. Downstairs you'll find a full-service bar, a busy oyster bar, a counter displaying fresh fish to go, and the friendly, casual Fish Market Restaurant. Be prepared to wait for a table (have a drink in the bar or visit the oyster bar for an appetizer). Seating overlooks the bay; the best tables are the ones on the outdoor patio, directly over the water. The menu features a huge selection of fresh-caught seafood prepared grilled, Cajun style, or fried, according to your preference. Fish is served with a side of rice or au gratin potatoes (a sinfully delicious choice) and steaming hot sourdough bread. For the money and bustling ambiance, the downstairs restaurant is the better bet. Upstairs, the more formal Top of the Market serves more exotic fresh seafood with more refined presentation and service and price tags to match. The list of offerings is astounding; you can tour the seven seas with Norwegian salmon, Alaskan halibut, New Zealand mussels, and Chilean sea bass, all flown in daily. The linen and candlelight setting is sublimely soothing; window tables present a romantic view of twinkling lights on boats floating in the bay. The wine list is excellent; servers will assist in matching grape and sea flavors. *$$ (Fish Market) $$$ (Top of the Market); AE, CB, DC, DIS, MC, V; no checks; lunch, dinner every day; full bar; reservations recommended for large groups; valet and self parking; map:M7* &

## French Pastry Shop / ★★

**5550 LA JOLLA BLVD, LA JOLLA; 858/454-9094** Reminiscent of neighborhood bakeries in Montparnasse or the Marais, this delightful restaurant features sit-down dining as well as a large takeout selection. Possible picnic fixings range from excellent pâtés (the coarse country variety is a standout) and a dozen types of bread to imported cheeses, assorted pastries, and gorgeous desserts. In addition to the informal dining room, there's an enclosed sidewalk patio that's just right for leisurely weekend breakfasts (our favorite meal here). Sit down with some good strong coffee, a selection of breakfast rolls or a fines herbes omelet (filled with fresh herbs like chervil, chives, parsley, and tarragon) and some of the cafe's fresh jam—then daydream your way all the way to the Right Bank. *$$; MC, V; checks OK; breakfast, lunch, dinner every day (closes by 6pm Mon); beer and wine; no reservations; self parking; www.frenchpastryshop.com; map:KK7*

## George's at the Cove / ★★★

**1250 PROSPECT ST, LA JOLLA; 858/454-4244** This popular restaurant on La Jolla's chic Prospect Street has been making local top-10 dining lists for more than a decade. Without a doubt, the three-level property has one of the finest views in the city—a panorama of La Jolla Cove and miles of Pacific coast. But unlike many a view restaurant in town, George's offers some terrific eating as well. The formal downstairs dining room is best for inventive fresh fish dishes that incorporate the flavors of California, France, and the Pacific Rim. The must-have starter is a smoked chicken and broccoli soup that's probably the most-requested recipe in the county (and yes, they'll share it). Follow that with the likes of crab cakes with shiitake "hash browns," diver-harvested scallops partnered with lobster risotto, or duck breast paired with buttery foie gras. Upstairs, in the bar (a top destination for singles) and on the rooftop terrace, the menu is a lower-priced affair that features excellent seafood salads, a gourmet meatloaf sandwich, very good focaccia, and splendid desserts. Two more reasons to drop by: the ever-changing collection of contemporary art in the main dining rooms, and owner George Hauer's thoughtfully chosen wine list. Note: Reservations aren't accepted on the upstairs terrace, which is open daily for lunch and dinner, but the open-air setting and throngs of swell-looking diners make it worth the wait. *$$–$$$; AE, DC, DIS, MC, V; no checks; lunch, dinner every day; full bar; reservations recommended downstairs; valet parking; www.georgesatthecove.com; map:JJ7* &

## The Grant Grill / ★★★

**326 BROADWAY (U.S. GRANT HOTEL), DOWNTOWN; 619/232-3121** With its dark-paneled walls, quaint hunting prints, and formally clad waiters, the Grant Grill resembles an old-fashioned gentlemen's club. Indeed, this hotel dining room, opened in 1910, once barred females from entering before 3pm. That all changed in 1969, when a group of San Diego women demanded a table for lunch. Since then, the restaurant has alternately thrived and languished as executive chefs have arrived, made their mark on the menu, and departed. These days, the Grant is on an upswing again, serving breakfast, lunch, and dinner items that are both generous and appealing. French toast made with banana bread, a delicious Monte Cristo sandwich served with a tangy berry sauce, a perfect Caesar salad, buttery seared foie gras with apples, and grilled wild salmon are just a few of the success stories we've sampled recently. Despite the changes in the kitchen over the past few years, the service remains consistently good, with an old-fashioned, courtly feel. The spacious booths are generally filled with businesspeople at lunch and concert- or opera-goers at night, so dress up a bit. An adjacent bar is every bit as handsome as the dining room, though it's modern enough to sport a wide-screen TV. The bar also offers a selection of sandwiches, pizzas, and salads for under $10. *$$$; AE, CB, DC, DIS, MC, V; checks OK; breakfast, lunch, dinner every day; full bar; reservations recommended; valet and self parking; map:N7 W*

## Greek Islands Cafe / ★★☆

**879 W HARBOR DR (SEAPORT VILLAGE), DOWNTOWN; 619/239-5216** Should you find yourself in tourist mecca Seaport Village, you're largely better off shopping than eating. Fortunately, there are a few exceptions to this rule. The friendly service and sunny bayfront patio at this modest Greek restaurant are bright enough to attract locals on their lunch hours, as well as out-of-towners with a yen for good gyros and pita bread. In addition to fat, juicy gyros and chicken sandwiches, the cafe offers a generous Greek salad and several combo plates. Order at the counter, then pick up your meal and choose a picnic table outside—or simply sit on the waterfront wall along the boardwalk. It's the best show around, with joggers, dog walkers, Rollerbladers, and conventioneers—not to mention a fabulous view of the harbor for the price of a $5 sandwich. *$; cash only; lunch, dinner every day; beer and wine; no reservations; self parking; www.greekislandscafe.com; map:M8* ⅋

## Gulf Coast Grill / ★★

**4130 PARK BLVD, UNIVERSITY HEIGHTS; 619/295-2244** If you like feisty, fun-loving Cajun food, head to Gulf Coast Grill, home to some mighty fine Southern cooking. This good-looking eatery captivates on a number of levels. There's the spacious dining area: a two-level arrangement with golden walls, whimsical fish sculptures, and paintings of jazz musicians. There's the convivial bar, home to expertly mixed martinis and more than a dozen food-friendly beers. And, of course, there's the hot stuff coming out of the kitchen, guaranteed to send you on a quick taste trip to the Big Easy. For starters, the barbecued shrimp in the shell are a messy must-have (dip into the spicy herb butter for maximum flavor). Signature entrees are pasta with fiery blackened prawns, smoked pork chops, and homey breaded catfish. Dessert, anyone? Might as well get fat on the bourbon-sloshed bread pudding. Mmmm good. *$$; AE, CB, DC, DIS, MC , V; no checks; lunch, dinner every day, brunch Sun; full bar; reservations recommended; street parking; gulfcoastgrill@cox.net; www.gulf coastgrill.com; map:P1* ⅋

## Hamburger Mary's / ★

**308 UNIVERSITY AVE, HILLCREST; 619/491-0400** There's rarely a dull moment at this Hillcrest watering hole, where a lively, largely gay crowd drops in for dining, drinking, and socializing. Given the name, it's no surprise that hamburgers dominate the menu, with about a dozen toppings and variations on tap. They're always dependable, but other highlights of the menu are the chicken breast sandwiches, the onion rings, and several salads (who could resist the "Carmen Miranda," a fruit number served in a pineapple shell?). Sunday brunch draws fans of the custom-made omelets, desserts, and free-flowing coffee, orange juice, and bubbly. Prime seating is on the patio, where people-watching is every bit as important as dining—maybe more so. At the adjacent Kickers bar, weekly events include karaoke, country-western dancing, and dance lessons. *$; AE, MC, V; no checks; breakfast, lunch, dinner every day, brunch Sun; full bar; no reservations; street parking; www.ham burgermarys.com; map:N2* &

## Hash House a Go Go / ★★☆

**3628 5TH AVE, HILLCREST; 619/298-4646** "Exuberant" pretty much sums up the cooking style at this Hillcrest hot spot, known for hulking portions and imaginative presentations of updated diner cuisine. Yes, there's classic fried chicken on this menu created by a former Midwesterner. But here, it's served on a stack of bacon-flavored waffles, drizzled with a maple glaze, and skewered with a rosemary spear for good measure. Other fun variations: a basic Caesar is gussied up with polenta croutons; fresh grilled fish arrives on vast beds of flavored mashed potatoes; meatloaf is served sandwich-style topped with mozzarella cheese. Even dessert gets an unusual spin: the signature bread pudding comes flavored with peanut butter and chocolate one night, Snickers candy bars the next. The dining room has a comfy, urban-meets-the-family-farm feeling, complete with an ancient wood-burning stove, trendy faux-finished walls, and old tools serving as wall decor. During warm weather, the back patio offers a nice alternative to the bustling dining room, which tends to be noisy. Tip: Unless you have the appetite of a sumo wrestler, spend the extra few dollars to split one of the massive entrees. *$$; AE, DC, DIS, MC, V; no checks; breakfast, lunch, dinner every day; beer and wine; reservations recommended; street parking; map: N3* &

## Hob Nob Hill / ★★☆

**2271 1ST AVE, DOWNTOWN; 619/239-8176** One of the city's longest-running success stories, Hob Nob Hill is a throwback to the good ol' days. You know the ones: when nobody counted fat grams, butter was the spread of choice, and cholesterol wasn't a household word. This proudly old-fashioned eatery has satisfied San Diegans for over 50 years, and while these days you can order an egg-white-only omelet, why would you bother? This is the place for corned beef hash with eggs over easy, or a big stack of pancakes with real bacon on the side. Breakfast isn't the only highlight; lunch and dinner feature roasted turkey with gravy, stuffed bell peppers, club sandwiches, and three-bean salad. Don't come by too late, though; the place closes up around 9pm. Service is pure diner, with efficient, fast-moving waitresses in sensible shoes who are always ready with a coffee refill and a smile. The decor probably hasn't changed since the place opened in the 1940s, and that's just fine. Hob Nob is a classic example of if it ain't broke, don't fix it. *$$; AE, CB, DIS, MC, V; checks OK; breakfast, lunch, dinner every day; beer and wine; reservations recommended; street parking; map:N5* &

## Hodad's / ★★

**5010 NEWPORT AVE, OCEAN BEACH; 619/224-4623** Hodad's hamburger shop in Ocean Beach may have served slightly fewer than a billion burgers, but it's almost as famous as the place with the Golden Arches. Here's why: the juicy, jumbo-size burgers come heaped with enough condiments to rate a half dozen napkins (you'll need twice that many for the infamous double bacon burger). The onion rings are fat and fresh-tasting, the french fries crisp and hot. And you can see why the place is especially popular with the surfing crowd: they can check the breaks around the O.B. Pier just by stepping out the door. As for the decor, it's pure seaside retro, consisting mostly of old license plates, surf memorabilia, and a booth fashioned from a VW bus. Servers are fast and friendly, the beer's always plenty cold, and the dress code, if you could call it that, is minimal. All in all, Hodad's is every bit as much a San Diego institution as the zoo. *$; AE, DC, DIS, MC, V; no checks; lunch, dinner every day; beer and wine; no reservations; street parking; map:B3*

## Ichiban / ★★

**1441 GARNET AVE, PACIFIC BEACH; 858/270-5755 / 1499 UNIVERSITY AVE, HILLCREST; 619/299-7203** A ceramic Korean good-luck cat beckons from the window—heed his call and enter. This update of the original Japanese restaurant in Hillcrest serves the same superb food in a spruced-up environment. Order at the counter before slipping into one of the big, comfortable, C-shaped black Naugahyde booths, or choose a tiny table for two. There are usually at least seven chefs, prep cooks, and servers bustling about the open kitchen, and two sushi chefs at the small bar. Everything at Ichiban (which means "number one" in Japanese) is delicious and authentic. The teriyaki chicken is an intense trio of chicken, fresh mushrooms, and zucchini in a thick, powerful teriyaki. It's accompanied by perfect sticky rice, a small seafood salad, marinated bean sprouts, and green salad with a delicious ginger dressing. The Fried Seafood Mixed has the same side dishes and arrives piping hot. Every day brings four new lunch and dinner specials, usually including a noodle dish and a sushi or sashimi combo.

The original Ichiban, in Hillcrest, serves equally delicious food in a more cramped setting, although now with an outdoor patio on busy Washington Street. It's sometimes hard to get a table, but one usually miraculously opens up just when you need it. *$; cash only (Ichiban PB); MC, V (Ichiban); lunch Mon–Sat, dinner every day (Ichiban PB); lunch, dinner every day (Ichiban); beer and wine (Ichiban PB); no alcohol (Ichiban); no reservations; street parking; map:KK7 and P2*

## Il Fornaio / ★★

**1555 CAMINO DEL MAR, DEL MAR; 858/755-8876 / 1333 1ST ST, CORONADO; 619/437-4911** These two branches are good representatives of an ever-growing chain (there's one at New York-New York in Vegas) that dazzles fans with stunning decor and interesting takes on gourmet pasta, pizza, and bread. The elegantly designed dining rooms are an instant transport to Italy with plenty of Carrara marble, terracotta flooring, vaulted ceilings, hand-painted trompe l'oeil friezes, and an open oven where meats and signature breads are baked to perfection (breads, pastries, and all food items are available for takeout). At times, the food doesn't live up to the

**59**

ambiance and prices. Most of the pasta dishes are good (ravioli di verdura al funghi is filled with Swiss chard, pine nuts, basil, Parmesan, and mixed mushrooms and topped with fresh tomatoes and artichokes), and the pizzas are nearly perfect (try pizza capricciosa with prosciutto cotto, kalamata olives, artichokes, and mushrooms). Other specialties include well-executed renditions of veal, steaks, chicken, and lamb. For dessert, the tiramisu is a must. The Del Mar restaurant sits atop Del Mar Plaza; the Coronado site has a large patio beside San Diego Bay. Regulars at both places choose outdoor tables with a view and order cappuccino and almond and anisette biscotti or wine and bread. *$$; AE, DIS, DC, MC, V; no checks; lunch, dinner every day, brunch Sun; full bar; reservations recommended; self parking; www.ilfornaio.com; map:GG7 and NN5;* &

## Indigo Grill / ★★★

**1536 INDIA ST, LITTLE ITALY; 619/234-6802** Chef Deborah Scott—the talent behind the fiery, multicultural cuisine at Kemo Sabe—has created another winner in this stunningly designed restaurant. Conceived as a salute to the indigenous cultures of the Americas, from Oaxaca to the Pacific Northwest, Indigo Grill offers a dazzling experience for the palate as well as the eye. The strongest influence on the menu is from Mexico, which means the chile is used in countless dishes here. However, Scott uses all those poblanos, serranos, and jalapeños to add complexity of flavor or a shimmer of heat, rather than all-out fire. So you won't need a flameproof palate to enjoy Scott's authentic beef enchiladas, delicate trout, slow-roasted pork ribs, or superb roasted baby chicken seasoned with sage and mole. Smooth-as-satin corn pudding, an offbeat Caesar salad fashioned with grilled romaine, and a rich portobello mushroom fettuccine are other signature dishes here. The decor is as artistic as the fare, with Oaxacan animal masks, Inuit carvings, and totem poles surveying the eclectic group of diners. At the entrance, a faux cypress tree spreads its branches in welcome, while behind the bar, water burbles soothingly down a wall. In addition to several high-quality tequilas and mezcals, there's an adequate wine list and some imaginative cocktail creations. *$$–$$$; AE, DC, DIS, MC, V; no checks; lunch Mon–Fri, dinner every day; full bar; reservations recommended; street parking; www.cohnrestaurants.com; map: M6* &

## Jake's Del Mar / ★

**1660 COAST BLVD, DEL MAR; 858/755-2002** Jake's has a laid-back rhythm, from the steady drumbeat of surf sounds to the endless parade of beachcombers seen through the big dining room windows. The owners have made a niche for themselves with Duke's on Oahu in Hawaii and Huntington Beach near L.A., and know how to create the quintessential place for a sunset cocktail followed by a hearty fish dinner. We find Jake's food to be less impressive than the sun and sand scenery. Order conservatively—it's the scene that matters, not the cuisine. Try the macadamia-nut-crusted calamari for a taste of Hawaii or ahi with a fiery chile crust. Other dinner entrees run the gamut from grilled chicken to roasted leg of lamb with herb Dijon mustard and mint-mango chutney. The great value here is Jake's happy hour (which occurs at odd times), when the bistro menu items are half-price. The deal is offered on Monday and Tuesday from 4pm to 9pm, Wednesday to Friday from 4pm to 6pm, and Saturday 2pm to 4pm. *$$–$$$; AE, DIS, MC, V; no checks; lunch Tues–Sun, dinner every day, brunch Sun; full bar; reservations recommended; self parking; www.hulapie.com; map:GG7* &

## Jasmine / ★★☆

**4609 CONVOY ST, KEARNY MESA; 858/268-0888** With seating for 800 diners, Jasmine at first glance might resemble a vast Chinese food factory. But don't be scared away. This handsome eatery specializing in Cantonese cooking manages to couple high quality with sheer quantity. Dim sum is served every day of the week, with the crowds peaking on Saturday and Sunday when the selection is at its most staggering. From sticky rice steamed in a lotus leaf to crispy chicken feet and barbecued pork, everybody's favorites show up on the fully laden carts. Dinner entrees include steamed fresh fish pulled live from large tanks just minutes before it hits your plate, excellent prawns the size of small lobsters, a marvelous shellfish stir-fry, and top-notch Peking duck. The place is equally popular with businesspeople and large families. While it's often packed, the skilled servers handle everyone with speed and aplomb. Need a quick lunch to go? Jasmine also operates a takeout counter right next door. *$; AE, MC, V; no checks; lunch, dinner every day; full bar; reservations recommended; self parking; map:JJ5*

## Jimmy Carter's Cafe / ★★☆

**3172 5TH AVE, HILLCREST; 619/295-2070** Jimmy Carter's (named for its local owner, not the former prez) is the kind of homey but hip cafe we'd love to see in every neighborhood. Alas, there's only one Jimmy Carter's, but it's worth a trip to Hillcrest and a wait for a table to sample a breakfast, lunch, or dinner here. The restaurant serves plenty of comfort food—corned beef hash, fluffy omelets, assorted flapjacks, terrific hamburgers and grilled cheese sandwiches—but you can also walk on the wilder side with dishes from the international portions of the menu. The savory dhosas (Indian crepes) filled with spicy vegetables are a signature dish; other ethnic fare here includes huevos rancheros, chilaquiles (a yummy tortilla casserole), even Mongolian barbecue. A lively, mixed crowd (families, singles, gay, straight, old, young) frequents the cafe, known for its fast service and low prices. Sit in the cozy main dining room, or in the slightly more spacious area that includes a smallish bar. Parking around here can be tight; check the side streets off Fifth Avenue for non-metered spots. *$; AE, MC, V; no checks; breakfast, lunch, dinner every day; beer and wine; no reservations; street parking; map:N4* &

## Joe's Crab Shack / ★★

**7610 HAZARD CENTER DR, MISSION VALLEY; 619/260-1111 / 4325 OCEAN BLVD, PACIFIC BEACH; 858/274-3474** One look at Joe's over-the-top nautical decor and wacky, fun-loving staff, and discriminating diners might assume that food takes a backseat to hilarity here. Wrong: the fish and seafood served in this every-day's-a-party place is fresh and carefully prepared. Settle in among the plastic seagulls, sports memorabilia, stuffed fish, and other junk, and start off with a bowl of buttery-rich clam chowder. Or choose the crab cakes or deep-fried spicy shrimp; both make fine snacking before you take a mallet and start attacking a big batch of steamed king crab legs. Equally tasty, but a lot less messy, are the grilled halibut, the salmon, and the crawfish étouffée. Staffers are cheerful and enthusiastic (especially when they break into a chorus or two of "Macarena"), and there's an ample beer and booze selection that might encourage you to join in as well. Both locations offer sunny patios for an offbeat business lunch—wouldn't you love to see the boss wearing Ray-Bans and a crab bib? *$$; AE, DC, DIS, MC, V; no checks; lunch, dinner every day; full bar; reservations recommended; self parking; www.joescrabshack.com; map: LL4 and KK7* &

## Jyoti Bihanga / ★★

**3351 ADAMS AVE, NORMAL HEIGHTS; 619/282-4116** Surprisingly, San Diego has only a handful of vegetarian restaurants, an odd situation in a town where health and fitness keep a pretty high profile. But just when you've decided there's a fast-food joint on every corner, you discover the soothing presence of Jyoti Bihanga, one of the city's oldest and best meat-free eateries. The serene, pastel-painted dining room has a definite New Age feeling that helps erase any type-A tendencies at the door. Settle in with one of the many metaphysical publications distributed here for free. Savor the simple, satisfying cuisine, which ranges from enormous salads and excellent smoothies to overstuffed veggie burritos and cornbread chili. We've been hooked for years on the Infinite Blue Salad, a meal in itself of green beans, brown rice, cucumbers, blue cheese, and veggies. Stir-fries and curries are other perennial favorites, and the place even offers some simple dairy-free dessert options such as pies and tofu-based cheesecake. The schedule here can change with little notice, so it's always best to call ahead. *$; AE, MC, V; checks OK; breakfast, lunch Mon–Sat, dinner Mon–Tues, Thurs–Sat; no alcohol; no reservations; street parking; map:LL4* &

## Kaiserhof / ★★

**2253 SUNSET CLIFFS BLVD, OCEAN BEACH; 619/224-0606** German food is done to perfection at this unpretentious biergarten just an oompah-pah from the beach. From authentic Wiener schnitzel to oh-so-tender beef rouladen to a dozen or so hearty side dishes, everything here is worthy of Oktoberfest in the old country. Portions are ridiculously large, and you may notice a waddle in your walk after a dinner that includes a choice of soup or salad, two side dishes, and plenty of bread. Of course, a number of German beers are available on tap, which makes up for a decided dearth of wine selections. Best seating is in the dining room with the fireplace or on the shaded patio, depending on the weather. Customers range from young couples on first dates to white-haired regulars who've been Kaiserhof fans for decades. *$$; AE, CB, DC, DIS, MC, V; no checks; lunch, dinner every day; full bar; reservations recommended; self parking; map:C2* &

## Karl Strauss Brewery & Grill / ★★

**9675 SCRANTON RD, SORRENTO VALLEY (AND BRANCHES); 858/587-2739** Part of a locally founded chain that's become wildly popular over the last decade, this casual brewery-restaurant is set in a deceptively elegant Japanese garden. Half the fun of visiting here is winding along the paths and through the greenery to the koi pond and inviting deck; the other is knocking back well-made ales (along with an impressive selection of wines by the glass) and chowing down on filling traditional bar fare. Specialties of the house include plump, spicy sausages, well-made burgers, sandwiches from Philly-style steak to portobello mushroom, filet mignon, and grilled salmon. Given the sizable business crowd that populates Sorrento Valley and the nearby Golden Triangle area, this can be heaven for yuppie singles, especially during happy hour. Keep in mind that the restaurant is closed on Saturdays, when it's often booked for wedding receptions and corporate parties. *$; AE, MC, V; no checks; lunch, dinner Sun–Fri (closed Sat for private parties); beer and wine; reservations recommended; self parking; www.karlstrauss.com; map:II7*

## Kemo Sabe / ★★☆

**3958 5TH AVE, HILLCREST; 619/220-6802** Forget any references to the Lone Ranger. In this part of town, Kemo Sabe simply means wow, referring equally to this eatery's spicy fusion fare and the chic, confident decor. From the metal-inlaid tables to the intricate ironworks inspired by primitive Native American art, the look is smashing indeed. The faint of palate need not drop by; chef Deborah Scott's cuisine is fashioned from the fiery personalities of Thailand, Mexico, and the American Southwest. Typical dishes include a grilled fish napoleon layered with pesto, goat cheese, and grilled vegetables; Asian-style dim sum served as a platter for two; and a grilled skirt steak that ought to be served with a fire extinguisher. A good selection of food-friendly wines and bold microbrew beers accompanies the food with style, and service is hip and accommodating. The location in a happening part of Hillcrest (near the Hillcrest Cinemas, one of the best movie theaters in town) keeps Kemo Sabe hopping; make reservations if you're looking to dine on the weekends. *$$; AE, DIS, MC, V; no checks; dinner every day; full bar; reservations recommended; street parking; www.cohnrestaurants.com; map:N2* &

## Kensington Grill / ★★

**4055 ADAMS AVE, KENSINGTON; 619/281-4014** Kensington Grill strikes just the right balance between a great neighborhood hangout and a hip hot spot—friendly and cool at the same time. The terrific bar, with a giant mirror to reflect the lively scene of 20- and 30-something professionals, features some great local microbrews and an extensive menu of wine by the glass. The purple-felt-covered pool table invites patrons to rack 'em up and shoot a few before dinner. Beyond the bar area is the main dining room, which has warm, butter-yellow walls that glow by candlelight. Deliciously spicy black linguine topped with grilled shrimp shares the menu with hearty mixed grills and burgers. Among the salads, opt for Mediterranean greens with an interesting combo of ingredients, including cranberries, pine nuts, and raisins. This place is crowded on the weekends, so it's best to call for reservations. But if you can't get a table, you can always snag a seat at the bar and order from the menu. An ideal spot if you're catching a movie revival at the Ken movie theater next door. *$$; AE, DIS, MC, V; no checks; dinner every day; full bar; reservations recommended; street parking; map:LL3* &

## King's Fish House / ★★★

**825 CAMINO DE LA REINA, MISSION VALLEY; 619/574-1230** Although this restaurant is part of a chain that includes San Diego's Royale Brasserie, the Water Grill in Los Angeles, and several other King's around the Southland, it has its own vibrant personality. Servers are smart and friendly, the decor is imaginative (with enormous mounted fish on the walls and Christmas lights in the bar), and the menu is lengthy and appealing. Brilliantly fresh seafood is the star of the show, appearing in soups and salads, appetizers, and, of course, main dishes and specials. New Orleans–style barbecued shrimp, deep-fried calamari, and spicy seafood chowder are the best ways to start out. Then move on to Chilean sea bass in a teriyaki glaze, plank-roasted salmon, pearly white halibut paired with tomato pesto, or simply grilled mahi mahi. Two side dishes are included with meals, as are soup or a salad. Oh, and don't forget the refreshing Key lime pie for dessert. We can guarantee you won't leave King's hungry. The warehouse-like main dining room is a popular choice for families (kids love looking at the stuffed fish, as well as the tanks of live lobsters) though it's certainly comfortable for grown-ups as well. The noisier bar area, where you can dine or simply have a drink, offers live rhythm and blues on the weekends. *$$; AE, DC, DIS, MC, V; no checks; lunch, dinner every day; full bar; reservations recommended; self parking; www.kingsfishhouse.com; map: LL4* &

### Ki's / ★

**2591 S COAST HWY 101, CARDIFF-BY-THE-SEA; 760/436-5236** Years ago, Ki's was just another hole-in-the-wall health-food cafe, where local surfers and the organic crowd congregated for smoothies, wheat grass juice, and Ki burgers. Though it later moved up to a prime ocean-view location just across from Cardiff Beach, Ki's has managed to up the ambiance and the menu considerably, while holding prices way down. Both indoor and patio seating are plentiful, though the best seats in the house are at the long upstairs bar facing the ocean. Place your order at the counter, then find a seat and await your meal. Organic fruits, veggies, and grains are incorporated into the mostly low-fat dishes, though cholesterol-laden eggs, avocados, and nuts are visible on the menu. The sizable chicken or salmon salads combine baby greens, roasted red bell peppers, tomatoes, and cucumbers, topped with either a grilled chicken breast or salmon fillet and orange-basil vinaigrette. Veggie lasagne remains a perennial favorite, and Mexican standbys such as burritos, tostadas, and fish tacos have been improved with whole wheat tortillas, organic rice, and lard-free beans. The fruit smoothies are filling, delicious, and healthy. *$; AE, MC, V; checks OK; breakfast, lunch, dinner every day; beer and wine; reservations recommended for dinner; self parking; map:EE7* &

### Kono's Cafe / ★

**704 GARNET AVE, PACIFIC BEACH; 858/483-1669** Fans of Kono's say it offers the best seaside dining in town, where the eye candy comes free with the meal. The high-profile location right on the boardwalk by Crystal Pier ensures diners a front-row view of enough beach babes, hunks, Rollerbladers, cyclists, and other characters to induce whiplash. This easygoing cafe also serves up darn good food, especially at breakfast, when you can always expect a wait on the weekends. Regulars swear by the breakfast burritos (stuffed with a scramble of eggs, bacon, cheese, and much more), as well as notable home fries. For lunch, we recommend the burgers and hot dogs, along with the BLT layered with avocado. An espresso stand offers a quick energy fix for those who don't have time to relax over a meal on the deck. Between the view and the quality fare, the proprietors could charge a small fortune for eating here, but Kono's is known for its cheap eats; it's hard to spend more than five bucks for your meal. *$; cash only; breakfast, lunch every day; no alcohol; no reservations; street parking; map:KK7*

## Korea House / ★★☆

**4620 CONVOY ST, KEARNY MESA; 858/560-0080** Although this popular ethnic restaurant serves a variety of entrees, the majority of diners prefer to feast on the traditional Korean barbecue. It's a strictly do-it-yourself affair, which is part of the charm. Settle into a comfy booth with a miniature grill right at the table, then cook flavorful strips of marinated beef exactly to your liking. The meat is served with a variety of accompaniments, including rice, assorted veggies, and kimchee—the fiery pickled cabbage that's used as a condiment. Along with beef, diners can order eel, tripe, and various kinds of fish (ask about any specials of the day). Some of the spiciest Korean fare in town can be found here, and the restaurant also offers such Japanese fare as sashimi and teriyaki dishes. This is a fine place for families; kids are intrigued by the barbecue process, and the staff is both gracious and helpful in explaining the menu. *$$; AE, MC, V; no checks; lunch, dinner every day; full bar; reservations recommended; self parking; map:JJ5*

## La Fresqueria / ★★☆

**550 WEST C ST, DOWNTOWN; 619/235-6816** Small enough to be dubbed a hole-in-the-wall, La Fresqueria is best known as a juice bar with fantastic smoothies. The place is a favorite of downtown workers seeking a healthy alternative to fast food. It's not strictly vegetarian, but offers several meat-free dishes and an emphasis on fresh, healthfully prepared foods. The smoothies alone can make a meal. Freshly blended with frozen fruit such as bananas or cantaloupe, they're smooth, slushy, and come in great combos like kiwi-orange and passion fruit–peach. On the more substantial side, the Chinese chicken salad with honey-sesame dressing is a winner. Sandwiches include subs, stuffed pita bread, and wraps, as well as tortas (Mexican-style sandwiches served on a thick roll called a *bolillo*). Torta lovers tout the Special—with avocado, cucumbers, cheese, and other good stuff—as the best sandwich downtown. The very narrow dining room offers limited seating, and there's a small patio out front, but most people grab lunch to go. *$; cash only; breakfast, lunch Mon–Fri; no alcohol; no reservations; street parking; map: M7*

## La Taverna / ★★☆

**927 SILVERADO ST, LA JOLLA; 858/454-0100** Good things indeed come in small packages, as this tiny Italian eatery proves time and again. There's seating for only about two dozen indoors, and you won't get much elbow room, but this family-operated place is big on value and personality. The well-priced lunches and dinners include perfectly prepared risottos (which change daily), superb salmon fettuccine with Parmesan cream, Parmesan-crusted chicken, and potato gnocchi served with a pungent but pleasing Gorgonzola sauce. Fennel-flecked sausage made fresh by the owner is another winner, and don't miss the bittersweet chocolate layer cake or the sky-high banana torte for dessert. In addition to the dining room, a compact but comfortable patio offers seating out front. No need to dress up; La Taverna has an informal, unpretentious air about it despite the gourmet-quality fare. *$–$$; DC,*

*DIS, MC, V; no checks; lunch Tues–Fri, dinner Tues–Sat (closed Sun); beer and wine; reservations recommended; street parking; map: JJ7*

**Laurel Restaurant & Bar / ★★★**

**505 LAUREL ST, DOWNTOWN; 619/239-2222** Laurel is so lovely and sophisticated you might think you've strolled into some chic new spot in San Francisco or New York. After you've valet-parked, make an entrance down the staircase into the main dining room and adjacent bar. Be graceful; this is the kind of place where heads turn each time the door is opens. While it's true that many come to Laurel simply for the panache of pricey furnishings, flattering light, and exquisite martinis, many more are drawn by the memorable fare. Although founding chef Doug Organ, who also oversaw the kitchen at the WineSellar & Brasserie (see review), has left the restaurant, his influence continues in the ever-changing mix of Mediterranean, North African, Provençal, and classic French cuisine served here. Longtime Laurel fans can still enjoy the rustic Provençal chicken stewed in a pot with a flurry of fragrant herbs, as well as a masterful duck confit with silken meat and crackly skin. Lamb and Moroccan spices, long-simmered osso buco, and a signature appetizer tart flavored with Roquefort and caramelized onions are also still present and well accounted for. An outstanding wine list offers many an unfamiliar bottle from various regions of France, although the list by the glass is somewhat lacking. Service is generally quite good, but it's the genial bartenders who really set the standard for Laurel's staff. Maybe that's why so many regulars drop by for a quick bite at the bar. *$$$; AE, DC, DIS, MC, V; no checks; dinner every day; full bar; reservations recommended; valet parking; www.laurelrestaurant.com; map:N5*

**Le Fontainebleau / ★★★**

**1055 2ND AVE (WESTGATE HOTEL), DOWNTOWN; 619/557-3655** Ever since stellar French chef Christophe Vessaire took command in 2001, this Versailles-inspired dining room has become a destination for serious foodies. The much-awarded Vessaire (whose credits include Michelin-starred restaurants in France and Switzerland) has created a menu that seamlessly blends classic French and updated California cuisine in one of the most elegant settings in town. The windowless room is opulent and appealing, with extravagant chandeliers, gorgeous wall treatments, a grand piano, and immaculately dressed tables. And the fare is divine, from the duck foie gras served with braised fennel and feathery fennel salad to the splendid seared halibut paired with fava beans and olives. Other tempting choices: artichoke soup infused with black truffles, butter-poached scallops with tender baby pea shoots, Sonoma duck breast complemented with an apricot compote, and escargot sautéed in fragrant Pernod. The chef takes special pride in his signature tasting menu featuring multiple courses of foie gras, but also offers more populist fare with a Friday-night seafood buffet and a Sunday Champagne brunch. The service is formal and correct, the ambiance definitely special occasion. *$$$–$$$$; AE, CB, DC, DIS, MC, V; checks OK; lunch Mon–Fri, dinner Mon–Sat, brunch Sun; full bar; reservations recommended; valet parking; www.westgatehotel.com; map:N7* ♿

## The Marine Room / ★★★☆

 **2000 SPINDRIFT DR, LA JOLLA; 858/459-7222** Between the unparalleled oceanfront location, the romantic ambiance, and the talents of executive chef Bernard Guillas, the Marine Room is a true original. Descend the staircase into this dining room built right on the sand, and you'll see why generations of San Diegans have come here for evenings of dining and dancing. The north and south dining rooms offer unrestricted views of the coastline; the central bar has the cozy buzz of locals relaxing over the week's gossip with a gin and tonic. Light-colored decor and crisp white linens create an airy, open feel. The cuisine came into its own when chef Guillas arrived on the scene a few years ago; today, a formerly good restaurant is outstanding. The French native infuses his brand of Mediterranean/Pacific Rim/California fare with imaginative flavors, from sambuca and fresh lavender to candied shallots and crunchy greens from the sea. Halibut, foie gras, ahi, and sweetbreads are some of the standouts on the menu, which changes according to the season and the chef's whims. Recent highlights have been the halibut poached in Pinot Noir, the dry-aged strip steak with truffle-based potatoes, and the goose liver paired with preserved cherries and cognac. Be sure to check out the restaurant's dramatic High Tide Breakfasts during the winter, complete with a luxurious buffet and waves misting the windows. Since the dining room is connected to the La Jolla Beach and Tennis Club, you'll see some casually clad folks here, but it's really much more fun to dress to the nines, make an entrance, and get the other diners wondering which who's who you're listed in. *$$$; AE, CB, DC, DIS, MC, V; no checks; lunch, dinner every day, brunch Sun; full bar; reservations recommended; valet parking; www.marineroom.com; map:JJ7*

## Market Cafe / ★★☆

**4000 CORONADO BAY RD (LOEWS CORONADO BAY RESORT), CORONADO; 619/424-4000** Locals fill this sunny cafe on Sunday mornings, since brunch doesn't get much better than this. Sushi, crab claws, giant shrimp, smoked salmon, pot stickers, carved lamb and roast beef, fresh blueberries and whipped cream—need we say more? OK. Unlimited fresh-squeezed orange juice and subtle French Champagne, served with a view of sailboats drifting through the Coronado Cays. Forget brunching here on Mother's Day, unless you make reservations weeks in advance. Be sure to make reservations no matter when you choose to serve yourself gourmet style. There are other meals to consider, and we're not talking typical hotel coffee-shop fare: the tortilla soup is a savory, spicy blend of chicken, tomatoes, avocado, and fried tortilla strips; the seafood-turkey Cobb salad is a work of art. The salmon is grilled to moist perfection; the surf-and-turf giant prawns and filet mignon can easily feed two. Kids tired of hotel fare are delighted to find crusty macaroni and cheese on the comfort-food menu. Even the club sandwich stands apart with its slices of white chicken, avocado, tomato, and crisp bacon strips. No matter what meal you eat (and you also must try Azzura Point, the hotel's fine dining room), you may be so sated you'll spend the night at the Loews—not a bad idea. *$$–$$$; AE, DIS, DC, MC, V; no checks; breakfast, lunch, dinner every day, brunch Sun; full bar; brunch reservations recommended; valet and self parking; map:NN5* ♿

## Mille Fleurs / ★★★★

**6009 PASEO DELICIAS, RANCHO SANTA FE; 858/756-3085** Possibly the most rarefied and romantic of all San Diego restaurants, Mille Fleurs manages to combine a fabulously lush atmosphere with spectacular cuisine. Tucked into a quiet courtyard in the heart of Rancho Santa Fe's little village, Mille Fleurs attracts with a seductive whisper rather than a flashy wink. Much of its allure is due to the winning team of Bertrand Hug, the legendary host/proprietor who never seems to forget a face, and Martin Woesle, the stunningly talented chef who's a stickler for using only the very finest ingredients. The cuisine leans toward updated French, with typical dishes including truffle-oil-dressed salads made from a variety of organic greens, sautéed sweetbreads, artful duck creations, and game specials such as venison and quail. One might start with delicate cream of parsley soup, fragrant as a patch of herbs, followed by sautéed soft-shell crab nestled on a salsa of local white corn and tiny tomatoes. Entree choices vary, but Woesle's best creations include venison medallions punched up with a juniper berry marinade, stuffed quail sauced with red currants, and monkfish flown in from France—and tastier than lobster. For dessert, there's a selection of imported cheese—surprisingly hard to find as a finale in this area—as well as pastries and sorbets often based on the season's best local fruit. Wine selections are limited only by your pocketbook, as Mille Fleurs offers one of the most impressive lists in town. The sophisticated service, understated Mediterranean decor, and welcoming piano bar all serve to show that, gastronomically speaking, at least, money can buy happiness. *$$$$; AE, CB, DC, MC, V; no checks; lunch Mon–Fri, dinner every day; full bar; reservations recommended; self parking; milfleurs@aol.com; www.millefleurs.com; map:EE5*

## Mimmo's Italian Village / ★★☆

**1743 INDIA ST, DOWNTOWN; 619/239-3710** Drop by this deli/restaurant during lunchtime, and it's busy enough to make you think they're giving food away. Well, they practically are—Mimmo's prices for deli salads and sandwiches are bargain basement, much like the decor in the dining room. Subs here are loaded with meats and cheeses heaped on good soft (but not too soft) rolls and start at less than $3. There's a vegetarian number too. But the very best value here is the sampler of four deli salads plus garlic bread for about $5.25. You have more than a dozen options, including freshly prepared pasta salads, excellent caponata, a seafood ceviche, and several meatless creations. Get lunch in a box to go, or brave the crowds and pick out a table near the battered but popular piano. If the playing isn't up to snuff, head out the back door to a pleasant patio. Whatever you do, don't miss Mimmo's if you're a connoisseur of cheap eats. *$; cash only; breakfast, lunch Mon–Sat; beer and wine; no reservations; street parking; map:M6*

## Mission Cafe & Coffee Shop / ★

**3795 MISSION BLVD, MISSION BEACH; 858/488-9060** Longtime fans of admittedly funky Mission Cafe don't mind the faded decor, the thrift-shop furnishings, or the tough parking situation during summer. They're interested in one thing: good food, and lots of it. The menu at this beachy eatery (just a block from the Mission Beach boardwalk) makes a big deal of breakfast—well worth a long, calorie-burning stroll afterwards. Pancakes, waffles, smoothies, breakfast burritos, and other morning foods shine; standouts include banana-blackberry pancakes, rosemary roasted potatoes, thick French toast, and low-fat fruit smoothies. Best of all, breakfast items are served until 3pm for you sleepyheads. Be prepared to wait quite a while on the weekends for a table, and don't dress up: sandals, tanks, and shorts fit this place to a tee. *$; AE, MC, V; no checks; breakfast, lunch every day; beer and wine; no reservations; street parking; map:LL7* &

## Mission Hills Cafe / ★★

**808 W WASHINGTON ST, MISSION HILLS; 619/296-8010** This bistro was a well-kept neighborhood secret until a glowing review by a popular food critic made it hard to get a table. Breakfast is reliably good; lunch features a menu of salads, sandwiches, and daily specials. You can't go wrong with half an eggplant, pesto, and provolone sandwich served with a cup of homemade carrot soup. Evenings, however, have a special buzz, when locals arrive for the bargain-price prix-fixe dinner menu that includes an appetizer, entree, and dessert, with choices in all three categories. On weekend evenings, there's a wait for the candlelit tables in two large dining rooms. It's tempting to fill up on the Italian flatbread, but do save room for the meal, which might begin with the Cambozola salad with strawberries and pears on a bed of baby lettuce. Entrees vary from fresh fish to osso buco and are served with your choice of rice or potatoes. When it's time for dessert, always opt for the crepes, which arrive filled with fruit or ice cream. A fair selection of domestic wines is available, along with bottled beers. *$$; AE, DIS, MC, V; no checks; breakfast, lunch, dinner every day; beer and wine; reservations recommended for dinner; street parking; map:M2* &

## MiXX / ★★★

**3671 5TH AVE, HILLCREST; 619/299-6499** Consistently one of San Diego's most exciting eateries, trendy MiXX is a place where innumerable culinary influences and ingredients blossom into a nightly kaleidoscope of flavors. The kitchen's goal, as stated on the menu, is "cuisine with no ethnic boundaries." That would explain executive chef Deborah Helm's bold mix of Southwestern, Pacific Rim, traditional French, Vietnamese, and fusion cooking that attracts a steady stream of customers to this lively, dinner-only establishment. Daily specials featuring lamb, pork tenderloin, or fish are always worth a try, but don't ignore the regular lineup: a French burnt walnut salad, peppered seared ahi, and duck ravioli helped make MiXX an instant hit on the local dining scene. The two-level restaurant offers a trio of seating options: the piano bar downstairs (see Nightlife chapter), a very see-and-be-seen dining room on the second level (with banquette seating and a fairly high noise quotient), and a plant-filled patio offering a bit more privacy at the back. In addition to the good-looking clientele, talented chefs, and skilled servers, MiXX is known as a showcase for contemporary art—much of it available for sale. *$$; AE, CB, DC, DIS, MC, V; no checks; dinner every day; full bar; reservations recommended; street parking; map: N3* &

## Montanas / ★★

**1421 UNIVERSITY AVE, HILLCREST; 619/297-0722** Ever since its splashy appearance on the dining scene some years back, Montanas has been packing 'em in with a sassy blend of spicy cooking, sleek environs, très cool crowd, and contemporary art. Business types often crowd the dining room during lunch, while an eclectic mix of young and old clad in anything from khaki pants to spandex keep the room busy right up to closing time. The appealing menu handles classic American cuisine with style, updating standards like grilled chicken and skirt steak with the flavors of the Southwest. Standout dishes include a New Mexican pork stew, barbecued ribs, chicken tossed with cilantro or jalapeño linguine, and a silky chocolate caramel tart. Large parties can reserve a semiprivate room lined with wine bottles; prime seating for couples or foursomes is in the front booths overlooking the sidewalk. Often noisy and always interesting, Montanas is a great stop for a single perfectly made martini or an entire meal. *$$; AE, DC, DIS, MC, V; no checks; lunch Tues only, dinner every day; full bar; reservations recommended; valet and street parking; www.montanas grill.com; map: P2* &

## Morton's of Chicago / ★★★☆

**285 J ST (HARBOR CLUB), DOWNTOWN; 619/696-3369** Welcome to the land of expense-account dinners, prime Midwestern beef, expertly shaken martinis, and baked potatoes almost the size of footballs. Morton's offers steak-house dining at its best, which means all the wood-paneled ambiance and waiterly ceremony you can handle. The crowd is much less formal, however; this national chain draws a mix of Hawaiian-shirted tourists, name-tagged conventioneers, and others dressed in everything from Gap to Gucci. Steaks, vegetables, and other items (including outsize live lobsters) are presented for your approval at the table before being turned into some truly top-notch all-American fare. Black bean soup and Caesar salad are the appetizers of choice; then it's a toss-up between the New York strip, the double-thick lamb chops, or the lightly breaded veal Sicilian as your main course. Portions are enormous, but you'll still want to indulge in one of the fabulous dessert soufflés or the Godiva chocolate truffle cake that takes the current rage for warm, gooey, melted-center desserts to new heights. A pricey but well-chosen wine list offers top California Cabernets and double magnums of premium Champagnes. Be ready to spend some money, and prepare for a splendid evening of excess. *$$$–$$$$; AE, CB, DC, DIS, MC, V; no checks; dinner every day; full bar; reservations recommended; valet and self parking; www.mortons.com; map:N8* &

## Nick's at the Beach / ★★

**809 THOMAS ST, PACIFIC BEACH; 858/270-1730** Nick's is really two restaurants in one, both of them fun. On the first floor, a small bar area and spacious dining room offer a wide variety of well-priced, well-prepared meals ranging from meatloaf to Cajun gumbo. We're certain that the mussels steamed with tomatillos and lime juice take top honors here, but the competition is stiff from Nick's Caesar salad, the quesadilla stuffed with garlic mashed potatoes, the well-seasoned crab cakes, and the fresh fish specials. The seafood pasta dressed with feta cheese and basil is also a special treat. Upstairs, a young crowd parties with a CD jukebox, four pool tables, lots of TVs, and a terrific late-night menu served daily till 1am. A recent remodel has added an ocean-view patio upstairs, while creating a needed bit of soundproofing and intimacy in the main dining room below. In addition to a stellar collection of beers on tap, the wine list offers lots of selections by both glass and bottle at user-friendly prices. No one under 21 is allowed upstairs. *$–$$; AE, DIS, MC, V; no checks; lunch, dinner every day (bar menu until 1am); full bar; reservations recommended; self parking; www.nicksatthebeach.com; map:KK7* &

## Nine Ten / ★★☆

**910 PROSPECT ST, LA JOLLA; 858/964-5400** Executive chef Michael Stebner, who earned plenty of kudos while cooking at Azzura Point, has turned the former Putnam's restaurant into a stylish (and pricey) new dining destination frequented by the who's who of La Jolla. The menu, based on the freshest seasonal produce and seafood the chef can obtain each day, leans toward luxurious items like an extra-rich lobster risotto spiked with truffle oil, soft-shell crabs done tempura style, and a roasted foie gras salad. Both full and half portions are available, so you can choose to make a meal of several different small dishes if you wish. For dessert, the molten-centered warm chocolate cake is a must. In addition to the dramatic-looking dining room and bar, where heads swivel each time someone new makes an entrance, seating is available on the sidewalk patio on Prospect Street and a quieter garden-view terrace. *$$$; AE, MC, V; no checks; breakfast, lunch, dinner every day; full bar; reservations recommended; street parking; www.grandecolonial.com; map: JJ7* &

## Old Town Mexican Cafe / ★★

**2489 SAN DIEGO AVE, OLD TOWN; 619/297-4330** For more than 20 years, this local institution has been packing 'em in with a combination of hefty margaritas, festive atmosphere, and filling, well-prepared Mexican food. Invariably crowded and frequently deafening, it's a favorite of both tourists and locals in search of good-size portions, party ambiance, and reasonable prices. The cafe has long been known for its tasty carnitas and carne asada, but other worthy choices include sizzling fajitas made with chicken, vegetables, or beef; heaping combo plates served with rice and beans; and chicken enchiladas topped with salsa verde. Over the years, the original restaurant has expanded to include several dining rooms, but there's still a lengthy wait for a table on most weekend nights. Watch the hard-working "tortilla ladies" plying their craft in the front window while you wait, or angle for a seat at the bar, which serves dozens of high-quality tequilas by the shot. The atmosphere is ultracasual, making this a popular spot for families with children, and the servers and bartenders are unfailingly pleasant. *$–$$; AE, DC, DIS, MC, V; breakfast, lunch, dinner every day; full bar; reservations accepted for 10 or more; street parking; www.oldtownmexcafe.com; map: J2*

## Old Venice Italian Restaurant Caffe & Bar / ★

**2910 CANON ST, POINT LOMA; 619/222-5888** The two best things about Old Venice are the pizza and the ambiance. The former has a delicious thin crust (both the recipe and the cooks came with the highly successful business when it was purchased in 1972 from Sicilian-American Vince Giacalone). The decor is simple yet elegant, with linen napkins and tablecloths—so what if the latter are covered with butcher paper? (A carton of markers on each table solves the butcher-paper mystery and provides recreation for the kids as they wait for the meal.) Lighting is furnished primarily by candles on the tables and in delicate wrought-iron sconces on the walls. The dining room gets a bit noisy when full; you can retire to the quieter back patio, dotted with potted plants. Avoid the house salad, which consists mainly of green-leaf lettuce, with a few red onion rings, one tomato chunk, and a bland house vinaigrette. Apart from the pizzas, the honey-glazed salmon is a good choice—tender and moist—and is accompanied by a medley of grilled veggies julienne. La Linguine di Kathleen is a powerful combo of sun-dried tomatoes, pine nuts, pesto, and feta on egg-and-pepper linguine, a bold (some might say brash) conglomeration of spices and flavors that's tasty, but not for the faint of palate. There's a fairly extensive wine list. Drinks come from the adjacent White Bar, under the same management; with the same graceful, airy decoration as Old Venice and a friendly clientele of Point Loma residents, it's is a comfortable, upscale version of the neighborhood bar. *$$; AE, MC, V; no checks; lunch Mon–Sat, dinner every day; full bar; reservations accepted for 10 or more; street parking; map:E7* &

### Olé Madrid / ★★☆

**755 5TH AVE, DOWNTOWN; 619/557-0146** One of the Gaslamp Quarter's most enduring clubs, Olé Madrid attracts an A-list crowd arriving late on Friday and Saturday to drink and dance the night away. On weekends, this is truly the home of the young and the restless. But although the sangria here is fabulous, the music cutting-edge, and the young male bartenders downright sexy, Olé Madrid manages to be a pretty good Spanish restaurant as well. Tapas range from basics like manchego cheese and chorizo to garlicky grilled shrimp and chicken croquettes. Main dishes include well-made paellas and grilled fish and meats, and the wine list features some noteworthy Spanish reds. The bar and dining rooms at this three-level hangout are attractive, with enormous flower arrangements, velvet curtains creating private spaces, and curving stairways. On balmy nights, the sidewalk patio offers a front-row view of the passing scene and the less fortunate in line waiting to get in. *$$; AE, MC, V; no checks; dinner Tues–Sun; full bar; reservations recommended; street parking; www.olemadrid.net; map:O8* &

### 150 Grand Cafe / ★★★

**150 W GRAND AVE, ESCONDIDO; 760/738-6868** Not known as a culinary haven, the North County city of Escondido does have a restaurant worth seeking out. This casual yet classy cafe is overseen by boyish-looking chef Carlton Greenawalt, who has a special way with what he calls New American cuisine. International recipes and ingredients are combined to create healthful dishes familiar to American palates. Dressed like New Age security guards in black trousers and Nehru shirts of subdued colors, attentive waitpersons deliver crusty bread from the Upper Crust bakery in Mission Valley. Move on to appetizers (try the excellent carpaccio) and a variety of yummy entrees with complex sauces and impressive presentation. Dessert here should be a priority, not an afterthought: the cinnamon chocolate cake glazed in orange ganache and topped with caramel mascarpone mousse is worth every calorie. Just a block from the California Center of Performing Arts, the cafe accepts reservations for even one person, which are certainly in order before a performance and on weekend evenings. The welcoming ambiance makes this a delightful spot to linger over California Chardonnay. *$$; AE, MC, V; no checks; lunch, dinner Mon–Sat; full bar; reservations recommended; self parking; map:CC2* &

## Ono Sushi / ★★

**1236 UNIVERSITY AVE, HILLCREST; 619/298-0616** Slide into one of the faux-leopard booths lining one wall, or perch on a stool around the two-sided sushi bar. Unobtrusive modern music will soothe you, as will the minimalist decor and soft lighting. You can start off with a big bowl of edamame—the steamed legume is a traditional appetizer—but don't fill up! Save room for a Hillcrest roll, which is a wrap of scallops, crab, and wasabi rice, or perhaps the sesame chicken salad: grilled chicken and sesame-ginger croutons on a bed of summer greens. In addition there are standard Japanese sushi choices, side dishes, and entrees of all types. On weekends well drinks are discounted, while Mondays after work there's a sushi happy hour special. *$$; AE, MC, V; no checks; lunch Sat–Sun, dinner every day; reservations accepted for 8 or more; street parking; map:O2* &

## Ortega's / ★★

**4888 NEWPORT AVE, OCEAN BEACH; 619/222-4205** Neighborhood Mexican restaurants abound in San Diego; this small cafe with barely a dozen tables is a local favorite. The Ortega family comes from Puebla, one of Mexico's culinary capitals, and they've created the perfect homeland ambiance by including much of the extended family in the operation. The family specializes in steamed tamales, which are served at a sidewalk stand in front of the restaurant during street fairs and farmers' bazaars. Sons and cousins work at an open grill by the front door, letting the savory smells of marinated pork, spiced shrimp, and corn tortillas tempt passersby. Regulars show up during off hours to feast on huevos rancheros drenched in salsa verde and melted cheese, enchiladas topped with mole (a blend of a dozen or more spices guaranteed to challenge the palate), and the best tacos al pastor (corn tortillas filled with grilled pork) this side of Tijuana. Specials include fresh tuna, calamari, or dorado and those incomparable tamales. *$; MC, V; no checks; breakfast, lunch, dinner every day; beer and wine; street parking; no reservations; map:B3*

## Pacifica Del Mar / ★★

**1555 CAMINO DEL MAR, DEL MAR; 858/792-0476** "Pacific Rim" may be a term that's getting a little tired, but the concept remains fresh and exciting at this ocean-view restaurant in Del Mar. Given the proximity to the sea, it's only fitting that seafood dominates the extensive menu. A clever "takoshimi" appetizer starring seared peppered ahi is one of the top dishes here. But don't rule out the likes of wok-seared catfish, ginger-marinated salmon, seafood pastas, a mixed seafood grill, and imaginative sandwiches, as well as some truly inspired Sunday brunch dishes. The dining room is pretty, but the real treat here is a seat on the patio. Don't drop by just for the food; the list of martinis and wines by the glass is impressive, and the singles scene in the eye-catching bar is legendary. Troll here on a Friday night and you might end up with the catch of the day. And no, we don't mean catfish. *$$; AE, CB, DC,*

*DIS, MC, V; no checks; lunch, dinner every day, brunch Sun; full bar; reservations recommended; self parking; www.pacificadelmar.com; map:GG7* &

## Pacific Coast Grill / ★★

**437 HWY 101, SOLANA BEACH; 858/794-4632** A winning combination of looks, food, personality, and location have made the PCG a favored hangout for upscale young North County residents. Out front, a shaded, lavender-surrounded patio inspires long lunches among the fragrant flowers; indoors, the clever surfer chic decor (complete with old photos, surfboards, and a giant seahorse) makes a great backdrop for lively conversation and cocktails. Tucked in a corner of the BeachWalk Center, the restaurant features a good-size bar area decked out with velvet couches and bar stools, as well as a spacious, often noisy dining room. The menu offers updated American favorites such as barbecued ribs, onion "strings," rotisserie chicken with mashed potatoes, fresh grilled ahi, and turkey meatloaf (all good choices) along with gloriously fattening desserts like the white chocolate bread pudding. Check out the wine list, chosen by the owners to spotlight some unfamiliar labels and lesser-known varietals. *$$; AE, DC, DIS, MC, V; no checks; lunch Mon–Sat, dinner every day, brunch Sun; full bar; reservations recommended; self parking; map: FF7*

## Pamplemousse Grille / ★★★☆

**514 VIA DE LA VALLE, SOLANA BEACH; 858/792-9090** High rollers, socialites, businessfolk, and trophy spouses abound at this stylish bistro across from the Del Mar racetrack. While many are no doubt drawn by the ambiance—a chic, sophisticated take on country French with beautiful people in every corner—others undoubtedly come for the imaginative fare. The food isn't always Triple Crown material, but the kitchen delivers artfully garnished, creatively conceived variations on nouvelle American and classic French cuisine. The foie gras usually served as a special is always outstanding, as are the grilled fish specials prepared with your choice of half a dozen sauces. Lamb stew, a very tender pork prime rib, and a roasted tomato–fennel soup are also perennial favorites. Salads and side dishes make fine use of the vegetables from Chino's produce farm (favored by chefs from L.A. and San Francisco) just down the road, and desserts—especially the semibaked, melting chocolate truffle cake or the trio of crème brûlées—are always worth an extra hour on the StairMaster. Pamplemousse is particularly busy during the racing season (linger in the bar and you might get a hot tip), but the prosperous mood and society gossip stay in the air year-round. *$$$; AE, CB, DC, DIS, MC, V; checks OK; lunch Wed–Fri, dinner every day, brunch Sun; full bar; reservations recommended; self parking; pgrille@pgrille.com; www.pgrille.com; map:FF7* &

## Panda Inn Chinese Restaurant / ★★

**506 HORTON PLAZA, DOWNTOWN; 619/233-7800** Hungry mall-goers and folks headed to nearby movie theaters or stage productions would be smart to remember this spacious Chinese restaurant on the top level of the Horton Plaza shopping center, where there's rarely a wait, even on weekend evenings. The decor is rather smashing, although casual attire is the norm, and the back dining room offers a view of downtown. Lots of families dine here (read: lots of kids), so the noise level tends to be high when the place is bustling. Check the blackboard at the reception desk for daily specials, which tend to feature fresh seasonal ingredients like green beans or eggplant. On the regular menu, standouts are the smoky pan-fried noodles topped with a variety of meats, any of the chicken-based stir-fries, sweet 'n' sour pork, and incomparable white-chocolate-dipped fortune cookies for dessert. Service is generally attentive and polite, and the reasonable prices and full bar may help to ease the pain of shoppers' maxed-out credit cards. *$$; AE, DC, DIS, MC, V; no checks; lunch, dinner every day; full bar; reservations recommended; self parking; www.pandainn.com; map:N7* &

### Parallel 33 / ★★

**741 W WASHINGTON ST, MISSION HILLS; 619/260-0033** Chef Amiko Gubbins, who made her name at Cafe Japengo, hit upon a novel concept with her own hip eatery. Realizing that San Diego sits at the same latitude as several exciting countries, Gubbins focuses on the flavors of the 33rd parallel. She mixes and matches spices and ingredients from California, Morocco, Lebanon, Japan, India, and several other countries with pleasingly successful results. For starters, try the Moroccan chicken with almonds, saffron, and raisins wrapped in phyllo and dusted with powdered sugar, the ahi poke with wasabi dressing, or the samosas with a tropical fruit sauce. The appetizer list is so inventive you may want to order a few selections, then share an entree. Go for the grilled flat iron steak rubbed with Moroccan spices. It's sliced and served atop mashed red potatoes with a kalamata olive sauce; the kitchen will divide the serving on two gorgeous plates. The servers are honest; one discouraged us from ordering the soft-shell crabs, saying they weren't as fresh as the Chilean sea bass or local ahi. Co-owner Robert Butterfield is equally helpful, stopping by the tables to suggest a wine pairing or helping diners choose between the chocolate crème brûlée or warm date madeleines with vanilla-rose ice cream. The room is sleekly decorated with bamboo screens and Indian textiles, though it can be noisy since there's nothing to absorb the chatter and laughter of your fellow diners. *$$; AE, MC, V; no checks; dinner Mon–Sat; beer and wine; reservations recommended; self parking; map:M2*

### Piatti / ★★

**2182 AVENIDA DE LA PLAYA, LA JOLLA; 858/454-1589** The fashionable neighborhood of La Jolla Shores makes the perfect setting for this ever-trendy Italian restaurant where air-kissing has developed into an art form. Dressed-up socialites, wealthy vacationers, casually clad regulars, and cell-phone-toting businessfolk keep the place hopping at lunch and dinner, and the bar and dining rooms can be cacophonous. Repeat visitors seeking a little peace and quiet ask to sit in the walled-in patio reminiscent of a Tuscan courtyard. Dominated by an enormous tree and loads of greenery, it's a charming spot to savor a Pinot Grigio or Barolo from the wine list. Consistent best-sellers include the simple but savory panini (sandwiches), fancy wood-fired pizzas, roasted chicken, risotto, vegetable lasagne, and beautiful salads. And for an appetizer, the garlicky bruschetta heaped with tomatoes and basil chiffonade can't be beat—it's one of the best versions in town. To fit in with the crowd, keep one eye on your plate, the other constantly surveying the room to see who's doing what with whom. *$$; AE, DC, MC, V; no checks; lunch, dinner every day; full bar; reservations recommended; street parking; map:JJ7* &

## Pizza Nova / ★★

**5120 N HARBOR DR, POINT LOMA (AND BRANCHES); 619/226-0268** The mountainous salads at Pizza Nova can easily be split between two diners—at least! Grilled chicken tops several variations, such as a chipotle-lime version sprinkled with yellow corn and roasted peppers. Pasta portions are also generous, and adding goat cheese (at less than a dollar it's a real bargain) to shrimp nested in tomato-basil angel hair yields rich veins of molten cheese. The Thai chicken pizza sports a colorful landscape of shredded carrots, peanuts, scallions, and cilantro in ginger sauce. Every pizza here gets a great head start thanks to spectacular dough that bubbles and crisps in a true wood-burning oven. Three other Pizza Nova branches have the same menu. The original location at Harbor Drive has the best view: its upstairs room overlooks San Diego Harbor. *$; AE, DIS, DC, MC, V; local checks only; lunch, dinner every day; beer and wine; reservations recommended; self parking; map:E6* &

## Pizza Port / ★★☆

**135 N HWY 101, SOLANA BEACH; 858/481-7332 / 571 CARLSBAD VILLAGE DR, CARLSBAD; 760/720-7007** Is this the area's best pizza? Probably. Is it the coolest pizzeria? For sure. It's close enough to the beach to attract the surf, skate, and sun-loving crowd, and the place also serves top-notch microbrew beers, made right on the premises. Pale ales, wheat beers, special seasonal brews, and more—they're all fresh and frosty and a perfect complement to pizza. And what pies these are: puff-crusted, chewy, and topped with goodies from trendy to traditional. Best bets are the spicy number topped with Canadian bacon and jalapeños; the seafood pizza loaded with clams, shrimp, and onions; and the more classic pie topped with artichoke hearts, olives, and mushrooms. You even get a choice of crusts, either traditional or whole-grain beer batter. The crowd here is predominantly young, but anybody is welcome: families, seniors, even yuppies, as long as they're into video games, surf films, brewskis, and good food. *$; MC, V; no checks; lunch, dinner every day; beer and wine; no reservations; street parking; www.pizzaport.com; map:FF7 and CC7* &

## Point Loma Seafoods / ★★☆

**2805 EMERSON ST, POINT LOMA; 619/223-1109** Generations of San Diegans have lined up at the counter of this seafood market, purchasing fresh fish to prepare for dinner or ordering takeout. The place is almost always jammed, and with good reason: year after year, the quality of the goods and service here are superior to anyplace like it in San Diego. Fish and seafood (including live clams, crabs, and lobsters) are expensive, but always divinely fresh. The shop is also known for moist, just-smoked fish (which makes terrific picnic fixings), appealing seafood salads, sourdough bread, and a decent selection of wine. Top takeout foods (which you can eat on the harborside patio) are the excellent clam chowder, seafood ceviche, fresh tuna sandwich, and shrimp or crab cocktails. Service is knowledgeable and cheerful, even during rush hours. The location adjacent to the busy sportsfishing docks can make parking a pain, but one bite of this restaurant's smoked swordfish or fried calamari and you'll be glad you dropped by. *$; no credit cards; local checks only; lunch, dinner every day (until 7pm); beer and wine; no reservations; self parking; map:E6* &

### Porkyland / ★

**1030 TORREY PINES RD, LA JOLLA; 858/459-1708 / 2196 LOGAN AVE, LOGAN HEIGHTS; 619/233-5139** Despite the lighthearted name, the people at this Mexican takeout spot turn out well-made, authentic fare. And the price is right, with lots of tacos, burritos, and tortas under $3. You'll find the usual south-of-the-border specialties here, like quesadillas and enchiladas, but it's pork that puts Porkyland in our culinary hall of fame. This is the place to find first-rate carnitas: the tender, long-cooked pork is heaven in a warm tortilla with onions and cilantro. Pork or chicken tamales are also outstanding, and Porky fans have been known to make pilgrimages across town for the pork al pastor. Service is fast, the setting ultra-casual with a do-it-yourself salsa bar. In addition to hot takeout, the shop sells fresh corn and flour tortillas and fixings like rice and beans. *$; cash only; lunch, dinner every day; no alcohol; no reservations; self parking; map:JJ7 and NN4* &

### The Prado Restaurant at Balboa Park / ★★

**1549 EL PRADO (IN THE HOUSE OF HOSPITALITY), DOWNTOWN; 619/557-9441** For too many years, this prime piece of real estate in Balboa Park housed a mediocre eatery and rather dusty bar. Then the Cohn family—proprietors of the Blue Point and Kemo Sabe eateries, among others—took over, and one of San Diego's most appealing dining destinations was born. Set off the lush courtyard in the House of Hospitality, the Prado has a spacious, multilevel dining room, separate bar, and a garden-view patio, all done up in modern hacienda decor. Start out with a trendy mojito or pisco sour to set the Latin tone, then choose just about anything on the ambitious Mexican- and Cal-cuisine-influenced menu; the chef is remarkably consistent. A few of the standouts: chicken tortilla soup, pork prime rib, and a clever combo of lemon-thyme grilled swordfish with butternut squash (prepared two different ways) and red beet-truffle purée. With its charming location, fun ambiance, and dependably good food and drink, the Prado is great for a leisurely lunch, a relaxed dinner date, or pretheater dining before heading across the plaza to a performance at the Globe or the Cassius Carter. The restaurant also offers catering and is the site for numerous indoor and outdoor weddings. *$$; AE, DC, DIS, MC, V; no checks; lunch, dinner every day; full bar; reservations recommended; valet and self parking; www.cohnrestaurants.com; map: O5* &

### The Prince of Wales / ★★★

**1500 ORANGE AVE (HOTEL DEL CORONADO), CORONADO; 619/522-8819** All the glamour of the Hotel Del's past comes to life in this elegant dining room, where strains of live jazz piano accompany leisurely meals. You can dine under the stars on the candlelit terrace, or view the sea from the long windows in the serene champagne-and-gold dining room. Reserve a booth for privacy, and order slowly. Start with a flute of imported bubbly with the osetra caviar parfait or oysters with sweet sake sorbet while you study the entrees and consider whether you want to experiment with the wild boar tenderloin or the yellowfin tuna with sautéed foie gras and truffle coulis. While a tie isn't mandatory, it certainly isn't out of place and makes for a nice change of pace in laid-back San Diego. This is the place to come for a special celebration—or just to revel in the good life for an evening. A wonderful wine selection complements the menu and impeccable service. *$$$$; AE, CB, DC, DIS, MC, V; no checks; dinner every day; full bar; reservations recommended; valet and self parking; map:NN5* &

### Qwiigs Bar & Grill / ★★

**5083 SANTA MONICA AVE, OCEAN BEACH; 619/222-1101** Snag a window table at sunset for the ultimate Ocean Beach dining experience, right across from the water. Qwiigs offers spectacular views of surfers, joggers, seagulls, and the O.B. Pier. Locals gather for steamed artichokes, bountiful house salads, fried calamari, and gourmet pizzas in the upper-level cocktail lounge or hover around the busy little sushi bar. The dining room features cozy ocean-view tables with prized window seats and raised U-shaped booths that also face the outdoor spectacle. The place is packed at sunset, naturally. Enormous fresh Cobb salads (we prefer the chicken version over the seafood salad) and thick burgers are good bets at lunch. Dinner specials might include rack of lamb or penne pesto with Japanese breaded chicken breast along with the fresh fish and blackened prime rib. A sit-down Sunday brunch includes average-to-good breakfast fare. The ambiance and service are fairly low-key; while some people show up in ties and work suits at lunch, this is definitely one of those come-as-you-are neighborhood haunts. Use the underground parking lot if possible; spots on the street can be tough to find. *$$; AE, DC, DIS, MC, V; no checks; lunch Mon–Fri, dinner every day, brunch Sun; full bar; reservations recommended; street parking; map:B2*

### Rancho Valencia Restaurant / ★★★

**5921 VALENCIA CIRCLE, RANCHO SANTA FE; 858/756-1123** Rancho Valencia, in the new-money enclave of Rancho Santa Fe known as Fairbanks Ranch, is far enough off the usual restaurant rows to feel like a secret destination. It could easily have been custom-built for lovers, boasting a secluded and exclusive setting in a world-class resort. The dining room is at once rustic and upscale, and although it's spacious, there's a definite intimacy to the place. Glowing fireplaces, artful flower arrangements, high-beamed ceilings, and highly polished service all complement the meals and add an air of effortless sophistication. Don't rush through a meal here. Instead, bask in the country-club ambiance while lingering over a well-chosen wine list and a menu inspired by France, California, and the Mediterranean. A number of notable chefs have passed through the kitchen here, each leaving a trademark dish or two. Steven Sumner, the personable executive chef at this writing, is especially fond of Asian dishes. His Hawaiian sashimi crisp is a to-die-for artful creation of finely diced ahi topped with a papaya-mango salsa, all wrapped in a spring roll taco. We ordered it two nights in a row during a recent stay at the resort. The quickly sautéed foie gras could hold its own in a French kitchen; other highlights are spicy sautéed crab cakes and veal with chanterelles. For dessert, choose the perfectly caramelized tarte Tatin. After dinner, take a stroll through the bougainvillea-bedecked courtyards. If you'd like to stay at the resort, call well in advance to book one of the private casitas here. Yes, it will cost a small fortune, but this verdant retreat is worth the extra green. *$$$–$$$$; AE, DC, MC, V; no checks; breakfast, lunch, dinner every day; full bar; reservations recommended; self parking; www.ranchovalencia.com; map:EE5* &

## Red Sails Inn / ★★☆

**2614 SHELTER ISLAND DR, SHELTER ISLAND; 619/223-3030** OK, so the decor is some of the oddest in town, complete with stuffed crabs and fish mounted on the walls and a vintage diving suit that looks left over from Halloween. Just don't let that or the humble '50s-esque setting sway you from trying some of San Diego's best old-fashioned seafood at decidedly old-fashioned prices. You won't find any fancy stuff, but the kitchen does a good job with grilled swordfish, mahi mahi, monkfish, and sea bass for under $20 a plate. That includes soup or salad and a baked potato on the side. In addition to the two spacious dining rooms, which feature a fireplace and harbor view along with those mounted fish, there's a delightful patio right on the water of San Diego Bay. Cheerful servers and basic breakfast and lunch items such as pancakes and tuna sandwiches make this a favorite of locals on the weekends. A huge fountain, boats coming and going, and lots of slumming seagulls keep kids entertained while you eat. *$$; AE, DC, MC, V; no checks; breakfast, lunch, dinner every day; full bar; reservations recommended; street parking; map:F7*

## Roppongi Restaurant, Bar, and Cafe / ★★☆

**875 PROSPECT ST, LA JOLLA; 858/551-5252** Local restaurateur Sami Ladeki, founder of the hugely popular, family-friendly Sammy's Woodfired Pizza chain, has gone upmarket with this flashy La Jolla endeavor. It's a sight to behold, from the expensive bric-a-brac to the spectacular aquarium with Day-Glo tropical fish. And the requisitely trendy menu, colored with influences from cutting-edge Pacific Rim to classic Americana, has plenty to dazzle as well—as long as you stick to the appetizers and skip the so-so entrees. The key to dining at Roppongi is to graze, tapas-style, through the list of superbly made starters. A multilayered crab napoleon; skewered scallops, plump and pretty as South Pacific pearls; fiery kung pao calamari; pot stickers filled with shrimp; and more—each is an exquisite, if expensive, little treat. The open dining room includes booth and table seating, as well as a semi-private dining room for large parties. Out front, a raised fire pit keeps diners comfortable on the coolest evenings. Service ranges from adept to iffy, and the wine list is overpriced, but those top-notch tapas keep us coming back. *$$$; AE, DIS, MC, V; no checks; lunch, dinner every day; full bar; reservations recommended; street parking; map:JJ7* &

## Royale Brasserie / ★★

**224 5TH AVE, DOWNTOWN; 619/237-4900** Although the cheeky Parisian decor often seems more authentic than the cuisine, this popular downtown bistro is a fun stop for diners in search of onion soup, escargot, and ambiance. The interior is sheer déjà vu for anyone who's visited Montparnasse, with a series of dining rooms done up with mosaic floors, banquette seating, gleaming paneling, and painted ceilings.

On the menu, decent versions of bouillabaisse, coq au vin, and cassoulet share space with grilled yellowfin or swordfish and a New York strip steak. Steamed mussels (cooked in white wine, beer, or fresh tomatoes) are a specialty of the house and come with the requisite *pommes frites* (french fries). Shellfish fans with deep pockets can share an oversize platter of fresh oysters, clams, shrimp, and crab for about $100, but we're perfectly happy with the excellent duck and pork pâté that's under $10. Service ranges from skilled to spacey; if you're in a hurry, it's generally best to duck into the bar for a beer and a quick bite. *$$; AE, DC, MC, V; no checks; dinner every day; full bar; reservations recommended; valet and street parking; www.royale brasserie.com; map: N8* &

## Roy's / ★★☆

**8670 GENESEE AVE, LA JOLLA; 858/455-1616** Grab your platinum cards—dining at this über-upscale chain founded by top Hawaiian chef Roy Yamaguchi doesn't come cheap. But it's a real treat, since the kitchen specializes in a winning blend of Asian, European, and Pacific Rim cuisine. Fresh fish in a variety of guises is a good bet, given this eatery's island roots; we're especially partial to cilantro-seared northern halibut and mahi mahi in a heady Cognac cream sauce. But other top contenders include pot stickers, grilled teriyaki scallops, roast lamb, and a delicious, unusual Mongolian pork pot roast. The vast, modish dining room, complete with exhibition kitchen, can be noisy, and prices for wines by the glass are often outrageous. Still, Roy's offers some terrific food, an intriguing sake-tasting menu, and a cool, moneyed atmosphere for anytime you're feeling flush. If you'd like to watch the chefs in action, ask for a seat at the counter; otherwise, relatively quiet tables are at the far edges of the room. At these prices, and with the relatively sophisticated preparations, you'll probably want to leave young children at home. *$$$; AE, DC, DIS, MC, V; checks OK; dinner every day; full bar; reservations recommended; self parking; lajolla@roysrestaurant.com; www.roysrestaurant.com; map: JJ6* &

## Rubio's / ★☆

**4504 MISSION BAY DR, PACIFIC BEACH (AND BRANCHES); 858/272-2801** What a success story: local boy visits Baja, falls in love with the fish tacos there, opens a tiny restaurant in Pacific Beach selling same, and gains fortune and fame. Millions of battered-and-fried fish tacos later, founder Ralph Rubio has extended the menu at this thriving chain of restaurants, which numbers more than two dozen in San Diego County alone and is rapidly spreading through the West. These days, you'll find fresh, flavorful takes on Mexican cuisine: everything from grilled mahi mahi tacos and shrimp burritos to Baja Bowls (a beans 'n' rice spin on the ubiquitous Asian rice bowl). A special HealthMex menu offers entrees with less than 22 percent of their calories from fat. But it's the original fish taco, made with a plump white fillet, a flurry of shredded cabbage, and a ranchlike dressing folded into a corn tortilla, that keeps Rubio's ardent fans coming back for takeout or a quick bite in the informal, sparkling-clean dining rooms. *$; AE, DC, DIS, MC, V; no checks; lunch, dinner every day; beer and wine; no reservations; self parking; www.rubios.com; map:KK7* &

## Ruby's Diner / ★

**1640 CAMINO DEL RIO N, MISSION VALLEY (AND BRANCHES); 619/294-7829**
Ruby's is that classic soda fountain from *It's a Wonderful Life* morphed into a sleek, modern diner straight out of the 22nd century. The snappy red-and-white decor makes for a cheery, welcoming feeling that's reinforced by the lengthy menu of old-time comfort foods. This is the place to bring the kids for real milk shakes, offered in a rainbow of flavors and served from the blender in all their slushy splendor. Then it's on to burgers, onion rings, and fries; club sandwiches and home-style meatloaf; fish and chips; even a turkey pot pie. In a nod to vegetarians, there's a decent garden burger on the menu. Ruby's is also good for lunch and a matinee at the nearby multiplex, or for a nostalgic hot fudge sundae after the show. Even if you don't have kids, it's worth dropping in for a taste of the past. The noise level rises in proportion to the number of young children in the crowd, but this diner still owns a little piece of our heart. There are two other Ruby's in North County, one right on the Oceanside Pier (1 Pierview Way, Oceanside; 760/433-RUBY) and the other in Carlsbad (5630 Paseo del Norte, Carlsbad; 760/931-7829). *$; AE, DC, DIS, MC, V; no checks; breakfast, lunch, dinner every day; beer and wine; no reservations; self parking; www.rubys.com; map:LL4, BB9, and CC7* ♿

## Saffron Noodles and Saté / ★★★

**3737 INDIA ST, MIDDLETOWN; 619/574-7737** Nobody has done more to introduce San Diegans to the pleasures of Thai cuisine than owner/chef Su-Mei Yu, who founded the tiny original Saffron next door (still a favorite takeout joint). Today, she's expanded her original rotisserie chicken shop into a full-scale noodle house, with dozens of choices that explore a range of styles from mild to incendiary. Classic noodle dishes such as pad thai and spicy noodles are done well, but it's the exotic daily specials flavored with pickled vegetables or fried shallots and the silken curries that are the true stars of this aromatic show. New specials are always popping up; each time Su-Mei travels to Thailand, she brings back additional regional recipes to tempt our palates. In addition to the artful food, the restaurant features works by glass artist Dale Chihuly and painter Italo Scanga. The place is a feast for the eyes as well as the palate, and the low prices make it an affordable treat. *$; MC, V; no checks; lunch, dinner every day; beer and wine; no reservations; street parking; map:L3 W*

## Sally's / ★★

**1 MARKET PL, DOWNTOWN; 619/687-6080** With a prime location in Seaport Village overlooking the harbor and Coronado, Sally's would probably draw plenty of business for the view alone. Between the outdoor tables lining the bayside boardwalk and the great vantage points in the bar, this is one of the prime places in town to watch the world go by. But Sally's doesn't depend solely on its looks; the seafood served up with Mediterranean, French, and Cal-cuisine influences can be inviting as well. Fresh oysters are a house specialty, and we've found their fresh, salty goodness is further enhanced by one of the frosty Bombay Sapphire martinis prepared by the resident mixologists. Main-dish salads topped with grilled fish or chicken are top sellers for good reason, as are seared scallops, a terrific tuna tartare, and swordfish dressed in an imaginative gazpacho sauce. Along with the patio seating and comfortable booths in the dining room, a chef's table in the kitchen may be reserved in advance for up to a dozen diners, who get to watch the staff whip up their custom-designed meal. *$$; AE, CB, DC, DIS, MC, V; no checks; lunch, dinner every day; full bar; reservations recommended; self parking; map:M8*

## Sammy's California Woodfired Pizza / ★★

**565 PEARL ST, LA JOLLA (AND BRANCHES); 858/456-5222** San Diego has never been the same since Sami Ladeki brought wood-fired pizza to town. Savor varieties such as Jamaican Jerked Shrimp (with cilantro and carrots), Artichokes (with tomato sauce, mozzarella, and Gorgonzola cheese), or Smoked Duck Sausage (with spinach, Roma tomatoes, garlic, and smoked Gouda). Other mouthwatering options include Norwegian salmon fillet, grilled chicken salad, and some exquisite pasta dishes (the four-cheese ravioli in cream sauce with wild mushrooms and spinach is an artery-clogging trip to heaven). The open kitchen lets you keep a close eye on your order. A full takeout menu is available. *$; AE, DC, MC, V; no checks; lunch, dinner every day; full bar; no reservations; self parking; www.sammyspizza. com; map:JJ7* &

## Santé Ristorante / ★★

**7811 HERSCHEL AVE, LA JOLLA; 858/454-1315** With a smart La Jolla address and a coterie of devoted fans, Santé has a New York neighborhood feel to it. It's the kind of place where the owner greets regulars and people tend to dress up—for San Diego, at least. Along with the rather formal dining room (which includes a fireplace), seating options include the intimate bar with a couple of tables, a courtyard lit with tiny lights, and two additional patios. The kitchen is known for a variety of veal specials—grilled chops, scaloppine sauced with lemon or topped, saltimbocca-style, with fresh herbs and prosciutto—as well as pastas such as fettuccine tossed with smoked salmon and finished with caviar. Wild game is occasionally featured on the menu, and both quail and breast of duck garnished with a rosemary glaze are especially well prepared here. Service is attentive, adding to the "everyone's a VIP" feeling. Whether you're looking for a classy place for a business dinner or a romantic setting for a hot date, Santé definitely delivers. *$$$; AE, CB, DC, DIS, MC, V; no checks; lunch Mon–Fri, dinner every day; full bar; reservations recommended; street parking; www.santeristorante.com; map:JJ7* &

## Sevilla / ★★

**555 4TH AVE, DOWNTOWN; 619/233-5979 / 3050 PIO PICO RD, CARLSBAD; 760/730-7558** After a long, hard day, downtown office workers unwind at this Spanish tapas bar in the Gaslamp district, and empty bar stools are a rarity after 5pm. The ambiance is the main draw. Bullfight posters and oil paintings of Andalusian beauties surround the mirrored bar, where slow-moving bartenders and waitresses dispense plates of Spanish olives stuffed with anchovy paste and glasses of Spanish and domestic wine. You can make a dinner of such tapas as tortilla española, fried calamari, or mushrooms in white wine garlic sauce at either of the two bars (serenaded by live flamenco guitar after 9:30pm). Or head to the dining room, El Patio Andaluz, which is dressed up like a courtyard from southern Spain. Wrought-iron grills and potted geraniums decorate make-believe windows, and a black light brings out a ceiling full of stars. The most popular dish here is traditional paella valenciana—seafood, sausage, and chicken in saffron rice—but you can also get seafood-only and vegetarian versions. Some of the desserts (all made on the premises) really do shine, like the sinful crema catalana, a chocolate espresso crème brûlée topped with whipped cream, with a bottom layer of chocolate chips. In the downstairs Club Sevilla, there's a different brand of live Latino music nightly, with samba lessons, Spanish rock, salsa, and, on Fridays and Saturdays, a dinner show (tango or flamenco) for $40. The Carlsbad restaurant has a more formal feeling, with several dark and cozy dining rooms and an upstairs bar. Advance reservations are required for the dinner shows here. *$$; AE, DC, DIS, MC, V; no checks; dinner every day; full bar; reservations recommended; street parking (downtown); self parking (Carlsbad); www.cafesevilla.com; map:O8, CC9* &

## Shakespeare Pub and Grille / ★

**3701 INDIA ST, MIDDLETOWN; 619/299-0230** The most authentic British pub in all of San Diego, the Shakespeare (or "Shakey's" to the regulars) draws a crowd of expats in search of a bit o' Britain. Families come with the kids in tow for Sunday dinner, while lads gather at other times of the week to catch soccer matches on the telly. Indoors at the wooden bar, British brews dominate the tap—sample the likes of Boddington's and Fuller's by the half- and full pint. On a sunny afternoon, the outdoor deck overlooking the airport and bay is a fine spot to while away a few hours. A full menu is available too, featuring bangers and mash, shepherd's pie, and, of course, chips (french fries) smothered with malt vinegar and salt. Sunday lunch is a feast of roast beef, but, in a nod to its American patrons, the management has added fish tacos to the menu. Check with the waitresses for the daily beer specials. Insiders like to welcome the new year at Shakey's, a time when kilted bagpipers march around at 4pm (midnight in England). Not to be missed. *$; AE, MC, V; no checks; lunch, dinner every day; full bar; no reservations; self parking; map:L3* &

## The Sky Room / ★★★½

**1132 PROSPECT ST (LA VALENCIA HOTEL), LA JOLLA; 858/454-0771** Saying La Valencia's The Sky Room is a romantic place to dine is like calling Placido Domingo a pretty good singer. This ocean-view dining room atop La Jolla's venerable pink palace of a hotel is *the* place in town to pop the question (whatever it might be), celebrate an important birthday or anniversary, or simply treat yourself to an evening of elegance and pomp. Gorgeous flower arrangements, tuxedo-clad servers, Wedgwood china, and long-stemmed roses for the ladies provide a feeling of old-world elegance and a lovely showcase for distinctly well-prepared California and French cuisine turned out by a cadre of experienced sous-chefs. Selections range from contemporary (free-range chicken with morels; fine Kobe beef imported from Japan) to classic (delicate smoked salmon paired with julienned cucumber; cream of mushroom soup; velvety foie gras). If they're offering the filet mignon finished with a Merlot demi-glace, it's a must-have. So is the dessert plate, a selection of sweets that generally includes tidbits of tiramisu, cookies, and sublime chocolate truffles. An extensive wine list is particularly strong in California Cabernet and Chardonnay, but high rollers will also find plenty of premium French labels, including vintage Champagnes. The courtly waiters and helpful sommelier, along with the rarefied ambiance, leave you feeling like royalty. Stop by the piano bar in the lobby after dinner for a nightcap of good music in one of La Jolla's loveliest rooms. *$$$–$$$$; AE, CB, DC, DIS, MC, V; no checks; dinner every day; full bar; reservations required; valet parking; www.lavalencia.com; map:JJ7* &

## Souplantation / ★

**3960 W POINT LOMA BLVD, MIDWAY (AND BRANCHES); 619/222-7404** Dedicated mainly to soup and salad when it opened in 1980, Souplantation has evolved into one of San Diego's most health-conscious smorgasbords. Among the six soups offered daily, you'll almost always find one vegetarian choice (perhaps vegetarian black bean, creamy potato leek, or vegetarian vegetable) as well as hearty vegetable beef. Brochures are available to spell out nutritional contents of the multitude of prepared salads, pizza, focaccia, pastas, and four kinds of homemade muffins. It's a favorite with families—kids enjoy concocting their own salads, selecting among chopped, shredded, diced, and sliced ingredients, and they live for preparing their own soft-serve or frozen yogurt desserts at the end of the meal. Parents love the pricing system: kids under 3 eat for free, 3- to 5-year-olds for just $1.49. The restaurant burned down in 2000, but was restored in essentially the same style: knotty pine paneling on walls and ceilings and a smattering of green plants as the only decorative elements. An army of young employees is on patrol to remove trays from tables and wipe up spills at the long salad bar. *$; DC, DIS, MC, V; no checks; lunch, dinner every day; no reservations; self parking; map:F2* &

## Spices Thai Cafe / ★★★

**3810 VALLEY CENTRE DR, DEL MAR; 858/259-0889 / 16441 BERNARDO CENTER DR, RANCHO BERNARDO; 858/674-4665** Locals tried valiantly to keep the original Spices, in Del Mar, an unofficial secret, but word spread rapidly and now the place is almost always packed. Nonetheless, the soothing dining room—decked out in pastel paint, black lacquer, and fresh flowers—still feels like a calm oasis. A bad meal here is unheard of, the service is gracious, and even the large lunch and dinner crowds don't diminish the serene vibes. Starters range from Thai spring rolls to dumplings, calamari, and tempura. The list of entrees is long and thought provoking, including myriad curries, vegetables, noodle and rice dishes (prepared with or without meat and fish), and seafood. House specialties include sizzling lemongrass chicken, roast duck in curry, and pineapple stuffed with chicken, shrimp, and cashews in a delicious special sauce. All dishes are individually prepared, MSG is a no-no, and you can regulate the spiciness by using the restaurant's 1-to-10 scale (10 is for fire-breathing dragons). The lunch specials are a terrific value, with soup of the day, green salad, steamed rice, spring roll, fried wonton, and choice of entree thrown into one very inexpensive package. Go after the power lunchers return to their cubicles. *$$; AE, DC, DIS, MC, V; no checks; lunch, dinner every day; beer and wine; reservations accepted for 7 or more; self parking; map:GG7, FF3* &

## Star of the Sea / ★★★

**1360 N HARBOR DR, DOWNTOWN; 619/232-7408** Since opening in 1966, this crown jewel in the Anthony's family restaurant chain has drawn a well-heeled crowd with its elegant seafood preparations. The dramatic wharfside location always kept the place busy, but over the last couple of years, both the cuisine and decor have taken a quantum leap forward. In 1999, the building received a complete renovation and stylish redesign. Architects transformed the dark, shingled dining room into a showcase, with floor-to-ceiling windows overlooking the bay, views from just about every table, lots of artistic flourishes (a jewelry designer created the silverware), and a dramatic over-the-water entryway. The kitchen has undergone changes as well. Chef Jonathan Pflueger, who drew raves when he arrived in 1995, has left, but the restaurant is in equally skilled hands with Brian Johnson, whose local cooking credits include the well-regarded El Bizcocho in Rancho Bernardo. At the Star, Johnson whips up dazzling combinations such as lobster with basil gnocchi, Norwegian salmon garnished with feta cheese and saffron sauce, and succulent scallops arranged on a bed of truffle risotto. Dessert, anyone? Order the puffy Belgian chocolate soufflé garnished with three sauces at least 20 minutes before you'd like to dig in. The wide-ranging wine list offers lots of fish-friendly Sauvignon Blancs and Chardonnays, along with a dozen lesser-seen whites and reds from California, Australia, France, Italy, and the Pacific Northwest. Not up for a full dinner? Grab a seat in the bar or the over-the-water patio and graze on appetizers. One caveat: this once-formal dining room no longer has a dress code, so you'll see more than your share of T-shirts and shorts along with evening dresses and suits and ties. *$$$–$$$$; AE, DC, DIS, MC, V; no checks; dinner every day; full bar; reservations recommended; valet parking; www.starofthesea.com; map:O9* &

## Sushi Deli One / ★
## Sushi Deli Too / ★

**828 BROADWAY AVE, DOWNTOWN; 619/231-9597 / 135 BROADWAY AVE, DOWNTOWN; 619/233-3072** The original Sushi Deli, at Eighth and Broadway, is noisy with '80s and '90s rock, the decor is decidedly low-budget, and it is located on the less fashionable end of Broadway. Yet Sushi Deli One receives a steady stream of the faithful young, tripping in after work or after working out and staggering out happy and full an hour or so later. Waiters glide among the mauve Formica tables and teal-cushioned chairs, delivering bar treats such as edamame (steamed soybeans), sunomono (a salad of clear noodles, cukes, and carrots), or chopped cucumbers with chili sauce. Sample many different dishes by ordering "small plates" (most under $4) such as the Dynamite, which includes red snapper, octopus, crab, and shrimp baked with a spicy cream sauce, or the fried gyoza (wonderfully ungreasy), fried pickles, or tofu teriyaki. Japanese paper lanterns cast a pink glow at the sushi bar, presided over by the slow but steady chef Amaya. At $12, the Shogun (a sampling of many different items) is the most expensive sushi plate. Sushi Deli Too, on lower Broadway, has a greater variety of cooked food, is a bit more expensive, and caters to the courthouse crowd. *$; MC, V; no checks; lunch Mon–Fri, dinner every day (Sushi Deli One); lunch Mon–Fri, dinner Mon–Sat (Sushi Deli Too); beer and wine; no reservations; street parking; map:O7 and N7* & *(Sushi Deli Too)*

## Sushi on the Rock / ★★☆

**7734 GIRARD AVE, LA JOLLA; 858/456-1138** After a move from its tiny original space on Prospect, this Cal-Asian sushi bar has a longer menu and room to accommodate a lot more fans. Good thing, since the place is generally packed on weekend evenings with a youngish, cell-phone-wielding crowd. They're obviously coming as much for the upscale-industrial setting and the affable, black-clad sushi chefs as the fare, since the menu ranges from merely average to outstanding. The lineup includes both classic and nouvelle-style sushi (both done quite nicely) as well as hot entrees. Best bets on this eclectic menu are the warm specialty sushis with fanciful names like Maui Wowie and Monkey Balls. The chilled vegetable-only rolls are also excellent, making this a vegetarian-friendly destination. Skip the limp tempura, however. The place is loud, with high, hard-edged ceilings and a concrete floor, and the animated conversations tend to drown out even the trendy music on the sound system. *$$; MC, V; no checks; lunch Mon–Fri, dinner every day; beer and wine; no reservations; street parking; sushiontherock@hotmail.com; map:JJ7* &

## Taste of Thai / ★★★

**15770 SAN ANDREAS RD, DEL MAR; 858/793-9695 / 527 UNIVERSITY AVE, HILL-CREST; 619/291-7525** This former bank building behind Del Mar's Flower Hill Mall is now the prettiest Thai restaurant in town. The whimsically decorated dining room is a visual feast, with squiggly cardboard lamps, colorful walls, and intricate tiled floors. Above, star-shaped cutouts in the ceiling change hue with the indirect lighting behind them. As for the fare, it's every bit as appealing as the setting. The lengthy menu ranges from the usual curries, soups, and appetizers to a number of stir-fries and grilled meats. Curries are particular standouts—try the panang version for a sweet 'n' spicy epiphany on what curry is all about. Seafood, noodles, and grilled or steamed fish are handled adeptly as well. A small wine list offers some spice-friendly selections like Gewürztraminer at very reasonable prices. In addition to the two main dining rooms, there's a heated patio and a tiny bar where you can wait for to-go orders. *$$; AE, MC, V; no checks; lunch, dinner every day (in Hillcrest, no lunch Sun); beer and wine; reservations recommended; self parking; www.tasteofthai sandiego.com; map:GG7 and N2* &

## Thee Bungalow / ★★★

**4996 W POINT LOMA BLVD, OCEAN BEACH; 619/224-2884** For 30 years, this family-run restaurant in a converted bungalow has kept a faithful clientele while attracting new fans all the time. Some diners stick with classics that have been on the menu since the beginning: roast duck garnished with green peppercorns or à l'orange, sea bass served in a luscious seafood sauce, and rack of lamb. Others are attracted by chef/owner Ed Moore's newer creations, which include superb steamed mussels, black-pepper-crusted salmon, and handsome grilled halibut. Since you get soup or salad with your entree (we adore the smoked tomato soup and the tarragon-dressed house salad), you don't need to order a starter. But if you're extra ravenous, do start with the simple cream-sauced tortellini. And wrap up the evening with a crackle-topped crème brûlée, a Bungalow specialty. The lengthy wine list earns praise for both depth of selection and excellent prices, and the restaurant regularly hosts reasonably priced, heavily attended wine dinners that are some of the liveliest around. Although the service and menu are a tad on the formal side, the setting is casual and comfy. Show up in jeans or in jewels—the good people of Thee Bungalow will welcome you just the same. Just across the street, Moore runs The 3rd Corner (see review), a new seafood eatery that we're sure will endure every bit as long as Thee Bungalow. *$$; AE, DC, DIS, MC, V; no checks; dinner every day; full bar; reservations recommended; self parking; bungalow@adnc.com; www.thee bungalow.com; map:C2* &

## The 3rd Corner / ★★★

**2265 BACON ST, OCEAN BEACH; 619/223-2700** This smart eatery across from Thee Bungalow in Ocean Beach is one of the most exciting new restaurants in town. Bungalow owner Ed Moore took over the old Belgian Lion, gave both the building and the menu a complete remodel, and a star was born. The mostly seafood menu, an artful blend of French and Mediterranean influences, features sampler-size "small plates" of classic dishes such as steamed or stuffed mussels, country pâté, ahi tartare, and scallops niçoise as well as full-size entrees. Consistency has been a hallmark of this new restaurant, both food and service-wise: staffers are unfailingly accommodating, and dishes such as cassoulet, bouillabaisse, roasted monkfish, roasted baby chicken, and lamb loin have scored high marks on every visit. The interior is chic yet casually inviting, with faux-finished walls, flattering lighting, and seating in both the dining room and the bar. The latter, which features a small fireplace, has become a popular spot for grazing at both the counter and a handful of tables. An offbeat wine list veers away from Chardonnay and Merlot in favor of an international lineup of whites and reds from Italy, Spain, Argentina, Chile, and France. *$$; MC, V; no checks; dinner every day; beer and wine; reservations recommended; self parking; www.thethirdcorner.com; map: C2* &

## Tip Top Meats / ★★

**6118 PASEO DEL NORTE, CARLSBAD; 760/438-2620** This North County butcher shop, grocery, and deli definitely deserves the moniker Tip Top. It's one of the few stores in the San Diego area that regularly carries prime-grade beef, and it's even better known as home to a great selection of freshly made sausages. This is where to find the best of the wursts: bratwurst, liverwurst, English bangers, Portuguese linguica, and more, along with excellent hot dogs. In addition to the butcher shop, an adjacent cafe offers made-to-order sandwiches, several deli salads, and rib-sticking entrees like meatloaf, stuffed cabbage, and barbecued ribs. There's plenty of seating, or you can get orders to go. Looking for some exotic groceries or imported beer? The market sells more than 100 varieties of beer from around the world, as well as lots of wine, imported condiments and cookies, and assorted crackers and fancy snacks. *$; AE, DIS, MC, V; checks OK; breakfast, lunch, dinner every day; beer and wine; no reservations; self parking; www.tiptopmeats. com; map:CC7* &

## Tony's Jacal / ★★

**621 VALLEY AVE, SOLANA BEACH; 858/755-2274** Family-owned and -operated since 1946, Tony's Jacal has obviously been doing everything right. Even if you overlook the autographed photos of celebrity diners, you can't miss the long lines—up to an hour on weekends and during Del Mar's racing season. Hang out at the bar with a margarita while listening for your name to be sung out over the loudspeaker. A waitress in blue ruffles will show you to an aqua-upholstered booth in a cavernous room with wood paneling, open beams, Mexican knickknacks, and half-moon-shaped stained-glass windows, or to a table on the outdoor patio with a small pond, gurgly waterfall, and flowering plants. Customary Mexican combination plates fill a big chunk of the menu, featuring pork and turkey along with the ubiquitous chicken. Special entrees include chili con carne, steak ranchero, and chicken mole, and the platillos speciales include various enchiladas, carnitas, tortas, quesadillas, and carne asada. $–$$; AE, MC, V; no checks; lunch Mon, Wed–Sat, dinner Wed–Mon (closed Tues); full bar; reservations recommended for 10 or more; self parking; map:FF7 W

## Top o' the Cove / ★★★

**1216 PROSPECT ST, LA JOLLA; 858/454-7779** Widely considered one of the county's most romantic restaurants, this La Jolla landmark attracts couples of all ages and is a notorious site for marriage proposals. With its lushly planted courtyard entrance, piano bar, and several tables overlooking the Pacific, Top o' the Cove is indeed a lovers' dream, as well as a top spot for upscale business dining. (A note for all you romantics: table 6 is considered the top spot for couples in love.) But there's more to the story than beauty; the kitchen's blend of classic French, Pacific Rim, and Mediterranean flavors is as impressive as the view. Over the past two years, the restaurant has undergone a couple of chef shuffles, but the kitchen manages to remain consistent. An appetizer of risotto and white truffles is exquisite (and should be, for the price). Entree-wise, grilled swordfish and salmon, often sauced with a Cabernet Sauvignon reduction that's perfect for these full-flavored fish, are our top choices. A rare-roasted Muscovy duck breast is another standout. The restaurant's wine list is breathtaking in depth and price; you can easily drop $100 or more on a bottle. Note that reservations are confirmed with a credit card; for parties of six or larger, you'll be charged unless you cancel 48 hours in advance of your reservation. $$$–$$$$; AE, CB, DC, MC, V; no checks; lunch, dinner every day, brunch Sun; full bar; reservations recommended; valet parking; www.topofthecove.com; map:JJ7 &

## Tori Tori New Japanese Cuisine / ★★

**1905 EL CAJON BLVD, UNIVERSITY HEIGHTS; 619/295-2902** This marriage of a fast-food joint and a traditional Japanese restaurant is a happy one indeed. Ignore the drab strip-mall setting, crowded parking lot, and simple decor; once you've sampled Tori Tori's sparkling fresh sushi, stir-fried noodles, and spicy curries, you'll be a convert. Especially at these prices: it's hard to spend more than $5 on a meal, unless you get carried away with sushi specialties like the caterpillar roll with eel. Most sushi items and appetizers (including terrific spicy scallop

## FRESH FROM THE SEA

San Diego's seafood restaurants rely on exotic imports for their menus, receiving fresh shipments of New Zealand mussels, Hawaiian swordfish, and Alaskan salmon and king crab. But residents keep local seafood calendars in mind when dining out or cooking at home. Pacific lobsters are in season from October through March; though less sweet than the Maine variety, these crustaceans bear meaty bodies with a tangy, saltwater taste. Yellowfin, bluefin, and albacore tuna swim by in the summer's warm waters; count on superb sashimi and seared ahi in July and August. Abalone were once common in local waters; now menus will occasionally have farm-raised abalone on their menus. The noble dorado (called mahi mahi on many menus) still leap and fight on the hook in area waters in late summer. Though some anglers deride what they call "bottom fish" (which require endurance at the reel), local bass and halibut make for fine eating in the winter months. Sometimes, when the moon, tides, and water temperatures coincide perfectly, a swordfish will snag its beak on a hook—an occasion for celebration among local cooks. Crustacean collectors know to be wary of poisons in local shellfish collected in spring and summer, so they treasure the winter months, when mussels and clams cling to easily accessible rocks and sand beds. Check out the local selection at Point Loma Seafoods before dining out, then order accordingly. Nothing beats the flavor of the catch of the day.

—*Maribeth Mellin*

rolls and yummy pot stickers) are between $4 and $5. Big spenders (here, that would be someone with six or seven bucks to spare) should choose one of the entrees like the ginger chicken or teriyaki chicken rice bowls, the Tori Tori fried rice, or the combo meals that come with three appetizers, a salad, and rice. To-go foods are just as carefully presented as those served on the premises, a boon for anyone in search of a nice take-home dinner. This is a no-tablecloths, no-frills kind of place, but the sushi chef is adept, the servers are pleasant, and the price is certainly right. *$; AE, DIS, MC, V; no checks; lunch, dinner Mon–Sat; beer and wine; no reservations; self parking; map:P1* &

## Trattoria Acqua / ★★★

**1298 PROSPECT ST, LA JOLLA; 858/454-0709** Opened in 1994, Trattoria Acqua is one of San Diego's best-known, best-regarded dining destinations. Part of the notoriety stems from a stunning setting; this indoor/outdoor restaurant, located in the Coast Walk building, is nestled into a La Jolla Cove hillside with ocean views that won't quit. But pretty views are a nickel a dozen in this seaside town; Acqua stands apart for actually delivering high-quality food and service too. The Mediterranean-influenced menu roams gracefully from Tuscany to Provence to Tangiers, with stops along the way for excellent designer pizzas, a variety of antipasti and salads, about a dozen pastas, and lots of grilled fish and meats. Start your meal with the complimentary spicy hummus dip while you peruse the lengthy wine list, where notable names from California and Italy are sold at most reasonable prices. Must-have dishes are the grilled portobello mushroom or bruschetta for starters; among the pastas, the lobster ravioli, penne Piemontese, or rigatoni with eggplant; and for main dishes, the veal shank or herb-crusted halibut. Prime seating is on the patio or one of the inside tables with a view of the water (reserve these well in advance). Validated parking is available in the garage under the building, or angle for a spot on busy Prospect Street. *$$; AE, MC, V; no checks; lunch, dinner every day; full bar; reservations recommended; self parking; www. trattoriacqua.com; map:JJ7* &

### Trophy's / ★

**7510 HAZARD CENTER DR, MISSION VALLEY (AND BRANCHES); 619/296-9600** Not your typical sports bar—the Trophy's chain has something to please everyone from serious fans to those who don't know a first down from a fumble. Sure, there's the requisite memorabilia and big-screen TV, along with cadres of baseball and football cognoscenti cheering for the home teams. But there's also a fun combination of friendly service and good food. Generous, fresh-tasting salads are always a fine choice, as are a variety of burgers, wood-fired pizzas, and some extra-spicy chicken wings. The house chili flavored with hot salsa is another winner. Of course, there's a full bar, with a multitude of beers and several decent wines. Servers tend to be young, cute, and perky—as well as hardworking and efficient. The ambiance is happy and noisy, with a thriving singles scene most nights. *$-$$; AE, MC, V; no checks; lunch, dinner every day; full bar; no reservations; self parking; map:LL4* &

### T's Cafe / ★★

 **271 N HWY 101, SOLANA BEACH; 858/755-7642** Locals have had a love affair with Mr. T's (as it's more commonly referred to) since it opened in 1978. Tucked unobtrusively as it is into one side of Solana Beach's rather uninteresting boardwalk, you'd never guess that lurking within are a spacious dining room with cozy bar area and small private function room (local artists' groups have staged Wednesday-morning breakfasts here for years). The woodsy feel and large open fireplace (blazing during the rare Southern California drizzle or foggy chill) lull patrons into dreams of Montana mountain lodges as they linger a salty breath away from the Pacific, enjoying enormous omelets with king crab, homemade chili, and roasted turkey, as well as various scrambles, Benedicts, bagels, pancakes, waffles, and potato skillet dishes. Although breakfasts are the claim to fame here (and are served until closing), the lunch menu offers a lengthy assortment of deli and veggie sandwiches, burgers, soups, and New York steak sandwiches. *$; AE, MC, V; no checks; breakfast, lunch every day; full bar; reservations accepted for 6 or more; self parking; map:FF7* W

### Turf Supper Club / ★

**1116 25TH ST, GOLDEN HILL; 619/234-6363** Why would you want to cook your own dinner at a restaurant grill? Because that's the way regulars have been doing it for decades at this neighborhood hangout. Burgers and steaks are served raw; patrons belly up to the coals and watch their meat sizzle while sipping Scotch or whiskey. The beef is marinated in garlic and oil (ask for more chopped garlic to lather on your steak and hunks of bread while grilling). Settle into a leatherette booth, check out the photos of '50s-era celebs by the rest rooms, throw a slab on the barbie, and chat with barflies who wouldn't drink anywhere else. *$; cash only; dinner every day; full bar; no reservations; self parking; map:Q7*

## Tutto Mare Ristorante / ★★☆

**4365 EXECUTIVE DR, LA JOLLA; 858/597-1188** The name means, basically, "everything from the sea," and that's what the menu at this glossy restaurant is all about. The fish fest starts with the appetizers: a delicate lobster salad with baby lettuces, deep-fried calamari, and slivers of salmon flavored with grappa, to name just a few. Next come pastas, many of them starring fish or shellfish (pasta stuffed with smoked trout is a standout, but the penne with duck sausage is no slouch either). Entrees include grilled chicken and New York steaks; grilled sea scallops, their sweetness highlighted by tiny artichokes; boutique pizzas topped with clams and shrimp; and the best pasta in the neighborhood: Maine lobster in a feisty tomato sauce. There's a well-selected wine list and a full bar for appropriate libations. A well-dressed business crowd tends to frequent Tutto Mare at lunch (prime seating on nice days is on the enclosed terrace), and many of the same people come back for dinner. The ambiance is stylish without being snobbish, with a sleek, contemporary look softened by displays of fresh ingredients like colorful handmade pastas hung to dry. Leave the little ones at home; Tutto Mare is meant for dates and power dinners. *$$$; AE, DC, MC, V; no checks; lunch Mon–Fri, dinner every day; full bar; reservations recommended; self parking; map:JJ7*

## The Vegetarian Zone / ★★☆

**2949 5TH AVE, HILLCREST; 619/298-7302** Previously known as Kung Food, this vegetarian restaurant underwent a name change a couple of years ago. But the menu hasn't been altered too much; this is still a mellow, meat-free eatery with an emphasis on healthful dining. The kitchen takes an international approach, offering dishes ranging from Indian to Mediterranean to Mexican. Greek spinach pie is one of the best dishes here, along with vegetable lasagne, several quesadillas (available with rennetless cheese, if desired), and a bean sprout salad. Soups change daily and are always worth ordering. The open dining room is pretty but can get a bit noisy; sit in the shaded patio out back when the weather allows. Although the service tends to be as laid-back as the clientele, wait staff are pleasant and well informed about meals and preparation methods. Along with the sit-down restaurant, an adjacent shop offers food to go and a fascinating array of books, music, jewelry, and skin-care products. *$$; DIS, MC, V; no checks; breakfast Sat–Sun, lunch, dinner Tues–Sat; beer and wine; no reservations; self parking; www.thevegetarianzone.com; map:N4*

## The Venetian / ★★

**3663 VOLTAIRE ST, POINT LOMA; 619/223-8197** Most of the peninsula's residents agree that the Venetian, near Point Loma High School, has the best thin-crust pizza in the city. First-generation Sicilian-American Vince Giacalone opened the business in 1965 as a small family pizza parlor. After years on Canon Street in Point Loma, he opened this second location, now run by sons Joe and

Frank. (The original location, sold in 1972, is now called Old Venice; see review.) Point Lomans and Obecians who ate here as kids now tuck their own offspring into the booths lining the walls of the original dining room, or they head for the peaceful covered patio in the back, with potted shrubs dusted in tiny white lights. If you're not in a pizza mood (unthinkable!), try the tasty seafood pasta: shrimp, clams, scallops, and calamari in a tomato-based sauce over linguine. *$; AE, DC, DIS, MC, V; no checks; lunch Mon–Fri, dinner every day; full bar; reservations accepted for 8 or more; self parking; map:E4* &

## Via Italia Trattoria / ★★★

**4705-A CLAIREMONT DR, CLAIREMONT; 858/274-9732** A chorus of *buona sera* greets customers who enter this Italian gem tucked into an otherwise unremarkable mall. The accents are authentic (the entire staff is Italian), and so is the cooking, much of it based on regional specialties rarely seen in San Diego. While the thin-crusted, wood-fired pizzas are certainly a fine reason to visit, the nightly specials set this little dining room apart. Look for venison simmered in brandy, polenta flavored with truffle oil, bread-spinach dumplings (called strozzapretti) in a lush porcini sauce, and a memorable dessert pairing mascarpone cheese and fresh berries run under the broiler. On the regular menu, the stewed Italian sausage, Gorgonzola-topped greens, and penne with pancetta and vodka lead an eclectic parade that mixes the familiar with the unusual. While the restaurant is small and plainly decorated, candles glow on every table and the service is warm and sincere, making otherwise informal meals feel like special occasions. It's smart to make reservations for dinner, as the nearby movie theater draws plenty of pre- and post-show diners. *$$; AE, MC, V; no checks; lunch, dinner every day; beer and wine; reservations recommended; self parking; map:KK6* &

## Vigilucci's / ★★

**505 S HWY 101, ENCINITAS; 760/942-7332** When Roberto Vigilucci opened his Italian restaurant in 1993, he not only brought his delectable hometown Milano recipes to North County, but also managed to turn one corner of an innocuous intersection into an elegant and intimate haven. Most afternoons and evenings the place is swamped with the well heeled looking to be well fed. Tables swathed in crisp linens and topped with fresh flowers are laden with gnocchi al Gorgonzola e nocchi (potato dumplings with Gorgonzola cheese sauce and walnuts), pollo alla florentina (chicken breast stuffed with spinach and ricotta cheese in a creamy white sauce), and saltimbocca alla romana (veal scaloppine topped with prosciutto, sage, and mozzarella in white wine sauce). Portions are large, and all entrees come with fresh vegetables and spaghetti aglio e olio. Lunch specials are quite reasonable, and the wine list is extraordinary, with generally reasonable prices and an outstanding selection of Italian reds and whites. The charming all-Italian staff remains much the same, offering unpretentious and welcoming service. *$$; AE, DIS, MC, V; no checks; lunch Mon–Fri, dinner every day; beer and wine; reservations accepted for 4 or more; self parking; www.vigiluccis.com; map:EE7* &

## Vivace / ★★★

**7100 FOUR SEASONS PT (FOUR SEASONS RESORTS—AVIARA), CARLSBAD; 760/603-6868** Be sure to request a window seat at this elegant, ultra-expensive dining room, so you can add a spectacular sunset view to your lavish splurge. Then forget about money and relish the dazzling floral arrangements, the golden glow emanating from wall niches lined with delicate glass objets d'art, and the superb Tuscan cuisine. Browse the menu while feeling ever so righteous as you sample the Caprese of vine-ripened tomatoes and mozzarella with black olive tapenade—one of the "alternative cuisine" calorie-conscious dishes on the menu. Then, toss calories out of the equation and have lobster risotto with grappa, or the rigatoni pasta with duck bolognese, or the salmon with salsify and polenta cake. Pasta dishes are served as entrees or appetizers, so you can more liberally sample the chef's specialties. Afterwards, sip a brandy or grappa in the hotel's comfortable bar while listening to live soft jazz. *$$$$; AE, DC, DIS, JCB, MC, V; checks OK; dinner every day; full bar; reservations recommended; valet parking; www.four seasons.com; map:CC7* &

## The Waterfront / ★

**2044 KETTNER BLVD, DOWNTOWN; 619/232-9656** A workingman's retreat since the 1930s, the Waterfront combines all the best qualities of dive bar, pool hall, burger joint, and neighborhood hangout. It's best known as a watering hole (and one that opens at 6am, at that), but savvy regulars know that the Waterfront offers darn good eatin' as well. Case in point: some of the best bargain burgers in town. They're a little bit greasy, but these half-pound beauties topped with grilled onions are some of the city's prime cheap eats. Fish tacos, excellent bean chili, and assorted sandwiches round out the menu, which also includes Mexican-style breakfasts on the weekends. Leave the little ones at home, and forget about asking for a wine list; the preferred accompaniment to anything you eat here is beer. Prime seating is at the open windows that survey the sidewalk, but no matter where you sit, you'll get cheery service and an eclectic crowd that ranges from well-dressed businessfolk at lunch to night-shifters coming in for breakfast and a brew. *$; AE, MC, V; no checks; breakfast, lunch, dinner every day; full bar; no reservations; street parking; map:M6*

## The Whaling Bar / ★★½

**1332 PROSPECT ST (LA VALENCIA HOTEL), LA JOLLA; 858/454-0771** Straight out of a Raymond Chandler mystery, the Whaling Bar is as close as San Diego gets to an old boys' club. The bar's character has hardly changed since the '50s, despite lengthy renovations in 1998. The tufted leather booths are cushier, the whaling mural has been restored, and the walls have a fresh rose-tinted glow. Though never trendy, the menu has been freshened a bit, offering upscale comfort food with a few twists. Oysters taste sparkling fresh with a dash of horseradish vinaigrette; baby spinach salads sport pistachios with their feta; truffle essence provides a soupçon of earthy flavor to veal. Loyalists swear by the steaks, sautéed calf liver, and crisp coating on the rack of lamb, and this may well be the best place in town to order swordfish. Tuck your knees under a red tablecloth, order a single-malt

93

Scotch, and watch maître d' Manny Silva—still a charmer after 30 years on the job—greet old friends. Makes you want to tuck a rosebud in your honey's lapel. *$$$; AE, DIS, MC, V; no checks; lunch, dinner every day; full bar; reservations recommended; valet parking; www.lavalencia.com; map:JJ7 W*

## When in Rome / ★★★

**1108 1ST ST, ENCINITAS; 760/944-1771** Restaurateurs Joe and Rosemary Ragone run this fine Italian restaurant the old-fashioned way, by doing just about everything themselves. They grow many of their own herbs, do much of the cooking, choose produce and meats with finicky precision, and even prepare their own breads and desserts. The results show in the perfect tomato and basil salad, the falling-off-the-bone osso buco (sometimes made with veal, sometimes with lamb), a velveteen fusilli with vodka, and each of the nightly fish specials. Particular treats include the sword-fish livornese dressed with capers and black olives, and the buttery sea bass matched with a saffron sauce. Desserts rate an equal rave, especially Rosemary's tiramisu, crème brûlée, and fluffy fresh fruit mousses. The spacious restaurant offers an especially cozy dining room with a fireplace, as well as a covered patio complete with bar and piano next to a larger room that's good for private parties. All in all, a visit to When in Rome means spending the evening in the company of very talented, very gracious people who make you want to return. *$$$; AE, MC, V; no checks; dinner every day; full bar; reservations recommended; self parking; map:EE7* &

## WineSellar & Brasserie / ★★★

**9550 WAPLES ST, SORRENTO VALLEY; 858/450-9576** Here's an upstairs/downstairs bit of heaven for wine connoisseurs and food worshippers alike. This nationally acclaimed restaurant may be miles from fashionable dining neighborhoods like downtown and La Jolla, but it's definitely center stage when it comes to the art of gastronomy. The incredible wine selection showcases little-known, hard-to-find boutique wines as well as heavy hitters from Bordeaux and Burgundy. The first floor of the restaurant, in fact, is a retail wine shop with an international selection; owner Gary Parker often buys entire cellars from collectors and offers many a rare bottle for sale. Upstairs, founding chef Doug Organ is no longer on the scene, having moved on to other projects. But the menu continues to impress diners with both traditional European and new-wave cuisine in a stylish, bistrolike setting with bar and table seating. Offbeat combos like foie gras sauced with lime and mangos or ginger-cured pork loin are every bit as good as classic roasted lamb with herbes de Provence. Other specialties include a luxurious soup made with local sweet corn, a pan-roasted veal chop nuanced with sorrel and mustard, and a rack of venison with sautéed cherries. *$$$; AE, CB, DC, DIS, MC, V; no checks; lunch Sat, dinner Tues–Sun; beer and wine; reservations required; self parking; www.winesellar.com; map:II7* &

## World Curry / ★

**1433 GARNET AVE, PACIFIC BEACH; 858/270-4455** With a selection of curries from Thailand, India, the Caribbean, and Japan, this informal eatery offers a veritable world of flavors. The generous portions of curries (served with rice) range from mild to fiery and can be ordered with choice of chicken, vegetables, or tofu. It's tough to pick a favorite, but the smooth, fragrant Japanese curry and the vegan Caribbean curry with black beans and a hint of pineapple both rate an honorable mention. Side dishes include jasmine-scented rice, freshly baked Indian breads, grilled chicken skewers, and refreshing salads. For dessert, chill your palate with an order of coconut ice cream. Eat in the vibrantly painted dining room, or order to go. Beer is the natural accompaniment for this spicy fare; the lineup includes labels from Singapore, India, Holland, and Japan. *$; AE, DIS, MC, V; no checks; lunch Mon–Sat, dinner every day; beer and wine; no reservations; street parking; www.worldcurry. com; map:KK6*

## Yoshino / ★★

**1790 W WASHINGTON ST, MIDDLETOWN; 619/295-2232** If you really love sashimi, forget all those sleek sushi bars and head to this luncheonette-style Japanese old-timer amid a centrally located (yet obscure) patch of offices and salons. Fresh tuna is Yoshino's forte. The chef chooses his catch with great wisdom, finding the perfect fillets for the thin, diagonal slices of rosy fish centered on a plain white plate. They're not chintzy here either—none of this charging by the slice. One serving with white rice and plenty of soy and wasabi fills you up. Keeping up with the times, Yoshino's has added an excellent sushi selection as well. Have your tablemate order the sesame chicken, a pile of chicken strips with a crisp, seed-filled crust, and share a great meal. Keep hold of your teacups, though; they tend to slip toward the edge of the slick plastic tables. *$; AE, MC, V; no checks; lunch Tues–Fri, dinner Tues–Sun; beer, wine; no reservations; self parking; map:L3* &

# LODGINGS

# LODGINGS

Location, location, location. It's the most important consideration when you're choosing accommodations in San Diego. During the week, downtown is largely the province of business travelers, conventioneers, and visitors using public transportation. The Gaslamp Quarter's exciting dining and nightlife scene now draws locals from all over the county who spend weekends in downtown hotels for a bit of urban immersion. Beware of added costs here—parking can cost upwards of $15 per night, and some hotels charge extra for use of their fitness facilities. Old Town's moderately priced inns and Mission Valley's modest chains and full-scale resorts are favorites with families. Boaters and bicyclists prefer the quiet feel of Shelter Island. Vacationers with sun and fun in mind head for Mission Bay. The more aesthetically minded prefer the Mediterranean flair of La Jolla and the small-town feeling in Coronado. Horse racing and hiking trails by the sea make Del Mar a sensible choice. Farther north, the coastal towns are popular with those seeking a subdued getaway or easier access to Disneyland and Los Angeles.

Trains, trolleys, and freeways connect much of the county; it's easy to stay even 60 miles outside the city and take day trips to Mission Bay, Balboa Park, and Old Town. There are a few tips to keep in mind when booking your room. Many hotels prohibit smoking in the rooms; most provide balconies, terraces, and ashtrays for outdoor smoking, and all have rooms or floors where smoking is prohibited. Some places will accept checks for reservations but require an additional deposit if you don't wish to leave a credit card imprint at the desk. More and more hotels have at least one room with a wheelchair-friendly shower—be sure to ask for one if you need it. Above all, make your reservations as early as possible. Rates tend to rise as availability decreases.

## Downtown

### Balboa Park Inn / ★★☆

**3402 PARK BLVD, DOWNTOWN; 619/298-0823 OR 800/938-8181** If you want to stay near the urban Eden of Balboa Park yet close to downtown, check out funky Balboa Park Inn. Located on the edge of the park, the inn has 26 rooms in a series of pink adobe mission-style buildings. Some rooms are truly charming, though others veer toward kitsch. If you prefer rooms in tasteful, soft pastels, ask for the Las Palomas suite, which boasts a roomy private balcony overlooking the park and a cozy glass-enclosed sunroom. The Casa de Oro suite is set up for guests with disabilities. Some rooms have working fireplaces, and many have whirlpool tubs. Rates include continental breakfast. Make reservations a month or two in advance. There's a seven-day cancellation policy. *$$–$$$; AE, DC, DIS, MC, V; checks OK (2 weeks in advance); self parking; info@BalboaParkInn.com; www.balboaparkinn.com; map:P3* &

## Courtyard by Marriott / ★★★

**530 BROADWAY, DOWNTOWN; 619/446-3000 OR 800/321-2211** The grand marble lobby of one of downtown's finest old bank buildings now serves as the entryway to a charming hotel. The painted coffered ceilings, brass teller's cages, and turnstile doors have all been restored to the grandeur they presented to bank customers in the 1930s. The Italian Romanesque revival building, designed by architect William Templeton Johnson when Broadway was in its heyday, stood vacant for many years when the focus of redevelopment turned to Horton Plaza and the Gaslamp. The hotel's designers managed to turn offices into 246 guest rooms and suites that suit the building's design, and guests feel as though they're staying in a venerable downtown inn. Check out the original vault in the basement, which now holds a meeting room. *$$$; AE, DC, MC, V; checks OK; valet and self parking; www.courtyard.com/sancd; map: M8* &

## Embassy Suites San Diego Bay / ★★

**610 PACIFIC HWY, DOWNTOWN; 619/239-2400 OR 800/362-2779** Families and conventioneers alike are enamored with this chain's sensible layout; the 337 suites all have separate living rooms, kitchenettes, and desk space outside the bedrooms. Though the rooms face a sky-high atrium, noise here is not a drawback; instead, the lively conversation from the lobby draws guests down to the complimentary breakfast buffet. Though the hotel lacks individuality, it more than makes up for that with its location, within steps of Seaport Village and the Gaslamp Quarter. Advance bookings are essential, no matter the time of year. The Embassy Suites chain also has a hotel in La Jolla. *$$$; AE, DC, MC, V; checks OK; valet and self parking; www.essandiegobay.com; map:M8* &

## Hilton San Diego Gaslamp Quarter / ★★★

**401 K ST, DOWNTOWN; 619/231-4040 OR 800/774-1500** You might expect a hotel located right across the street from the convention center to be enormous and frantically busy. Instead, this 275-room gem has the ambience of a boutique hotel. In the Enclave section, the rooms are designed much like artist's lofts with high windows letting in streams of natural light that illuminate velvety couches and cushy beds draped with Frette linens. The brick and steel Bridgeworks building, which houses the hotel and other businesses, has a contemporary feel that's enhanced by the use of original glass objets d'art placed around a blazing fireplace in the lobby. Guests unwind after business meetings at the soothing Artesia spa or work off their tensions in the fitness center, then stroll to excellent restaurants in the building or the Gaslamp Quarter. *$$$; AE, DC, DIS, MC, V; checks OK; valet and self parking; www.hilton.com; map:N8* &

## Horton Grand Hotel / ★★

**311 ISLAND AVE, DOWNTOWN; 619/544-1886 OR 800/542-1886** The Horton Grand Hotel offers a touch of Victorian-era gentility in the heart of the historic Gaslamp Quarter. Comprising two historic Victorian hotels, the Horton Grand has quite a colorful history. Wyatt Earp slept here when he lived in San Diego, and the restaurant is named in honor of Ida Bailey, a notorious turn-of-the-century madam whose bordello once occupied this site. All 132 rooms are decorated with period antiques, lace curtains, and working gas fireplaces. But we'll bet Wyatt Earp never had a microwave or a hair dryer. For more space, request one of the 600-square-foot minisuites. While the hotel has plenty of quirky charm, its location is the real bonus. You can live it up at the Gaslamp's many clubs and bars, then stroll or catch a pedicab back to the hotel. *$$$; AE, DC, DIS, MC, V; checks OK; valet and self parking; horton@connectnet.com; www.hortongrand.com; map:N8* &

### La Pensione Hotel / ★★

**1700 INDIA ST, DOWNTOWN; 619/236-8000 OR 800/232-4683** This modern, architecturally innovative hotel is a boon for budget travelers. Most of the 80 rooms have kitchen facilities and large tables or desks; some have views of San Diego Bay; all have windows opening to sea breezes and sunlight, and high ceilings that add a sense of space. Laundry facilities, a tiled courtyard, a marble fireplace in the lobby, and two adjacent restaurants are added perks, as is the colorful cast of multilingual travelers. The hotel is in the midst of the redevelopment activity in Little Italy. The neighborhood has good Italian restaurants and bakeries, and the trolley runs nearby. *$; AE, DC, DIS, MC, V; no checks; la-pensione@travel base.com; self parking; www.lapensionehotel.com; map:M6* &

### The Westgate Hotel / ★★★★

**1055 2ND AVE, DOWNTOWN; 619/238-1818 OR 800/221-3802** Versailles meets SoCal in the lobby of this elegant hotel, financed in 1970 by San Diego's legendary character C. Arnholt Smith. Banker, politician, and misguided visionary, Smith poured more than $16 million into the white palace with gold-tinted windows and gave his wife carte blanche to tour Europe, collecting Louis XV chairs, couches, and Baccarat chandeliers. The lobby remains a gracious museum staffed by courteous courtiers. The Westgate's 223 rooms and suites could be considered a bit stuffy. Satin negligees and silk pajamas are in order here; a gold-and-white color scheme prevails; antique chairs demand proper use; and armoires hide the TVs. Cocktail dresses and suits are the attire of choice in Le Fontainebleau restaurant, where lunch, dinner, and Sunday brunch are served with subdued elegance. The hotel's facilities include a fitness center and spa, barbershop, and gourmet deli. *$$$–$$$$; AE, DC, MC, V; no checks; valet parking; info@westgatehotel.com; www.westgatehotel.com; map:N7* &

### Wyndham U. S. Grant Hotel / ★★★

**326 BROADWAY, DOWNTOWN; 619/ 232-3121 OR 877/ 999-3223** Ulysses S. Grant Jr. thought of San Diego as a grand spot for a monument to his more famous dad, and commissioned Harrison Albright to design an Italian Renaissance palace in the heart of downtown. The hotel opened in 1910 amid much fanfare; after all, how many urban inns could boast a saltwater swimming pool and ladies' billiard hall amid marble pillars? Fortunes rose and fell in this hotel over the decades. It seems anyone who purchased the property felt like the poor offspring of a British duke saddled with the family mansion. The 285 rooms and 60 suites are visions of far nobler times, with two-poster beds, Victorian chairs, and fireplaces (in

## SLEEPING ON A SHOESTRING

There's no way around it—hotel rooms are expensive in San Diego. The small inns with budget rates have all raised their prices for the summer vacation season and holidays, and it's hard to find a room for under $100. Fortunately, there are a few hostels, and you needn't be a student or young backpacker to claim a room or bunk. Hostelling International (www.hostelweb.com/sandiego) runs two facilities in central San Diego. Its **POINT LOMA HOSTEL** (3790 Udall St; 619/223-4778) is located in a residential neighborhood on the bus line, near a public library (where you can check your e-mail), laundromat, and grocery store. The hostel has six private rooms with double beds, as well as the traditional separate-sex dorms with bunk beds. All rooms have shared baths, and there are kitchen facilities. The **DOWNTOWN HOSTEL** (521 Market St; 619/525-1531) has both private rooms and dorms, kitchen facilities, and a great location in the Gaslamp Quarter. The **OCEAN BEACH INTERNATIONAL HOSTEL** (4961 Newport Ave; 619/223-SURF, 800/339-SAND; e-mail obihostel@aol.com) is a private, 60-bed facility that only accepts international travelers with passports and visas. It's right in the middle of Ocean Beach's main drag and has a big front porch where travelers write postcards and exchange travel tips while watching the street scene.

—*Maribeth Mellin*

some suites). The lobby and bar are popular gathering spots for San Diegans, and the restaurant is a treasured landmark. *$$$; AE, DC, MC, V; checks OK; valet and self parking; www.wyndham.com/USGrant; map:N7* &

# Airport Area

### Sheraton San Diego Hotel and Marina / ★★
**1380 HARBOR ISLAND DR, HARBOR ISLAND; 619/291-2900 OR 888/625-5114**
This well-situated Sheraton is a good choice if you want to stick close to the airport and use taxis for transportation to downtown. The hotel's two towers hold 1,045 rooms of varying sizes. Those on the upper floors on the bay side have fabulous views of downtown. The lobby in the east tower is particular impressive, with ceiling frescoes lit by a computerized system that replicates the sky at various times of the day. The spa and fitness center are large, and body treatments and massages are reasonably priced. Other pluses are bayside pools, tennis courts, bike and boat rentals, and trails leading along the island's edge to Spanish Landing, a long, narrow park beside San Diego Bay. The restaurants, while not stellar, are very good, and quick meals at the lobby Aroma Cafe keep dining costs down. *$$$; AE, DC, DIS, MC, V; checks OK; valet and self parking; www.sheraton.com; map: I6* &

# Coronado

### El Cordova Hotel / ★★☆

**1351 ORANGE AVE, CORONADO; 619/435-4131 OR 800/229-2032** In a beach town dominated by grand resorts, El Cordova Hotel is an affordable alternative. The salmon adobe building presiding over Coronado's bustling Orange Avenue is redolent of California in the 1930s. The airy, terra-cotta-tiled lobby sets just the right tone with a melodious fountain, intricate tile work, rustic carved-wood furnishings, and wrought-iron decorative touches. The inn's 40 rooms have a simple decor with carved wood furniture and Mexican tiles. Most rooms are accessed from the lush inner courtyard. We have a couple of quibbles, though. Noise is a factor, emanating from both busy Orange Avenue and the patio tables of Miguel's Cocina, which occupies El Cordova's courtyard. The inn also has a dinky pool, so plan to hit the beach instead. *$$; AE, DIS; MC, V; no checks; self parking; www.elcordovahotel.com; map:NN5*

### Glorietta Bay Inn / ★★★

**1630 GLORIETTA BLVD, CORONADO; 619/435-3101 OR 800/283-9383** John Spreckels, the sugar baron fond of all things grand and glorious for his vision of Coronado, hired architect Harrison Albright to design his family mansion on a sloping lawn facing the bay in 1908. The mansion now houses 11 of the hotel's rooms; the rest are in less glamorous (and less expensive) buildings with balconies and gardens above the bay. The original house is a wonder of polished wood, brass, glass, swooping marble stairways, and eye-boggling antiques. The rooms are the perfect beginning for a tour through Coronado's history. The hotel attracts an amiable clientele, and guests tend to linger in the Music Room exchanging vacation tips while eating the complimentary continental breakfast. The staff has justifiably garnered several awards for service—guests tend to feel quite at home here. *$$$; AE, DC, DIS, MC, V; checks OK (2 weeks in advance); self parking; www.gloriettabayinn.com map:NN5* &

### Hotel del Coronado / ★★★★

**1500 ORANGE AVE, CORONADO; 619/435-6611 OR 800/HOTEL-DEL** Opened in 1888, this sprawling, white-frame Victorian confection of red-roofed turrets, stained glass, and crown-shaped chandeliers is a National Historic Landmark that has hosted just about every dignitary and celebrity to roll through town, including 14 U.S. presidents. It also played a starring role—alongside Marilyn Monroe, Jack Lemmon, and Tony Curtis—in *Some Like It Hot*. If you like the bustling activity of a full-service resort, with its scheduled activities, shopping arcade, and such, the Del should fit the bill. Many of the rooms in the original building overlook the lovely Windsor Lawn, with plenty of benches for admiring the sunset. Eight new beachfront cottages set right above the sand command high nightly rates, though their decor is rather motel-like. The Babcock & Story Bar is a great spot for sunset cocktails, and the new spa is a welcome addition. Locals and tourists mob the Crown Room for Sunday brunch—make advance reservations. If the bustle in the Del's main building sounds overwhelming, look to the Ocean Tower, a high-rise building set south of the pool area. Its spacious, comfortable rooms overlook the Pacific or the bay, and have been decorated like country cottages in shades of blue and green; the tower has its own pool and a nice stretch of beach. *$$$; AE, DC, DIS, MC, V; checks OK; valet and self parking; www.hoteldel.com; map:NN5* &

## Loews Coronado Bay Resort / ★★★☆

**4000 CORONADO BAY RD, CORONADO; 619/424-4000 OR 800/235-6397**
Far removed from the bustle of downtown, the self-contained compound sprawls beside San Diego Bay at the southern end of Coronado. Silver Strand State Beach is right across the street. The resort's Azzura Point and Market Cafe restaurants are both excellent. Energized souls sign up at Action Sports for sailboats, paddleboats, and bikes; lovers drift under the setting sun in gondolas. The 438 rooms and suites all have water views and balconies; the best sit at the tip of the resort facing the 80-slip marina. Kids get rubber ducks and bubbles in the giant bathtubs—although first they have to kick out the grown-ups. Chairs, couches, and beds are all comfy; it's hard to leave them for the padded pool chairs—though the idea of Häagen-Dazs bars sold poolside is enticing. When the hotel's spa construction is completed in early 2003, there will be yet another reason to stay put. Why leave when you're stranded in paradise?

If you must go out, shuttles run regularly to Coronado's shopping area and downtown's Horton Plaza. *$$$; AE, DC, MC, V; checks OK; valet and self parking; www.loewshotels.com; map:NN5* &

# Point Loma/Shelter Island

## The Bay Club / ★★

**2131 SHELTER ISLAND DR, SHELTER ISLAND; 619/224-8888 OR 800/833-6565**
Rattan furnishings, tropical fabrics, and plenty of windows open to the sea air make this 105-room low-rise hotel a good choice for adults on a grown-up getaway. Rooms face the yacht basin or the bay, though views from those on the ground level, street side, are obstructed by traffic. Guests mingle at the complimentary breakfast buffet and beside the shaded pool when not off on excursions around the city. Service is personal, friendly, and accommodating; you can arrange nearly anything with the concierges. *$$–$$$; AE, DC, DIS, MC, V; checks OK; www.ba yclubhotel.com; map:F7*

## Shelter Pointe Hotel and Marina / ★★☆

**1551 SHELTER ISLAND DR, SHELTER ISLAND; 619/221-8000 OR 800/566-2524** Tiki torches and mai tais were mainstays at this island resort when it opened as the Kona Kai in 1952. The renovated Mediterranean-style resort faces a private marina; rooms on the street side face the bay, Coronado, and downtown. A waterfront sidewalk runs the length of the property, past low-rise buildings housing the rooms and suites. The two-story units are particularly spectacular. Breakfast in the king-size bed in the second-story master bedroom comes with a water view, while downstairs living rooms, sleeper sofas, and full kitchens give families plenty of room to spread out in comfort. Even the regular rooms are satisfying, with their terraces on the lawn within steps of the pool. Tennis courts, a fitness club, decent restaurants, and marina facilities provide entertainment; walkers and joggers appreciate the paths along the edge of Shelter Island. *$$$; AE, DC, DIS, MC, V; checks OK (if mailed in advance); www.shelterpointe.com; map:E8*

# Old Town and Mission Valley

## Best Western Hacienda Suites / ★★

**4041 HARNEY ST, OLD TOWN; 619/298-4707 OR 800/888-1991** White stucco buildings are staggered down a steep hill at this compact 169-room hotel, where it takes some time to figure out which stairway or ramp leads to the pool and your room. The rooms don't rate as suites in our book, and fold-out couches and writing tables take up space. A Southwest style (think wood, striped fabrics, and clay ornaments) prevails, and all rooms are stocked with microwave ovens, coffeemakers, VCRs, and refrigerators. There's limited room service from the adjacent Acapulco restaurant (a good spot for sunset cocktails). The street is fairly quiet, and all of Old Town's attractions are within walking distance. Save energy for the hike back to your room. *$$–$$$; AE, DC, DIS, MC, V; no checks; self parking; www.haciendahotel-oldtown.com; map:J2*

## Comfort Inn and Suites / ★★

**2201 HOTEL CIRCLE S; 619/291-2711 OR 800/772-6318** Mission Valley has many chain motels for budget travelers who care more about price than luxury. This small inn is one of the nicest, since it is set back a bit from Interstate 8. Don't be thrown by the name; this used to be called the Hotel Circle Inn, and many of the longtime staff members are still around. The inn's 220 rooms were renovated in 2001 and are surprisingly comfortable; those at the far back are the quietest. All rooms have satellite TV with movie channels; rooms with kitchenettes are nearly twice as expensive as those without. There's a new pool area with a wading pool for kids, and a laundry room for guests. We think this is one of the best family-oriented bargains in town, and it's also good for business travelers who prefer friendliness over anonymity. Make reservations way in advance of your stay, since prices rise as room supply diminishes. *$$; AE, CB, DC, DIS, MC, V; checks OK (if mailed in advance); self parking; www.hotelcircleinn.com; map:K1* &

## Doubletree San Diego Mission Valley / ★★

**7450 HAZARD CENTER DR, MISSION VALLEY; 619/297-5466 OR 800/222-8733** Located in a residential and business sector in Mission Valley away from the interstate, the Doubletree faces a small dining and shopping plaza called Hazard Center. Fashion Valley and Mission Valley malls are nearby, as are Highway 163 and a trolley stop. The 294 rooms and six suites are spacious and decorated in light pastels; in-room coffeemakers, irons and ironing boards, large work tables with good lighting, and modem phone lines are assets for business travelers. Suites on the executive floors all have balconies, as do some of the standard rooms. Families enjoy the hotel's light, airy style, the indoor and outdoor pools and hot tub, and the free giant chocolate chip cookies. The neighborhood isn't particularly scenic, but there are shopping and dining options galore. Best of all, the trolley stops just across the street from the hotel, so guests can tour around without driving. *$$$; AE, DC, DIS, MC, V; no checks; valet and self parking; map:LL4* &

### Heritage Park Inn / ★★★

**2470 HERITAGE PARK ROW, OLD TOWN; 619/299-6832 OR 800/995-2470** Nestled in a cluster of lovingly restored Victorian homes overlooking Old Town, Heritage Park Inn is true to its elegant, old-time roots. Twelve rooms are contained in two historic homes—the circa 1889 Christian House and the Italianate Bushyhead House. With a formal Victorian parlor (where classic films are screened every evening) and period antiques and stained-glass windows throughout, it doesn't take long to let the ambience slow your pace. We recommend the romantic Turret Room overlooking the gardens, or the Garret, with its own secret staircase. For more luxury, reserve one of the three rooms in Bushyhead House, with whirlpool tubs for two. Rates include a gourmet breakfast, served by candlelight in the dining room, plus a filling afternoon tea of finger sandwiches and sweets. The location is a short stroll from Old Town's shops and restaurants and the trolley stop. *$$–$$$; AE, DC, DIS, MC, V; checks OK; self parking; innkeeper@heritageparkinn.com; www.heritageparkinn.com; map:J2*

### Red Lion Hanalei Hotel / ★★

**2270 HOTEL CIRCLE N, MISSION VALLEY; 619/297-1101 OR 800/882-0858** One of the better choices in the busy Mission Valley area, the Hanalei is Polynesian through and through. Guests who delighted in the tropical scene were concerned when the hotel was remodeled in 1998. But the fresh pale cream exterior and updated edifice don't detract from the palms, hibiscus flowers, waterfalls, koi ponds, and tiki torches. With 402 rooms and 14 suites in high-rise towers, the hotel isn't exactly peaceful. Noise rises from the pool area and nearby freeways, causing recluses to shut their windows and crank up the AC. Guests become instant friends while lounging by the pool, and can schedule tours to all the local highlights using tips from the friendly staff. *$$; AE, DC, DIS, MC, V; checks OK (if mailed in advance); www.hanaleihotel.com; map:LL5* &

# Mission Bay

### Dana Inn / ★★

**1710 W MISSION BAY DR, MISSION BAY; 619/222-6440 OR 800/445-3339** Among the expensive resorts at Mission Bay, this simple hotel stands out as a family-friendly and affordable hangout. The 196 rooms are spread about the property in two-story wood buildings facing parking lots, the bay, and the pool. Sensible rather than picturesque, the rooms all have small refrigerators, coffeemakers, and single or double beds; the wood-veneer and plastic furniture is designed to withstand sandy bodies and wet towels. All family members stay entertained with shuffleboard and tennis courts; two pools; bike, skate, and water-sports rentals; and all the parks and playgrounds on the bay. Sea World sits just across the water (there's a shuttle from the hotel), providing free entertainment with the nighttime fireworks exploding overhead. Guests who want peace and quiet opt for the bayside rooms, which have all been refurbished. The coffee shop does a decent job with home-style meals. Rooms book quickly in summer and get more expensive as supply diminishes. This is one of our favorite places to accommodate visiting relatives. *$$; AE, DC, DIS, JCB, MC, V; checks OK (if mailed in advance); self parking; map:LL6*

## Hilton San Diego Resort / ★★★

**1775 E MISSION BAY DR, MISSION BAY; 619/276-4010 OR 800/221-2424** Craving action and adventure with massage and spa treatments on the side? You belong at this swath of beach, bike paths, lawns, and private terraces beside Mission Bay. Hotel facilities include several swimming pools, tennis courts, fitness center, and equipment rentals for nearly every water or land sport you can imagine. The 357 tropical-style rooms and suites, with tables and chairs for group snacks and games (or laptops if you must), are scattered through Mediterranean-style low-rise buildings (complete with terraces and balconies) beside the bay and one eight-story building facing Interstate 5. Rollerbladers whiz by from dawn to dusk, following trails for miles along the bay. Kites of every shape float in the sky. Multigenerational families celebrate weddings, birthdays, and sunny Sundays with elaborate picnics all around the hotel, and visitors are completely immersed in the SoCal scene. *$$$; AE, DC, MC, V; checks OK; valet and self parking; map:LL5* &

## Paradise Point Resort / ★★★

**1404 W VACATION RD, MISSION BAY; 858/274-4630 OR 800/344-2626** Originally opened by a Hollywood producer in the 1960s as Vacation Village South Seas Paradise, this sprawling 44-acre resort has gone through several transformations. The 462 rooms and suites are housed in single-level buildings and have private patios, refrigerators, and coffeemakers. Most have dark patterned carpeting (to hide the marks of sandy feet); red, white, and blue linens; and marble baths. Guests are kept ultra-busy with the four swimming pools, 18-hole putting course, tennis courts, and volleyball nets on the sand. The marina offers water sport rentals; the activities center provides bikes for those wishing to cruise the bay on land. The luxurious spa is a major plus in our view—you can always sneak away for a Balinese massage while the kids are playing. Restaurants include the ever-popular Barefoot Bar on the sand along with the upscale Baleen dining room. Rooms are spread far enough apart that honeymooners can feel they're on a romantic escape. Mission Beach, Sea World, Old Town, and other attractions are just a few minutes away. *$$$; AE, DC, DIS, MC, V; checks OK (if mailed in advance); valet and self parking; www.paradisepoint.com; map:LL6* &

# Pacific Beach

## The Catamaran Resort Hotel / ★★★

**3999 MISSION BLVD, PACIFIC BEACH; 858/488-1081 OR 800/422-8386** Another venerable resort on Mission Bay, this self-contained oasis has a tropical South Seas style. The aquariums, rare plant gardens, waterfalls, and ponds provide a cool, shaded retreat from the Pacific Beach scene, yet those staying in one of the 312 rooms and suites can walk to most of PB's restaurants and attractions. The hotel's 12-story tower rises above busy Mission Boulevard; though ocean views are spectacular from the top floor, street noise and helicopter lights can distract from a peaceful retreat. The rest of the rooms in the tower and cottage-type buildings face gardens, pools, and a quiet stretch of Mission Bay. The rooms echo the hotel's tropical decor, with pastel fabrics and light wood furnishings, and feature such vacation necessities as refrigerators, coffeemakers, and irons and ironing boards. The bars and restaurants are popular with locals and guests, and the activities center offers kayaks, boogie boards, Wave Runners, sailboards, and tandem bikes with baby seats. Park your car, rent a bike, and live like a beach bum in paradise. *$$$; AE, DC, DIS, MC, V; checks OK (if mailed in advance); valet and self parking; www.catamaranresort.com; map:KK7* &

### Crystal Pier Hotel & Cottages / ★★★★

**4500 OCEAN BLVD, PACIFIC BEACH; 858/483-6983 OR 800/748-5894** Drive your car across the boardwalk and onto the pier. Park in front of a blue-and-white country cottage with flowers abloom beneath shuttered windows. Open the front door; gaze across the living room and kitchen to your back porch perched over the sea. Check out the bedroom; lie flat on your back atop a patchwork quilt. Feel the surge of the surf and sense the white noise of water and wind. Return to the hotel's office and request another night or more. The 26 Crystal Pier cottages are claimed months in advance by families from Arizona to Canada who set out barbecue grills, fill the fridge, and hang their beach towels over lounge chairs and wood railings. The scene is more peaceful during the off seasons, when couples and singles claim the cottages as private escapes. Winter nights are particularly exciting when the surf is high and the air has a salty chill. One longs for a fireplace to complete the ambience; sadly, there aren't any. The boardwalk scene is just a few steps away if you want to grab a great meal, rent a bike or boogie board, or mingle with humanity. After all, you'll be over the water from dark to dawn, sleeping above the sea. Advance reservations are absolutely essential in summer. *$$$; AE, MC, V; no checks; www.crystalpier.com; map:KK7* &

# La Jolla

### The Bed & Breakfast Inn of La Jolla / ★★☆

**7753 DRAPER AVE, LA JOLLA; 858/456-2066 OR 800/582-2466** It's easy to miss the ivy-covered entrance to this pleasant hideaway just a few blocks from busy Prospect Street. Designed by architect Irving Gill in 1913 as a private home, it's a historic treasure once occupied by John Philip Sousa in the '20s. Kate Sessions, San Diego's grande dame of horticulture, designed the original gardens. Today, the 16 rooms offer a taste of genteel living. You'll find plenty of nice touches—fresh flowers, sherry, and fruit in the rooms; antiques and original artworks that lend the air of a private home. The Holiday Room is a romantic retreat with a four-poster bed and working fireplace. If you want a view of the water, reserve the Irving Gill Penthouse Suite, which has a private deck. The upstairs Peacock Room has a private balcony for sunbathing—you'll feel like you're at an elegant Côte d'Azur pension. Breakfast is served on Royal Albert bone china in the dining room or by the fountain on the patio. *$$; AE, MC, V; no checks; bed+breakfast@innlajolla.com; www.innlajolla.com; map:JJ7*

## SPAS AND SALONS

Pampering is as popular as surfing in San Diego, home to some of the nation's most prestigious spas. The **GOLDEN DOOR** (777 Deer Springs Rd., San Marcos; 760/744-5777 or 800/424-0777; www.goldendoor.com) has catered to spa aficionados since 1958. It sets the standard for privacy, mind-body awareness, and physical challenges, and is favored by the elusive elite. Located 40 miles northeast of downtown San Diego, near the beach community of Carlsbad, the spa looks like a rambling Japanese garden and exudes a privileged ambience. Women reign at the Golden Door most of the year. Men are only allowed stay here five days a year; couples are allowed entry four weeks each year. The rest of the time, women stay in the 40 single rooms designed with serenity in mind.

Located in the same part of San Diego's backcountry, **CAL-A-VIE** (2249 Somerset Rd., Vista; 760/945-2055 or 866/772-4283; www.cal-a-vie.com) also caters to a well-heeled clientele. Capacity is limited to 48 guests per week, and the emphasis is on yoga, healthy nutrition, fitness, and weight loss. Guests relax in cottages tucked beside citrus trees and hiking trails ramble through the 220-acre property (which includes a golf course) and indulge in wraps and massages after vigorous workouts. A computerized fitness evaluation sets the tone for the week; diet and exercise plans are designed to optimize weight loss and fitness.

Professional tennis and golf players frequent the courts and courses at **LA COSTA RESORT & SPA** (Costa del Mar Rd, Carlsbad; 760/438-9111 or 800/854-5000). Recent renovations have updated rooms and facilities at this venerable 400-acre property, where guests have long enjoyed diet and exercise programs, spa treatments, and plenty of sporting options. The resort is now home to the **CHOPRA CENTER** (www.chopra.com), headed by San Diego's famed wellness guru Deepak Chopra. Medical programs are combined with techniques for spiritual, physical, and emotional health, and the center offers both a day spa and longer workshops. Eastern and Western philosophies are incorporated in individual plans, which include meditation, massages, yoga, and diet.

Just south of the border is the famed **RANCHO LA PUERTA** (Km. 5 Carretera Federal, Tecate, Baja California) 760/ 744-4222 or 800/443-7565; www.ranchola-puerta.com). The ranch is set amid boulders and stark hillsides 35 miles southeast of San Diego and three miles across the border. Cottages, haciendas, and villas house up to 150 guests each week; those in the know book their rooms and treatments several months in advance. Fitness programs include hiking and 60 exercise classes, and workshops on health topics including menopause, supplements, and cancer prevention are offered daily. There's time for pampering spa treatments and siestas poolside as well.

Many of San Diego's resort hotels have full-service spas. Among the best are those at the **FOUR SEASONS AVIARA, PARADISE POINT, L'AUBERGE DEL MAR, RANCHO BERNARDO INN** and the **HOTEL DEL CORONADO** (See Lodgings Chapter). If you're not staying at a spa hotel, sign up for a treatment and spend several hours using the facilities.

Day spas and beauty salons combine pampering with the usual maintenance treatments; most offer day packages that leave you with a satisfied glow. At the **ARTESIA DAY SPA AND SALON** (240 Fifth Ave, downtown; 619/338-8111), office workers indulge in lunchtime pedicures and massages. The spa is located in the same complex as the **HILTON SAN DIEGO GASLAMP QUARTER**, just across the street from the Convention Center. Set amid La Jolla's chic boutiques and cafes, the **GAIA DAY SPA** (1299 Prospect St, La Jolla; 858/456-8797; www.gaiadayspa.com) sets the mood with private suites containing saunas, showers, and soaking tubs. Feng shui principles are used in the spa's design, and treatments include thalassotherapy, Vichy salt glows and showers, and herbal wraps. **BEAUTY KLINIEK DAY SPA AND WELLNESS CENTER** (3268 Governor Dr, Golden Triangle; 858/457-0191; www.beautykliniek.com) has been one of San Diego's most popular day spas for more than 18 years. The 5,000-square-foot spa's specialty is aromatherapy, but there are tons of specialized treatments, including massage and pedicures for couples. At the front of the spa, French bath and body care products are sold; most are based on botanicals. Formerly called Primo, the **TOWN & COUNTRY SALON AND DAY SPA** (500 Hotel Circle N, Mission Valley; 619/220-0014) is another longtime beauty facility offering mad wraps, massages, and beauty services. **WALDEN ASHE** (930 W Washington St, Mission Hills; 619/295-7302; www.waldenashe.com) is known for its facials, peels, and esthetic services.

—*Maribeth Mellin*

## Hotel Parisi / ★★★

**1111 PROSPECT ST, LA JOLLA; 858/454-1511 OR 877/4PARISI** More urban and hip than what you'd normally expect in San Diego, the Parisi is a 20-room boutique property in the heart of La Jolla. The spare, contemporary high-design concept seems to float above the hubbub of Prospect Street. Indeed, the hotel occupies the top floor of a mixed-use retail building. Guests are greeted by a calming lobby with a natural stone fountain and a fireplace, in keeping with the elements of feng shui that were incorporated in the design. The rooms are restful cocoons in shades of sand and taupe, outfitted with simple custom-made furnishings and beds dressed in inviting white-linen-covered duvets. Flame-cut steel and wood nightstands are offset by cozy slipcovered chairs; the overall effect is serenely uncluttered without being cold. Rooms overlooking Prospect Street have a view of La Valencia Hotel just across the street, as well as a partial ocean view. *$$$$; AE, DIS, JCB, MC, V; no checks; www.hotelparisi.com; map:JJ7* ♿

## La Jolla Cove Suites / ★★

**1155 COAST BLVD, LA JOLLA; 858/459-2621 OR 888/525-6552** It never ceases to amaze locals and visitors alike that such a plain motel-like structure should sit right across from beautiful La Jolla Cove. All the better, we say. The simplicity of the accommodations allows for some of the lowest room rates you'll find in La Jolla, yet many rooms have direct views of magnificent Ellen Browning Scripps Park and the sea. There are 117 rooms and suites in a compound of drab buildings; the best have water views, kitchenettes, and a separate bedroom. Free parking is available—a major treat in this clogged area. The pool is a simple, square affair, and there is no restaurant (though continental breakfast is served on the rooftop terrace). But all of La Jolla's excellent restaurants, shops, museums, and clubs are within easy walking distance, and nothing beats the serenity of sleeping right by the sea. Rates drop considerably from January to May. *$$$; AE, DC, DIS, MC, V; no checks; self parking; map:JJ7*

## La Valencia Hotel / ★★★★

**1132 PROSPECT ST, LA JOLLA; 858/454-0771 OR 800/451-0772** To many residents and visitors, La Valencia Hotel *is* La Jolla. The Mediterranean-style "Pink Lady" has reigned over Prospect Street since 1926, and it's always been a hub of activity for well-heeled guests and local bigwigs. The hotel's 117 rooms, suites, and villas are individually decorated. Some have a green floral motif; others boast a beachy blue-and-white seashell theme. Naturally, rooms with million-dollar views of La Jolla Cove are the most desirable, though guests with ample discretionary cash opt for the 17 smashing villas (rates start at $550 per night). Private butlers stock the villas' fridges with the guests' favorite treats—a sampler of pâtés and cheeses, perhaps, or just the right bubbly. The butlers also unpack your luggage, draw your bath, take your shoes to be shined, and do whatever you desire (within reason). "La V" is delightfully old-fashioned in that its public spaces are well trafficked, which gives the place a pleasant hum of activity. Every afternoon, the Mediterranean Room patio is filled with ladies who lunch, and the Whaling Bar is a favorite local hangout. At sunset, head to La Sala Lounge, sink into a sofa, and enjoy the view. Be sure to check out the hand-painted ceiling overhead. *$$$$; AE, DC, DIS, MC, V; checks OK; info@lavalencia.com; www.lavalencia.com; map:JJ7* &

## The Lodge at Torrey Pines / ★★★★

**11480 N TORREY PINES RD, LA JOLLA; 858/453-4420 OR 800/656-0087** Architects and interior designers are riveted by this California Craftsman–style hotel. Guests have the good fortune to stay in rooms that faithfully replicate the style of the 1920s, with leather furnishings and a mountain lodge comfort. Stone walls, high wood-beamed ceilings, and original Stickley furnishings in the public spaces were designed for historical accuracy. The lodge feels like a classic Craftsman home, albeit larger. But it's also designed to satisfy the needs of modern travelers, with all the essential business and comfort amenities in the rooms, a full spa, lots of meeting space, and two restaurants. It's located beside the famed Torrey Pines golf course, home to major tournaments. The room rates at the lodge are high. If you'd like to see more representations of the Craftsman style, wander the back streets of

Mission Hills, an older neighborhood near downtown. *$$$$; AE, DC, DIS, MC, V; checks OK; valet and self parking; www.thelodgeattorreypines.com; map:HH7* &

## Scripps Inn / ★★

**555 COAST BLVD S, LA JOLLA; 858/454-3391** Guests check in to this tiny hotel for weeks, setting up housekeeping just steps from the coastline and stately Ellen Browning Scripps Park. Two buildings face each other in a narrow lot; some privacy is lost, but the location and reasonable room rates are worth the close quarters. Most of the 14 rooms have views of the sea; the best have working fireplaces and ocean-view balconies. Rooms and suites (some with two bedrooms) have refrigerators, sitting areas, and fold-out sofas; white walls, pale tan furnishings, and French doors lend a breezy, relaxed feel. A complimentary breakfast of pastries and coffee is served on the lobby terrace. There's no pool—but who needs one when the best snorkeling spot on the coast is just a few steps away? Book a room at this little gem way in advance of your trip, and consider splurging on rooms 6 or 12, both with fireplaces and full views. *$$$; AE, DIS, MC, V; checks OK; self parking; www.scrippsinn.com; map:JJ7*

## Sea Lodge / ★★★

**8110 CAMINO DEL ORO, LA JOLLA; 858/459-8271 OR 800/237-5211** Lucky are those who happen upon this hidden beachfront hotel, tucked down a side street at La Jolla Beach. Low-rise tiled-roof buildings frame a central courtyard and pool; Mexican painted tiles and terra-cotta fountains add a Spanish air to the 128-room complex. Floral plants and light rattan furnishings lighten up the rooms facing the courtyard; those with a view of the sea are filled with sunlight. The restaurant has a full ocean view, and a sidewalk just outside the door leads to a playground area and the beach. The staff is like family to the many returning guests, who don't mind a bit of sand in their carpets and a casual ambiance. The courtyard pool is a cool retreat from the beach, and underground parking protects cars from the salt air. The hotel's restaurant is overseen by Bernard Guillas, the star chef at the nearby Marine Room (see the Restaurants chapter). Some folks in the neighborhood are so fond of his selection of reasonably priced dishes that they dine here weekly. There's a five-night minimum stay during the summer. *$$$; AE, DC, DIS, MC, V; no checks; self parking; www.sealodge.com; map:JJ7* &

# Del Mar

## L'Auberge Del Mar / ★★★★

**1540 CAMINO DEL MAR, DEL MAR; 858/259-1515 OR 800/505-9043** This deluxe 120-room resort may be right on Del Mar's main drag, but you'll find ample privacy for any rendezvous. Small and wonderful, L'Auberge has all the elements of a great getaway. Rooms are decorated in an upscale Provençal coastal cottage theme, and all have a private balcony or patio. Bring your swimsuit, because the inn has two pools—one for lounging, another for lap swimming—and the beach is a short stroll away. There are also tennis courts, a small but well-equipped fitness room, and a terrific little spa where you'll want to indulge in a treatment or two. L'Auberge's central location means you can explore Del Mar's shops and restaurants on foot—but you'll likely eat at the inn's J. Taylor's restaurant frequently. For the most privacy, request a top-floor corner room from which you can gaze at the treetops and get a glimpse of the Pacific. *$$$; AE, DC, DIS, MC, V; checks OK; valet and self parking; www.laubergedelmar.com; map:GG7*

## Les Artistes / ★★

**944 CAMINO DEL MAR, DEL MAR; 858/755-4646** This rambling adobe inn just south of Del Mar's village center is a favorite of those who like quirky, personable lodgings. Behind the magenta bougainvillea, purple wisteria, and gurgling fountains out front, the 12 rooms boast creative tile work and prints, objets d'art, and original paintings in various themes. Seven "designer" rooms are larger than standard accommodations, and each is decorated to commemorate a different artist. The Diego Rivera room is a large upstairs unit with an ocean view and cozy, rustic Mexican decor. Similarly, with its wood beams and white stucco walls, the spacious Georgia O'Keeffe room befits its namesake. The hotel is walking distance from Del Mar's hopping restaurants and shops. If you like your accommodations on the bohemian side, you'll appreciate Les Artistes' offbeat charm. *$$–$$$; AE, DIS, MC, V; no checks; self parking; www.lesartistesinn.com; map:GG7*

# Rancho Santa Fe

## The Inn at Rancho Santa Fe / ★★

**5951 LINEA DEL CIELO, RANCHO SANTA FE; 858/756-1131, 800/654-2928, OR 800/843-4661** In the heart of Rancho Santa Fe's tony but low-key village, The Inn at Rancho Santa Fe is an unassuming charmer that doesn't rush to embrace every trend. Eighty-seven rooms are spread throughout a cluster of cream-colored adobe buildings and cottages, surrounded by carefully manicured grounds. The inn's cool, wood-beamed main building was designed in 1923 by Lillian Rice, the architect responsible for Rancho Santa Fe's genteel Spanish-colonial look. All rooms are individually decorated with gingham couches and Windsor chairs in a retro-1940s take on American colonial. For extra privacy, request one of the garden cottages with a private patio. Still, you'll want to hang out on a chaise longue by the pool or borrow equipment for a rousing round of croquet on the front lawn. Boutiques and more fine restaurants are a short stroll away. If you want to put in some time at the beach, the inn maintains a private day cottage on the sand in nearby Del Mar. *$$–$$$; AE, DC, MC, V; no checks; valet and self parking; www.theinnatranchosantafe.com; map:EE5* ♿

## Rancho Valencia Resort / ★★★★

**5921 VALENCIA CIRCLE, RANCHO SANTA FE 858/756-1123 OR 800/548-3664** You never know whom you might see on the tennis court or in the dining room at this deluxe hideaway—maybe Regis Philbin or an oil tycoon on an extended vacation. They're among the well-heeled regulars who come for the resort's first-rate pampering and bucolic setting. City lights don't obstruct the clear night skies; pollution doesn't mar the view of hot-air balloons drifting by at sunset. The fragrance of citrus blossoms is a nearly constant presence—there are 1,000 citrus trees on the property. Naturally, days begin with fresh-squeezed orange juice and morning newspaper left just outside your door.

The 43 suites here are no bargain, but the setting is utterly lovely. The smaller Del Mar suites are each a roomy 850 square feet of airy, Mediterranean elegance—terracotta floors, gas fireplaces, high-beamed ceilings, custom-made furnishings, and spacious private patios. The one-bedroom Rancho Santa Fe suites offer even more room to relax. New casitas have private hot tubs, rain-forest showerheads, and televisions in the bathrooms. Rancho Valencia began as a tennis resort, and it constantly ranks in *Tennis* magazine's top lists. The 18 tennis courts and first-rate teaching staff make this a dream escape for tennis buffs; players not staying at the inn can use the courts or take classes for a fee. If you're lucky, you'll get to join in a croquet tournament on the lawn—be sure to bring along white play clothes. There's no spa, but you can have excellent massages and facials in your suite. Breakfast is served in a sunroom walled with yellow and blue tiles or on a terrace overlooking the tennis courts. The dining room is both comfortable and romantic, and the food is superb (see the Restaurants chapter). *$$$$; AE, CB, DC, MC, V; checks OK; valet and self parking; www.ranchovalencia.com; map:EE5*

# Cardiff-by-the-Sea

## Cardiff-by-the-Sea Lodge / ★

**142 CHESTERFIELD, CARDIFF-BY-THE-SEA; 760/944-6474** There are precious few hotel rooms near the awesome beach in Cardiff. This B&B is artfully squished into a residential block just across the sand from Highway 101. The wood-shingled buildings hold 17 rooms of varying design and comfort; seven have ocean views. The rooftop terrace has a whirlpool tub, a gas fire ring, and plenty of room for relaxing or mingling. Returnees book their favorite rooms and dates months in advance, and wedding parties sometimes fill the place. You can walk to the beach and a good market from the inn. *$$–$$$; AE, DC, MC, V; checks OK in advance; self parking; www.cardifflodge.com; map:EE8*

# Carlsbad

## Beach Terrace Inn / ★

**21775 OCEAN ST, CARLSBAD; 760/729-5951 OR 800/433-5415** The motel-like buildings of this somewhat battered 49-room inn fade from view as you walk from your room to the sand without crossing a street or touching pavement. The pool is a simple affair, steep steps lead to various styles of rooms, and there's no restaurant on the property. You can't even see the sea from some rooms. Who cares? You can hear it like a crashing lullaby in the background, and feel its dampness on your skin (and clothes). Summer weekends book up fast, but visitors without reservations are sometimes pleasantly surprised. *$$–$$$; AE, DC, MC, V; checks OK in advance; self parking; www.beachterraceinn.com; map: CC9*

## Carlsbad Inn Beach Resort / ★★

**3075 CARLSBAD BLVD, CARLSBAD; 760/434-7020 OR 800/235-3939** This gem right in the heart of Carlsbad is just across the street from the beach, yet it feels like an urbane European inn. The Tudor-style facade gives way to a peaceful carpeted lobby, with curved stairways leading to upper-floor rooms (there's also an elevator). Peaked, shingled roofs and wooden balconies continue the European theme in buildings framing the pool and a broad lawn. The 62 rooms in the main building are cozy and reminiscent of the inn's origins as a 1920s mansion. Those in the wing buildings have varying shapes and sizes; some are used as time-share units (sometimes available as hotel rooms) and have kitchenettes or kitchens and separate bedrooms. Hotel guests can participate in activities designed for the time-share owners—day trips to San Diego attractions are sometimes offered, as are wine and cheese parties and live music on the lawn. The hotel has a beach club just across the street. *$$$; AE, DC, MC, V; checks OK in advance; self parking; www.carlsbadinn.com; map: CC9*

## Four Seasons Resort–Aviara / ★★★★

**7100 FOUR SEASONS PT, CARLSBAD; 760/603-6800 OR 800/332-7100** Yes, the Four Seasons is sleek, swank, and serene. But we love it best for its beds, which feel like fluffy clouds. Soft green walls, understated furnishings (including a large desk with comfortable chair), and marble baths with soaking tubs make it hard to leave the room, though it is nice to settle on the private balcony's cushioned deck chairs for sunset cocktails. There are plenty of other diversions in this 329-room hotel overlooking Batiquitos Lagoon and the ocean. The recently enlarged spa is filled with sensory delights from gentle citrus sugar scrubs to avocado wraps and will also send a masseuse to your room for pampering. The Jose Eber Salon is the perfect place to primp for dinner at Vivace, where chef Pascal Vignau presents Tuscan culinary wonders in a Mediterranean-style, ocean-view dining room (see the Restaurants chapter). A to-die-for brunch (with a separate serving table overflowing with treats for kids) is displayed at the California Bistro, which also hosts a Friday-night seafood buffet that's often sold out days or weeks in advance. Afternoon tea is graciously presented in the flower-filled Lobby Lounge.

Golfers rave about the Arnold Palmer–designed Aviara Golf Course that sprawls over 180 acres of canyons and lagoons. Tennis buffs head for the six lighted courses; swimmers delight in a seemingly endless pool (there's a quiet pool separate from the one for families). Though the hotel is lush and luxurious, children aren't ignored: the Kids for All Seasons program is excellent, and there are PlayStations in all rooms. Special programs include a jazz series on summer nights. *$$$; AE, DC, DIS, JCB, MC, V; checks OK; valet parking; www.fourseasons.com; map:CC7* &

# Oceanside

## Oceanside Marina Inn / ★★

**2008 HARBOR DR N, OCEANSIDE; 760/722-1561 OR 800/252-2033** Front-row rooms face the open ocean held at bay by a rock jetty. The back rooms face the Oceanside Marina. Yachties spend weeks on end at this comfortable, hidden hotel. It sits at the very end of the marina road, across the water from the north end of Oceanside's fabulous beach. The hotel ferries guests to the sand in a motorized boat on summer weekends. It's tempting to spend upwards of $300 a night for an oceanfront suite with a full kitchen, separate bedroom with tall four-poster bed, and fireplace. But even with an obstructed view and more modest amenities, you'll have the sea near your door. You can't swim in the ocean here, or even walk on the sand; still, the pool, hot tub, and sauna are heated and inviting. While the 64 rooms and suites vary in decor, all have full kitchens, fireplaces, and balconies. Continental breakfast is included in the rate. *$$; AE, DIS, MC, V; no checks; self parking; www.omihotel.com; map:DD9* &

# Rancho Bernardo

## Rancho Bernardo Inn / ★★★★

**17550 BERNARDO OAKS DR, RANCHO BERNARDO; 858/675-8500 OR 800/770-7482** Gourmands, golfers, business bigwigs, and vacationing families all feel at home in this hacienda-style inn set amid rolling fairways and clear valley air. Sculptures, fountains, and flowers mark the entrance to the lobby, where hand-painted tiles, hardwood beams, and blazing fireplaces evoke early California style at its most gracious. The best of the 288 rooms and suites have living room fireplaces, bedroom whirlpool tubs, and patios the size of an urban backyard. The rest are comfortable, though it's best to ask for one with a view of the grounds or distant mountain peaks. Guests in the know make time for at least one dinner and Sunday brunch at El Bizcocho, one of the county's finest restaurants (see the Restaurants chapter). Ask about the Gourmet Getaway package that includes a five-course dinner at the restaurant. You can always work off the calories at the inn's championship golf course (along with four others in the neighborhood), 12 tennis courts, and fitness center, or vegetate in the spa or beside the two pools, both so ensconced in flowering bushes and trees they feel like country lakes. The Wild Animal Park, several wineries, and the mountains and desert are all nearby, and downtown San Diego is just a 25-minute drive south. *$$$; AE, DC, DIS, MC, V; no checks; valet parking; www.ranchobernardoinn.com; map:FF3*

# Julian

## The Artists' Loft / ★★☆

**4811 PINE RIDGE AVE, JULIAN; 760/765-0765** Owner/artists Nanessence and Chuck Kimball's serene 11-acre oasis outside the town of Julian is just the place to kick back and listen to the wind rustle through the manzanita trees. Two rooms in the main house are decorated with rustic antiques, Persian rugs, and, of course, the Kimballs' own artwork. The Manzanita Room comes complete with a working antique parlor stove. The Gallery Room is a spacious, cheerful, yellow-hued hideaway. The Cabin at Strawberry Hill, named for the wild strawberries that surround it, boasts an inviting couch, a wood-burning stove, a king-size bed, and a fully equipped kitchen. The cabin's huge screened porch is a special treat on warm summer evenings. The 70-year-old Big Cat Cabin is named for a mountain lion that hides nearby in the wilds, far from view. They've lavishly remodeled this one-bedroom gem, which features a massive stone fireplace, fully equipped kitchen with countertops made of local oak, and a bathroom with a wood-paneled shower and a vintage cast-iron tub. You'll drift to sleep in an antique Balinese wedding bed, and the bedroom's screened study area is the ideal spot to curl up with a book. *$$; MC, V; checks OK; self parking; mail@artistsloft.com; www.artistsloft.com*

# Borrego Springs

## La Casa del Zorro / ★★

**3845 YAQUI PASS RD, BORREGO SPRINGS; 760/767-5323 OR 800/824-1884** There's no need to suffer and sweat in the desert. Instead, book a room or casita at this lush oasis buried in date palms set against a mountain backdrop. The casitas, with one to four bedrooms, are spread about in clusters throughout the 42-acre property. Some have fireplaces and private pools; all have kitchen facilities and living and dining rooms. Families book large casitas for reunions; couples hide out in one-bedroom settings with private hot tubs. Two-story white buildings with tiled roofs house the large, lodgelike guest rooms, most with fireplaces (the desert gets mighty chilly on winter nights). Several pools, one reserved for adult use only, are scattered about the gardens, and a river flows over boulders between the buildings. Prices are high in the restaurant, but you can get lots of touring tips from the staff. Big-name jazz groups play on summer weekends. Tours of the desert are available, in jeeps or on foot. Visit in spring when ocotillo plants thrust spires of red blossoms into the sky. Rates here drop considerably in summer. *$$$; AE, DC, DIS, MC, V; no checks; valet and self parking; www.lacasadelzorro.com* ♿

# EXPLORING

# EXPLORING

## Top 25 Attractions

### 1) Balboa Park

**2125 PARK BLVD, DOWNTOWN; 619/239-0512** Spread over 1,200 acres in the heart of San Diego, Balboa Park has been an exemplary setting for city planners since 1909, when the first jacaranda and pepper trees appeared atop canyons and mesas just east of downtown. Garden lover Kate Sessions, long dubbed the "mother of Balboa Park," was given the honor and responsibility of turning a barren tract of seemingly uninhabitable land into a park, and her early plantings remain among the city's many treasures.

Today, more than 14,000 trees representing 350 different species grow here amid rolling lawns; the twisted limbs and gnarled roots of the 60-foot-tall Moreton Bay fig, north of the Natural History Museum, create natural works of art. The **BOTANICAL BUILDING,** a large wood lath structure located on El Prado west of the Museum of Art, houses thousands of tropical plants as well as seasonal flowers. Just south of the Botanical Building children peer into the **LILY POND,** looking for goldfish, turtles, and frogs (left in the pond by errant pet owners). The **ALCAZAR GARDEN,** with its ornate fountains adorned with turquoise, yellow, and green tiles, is replanted seasonally; the **INEZ GRANT PARKER MEMORIAL ROSE GARDEN** makes an idyllic wedding backdrop; and the **ZORO GARDEN,** a stone grotto planted with lantana, pincushion flowers, and verbena, is a paradise for monarch, sulphur, and swallowtail butterflies.

Best known as the home of the superb **SAN DIEGO ZOO,** Balboa Park is also the soul of San Diego's cultural legacy. Many of its buildings date back to the 1915–1916 Panama-California Exposition, held to honor the completion of the Panama Canal (and, domestically, to boost the new city's image among potential investors). Yellow and blue tiles gleam in the sun atop the ornate **CALIFORNIA TOWER,** a fine example of the Spanish colonial revival style of architecture favored by the exposition's sponsors. A second burst of construction occurred prior to the 1935–1936 California Pacific International Exposition, which led to another financial boom for San Diego. Many of the park's 12 museums are housed in decades-old buildings covered with bas-relief carvings and baroque stone ornamentation. They weren't designed to last this long, but generations of San Diego families and civic entities have labored and lobbied to ensure their survival. Today, the city's Park and Recreation department does a commendable job of maintaining and restoring these marvelous old structures.

For the culturally minded and the artistically inclined, Balboa Park's attractions are varied and diverse. Start your sojourn at the **VISITORS CENTER,** located at the **HOUSE OF HOSPITALITY** near the middle of the park. Pick up a map and purchase a Passport to Balboa Park coupon book, valid for one week and entitling the bearer to admission to 13 park attractions. Ask about free garden tours and the cultural activities going on at the **HOUSE OF PACIFIC RELATIONS** and Spanish Village, a cluster of artists' studios. If you happen to visit on a Sunday afternoon, go by the

## TOP 25 ATTRACTIONS

1. Balboa Park
2. San Diego Zoo
3. Gaslamp Quarter
4. La Jolla Cove
5. Cabrillo National Monument
6. Mission Bay Park
7. Hotel del Coronado
8. Downtown Waterfront
9. Wild Animal Park
10. Sea World
11. Horton Plaza
12. Reuben H. Fleet Space Theater
    & Science Center
13. Old San Diego Town State
    Historic Park
14. Birch Aquarium at Scripps
15. Historic Highway 101
16. Torrey Pines State Reserve
17. Silver Strand State Beach
18. Boardwalk and Belmont Park
19. Mission Trails Regional Park
20. San Diego Museum of Art
21. Ocean Beach
22. San Diego Museum of Man
23. Quail Botanical Gardens
24. Mission Basilica San Diego de Alcalá
25. Legoland California

**SPRECKELS ORGAN PAVILION,** home to one of the world's largest outdoor pipe organs, and treat yourself to a free concert. Performances are held from 2pm to 3pm.

When the kids tire of the museums, take them for a ride on the **CAROUSEL,** located near the zoo. Built in 1910, the carousel has been at the park since 1922. Riders whirling around on tigers and ostriches hand-carved by European craftsmen try to catch the brass ring and win another go-round. From the third week in June through Labor Day, the carousel runs daily from 11am to 6pm. Winter hours are Saturdays, Sundays, and school holidays, 11am to 5:30pm. The price of a ticket is $1.50.

When hunger strikes, there are several remedies. The **GALILEO CAFE** at the Reuben H. Fleet Science Center has tables set out next to the fountain; sandwiches, soups, and pastries are available daily after 9:30am. After years of neglect, **THE PRADO RESTAURANT AT BALBOA PARK** (see the Restaurants chapter) in the House of Hospitality has become an exciting dining venue. Tea, miso soup, and noodle dishes are served in the **TEA PAVILION** at the Japanese Friendship Garden daily from 10am to 4pm. *Every day (Visitors Center open daily 9am–4pm); http://balboapark.org; map:P5* &

### 2) San Diego Zoo

**2920 ZOO DR, BALBOA PARK, DOWNTOWN; 619/234-3153** Nestled on 100 acres in the heart of Balboa Park, the world-famous San Diego Zoo began humbly with a handful of animals left over from Balboa Park's 1915–1916 Panama-California Exposition. A local surgeon, Harry M. Wegeforth, sought to protect lions, tigers, and bears left behind when the exhibits closed and spearheaded the Zoological Society of San Diego in 1916. This not-for-profit organization has grown into one of the finest examples of its kind in the world while overseeing the zoo and its sister attraction, the San Diego Wild Animal Park (see Attraction number 9).

The zoo's rare and exotic creatures flourish in San Diego's temperate climate. Among the most unusual and popular specimens are giant pandas Bai Yun and Shi Shi, on long-term loan from the People's Republic of China. The zoo is also home to one of the largest colonies of koalas outside Australia.

Recently designed enclosures resemble the natural homes of the animals, with moats or thick glass to protect them from us. The **POLAR BEAR PLUNGE** simulates the arctic tundra with polar bears, Siberian reindeer, and arctic foxes in residence. A 130,000-gallon pool—cooled to 55 degrees—is a playground for the frolicsome bears; a special indoor underwater viewing room, with a 5-inch-thick acrylic panel, allows an unusual perspective on their agile antics. **HIPPO BEACH** features a similar observation room, this one for viewing the surprisingly graceful 2-ton hippos as they slowly bounce along the bottom of their pool at viewers' eye level. **GORILLA TROPICS** transports you into an African rain forest, haven to a gregarious troop of western lowland gorillas and thousands of jungle plants. Nearby is the **SCRIPPS AVIARY**, like a giant birdcage with splashing waterfalls, exotic plants, and hundreds of native African birds.

If scales and forked tongues are your forte, check out the **REPTILE HOUSE**. Slithering safely behind glass is a wondrous collection of snakes and lizards. A huge albino python hangs out in its tree or wallows lazily in its mini-pool. Thelma and Louise, an aptly named two-headed corn snake, elicits shrieks of amazement from the kids. Just past the Reptile House, the **CHILDREN'S ZOO** has several nurseries where you can watch a hairy baby with its bottle. Visit the petting paddock and come face to snout with a potbellied pig.

A good introduction to the zoo is the 40-minute bus tour; informative and entertaining drivers are your guides. Double-decker buses leave the station every few minutes for the meandering 3-mile journey through much of the park, giving you a good idea of what warrants your further investigation and how far you'll have to hoof it to get there. If you don't suffer from acrophobia, try the Skyfari, an aerial tramway dangling 180 feet above ground.

General admission for adults is $19.50, $11.75 for children ages 3 to 11; children 2 and under are free. Deluxe admission, which includes the bus tour and Skyfari aerial tram ride, is $32 for an adult and $19.75 for a child. If you are also interested in visiting the Wild Animal Park, a Two-Park Ticket (admission to both attractions) costs an adult $46.80; for a child it's $31.40. Parking at the zoo is free. *Every day, hours vary; www.sandiegozoo.org; map:P4* ♿

### 3) Gaslamp Quarter

**BORDERED BY W HARBOR DR, BROADWAY, 4TH AVE, AND 6TH AVE, DOWNTOWN; 619/233-5227 (GASLAMP QUARTER ASSOCIATION)** Covering a stretch of more than 16 downtown blocks, the Gaslamp is a living reminder of turn-of-the-century San Diego—and a wildly successful redevelopment project. At one time it was a red-light district known as the Stingaree, where Wyatt Earp is said to have operated three gambling halls in the 1880s. Today's Gaslamp contains some of San Diego's finest Victorian-style buildings, constructed between the Civil War and

World War I. The **GASLAMP QUARTER HISTORIC FOUNDATION**, protector of this priceless pocket of history, is located in the historic Cape Cod–style **WILLIAM HEATH DAVIS HOUSE** (410 Island Ave; 619/233-4692). The house contains a museum with old photographs and room displays, and offers audiocassette rentals for self-guided tours of the neighborhood. Call in advance for opening times, as the house is staffed by volunteers and sometimes closes unexpectedly.

The Gaslamp has become San Diego's most happening nightlife center, a place where crowds of dressed-to-impress revelers party into the wee hours on weekends. This phenomenon surprised San Diegans, who just two decades ago were inclined to view downtown's oldest neighborhoods as run-down and dangerous. But visionaries and preservationists fiercely defended their city's oldest buildings, and the quarter was declared a National Historic District in 1980. Perhaps evoking the spirit of Wyatt Earp, modern-day gamblers renovated down-at-the-heels Victorian, frontier, Italian Romanesque, and Spanish Renaissance buildings, transforming them into restaurants, shops, and office buildings, and awaited success with determination. Their bet paid off handsomely, though it took several years to lure San Diegans downtown after dark.

**FIFTH AVENUE**, downtown's original Main Street, has developed into the hub of San Diego's nightlife scene, with gaslamp-style street lamps illuminating hordes of stylish pedestrians. **FOURTH AND SIXTH AVENUES** are nearly as crowded. Throughout the neighborhood, diners enter intimate indoor spaces or sit at sidewalk cafes to catch a view of the passing crowds. And crowded it is, especially on weekend nights; lines are long and reservations are wise. Infectious rhythms of swing, country, jazz, and rock spill from the doorways as popular groups perform in bars and nightclubs. Shop and gallery windows beckon browsers. It's best to circle the neighborhood a few times before settling on a restaurant or nightclub—check our Restaurants and Nightlife chapters for ideas. If you reach humanity overload, drop into **GASLAMP STADIUM 15** (701 5th Ave; 619/232-0400), which shows films from noon till midnight.

Driving and parking in the Gaslamp are nightmares best avoided, especially on weekends. A new 500-space garage at Sixth and Market called Park It on Market has helped, and there are several public lots on Island Avenue and Market and G Streets. Horse-drawn carriages and bicycle-powered coaches called pedicabs ply the streets, offering rides through downtown and the waterfront. *Map:N7–O7*

## 4) La Jolla Cove

**1100 COAST BLVD, LA JOLLA; 619/221-8900** True beach connoisseurs think they've reached nirvana at La Jolla Cove. This 150-foot-long smidgen of sand carved beneath crumbling sandstone cliffs is arguably one of the most beautiful beaches on the California coast. **ELLEN BROWNING SCRIPPS PARK** (see Beaches and Parks) creates a tableau of soul-satisfying lawns, twisted pines, and sky-high palms between the cove and the street. Million-dollar condos and homes pack every inch of turf on the hillside between Coast Boulevard and Prospect Street, the center of tony La Jolla's shopping and dining district. Rocks, boulders, spits of sand, and tide pools sculpt the coastline from the north-facing cove to La Jolla Shores. During the summer, La Jolla Cove is jam-packed with bodies by noon; arrive early and stake your turf near the cliffs. At high tide, the calm water edges upward and swallows towels and gear set close to its edge. The cove is a favorite launching site for scuba divers, who can be seen surreptitiously wiggling into their wet suits on Coast Boulevard above the beach. On a good day, underwater visibility reaches 30 feet; scuba divers and snorkelers use those stellar conditions to investigate the **SAN DIEGO–LA JOLLA UNDERWATER PARK.** Created in 1970, this 6,000-acre underwater sanctuary extends from La Jolla Cove north to the Torrey Pines State Reserve. Included in the park are an **ECOLOGICAL RESERVE** and a **MARINE LIFE REFUGE,** designed to protect the native marine and geological resources. Fishing is allowed farther offshore but not in the ecological reserve, where "look but don't touch" is the prevailing dictate. Golden garibaldis, blue neons, angelfish, and the occasional misguided seal are at home in the preserve's safe waters, and grow in size and numbers as they would in a giant aquarium.

Lifeguards are on duty at the cove year-round but the hours vary. There are rest rooms and showers by the steps down to the sand, next to the private **LA JOLLA SHUFFLEBOARD CLUB,** an idyllic wedding setting. Parking will probably be the most frustrating part of your day. Places on the street fill up fast, so bone up on your parallel-parking skills and cruise the residential streets nearest the beach. *Every day; map:JJ7*

## 5) Cabrillo National Monument

**AT THE END OF CABRILLO MEMORIAL DR, POINT LOMA; 619/557-5450** Few vistas compare with those from atop the cliffs of Point Loma, jutting into the Pacific on the north side of San Diego Bay. Telescopes, charts, and hiking trails enhance the views at Cabrillo National Monument at the very tip of the point, 400 feet above sea level. The park was a scant half acre when established by President Woodrow Wilson in 1913; today it covers more than 80 acres of relatively undisturbed coastal habitat.

Set on the highest point in the park is the Cape Cod–style **OLD POINT LOMA LIGHTHOUSE,** which served as the southernmost beacon along the U.S. Pacific Coast from 1855 to 1891. The lighthouse is closed to the public, but its dramatic architecture and setting serve as a focal point for the park. Nearby is the visitor center, where slide shows on whales, tide pools, and other oceanic subjects are presented throughout the day. The gift shop next door is one of the best in San Diego, with a plethora of books on boating and sea creatures, as well as souvenirs in every imaginable sea theme.

Behind the building is a lookout point with telescopes and charts describing the naval vessels in the bay. **NORTH ISLAND NAVAL AIR STATION** on Coronado is directly across the water; carriers, subs, destroyers, and all sorts of monstrous gray ships sit peacefully in the water off the island as fighter jets and helicopters lift off on maneuvers. On a clear day the view encompasses downtown, Coronado, and the sea as far as Mexico; in the winter months visitors sometimes catch glimpses of spouting gray whales migrating south from the Bering Sea to the birthing grounds in Baja California.

The best part of the park for nature lovers is the **BAYSIDE TRAIL,** a winding path down the cliff past native plants. At the west side of the park, Cabrillo Road leads down to more hiking trails above natural tide pools. Most of Point Loma near the monument is controlled by the U.S. Navy, but the public is welcome to wander the lawns at **FORT ROSECRANS NATIONAL CEMETERY,** where solemn lines of white headstones spread for 71 acres overlooking San Diego Bay. Admission to Cabrillo Monument is $5 per car or $2 per person for walk-ins; the pass into the park is good for seven days. *Every day 9am–5:15pm; www.nps.gov/cabr/index.htm; map:OO6*

## 6) Mission Bay Park

**BORDERED BY I-5, I-8, GRAND AVE, AND MISSION BLVD, MISSION BEACH; 619/221-8901** Back before World War II, Mission Bay Park was a swamp, originally named False Bay by the Spanish conquistadors. After the war, which vastly increased the military presence in San Diego and changed its character and landscape forever, the Army Corps of Engineers diverted the river, dredged channels, and carved a 4,600-acre swath of lawns and beaches between Interstate 5 and the ocean. The park has since evolved into a giant playground for all manner of San Diegans. Boaters and anglers head for Quivira Basin (Quivira Rd) within a stone's throw of Ocean Beach and Sea World. Charter boats carry herds of anglers from the marina at **SEAFORTH SPORTFISHING** (1717 Quivira Rd; 619/224-3383; www.seaforthlanding.com); boats bring back the catch around noon and 4pm. **THE LANDING** (1729 Quivira Rd; 619/222-3317), where crews fuel up on hearty pancakes, ham and eggs, and burgers, is a good place to listen to fish tales, as is **SPORTSMEN'S SEAFOODS** (1617 Quivira Rd; 619/224-3551), where seagulls beg for scraps at patio tables.

**SEA WORLD** (see Attraction number 10) sprawls along the southeast side of the bay; its frequent fireworks can be spotted from nearly everywhere in the park. **FIESTA ISLAND** (Fiesta Island Rd at Sea World Dr) is a man-made plot of dredged dirt and sand that serves as party central for jet-boaters, water-skiers, and powerboat fanatics. Eucalyptus groves, quiet picnic areas, and lawns favored by kite flyers lie along the south edge of the bay; here, kids delight in the latest play equipment at **TECOLOTE PLAYGROUND,** the largest disabled-accessible play area in the city.

Mission Bay's main entrance and **VISITOR INFORMATION CENTER** are located just off Interstate 5 at the East Mission Bay Drive exit; on summer weekends, huge awnings and tents provide shade for corporate picnics and waterfront weddings around the center. Cyclists, roller skaters, joggers, and power walkers love this section of the park, with its wide sidewalks swooping past the action around the **HILTON SAN DIEGO RESORT** (see the Lodgings chapter; 1775 E Mission Bay Dr; 619/276-4010 or 800/221-2424). Families and friends set up daylong carne asada and hot dog barbecue parties with volleyball games and bonfires (in cement fire rings), presenting all the SoCal action one could desire. **CROWN POINT** (Crown Point Dr at Ingraham St) also has fire rings, playgrounds, and idyllic picnic areas facing Sea World.

The shoreline curves around Crown Point, cupping the calm waters of **SAIL BAY** (near Briarfield Dr) and backed by private homes lining **BAYSIDE WALK**. Kayaks, canoes, windsurfers, and other water toys are clustered about **SANTA CLARA POINT,** where classes and rentals are available at **MISSION BAY SPORTCENTER** (1010 Santa Clara Pl; 858/488-1004). The newest sport attracting thrill seekers is kiteboarding, which involves steering a large kite while balancing on a surfboard.

West Mission Bay Drive parallels the most populated areas of the park close to Mission Beach, where wheel-borne sightseers run into traffic jams on the approach to Belmont Park.

The entire Mission Bay area becomes utterly congested on holidays throughout the year—what could be more San Diegan than Christmas amid palms and kites? On some summer weekends, the park's 700 parking spots fill by noon; locals arrive at dawn to stake out prime party spots. Some areas can be reserved in advance. Check with the officials at the **MISSION BAY PARK HEADQUARTERS** (2581 Quivira Ct; 619/221-8901) for information on permits and maps; the office is open Monday through Friday 8am to 5pm. Admission is free. *Every day; www.sannet. gov/park-and-recreation/parks/missbay; map:LL6* &

## 7) Hotel del Coronado

**1500 ORANGE AVE, CORONADO; 619/435-6611** The red-shingled turrets, dormers, and peaked roofs of the Hotel del Coronado are a point of pride for all San Diegans, who delight in the oohs and aahs of first-time visitors. Designed by architects James and Merritt Reid in the late 1800s for visionary developers Elisha Babcock and H. L. Story, the hotel was meant to be the most lavish resort on the Pacific Coast. One could argue that it still is; filmmakers certainly find it the perfect backdrop. Billy Wilder chose the hotel as the idyllic headquarters for the antics of Marilyn Monroe, Tony Curtis, and Jack Lemmon in *Some Like It Hot;* Peter O'Toole dangled from its turrets in *The Stunt Man*. More recently, the hotel served as a suitable backdrop when the Travel Channel named Coronado Beach one of the 10 best beaches in the United States.

Begin your tour in the magnificent lobby, where walls of Illinois oak and Honduran mahogany gleam in the glow from crystal lights. Take a peek at the **CROWN ROOM**, with its sugar-pine-domed ceiling and crown-shaped chandeliers (the original chandeliers were designed by L. Frank Baum of Dorothy and Oz fame). Consider booking a table for Sunday brunch, an overpriced but lavish affair that entices guests to dress to the nines and act like royalty. Stroll through the central courtyard, beloved by brides, who pose in the white gazebo surrounded by roses and palms.

The hotel has undergone a $55 million renovation in the past few years, and it's looking marvelous once again. The unsightly tennis courts that once stood between the original building and the beach were replaced by a pretty patch of grass called the **WINDSOR LAWN**. The original birdcage brass elevator in the lobby is constantly buffed to a high sheen, and the rows of white umbrellas by the pool look like a windblown chorus line. Sip a martini in the **BABCOCK & STORY BAR** at sunset and imagine conversing with your favorite dignitaries. It seems they've all stayed here at least one night. For information on adding your name to the guest roster, see the Lodgings chapter. *Every day; www.hoteldel.com; map:NN5*

## 8) Downtown Waterfront

**N HARBOR DR AND ASH ST TO W HARBOR DR AND 5TH AVE, DOWNTOWN** The indigenous Kumeyaay Indians, living in simple camps by the water, might well have considered San Diego Bay to be the region's downfall. Were it not for this placid deep-water pool protected from winds by Point Loma, European explorers might have continued north without stopping to plant the Spanish flag on the bay's shores. But Juan Rodriguez Cabrillo found the bay in 1542, and less than a century later settlers and missionaries were building forts and missions on hills overlooking the water. Today, the natural curve of land against blue water is the focal point of downtown's revitalization and one of the most exciting parts of the city.

A waterfront walkway called the **EMBARCADERO** runs along the water's edge beside Harbor Drive. The first focal point is the **MARITIME MUSEUM** (N Harbor Dr at Ash St; 619/234-9153), home to the noble *Star of India,* a square-rigged, three-masted, steel-hulled ship that circled the globe many times after its construction in 1863. Sails unfurled, it's a stunning sight to visitors, who are welcome to explore belowdecks. The ship is preserved (and occasionally taken out to sea) by devoted volunteers. The museum also maintains the *Berkeley,* an ornate 1898 ferry built to shuttle passengers from Oakland to San Francisco. The museum's offices are on the ferry's first deck.

Across Harbor Drive from the ships is one of San Diego's most beautiful buildings, the **SAN DIEGO COUNTY ADMINISTRATION CENTER** (1600 Pacific Hwy; 619/531-5880), dedicated by FDR in 1938. Architect Sam Hamill designed the structure in a colonial/Beaux Arts fashion; sculptor Donal Hord created the *Guardian of the Water* statue of a woman bearing a water jug, which rises gracefully from the lawn.

The Embarcadero becomes packed with office workers striding in suits and sneakers during their lunch hours; those who arrive early enough stop by casual waterfront eateries for lunch. Visitors with plenty of time to spare escape the crowds by boarding a boat tour offered by **SAN DIEGO HARBOR EXCURSION** (1050 N Harbor Dr; 619/234-4111). If you're too short on time for a complete tour, take the **CORONADO/SAN DIEGO FERRY** (1050 N Harbor Dr; 619/234-4111).

At the **CRUISE SHIP TERMINAL** (N Harbor Dr at B St) you'll likely see a Princess or Holland America cruise ship tied up for the day. Both lines include San Diego in their regular stopovers. Because the cruise trade is booming in San Diego, the terminal building is scheduled to be enlarged. The cruise area is part of an overall section of the waterfront slated for redevelopment. There's a move afoot to dock the **USS MIDWAY,** a retired aircraft carrier, just south of Broadway. Backers would like to make it a floating museum, reflecting the U.S. Navy's strong presence in San Diego. At present, the area is parklike, with pathways and benches. Harbor Drive continues past the G Street Mole, once a working fishing pier that's now home to a huge parking lot and a restaurant.

Farther along the shore, **SEAPORT VILLAGE** (849 W Harbor Dr; 619/235-4013) comes into view, with picturesque shops, restaurants, and a carousel. A bandstand in the middle of the village is the site of magic shows, clown acts, and free musical performances. Visitors eat ice cream cones, wander in and out of shops, and stroll toward the marina filled with handsome yachts at the **MARRIOTT HOTEL AND MARINA** (333 W Harbor Dr; 619/234-1500), a mirrored, double-towered building that was one of the first hotels constructed on the downtown waterfront. It's now joined by the **MANCHESTER GRAND HYATT SAN DIEGO** (1 Market Pl; 619/232-1234), a luxury hotel that provides a stunning view of the city from its 40th floor.

Looking south and east, you'll see the source of downtown's revitalization and ongoing redevelopment—the **SAN DIEGO CONVENTION CENTER** (111 W Harbor Dr; 619/525-5000; www.sdccc.org), topped with enormous Teflon-coated sails. The center opened in 1990; in less than a decade city leaders began pushing for an expansion, which was completed in 2001. Now the bulldozers and cranes are busy farther east on Harbor Drive, where construction of a much-disputed ballpark is under way. The ballpark is scheduled to open for the 2004 baseball season, as is the centerpiece of the **EAST VILLAGE** redevelopment district.

The San Diego Trolley runs along Harbor Drive across from the convention center. **MARTIN LUTHER KING PROMENADE,** a pleasant linear park lined with sculptures, benches, and trees, borders the tracks. The park and tracks lead to the East Village; someday soon, conventioneers will be able to take a break from their work and walk to the ballpark for an afternoon game. *Map:L6–O9*

## 9) Wild Animal Park

**15500 SAN PASQUAL VALLEY RD, ESCONDIDO; 760/747-8702** The closest you may ever come to the African plains or the Mongolian steppe is just 30 miles north of downtown. The "WAP," with more than 3,200 mammals and birds, ranges over 1,800 acres in northern San Diego County. This part of the prestigious San Diego Zoological Society serves as a wildlife refuge and breeding center for endangered and rare animals that appear to thrive in surroundings replicating their natural homes.

There are several ways to appreciate the distinct environments carved into North County's dry, hot terrain. One is the slow-moving **WGASA BUSH LINE MONORAIL,** an elevated, electricity-driven journey around 5 miles of African- and Asian-style habitats where herds of antelopes, rhinoceroses, and giraffes roam in illusionary freedom. Drivers narrate the 55-minute trip with tasty tidbits of information. Did you know an elephant has 100,000 muscles in its trunk? Ever seen a white rhino? The WAP's Center for Reproduction of Endangered Species has bred 85 white rhinos; small herds of the beautiful and rare Przewalski's horse have also been successfully reproduced and returned to the Mongolian range.

At the **HEART OF AFRICA** exhibit, a circuitous trail leads hikers through varying African-style terrains. Forest hides shy opaki, kin to the giraffe. Lower wetlands reveal hairy warthogs and bat-eared foxes. Two crashing waterfalls empty into a large lagoon with five islands, each harboring its own animal population. The center island, accessible by a floating bridge, has an interactive research center and simulated field camp.

The shows are always a hit with the kids. There are amusing and educational bird performances, and others with those ever-popular elephants. If birds are your bag, feed the parrot-like lorikeets at Lorikeet Landing. Some visitors ignore the creatures and study the WAP's accredited botanical garden with more than 4,000 species of plants, seeking out the North African cypress, one of 153 left in the world. There are 10 specialty gardens in the northeast corner of the park; the Bonsai Pavilion, Fuchsia House, and Old World Succulent Garden are especially fascinating.

**NAIROBI VILLAGE,** close to the entrance, contains most of the visitor amenities. The Thorn Tree Terrace serves up hamburgers, sandwiches, and salads. The shops stock an irresistible array of Asian and African art, animal photos, cards, books and toys, and other gifts worth browsing.

The WAP offers still other temptations. The **PHOTO CARAVAN** tour takes visitors in open-backed trucks into the animal habitats for once-in-a-lifetime shots of giraffes, lions, and gazelles. Other behind-the-scenes educational tours and programs include the Roar n' Snore overnight camping program available from mid-April through October. For reservations for special programs call 619/718-3000. Adult admission is $26.50; ages 3 to 11, $19.50; ages 2 and younger are free. Parking is $6 per vehicle. *Every day, 9am to seasonal closing times (call for information); www.sandiegozoo.org; map:CC2* &

## 10) Sea World

**500 SEA WORLD DR, MISSION BAY; 619/226-3901** Never content to rest on Shamu's laurels, the corporate owners of this 150-acre aquatic park constantly add exhibits and rides to its repertoire, reeling in locals bearing annual passes and tourists who wouldn't dream of a San Diego vacation without a visit. In 2002, the park presented new expansion plans to the public and multiple government agencies. Among the most controversial are plans for amusement-park-style rides.

Sea World started moving in this direction in 1999 with **SHIPWRECK RAPIDS,** a ride that has passengers swirl about in inner-tube vehicles during a simulated storm at sea. Hardy types then visit the 1,000-seat **SHIPWRECK CAFE,** where real-life penguins and sea otters wander under the buffet. Other rides captivate some, but the real joys at the park come from watching white-tipped sharks glide by in the **SHARK ENCOUNTER AQUARIUM,** emperor penguins strutting about in the glass-enclosed icy **PENGUIN ENCOUNTER,** and bat rays and eels slinking through the **FORBIDDEN REEF.** Visitors stand in line patiently for a chance to pet the slippery snouts of bottlenose dolphins at **ROCKY POINT PRESERVE** or sling slimy fish to barking sea lions at the **FEEDER POOL.** One lucky kid gets chosen to pet a 10,000-pound orca during each **SHAMU THE ADVENTURE SHOW,** which never fails to thrill onlookers (and drench those in the front rows).

You can easily spend a full day and evening at Sea World and still feel there wasn't enough time to watch sea otters at play, gaze at graceful sea turtles swimming in shallow tanks, and study cumbersome manatees with gentle faces. Park hours vary with the season; if you've got only one day, start when the park opens and stay till the fireworks show (every summer evening) at the end. Kids can unleash their energies at several theme playgrounds while parents sprawl on benches and catnap. Sit-down restaurants serve barbecued ribs, grilled seafood (horrors!), and decent Italian cuisine. For an additional fee, you can splurge on **DINING WITH SHAMU** and eat with the whale trainers beside the leviathans' pool. Admission is $42.95 for adults, $32.95 for children 3 to 11, and $39.95 for seniors; parking is $7. *Every day, hours vary; www.seaworld.com; map:F1*

## 11) Horton Plaza

**ENTRANCES ON BROADWAY, 4TH AVE, G ST, AND 1ST AVE, DOWNTOWN; 619/238-1596** A Disneyesque group of pink and purple buildings with Spanish domes and medieval banners, Horton Plaza was one of the prime catalysts for the regrowth of downtown. The plaza opened in 1985 beside a statue of city founder Alonzo Horton at the center of Broadway. The architecture was outlandish, but it brought curious locals downtown and became an instant gathering spot for visitors from all over the world.

The plaza was purchased by an enormous conglomerate that's gobbling up many malls in Southern California, and the name has officially been changed to Westfield Shoppingtown Horton Plaza—an awkward moniker sure to be ignored by locals. The current anchor department stores are **MACY'S** (619/231-4747), **MERVYN'S** (619/231-8800), and **NORDSTROM** (619/239-1700); all have escalators and elevators you can use as shortcuts to the various mall levels. Given the plaza's theme-park appeal, several big names have fittingly entered the scene and are magnets for kids. Shops specializing in toys, gadgets, fine jewelry, designer clothing, housewares, and other indulgences abound.

If you're not into shopping, you can duck into the **UNITED ARTISTS THEATRE** (619/234-4661) with 14 movie screens on the plaza's fourth level. For stage plays, the underground **LYCEUM THEATER** (619/544-1000) is home to the San Diego Repertory Company and occasional matinee concerts.

In Horton Plaza, there is always music in the air and a sense of confused bedazzlement among first-time shoppers. It's hard to find your way around the plaza's mazelike configuration: you can stand on one level and see the store you want . . . and have no idea how to get there. The elevators at each end of the mall are tiny and slow; the designers made sure visitors would pass by every establishment while following ramps, bridges, and stairways tucked beside plants and trees.

One highlight: the irresistible sugary aroma escaping from **CLAUDIA'S CINNAMON ROLLS** (619/233-1529). It's right next to the movie theaters, along with a dozen other fast-food outlets serving Greek, Mexican, and all-American treats that attract a younger crowd. On other levels, restaurants for mature tastes abound.

Horton Plaza's parking garage is another puzzle—even for frequent visitors. It's important to remember whether you parked at "tomatoes" or "avocados," "beets" or "pineapples"—and whether you're on the Fourth Avenue side or the G Street side. (When all else fails, security staff will drive you around until you find your car.) Three-hour validation is available at all plaza businesses; theaters have four-hour stamps. After that, the fees add up quickly. *Every day; http://hortonplaza.shoppingtown.com; map:N7* &

## 12) Reuben H. Fleet Space Theater & Science Center

**1875 EL PRADO, BALBOA PARK, DOWNTOWN; 619/238-1233** A space-age theater, child-size interactive exhibits, and an irresistible gift shop draw hordes to one of the most exciting museums in Balboa Park. Gadgets, gizmos, and computerized games fascinate the scientifically inclined at the **SCIENCE CENTER**, where even those who can't tell a computer from a calculator are hooked by whisper chambers, bolts of electricity zapping across terminals, and giant kaleidoscopes. The museum's resident astronomer, Dennis Mammana, displays his photographs of streaking stars and planets in the **SKYSCAPES** gallery on the second floor, rotating his favorite shots through the exhibit. The biggest draw is the domed **SPACE THEATER**, one of the first built in the world. Dizzying IMAX films take viewers up

Mount Everest or into the depths of shark-filled seas; don't sit in the front rows if you tend toward vertigo. The middle rows actually provide better viewing, and you needn't get a crick in your neck trying to take in the highest images.

Try keeping your wallet in your pocket while touring the **NORTH STAR SCIENCE** retail shop; chances are you won't succeed. You needn't splurge on a $10,000 telescope, but you might want an old-fashioned gyroscope, a wall-size poster of planets and stars, or a watch showing the phases of the moon. Plan on spending considerable time in this space-age complex; if it all gets to be too overwhelming, you can always wander out the front door and gaze at Balboa Park's centerpiece fountain, then return for more stimulation. Admission is $6.75 for those 13 and older; $5.50 for kids 3 to 12. Packages are available for visiting the exhibits plus one or two IMAX films. *Mon–Tues 9:30am–5pm, Wed 9:30am–7pm, Fri–Sat 9:30am–8pm, Sun 9:30am–6pm; www.rhfleet.org; map:O5* &

## 13) Old Town San Diego State Historic Park

**TWIGGS ST AT JUAN ST, OLD TOWN; 619/237-6770** Old Town is at once San Diego's humble historical birthplace and a thriving tourist attraction. **OLD TOWN SAN DIEGO STATE HISTORIC PARK** is a six-block area featuring the original restored 19th-century structures. It looks like a Wild West movie set, but these buildings are the real McCoy and offer a glimpse of the way life was for the city's first residents. Especially charming, **LA CASA DE ESTUDILLO** (4001 Mason St; 619/220-5422) is a traditional Mexican hacienda built in 1829 that's been restored to its original glory. Rooms furnished with period items open onto the central courtyard. Right across from La Casa de Estudillo, **CASA DE BANDINI RESTAURANT** (2754 Calhoun St; 619/297-8211) is a wildly popular Mexican eatery (i.e., prepare for a wait and expect high-volume cooking) housed in the circa 1829 mansion of the Bandini family. The stately, two-story **WHALEY HOUSE** (2482 San Diego Ave; 619/298-2482), built in 1857, is said to be haunted; take a docent-led tour for the ghost stories.

San Diego Avenue, the main road through Old Town, is home to several excellent restaurants (see the Restaurants chapter) and tiny **EL CAMPO CEMETERY,** final resting place of some of the city's early denizens. Just off Juan Street, **HERITAGE PARK VICTORIAN VILLAGE** (247 Heritage Park Row; 619/565-3600) is an enclave of seven lavishly restored Victorian homes that look like colorful dollhouses. Now housing shops, law offices, and a fine bed-and-breakfast inn, these fanciful structures are a departure from the Spanish colonial buildings that dominate Old Town. Sitting above Old Town and worth the short trek up Presidio Drive, **PRESIDIO PARK** stands guard over the city. This is California's birthplace, where Father Junipero Serra established his first mission in 1769. The original mission is long gone (though you can watch archaeologists excavate its remains); the gleaming white adobe building on the hill is a replica that was built in 1929. Inside, check out the historic objects and exhibits of the **JUNIPERO SERRA MUSEUM** (2727 Presidio Dr; 619/297-3258).

At the heart of Old Town is its most popular attraction, **BAZAAR DEL MUNDO** (2754 Calhoun St; 619/296-3161), built on the remains of an authentic 19th-century Mexican casa. The bazaar is a parade of 18 interconnected stores surrounding a courtyard where mariachis strike up festive tunes and colorfully costumed dancers perform on weekends. Yes, it's a tourist trap, but it can be hard to resist the charms of this pseudo-Mexican village. Blazing scarlet bougainvillea tumbles over white stucco cottages framing a broad lawn where folkloric dancers twirl about the central gazebo, their ruffled blue and yellow skirts fluttering. Marimba and mariachi musicians compete for attention beside fiesta-themed restaurants; parrots and macaws squawk from their perches in giant cages; and the aromas of fresh tortillas, sautéed chiles, and steaming hot chocolate fill the air. San Diegans looking for that special gift know they can rely on the Bazaar's excellent (if expensive) stores displaying Italian platters and bowls, Guatemalan fabrics and clothes, and Mexican tin-framed mirrors and fanciful hand-carved dragons, called *alebrijes* in Oaxaca.

Giant margaritas are a major draw at Bazaar del Mundo's restaurants; diners stand in line up to an hour for a table at **CASA DE PICO** (619/296-3267). Other restaurants are tucked in corners about the bazaar; take a break from shopping and order hot chocolate and *pan dulce* (Mexican pastries) from **LA PANADERIA** (619/291-7662).

Though there are several free lots in the Old Town area, parking can be horrendous. Consider taking the trolley from Mission Valley or downtown. *Every day 10am–9pm; www.bazaardelmundo.com/ map:J1* &

## 14) Birch Aquarium at Scripps

**2300 EXPEDITION WY, LA JOLLA; 858/534-3474** Fond of fish? Glad about groupers? Ecstatic about eels? Well then, the Birch Aquarium at Scripps is just the place for you. Set high above the shores of the Pacific Ocean in La Jolla, the aquarium offers a fascinating look into the wet and wavy part of our planet. Start your aquatic adventure in the cool, dark **HALL OF FISHES,** with 33 tanks full of various sea life categorized by region. Pacific salmon and a giant Pacific octopus occupy the **NORTHWEST COAST** exhibit; a 150-pound grouper floats along in the warm water of **MEXICO'S GULF OF CALIFORNIA TANK;** and 10-inch-thick glass holds back 70,000 gallons of water in the massive **KELP FOREST** showcase exhibit. The latter is the only tank open at the top, a feature necessary for the kelp, which can grow a phenomenal 10 inches a day. Wander around and see the hilarious garden eels, their bottom halves burrowed in the sand, their upper halves up and waving at each other like silent guests at an underwater tea party. Darling little sea horses and brown polka-dotted clown triggerfish bring squeals of delight from the hordes of children visiting on school field trips.

Outside at the **PREUSS PLAZA,** tear yourself away from the fabulous ocean view to check out the demonstration tide pool, stocked with local marine plants and animals. Children aren't allowed to touch these creatures, but are encouraged to gently handle the sea cucumber and starfish in a nearby tank. Finish up your visit with a walk through the other side of the aquarium housing the **BLUE PLANET THEATER,** learning center, and educational hands-on exhibits. The **NEW PERSPECTIVES GALLERY** features short-term exhibits and traveling collections from around the world. Aquarium admission is $8.50 for adults, $5 for children 3 to 17, ages 2 and younger free. *Every day 9am–5pm (except major holidays); www.aquarium.ucsd. edu/; map:JJ7* &

## 15) Historic Highway 101

**DEL MAR TO OCEANSIDE, NORTH COUNTY** San Diego County's historic Coast Highway 101 between Del Mar and Carlsbad seems an odd sort of back road. In the 1960s, Interstate 5 opened in the hills to the east, and this once-bustling stretch between L.A. and San Diego slipped into a slumber. Few travelers used it other than surfers in search of a better break, locals on errands, or curious travelers. Leucadia, Encinitas, Cardiff-by-the-Sea, and Solana Beach fell into a hippie-ish beach funk. Today, a drive along this same route (about 23 miles) juxtaposes funkiness, extraordinary prosperity, and long glimpses of unobstructed beach. The towns now sport hip cafes, ethnic eateries, shops, galleries, and—alas—a few chain stores and restaurants.

The drive begins north of Del Mar (see the Neighborhoods section). The first town, **SOLANA BEACH,** is home to the **CEDROS DESIGN DISTRICT** (see "Designer Shopping" in the Shopping chapter). The east side of 101 is bordered only by a bike path adjacent to the train tracks (which run out of sight in a deep trench). One of the north coast's most intimate beach parks is at the foot of Lomas Santa Fe Drive. **FLETCHER COVE BEACH PARK** (858/755-1569 for information), bounded by tall cliffs, is a gem for safe swimming and beach walking. At low tide, you can walk a mile or more in either direction beneath wind- and wave-sculpted cliffs. Notice the ancient layers of fossilized oyster shells, a reminder of a time when most of the San Diego coast was the bottom of a shallow sea.

Freshwater and tidewater meet at **SAN ELIJO LAGOON,** alive with fish, insect life, and wading birds like herons and curlews. Thousands of migratory wildfowl drop in every winter as they ply the Pacific Flyway to Central and South America. The county's best lagoonside hiking trail skirts San Elijo's southern edge to eroded sandstone cliffs behind a eucalyptus grove.

**CARDIFF-BY-THE-SEA** borrowed its name from Wales; the developer also gave most of the streets British Isles place names. Cardiff's main attraction, **SAN ELIJO STATE BEACH** (S Hwy 101 at Chesterfield Dr; 760/753-5091), offers excellent camping, swimming, and tide pooling along a wide beach beneath crumbling bluffs. A parking lot at the north end of the camping area is available for day use only. Prowl around the little town by taking Chesterfield Drive east one block from San Elijo State Beach. **SEASIDE MARKET** (2087 San Elijo Ave; 760/753-5445) is a real find for beach picnic necessities like salads, sandwiches, and cold cuts.

Highway 101 continues north to **ENCINITAS.** At the south edge of town, the **SELF-REALIZATION FELLOWSHIP** (939 2nd St; 760/436-7220) shimmers like an Eastern mystic's vision with its lotus-blossom-shaped towers and mysterious inner gardens. Visitors are welcome—the gardens are quite beautiful. Surfers gave a park on a coastal point just south of the Fellowship grounds the somewhat irreverent, but now accepted, local name of **SWAMI'S** (Hwy 101, 1 block south of K St; 760/633-2750). Downtown Encinitas hasn't changed much since the 1930s. Cars park at an angle by the classic theater, **LA PALOMA** (471 S Hwy 101; 760/436-5774), which hosts everything from movies and surf film festivals to folksingers.

**LEUCADIA'S** spectacular grove of giant eucalyptus trees paralleling Highway 101 recalls the community's reputation among a group of British spiritualists who named it "the sheltered place" (from the Greek). It's managed to remain a mellow place where small family businesses thrive.

The stark buildings of the Encina Power Plant mar the lagoon and sea view at South Carlsbad State Beach, but it's still a fabulous stretch of soothing scenery leading to the Tudor-style center of **CARLSBAD** (see the Neighborhoods section). Take a break here for ice cream at **COLD STONE CREAMERY** (2967 Carlsbad Blvd; 760/720-2974).

The surroundings turn more commercial as you enter **OCEANSIDE,** as much an adjunct to Camp Pendleton Marine Base to the north as it is an ever-growing beach town. **CAFE 101** (631 S Coast Hwy; 760/722-5220; www.101cafe.net) is the seat of the movement that made 101 a historic landmark. A stop here is absolutely essential to the experience. Order breakfast or a cup of coffee and study the walls, filled with memorabilia. You might even splurge on an authentic Historic Highway 101 sign. Oceanside's pier, marina, and long, long beach are all worth a stroll, and savvy travelers stay here if they're headed to Disneyland and other attractions in Orange County.

For information on the North County cities contact the **SAN DIEGO NORTH CONVENTION & VISITORS BUREAU** (800/848-3336; www.sandiegonorth.com). *Take the Villa de la Valle exit from I-5, and travel along Highway 101 (also called S21) for approximately 24 miles to Oceanside; map:GG7–GG9.*

### 16) Torrey Pines State Reserve

**11000 N TORREY PINES RD, LA JOLLA; 858/755-2063** Once owned in part by one of San Diego's most generous philanthropists, Torrey Pines State Reserve has been part of California's park system since 1959. Ellen Browning Scripps, a remarkable and magnanimous woman who died in 1932 at age 95, was instrumental in the formation of this natural preserve.

Native only to this strip on the San Diego coast and on Santa Rosa Island (off the coast of Santa Barbara), the Torrey pine is one of the rarest pines in the world. It grows in abundance here amid a rich plant community rife with brilliant wildflowers in the spring. Seven miles of authorized trails lead through the reserve, and visitors are warned against leaving the sanctioned paths, to guard against erosion of crumbling earth or a disastrous tumble from an unstable cliff. Glorious views of the beach below and the ocean beyond can be seen from the safe havens of **YUCCA** and **RAZOR POINTS**, both of which can be accessed from trails intersecting with the popular Beach Trail.

Near the top of the road that climbs up into the reserve are a parking lot and the visitor center. Built as a restaurant in 1922 and known as the **TORREY PINES LODGE**, this adobe brick structure now houses the ranger station. A cozy little fire warms the central room during the winter months, and guests are encouraged to wander around the exhibits. Kids get a kick out of the "Please Touch" signs next to the genuine (albeit stuffed) coyote, mountain lion, and red-tailed hawk; a sleek, plump stuffed skunk stands sentry on the greeter's desk near the door. The rangers here are friendly and happy to answer questions. Guided tours that last about two hours leave from the visitor center weekends and holidays at 10am and 2pm. Park admission is $2 per car. *Every day 8am–sunset; map:HH7*

## 17) Silver Strand State Beach

**5000 HWY 75, CORONADO; 619/435-5184** This could be considered the quintessential Southern California beach, with its three miles of sand along the ocean and an array of laudable characteristics. A state park since 1932, Silver Strand derives its name from the tiny silvery seashells found in great numbers near the water. Parents of young children prefer this spot to other county beaches, as the waves are generally calm. The same feature attracts surf fishermen hoping to catch a California halibut, white croaker, or perch for dinner. Unfortunately, the water is sometimes polluted: obey warning signs when fishing or swimming.

**GRUNION**—funny little fish that flounce onto the sand to mate after dark—are found in abundance during the spring and summer months. The best time to spot them is at high tide four days after a full or new moon (check the events page of the local paper). Their capture is permitted with bare hands only. Hot summer days find teenagers flocking around the snack stand or chasing a volleyball on the sand. State lifeguards protect beachgoers all year round. Camping aficionados can bring in an RV and stay overnight for a $12 fee. *Every day; map:NN5*

## 18) Boardwalk and Belmont Park

**SOUTH MISSION BEACH PARK TO LAW ST, MISSION AND PACIFIC BEACHES** Bikini-clad bicyclists, tattooed oglers, roller skaters in neon spandex, and cops in shorts populate the 3-mile-long concrete boardwalk running between the ocean and the communities of Mission Beach and Pacific Beach, creating a classic SoCal beach scene. The walk begins in South Mission Beach, where pricey private homes built on postage-stamp lots face beach areas with fire rings and sand volleyball courts. An enormous parking lot separates the homes from **BELMONT PARK** (3146 Mission Blvd; 858/488-0668), the only survivor from the post–World War I era of elaborate theme parks on area beaches, replete with seawater pools and flashy ballrooms. Though it's been transformed into a shopping, dining, and amusement center, the park has retained its centerpiece, the 1925 **GIANT DIPPER** roller coaster (www.giantdipper.com). The coaster is modest by modern standards, but screams echo throughout nearby streets as the cars dip and swerve on wooden tracks. Also preserved is the **PLUNGE** (3115 Ocean Front Walk; 858/488-3110), a 175-foot-long swimming pool encased in a Spanish Renaissance palace. Other amusement rides, fast-food stands, and souvenir shops are clustered about the commercial area of the park, which is in need of a facelift. City leaders and developers are in the midst of debates over its future, but the roller coaster and pool are sure to be protected by vociferous fans. This area is a fine spot for family fun during daylight hours, but can be a bit risky at night. Hold on to your possessions no matter what the hour, and take the kids home before dark.

The boardwalk's main action begins at the intersection of Mission Boulevard, West Mission Drive, and Ventura Place. Day-trippers pick up rental bikes and skates at **MISSION BEACH CLUB** (704 Ventura Pl; 858/488-5050), formerly known and still referred to as Hamel's. First-timers should approach the stream of traffic on the boardwalk with respectful temerity. Though the city imposed an 8mph speed limit on wheel-borne traffic in 1994, novices still feel like they're entering a speedway. The congestion along this stretch is incredible on summer days; if you're not a confident, savvy athlete, stick to your feet and pass by the rental houses crammed with eager customers eyeing the babes on the beach.

Classic bars like **THE GREEN FLASH** (858/270-7715) attract bronzed and buff sunbathers with cold beer, iced tea, moderately priced eats, and shaded tables overlooking the scene. If you're hungry, check out **KONO'S CAFE** (858/483-1669; see Restaurants chapter) at the foot of **CRYSTAL PIER**. The 400-foot-long wood pier first opened in 1925, and led the way to the Crystal Ballroom perched atop the waves. The ballroom disappeared early on, as the sea proved too powerful for such lavish construction, but the pier remains one of the most treasured landmarks in Pacific Beach. The New England–style cottages of the **CRYSTAL PIER HOTEL & COTTAGES** (4500 Ocean Blvd; 858/483-6983) now line the wood slats to the end T, where anglers dangle their lines in hopes of catching mackerel or sea bass.

The boardwalk action quiets down north of the pier, and walkers can actually link arms and lower their speed to a stroll as they approach the end of the walkway at **PALISADES PARK**, a small pocket of grass and benches perfect for watching the sun drop into the sea. *Every day; map:LL7* &

## 19) Mission Trails Regional Park

**1 FATHER JUNIPERO SERRA TRAIL, TIERRASANTA; 619/668-3275** Just 8 miles northeast of downtown San Diego, Mission Trails Regional Park is reminiscent of an era before urban sprawl and freeway crawl, when much of San Diego County was the domain of the Kumeyaay Indians. At 5,760 acres (one of the largest urban parks in the country), this unpolished gem is a well-kept secret, surprisingly enough, even to most locals. Those in the know start their day's adventure at the marvelous and modern **VISITOR AND INTERPRETIVE CENTER**, open every day from 9am to 5pm. An architectural delight set amid native chaparral and sagebrush, the center features an auditorium, library, and small gift shop with authentic local Kumeyaay Indian crafts for sale. Interactive exhibits instruct young and old alike about the geology, history, plants, and animals of the area. Beyond a wall of windows to the northeast is a stunning view of Cowles and Fortuna Mountains, sliced down the middle by Mission Gorge and the San Diego River. Maps showing biking and hiking trails and their respective degrees of difficulty, as well as information on the best fishing holes in the park, are also provided. Helpful volunteers and park rangers can direct you to the **OLD MISSION DAM**, a National Historic Landmark, where Spanish missionaries enlisted the Kumeyaays' help in building the dam to provide water for the **MISSION BASILICA SAN DIEGO DE ALCALÁ** (see Attraction number 24, below) in the early 19th century. Also part of Mission Trails Regional Park is nearby **LAKE MURRAY** (619/465-3474), where fishing and boating are permitted on Wednesday, Saturday, and Sunday. If golf is your game, **MISSION TRAILS GOLF COURSE**, an 18-hole, par-71 course, is included in the park. Call 619/460-5400 for more information. *Every day; map:JJ2*

## 20) San Diego Museum of Art

**1450 EL PRADO, BALBOA PARK, DOWNTOWN; 619/232-7931** The largest visual arts museum in "America's Finest City," the San Diego Museum of Art started off as a small community art gallery more than 75 years ago. Its 12,000-piece collection is now presided over by the youthful Don Bacigalupi, wooed from the Blaffer Gallery of Houston in the summer of 1999. The lovely, Spanish colonial revival building houses a California room, Japanese and Chinese art, and an extensive collection of South Asian paintings. Second-floor galleries are home to 14th- through 19th-century European art, lit by frosted-glass skylights and well-placed track lighting. Explanatory information is in both Spanish and English. Spring brings the well-loved "Art Alive" exhibit, when local professional and amateur horticulturists reinvent some of the museum's best paintings and sculptures in unique floral arrangements. Access the IMAGE Interactive computers to read about your favorite artists or paintings, or to create your very own self-guided tour. Free docent-led tours are available daily. The museum also sponsors lectures, performances, and classes and a popular jazz series. Stop in at the gift shop, which has jewelry, cards, and postcards in addition to a fabulous collection of art books. View the sculptures by Rodin and Miro in the outdoor May S. Marcy Sculpture Court. The museum is closed Monday, open 10am–9pm on Thursday and 10am–6pm Friday, Saturday, and Sunday. Admission is $8 for adults; $6 for seniors, military, and ages 18 to 24; $3 for students 6 to 17; kids under 6 free. *Tues–Sun 10am–4:30pm; www.sdmart.org; map:O5* &

### 21) Ocean Beach

**THE END OF I-8 AT SUNSET CLIFFS BLVD; 619/224-4906** There are fabulous beach towns all along San Diego's coastline. We're particularly keen on Ocean Beach, a cult destination and home to independent souls of every age who happily say they're Obecians. The town is a little bit funky (it attracts bikers, druggies, and the down-and-out), and the roar of airplanes taking off from nearby Lindbergh Field detracts from the ambiance. But it's a solid community where generations of families attend the same schools and churches, march in parades, and exchange greetings in the street.

OB begins at the intersection of Interstate 8, Sea World Drive, and Sunset Cliffs Boulevard, said to be the westernmost point in the continental United States. Those bound for the beach follow West Point Loma Boulevard to the parking lot beside the river channel, where bird-watchers delight in sighting herons and egrets. Swimmers, boogie boarders, and body and board surfers congregate at various points along the sand, where cement fire rings are loaded with wooden pallets as groups claim sunset seats.

The ocean pounds with all its might on the sand and against the pilings under the **OCEAN BEACH PIER** at the intersection of Abbott Street and Newport Avenue. The pier stretches a half mile over a prime surf break, and is favored by photographers shooting neon-clad surfers atop wave-slicked boards. Families set up coolers along the pier railings and dangle lines and hooks into the surf. Cod, sea bass, perch, and the occasional sandal or wad of kelp are their rewards. (No fishing license is required here, but the catch limit is enforced.) At the **OCEAN BEACH PIER CAFE** and the **BAIT SHOP** (near the end of the pier; 619/226-3474; open daily 8am–8pm) slippery anchovies, squid, and shrimp fill the bait tanks; the shop sells everything from sunblock to soda. The pier is closed when the surf reigns supreme.

**NEWPORT AVENUE,** running southeast from the beach up into the hills of Point Loma, is OB's main drag. A cluster of beach bars and surf shops lines the first block.

The next is home to a Starbucks (look for "No Starbucks in OB" bumper stickers), hair and piercing salons, restaurants, and the **STRAND THEATRE** (4950 Newport Ave; no phone), recently purchased by a souvenir shop. Antique malls have gained hold over mom-and-pop shops throughout the four-block downtown stretch, much to the dismay of those who loved walking from home to pick up stationery supplies, five-and-dime trinkets, and current books. Still, the blocks are packed with Greek, Chinese, Mexican, and all-American cafes, and regulars beat the beach crowds to breakfast most every morning.

Newport intersects Sunset Cliffs Boulevard, which leads past mini-malls to **SUNSET CLIFFS,** a scenic wonder of golden sandstone ridges over rock-strewn coves. Surfers haul their boards down the cliffs to the few safe entry points into the sea; only the best tangle with the high waves crashing against boulders and caves. Still one of the priciest neighborhoods in San Diego, Sunset Cliffs is home to the plantation-style pink 1926 **MILLS MANOR,** a true tribute to excess.

Other pockets of OB are also well worth exploring. **OB PEOPLE'S NATURAL FOODS** (4765 Voltaire St; 619/224-1387) is a flash-to-the-past, a 1960s food co-op that has maintained a faithful following for three decades. Where else can you listen to Joni Mitchell while picking up carrot juice, tabbouleh salads, organic grains, and veggies? Check it out, grab a snack, then drive to the top of Narragansett or Newport Street and look for the green parrots and blue macaws that nest in high palm trees and billboards. They know a good home when they see it. *Map:MM6*

## 22) San Diego Museum of Man

**1350 EL PRADO, BALBOA PARK, DOWNTOWN; 619/239-2001** Pleasing to the eye and intellect, the San Diego Museum of Man is one of Balboa Park's greatest treasures. Its edifice alone is worthy of close examination—from the 200-foot-high **CALIFORNIA TOWER** to the stone-carved likenesses of California's founders in the facade. The buildings now housing the museum were designed by Bertram Goodhue and Carleton Winslow as the entryway to the 1915–1916 Panama-California Exposition; their Spanish colonial/baroque theme set the architectural standard for dozens of historic buildings scattered about the park.

The museum's collection began with artifacts displayed at the exposition and has grown to encompass cultures from around the world. Though the largest permanent exhibit is called **LIFE AND DEATH ON THE NILE** and features a genuine Egyptian mummy, much of the museum's focus is on the Americas. Rotating exhibits feature folk art and artifacts from Peru, Venezuela, Mexico, and other Latin countries. The annual **SAN DIEGO AMERICAN INDIAN CULTURAL DAYS** in late spring brings tribal leaders, musicians, dancers, and artists to the cement courtyard between the museum's buildings and the arched portals leading to Alcazar Gardens. The gift shop is excellent for memorable souvenirs, from Guatemalan purses to Egyptian cloth. Admission is $6 for adults, $5 for seniors, $3 for children 6 to 17, children under 6 free. *Every day 10am–4:30pm; www.museumofman.org; map:O5*

### 23) Quail Botanical Gardens

**230 QUAIL GARDENS DR, ENCINITAS; 760/436-3036** Eucalyptus groves, native-plant gardens, and one of the largest bamboo collections in the United States cover 30 acres at San Diego's largest public garden in coastal North County. Quail Gardens was established as a county park in 1971; in 1991 it became a private nonprofit entity with hundreds of plant-savvy volunteers. There are 24 representative gardens, from tropical to desert and everything in between. A map in the gift shop will direct you to the plants in bloom at the time of your visit. The annual plant sale in October attracts flocks of amateur and professional gardeners. Admission is $5 for adults, $2 for children 5 to 12, free for children under 5. *Every day 9am–5pm; www.qbgardens.com; map:EE7*

### 24) Mission Basilica San Diego de Alcalá

**10818 SAN DIEGO MISSION RD, MISSION VALLEY; 619/281-8449** A peaceful retreat at the edge of the once-fertile Mission Valley, Mission San Diego de Alcalá is San Diego's oldest parish church and the oldest mission in California. The classic **CAMPANARIO** (bell tower) with five iron-cast bells set in white arches rises 46 feet above the grounds where Spanish Franciscan missionaries and indigenous Kumeyaay laborers farmed corn in the 18th century. The locals never developed a fondness for their patrons; California's first Christian martyr was killed here during a 1775 uprising.

The small **FATHER LUIS JAYME MUSEUM** on the mission grounds includes the original records of disputes that still linger. Archaeologists and Native Americans who say the mission was built on sacred turf now explore Indian burial grounds. The church still has an active congregation; Sunday mass in the simple wood pews can evoke a sense of serenity. A statue of Saint Francis of Assisi sits amid gardens of native shrubs that attract hummingbirds and butterflies.

If your interest in missions is sparked at Alcalá, be sure to check out **MISSION SAN LUIS REY** (www.sanluisrey.org; see the Neighborhoods section) in Oceanside. Admission to the museum is $5 for adults, $2 for ages 6 to 14. *Tues–Sun 10am–4:30pm; map:KK3*

### 25) Legoland California

**I LEGO DR, CARLSBAD; 760/918-5346** Young kids enamored with those knobby yellow, blue, green, and red plastic bricks (which originated in the tiny country of Denmark) are captivated by San Diego County's latest theme park. Spread over 128 acres in Carlsbad, Legoland California opened in the spring of 1999 and the expected capacity-level crowds arrived. The fanfare has died down, and the park was closed on Tuesdays and Wednesdays in the winter and spring of 2002. The park has a narrow niche market—basically kids between 3 and 8 years old who love Legos—and the admission prices are outrageously steep. Local admirers spring for an annual pass to save big bucks.

Parents with toddlers in tow ride the **KID POWER TOWER,** with its seats built from real Legos and its 30-foot free-fall drop, or push strollers past miniature power brokers striding to work in Washington, D.C., one of five U.S. regions depicted in **MINILAND.** It's astonishing to realize that every piece of the park is constructed from

EXPLORING

the same pieces kids use at home; reality hits home when the young ones enter the **BIG SHOP** and peruse the Lego selection, intent on building the city of their dreams. Science-oriented displays incorporating Legos with computer programs are a hit with kids who might be bored elsewhere. Admission is $39 for adults, $33 for seniors and children 3 to 16; ages 2 and younger are free. Parking is $4. *Hours vary with the season (call for information); www.lego.com; map:CC7* &

# Neighborhoods

## Coronado

Just across the bay from downtown's skyscrapers, Coronado is an old-fashioned oasis of small-town living that marches at its own graceful pace. It's blessed with fine beaches, from which you can glimpse dolphins in the surf and watch Navy planes make their long, low descent to the **NAVAL AIR STATION AT NORTH ISLAND**. The military base, which amiably shares this golden isthmus with residents, has a special place in aviation history—in 1927 Charles Lindbergh departed from North Island on the first leg of his historic solo flight across the Atlantic.

No exploration of the town is complete without a turn through the **HOTEL DEL CORONADO** (1500 Orange Ave; 619/435-6611, see Top 25 Attractions). To learn more about the town's past, spend an hour in the **MUSEUM OF HISTORY AND ART** (1100 Orange Ave; 619/435-7242), or join **CORONADO TOURING** (619/435-5993) for a 90-minute stroll through the island's historic neighborhoods. Tours depart from the music room of the **GLORIETTA BAY INN** (1630 Glorietta Blvd; 619/435-3101), formerly the mansion of sugar magnate John D. Spreckels, who considered the grand Italianate estate overlooking Glorietta Bay to be, well, modest.

On busy Orange Avenue, join the locals at a number of favored hangouts. **CLAYTON'S COFFEE SHOP** (979 Orange Ave; 619/435-5425) serves diner fare alongside original 1950s tabletop jukeboxes. **CAFE 1134** (1134 Orange Ave; 619/437-1134) is the local coffeehouse that's taking on Starbucks up the street. For Mexican food, find a patio table at **MIGUEL'S COCINA** (1351 Orange Ave; 619/437-4237), hidden away in the shaded courtyard of El Cordova Hotel.

But don't miss the action on Coronado's bay side. **FERRY LANDING MARKETPLACE** (1201 1st St) is the place to go at the end of the day, when the setting sun paints the high-rise buildings of downtown in fiery golden hues. Stop for a cocktail and coconut shrimp appetizer at **PEOHE'S** (1201 1st St; 619/437-4474). Or, for a completely unobstructed view of sunset on the bay, have a cappuccino on the glassed-in patio at **IL FORNAIO** (1333 1st St; 619/437-4911). Check out the farmers market at the ferry landing on Tuesday evenings.

Coronado may be a casual resort community, but residents know how to step out in style. For fine dining, make reservations at Loews Coronado Bay Resort's signature restaurant **AZZURA POINT** (4000 Coronado Bay Rd; 619/424-4000). For a romantic French dinner, book a table at **CHEZ LOMA** (1132 Loma Ave; 619/435-0661), housed in a historic Queen Anne cottage.

For entertainment, Coronado has two live stage theaters. The intimate **CORONADO PLAYHOUSE** (on Silver Strand; 619/435-4856) stages amateur theatrical pro-

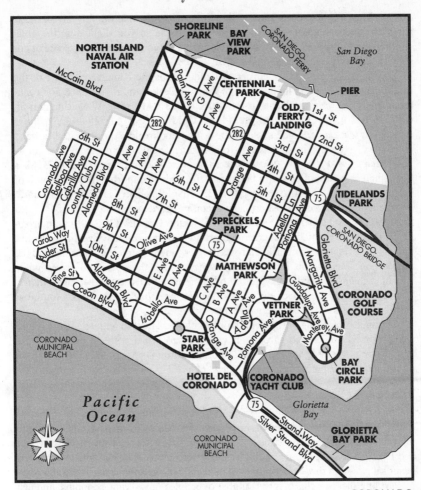

CORONADO

ductions, while the professional repertory company, the **LAMBS PLAYERS THEATRE** (1142 Orange Ave; 619/437-6000), offers revivals and new plays on a stage in the remodeled Spreckels Building. *Map:NN5*

## Mission Hills

House-proud residents guard a rich architectural heritage of Craftsman bungalows, Spanish colonial–style estates and Italianate mansions in this old, upscale neighborhood. The first residents came in the 19th century, when savvy Captain Henry James Johnson sold parcels overlooking the bay to wealthy East Coasters. These new San Diegans commissioned well-known architects including Irving Gill and Richard Requa, to design the lovely homes that give the neighborhood an aura of wealth and history. Most of these houses are visible from the street, making this an appealing neighborhood to explore. Do so on foot or bicycle so you don't miss the quiet charms—carefully tended gardens, a cat lounging on an inviting porch, a cafe or gift shop tucked away on a residential road.

Washington Street, at the corner of Goldfinch, is the commercial heart of the neighborhood. Here you'll find a mix of shops, galleries, and restaurants. For a generous breakfast, join the locals at **MISSION HILLS CAFE** (808 W Washington St; 619/296-8010). **A LA FRANÇAISE** (4029 Goldfinch St; 619/294-4425) draws crowds on weekends. Some settle in for a leisurely breakfast; others grab a flaky croissant or other fresh-baked sweet to go. French treats of a different sort can be purchased at **MAISON EN PROVENCE** (820 Fort Stockton Dr; 619/298-5318), a Craftsman bungalow filled with linens and furnishings imported from the south of France. The **FRENCH GARDEN SHOPPE** (3951 Goldfinch St; 619/295-4573) has an equally tempting selection of European decor and garden wares.

**MISSION HILLS NURSERY** (1525 Fort Stockton Dr; 619/295-2808) is an urban jungle that has delighted local green thumbs for nearly a century. Even if you're not buying, it's a treat to stroll through rows of trees, flowers, and fountains. Behind the nursery on Washington Place, locals lounge under the eucalyptus trees while watching their kids in the playground of diminutive **PIONEER PARK** (Washington Pl and Randolph St). Check out the cluster of gravestones in the park's southeast corner, remnants of the cemetery that once occupied this space.

Continue west along Fort Stockton or West Lewis Street to admire Mission Hills' well-groomed homes and gardens. If you want to refuel with cappuccino and a pastry, pop into **ESPRESSO MÍO** (1920 Fort Stockton Dr, Ste B; 619/296-3037). Sit on the small back patio for a canyon view. *Map:K1*

## Hillcrest

Hillcrest may be the heart of San Diego's gay and lesbian community, but it charms everyone with an eclectic blend of shops and cafes. Mainstream meets cutting edge in this busy neighborhood that stretches east on University Avenue between First Avenue and Park Boulevard. It borders the west edge of Balboa Park and gives way to the beautiful two- and three-story homes of Bankers' Hill, at downtown's northern edge.

Part of Hillcrest's charm is the number of people out walking, shopping, and just hanging out. Watch the passing parade from a sidewalk table at **BREAD & CIE** (350 University Ave; 619/683-9322), where the aroma of fresh gourmet bread is a powerful draw. From there, walk over to **COLUMN ONE** (401 University Ave; 619/299-9074) to browse through neoclassical plaster objets d'art and statuary. A few doors up, **BABETTE SCHWARTZ** (421 University Ave; 619/220-7048) has the latest in hip kitsch tchotchkes, and **CATHEDRAL** (435 University Ave; 619/296-4046) offers scented candles and accessories in a romantically gothic setting. Continue one more block for a great selection of reading material at **HILLCREST NEWSSTAND** (529 University Ave; 619/260-0492).

Many come to Hillcrest for its abundance of restaurants. One of the best loved for its low prices and comfortable atmosphere is **KAZUMI SUSHI** (3975 5th Ave; 619/682-4054). The stalwart **CITY DELICATESSEN & BAKERY** (535 University Ave;

# A MAZE OF NEIGHBORHOODS

San Diego is composed of a series of small towns and neighborhoods connected by a maze of highways and surface streets. The city blends into San Diego County without warning. Boundaries are indistinct in many cases; in others, street signs proclaim a community's sense of pride. Personality-filled neighborhoods packed with shops, attractions, and restaurants are described in this chapter. But don't miss the gems that are tucked in less distinguished enclaves.

India Street runs north of downtown into **LITTLE ITALY** (also known as Middletown), a pocket of commercial and residential streets that are home to fine Italian restaurants. From there, Washington Street climbs through Mission Hills to **UNIVERSITY HEIGHTS, NORMAL HEIGHTS,** and **NORTH PARK;** look for Asian eateries and antique shops.

Broadway travels east of downtown to **GOLDEN HILL,** where streets are lined with fine old Victorian houses and some notable nightlife spots. Follow Interstate 94 out of downtown to **EAST SAN DIEGO** (check out the ethnic markets) and **LEMON GROVE** (home to one of the best bakeries in all San Diego). Interstate 8 provides an eastern link to **MISSION VALLEY** (think shopping malls) and **LA MESA** and one of several entrances to Lake Murray and Mission Trails Regional Park, which sprawl north to Tierrasanta.

Harbor Drive runs along the north edge of San Diego Bay and then wraps southward to **HARBOR** and **SHELTER ISLANDS** and **POINT LOMA,** where hills rise from the bay to Cabrillo National Monument. Neighborhoods spread beneath Point Loma, with businesses concentrated around the Midway Drive area. Interstate 5 runs north and south, skirting the lawns and playgrounds of Mission Bay. Though beach dwellers joke that there's no life east of Interstate 5, off-ramps lead in that direction to **BAY PARK,** where markets and bars cater to an eclectic crowd. Take Balboa Avenue and climb east to **CLAIREMONT** and **KEARNY MESA,** with several good restaurants and interesting shops.

La Jolla also has spawned popular offshoot communities east of the coast: **UNIVERSITY CITY, GOLDEN TRIANGLE, SORRENTO VALLEY,** and **SORRENTO MESA** (all east of I-5) are filled with upscale hotels, malls, and fine restaurants. Farther east, Interstate 15 runs past the golf courses and inns of **RANCHO BERNARDO** to **ESCONDIDO,** home of the Wild Animal Park. Dozens of other communities beckon the curious; grab a map and start cruising.

—*Maribeth Mellin*

619/295-2747) stays open till the wee hours for the late-night crowd. **CALIFORNIA CUISINE** (1027 University Ave; 619/295-2747) was thrust into the limelight as the place where Andrew Cunanan, the serial killer who slew fashion designer Gianni Versace, ate his last meal in San Diego. Don't let that put you off—the back patio is still a romantic dinner spot. Fifth Avenue's small restaurant row offers exotic fusion fare at **KEMO SABE** (3958 5th Ave; 619/220-6802) and great Indian food at **BOMBAY** (3975 5th Ave; 619/298-3155). Before dining, pop into the **WINE LOVER** (3968 5th Ave; 619/294-9200) to sample some California vintages, or catch an arty flick at the **HILLCREST CINEMAS** (3965 5th Ave; 619/299-2100), across the way.

More great home-furnishing stores and restaurants line University Avenue as you head toward Park Boulevard. In the **UPTOWN DISTRICT,** a model of low-hassle living, more than 300 apartments share space with Ralph's and Trader Joe's grocery stores, gift shops, and restaurants.

Hillcrest isn't all shopping and eating. The streets south of Balboa Park are lined with enchanting edifices—from Victorian to Spanish revival and Craftsman—some now converted to office buildings. There are churches as well, including a romantic, soaring building at Fifth Avenue and Olive. Built in 1910 as a Methodist church, it was converted to **THE ABBEY** (2825 5th Ave; 619/686-8700) restaurant in the 1980s. The restaurant is currently open only for group functions. The gold statue atop its beautiful dome can be seen for blocks around.

On the other side of Hillcrest, check out the **VERMONT STREET PEDESTRIAN BRIDGE** (foot of Vermont St), which spans Washington Street to link Hillcrest with University Heights. Built in 1994, it's a charismatic piece of functional public art. Pithy quotations from Dr. Seuss and Kate Sessions (San Diego's grande dame of horticulture) are inscribed into its panels of steel and glass, casting a cobalt blue light onto the footpath. "I am thankful that I wear sensible shoes and can walk with comfort all day long," Sessions comments. Good advice for anyone exploring this charming neighborhood. *Map:N2*

## Kensington/Adams Avenue

Perched on the hills above the intersection of Interstates 805 and 8, Kensington and busy Adams Avenue are throwbacks to an earlier era. In the 1920s, Kensington was a fashionable address. Silent film star Norma Talmadge and her sisters bought some property in the neighborhood, and the streets Norma, Constance, and Natalie Drives still bear their names. Today, this area, called Talmadge, is home to a diverse population of artists, writers, young families, professionals, and longtime residents. Adams Avenue is the neighborhood's main artery. Working your way east, there's plenty to catch your attention. The avenue offers a compelling mélange of antique stores, used-furniture shops, vintage clothing boutiques, bookshops, and cafes. The greatest concentration of antique stores lies between 30th and 40th Streets. They are loosely allied, and most have handy a brochure listing their competitors down the way. Two of the dozens of worthwhile stores are **QUICKSILVER STAINED GLASS & ANTIQUES** (2946 Adams Ave; 619/283-3638) for treasures sold on consignment and **PRINCE AND THE PAUPER** (3201 Adams Ave; 619/283-4380) for collectible children's books.

Restaurants run from the hip **KENSINGTON GRILL** (4055 Adams Ave; 619/281-4014) to **JYOTI BIHANGA** (3351 Adams Ave; 619/282-4116), serving inexpensive vegetarian fare. It seems there are almost as many coffeehouses on Adams as there are antique shops, including the wonderfully named **LESTAT'S** (3343 Adams Ave; 619/282-0437), offering live music nightly in a wide range of genres.

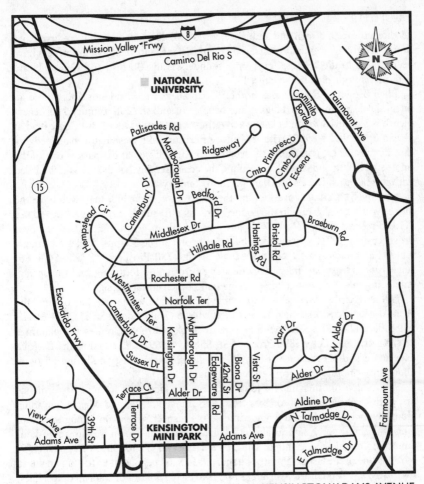

KENSINGTON/ADAMS AVENUE

Order that latte to go and segue from the business district to the residential streets. From Adams Avenue, walk north on Marlborough Drive into a network of winding roads lined with delightful Spanish-style bungalows, Tudor-style villas, and other architectural gems—all fronted by manicured lawns, of course. With street names like Hempstead Circle, Canterbury Drive, and Bristol Road, there's little doubt Kensington's developers were serious Anglophiles.

Movie buffs are fond of the somewhat dilapidated **KEN THEATER** (4061 Adams Ave; 619/283-5909), which has been entertaining San Diegans with classic and modern art-house films since the 1940s. Next door, **KENSINGTON VIDEO** (4067 Adams Ave; 619/584-7725) boasts an enormous and diverse selection of videos and DVDs that puts the likes of Blockbuster to shame. *Map:LL4*

# La Jolla

Mediterranean in design and ambiance, La Jolla is genteel and trendy, reserved and brash, yet always refined. Artists, writers, musicians, and wealthy landowners have been drawn to the "village" ever since founders Frank Bosford and George Heald laid out its floor plan in the late 1880s.

Ellen Browning Scripps, the mother of San Diego's garden landscape, played an integral role as landscape designer and benefactor into the 20th century. Her benevolence is memorialized in **ELLEN BROWNING SCRIPPS PARK** (1180 Coast Blvd at Ocean St; 619/221-8900) with its fringe of century-old Washington palms edging the waterfront. **LA JOLLA COVE** (see Top 25 Attractions) at the park is one of the finest snorkeling and diving spots along the coast. Its tiny beach is checkerboarded with bright beach towels by 10am on sunny Sundays.

**PROSPECT STREET,** overlooking the sea from a slight hill, may well have the highest-priced real estate in the county. Pink as a flamingo, **LA VALENCIA HOTEL** (1132 Prospect St; 858/454-0771) has presided like a gracious grande dame over Prospect since 1926. More modest but equally precious is Scripps' Wisteria Cottage, which has housed **JOHN COLE'S BOOK SHOP** (780 Prospect St; 858/454-4766) since 1966. Heavy lavender blossoms dangle from a 60-foot-long trellis in spring, enhancing the beauty of architect Irving Gill's beach cottage design.

Gill and Scripps were also responsible for the 1916 estate that has become the **MUSEUM OF CONTEMPORARY ART SAN DIEGO** (700 Prospect St; 858/454-3541). Art galleries line Prospect Street; be sure to check out the sculptures and paintings at **TASENDE GALLERY** (820 Prospect St; 858/454-3691). Essential to the La Jolla experience is dinner at one of San Diego's finest restaurants; you'll find an over-abundance of options in our Restaurants chapter.

Shopping is another fine La Jolla tradition—in fact, it's a form of performance art, with sleek boutique-browsers from Argentina, France, and Mexico parading along shady streets. Girard Avenue intersects Prospect Street, continuing the shopping and dining scene several blocks inland. A few homegrown treasures stand out amid the designer-name shops. The **COVE THEATRE** (7730 Girard Ave; 858/459-5404) is one of the last neighborhood theaters in San Diego; **ADELAIDE'S FLOWERS AND GIFTS** (7766 Girard Ave; 858/454-0146) displays a riot of colorful tulips, lilies, daffodils, and roses along the sidewalk. Book lovers head to **WARWICK'S** (7812 Girard St; 858/454-0347) and the **WHITE RABBIT** (7755 Girard St; 858/454-3518), a fanciful haven for kids.

La Jolla's jewel-like facets aren't confined to the village. Stroll south from the main beach at **LA JOLLA SHORES** (8200 Camino del Oro, La Jolla; 619/221-8900) to reach a park and playground, a great place to stop for lunch. Farther along, you may be able to search for anemones in the tide pools near the **MARINE ROOM** (2000 Spindrift Dr; 858/459-7222) unless the tide is so high waves are crashing against the restaurant's windows. In that case, visit the "mock" tide pools at the **BIRCH AQUARIUM AT SCRIPPS** (see Top 25 Attractions). *Map:JJ7*

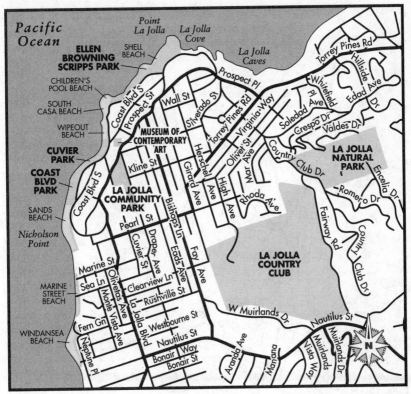

LA JOLLA

## Del Mar

Del Mar has always attracted those who love sojourning at the beach. Situated on the sloping western side of a 2-mile-long sandstone mesa, the town of about 6,000 was designed like a row of bleachers oriented toward every spectacular sunset. First plotted in 1885 by founder Jacob Taylor, it quickly attracted vacationers and residents. Many came to frolic in the waves or swim in a unique "natatorium": a concrete-walled enclosure that extended far out into the waves. Today, although the natatorium and other fin de siècle beach-resort ventures are gone, Del Mar remains the quintessential beach town.

The 2½-mile-long stretch of sand from Torrey Pines State Reserve north to the mouth of the San Dieguito River (near the Del Mar Fairgrounds) is one of the best public strands in Southern California for walking, swimming, surfing, or simply lazing under an umbrella. Most beachgoers access it from the neighborhood between 18th and 29th Streets. **SEAGROVE PARK** (5th St and Ocean Ave) overlooking the beach at the foot of 15th Street is perfect for picnicking and sunset watching; small summer concerts and other events are held here.

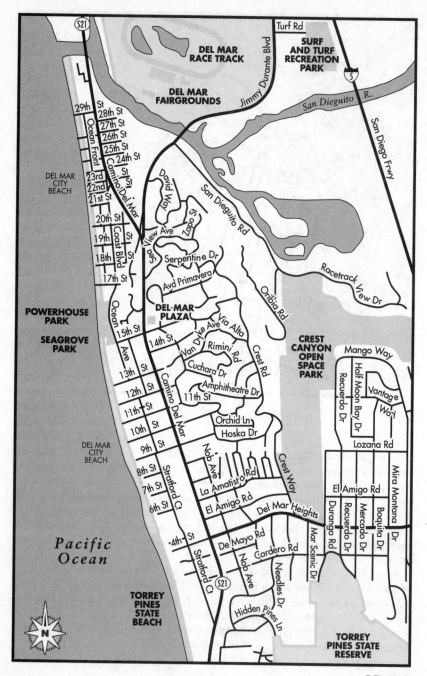

DEL MAR

Del Mar's compact town center lies at the intersection of Camino Del Mar and 15th Street. Walk southward along Camino Del Mar to 12th Street to window-shop at the town's eclectic shops. Notable among the independents are **EARTH SONG BOOKSTORE** (858/755-4254) and **OCEAN SONG MUSIC OF DEL MAR** (858/755-7664), sharing the same space at 1438-1440 Camino Del Mar. The first is an excellent neighborhood bookseller with an emphasis on spirituality and self-help, the other an art, gift, and music shop with a Latin American flair.

**DEL MAR PLAZA** (1555 Camino Del Mar; 858/792-1555), designed to resemble an Italian hill town, shouldn't be missed. Among its upscale shops and restaurants, you'll have to hunt for **ESMERALDA BOOKS & COFFEE** (858/755-2707), but this small shop is a real gem with an impressive book selection, a coffee bar serving pastries and light meals, and indoor and outdoor seating. The plaza's grandest feature is its huge terrace overlooking the ocean. You can sit in this public space as long as you please in comfortable Adirondack chairs and feel as though you are on Del Mar's "front porch." The plaza's pay parking lot is a blessing in this congested area.

The **DEL MAR FAIRGROUNDS** (I-5 at Via de la Valle, main entrance on Jimmy Durante Blvd; 858/792-4252, 858/793-5555 for 24-hour event hotline; www.delmarfair.com) hosts one of California's best fairs during the last two weeks of June through July 4. The **DEL MAR THOROUGHBRED CLUB** (858/793-5555) hosts a racing season every summer, late July through early September, that's legendary not only for its founder, Bing Crosby, but also for a grand slogan: "Where the Turf Meets the Surf." Horse-racing honchos nearly take over **L'AUBERGE DEL MAR** (1540 Camino Del Mar; 858/259-151), which feels like a country hideaway though it's at the busiest intersection in town.

If you crave hiking, clamber through the Del Mar side of **TORREY PINES STATE RESERVE** (see Top 25 Attractions); park with the surfers at the south end of Camino Del Mar. If you'd rather stroll along the sand while admiring multimillion-dollar mansions, walk north along the beach from the foot of Seagrove Park to the San Dieguito River. Look east, away from the sea, if you're walking in late afternoon: you may see hot-air balloons drifting above canyons and neighborhoods. For further information, call or visit the **DEL MAR REGIONAL CHAMBER OF COMMERCE** (1104 Camino Del Mar; 858/755-4844; www.delmarchamber.org). *Map:GG7*

## Rancho Santa Fe and Environs

Hardly anyone even knew Rancho Santa Fe existed—let alone that it's one of the country's wealthiest enclaves—until 1997, when the Heaven's Gate cult members chose it as the perfect spot for their mass suicide. In fact, this eucalyptus-shrouded, super-exclusive community has, since the 1920s, been the coveted home of a crowd of celebrities, tycoons, and politicians.

"The Ranch," as it's known to its denizens, had an illustrious beginning and easily grew into its tight-as-a-fresh-face-lift skin. Designed by esteemed architect Lillian Rice, who used Spanish villages as her inspiration, the community evolved into a genteel grouping of Spanish colonial revival buildings surrounded by huge estates (many with fruit groves and horse paddocks), golf courses, and riding trails. Once you've driven around the winding roads, ogling the mansions and taking in the coun-

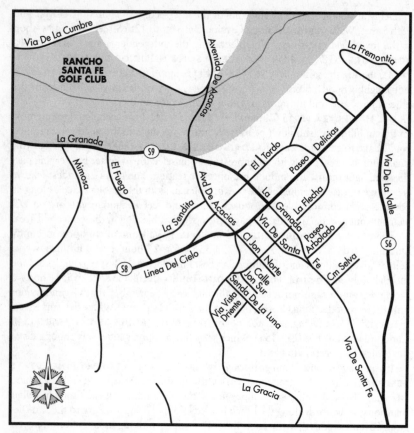

RANCHO SANTA FE AND ENVIRONS

trified atmosphere, return to "town" and park your wheels—this tiny village is best explored on foot. The village hub is dominated by real estate offices, though there is an array of chic boutiques, jewelers, and art and antique dealers in and around Paseo Delicias, the main drag. Wise shoppers stop by the **COUNTRY FRIENDS SHOP** (Avenida de Acacias at El Tordo; 858/756-1192), packed with donated or consigned furniture, crystal, silver, paintings, and all manner of objets d'art.

Wander over to the historic **INN AT RANCHO SANTA FE** (5951 Linea del Cielo; 858/756-1131), onetime hangout for Errol Flynn, Bette Davis, and Bing Crosby. The present-day inn was Lillian Rice's first building—a 12-room house constructed in 1922, now incorporated into the peaceful, parklike 20-acre property where guests bed down in private casitas and play croquet on the lawn.

For excellent (and expensive) French cuisine, book a table at Bernard Hug's **MILLE FLEURS** (6009 Paseo Delicias; 858/756-3085), with its romantic French atmosphere. **DELICIAS** (6106 Paseo Delicias; 858/756-8000) is another good choice, with California cuisine and a country French setting. Even if you can't afford to eat out, you can buy the same exotic produce, baby veggies, and gourmet herbs as many of the top chefs at **CHINO'S VEGETABLE SHOP** (6123 Calzada del Bosque, at Via de Santa Fe; 858/756-3184). Though it might look like just another roadside stand (don't be deceived by the simple Vegetable Shop signs), many of California's culinary artists (including Alice Waters, who started the whole California cuisine commotion) wouldn't dream of handpicking their ingredients anywhere else when they're in town.

Tucked down a quiet country road amid citrus groves is the ultra-chic **RANCHO VALENCIA RESORT** (5921 Valencia Circle; 858/756-1123). This exclusive hideaway is a favorite escape for celebrities and racehorse owners following the action at the Del Mar track. The restaurant is fabulous—make reservations for dinner and hobnob with the stars.

Douglas Fairbanks Sr.'s sprawling old ranch, across the river valley from Rancho Santa Fe, has metamorphosed into Fairbanks Ranch, a distinctive area of more exclusive estates, golf courses, and riding stables. The **RANCHO SANTA FE POLO FIELD** (14555 El Camino Real; 858/481-9217) is just a trot away. Polo matches are held every Sunday from early June to the end of September. General admission is $5. Pet lovers should stop by the **HELEN WOODWARD ANIMAL CENTER** (6461 El Apajo Rd; 858/756-4117). The esteemed nonprofit organization has an adoption center for dogs, cats, and other pets, an equine hospital, educational programs, a kids' camp, and a shop. *Map:EE5*

# Museums

Photography, astronomy, natural history, and dozens of other special interests are honored with museums in San Diego. Balboa Park alone has about a dozen; many participate in the free Tuesdays program, which offers free admission at different museums on rotating Tuesdays. Most museums are housed in architectural monuments, from the ornate Spanish-style Museum of Man in Balboa Park to the modernistic San Diego Museum of Contemporary Art in La Jolla. Many offer special programs, from lectures to nature hikes.

## California Surf Museum

**223 NORTH COAST HWY; OCEANSIDE; 760/721-6876** Learn about surfing lore and the legends who popularized the sport, from the earliest innovators to today's cutting-edge kids. Many of the objects displayed are loaned from these legends themselves for rotating exhibits; there is one major show each year and several smaller ones. In addition to these changing exhibits there is a permanent show of surfboards and gear, and photos and drawings of beautiful waves and beautiful people. The museum store sells T-shirts, posters, videos, and surfer mags. Admission is free; donation suggested. *Thurs–Sun 10am–4pm; www.surfmuseum.org; map:BB9*

## Children's Museum/Museo de los Niños

**200 W ISLAND AVE, DOWNTOWN; 619/233-5437** The children's museum, at its best, is a hands-on, "kids-are-king" kinda place. At present, it's a rather disappointing collection of exhibits—but there's always room for improvement. Museum leaders are constantly seeking funding and sources for innovative, temporary exhibits to increase the excitement level. Children can create high towers of connectable cardboard boxes and improvise skits or dance on a small stage. One area has blocks and other toys for younger kids; in fact, most of the exhibits seem geared to please children up to about age 4. Children can also paint or work with clay. The museum store has a variety of educational toys for sale. The museum may be closed when you're in town. It's located in an area scheduled for redevelopment. Call before visiting. Admission is $6 per person. *Tues–Sat 10am–4pm; www.sd childrensmuseum.org; map:N8* &

## Computer Museum of America

**640 C ST, DOWNTOWN; 619/235-8222** Computer nuts will love this large collection of hardware, which details the amazing advances in computer science since before the Cold War. Some of the exhibits are quite rare and cost tens of thousands of dollars when they were unveiled as the cutting edge of computer technology. Samples of what you'll find here are Apple's first PC-type computer, the Apple Lisa, and a 1920s Burroughs comptometer. This is a real reality check for those who constantly whine for upgrades. Admission is free; donations suggested. *Tues–Sun 10am–5pm; www.computer-museum.org; map:O7*

## George White and Anna Gunn Marston House

**3525 7TH AVE, DOWNTOWN; 619/298-3142** This lovely example of turn-of-the-century, Arts and Crafts–style architecture is listed in the National Register of Historic Places. Built in 1905 by renowned San Diego architects Irving Gill and William Hebbard, it sits on 5 acres of landscaped grounds and has a formal English garden. Rooms are furnished in the Arts and Crafts style, with Stickley, Ellis, and Roycroft furniture; Tiffany lamps; and Native American art. All visits are by 45-minute guided tours leaving on the hour. Admission is $5 for adults; $4 for seniors, military, and students; $2 for ages 6 to 17. *Fri–Sun 10am–4:30pm; map:N3*

## Mingei International Museum

**1439 EL PRADO, HOUSE OF CHARM, BALBOA PARK, DOWNTOWN; 619/239-0003** Mingei is a combination of the Japanese words *min* (all people) and *gei* (art). The museum promises—and delivers—art by and for and about people. Although the more traditional examples of folk art are decorated utilitarian objects from around the world, some pieces border on the purely aesthetic. Located outside near the front entrance, Niki de Saint-Phalle's bold, bright "Niki-Gator" of polyester resin definitely leans toward the decorative. Exhibits combine the museum's collection with loaned items. The facility also has a theater, research center, and multimedia center. The museum store sells unusual jewelry, ethnic artifacts, and contemporary American crafts. In Escondido, work has begun on a satellite museum just a block from the California Center for the Arts at 155 W Grand Avenue. Scheduled for completion around winter of 2002, the 5,000-square-foot museum will provide much-needed space for some of the museum's 12,000 artifacts from 100 countries. Museum admission is $5 for adults, $2 for children 6 to 17 and students with ID. *Tues–Sun 10am–4pm; www.mingei.org; map:O5* &

## Museum of Contemporary Art San Diego (MCA)

**700 PROSPECT ST, LA JOLLA; 858/454-3541 / 1001 KETTNER BLVD, DOWN-TOWN; 619/234-1001** Designed by Irving Gill in 1916 and originally the home of nature preservationist Ellen Browning Scripps, the La Jolla MCA hosts temporary shows in addition to its permanent 3,000-piece collection. Contemporary works run the gamut of media, with particular emphasis on installation and conceptual art, minimalism, and pop art. Expanded and renovated in 1996, the solid, simple building has lots of unadorned columns and arches and, more important, 60,000 square feet of exhibition space, including the Edwards Sculpture Garden. Private parties and group meetings are held in rooms overlooking the Pacific; symposiums and lectures are presented regularly at **SHERWOOD AUDITORIUM.**

The museum's downtown venue is located within the triangular **AMERICA PLAZA** across from the Santa Fe train depot. Currently under construction are several new gallery spaces, including a total renovation of the train depot's baggage claim area. The 38-foot ceiling of this historic edifice makes it the perfect venue for installation art and the display of large works of art. Construction should be completed by 2004.

Both museum stores have an eclectic assortment of trendy gifts as well as books about architecture, photography, and contemporary art. In La Jolla, adult admission is $4; students, seniors, and military pay $2; members and children under 12 are free. There is no charge to visit the downtown venue. *Closed Wed; La Jolla: Fri–Tues 11am–5pm (until 8pm in summer), Thurs 11am–8pm; downtown: Thurs–Tues 11am–5pm year-round; www.mcasd.org; map:JJ7 and M7* &

## Museum of Photographic Arts (MoPA)

**1649 EL PRADO, CASA DE BALBOA, BALBOA PARK; DOWNTOWN; 619/238-7559** Featured among the museum's 4,000 photographs are some of Ansel Adams' glorious nature stills; MoPA's strength, however, is social documentary, including works by Sally Mann, Weegee, and Margaret Bourke-White. The 1995 "Points of Entry" exhibit generated discussion of U.S. immigration issues among San Diegans. Other important works include photos by prominent Latin American photographers (Alvarez Bravo and Graciela Iturbide) and documentary images from the USSR in the Stalin era.

Finished in March 2000, a yearlong expansion created a print-viewing room and a 25,000-tome library. Several new galleries permit three or four simultaneous exhibitions. The 240-seat theater shows art films and videos several nights a week. MoPA's museum store has a good selection of photography books. General admission is $6; $4 for students, seniors, and military; free for children under 12 accompanied by an adult. *Every day 10am–5pm (Thursdays until 9pm); www.mopa.org; map:O5* &

## Museum of the San Diego Historical Society

**1649 EL PRADO, CASA DE BALBOA, BALBOA PARK, DOWNTOWN; 619/232-6203** Exhibits are changed twice yearly at this history museum showing regional art, historical photographs, and memorabilia as well as national and international traveling shows. Scholars and history buffs can access the nearly 2 million photographic images in the historical society's archives (open Thurs–Sat 10am–4pm), as well as manuscripts, public records, architectural drawings, and oral histories. Museum admission is $5 for adults, $2 for ages 6 to 17. *Tues–Sun 10am–4:30pm; www.sandiegohistory.org; map:O5* &

## San Diego Aerospace Museum

**2001 PAN AMERICAN PLAZA, BALBOA PARK, DOWNTOWN; 619/234-8291**
More than 60 restored, reproduction, and model aircraft and spacecraft are exhibited in the circular 1935 Ford Building with its strip of blue neon lighting the night sky. Check out the original Pietenpol Air Camper, with its 1928 Model-A Ford automobile engine and radiator, and the Piper J-3 Cub, the first "everyman's" airplane, mass-produced in the early 1930s. Other originals include the Stearman N2S-3 Kaydet, in which most World War II aviators learned to fly. Full-size reproductions include the *Spirit of St. Louis* and the Messerschmitt Bf-109G-14, whose brilliant German design cost many Allied aviators their lives in the Second World War. The Hall of Fame displays oil paintings, bios, models, and memorabilia describing the history of aviation. Lecture series host speakers such as Erik Lindbergh, grandson of the famous aviator. Kids interested in aeronautics can attend a weeklong math and science camp in the summer. Admission is $8 for adults, $6 for seniors, $3 for children 6 to 17. *Every day 9am–5:30pm (summer), 10am–4:30pm (winter); www.aerospacemuseum.org; map:O5* &

## San Diego Automotive Museum

**2080 PAN AMERICAN PLAZA, BALBOA PARK, DOWNTOWN; 619/231-2886**
Lovers of vintage cars should not miss this museum. Exhibitions change at least four times a year, giving devotees the chance to view vintage motorcycles, race cars, stadium trucks, and priceless antiques. You might see the sexy black 1931 Lagonda, sparkling Model T's, and a 1909 International Harvester "Farm Wagon." The museum's library and resource center are invaluable resources for car aficionados and offer manuals, reference books, vintage car magazines, photos, and vintage films on video. The museum store carries—you guessed it—automobile-related gifts. General admission is $7 for adults, $6 for seniors and military, $3 for children 6 to 15. *Every day 10am–4:30pm; www.sdautomuseum.org; map:O5* &

## San Diego Hall of Champions Sports Museum

**2131 PAN AMERICAN PLAZA, FEDERAL BLDG, BALBOA PARK, DOWNTOWN; 619/234-2544** Sports fans love the interactive exhibits at the Hall of Champions, which moved in the summer of 1999 to the refurbished Federal Building, built for the 1935–1936 exposition. Test your sportscasting skills at the Broadcast Booth, or rate your strength, flexibility, and other athletic abilities in the Sportsability Center. Parents snap their kids' pictures in the Locker Room as the little darlings dress up in different athletic uniforms. See what's happening in the Center Court: there might be a mini-Chargers' football training camp or a rock-climbing-wall demonstration. The art gallery shows work by athlete/artists, including the oil paintings of soccer player and San Diego resident Juli Veee. Admission is $4 for adults; $3 for seniors, military, and students; and $2 for children 7 to 17. *Every day 10am–4pm; www.sandiegosports.org; map:O5* &

## San Diego Model Railroad Museum

**1649 EL PRADO, CASA DE BALBOA, BALBOA PARK, DOWNTOWN; 619/696-0199** Kids weary of art or history exhibits revel in this museum, which boasts the largest permanent operating scale model and toy train display in the country. Trolleys and narrow- and standard-gauge trains run through landscapes portraying real and make-believe towns, mountains, rivers, and valleys of the South-west. While most of the trains are run by overgrown kids belonging to various San Diego model railroad clubs, your little ones can play in the Toy Train Gallery near the back of the museum. Club members patrol their train-filled worlds and answer the questions of both neophytes and model railroad aficionados. Admission is $4 for adults, $3 for seniors, $2.50 for students with ID, and free to children 15 or under when accompanied by an adult. *Tues–Fri 11am–4pm, Sat–Sun 11am–5pm; www.sdmodelrailroadm.com; map:O5* ♿

## San Diego Natural History Museum

**1788 EL PRADO, BALBOA PARK, DOWNTOWN; 619/232-3821** Facing the large fountain on the Prado, the natural history museum is a work in progress. A new wing houses the "Natural Treasures" exhibit, a collection of favorite things from the original building, which is undergoing total reconstruction and renovation. The exhibit features live bugs and snakes and information on whales and other California fauna and flora. The new wing also houses "Desert and Sea," a photographic exhibit depicting Baja California wildlife. In the traveling exhibition hall, there's a new show every trimester; look on the Internet to see what's up.

Renovations of the old wing will be ongoing as funds are raised. The first exhibit to open is the **DISCOVERY ROOM**, where kids and adults can conduct experiments, look through microscopes, ask questions, touch things, and even get dirty if they choose. Future exhibits will include a walk-through diorama showing San Diego's different ecosystems and a fossil mysteries exhibit.

But even better than the Natural History Museum's displays and exhibits are the educational programs it offers. Kids love the **WACKY SCIENCE SUNDAYS**, meant to both enlighten and entertain. In the summer, **DAY CAMPS** get kids off the couch and into the countryside, and there are camping trips, photo expeditions, and conservation programs for members and nonmembers. **CANYONEERING HIKES**, offered all year except summer, include dozens of different hikes with knowledgeable guides. This museum's gift shop is one of the park's best, with lots of toys for both kids and adults. Admission is $7 for adults; $6 for seniors, military, and students with ID; $5 for children 3 to 17. Admission price may increase for certain exhibits. *Every day 9:30am–4:30pm; www.sdnhm.org; map:O5* ♿

## Timken Museum of Art

**1500 EL PRADO, BALBOA PARK, DOWNTOWN; 619/239-5548** Financed by the wealthy Putnam sisters of Vermont, this small, pink-wallpapered museum opened in 1965 on Balboa Park's El Prado, which is Spanish for "a pleasant place to stroll." San Diego's one free art museum, the Timken has a collection of more than a hundred works of art spanning five centuries. The city's only Rembrandt painting is here, part of a collection of European masters and medieval religious paintings. Among the most impressive holdings are the European masterpieces, including Niccolo di Buonaccorso's *Madonna and Child*, two small triptychs that are extremely rare 14th-century pieces of tempera and gold on wood, and the Russian religious paintings. Admission is free. *Tues–Sat 10am–4:30pm, Sun 1:30–4:30pm (closed Sept); map:O5* ⊛

# Art in Public Places

For all its kicked-back and outdoorsy character, San Diego has an inherent conservatism—it's not as innovative as Los Angeles or as footloose as Northern California. Such conservatism may be one reason it took until 1990 for the city of San Diego to commit to a serious public arts program. Since then, however, its public art policy has been recognized nationally as a model of community development. The city offers matching grants and other incentives to encourage grassroots involvement in neighborhoods and communities.

Among the most colorful projects resulting from the program are the bright and whimsical **SEA GODS** (west end of Newport Ave, Ocean Beach; map:B3) by local artists Jill Moon and Matthew Welsh. The painted enamel-on-steel sculptures guard Ocean Beach's beachfront public parking lot. San Diego's ethnic diversity is celebrated in Jean Cornwell's **TO LIGHT THE WAY**, a colorful tile mosaic on the exterior walls of the Malcolm X Library (5148 Market St; map:MM3) in southeast San Diego.

The unique **VERMONT STREET PEDESTRIAN BRIDGE** (see Hillcrest in Neighborhoods section), won both the American Planning Association's Outstanding Planning Award and the American Institute of Architects' Orchid Award. **WATER MARKS**, a 200-foot-long mosaic of stone, colored concrete, tile, and bronze, was built to partially obscure the pump station within Mission Trails Regional Park (1 Father Junipero Serra Trail, Tierrasanta). The project by San Diego artists Lynn Susholtz and Aida Mancillas was one of four San Diego winners of the Metropolitan Water District's 2001 "Liquid Art" contest, drawing attention to regional water conservation.

Some of San Diego's North County communities are involving the public in appreciation of the arts. Escondido, once a tiny agricultural town, is now one of North County's most dedicated patrons of the arts. Its program for public art has commissioned some 20 works since 1986. One of the most ambitious is **MONUMENTS TO TIME IN THE CORRIDOR OF LIFE, ART, AND CULTURE,** a series of pieces, some with musical accompaniment, beginning at the California Center for the Arts and lining Grand Avenue, in the city's old downtown section. Prolific artist Niki de Saint Phalle is, at press time, working on a huge outdoor sculpture garden, "Queen Califia's Magical Circle." Celebrating California's cultural history, it should be completed by late 2003. Escondido residents can tour galleries and studios during **ART WALK,** held the second Saturday of each month. The city of Oceanside combines fund-raising with public art in its **ARTS ALIVE** program. Between February and June, 40 or more banners, painted mainly in acrylics, adorn downtown Oceanside. At the end of the event they are auctioned off to raise funds for aesthetic improvements to the downtown area.

At the opposite end of the county, the community-generated murals at **CHICANO PARK** (National Ave at Crosby St, Barrio Logan; map:Q9) embody the spirit of San Diego's Chicano and Latino communities. Huge likenesses of everyday people and heroes from Chicano and Latino cultures adorn the supports of the San Diego–Coronado Bay Bridge in Barrio Logan. Raw, organic, and powerful, they reflect a combination of hope, anger, spirit, and community activism that is a source of inspiration for the adults who watch their kids climb on the playground equipment in the unassuming park below. The murals have been defaced with racist graffiti, an incident that united the whole city in protest against ignorance.

On Shelter Island, other ethnicities have made their mark. Franco Vianello's giant **TUNAMAN'S MEMORIAL** (Shelter Island Dr; map:E7) is a tribute to San Diego's now-extinct tuna fishing fleet, the pride of Point Loma's Portuguese community. Further west along Shelter Island Drive, near the harbor police substation, the **YOKO-HAMA FRIENDSHIP BELL** (Shelter Island Dr; map:E7) nestles under its tiny pagoda roof. The cast bronze bell was a gift of San Diego's sister city in Japan in 1960. Adjacent to the friendship bell, bright mosaic tiles form the **PEARL OF THE PACIFIC** (1401 Shelter Island Dr; map:E8), with tigers, dragons, and flower motifs adorning a ground-level fountain backed by delicate concrete and iron structures. James T. Hubbell created this monument to intercontinental cooperation with the help of architecture students from China, Russia, and Mexico.

The **INSITE** exhibitions, held in San Diego and Tijuana approximately every three years, are another form of intercultural collaboration. Initiated in 1992, this binational partnership between the San Diego–based, nonprofit Installation Gallery and Mexico's National Fine Arts Institute is still evolving. For the 2000 event, 34 artists from North and South America created 27 works of art: everything from performance art to mobile puppet shows. One installation featured the artist, dressed as a border patrol agent, posing for tourists' pictures atop a zebra-striped burro—a clichéd image of tourism in the Mexican border zone. The next show is scheduled for 2005.

Some of the city's most treasured public art, tucked away on the campus of the University of California at San Diego (Gilman and La Jolla Village Drs, La Jolla; 858/534-2230; map:JJ7), remains undiscovered by most San Diego residents. A center for conceptual and avant-garde art since its inception in 1960, UCSD's 1,200-acre campus is home to the **STUART COLLECTION,** a thought-provoking series of site-specific sculptures. Alexis Smith's *Snake Path* is a visual representation of the nature-versus-culture conundrum; its 10-foot-wide path meanders 560 feet though the campus, passing a giant book identified as Milton's *Paradise Lost* and ending at the entrance to the Geisel Library. Niki de Saint Phalle's colorful, 14-foot *Sun God* (between Mandeville and the Faculty Club) is perched atop a 15-foot concrete arch on a grassy knoll. This giant bird was de Saint Phalle's first large outdoor work in the United States. Pick up a walking map of the collection's 15 pieces at the Gilman Drive or North Point information kiosks, or get it on the web site at http://stuart-collection.ucsd.edu.

# Galleries

San Diego's galleries are primarily in La Jolla and downtown, although there are plenty sprinkled throughout the county. Many of the smaller galleries have reduced hours but also show by appointment; call ahead for schedules. A fine time to reacquaint yourself with fine art is during April's ArtWalk, when dozens of downtown and Little Italy galleries host special arts and music programs, and the artists are on hand to talk about their work. Another opportunity to check out San Diego artists at work is during the September Open Studios Tours, when patrons can visit private studios and showrooms of artists throughout the county.

## Africa and Beyond

**1250 PROSPECT ST, LA JOLLA; 858/454-9983** Once *the* place to buy African beads, this gallery shop now sells Shona sculpture, Ethiopian Coptic crosses, Ashanti fertility dolls, Berber prayer boxes from Morocco, and more. An expansion of the premises now provides space for clothing and textiles as well as more artifacts. *Every day; map:JJ7*

## Alcala Gallery

**950 SILVERADO ST, LA JOLLA; 858/454-6610** Sashay into this small, stylish La Jolla gallery if you're looking for early California art (mid-1800s to 1940s) in fancy gilt frames. The other specialty here is pre-Columbian art, primarily Mayan work and pieces from Mexico's west coast. Additionally, the store sells ancient Asian art, furnishings, decorative arts, and porcelain. *Every day; www.bauerart.com; map:JJ7*

## The Artists Gallery

**7420 GIRARD AVE, LA JOLLA; 858/459-5844** Longtime La Jolla watercolorist Georgeanna Lipe features the work of more than 30 local artists. Tourists might buy paintings as a keepsake here, yet there's enough quality and variety to keep regular collectors interested as well. Most of the work is representational and the sales staff friendly. There's free parking. *Tues–Sat; www.artists-gallery.com; map:JJ7*

## Athenaeum

**1008 WALL ST, LA JOLLA; 858/454-5872** La Jolla's lovely music and arts library, built in the 1920s by William Templeton Johnson, has frequent juried fine-art exhibits and also presents lectures and hosts art classes. *Tues–Sat; map:JJ7*

## David Zapf Gallery

**2400 KETTNER BLVD, DOWNTOWN; 619/232-5004** The Studio Building, a converted warehouse filled with art studios and galleries, is home to this gallery representing mainly San Diego artists. Works include the colorful, spiritual landscapes of Nancy Kittredge, lushly painted figurative acrylics by David Baze, and the soft, earth-toned photography of Eric Blau. Furniture maker Paul Henry also exhibits here. *Thurs–Sat and by appointment; map:M5*

## Debra Owen Gallery

**354 11TH AVE, DOWNTOWN; 619/231-3030** Debra Owen, formerly of Dos Damas Gallery on Market Street, relocated in 1997 to the ReinCarnation Project. Ubaldo

Spagnolo and architect Wayne Buss collaborated to restore the old Carnation Dairy Building in downtown's latest redevelopment district. Owen's L-shaped venue features contemporary art by local artists, including fabulous local painters Maura Vazakas and Marcelina Kim. The multiuse ReinCarnation building is also home to a community media center and outdoor stage, private lofts and art studios, and the Sushi Performance Gallery. *Fri and Sat and by appointment; map:O8*

### Fingerhut Gallery

**1205 PROSPECT ST, LA JOLLA; 858/456-9900** Smack in the middle of La Jolla's prominent promenade, this upscale gallery has among its compelling artists Jiang Tiefeng, creator of brilliant stylized serigraphs and oil paintings and one of the originators of the Hunan school of painting. Other artists represented are Joanna Zjawinska, Peter Max, and Ted Geisel (Dr. Seuss). A few etchings and lithos by Chagall, Renoir, Picasso, Rembrandt, and other masters are always on hand for the collector of fine European art. One of the gallery's newly signed artists is Russian Sergey Smirnov, who paints haunting images—many of wan, serious female faces—in oil on linen. The gallery is open until 10pm Tuesday through Sunday. *Every day; www.fingerhutart.com; map:JJ7*

### Gallery Alexander

**7925 GIRARD AVE, LA JOLLA; 858/459-9433** This fanciful art gallery almost always makes one smile and is an excellent source for one-of-a-kind gifts, including those with Jewish motifs. Glass, metal, wood, and ceramics are pressed, carved, and otherwise molded into utilitarian and decorative objects such as garden art that doubles as lawn furniture. Every two or three months the gallery hosts a special showing. *Every day; www.galleryalexander.com; map:JJ7*

### Gallery Eight

**7464 GIRARD AVE, LA JOLLA; 858/454-9781** There's a wonderful feeling of space in this gallery. Every item is beautifully showcased no matter what the price. In addition to handcrafted jewelry, ceramics, eclectic furniture, and glass, they sell beautiful clothing, and ribbon by the foot. Smaller items reign—it's a great source for gifts. The gallery was started by eight women as a nonprofit to benefit the UCSD International Center, hence the name. It's now strictly a business venture, with two of the founding artists still involved. The entire inventory goes on sale in late January, at 25 percent off. *Mon–Sat; map:JJ7*

### La Jolla Fiber Arts

**7644 GIRARD AVE, LA JOLLA; 858/454-6732** Here you'll find wonderful woven stuff—everything from baskets, clothing, scarves, and throws to three-dimensional sculpture, dolls, and wall hangings. Prices reflect the painstaking work that goes into the individually designed and executed pieces. *Every day; www.lajollafiber arts.com; map:JJ7*

### Nofufi Garden Gallery

**90-C NORTH COAST HWY, ENCINITAS; 760/635-0556** This charming gallery showcases landscape sculpture and garden furnishings, accessories, water features, and fountains. The works of individual artists are displayed in periodic shows, and gallery programs include guest lectures and classes in tile art and other groovy genres. *Every day; www.nofufi.com; map:EE7*

## Parisi Gallery and Sculpture Garden

**2002 JIMMY DURANTE BLVD, STE 308, DEL MAR; 858/259-0490** This sculpture garden and art gallery has featured the works of prominent U.S. artists since 1998. Bronze, glass, and ceramic pieces from small to monumental dot the outdoor garden; others are housed in the intimate indoor gallery, where you'll also find contemporary oil paintings and photography. International artists represented here include New Yorker Albert Paley, whose ornamental, hand-tooled steel gates enclose the Renwick Gallery at the Smithsonian. Lucia Eames, daughter of furniture designers Ray and Charles Eames, creates functional gates and benches in steel. Curator Betsy Lane works with patrons as well as interior designers to recommend art for private and public spaces. *Tues–Sat; www.parisiportfolio.com; map:GG7*

## Pratt Gallery

**2400 KETTNER BLVD, DOWNTOWN; 619/236-0211** Some of the artists represented by Doug Pratt do wonderful plein-air works; others interpret the urban landscape in acrylics or oils. Robert Goldman has long contributed his landscapes and cityscapes. Bill Mosley, another local artist and teacher, paints contemporary cityscapes in oil and pastel. He attributes influence and inspiration to the work of Wayne Thiebaud and Richard Diebenkorn. Wade Cline has a penchant for painting foggy mornings, rainy days, and other atmospheric portrayals. *Wed–Sat and by appointment; map:M5*

## Quint Contemporary Art

**7661 GIRARD AVE, LA JOLLA; 858/454-3409** Quint is one of San Diego's oldest galleries, and owner Mark Quint is considered a local authority on issues of contemporary art. The gallery has monthly exhibitions featuring museum-quality contemporary art by internationally recognized and regional artists. *Tues–Sat; www.quintgallery. com; map:JJ7*

## Robson Gallery

**535 4TH AVE, DOWNTOWN; 619/234-7356** Emerging and established artists shown here represent mainly impressionism and realism—from Pam Ingalls-Cox's small "slices of life" on canvas to Teresa Cherney's bronze nudes. The bookstore sells how-to books as well as coffee-table books on the world's great artists. *Tues–Sat and by appointment; www.robsongallery.com; map:O8*

## San Diego Art Institute

**1439 EL PRADO, HOUSE OF CHARM, BALBOA PARK, DOWNTOWN; 619/236-0011** A friend to the emerging artist, the institute hosts a new juried exhibit every five weeks, each with a different guest juror. Exhibitions feature the work of San Diego artists, showcasing a particular artist of special merit. The variety of styles and media include assemblages, mixed media, watercolors, painting, and photography. If the fine art in Balboa Park's museums inspires you to buy, you can stop at the House of Charm and purchase original pieces at reasonable prices. *Tues–Sun; www.sandiego-art.org; map:O5*

### San Diego Watercolor Society Showcase Gallery

**2400 KETTNER BLVD, DOWNTOWN; 619/338-0502** San Diego Watercolor Society's gallery, next to David Zapf on Kettner Boulevard, is the place to shop for watercolors and gouaches. Juried group shows change monthly, and although most of the work is representational, there's a nice variety of styles. The Watercolor Society also sponsors workshops and classes. *Wed–Sat; map:M5*

### Susan Street Fine Art Gallery

**415 S CEDROS AVE, STE 160, SOLANA BEACH; 858/793-4442** One of North County's most prestigious galleries shows the work of talented emerging artists as well as those whose work carries a higher price tag. Look for paintings and prints in classic and more contemporary flavors. The shop is located within the Cedros Design District. *Mon–Sat; susanstreetfineart.com; map:FF7*

### Tasende Gallery

**820 PROSPECT ST, LA JOLLA; 858/454-3691** San Diego's provider of high-end painting and sculpture, Jose Tasende shows modern and contemporary artists of international fame. With an emphasis on large-format sculpture for open spaces, the gallery represents Basque-born Eduardo Chillida, who creates sculpture of steel as well as granite. Other sculptors are England's Lynn Chadwich, who works in bronze, and Niki de Saint Phalle, whose painted polyester sculptures can be seen around San Diego, including on the UCSD campus. Other international talent includes Roberto Matta, the youngest member of Andre Breton's surrealist group, and Mexico's José Luis Cuevas, best known for his pen-and-ink work. So strong is Tasende's international focus that Barbara Weldon's May 1999 show of oils, acrylics, and encaustic paintings represented the first San Diegan showing in the gallery's 20-year history. *Tues–Sat and by appointment; map:JJ7*

# Gardens

San Diego may have originally been a vast, dry wasteland, but designers and developers have consistently scraped away scrubby chaparral and planted tropical landscapes beneath sky-high palms. Even the freeways are edged with bubblegum-pink ice plant, the ubiquitous succulent that turns barren hillsides into vivid fields of delicate blooms. All of San Diego is a garden, which may explain why there are so few public gardens outside Balboa Park. Instead of plotting formal landscapes, San Diegans have always considered the overall scenery. Jacaranda trees shed delicate lavender blossoms along the sidewalks of downtown, Hillcrest, and Mission Valley. Orange trees flavor the air with their sweet scent throughout residential neighborhoods. Startling red poinsettias wave from leggy bushes during the Christmas season—San Diego is one of the country's leading producers of this holiday favorite. Orange and blue bird-of-paradise peers through broad leaves throughout the year. Blue delphiniums, white foxgloves, and rosy hollyhocks peek above daffodils and violet swaths of lobelia in Coronado's front gardens during the annual Flower Show Weekend in April, where homeowners fervently compete for awards.

Agriculture is one of San Diego's leading industries; avocados star in the annual Fallbrook Avocado Festival in North County, while the Grapefruit Queen reigns over the Borrego Springs Grapefruit Festival in the desert. Most major flower and produce shows occur in April and early May. The largest celebration occurs in Carlsbad, where stripes of yellow, red, and white ranunculus buds cover 50 acres at the Flower Fields at Carlsbad Ranch. Encinitas, home to several private commercial nurseries, holds an annual Flower Celebration in early June—a rare opportunity for gardening fanatics to see how the pros grow such gorgeous roses, poinsettias, begonias, and fuchsias. San Diego also has a number of fine commercial plant nurseries that rival any public gardens; see the Shopping chapter for the best.

The following public gardens offer seasonal delights.

### The Flower Fields at Carlsbad Ranch

**PASEO DEL NORTE, OFF I-5 AT PALOMAR RD, CARLSBAD; 760/431-0352** A family flower farm turned tourist attraction, Carlsbad Ranch's natural exhibit, called The Flower Fields, has become one of North County's leading draws in just a decade. Its 50 acres of blooming ranunculus attract considerable attention during April and May, when hillsides are striped with eye-popping red, yellow, and orange blossoms. Historic biplanes and hot-air balloons putter and float over crowds of flower fans; more than 150,000 visitors wander through the gardens during the blossoming season. The ranch also has a walk-of-fame rose test garden, where gardeners can see new varieties in bloom. The ranch's owners come up with new ideas every year to please their ever-growing crowds. Sometimes they plant fields of sunflowers; other times they have artists create floral landscape paintings. The gift shop has a good selection of bulbs and gardening paraphernalia. When the flowers are in full bloom (usually mid-March through May), the ranch is open from 9am to dusk. Admission for adults is $5, $4 for seniors, and $3 for children 3 to 10. *Every day; www.theflowerfields.com; map:CC8*

### Self-Realization Fellowship

**939 2ND ST, ENCINITAS; 760/753-2888** Indian yogi Paramahansa Yogananda (author of *Autobiography of a Yogi*) founded the fellowship in 1920, and created this magical temple and gardens on prime turf above the sea in Encinitas. Visitors can stroll past koi ponds and along the cliffs over the sea, where the yogi began gardens of native plants and trees in 1936. The setting is serene and refreshing. Admission is free. *Tues–Sat 9am–5pm, Sun 11am–5pm; map:8EE*

# Beaches and Parks

Gloriously endowed with one of the most temperate climates in the world, San Diego is the perfect place to explore marvelous beaches and parks. No matter what your fancy—surfing (Tourmaline or Windansea), family (Coronado or Ocean), or hip and happening (Mission or Pacific)—you'll want to check out as many as you can.

Balboa Park, first established in 1868, is queen of the city's park system, with 1,200 acres and more than 12 million visitors a year. While it may be the star, it is by no means the whole show. More than 32,000 acres of developed parks and undeveloped open space serve the citizens of San Diego. Parks range from kid-friendly (Mission Bay/Tecolote Playground) to recreational (Mission Trails Regional Park) to just plain beautiful (Ellen Browning Scripps Park). Watch a sunset from Kellogg

Park, ride your horse at Mission Trails Regional Park, or quietly scout for elusive birds at Mission Bay. For more information about parks or beaches within the city, call 619/221-8900. For information regarding state parks, call 800/777-0369.

Many parks are mentioned in either the Top 25 Attractions or the Neighborhoods sections; be sure to check them out for more details.

## Black's Beach

**2800 TORREY PINES SCENIC DR, AT N TORREY PINES RD, LA JOLLA; 619/221-8900** Black's Beach is the unofficial home to nude sun lovers. Formally unsanctioned yet judicially ignored, nudism prevails at the northernmost 2-mile-long section of sand beneath towering cliffs north of La Jolla. Hang gliders launch their colorful crafts into the updrafts from the glider-port atop the cliffs for a swirling ride over the ocean, where superb swells on the southern end of the beach attract the cream of the surfing crowd. Accessing Black's Beach is a challenge; one obvious way is hiking down the 300-foot-high bluffs. Although there are plenty of strongly worded signs warning people away from the unstable cliffs, scores of people gingerly make their way down every day. A safer approach is to walk along the sand from adjacent beaches to the north and south, but these routes may be obstructed at times by high tides. Although there are no permanent stations at this beach, lifeguards patrol year-round. No rest rooms exist on the beach, nor is there a snack stand or equipment rental establishment in sight. While amenities are absent, the incredible beauty of the spot more than compensates. Free parking is available at the glider-port and at the public lot at La Jolla Shores. There are also 450 pay-parking spaces at Torrey Pines State Beach. *Map:HH7*

## Children's Pool Beach

**850 COAST BLVD, AT JENNER ST, LA JOLLA; 619/221-8900** Safeguarded by a man-made seawall and originally intended as a beach for children and the swimming-impaired, this small beach in La Jolla with its beautiful panoramic view is now domain to a large group of federally protected harbor seals. Deemed unsafe for swimming in 1997 because of high bacterial levels, Children's Pool Beach has long been a political hot potato, pitting people against pinnipeds. Advocates of the seals were delighted when a recent state Coastal Commission vote went their way; the area will remain a reserve, and the chubby, blubbery mammals can stay. It is estimated that 80,000 people a month come to watch the seals. Pupping season is from mid-February through April. Parking is limited; there are no public lots at the beach, and a vacant place on the street is cause for celebration. *Map:JJ7*

## Coronado Municipal Beach

**OCEAN BLVD AT MARINA AVE, CORONADO; 619/522-7342** Your choice of scenery at Coronado Municipal Beach is varied. You can plop your towel down near the east end and enjoy the fabulous Hotel del Coronado as your backdrop (the Travel Channel rated this stretch among the top 10 U.S. beaches in 2002). Or head farther down Ocean Boulevard to the west end of the beach and watch huge airplanes roaring to and from their home at the Naval Air Station at North Island. With 1½ miles of wide shoreline, you are certain to find a patch of sand to call your own. This is a popular place for families to bring their children

## TIDE POOL TANGO

The small animals that inhabit coastal tide pools are some of the most adaptive and tenacious on the planet. Living in an environment that undergoes tidal changes four times a day, these little creatures are the commandants of compromise. At low tide their watery sanctuary disappears, exposing them to the broiling sun, increased salinity, and hungry predators. To survive, mussels collect seawater inside their bodies, then slowly release it to cool by evaporation. Sea anemones fold inward, trapping tiny drops of water to sustain themselves until the flow of water returns. At high tide, they are once again flooded, with rough swirls of seawater threatening to evict them from their homes. Barnacles hold on to rocks for dear life or risk being hurled up on the beach or out to sea. Sea urchins stay put by burrowing their spines deep into the rocks on which they live. There is also a constant threat of being eaten by a neighbor. Clams, scallops, and oysters are the favored dinner of the carnivorous sea star, which in turn makes a fitting snack for a gull or a crow. If this wet, miniature-scale drama sounds interesting, San Diego has several prime spots for front-row viewing. Put on your rubber-soled tennis shoes and head for Bird Rock, La Jolla Cove, and the tide pools located on the western side of Point Loma, near Cabrillo Monument. Birch Aquarium at Scripps (see Top 25 Attractions in this chapter) offers classes on tide-pooling and can provide information on the best times for viewing. Call 858/534-7336 for more information.

*—Susan Humphrey*

during the summer; the waves are gentle and the lifeguards plentiful. There is a ramp to the sand for wheelchairs. Even the canine member of the family is welcome at the most westerly end of the beach, near the Navy enclave. Rover can romp joyously amid the clumps of palm trees on ice-plant-covered dunes or in the waves. Sturdier souls enjoy the chilly beach during winter months; with some luck and a good pair of binoculars directed toward the ocean, you may spot California gray whales migrating south toward Baja California, Mexico. Parking is available on Ocean Boulevard and the residential streets farther inland. *Map:NN5*

### Ellen Browning Scripps Park

1180 COAST BLVD, AT OCEAN ST, LA JOLLA; 619/221-8900 One of San Diego's most beautiful landscapes, Ellen Browning Scripps Park hugs the bluffs overlooking the Pacific Ocean in La Jolla near the cove. Extending from palm-lined Coast Boulevard to a paved walkway paralleling the cliffs, this grassy stretch is a perfect place for a leisurely afternoon picnic or a rousing game of croquet. A gentle breeze on a hot summer day makes for a delightful study hall; students come to read, sprawling beneath gnarled cypress trees. Children crowd into the open-air wooden shelters precipitously perched at the park's edge and cautiously peer down at the waves crashing on the rocks below. Plan a barbecue for a Sunday afternoon when the La Jolla Town Council presents one of its summer Sunday-afternoon concerts (call 858/454-5718 for scheduling information). As always in this area, parking is a headache. Your best bet is a vigilant and slow prowl of the residential zones adjacent to the park, or use one of the pay lots in La Jolla village. *Map:JJ7*

## Embarcadero Marina Park

**END OF KETTNER BLVD, AT HARBOR DR, DOWNTOWN; 619/686-6200** Located between Seaport Village to the north and the San Diego Convention Center to the south, Embarcadero Marina Park is a green haven between bustling crowds. Take a break from a hectic day of shopping at the village or a demanding round of meetings at the center to enjoy a bite to eat while you watch huge ships making their way through San Diego Bay. The view of the San Diego–Coronado Bay Bridge is excellent from here. Be sure to check out the large, black granite sculpture entitled *Morning* by the late Donal Hord, a renowned, San Diego–based artist. It is located on the lawn near the entrance cul-de-sac. The park also features basketball courts, gazebos, and bike and jogging paths. There is a large parking lot at Seaport Village (a purchase at one of the shops gets you two free hours of validated parking) and at the cruise-ship pier. *Map:N8*

## Fiesta Island

**FIESTA ISLAND RD, AT E MISSION BAY DR, MISSION BAY; 619/221-8900** The most undeveloped part of Mission Bay Park, Fiesta Island is a favored launching site for water-sports enthusiasts who roar around in their powerboats or zip past on Jet Skis. It is also one of the rare places in San Diego where Fido can roam without his leash. The annual Over the Line tournament is held here over two weekends in July. Not for the faint of heart, it's a raucous, rowdy softball-type event, with team names of a decidedly ribald nature. Don't bring the children! *Map:LL6*

## Imperial Beach

**SEACOAST DR, AT PALM AVE, IMPERIAL BEACH; 619/423-8328** Meandering along the municipal pier at Imperial Beach, you may encounter an unusual sight suggestive of Robin Hood and his followers. It's not the Merry Men, however, but lighthearted fishermen employing bow and arrow to spear their catch. Upon completion of a safety course sponsored by the city of Imperial Beach, this unusual method of sportfishing is permitted from the 1,500-foot pier. Along with the archers, you will find more conventional anglers vying for barracuda, bat rays, or the more ordinary bass and croaker. No license is required to fish. A major renovation at the foot of the pier in 1999 added picnic tables, a playground, rest rooms, shops, and a large sculpture called *Surfhenge,* designed by La Jolla artist Malcolm Jones. The beach in Imperial Beach (which bills itself as the "Most Southwesterly City in the Continental United States") is long and wide, with 3 miles of surf breaks; three-quarters of a mile is lifeguarded for swimming. Surfing is allowed in designated areas, with an especially fabled break called the Slough. Always check with the lifeguards before splashing into the spray; unfortunately, the greenish blue water is often foul with sewage coming up from Tijuana. The opening of a sewage-treatment plant near the border has cut down on the contamination problem, but it's still a good idea to consult the experts before entering the water. One of the summer highlights is the annual sand castle competition, usually held in late July. Upwards of 200,000 people come to enjoy the weekend of parades, parties, and fabulous creations made from sand. *Map:QQ4*

## Kate Sessions Memorial Park

**SOLEDAD RD, AT LORING ST, PACIFIC BEACH; 858/581-9927** Dedicated in 1957 to San Diego's remarkable gardener extraordinaire and prolific planter of trees, Kate Sessions Memorial Park is a lovely park in the neighborhood of Pacific Beach. People come with their picnic baskets and pooches, as do parents whose children clamber to the top of the rocket-ship slide at the small playground near the bottom of the park. The arboreal collection on the park's 80 acres would do Ms. Sessions proud: clumps of evergreens, giant eucalypti, and hardy pepper trees provide lots of shade on warm summer days. Climb to the top of the grassy slope for a splendid view of San Diego Bay and the Pacific. Summer nights attract fireworks fans, who watch the pyrotechnics exploding from Sea World. Parking here is adequate; finding a spot will not likely be a problem except on the busiest summer weekends. *Map:KK6*

## La Jolla Shores

**8200 CAMINO DEL ORO, LA JOLLA; 619/221-8900** Picture-postcard perfect, La Jolla Shores is what you imagine a beach should be: a mile-long stretch of powdery sand under bright blue skies, crowded with bronzed locals, scads of frolicsome kids, and lissome surfers with bleached-blond hair. The waves here are generally gentle, although children and weak swimmers should be wary of possible rip currents. The tame waves and the shore's gradual declining slope draw scuba divers to formal classes and informal dives. Divers can explore the adjacent San Diego–La Jolla Underwater Ecological Reserve. Scripps Pier and the prestigious Scripps Institute of Oceanography border the north side of the Shores. Small boats, kayaks, and canoes float in the surf at the foot of Avenida de la Playa, the only beachfront boat launch within city limits. A four-wheel-drive vehicle is recommended, as the launch is simply sand. The lifeguard station is at the foot of Calle Frescota, as is the 350-space parking lot teeming with idling autos canvassing for a place to park during the busy summer months. A quarter-mile walkway separates the beach from Kellogg Park, a grassy area lined with tall palms, ideal for picnics, Frisbee tosses, and ogling the mansions on the hillside. Flanking the park are the rest rooms. Bring a sweatshirt and some firewood and stay past sunset; portable containers for beach fires are generally provided during the summer and are available on a first-come, first-served basis. *Map:JJ7*

## Mission Beach

**3141 OCEAN FRONT WALK, AT MISSION BLVD, MISSION BEACH; 619/221-8900** Do you enjoy a mass of humankind, lots of noise, sun and surf, and plenty of people-watching? Then Mission Beach in mid-July may be the place for you. This section of sand between Pacific Beach and the Mission Bay channel entrance is a local favorite. The 12-foot-wide cement boardwalk that parallels the beach is a hotbed of sizzling activity: bikini-clad women race by on Rollerblades; guys in sagging, gravity-defying shorts zoom around on skateboards; and bicyclists pedal past. There is an 8mph speed limit, often ignored. When it's crowded, it's chaos; pay attention as you stroll. Should the frenzied pace of the boardwalk be too much for you, wander toward the southern section of the beach and watch a pickup game of volleyball or a variation of softball called Over the Line. If you forgot your sporting equipment, rental establishments are on hand. Surfing and swimming are both permitted in the ocean, with clearly delineated and enforced zones. There are plenty of lifeguards, rest rooms, shops, and restaurants. There's even a wonderful refurbished wooden roller coaster at Belmont Park at Ventura Place. Alas, the only thing there is never enough of is parking. Try your luck at the public lots on either side of Belmont Park or at the foot of West Mission Bay Drive. *Map:LL7*

## Mount Soledad Natural Park

**INTERSECTION OF LA JOLLA SCENIC DR S AND VIA CAPRI, LA JOLLA; 619/221-8900** Situated on one of the highest points within the city limits, Mount Soledad offers an incredible, panoramic vista of San Diego, from the ocean to the west to the mountains in the east. Situated at the peak of the park is a half-acre, privately maintained war memorial, with a 43-foot white cross and six concentric walls with granite plaques bearing the names of war veterans. The park is open daily 5am–midnight. For $34.50, the city will grant a permit for individuals wishing to have their nuptials in this awe-inspiring setting. *Map:JJ6*

## Ocean Beach

**1950 ABBOTT ST, OCEAN BEACH; 619/221-8900** Ocean Beach has the same free and easy air as the community that shares its name. Wedged between the Ocean Beach Pier to the south and the Mission Bay channel entrance to the north, this city beach exudes a come-join-us attitude; there's always room for one more towel or a couple more toddlers at the shoreline. Summertime finds families, surfers, locals, and camera-toting tourists sharing the wide, sandy seashore. The most northern part of the beach, aptly called Dog Beach, is the only city beach where dogs can run in the surf without a leash. Owners are required to clean up the inevitable canine droppings, but it is still wise to watch where you put your bare feet. South of Dog Beach, buff men and women compete in pickup volleyball games and formal tournaments. Showers and rest rooms are located near the main lifeguard station at 1950 Abbott Street. Lifeguards are on duty year-round at this main tower; summer months bring additional crews to staff seasonal towers set up along the sand. They are kept busy with water rescues, as there is a strong rip current offshore. If you tire of baking on the beach, stroll down the quarter-mile-long Ocean Beach Pier (see Top 25 Attractions). Finding a place to park is a snap at Ocean Beach. There is a 300-car lot off West Point Loma Boulevard and another 110 spaces in the lot near the pier off Newport Avenue. If these are full, you can usually find a spot in the residential areas nearby. *Map:MM6*

## Pacific Beach

**950 GRAND AVE AT OCEAN BLVD, PACIFIC BEACH; 619/221-8900** Three miles of sand teeming with humanity, Pacific Beach is one of San Diego's most popular beaches. With La Jolla bordering the north and Mission Beach to the south, intersected by the enchanting Crystal Pier at Garnet Avenue, it typifies the Southern California beach scene. In the northernmost section, under towering, tan cliffs, is Tourmaline Surfing Beach, its medium-size parking lot full of cars with surf racks. Whether it's wonderfully warm or blustery cold, the surfers are always here, nearly naked in baggy shorts or shivering in wet suits, riding the waves and then rinsing off at the colorfully painted showers at the foot of the parking lot. About a mile south of Tourmaline is Crystal Pier, a public fishing pier and home to the Crystal Pier Hotel. South of the pier are another two miles of Pacific Beach's powdery sand and rolling surf, replete with sunbathers, families with kids, bodysurfers, and boogie boarders. Paralleling the beach is a cement boardwalk, where bicyclists evade joggers and Rollerbladers dodge those on foot. There are rest rooms at Tourmaline Surfing Beach, at the foot of Grand Avenue by the lifeguard station, and at Pacific Beach Drive. The beach is well staffed by lifeguards. Aside from the public parking lot on Tourmaline Street, you're on your own with the street-parking hunt. *Map:KK7*

## Spreckels Park

**601 ORANGE AVE AT 6TH ST, CORONADO; 619/522-7342** This clean, boxy little park in the heart of Coronado exudes a feeling of America gone by, with its old-fashioned gazebo, luxuriant green lawns, and spreading shade trees. It's the center of Coronado's family gatherings, much like a central plaza in a Mexican village. Kids gather at the swing sets, parents sip cocktails (served from the disguise of thermoses) at picnic tables, and artists set up their easels in view of memorable scenes. The park is headquarters for frequent art and garden shows. Coronado Promenade Concerts has been putting on shows here for 25 years, with music ranging from jazz to the sounds of the U.S. Navy Concert Band. The series begins in June and runs through August, Sunday evenings at 6pm. Call 619/437-8788 for more information. *Map:NN5*

## Tidelands Park

**GLORIETTA BLVD AT 4TH ST, CORONADO; 619/686-6200** Under the jurisdiction of the Port of San Diego, this 22-acre park along San Diego Bay and under the Coronado Bay Bridge has recreational fields, play areas for the kiddies, a recently opened skate park (admission is charged), and a soft sand shore where boaters stash their rafts and rowboats while collecting supplies onshore. A bike path runs under the Coronado Bay Bridge to the edge of the golf course. The Ferry Landing, a collection of shops, restaurants, and sports-rental stands, sits just north of the beach; mainlanders can catch the ferry from downtown and be on the beach in just minutes. Parking is free, but often scarce. *Map:NN5*

## Torrey Pines State Beach

**12600 N TORREY PINES RD, LA JOLLA; 858/755-2063** Torrey Pines State Beach has 4½ miles of shoreline, stretching from Del Mar past the marshy Los Peñasquitos Lagoon to the lofty sandstone cliffs of Torrey Pines Mesa. Crowning the cliffs like a jewel is the Torrey Pines State Reserve. During the cooler winter months, this beach is popular with surfers, especially when the swell arrives in good form from the south. Sun lovers jam the beach during the warmer months, and picnic baskets crammed with goodies dot the tables near the North Torrey Pines Road entrance. The rest rooms and showers are located here too; take the opportunity to rinse off those sandy children before hopping in the car for the ride home. State lifeguards keep vigil year-round. A large parking lot at the north end of the beach will meet your parking needs for a $2 fee. A smaller lot can be found off Carmel Valley Road. Parking on North Torrey Pines Road is free but hard to acquire. *Map:HH7*

## Windansea Beach

**6800 NEPTUNE PL, LA JOLLA; 619/221-8900** A Southern California surfing classic, Windansea Beach in La Jolla is for serious board jockeys only. Waves here tend to be bigger than those at other beaches in the area, and an underwater reef makes them break hard at the shore; entrance to the ocean should be accomplished with caution. Local surfers have a reputation for thinly veiled inhospitality toward newcomers who don't know their curls; those who can't appreciate their way around a "left shoulder" might want to try a less challenging surfing spot out of the way of the pros. If you just want to watch, set your beach chair on one of the large sandstone rocks that form much of the shore. Check out the thatched hut built on the sand and lovingly maintained by the Windansea Surf Club. One fully expects to see Frankie Avalon and Annette Funicello snuggling towel to towel beneath the palm fronds. Lifeguards are on duty in the summer but not necessarily in the winter; call to find out the staffing schedule. Other than the lifeguards, this beach is au naturel, with no showers or rest rooms. There is one small parking lot, or you can try your luck on Neptune Place. *Map:JJ7*

# Organized Tours

To capture the true spirit of San Diego, start your visit in that wonderful microcosm, Balboa Park. Free tours encompassing history, architecture, theater, and natural attractions are available; whether you're an avid birder or a culture buff, you'll find a tour geared to your tastes. The **COMMITTEE OF 100**, a nonprofit organization devoted to preserving the Spanish colonial architecture in Balboa Park, gives one-hour tours on the first Wednesday of each month at 9:30am; call 619/223-6566 for more information. For the thespian-minded, the **GLOBE THEATRES** offers a behind-the-scenes perusal of its three stages, as well as a glimpse into the costume shop and craft areas. Tours are given most Saturdays and Sundays at 10:30am and cost $3 for adults, $1 for children; call 619/231-1941 for information. If the great outdoors calls, join a **NATURAL HISTORY MUSEUM'S CANYONEERS** nature walk. Volunteer naturalists trained in local flora, fauna, and geology lead groups through San Diego's diverse habitats, including mountain, canyon, and desert terrains. The walks range from 1½ to 6 hours long. Call 619/232-3821, ext. 7 for scheduling information.

## SPECIAL TOURS

The military is a major presence in San Diego, with Navy and Marine facilities and personnel; some interesting and informative public tours are often available. **CAMP PENDLETON** in Oceanside, the Marine Corps' largest amphibious assault training facility, offers a self-guided driving tour daily from 8am to 5pm. Visitors show up at the gate with proof of insurance, registration, and a valid driver's license and are allowed to motor through the camp. (At press time, this tour option was not available due to heightened security; call 760/725-5727 to check the status.) A more up-close tour is available on the second Tuesday and fourth Thursday of every month, with minimum 60-day advance reservations required for groups of 25 or more; call for information.

Host ships offer tours of **NAVY VESSELS** at the Broadway Pier and also at the 32nd Street Pier. Tours are suspended during times of international conflict; call the Navy Public Affairs Office at 619/532-1430 to find out if tours are available.

## ARCO Training Center

**2800 OLYMPIC PKWY, CHULA VISTA; 619/656-1500** Sports enthusiasts enjoy visiting the ARCO Olympic Training Center, where up to 60 athletes live on-site and many more have access to the facilities. The one-hour guided tour begins with a short video, followed by a walk through the state-of-the-art center. Visitors watch athletes training on the 400-meter track, the world-class field hockey and soccer fields, and the largest permanent archery range in North America. Tours are offered every day, Monday through Friday from 10am to 4pm, Saturday from 9am to 4pm, Sunday 11am to 4pm; hours vary with the season. Groups of 10 or more must make reservations four weeks in advance. *www.olympic-usa.org; map:OO2* &

## AIR TOURS

### Aviation Adventures, Ltd.

**2160 PALOMAR AIRPORT RD, CARLSBAD; 800/759-5667** Operating from the McClellan-Palomar Airport, this company offers aerial tours over San Diego's coastline and some of the more interesting sights inland. A 30-minute flight takes you down the coast from Carlsbad to Del Mar, then inland for a swoop over the opulent mansions of Rancho Santa Fe; another, called the Sunset Snuggler, takes you up an hour before sunset. As the pilot increases altitude you can watch the sun set over and over. If you like stomach-churning aeronautics, the Red Baron Thrill Ride provides a one-hour mock combat adventure. Prices vary, but range from about $200 to $500. *www.barnstorming.com; map:CC8*

### Civic Helicopters

**192H PALOMAR AIRPORT RD, CARLSBAD; 760/438-0451** This company, located at the McClellan-Palomar Airport, offers helicopter tours of the area starting at $100 per person for a half-hour flight; customized tours are available. *www.civic helicopters.com; map:CC8*

## BOAT TOURS

### Bahia Sternwheelers

**998 W MISSION BAY DR, MISSION BAY; 858/539-7779** A Victorian-style sternwheeler, the *Bahia Belle* features an open-air upper deck and two interior decks with oak walls, etched glass, and deep red curtains. Live music and a dance floor add to the entertainment as the paddle wheeler churns through Mission Bay on Friday and Saturday evenings throughout the year. Wednesday and Thursday tours are added during the summer. Call for exact departure times. Tickets cost $6 for adults, $3 for children. *www.sternwheelers.com; map:LL6*

## Classic Sailing Adventures

**2051 SHELTER ISLAND DR, DOWNTOWN; 619/224-0800** Various boating experiences are offered aboard a 38-foot sailboat, the *Soul Diversion,* with a six-passenger maximum. The afternoon cruise from 1pm to 5pm, sunset champagne cruise from 5:30pm to 7:30pm, and seasonal whale-watching expeditions cost $50 per person. The boat is anchored at the Shelter Island Marina at the Island Palms Hotel. *www.classicsailingadventures.com; map:F7*

## Hornblower Cruises & Events

**1066 N HARBOR DR, DOWNTOWN; 619/686-8700** Nightly dinner and dancing as well as a Sunday Champagne brunch are offered aboard Hornblower's fleet of ships. Cruise the harbor while the chefs prepare your meal, then dance belowdecks or go up top to watch the twinkling lights of the city drifting by. Nightly cruises are 7pm to 10pm and cost $56.50 per person. The Sunday brunch cruise is 11am to 1pm and is $35.50 per person. One- and two-hour harbor tours and whale-watching expeditions are also available. *www.hornblower.com; map:M7*

## San Diego Harbor Excursion

**1050 N HARBOR DR, DOWNTOWN; 619/234-4111 OR 800/442-7847** One- and two-hour harbor tours are available daily. Mini cruise ships take you past huge Navy ships and up to Cabrillo Monument; the longer tour continues past Harbor and Shelter Islands to the San Diego–Coronado Bridge. Departure times are seasonal; call for a schedule. The one-hour tour is $13 for adults, $6.50 for ages 4 to 12; the longer cruise costs $18 for adults and $9 for the kids. Whale-watching expeditions are also available during the gray whales' migration south (December through April). *www.sdhe.com; map:M7*

## MOTOR TOURS

### Old Town Trolley Tours of San Diego

**2115 KURTZ ST, OLD TOWN; 619/298-8687** Tootling all over the city, these open-air red and green motorized trolleys are driven by jocular conductors who provide historical anecdotes on a two-hour jaunt. Passengers can depart the trolley at eight stops for a more thorough investigation, then reboard the next time a trolley rolls by. Trolleys come by each stop every 30 minutes, starting at 9am and ending in early evening; hours vary with the season. Locals who pay for the tour once annually are eligible for a Hometown Pass allowing them to ride free with a paying passenger. Tickets are $24 for an adult, $12 for ages 4 to 12, and free for children 3 and under. *www.trolleytours.com; map:J3*

### Seal Tours

**KETTNER BLVD AT HARBOR DR, SEAPORT VILLAGE; 619/298-8687** A bit of a motor tour, a bit of a water tour, the San Diego Seal excursion is a fun combination of both. Seating 47 people, the amphibious *Hydra-Terra* starts its voyage at Seaport Village, then makes its way to Mission Bay, where it splashes into the water for a scenic cruise. Venturing back to land, you're off to San Diego Bay for a narrated tour of that watery locale. The trip takes about 90 minutes (depending on traffic and wave conditions) and costs $24 for adults and $12 for children 4 to 12. *www.sealtours.com; map:M8*

## WALKING TOURS

### Art Tours

**5701 LA JOLLA BLVD, LA JOLLA; 858/459-5922** For a different perspective on San Diego's scenery, join a five-hour art class and create your own vision of San Diego with guidance from a professional artist. Art Tours provides all the supplies and a gourmet lunch. Budding artists meet at visually appealing spots at Balboa Park, Presidio Park, or La Jolla Cove, among others. The cost is $185 per painter. Call for reservations. *Map:JJ7*

### Coronado Walking Tour

**1110 ISABELLA AVE, CORONADO; 619/435-5993** To visit some of Coronado's most interesting historical sites, join the Coronado Walking Tour for a 90-minute stroll that includes the Glorietta Bay Inn (former mansion of sugar baron J. D. Spreckels), the "Hotel Del," and the Cottage of the Duchess of Windsor. Tours leave Tuesday, Thursday, and Saturday at 11am from the Glorietta Bay Inn and cost $8. Call 619/435-5993 for more information. *Map:NN5*

### Gaslamp Quarter Historical Foundation

**410 ISLAND AVE, DOWNTOWN; 619/233-4692** Headquartered in the William Heath Davis House, this nonprofit corporation promotes the historic and cultural development of downtown's 16-block Gaslamp Quarter, listed on the National Register of Historic Places. The organization offers two-hour tours, rain or shine, through a portion of the restored district every Saturday at 11am; cost is $8. *Map:N8*

### Urban Safaris

**2282 CAMINITO PAJARITO #154, OCEAN BEACH; 619/944-9255** Walking tours in eight of San Diego's unique neighborhoods are conducted by Patty Fares, a 25-year resident of San Diego and travel and tourism instructor at a local community college. The groups are limited to 10 people and usually begin at an area coffee shop; the areas trodden are Ocean Beach, Point Loma, Hillcrest, the Gaslamp, Bankers Hill, East Village, South Park, and University Heights. The jaunts are scheduled for Saturday mornings from 10am to noon. Advance reservations are required and the cost is $10 per person. Special tours for groups or small parties can be arranged during the week. *urbansafaris@yahoo.com; www.walkingtoursofsandiego.com; map:E3*

### Walkabout International

**835 5TH AVE, RM 407, DOWNTOWN; 619/231-7463** Volunteer guides conduct Walkabout International tours, which include everything from a leisurely loop around Mission Bay to a hardy hike along the trails of Palomar Mountain. Tours are conducted morning, noon, and night and offer enough variety to please walkers of all persuasions and abilities. Call for schedules and tour descriptions. *Map:O7*

# SHOPPING

# SHOPPING

We've got everything from Armani suits to zories (aka flip-flop sandals) up for grabs in San Diego. The malls and neighborhoods listed below cover most needs, though some of the best shops are scattered to the far ends of the county. To shop like a master, study your options, map your trail, and combine touring with splurging. To help along the way, see the Neighborhoods section in the Exploring chapter. We've included San Diego's one-of-a-kind, family, and quirky businesses, eschewing most chains. You can find all the big names here—Home Depot, Tower Records, Tiffany, Godiva, Borders Books—but you'll be able to stumble upon them on your own. The shops listed here are harder to find, and often more interesting.

## Neighborhoods and Malls

### DOWNTOWN SAN DIEGO

It's easy to satisfy most of your shopping demands within the confines of downtown and come up with a few rare finds. **SEAPORT VILLAGE** displays kites and porch swings (great vacation mementos); **WESTFIELD SHOPPINGTOWN HORTON PLAZA** runs the gamut from Disney characters to serious designer boutiques; the **GASLAMP DISTRICT** presents a mélange of specialty shops and galleries. For more information about these three shopping areas, see Top 25 Attractions in the Exploring chapter.

### HISTORIC DISTRICTS

A theme-park ambiance prevails amid adobe cottages and turn-of-the-century barns in **OLD TOWN** and **BAZAAR DEL MUNDO** (see Top 25 Attractions in the Exploring chapter).

### NEIGHBORHOODS

Trendy shops line the main streets in **HILLCREST,** San Diego's alternative-lifestyle neighborhood. Couples gay and straight browse hand in hand while seeking the perfect objets d'art for their stylish flats. The best shops are on Fourth and Fifth between Pennsylvania and University; park in a lot on University or Washington. Nearby **MISSION HILLS** is far more refined, with an emphasis on French country furnishings for the chic elite. Small antique, book, and video shops line **UNIVERSITY AVENUE** and **ADAMS AVENUE** from Hillcrest to Kensington, long an outpost for those who love historic homes buried in jacaranda blossoms.

The beach cities offer a whole different perspective, featuring bikinis, sunglasses, surfboards, and aloha shirts. **CORONADO** favors refined bookshops, florists, high-end sportswear boutiques, and small gift purveyors along Orange Avenue. The village neighborhood of downtown **LA JOLLA,** the grande dame of style, is practically an open-air mall. Virtually all major international designers are featured in boutiques and galleries, and window-shopping is a lifestyle among locals and guests. Despite the rather snobbish air in the streets, the village also has garnered its fair share of chain stores, from Victoria's Secret to the Gap. Prospect and Girard are the hottest shopping strips; look for one-of-a-kind gift shops on the side streets.

Between the two stylish beaches lie the commoners' enclaves, each with a distinct character. **OCEAN BEACH** has a succession of antique malls jam-packed with collectibles all along Newport Avenue. Swimsuits, bikes, water toys, and beach togs predominate in shops along Mission Boulevard in **MISSION BEACH**. Chain stores like Pier One and Trader Joe's sit beside tattoo parlors, costume and vintage clothing shops, and used-furniture havens on Garnet Avenue in **PACIFIC BEACH**.

## SHOPPING DISTRICTS

Being a tourist town, San Diego has an abundance of shopping/dining/entertainment theme parks filled with specialty shops. **VILLAGE HILLCREST** (Washington St and 5th Ave, Uptown; map:N2) specializes in small boutiques; the nearby **UPTOWN DISTRICT** (University Ave between Washington and Richmond Sts, Uptown; map:O2) has large grocery stores and some specialty shops. **DEL MAR PLAZA** (1555 Camino Del Mar, Del Mar; map:GG7) is beyond upscale, with excellent galleries, home furnishings shops, and clothing boutiques.

## MALLS

Nothing compares with downtown's **WESTFIELD SHOPPINGTOWN HORTON PLAZA** (Broadway at 4th Ave, downtown; map:N7; see Top 25 Attractions in the Exploring chapter) when it comes to sheer architectural audacity and state-of-the-art shopping. But San Diego's more traditional malls have taken giant strides to become hip, user-friendly, and entrancing. **FASHION VALLEY** (707 Friars Rd, Mission Valley; 619/688-9113; map:LL5) has the best Nordstrom in town, along with great branches of Gap, Aveda, Crate and Barrel, Pottery Barn, and Godiva. **WESTFIELD SHOPPINGTOWN MISSION VALLEY** (1640 Camino del Rio N, Mission Valley; 619/296-6375; map:LL4) is more mid-brow, with giant branches of Nordstrom Rack, Macy's, and a brand-new Target store. Its movie-theater complex is a big draw, as are several trendy restaurants. The Golden Triangle and inland La Jolla area have **WESTFIELD SHOPPINGTOWN UTC** (4525 La Jolla Village Dr; 858/546-8858; map:JJ7) and **LA JOLLA VILLAGE SQUARE** (8657 Villa La Jolla Dr; 858/455-7550; map:JJ7).

# Shops from A to Z

## ANTIQUES

### The Antique Radio Store

**8280 CLAIREMONT MESA BLVD, STE 114, CLAIREMONT; 858/268-4155** Tucked into a small corner of a nondescript shopping center, this store has more than 100 styles of old radios for sale. Most have been reconditioned and all work. A Bakelite radio from the 1940s sells for about $75. *Mon, Wed evenings, all day Sat; antrad@ juno.com; map:JJ5*

### Architectural Salvage of San Diego

**1971 INDIA ST, MIDDLETOWN; 619/696-1313** With a background in art and a building contractor father, native San Diegan Elizabeth Scalice had the entrepreneurial savvy to open this fabulous storehouse of vintage and antique building materials in 1996. Since then it has grown in both size and popularity as San Diegans search for leaded glass, claw-foot bathtubs, decorative molding, chandeliers, and old heater grates. There are glass building blocks from the 1940s and '50s and a bucket of rusty square nails from the 1800s. It's worth a trip just to admire the beautiful collection of doorknobs. *Every day; map:M6*

## The Corner Stone

**7501 GIRARD AVE, LA JOLLA; 858/456-7517** Described as purveyors of "shabby chic," the owners of this airy boutique sell a unique mix of primitive, rustic, and cottage furniture and garden pieces. You'll find trundle tables that have been repainted and then distressed, and plenty of dressers, cabinets, and seating from the '40s and '50s. Also on hand are antique and vintage garden accessories, Bauer bowls, and other small period pieces. The inventory includes pieces from England, France, and beyond. *Every day; map:JJ7*

## D. D. Allen Antiques

**7728 FAY AVE, LA JOLLA; 858/454-8708** With a strong reputation throughout the antiques community, this small store has 18th- to 20th-century furniture, linens, porcelain, and decorative art. The authenticity of each piece is guaranteed. Some vintage wares are also for sale. *Every day; www.ddallen.com; map:JJ7*

## Glorious Antiques

**7643 GIRARD AVE, LA JOLLA; 858/459-2222** This not-for-profit store is one of the few charity outfits that sells antiques, including estate jewelry, linens, and Asian and European collectibles. The beneficiaries of sales are the SPCA and the San Diego Humane Society, making this a worthwhile place to spend your cash. *Mon–Sat; map:JJ7*

## JP and Company

**7844 HERSCHEL AVE, LA JOLLA; 858/456-7688** Selling both reproductions and antique furnishings and accessories on consignment and outright, this enormous shop has a warehouse feel. It's fun to wander among the enormous cast-metal gorillas and alligators that share the floor with water-buffalo leather couches, animal-print settees, and hassocks, lighting, and accessories. Large-format framed art hangs on the wall. *Every day; map:JJ7*

## King and Company

**7470 GIRARD AVE, LA JOLLA; 858/454-1504** Owner Candace King and her associates stock a varied selection of English, American, and Continental furniture and accessories in a warm, unpretentious atmosphere. This long, deep store contains mainly antique furniture and decorative art from the 1700s to early 1900s. The fact that the associates are principally designers and artists themselves makes this a favorite stop for the county's interior design mavens. King and Company also offers home consultations. *Mon–Sat; map:JJ7*

## Ocean Beach Antiques Mall / Empire Enterprise

**4878 NEWPORT AVE, OCEAN BEACH; 619/223-6170; 619/224-9216** Of Ocean Beach's many antique stores along Newport Avenue, this one is airy and well organized, with calming music in the background. It's a great place for gift shopping, with a large selection of jewelry and porcelain. The majority of the items are "smalls," including household and kitchen accessories. Within the Ocean Beach Antiques Mall you'll also find **EMPIRE ENTERPRISE**. Friendly owner Ken Freeman is both super-knowledgeable and generous with his time. The former elementary school teacher has the ability to educate without making you feel dim. The shop specializes in old ivory pieces, vintage gold and silver jewelry, and sterling silver hollowware. *Every day (OB Antiques Mall), Tues–Sun (Empire Enterprise); map:B3*

### Pied-à-Terre

**7645 GIRARD AVE, LA JOLLA; 858/456-4433** Owner Javid Nazarian has been collecting for more than 15 years. Treasure hunters will love searching through the overwhelming jumble of 17th- to 19th-century pieces, although claustrophobes may need to dash outside occasionally for air. This La Jolla shop's name is French for "second home," or "where your foot rests on the earth." In the spirit of decorating a cozy pied-à-terre, the store has a good mix of lighting, indoor and outdoor furniture, and tchotchkes, mainly Oriental and European. *Mon–Sat; map:JJ7*

### Rusty Spokes Vintage Bicycles

**1344 GARNET AVE, PACIFIC BEACH; 858/581-1931** Rusty Spokes specializes in antique and vintage push-bikes and motorbikes from as far back as the 19th century. If you can't justify buying an unrestored Pope Columbia shaft-drive bike for $3,000, or another of the really outrageous antique beauties, you can have your cherished but dilapidated Elgin or Schwinn refurbished and consider it a sound investment. *Tues–Sun; www.rustyspokes.com; map: KK7*

## APPAREL

### Ariana

**2754 CALHOUN ST, BAZAAR DEL MUNDO, OLD TOWN; 619/296-4989** This eclectic store sells bold and colorful women's styles with an ethnic flair. Southwest designs are popular, but you're just as likely to find handcrafted dresses from Indonesia or Europe. Hand-painted silks are a specialty as well. The prices are surprisingly reasonable. Don't miss Ariana's Bargain Bazaar downstairs, where you can find deals from several of the Bazaar's shops. *Every day; map:J2*

### The Ascot Shop

**7750 GIRARD AVE, LA JOLLA; 858/454-4222** As the name implies, this iconic La Jolla men's clothing store features traditional and elegant wear. Labels such as Hickey-Freeman and Talbot are featured. But there's more than traditional knitwear; the store stocks everything from socks and underwear to suits and ties and has an in-house tailor, making this a perfect spot for one-stop shopping. *Mon–Sat; map:JJ7*

### Atomic Trading Company

**1036 GARNET AVE, PACIFIC BEACH; 858/272-8822** Owner Eric Kramer describes the store's offerings as "futuristic sport utilitarian." That translates to sporty styles with big pockets for the happening Gen-Xer. Wild plastic light fixtures help give the

## DESIGNER SHOPPING

What began as a light-industry neighborhood hidden beside the railroad tracks in Solana Beach has become one of Southern California's premier design districts. The **CEDROS DESIGN DISTRICT** is the offspring of a neighborhood association of merchants who breathed new life into a quarter-mile section of South Cedros Avenue. The district's gateway (signaled by arching signs over the roadway) lies at Lomas Santa Fe Drive, one block east of the main coast route, Highway 101.

Attracted by low rents in a block-long Quonset-like building and by light-filled spaces inside a 1950s moderne-style electronics factory, the bohemian fringe moved in during the 1980s. Artists, furniture and antique dealers, importers, and high-end gift retailers have now completely taken over the neighborhood. Shedding its blue-collar architectural origins, Cedros Design District has grown into a hip, attractive, and remarkably pedestrian-friendly neighborhood where shoppers stroll beneath vine-covered trellises, wander from shop to shop, and pause to sip coffee and nibble lemon-pecan cookies on the patio of **CAFE ZINC** (132 S Cedros Ave; 858/793-5436) beneath umbrella-like pepper trees. Allow yourself at least two hours to visit some of the district's highlights, including **KERN & CO.** (858/792-7722), with its Indonesian-made furniture and other designer finds; **ADVENTURE 16** (858/755-7662), offering expedition-quality outdoor equipment and clothing; **BIRDCAGE** (858/793-6262), for casual-chic gifts and decor; and, anchoring it all, the **BELLY UP TAVERN** (143 S Cedros Ave; 858/481-9022), which has brought headliner bands into town since 1975, when the tavern pioneered the district's makeover. (All are located in the neighborhood's longest building at 142 S Cedros Avenue.) On the east side of the street, don't miss **CASSIDY WEST** (112 S Cedros Ave; 858/755-2728), for Southwest furnishings, and **TRIOS GALLERY** (130 S Cedros Ave; 858/793-6040), one of the county's best showcases for fine arts, crafts, and jewelry.

Although not much bigger than a large closet, nearby **MISTRAL LA COMPAGNIE DE PROVENCE** (146 S Cedros Ave; 858/755-3613) packs every inch of its shop with soaps, oils, and other bathing paraphernalia, all imported from southern France. **THE ANTIQUE WAREHOUSE** (212 S Cedros Ave; 858/755-5156) fits dozens of small dealers' booths into a tidy mall of collectibles, while **SOLO** (307 S Cedros Ave; 858/794-9016) features multiple independent importers of new crafts and furnishings from Mexico, Africa, Indonesia, and Europe. **CEDROS GARDENS** (330 S Cedros Ave; 858/792-8640) is a fine little nursery and more—step inside to browse their garden gifts.

—Peter Jensen

store a retro look. Some of the nostalgic styles are kitschy, with plenty of references to the '50s and '60s, but it's not novelty wear. Kramer says he aims for "cool and different cuts." Atomic also has the footwear and hip glasses to complete the perfect club-hopping ensemble. *Every day; map:KK7*

## Cream of the Crop

**4683 CASS ST, PACIFIC BEACH; 858/272-6601** Fashionistas on a budget will love this resale boutique that offers an ever-changing selection of women's clothing and accessories. Finds here might include purses from Chanel, Louis Vuitton, and Dooney & Bourke; cocktail dresses from top designers; vintage costume jewelry; and new-looking leather jackets and shoes. *Every day; map: KK7*

## Encore of La Jolla

**7655 GIRARD AVE, LA JOLLA; 858/454-7540** You'd never guess this is a used clothing store; the atmosphere is classic Beverly Hills boutique. But instead of castoffs, it specializes in gently used top designer labels for men and women, including Armani, Chanel, and Versace. There is a plentiful selection of contemporary men's suits. If you're lucky, you'll find heavily discounted Prada bags and Ferragamo shoes. *Every day; map:JJ7*

## Nicole Miller

**1275 PROSPECT AVE, LA JOLLA; 858/454-3434** When La Jolla's society prepares to gather, this is where the women go to dress. Miller, the New York–based high-end designer, specializes in cocktail dresses and evening wear, although many rave about her sportswear too. For something different, check out her men's silk novelty ties. *Every day; map:JJ7*

## Pilar's Beachwear

**3745 MISSION BLVD, MISSION BEACH; 858/488-3056** California bikini styles tend to be a bit more conservative than the daring down-to-there ones on the Caribbean or French Riviera. Pilar's offers a full line of the latest and hottest SoCal designs, as well as many of the big-name international lines such as Oscar de la Renta. It also goes beyond the latest waif-wear to offer a wide variety of sizes. Mission Beach can get crowded, but parking is available in the back. *Every day; map:LL7*

## Ron Stuart Men's Clothing

**1110 5TH AVE, HILLCREST; 619/232-8850** In the downtown area, this well-stocked men's store offers stylish wear for both an afternoon at the country club and an evening dinner party. It focuses on the European styles of such designers as Joseph Abboud and Jhane Barnes, but you can also go more traditional with Chequers. Best of all, there's a tailor on-site for fashion emergencies. *Mon–Sat; map:N7*

# BAKERIES

## A La Française

**4029 GOLDFINCH ST, MISSION HILLS; 619/294-4425** If you're looking for a quiet spot to pick up a flaky croissant and peruse *Le Monde*, look no more. Nestled in a corner a block off Mission Hills' main drag, in the heart of a nice little antiques enclave, the shop has a small outside patio that captures the morning sun. The fresh breads, pastries, and strong coffee keep people coming back; so does the array of European desserts. *Every day; map:M2*

## Baked by Etta

**3085 REYNARD WY, MIDDLETOWN; 619/293-7650** The unassuming exterior of this small bakery conceals a wonderland of home-style desserts inside. Etta Miller is a charming hostess, and she's more than willing to give you a personal tour of her fresh-baked treats. Chocolate meltaways, sugar-free apple turnovers, low-fat (and delicious) brownies, and cappuccino caramel cheesecake are among her specialties. During the holidays she prepares special Christmas-tree cookies and cakes, and she fashions gorgeous custom-made wedding cakes. *Mon–Fri; map:L3*

## Bread & Cie

**350 UNIVERSITY AVE, HILLCREST; 619/683-9322** Owner Charles Kaufman toured Europe in search of the perfect bread before opening this business, and his legwork shows: the beauties baked here taste as divine as they look. Each day 12 to 15 types are baked fresh, including such exotic flavors as rosemary olive oil, kalamata olive, and jalapeño cheese. Buy loaves to go, or settle into the cafe for a sandwich, a caffè latte, and one of the bakery's fabulous Paradise bars for dessert. *Every day; map:N2*

## European Cake Gallery

**3661 VOLTAIRE ST, POINT LOMA; 619/222-3377** Longtime Point Loma residents rave about this old-world bakery, which specializes in special cakes for special occasions. The Swiss Black Forest cake is one of the most popular, along with the German chocolate and carrot cakes. During the holidays, try the special mouthwatering stollen. *Wed–Sat; map:E4*

## Grove Pastry Shop

**3308 MAIN ST, LEMON GROVE; 619/466-3277** San Diegans have been buying birthday and wedding cakes here since 1953. The whipped-cream icing alone is worth the drive to this inland community about 15 minutes from downtown. *Mon–Sat; map:MM2*

## Homie's Cinnamon Rolls

**735 SANTA CLARA PL, MISSION BEACH; 858/488-2354** From Awesome Apple and Pecan Pleasure to the original Homie's Cinnamon Rolls, these buns are downright addictive. Outsize, wonderfully fragrant, and packed with flavor (and, no doubt, calories), these fresh-baked rolls get our vote for the best in San Diego. Take a batch home, or enjoy one with coffee on the small patio in front of the bakery. *Every day; map: LL7*

## Karen Krasne's Extraordinary Desserts

 **2929 5TH AVE, MIDDLETOWN; 619/294-7001** Sure, a slice of cake can run $3 or more, but price be damned: Krasne bakes up the best, and prettiest, desserts in town. Tortes, tarts, even simple oatmeal cookies and lemon bars are made from the finest ingredients. Forget taking wine to your host's dinner; pick up one of these babies and you'll be swamped with invites forevermore. *Every day; info@extraordinarydesserts.com; www.extraordinarydesserts.com; map:N4*

## Michele Coulon Dessertier

**7556 FAY AVE, LA JOLLA; 858/456-5098** For years, pastry chef Michele Coulon supplied desserts to some of the finest restaurants in town. Now she's opened her own bakery, and her signature cakes and confections are available to the public. Everything she bakes is swoon-worthy, but top picks here are the rum walnut torte, white chocolate mousse cake, and anything made with Belgian chocolate. Custom orders are available. In addition to desserts, Coulon and her son prepare a tempting selection of salads, breakfast pastries, soups, and light entrees that can be savored inside the cozy bakery or on the tree-lined patio out front. *Mon–Sat; www.dessertier.com; map: JJ7*

## Solunto Baking Company

**1643 INDIA ST, MIDDLETOWN; 619/233-3506** Italian delis all over the city buy their bread from this old-time bakery in Little Italy. Regulars stop by several times a week for that same bread as well as deli sandwiches, cannoli, and a huge variety of Italian cookies. *Mon–Sat; map: M6*

# BODY CARE

## AVEDA LIFESTYLE STORE

**7007 FRIARS RD, FASHION VALLEY CENTER, MISSION VALLEY; 619/220-8518** Proudly eschewing nonrenewable resources, Aveda makes beauty products with organically grown herbs and botanicals. One of the two perfume lines was developed to coincide with and stimulate the body's seven chakras. The saleswomen will help you blend your own fragrance, which can then be mixed into a full line of hair, body care, and beauty products. *Every day; www.aveda.com; map:LL5*

## La Compagnie de Provence

**3870 5TH AVE, HILLCREST; 619/295-8322** Owner Pierre Monnoyer's one-of-a-kind body and fragrance store specializes in bath and body products from the south of France. His suppliers are mainly family-owned businesses from Provence, such as Molinard, which has been fabricating natural soaps since 1849, and Fragonard, a beauty soap maker since 1900. Monnoyer also sells candles, tablecloths, and handmade ceramics from southern France. *Every day; www.frenchbeautystore.com; map:N2*

## Sephora

**4545 LA JOLLA VILLAGE DR, STE 16C, UNIVERSITY TOWNE CENTRE, GOLDEN TRIANGLE; 858/457-1983 / 7007 FRIARS RD, STE 314, FASHION VALLEY CENTER, MISSION VALLEY; 619/220-0771** A French company with retail stores around the world, Sephora now has two branches in San Diego. Its sales techniques are low pressure and hands-on. In addition to multinationals such as Estée Lauder and Lancôme, Sephora sells its own line of cosmetics, as well as niche brands often unavailable outside their normal distribution areas. *Every day; www.sephora.com; map:JJ6*

## U.S. House Apothecary and Soap Shop

**2765 SAN DIEGO AVE, OLD TOWN; 619/574-1115** What at first glance appears to be a cutesy soap shop in historical Old Town is, on closer inspection, a fabulous apothecary. Owners Mike and Jeri Packard create all of their own products from scratch, including dozens of scented soaps and creams and more than a dozen varieties of Epsom salts. Certified aestheticians are on staff to suggest products compatible with your skin or for specific problems. Don't forget to sniff the herbal pillows in the back room, some of which are meant to be microwaved. *Every day; www.ritchartoils.com; map:I1*

# BOOKS AND PERIODICALS

## Barnes & Noble Booksellers

**7610 HAZARD CENTER DR, MISSION VALLEY (AND BRANCHES); 619/220-0175** Yes, B&N is one of the country's largest booksellers and the bane of small shops. But it does have an astounding selection of titles in a comfortable setting with plenty of tables and chairs for browsers. Book signings are held at all branches; look for the big-name authors here. *Every day; www.barnesandnoble.com; map:LL4*

## Bay Books

**1029 ORANGE AVE, CORONADO; 619/435-0070** Don't think about stopping by this entrancing shop unless you have time to spare. The selection of travel tomes, best-sellers, and Spanish-language novels is overwhelming. Fortunately, the staff is beyond helpful and customers are welcome to browse through their selections in the quiet reading room. Author signings are held regularly. *Every day; bay books@pacbell.net; www.baybookscoronado.com; map:NN5*

## Bookstar

**3150 ROSECRANS PL, POINT LOMA; 619/225-0465 / 8650 GENESEE AVE, LA JOLLA; 858/457-7561** The Loma Theater, once one of San Diego's grandest movie palaces, has been transformed into this enormous bookstore, with magazines and cards packed in the lobby and shelves lining the sloping amphitheater toward the stage. Members receive a discount on all purchases, but the selection is fairly mainstream. The La Jolla location is frequented by students from nearby UCSD. *Every day; map:G3 and JJ6*

## Borders Books & Music

**1072 CAMINO DEL RIO N, MISSION VALLEY (AND BRANCHES); 619/295-2201** Even those who boycott most large booksellers can't resist Borders' excellent selection of books and music presented in a sensible layout. The staff is quite well informed, and Borders has become one of the main venues in town for signings by top-name and new authors. Other Borders are in El Cajon (159 Fletcher Pkwy; 619/593-5119) and Carmel Mountain (11160 Rancho Carmel Dr, 858/618-1814). *Every day; www.borders.com; map:LL4*

### Casa del Libro

**1735 UNIVERSITY AVE, HILLCREST; 619/299-9331** Spanish-language novels, dictionaries, and classics are stocked at this small shop favored by students and San Diego's large bilingual population. *Every day; map:P2*

### Controversial Bookstore

**3021 UNIVERSITY AVE, UNIVERSITY HEIGHTS; 619/296-1560** Feeling metaphysical, psychic, or downright mystical? Stop by this incense-scented shop, which has been in business for more than three decades—well before the New Age movement took off. You'll get sensible advice from those who can separate authentic spirituality from the fads. *Every day; map:MM4*

### Hillcrest Newsstand

**529 UNIVERSITY AVE, HILLCREST; 619/260-0462** Every imaginable social trend is covered in the magazine selection at this busy stand located near several coffeehouses and cafes. It's also close to two large hospitals, providing a welcome break for visitors seeking diversion or gifts for patients. *Every day; map:N2*

### John Cole's Book Shop

**780 PROSPECT ST, LA JOLLA; 858/454-4766** Gnarled vines laden with clusters of lavender blossoms twine through the arbor leading to Wisteria Cottage, the historic home of the Scripps sisters, doyennes of early La Jolla. The Irving Gill architecture alone is worth the trip; the bookstore inside is a romantic's dream. Piles of new and treasured used books tumble about; the section of old Mexico and San Diego travel books is a delight. Bedrooms, dens, and sitting rooms are devoted to art, architecture, and classics. Readers' collectibles are scattered throughout. Zach's Music Corner in a side room is a collector's haven, with rare jazz albums and what's said to be the largest selection of harmonicas on the West Coast. *Tues–Sat; map:JJ7*

### Libros

**2754 CALHOUN ST, BAZAAR DEL MUNDO, OLD TOWN; 619/299-1139** Gorgeous hardbound architecture, art, and travel books line one wall of this shop, where kids can't resist the back room devoted to their interests. Those who collect greeting cards as if they were fine art should plan to spend major bucks here. *Every day; map:I1*

### Newport News

**4949 NEWPORT AVE, OCEAN BEACH; 619/225-2300** Comic books, surfing magazines, and Latin American periodicals attract a colorful clientele to this Ocean Beach shop, which also displays a tempting array of Brazilian foodstuffs. *Every day; map:B3*

### Paras Newsstand

**3911 30TH ST, NORTH PARK; 619/296-2859** The selection of out-of-town and international periodicals here far exceeds that of your typical public library; homesick newcomers catch up on their news from back home while scouring papers from Seattle to Singapore. Fashion mags from France, travel mags from China—you name it, Paras has it. *Every day; map:MM4*

SHOPPING

## Rand McNally Map & Travel Store

**243 HORTON PLAZA, DOWNTOWN; 619/234-3341** Globes, atlases, and maps galore delight world travelers, who also can't resist highly detailed tomes describing their favorite destinations. The selection of magnifying glasses, compasses, and travel gear is equally impressive. *Every day; map:N7*

## Upstart Crow Bookstore & Coffeehouse

**835 W HARBOR DR, SEAPORT VILLAGE, DOWNTOWN; 619/232-4855** Conventioneers in need of distraction stop by this cozy shop for magazines, novels, and mysteries from the bookshelves by the coffee stand. The selection is fairly mainstream, but you'll find plenty of local lore. *Every day; info@upstartcrow trading.com; www.upstartcrowtrading.com; map:M8*

## Wahrenbrock's Book House

**726 BROADWAY, DOWNTOWN; 619/232-0132** Dusty treasures tumble and topple from shelves in this three-story literary paradise beloved by collectors of antiquarian and rare used books. Owner Chuck Wahrenbrock and his staff can point the way to almost anything you need (and some things you didn't know you had to have). They'll also track down titles not in stock. *Every day; map:N7*

## Warwick's

**7812 GIRARD AVE, LA JOLLA; 858/454-0347** Staff members memorize their customers' names and interests at this long-standing neighborhood shop, which first opened in 1896. Generations of La Jollans have established accounts here, relying on the stationery staff to supply perfect party invitations and personalized note cards. The selection by local authors may be the best in the county, and signings by best-selling celebrities attract long lines of fans. *Every day; map:JJ7*

## The White Rabbit

**7755 GIRARD AVE, LA JOLLA; 858/454-3518** What a magical hole you fall into after passing a 4-foot-high rabbit at the front door. This wonderland is devoted completely to children's interests, with something for all ages from infant to teen. Devoted aunts and uncles find valuable guidance when seeking the perfect gift; parents delight in the weekly story time and the opportunity to encourage a love of books. Call for a copy of the newsletter—it's a treasure trove of information for young readers. *Every day; map:JJ7*

# CANDY AND CHOCOLATE

## Make Mine Sweet

**4705 CLAIREMONT DR, CLAIREMONT; 858/273-8234** Ten "candy art" pieces spoofing artistic masterpieces are a sign of the candy makers' quirkiness. You'll also find a bottle of champagne made of pure milk chocolate adorned with a label featuring the Coronado Bridge and boxes of chocolates wrapped in a watercolor of the Carlsbad flower fields. Sample the sugar-free specialties. You can buy 200 candies by the pound. *Every day; www.makeminesweet.com; map:JJ6*

## See's Candies

**107 HORTON PLAZA, DOWNTOWN (AND BRANCHES); 619/ 233-5450** They give you a free piece of candy for buying something at this candy-shop chain displaying old-fashioned nut chews, creams, and mints encased in dark and milk chocolate. Gift boxes are flown all over the country during holidays as former San Diegans request caramel lollipops, sour balls, and pounds of assorted candies. Other locations are in the North County Fair, Plaza Camino Real, Fashion Valley, and Grossmont Center malls. *Every day; www.sees.com; map:N7*

## Sweet & Sugar Free

**4425 GENESEE AVE, CLAIREMONT; 858/874-4365** What a terrific concept: tasty cheesecakes, candies, chocolates, cookies, and assorted desserts, all made without sugar and suitable for diabetic and low-carb diets. Other items on sale include sugar-free bagels, breads, cakes, and frozen yogurt. The knowledgeable owners are happy to explain various ingredients and recipes and will also assemble customized gift baskets. *Every day; map: KK5*

# COFFEE AND TEA

## The Coffee Bean & Tea Leaf

**3865 5TH AVE, HILLCREST (AND BRANCHES); 619/293-5908** This California-based company has six stores in San Diego. The most popular bean is the Viennese dark roast. The selection of teas from China, Formosa, India, and Ceylon can be boggling. Straightforward brochures give the origin and price of each coffee or tea and describe its special characteristics. For mail-order coffee and teas, call 800/832-5323. *Every day; http://coffeebean.com; map:N2*

## Pannikin Coffee and Tea

**675 G ST, DOWNTOWN (AND BRANCHES); 619/239-7891** San Diego's most tenacious coffee and tea purveyor (now owned by former employees of the Pannikin founder) is located in a turn-of-the-century red brick building in the heart of the city. There are coffees from four continents—dark roasts, espresso roasts, blends, decaf, and organics—in addition to an outstanding collection of teas. An eclectic collection of ethnic baskets, mugs, and small kitchen utensils is available, as well as teapots, thermoses, and European coffeemakers. Order beans and teas by calling 888/290-1996. *Every day; map:N8*

## Peet's Coffee & Tea

**350 UNIVERSITY AVE, HILLCREST; 619/296-5995**
**8843 VILLA LA JOLLA DR, LA JOLLA; 858/678-0806** Peet's was born in the '60s in Berkeley, California, before gourmet coffee became part of the middle-class lexicon. The espresso counter serves the usual brews, with juice and some baked goods; get a free cuppa joe when you buy a pound of beans. The airy, open salon—with seating in the form of wooden church pews, polished stone bar tables, and a bar facing the comings and goings along University Avenue—makes for a pleasant rendezvous spot. *Every day; www.peets.com; map:N2 and JJ7*

### San Diego House

**2767 SAN DIEGO AVE, OLD TOWN; 619/297-6892 OR 888/624-8000** In the heart of historic Old Town, this building has been remodeled several times since its construction in the 19th century. The owner proudly displays freedman's papers for previous tenant and former slave Allen Light, which found during one of the building's upgrades. If tutti-frutti or bubble-gum tea and peaches-and-cream or maple-walnut coffee appeal to you, you'll be in java heaven here. There are more traditional beans from Africa, Central and South America, and Hawaii as well, plus coffee and tea accessories. *Every day; www.sdhouse.com; map:J2*

## ETHNIC MARKETS

### Andres Latin American Market

**1249 MORENA BLVD, BAY PARK; 619/275-6523** Devotees of all things Latin are thrilled with this tiny market, where black beans, yellow rice, Mexican cheeses, and tamarind paste are displayed amid candles bearing the images of saints. The small restaurant next door (619/275-4114; closed Sundays) serves authentic Cuban sandwiches, soft rolls packed high with cheese, meat, pickles, lettuce, and secret sauce. *Every day; map:LL5*

### Assenti's Pasta Company

**2044 INDIA ST, MIDDLETOWN; 619/239-5117** Opened in 1980 by Adriana Assenti, an immigrant from Italy's Adriatic coast, this wonderful pasta shop is now run by sons Roberto and Luigi. Pastas come in 13 shapes and exotic flavors including squid ink, black bean, and chipotle chile. Fresh pasta sauces are sold by the pound or half pound, along with imported and domestic olive oil, cheeses, deli meats, and more. *Mon–Sat; map:M6*

### Caravan Market

**3200 ADAMS AVE, STE 101, NORMAL HEIGHTS; 619/280-2330** East European products, including salt cod, sardines in oil, cacao powder, pelmeni (dumplings of meat or potatoes and apples), and Polish deli meats are on display in this neighborhood shop. They also sell farina, kasha, kefir, farmer cheese, and jars of taramasalata. *Every day; map:LL4*

### Filippi's

**747 INDIA ST, MIDDLETOWN; 619/232-5094** Although best known for its wonderful pizzas, Filippi's sells cheeses, deli meats, olives, capers, sardines, packaged pastas, olive oil, and wine—both domestic and imported from Italy, Portugal, and Spain. *Every day; map:M6*

### French Accent

**8935 TOWNE CENTRE DR, STE 105, LA JOLLA; 858/320-0050** Splurge on fine wines, Cognac, truffles, goose-liver mousse, and the seasonings and spices needed for French recipes and surprising your guests. Better yet, just pick up French deli items for a fabulous picnic. *Every day; www.frenchaccentsd.com; map: JJ7*

## Hoa Hing

**4149 UNIVERSITY AVE, EAST SAN DIEGO; 619/280-2132** Enter this Vietnamese grocery and get a blast of contradictory smells. The butcher shop has stacks of pig's tongues and live shell oysters. The produce section displays mangoes, eggplant, mint, bamboo shoots, ginger, and more. All the necessary ingredients for a Vietnamese feast are available, along with a small selection of Mexican ingredients. *Every day; map:MM3*

## International Groceries of San Diego

**3548 ASHFORD ST, KEARNY MESA; 858/569-0362** As befits the name, this store sells products from around the globe: New Zealand lamb, Indian naan, Persian-style lavash, Turkish jams, relishes from Bulgaria, and flavored tobacco from Egypt. Rich Egyptian hennas, coffee beans, nuts, seeds, grains, and spices overwhelm and delight shoppers. They even have a video transfer service to copy foreign films to VHS format. *Every day; map:KK5*

## Mona Lisa Italian Delicatessen

**2061 INDIA ST, MIDDLETOWN; 619/239-5367** In addition to imported Italian pastas and olive oil, the Brunetto family sells fresh pizza dough and egg pastas (linguine, fettuccine, and spaghetti) and ready-to-bake, homemade lasagne. At the deli counter, Italian-speaking matrons inspect vats of Cerignola olives and sheets of baccalà (salt cod). Fresh artichoke and octopus salads and deli sandwiches make great take-out meals. *Every day; map:M6*

## 99 Ranch

**7330 CLAIREMONT MESA BLVD, CLAIREMONT; 858/565-7799** In most Asian cultures, the number 9 is a harbinger of good luck; thus the odd-sounding name of this Asian-food emporium. Fast-food eateries here serve Vietnamese, Taiwanese, and Chinese food; a juice bar offers grass jelly, almond tofu, and coconut milk. The Taiwanese snack shack displays salty duck eggs, simmered seaweed, and other delicacies. The store itself has live geoduck clams, Dungeness crab, striped bass, and catfish on ice. Chefs from the finest restaurants shop here alongside happy immigrant families. *Every day; map:JJ5*

# FLORISTS AND NURSERIES

## Adelaide's

**7766 GIRARD AVE, LA JOLLA; 858/454-0146** Living works of art are created at this fashionable florist, long the mainstay of La Jolla patrons. Snow-white tulips, fragile ferns, and sprigs of pussy willow are transformed into sculptures so gorgeous they're used as backdrops for wedding portraits. Bet you can't leave without a few blooms for your room. *Every day; map:JJ7*

## Floral Fantasia

**4993 NIAGARA AVE, OCEAN BEACH; 619/224-6404** The shop may be tiny, but the arrangements designed inside are spectacular. A small selection of emerald, sapphire, and crystal-clear vases inspire creativity, and the young, innovative florists are eager to experiment with colors and shapes, turning a simple bunch of roses into a masterpiece. *Every day; map:B3*

## Mission Hills Nursery

**1525 FORT STOCKTON DR, MISSION HILLS; 619/295-2808** Care to present a blooming gardenia bush or Victorian birdbath as a wedding gift? Then skip the trays of perennials by the sidewalk and wander the backyard at this historic nursery, first opened by renowned local gardener Kate Sessions in 1910. The surrounding neighborhood has some of the most gorgeous old gardens in the city—perfect inspiration for a living Monet in your yard. *Every day; map:L2*

## Walter Andersen Nursery

**3642 ENTERPRISE ST, POINT LOMA; 619/224-8271 / 12755 DANIELSEN CT, POWAY; 858/513-4900** Impeccably healthy pansies, lobelia, snapdragons, and poppies sit ready for planting; baskets of purple fuchsias hang above pure white calla lilies. Cacti, succulents, and herbs abound in the native plants section, and all about the nursery are jungles of tree ferns, mini-orchards of citrus trees, and ponds filled with floating plants. Someone is available to answer nearly any question and suggest unusual combos for your flower patch. *Every day; www.walterandersen.com; map:I2*

## Weidner's Gardens

**695 NORMANDY RD, ENCINITAS; 760/436-2194** Seasonal sales at this enormous flower farm attract hundreds of buyers seeking rare fuchsias blooming in hanging baskets or cropped into toparies. Geraniums in every imaginable color and scent, begonias like rare tropical plants, and an overabundance of blooms you've never seen keep gardeners returning regularly for a view of Weidner's latest find. *Wed–Mon (closed Jan–Mar and Oct); map:EE7*

# GIFTS

## Apache Trading Post

**2802 JUAN ST, OLD TOWN; 619/298-4106** A staple of the touristy Old Town district, this unusual store is packed with interesting, top-quality Native American arts and crafts from throughout the Southwest, including handmade moccasins, belts, and woven baskets. *Every day; map:I1*

## Babette Schwartz

**421 UNIVERSITY AVE, HILLCREST; 619/220-7048** There is a definite flair to a store that combines *Gilligan's Island*–inspired paraphernalia with Mexican Day of the Dead icons. A wide selection of cards and classic toys is also available. *Every day; babette@babette.com; www.babette.com; map:N2*

## The Black

**5017 NEWPORT AVE, OCEAN BEACH; 619/222-5498** In less polite society, this would be called a head shop. But beyond the smoking paraphernalia, the store offers one-stop shopping for countercultural gifts. It's one of the few places to find lava lamps, black lights, and a vast selection of classic psychedelic posters. One part of the store is devoted to unusually chic biker-wear and jewelry. *Every day; map:B3*

## Bo Danica

**7722 GIRARD AVE, LA JOLLA; 858/454-6107** A sophisticated contemporary atmosphere permeates this store, displaying crafts, art, and pottery from American and European artists along with soaps, candles, and lamps. The fine china and crystal make it a popular bridal registry. *Every day; map:JJ7*

## The Collector

**7100 FOUR SEASONS PT, CARLSBAD; 760/603-9601** Colorful gemstones beckon from the cases of this unusual jewelry store in the Four Seasons–Aviara Resort. There are crystals, geodes, fossils, and stones, some from the store's own tourmaline mine in Mesa Grande. Lapidary and stone cutting are available. *Every day; map:CC7*

## F Street Bookstore

**751 4TH AVE, DOWNTOWN; 619/236-0841** Brightly lit and across the street from Horton Plaza, this adult store is full of naughty toys and gifts for lovers, everything from sexual aids to board games. *Every day; map:N7*

## French Garden Shoppe

**3951 GOLDFINCH AVE, MISSION HILLS; 619/295-4573** A taste of provincial luxury is the ticket here, with an emphasis on pottery, fluffy towels, soaps, and everything French. Custom floral arrangements are available as well. *Mon–Sat; map:M2*

## Great News Cooking Supplies

**1788 GARNET AVE, PACIFIC BEACH; 858/270-1582** The prices on professional-level cooking supplies are better here than at most of the chains, and the emphasis is on utensils, books, and spices used by real cooks. Staff members know what they're talking about—this is also a cooking school. *Every day; www.great-news.com; map:KK7*

## The Healthy Back Store

**1201 UNIVERSITY AVE, HILLCREST; 619/299-2225 / 8715 VILLA LA JOLLA DR, LA JOLLA; 858/623-0055** Anyone with an aching back will love this store. It stocks everything from ergonomic office chairs to therapeutic mattresses to neck-support pillows and books on stretching. A car-seat lumbar support makes a perfect gift for a commuter. *Every day; www.healthyback.com; map:O2 and JJ7*

## Le Travel Store

**739 4TH AVE, DOWNTOWN; 619/544-0005 OR 800/713-4260** Joan and Bill Keller have been running a store for "international independent" travelers in San Diego since 1976. Now conveniently located across the street from Horton Plaza, their store is packed with books, backpacks, and essential accessories. You can also purchase their travel gear online. *Every day; www.letravelstore.com; map:N8*

## Panache

**7636 GIRARD AVE, LA JOLLA; 858/454-4220** A classy gift shop long favored by La Jolla's most stylish, the store lives up to its name with fine crystal and silver decorations for the home. It also usually features the jewelry creations of several local artists. A bridal registry is available. *Mon–Sat; map:JJ7*

## Patina

**1310 ROSECRANS ST, POINT LOMA; 619/224-1491** This store is a delight to explore, full of scented pillows, jewelry boxes, linens, and books. It is clear the items are specially selected, with little of the fodder typical in gift stores. An alcove holds unusual baby gifts. *Tues–Sat; map:E6*

## San Diego Harley-Davidson

**5600 KEARNY MESA RD, CLAIREMONT; 858/616-6999** You don't have to ride a chopper to appreciate the cool Harley accessories here. The classic Harley logo appears on everything from key chains and lighters to authentic leathers. *Every day; www.sandiegoharley.com; map:JJ4*

## The Silver Skillet

**2690 VIA DE LA VALLE, FLOWER HILL MALL, DEL MAR; 858/481-6710** As soon as you walk through the door, you know how Martha Stewart equips her kitchen. Two floors are stocked with everything from terra-cotta tortilla steamers to fondue sets to colorful dinnerware imported from Italy. Shiny stainless steel pots and pans gleam from the racks. Vases, pillows, and glasses from top European designers are sprinkled among the shelves. Gift wrapping is free; they'll also ship. *Every day; map:GG7*

## Stacey Himmel Stationery

**3997 FALCON ST, MISSION HILLS; 619/295-4764** Just when you think you're in a typical stationery store, you find a section with fine leather journals or another area packed with boxes of unusual paper stocks. The in-house printing department can handle all sorts of orders, including custom invitations and announcements. *Mon–Sat; map:M2*

# HARDWARE

## Hillcrest Ace Hardware

**1007 UNIVERSITY AVE, HILLCREST; 619/291-5988** Not just a hard-core hardware store here—you're more likely to find stylish teakettles in the entryway than boxes of nails. The two floors offer plenty of the basics, but there is also a healthy emphasis on home redecoration and fix-it-up suggestions, pool and pet supplies, and more. Delivery available. *Every day; www.hillcresthardware.com; map:O2*

## Ocean Beach Paint and Hardware

**4851 NEWPORT AVE, OCEAN BEACH; 619/223-3083** This little store on Ocean Beach's main drag has been helping locals fix their toilets and faulty light switches since 1919. You won't find a gardening department or rows of bathroom fixtures, but you will find key items for electrical, plumbing, painting, and other household repairs. *Every day; map:B3*

### San Diego Hardware

**840 5TH AVE, DOWNTOWN; 619/232-7123** San Diego's oldest hardware store is a tourist attraction in its own right, a throwback to a different era with its old wood floors and a Victorian pressed-tin ceiling. It's also fun to explore, offering 50,000 items, including decorative hardware you won't find in Home Depot. The basement is where you'll find the fasteners, chicken wire, and other nuts-and-bolts supplies. *Mon–Sat; www.sandiegohardware.com; map:N7*

## HEALTH FOOD

### Henry's Market Place

**1260 GARNET AVE, PACIFIC BEACH; 858/270-8200** In addition to an amazing variety of dietary supplements, organic produce, beauty products, and bulk grains and nuts, Henry's offers a deli, meat counter, wine department, and freshly baked breads. You'll also find ready-to-cook entrees such as beef fajitas and stuffed chicken breasts. *Every day; map:KK6*

### In Harmony

**4808 SANTA MONICA AVE, OCEAN BEACH; 619/223-8051** Dubbed one of the 10 best herb stores in the United States by *Self* magazine, this place is worth a visit for the aromas alone. It offers more than 250 herbs and spices, many organically grown. There's also a wide selection of aromatherapy products. Order herbs by calling 800/51-HERBS. *Mon–Sat; www.inharmonyherbs.com; map:B3*

### People's Organic Foods Market

**4765 VOLTAIRE ST, OCEAN BEACH; 619/224-1387** A good ol'-fashioned co-op, this market is consistently well stocked with top-quality, organically grown vegetables and herbs. The vitamin selection is one of the best around. Beyond food, you can stock up on natural beauty-care products, including handmade scented soaps, real herbal shampoos, and a variety of products developed without animal research. *Every day; map:C2*

### Vegetarian Zone

**2949 5TH AVE, HILLCREST; 619/298-7302** The companion gift shop to the popular restaurant (see Restaurants chapter) primarily stocks gifts such as crystals and wind chimes; there's also a good selection of teas and breads and an excellent range of vegetarian cookbooks. *Tues–Sun; www.vegetarianzone.com; map:N4*

## HOME FURNISHINGS

### Circa a.d.

**3867 4TH AVE, HILLCREST; 619/293-3328** This marvelous shop with its large and eclectic array of decorative art, antiques, and furnishings would inspire anyone to redecorate. Byzantine icons and Japanese kimonos mix and mingle with hand-carved containers, rattan balls, unique fountains, African masks, laquerware, religious decor, and an orchard's worth of wooden fruit. Don't overlook the jewelry case. *Every day; www.circaad.com; map:N2*

## Column One

**401 UNIVERSITY AVE, HILLCREST; 619/299-9074** This large corner shop features a terrific collection of fountains (including some in column and block forms), garden decor, metal sculptures, ornate corbels, outdoor lights, sun gods, and wind chimes. Statuary runs the gamut from Saint Francis sheltering a bird to reclining cherubs and exhibitionist nudes. *Every day; map:N2*

## Everett Stunz Company Ltd

**7624 GIRARD AVE, LA JOLLA; 858/459-3305** Since the early 1960s, this shop has been a prime source for beautiful, classy, imported bath towels and bedding such as imported Italian bedroom ensembles featuring 600-thread-count sheets and exquisite workmanship. Cashmere blankets, bath oils, and silk pajamas round out the luxurious selection; DUX and adjustable beds are also for sale. *Mon–Sat; www.everett stunz.com; map:JJ7*

## Genghis Khan

**1136 MORENA BLVD, BAY PARK; 619/275-1182** Walking through the door here is like taking a trip to the Orient. Exotic accent pieces include stone fountains, stoic Buddhas and various deities in all sizes, ceremonial tea sets, birdcages, mirrors, carvings, and miniature pagodas. The ornate doors, gates, and relief carvings are particularly fascinating. *Every day; map:LL5*

## Highlights

**301 4TH AVE, DOWNTOWN; 619/232-6064** Light up your life and home with contemporary lamps and fixtures. Only the foremost European and American designers and manufacturers are represented, and the staff is happy to assist with selections. Collectors will drool over the Memphis, Venini, and VeArt designs. *Mon–Sat; map:N8*

## Home Accents of La Jolla

**7840 GIRARD AVE, LA JOLLA; 858/454-0442** This very ornate shop displays hand-painted birdcages, hand-carved Arabian trunks, handblown glass scepters, elegant vases, unusual lamps, glyph panels, fringed tassels, tapestry cushions, limited-edition prints, marble turtles, and onyx eggs. *Every day; map:JJ7*

## Lamp Shades Unlimited

**1022 W MORENA BLVD, BAY PARK; 619/276-6530** With a stock of more than 10,000 shades, you'll find a suitable covering for any lamp imaginable—from a transformed Chianti bottle to a piece of rare antique porcelain. *Mon–Sat; map:LL5*

## Maidhof Brothers

**1891 SAN DIEGO AVE, OLD TOWN; 619/574-1891** Maidhof Brothers claims to be one of the state's longest-operating purveyors of nautical salvage and fine chandlery. Every boating accessory imaginable is stashed within this salty warehouse—genuine *Titanic* posters, engine equipment, old prints, lamps, mastheads, bells, anchors, lanterns, ships inside bottles, and more. *Mon–Sat; map:K3*

## Maison en Provence

**820 FORT STOCKTON DR, MISSION HILLS; 619/298-5318** Enter the heavenly world of rural France in this enchanting shop filled with such Provençal delights as imported French pottery, quilts, cushions, brooms, dishes, crockery, table linens, fine fabrics, and hand-milled and molded soaps. The Barbotine pitchers are created from the original 14th-century molds. *Tues–Sun; map:M2*

# MEAT AND FISH

## Point Loma Seafoods

**2805 EMERSON ST, POINT LOMA; 619/223-1109** Locals stop by for a cup of clam chowder and a calamari sandwich, but primarily this place sells dozens of varieties of fresh fish from all over the world. You're likely to find green-lipped mussels from New Zealand, king salmon from the Northwest, and black sea bass from Mexico. You can choose your own shellfish from saltwater tanks. Sushi lovers appreciate the sashimi-grade ahi. *Every day; map:E6*

## Siesel's Old-Fashioned Meats

**4131 ASHTON ST, BAY PARK; 619/275-1234** For 31 years Marv Siesel has been preparing choice cuts for meat lovers. He takes pride in offering prime USDA choice, and the helpful staff will gladly make suggestions for the right steak for the right occasion. For something out of the ordinary, try one of the 35 different marinades. *Every day; map:LL5*

## Sportsmen's Seafood

**1617 QUIVIRA RD, MISSION BAY; 619/224-3551** Fresh sea bass, shark, cod, and other local delicacies are taken right off the boats and into the cases of this local icon, owned and operated by the Busalacchi family, well-known San Diego restaurateurs since 1960. Sportsmen's is famous for its smoked fish, including smoked albacore and salmon. It also makes its own tuna jerky. *Every day; map:D1*

## Tip Top Meats

**6118 PASEO DEL NORTE, CARLSBAD; 760/438-2620** Looking for English bangers or German wursts? This well-stocked butcher shop and grocery specializes in sausages of every stripe, as well as just about any type of meat or poultry you can imagine. Choice and prime grade beef is available here, and the staff will be happy to order specialty meats or game with advance notice. The catering department features ready-made dinners such as barbecued ribs, stuffed pork chops, roast turkey, and chicken cordon bleu. *Every day; www.tiptopmeats.com; map: CC7*

# MUSIC (CDS, RECORDS, AND TAPES)

## Art-Te Company

**945 BROADWAY, DOWNTOWN; 619/232-7231** Ninety-nine percent of the music sold here is in Spanish. The genres vary, however, from mariachi to merengue, rock en español to Mexican polka tunes. The store's strength is popular music—música grupera, música de banda, norteña, and just plain "pop" (say that with a Latino accent), in addition to tropical tunes, including cumbia, son, and salsa. *Mon–Sat; map: O7*

### Blue Meannie Records

**916 BROADWAY, EL CAJON; 619/442-2212** In business for 25 years, this music store specializes in new and used, domestic and imported, classic rock, punk, heavy metal, and hard core. Almost anything in print can be special-ordered in a few days. The huge selection of vinyl includes many 45s. The Meannie buys clean used CDs and cassette tapes, along with some vinyl, and also sells posters, buttons, stickers, and magazines. *Every day; www.bluemeanniemetal.com; map:KK1*

### Cow

**5029 NEWPORT AVE, OCEAN BEACH; 619/523-0236** Owner Greg Hildebrand lucked out when he scored the entire inventory of Jerry's Records on Newport for $2,500. Since then he's turned a good profit selling used vinyl, cassettes, and CDs. New competition from the Music Trader chain up the street has Hildebrand offering more collectibles and rare items, such as gatefold, signed, and promotional albums. Although rock is his biggest seller, he makes a point of carrying jazz, country, classical, rap, and reggae. Ask for a card that turns into a $10 gift certificate after $100 in purchases. *Every day; map:B3*

### Folk Arts Rare Records

**3611 ADAMS AVE, NORMAL HEIGHTS; 619/282-7833** Owner and music historian Lou Curtis has done discographic work for the Smithsonian and the Library of Congress. His personal collection of rare recordings totals an astonishing 90,000 hours of music—favoring but not limited to folk, blues, jazz, and country. His shop offers vintage LPs, 45s, and 78s, with an emphasis on artists from the teens, '20s, and '30s. Customers can order custom cassettes, CDs, or reel-to-reel tapes with compilations from the song catalog. Curtis founded and coordinates the San Diego Folk Festival (now the Adams Avenue Roots Festival) and is involved in the yearly Adams Avenue Street Fair. He also has a radio show on KSDS radio, featuring jazz roots from the '20s and '30s. *Every day; map:LL3*

### Nickelodeon Records

**3335 ADAMS AVE, NORMAL HEIGHTS; 619/284-6083** Owners Ruth Bible and Elizabeth Scarborough have been selling vintage vinyl—and *only* vinyl—since 1984. Their specialty is movie sound tracks and off-the-wall recordings by comedians and personalities (for example, old TV or movie stars dabbling in music careers—think Leonard Nimoy crooning to a crowd of Vulcans). Bible and Scarborough also go for unusual cover art from the '50s and '60s. Check out the "smoking section," where each cover pictures someone smoking. *Mon–Sat; www.nickelodeonrecords.com; map:LL4*

### Off the Record

**3849 5TH AVE, HILLCREST; 619/298-4755** In business for more than 20 years, this record store is a long, deep emporium in the heart of Hillcrest. Specializing in hard-to-find music, the store has an excellent, eclectic selection of used CDs, cassettes, and albums. Featured is a wide range of today's musical styles—everything from industrial/techno to jump blues and dance tunes—any of which may be playing at a vigorous volume as you shop. *Every day; www.otrvinyl.com; map:N2*

## Trade Roots Reggae

**3804 ROSECRANS ST, MIDWAY; 619/299-7824** In addition to Bob Marley bumper stickers, incense, and other rockin' paraphernalia, you can get a good selection of reggae music in the form of new CDs, records, and cassettes. *Every day; map:H2*

# OUTDOOR GEAR

## Adventure 16

**4620 ALVARADO CANYON RD, COLLEGE AREA; 619/283-2362 / LOMAS SANTA FE AT HWY 101, SOLANA BEACH; 858/755-7662** A-16 is one of those stores that's easy to love. The sales staff is helpful but not pushy, and always gracious about returns. The company stocks made-in-America and recycled products, such as Patagonia's PCI Synchilla alpine hat, made of recycled soda-pop bottles. It's a no-holds-barred camp and travel shop, selling popular brands of adventure-style clothing, luggage, shoes, maps, and camping equipment. You can rent camping and sports equipment with an option to buy. The quarterly newsletter lists free and inexpensive activities including slide shows, clinics, classes, and wilderness trips. *Every day; www.adventure16.com; map: KK3, FF8*

## Cal Stores

**4030 SPORTS ARENA BLVD, MIDWAY; 619/223-2325** They have a little bit of most things, but not a lot of any one type of sports equipment or clothing. But the selection of walking, running, and hiking shoes is huge, and prices on most items are lower than at trendier specialty stores. *Every day; map:F1*

## The Diving Locker

**1020 GRAND AVE, PACIFIC BEACH; 858/272-1120** Chuck Nicklin opened the Diving Locker in 1959 and since then has segued from diving instructor to underwater photographer and filmmaker. You can still get scuba certification through the shop, which also rents, repairs, and of course sells scuba gear. The store's Nautilus Club sponsors Saturday-morning dives, lectures, slide presentations, photo workshops, kelp-bed and wreck dives, and trips to such exotic destinations as Thailand, Fiji, and Hawaii. *Every day; www.divinglocker.com; map:KK7*

## GI Joe's Army-Navy Surplus

**555 MARKET ST, DOWNTOWN; 619/531-1910** On the first floor are surplus foul-weather gear, duffel bags, pocket knives, and a limited amount of camping supplies. There's also an impressive array of straps in varying widths (sold by the foot) and buckles. In the basement you'll find racks of used Wellingtons and regulation leather boots, military shirts, jackets, and trousers. No cash refunds. *Every day; map:O8*

## Hook, Line & Sinker

**1224 SCOTT ST, POINT LOMA; 619/224-1336** Though there are larger sportfishing shops in San Diego proper, this one is near the marinas of Shelter and Harbor Islands and has lots of info on local conditions. It's also a reliable standby for high-quality rods and reels as well as videos on major fishing areas around the world. *Every day; map:E6*

### Mission Beach Club

**704 VENTURA PL, MISSION BEACH; 858/488-5050** Brothers Dan and Ray Hamel opened this beachside store 32 years ago, renting Sting Ray bikes, rubber rafts, and giant surfboards for beach and boardwalk fans. They sold the store in 1999, but the new owners rent much of the same merchandise, including surfboards and body boards, beach umbrellas, baby joggers, and in-line and old-fashioned roller skates. A limited selection of skating clothing is also sold. *Every day; map:LL7*

### Norpine Mountain Sports

**3045 CLAIREMONT DR, CLAIREMONT VILLAGE SHOPPING CENTER, CLAIRE-MONT; 619/276-1577** Owner Jim Foxworthy sells and rents cross-country, telemark, and backcountry ski equipment—no snowboarding or downhill. The shop is open only during ski season (usually from the beginning of November through the end of April), when gear can also be purchased mail-order. Foxworthy asserts that the majority of cross-country ski equipment sold in the southern half of the state comes from his store, and that on any given Saturday 75 percent of his customers will be from outside San Diego. *Mon–Sat, Nov–Apr; www.norpine.com; map:KK5*

### Performance Bicycle Shop

**3619 MIDWAY DR, MIDWAY; 619/223-5415** This bike shop offers service as well as sales, and it will beat any other San Diego shop's price on equipment. They have road, mountain, and racing bikes as well as accessories: clothing, pumps, helmets, sunglasses, and watches. Those who spend $200 a year on biking equipment should join Team Performance, wherein a $20 yearly membership fee earns points worth a 10 percent discount on future purchases. Members also receive a quarterly newsletter and invitations to special sales. *Every day; www.performancebike.com; map:G2*

### Play It Again Sports

**1401 GARNET AVE, PACIFIC BEACH; 858/490-0222 / 8366 PARKWAY DR, LA MESA; 619/667-9499** Here you can rent or buy a wide variety of new and used sports equipment. The store's strength is equipment for individual action sports, including in-line skates, fitness equipment, surfboards and wetsuits, snowboards and skateboards, and golf clubs. You will also find a range of team sports equipment for hockey, softball, baseball, and more. About 30 percent of sales are in used items; trade-ins are welcome. Much of the inventory is also available for rent. *Every day; www.playitagainsd.com; map:KK7 and LL2*

### Recreational Equipment, Incorporated (REI)

**5556 COPLEY DR, KEARNY MESA; 858/279-4400** Now the largest retail co-op in the country, REI was formed in 1938 in the Pacific Northwest as a way for the founders to import quality climbing gear. REI sells outerwear (North Face, Marmot, Patagonia, and REI labels), foul-weather gear, and a large selection of hiking boots in addition to comfortable, casual clothing. Co-op members receive annual dividends, can rent camping equipment, and get special prices on some equipment repair and sale items. REI also has a 100-percent-satisfaction return policy. *Every day; www.rei.com; map:JJ5*

## GROWTH AND DREAMS

California became the 31st U.S. state in 1850. Since then, San Diego's history has been a slow, steady tale of economic dreams and growth. The city's year-round warm climate, the best harbor south of San Francisco, and a brief gold rush in Julian during the 1870s started a constant population gain and intermittent bursts of development.

Perhaps the greatest influence on growth was the arrival of the U.S. Navy's Great White Fleet in 1908. World War II and the Pacific Theater turned San Diego into an anthill of airplane factories and shipping. Today, San Diego Harbor is still home port to tens of thousands of servicemen and -women; hordes of these part-time San Diegans decide to stay when their service ends.

Ultimately, San Diego's most valuable commodity has always been space to grow. By the 1950s, San Diego city and county had become a modern metropolis of freeways, suburbs, and outlying rural areas. New, self-contained cities served as models for other growing states; prime turf was carved into exclusive enclaves. Today developers continue to ride crests; highways and full-scale communities continually reshape the landscape. But San Diego still doesn't feel like Los Angeles, thanks in large part to the natural landscape. Not only is it buffered from Orange County's growth by the huge Camp Pendleton Marine base, but San Diego's many stream-cut canyons and steep-sided mesas make for an endlessly varied topography. The county is really a series of self-reliant, independent districts, towns, and cities intertwined under a unique identity.

—*Peter Jensen*

### Seaforth Sportfishing

**1717 QUIVIRA RD, MISSION BAY; 619/224-3383** Stop by in the evening and mingle with anglers headed out on long-range fishing trips in search of tuna, dorado, and the occasional marlin. The shop sells all the gear you could possibly need to jump right on a boat, from high wader boots to wide-brimmed straw hats and warm windbreakers. Oh yes, they also have rods, reels, hooks, lures . . . you name it. *Every day; map:D1*

### South Coast Surf Shop

**5023 NEWPORT AVE, OCEAN BEACH; 619/223-7017 / 740 FELSPAR ST, PACIFIC BEACH; 858/483-7660** Surf shops have come a long way since long boards and woodies were in style. Actually, long boards are in again, but shops now also stock sunglasses, tons of casual sporting wear, darling bikinis, skateboards, beach towels, animal-print flip-flops, and Sex Wax. Unlike those at some other surf shops, the sales clerks at South Coast are generally willing to help neophytes and other non-hardcore surfers. Four doors down toward the ocean on Newport, the affiliated South Coast Long Board Shop is longer on sticks and shorter on accessories. In Pacific Beach, the South Coast Wahine store (4500 Beach Blvd, at the end of Garnet;

858/273-7600) has lots of foxy girls' and women's surf wear, thongs (both bathing suits and footwear), wet suits, and boards for the female of the surfer species. *Every day; www.southcoast.com; map:B3 and KK7*

## TOYS

### Brad Burt's Magic Shop

**690 CONVOY ST, CLAIREMONT; 858/571-4749** Houdini wanna-bes will find all the basics in this friendly little shop in the Aaron Brothers shopping center. Supplies for the hidden rope trick or the invisible deck are available, but you'll have to supply your own rabbit for any hat tricks. *Every day; map:JJ5*

### Discount Hobby Warehouse

**7750 CONVOY CT, CLAIREMONT; 858/560-9636** For 25 years local hobbyists have been flocking to this store for their essential supplies. Model builders will find rare kits, paints, and specialty tools. There is also an impressive selection of remote-control boats, helicopters, and planes. *Every day; map:JJ5*

### Gepetto's

**7007 FRIARS RD, FASHION VALLEY CENTER, MISSION VALLEY (AND BRANCHES); 619/294-8878** The decor may go a little heavy on the old-toy-maker theme, but the store comes through with handcrafted wooden puppets and other traditional favorites. There is also a wide selection of Steiff teddy bears, books, and unusual puzzles. Other locations are in the Bazaar del Mundo in Old Town (619/291-4606) and at the Hotel del Coronado (619/435-8871). *Every day; map:LL5, I1, M9*

### Reed's Hobby Shop

**8039 LA MESA BLVD, LA MESA; 619/464-1672** It's a little out of the way, but this little store has everything for the electric-train enthusiast. Besides rare engines and cars in all gauges, there are shelves full of different landscapes, model villages, and tunnels. If they don't stock a tool or a rare caboose, they'll know where to find it. For the hard core, the employees will custom-paint trains. *Every day; map:LL2*

### Thinker Things

**670 VIA DE LA VALLE, DEL MAR; 858/755-4488** Kids love to wander the aisles of this playful store, which features few of the alien creatures and gun-toting villains of chain stores. Instead the nooks and crannies are packed with fun, creative toys that can fuel a child's imagination. In addition to wonderful stuffed animals and dolls, there are intriguing science kits and puzzles. *Every day; map:GG7*

## VINTAGE/RETRO

### Anatomic Rag

**979 GARNET AVE, PACIFIC BEACH; 858/274-3597** Geared toward eclectic and imaginative San Diegans, this store carries a wonderful selection of vintage clothing, including some Victorian pieces, plus lots of faded blue jeans and a sprinkling of new items. Prices are reasonable, but there are no exchanges or refunds—no exceptions. *Every day; map:KK7*

## Boomerang for Modern

**2040 INDIA ST, MIDDLETOWN; 619/239-2040** Period originals—mainly from the '50s, '60s, and '70s—are artfully arranged in this light-filled space in Little Italy. Owner David Skelley may give you a lecture if you confuse his pieces with "retro," which are modern copies of period pieces. He does represent Herman Miller, selling reissues of classic designs, but his focus is vintage seating, coffee tables, and dining sets by companies such as Eames and Knoll. The store usually has a good selection of Danish modern furnishings, period lighting, rugs, Rosenthal vases, and colorful handcrafted Blenko glassware. *Mon–Sat; www.boomerangformodern.com; map:M5*

## Cream of the Crop

**4683 CASS ST, PACIFIC BEACH; 858/272-6601** Although the shop handles mainly designer labels sold on consignment, some vintage items creep into the inventory in this women's resale boutique, which has loads of jewelry. The shop is well organized and the clothes are in good condition—offering up good things for those who hunt well. *Mon–Sat; map:KK7*

## Flashbacks Recycled Fashions

**3847 5TH AVE, HILLCREST; 619/291-4200** Colored freak wigs decorate one wall in this secondhand shop in the heart of Hillcrest. Although vintage clothing shares the stage with more recently worn glad rags, there are bubble-plastic purses, funky hats, furry coats, and lots of big, black shoes and boots. *Every day; map:N2*

## Hot Topic

**1640 CAMINO DEL RIO N, MISSION VALLEY CENTER, MISSION VALLEY; 619/542-8450** Teens and twentysomethings appreciate the inexpensive gifts and trendy and retro attire found in this mall-based, music-oriented chain clothing store. The tragically hip shop here, whether moved or motivated by grunge, Goth, punk, or other music genres. There's club-wear and the chain's own line of clothing, Morbid Threads. Also jewelry, handbags, shoes, glitter makeup, and, of course, vinyl clothing for men and women. *Every day; www.hottopic.com; map LL5*

## Indigo Way

**437 MARKET ST, DOWNTOWN; 619/338-0173** Vintage men's clothing is the order of the day here, including old-fashioned bowling and Hawaiian shirts, sporting attire from the '30s through the '60s, and a large selection of faded Levi's blue jeans and jean jackets. Owner Pascal Loupias also sells his own line of handcrafted leather belts. *Every day; map:O8*

## Karen's Consignment Gallery

**4051 VOLTAIRE ST, OCEAN BEACH; 619/225-8585** The showroom is full of elegant, hardly worn contemporary furniture, and surprises await those willing to hunt through the rooms. There are few real bargains to be found in this gallery, but it has long been a favorite of local interior designers. *Every day; map:D3*

## Revivals

**3320 ADAMS AVE, NORMAL HEIGHTS; 619/284-3999** The owner buys constantly from area estate sales to keep this 5,000-square-foot store well stocked with furniture, art, rugs, china, and glassware. When you walk in, it's not unusual to find books and knickknacks piled to the ceiling; antiques can be found as well as vintage and collectible items. Large set pieces from the Old Globe Theatre in Balboa Park give the store a fantasy atmosphere. Bargains abound. *Every day; map:LL4*

## Shake Rag-Epicenter

**440 F ST, DOWNTOWN; 619/237-4955** Underneath Croce's at Fifth and F Streets are 4,000 square feet of nostalgia. There's a great selection of everything vintage, including hard-to-find little kids' clothing. Exposed heating ducts and lilac walls define the large space, and track lighting illuminates the '40s- to '70s-era clothing. *Every day; map:N7*

## Wear It Again Sam

**3823 5TH AVE, HILLCREST; 619/299-0185** In business for more than 20 years, Wear It Again Sam has la crème de la crème of hats, boots, jewelry, accessories, and clothes that make you wonder how and where they found them. Everything from turn-of-the-last-century through the 1950s is represented, with emphasis (when they can get them) on nice men's suits from the '40s and '50s, plus vintage women's shoes. High-quality reproduction items are sometimes stocked as well. *Every day; map:P2*

# WINE AND BEER

## Barons

**4001 W POINT LOMA BLVD, POINT LOMA; 619/223-4397 / 3545 DEL MAR HEIGHTS RD, DEL MAR; 858/481-2323** These two well-stocked shops feature a vast selection of domestic and imported wines, with prices ranging from cheap to exorbitant. Aisles and bins are crammed with picnic items such as cheeses, crackers, nuts, sweets, and other delicacies, plus breads and gourmet coffee. *Every day; map:F2 and GG6*

## Beer King

**7150 CLAIREMONT MESA BLVD, CLAIREMONT; 858/292-9210** Serious party animals head here for kegs and cases of favorite domestic and imported brands. Ice, dry ice, cups, jockey boxes, dispenser rentals, and picnic pumps are all on tap. And best yet, Beer King delivers. *Every day; www.beerking.com; map:JJ5*

## Crest Liquor

**3787 INGRAHAM ST, PACIFIC BEACH; 858/274-3087** In operation since 1947, Crest is well known among locals for the stock of premium wines, spirits, and microbrews housed within its 7,000-square-foot space. If for some reason you can't find that special brand, Crest offers a wine and spirits search service. Cigars, a deli, and catering services are added perks. *Every day; map:KK7*

## San Diego Wine Company

**5282 EASTGATE MALL, MIRA MESA; 858/535-1400** The knowledgeable, enthusiastic store owner delights in finding wines from around the globe that offer great value along with good taste. This is a great place to pick up little-known Spanish or Italian imports, brand-new finds from New Zealand and Australia, and, of course, plenty of fine labels from California vineyards. You'll find scores of excellent wines for under $8. Tastings of several selections are generally offered on Saturdays for a small fee. *Every day; map: II5*

## Spirits of St. Germain Liquors

**3251 HOLIDAY CT, LA JOLLA; 858/455-1414** Not a chance you'll go away empty-handed after scouring the stock of around 1,000 bottles of California and European wines, 600 different kinds of spirits, and more than 330 varieties of beer. Wine prices range from an affordable $4 per bottle up to a $250 sky-high splurge. *Every day; map:JJ6*

## Vintage Wines Limited

**6904 MIRAMAR RD, STE 101, MIRA MESA; 858/549-2112** One of San Diego's favorite wine shops for more than a decade, Vintage Wines features a helpful, wine-savvy staff and a carefully picked selection of varietals and vintages. Here you'll discover France's top Burgundies, Champagnes, and Bordeaux, along with rare California Cabernets and Chardonnays, top-notch vintage port, hard-to-find dessert wines, and much, much more. Be sure to ask for a schedule of the shop's upcoming tastings. *Every day; info@vintagewinessd.com; www.vintagewinessd.com; map: II5*

## Wine Bank

**363 5TH AVE, DOWNTOWN; 619/234-7487** Close to convention hotels, on the edge of the trolley tracks, this brick warehouse is packed with inexpensive wines from all over the world, along with expensive wines and liquors. *Every day; map:N8*

## The Wine Connection

**2650 VIA DE LA VALLE, FLOWER HILL MALL, DEL MAR; 858/350-9292** This store has a large assortment of high-end domestic and imported wines, fine Cognac and Scotch, Riedel glasses, and accessories such as wine bags, iceless chillers, screw pulls, and vacuum stoppers. All case wine purchases are discounted, and temperature-controlled wine storage is available on the premises. *Every day; map:GG7*

## WineSellar & Brasserie

**9550 WAPLES ST, STE 115, SORRENTO VALLEY; 858/450-9557** The location is a bit off the beaten path, but well worth the search. The reward: thousands of bottles of hand-selected wines, including domestic labels, bottlings from small European producers of Bordeaux and Burgundy, and rare classics. Storage, appraisals, and tastings are part of the service at this highly esteemed fine wine shop. *Mon–Sat; www.winesellarandbrasserie.com; map:II7*

# PERFORMING ARTS

# PERFORMING ARTS

## Theater

The theater scene in San Diego is a marvel to behold. It's been booming for the past dozen years and shows no signs of slowing down. The La Jolla Playhouse has sent numerous productions to Broadway, garnering several Tony awards and nominations. "The Playhouse keeps setting up new plays as fast as you can enjoy them," says one local critic. The Globe Theatres continue to challenge and satisfy audiences with world-class dramas and musicals, as does the San Diego Repertory Theatre. Even the Lamb's Players, a small homegrown troupe, made it to Cambridge in 1998 to stage *Till We Have Faces* by C. S. Lewis. All this action is heartily supported by San Diegans and theatergoers from throughout Southern California. If you're determined to see a particular production, buy your tickets in advance. If you're more interested in checking out the overall theater community, purchase last-minute tickets at discounted prices from some theaters (call ahead) and Arts Tix (see "Ticket Alert" sidebar in this chapter).

### Avo Playhouse

**303 MAIN ST, VISTA; 760/724-2110** This 382-seat theater was once the town's sole movie theater. It has been renovated as an indoor venue for Moonlight Stage Productions (see Moonlight Amphitheater), as well as for community organizations and events. *www.ci.vista.ca.us/avo; map:AA6* ⚓

### California Center for the Arts, Escondido

**340 N ESCONDIDO BLVD, ESCONDIDO; 760/839-4100 OR 800/988-4253** This elaborate cultural center was the dream of Escondido civic leaders who wanted to bring up-to-date plays, musical performances, and art to North County. Classic in style, the California Center for the Arts, Escondido, occupies 12 acres adjacent to historic Grape Day Park, site of several historical museums. Its 1,500-seat concert hall easily accommodates music festivals as well as Broadway plays, major dance productions, and community gatherings, while the 400-seat Center Hall is booked for dramas and more intimate musical performances. It has served as the impetus for the town's burgeoning culture and dining scene, even stirring downtown denizens from their urban digs. *www.artcenter.org; map:CC2* ⚓

### Coronado Playhouse

**1775 STRAND WY, CORONADO; 619/435-4856** This small, run-down building on Glorietta Bay (across from the Hotel del Coronado) was used as a WAVES barracks during World War II. Currently serving as a community theater, this small venue seats 104, cabaret style, and presents musicals, comedies, and mysteries. The management found Friday-night dinner theater buffets ($15 over the usual ticket price of $20) so successful, they added Sunday brunches. The Playhouse stages free performances of Shakespeare's plays on the outdoor grassy area by the bay on weekends at 8pm from August to September. *www.coronadoplayhouse.com; map:NN5* ⚓

## TICKET ALERT

Tickets for most of the concert and performing arts venues can be purchased through **TICKETMASTER.** Call 619/220-8497 or visit the web site at www.ticketmaster.com for locations. Many of the Wherehouse and Robinsons-May stores around town have Ticketmaster outlets. The San Diego Performing Arts League's **ARTS TIX** booth, just outside Horton Plaza, offers half-price tickets for many San Diego–area theater, music, and dance performances. These tickets are for the date of purchase on a cash-only basis. Call 619/497-5000 or visit the web site at www.sandiegoperforms.com for more information. The Arts Tix booth is also a Ticketmaster outlet selling full-price tickets.

—*Susan Humphrey*

### East County Performing Arts Center

**210 EAST MAIN ST, EL CAJON; 619/440-2277** Performers and audience members alike appreciate the acoustics in this 1,142-seat theater, where the back row is only about 100 feet from the stage. During a performance in 1998, Tony Bennett asked for all amplification to be turned off when he belted out a song that resonated throughout the theater. Each season, the concert hall hosts a wide variety of performers, from Steve Lawrence and Eydie Gorme to the Inbal Dance Theater, Tommy Tune, Directions in Music with Herbie Hancock, and chamber music concerts. *www.ecpac.com; map:KK1* &

### The Globe Theatres

**EL PRADO, BALBOA PARK, DOWNTOWN; 619/239-2255** The Old Globe Theatre in Balboa Park has been a San Diego tradition since it opened in 1935 as a charming little replica of the Old Globe in London. At first the performances were hour-long versions of Shakespeare's plays. Today the Globe is part of an umbrella organization called the Globe Theatres, which encompasses three theaters (the Old Globe, the Cassius Carter, and the outdoor Lowell Davies Festival Stage), and Shakespeare is only one of many playwrights given a hearing.

Works by Edward Albee, Thornton Wilder, Stephen Sondheim, and Neil Simon have had their turn on the stage. Stage and screen actors consider starring at the Old Globe a rite of passage—one worth revisiting. Jon Voight, Sada Thompson, David Ogden Stiers, Victor Buono, Kelsey Grammer, and Christopher Reeve have all starred here. The Globe now ranks as the longest-established professional theater in California.

In 1978 the main theater burned to the ground. Some say the fire was set by an actor who disliked the acoustics—which were bad. No such problems exist now. The citizens of San Diego devoted millions of dollars and hours to the Globe's reconstruction, and it reopened in 1982 with three distinct structures. The Lowell Davies Festival Stage is especially fun, as the outdoor stage and seats border the San Diego Zoo. *Night of the Iguana* and *Henry the IV* (with John Goodman) both played well here, with a background of chirping birds. The Festival Stage was destroyed by a fire in 1984, but quickly returned.

In 1981, the Globe established a talented triumvirate to guide the theaters into prominence. Craig Noel (who first acted at the Globe in 1937) became executive producer, Jack O'Brien was named artistic director, and Thomas Hall took the role of managing director. Hall has moved on, but during his tenure the Globe's revival of *Damn Yankees* made its way to Broadway. All in all, nine of the Globe's productions have gone on to the bright lights of Broadway. The theater regularly produces a season of at least 12 main-stage productions. At the height of its season, the company consists of 250 artistic and administrative staff and more than 1,000 volunteers. *www.theglobetheatres.org; map:O5* &

## Horton Grand Theatre

**444 4TH AVE, DOWNTOWN; 619/234-9583** This modest theater in a historic building has been running *Triple Espresso,* a comedy that's become an institution in several cities. The brick building, around the corner from the Horton Grand Hotel, once housed the Gaslamp Theatre Company, a venue for new plays and playwrights. Weary travelers benefit from a nice dinner in the Gaslamp and a few chuckles and guffaws at the play. *www.tripleespresso.com; map:N8* &

## La Jolla Playhouse

**2910 LA JOLLA VILLAGE DR, LA JOLLA; 858/550-1010** Gregory Peck, Dorothy Maguire, and Mel Ferrer liked hanging around La Jolla in the 1940s, and developed a reason to stay by forming the La Jolla Playhouse in 1947. In many ways, they were the inspiration for San Diego's thriving theater scene. Lack of funding caused the Playhouse to close in 1964; it was resurrected as the Mandell Weiss Center for the Performing Arts on the campus of the University of California at San Diego in 1983. There are now two theaters at UCSD under the La Jolla Playhouse banner: the Mandell Weiss Theater, where large productions are presented, and the more intimate Forum. Theater critics from New York and London pay close attention to Playhouse schedules; several local productions have made it to Broadway and beyond.

Des McAnuff, the first director of the current Playhouse, took local productions of *Big River, A Walk in the Woods, The Who's Tommy,* and *How to Succeed in Business Without Really Trying* to Broadway. He then handed the baton to Michael Greif, best known as director of the Tony- and Pulitzer-winning show *Rent.* Greif brought *Rent* with him for its West Coast premiere, and went on to direct Randy Newman's *Faust.* During Greif's tenure, the Playhouse won the 1993 Tony as America's Outstanding Regional Theater. Des McAnuff returned as artistic director in 2001.

Classical plays, each with an unusual twist, alternate with new productions that are constant surprises. Plays are given elaborate productions, with no theatrical holds barred. Playwrights, musicians, set designers, and stars challenge their boundaries during the May-to-November six-play series. The 2001–2002 season included *Tartuffe, Feast of Fools, When Grace Comes In,* and *Adoration of the Old Woman.* *www.lajollaplayhouse.com; map:JJ6* &

## Lamb's Players Theatre

**1142 ORANGE AVE, CORONADO; 619/437-0600** A full-time, long-term company of actors, directors, playwrights, and designers, Lamb's is the only San Diego theater with a year-round repertory company. It performs in the historic Spreckels Building in downtown Coronado, which has no seat more than seven rows from the stage. The resident theater offers five main-stage productions from February through November, with a Christmas production in December. The troupe also presents a Christmas show at the Hotel del Coronado and one production during the summer at the Lyceum Theatre in Horton Plaza.

The company came together in the early 1970s as a Christian street theater troupe. In its 30 years, it has become one of Southern California's leading professional nonprofit theaters, with a year-round staff of 42 and an annual budget of $3.7 million. Though no longer Christian based, the troupe aims to please everyone with humorous takes on the human condition such as *Joyful Noise* and *Till We Have Faces* and the musical revues *Boomers* and *American Rhythm*. Productions are geared to the 8,000 subscribers; plays are challenging but not outrageous, and the old chaste image is fast disappearing. *www.lambsplayers.org; map:NN5* &

## Moonlight Amphitheater

**1200 VALE TERRACE DR, VISTA; 760/724-2110** After two decades in operation, Moonlight Stage Productions in Vista has become one of the most important venues in North County. Its 2,000 seats combine reserved seats and general-admission lawn seating—meaning plenty of grass for picnic blankets. Patrons are encouraged to bring their own alfresco meal or purchase snacks and full-course dinners at the concession stand. The season runs June through September, opening with a youth theater production followed by four Broadway-style musicals. *www.moonlightstage. com map:AA6* &

## Mystery Cafe Dinner Theatre

**505 KALMIA ST, DOWNTOWN; 619/544-1600** Dinner guests mingle with actors performing tales of blackmail, deceit, and murder. It's all tongue-in-cheek, but the impact is considerable when you find the person sitting next to you is the killer. You might even have a starring role. Includes a four-course dinner and show, with informal group seating Friday and Saturday nights at Imperial House Restaurant. *www.mysterycafe.org; map:N5* &

## North Coast Repertory Theatre

**987-D LOMAS SANTA FE AVE, SOLANA BEACH; 858/481-1055** This intimate 194-seat theater has produced more than 125 high-quality plays in 20 seasons. The company focuses on neglected plays of merit, both contemporary and classical, and those that address social issues. An audience of more than 30,000 annually views award-winning plays and West Coast premieres of plays not otherwise staged in the area. In addition, the organization hosts an Off-Night Series, with a wide variety of performances, and Theatre School productions. The theater was founded by Tom and Olive Blakistone with a group of dedicated volunteers and is under the artistic direction of Sean Murray. It employs a full-time staff of seven, with more than 300 volunteers. Year-round, the schedule aims for seven main-stage plays from June through May. *www.northcoastrep.org; map:FF7* &

## Poway Center for the Performing Arts

**15498 ESPOLA RD, POWAY; 858/748-0505** This stunning building, with a 30-foot window-wall along the full length of the east side of the lobby providing views of the surrounding countryside, is an excellent venue for performances by big-name touring artists, entertainers, and ensembles, as well as a user-friendly environment for community- and school-based productions. Recent performers include Manhattan Transfer, Trinity Irish Dance Company, Arturo Sandoval, and the Reduced Shakespeare Company. *www.powayarts.org; map:FF2* &

## San Diego Civic Theatre

**202 C ST, DOWNTOWN; 619/615-4100** This large venue (almost 3,000 capacity with a 123- by 60-foot stage) is part of the downtown San Diego Community Concourse, which was formally dedicated in 1965, the year the theater played host to the first staging of the San Diego Opera (*La Boheme*). In addition to the five operas presented annually, Broadway/San Diego (619/231-8995; www.broadwaysd.com) has presented its shows of late exclusively at the San Diego Civic Theatre. Under the Broadway/San Diego banner, San Diegans get everything from rock concerts and dance performances to blockbuster musicals and legitimate drama. The theater is praised by performers for its performer-friendly acoustics. *www.sdccc.org; map:N7* &

## San Diego Repertory Theatre

**79 HORTON PLAZA, DOWNTOWN; 619/544-1000** This energetic nonprofit company is in its 27th year in San Diego and its 17th at the Horton Plaza Lyceum Theatre. There are two spaces at the Lyceum: the 550-seat Stage and the 260-seat Space. The Rep, as it's called, stages six plays a subscription season (September to June), an annual production of *A Christmas Carol,* and two festivals: the Kuumba Fest, showcasing local African-American performers, and the Lipinsky Family San Diego Jewish Arts Festival. Artistic director Sam Woodhouse chooses musicals, comedy, drama, new plays, and classics to fill his demanding schedule. Edward Albee's *Who's Afraid of Virginia Woolf?* was featured in 2001. Latin American playwrights are treated with respect by the Rep, and you can always count on at least one twisted production each season. *Six Women with Brain Death* was one of the longest-running shows in Rep history, and the intellectual side of Steve Martin was showcased in *Picasso at the Lapin Agile* in 1999. *www.sandiegorep.com; map:N7* &

## Sledgehammer Theatre

**1620 6TH AVE, DOWNTOWN; 619/544-1484** The name says it all. Known for powerful, controversial productions, the Sledgehammer professes "an intense dedication to the development of new American voices in the theater." The company's actors spent most of their early years as urban gypsies, alternating between sites ranging from San Diego's Old Carnation Milk Factory to a variety of now-abandoned or destroyed warehouses (though they had one fling at New York's Whitney Museum of American Art). Now in its 17th year, Sledgehammer has also provided graduates and undergraduates from the University of California at San Diego with their first professional credits. Notorious productions include a five-hour uncut *Hamlet, Demonology, Peter Pan* (with a twist), and *Sweet Charity* (with an ultrafeminist slant). More recently, the group has concentrated on ensemble-created and -generated pieces such as *The Frankenstein Project, The Devil's River,* and *The Universal Monster Show.* Since 1992, Sledgehammer Theatre has made its home in a converted funeral chapel, Saint Cecilia's, formerly the Sixth Avenue Playhouse. *www.sledge hammer.org; map:O6* &

## Starlight Theatre

**2005 PAN AMERICAN PLAZA, BALBOA PARK, DOWNTOWN; 619/544-7827** The Starlight Theater in Balboa Park is a San Diego tradition. For 56 years theatergoers have flocked to its 4,000-seat amphitheater, bringing picnic boxes and a thirst for good music and drama. Unfortunately, the theater is directly in the flight path of planes landing at Lindbergh Field, so the action freezes onstage when a plane zooms overhead and then resumes when all is clear. Audiences have become accustomed to this odd method of performance, but Starlight aficionados have long wished for an indoor venue. Recent productions include *1776, My One and Only, Annie,* and *Jekyll and Hyde.* Children 12 and under get in free when accompanied by an adult on Thursdays and Sundays. *www.starlighttheatre.org; map:O5* &

## Theatre in Old Town

**4040 TWIGGS ST, OLD TOWN; 619/688-2494** Located in the heart of Old Town San Diego State Historic Park, this professional theater company specializes in bringing Broadway and off-Broadway musicals and comedies to life. These year-round, open-ended productions have included *Beehive, Forever Plaid,* and *Forbidden Broadway.* *www.theatreinoldtown.com; map:J2* &

## University of California at San Diego Theatre

**2910 LA JOLLA VILLAGE DR, LA JOLLA; 858/534-4574** The UCSD Department of Theatre and Dance is the third-ranked graduate theater training program in the nation. It shares facilities with La Jolla Playhouse at the Mandell Weiss Center for the Performing Arts; MFA students in acting, design, directing, and stage management get at least one professional residency with the La Jolla Playhouse company. The department produces 10 main-stage shows a year, with eight at other venues on campus. The selections are from Shakespeare, Greek tragedy, cutting-edge drama and comedy, and theater/dance. The season is from fall to June. Tickets to UCSD's main-stage shows are a good bargain, and half-price for students. *www-theatre.ucsd.edu; map:II6* &

## Welk Resort Theatre

**8860 LAWRENCE WELK DR, ESCONDIDO; 760/749-3448** Yes, it's Lawrence Welk's old haunt, built in 1981. The theater is part of the Welk Resort Center, which includes a hotel, golf course, and shopping center. Until he died in 1992, the champagne-and-bubbles host lived nearby. The 339-seat theater stages five productions a year—four established musicals and one regular Christmas show featuring ex-Welk stars and plenty of music. The cost includes dinner at a nearby Welk Resort restaurant. *www.welkresort.com; map:BB4* &

# Fringe Theaters

San Diego has a number of fringe theaters with loyal audiences. The **FRITZ THEATRE** (619/233-7505; www.fritztheatre.com; map:N8) hosts the annual Fritz Blitz of New Plays by California Playwrights in June and July. The rest of the year-round schedule includes works from off-Broadway, classics, and eclectic choices presented in venues such as the Lyceum Theatre, Sushi Performance and Visual Art, 6th@Penn (3704 6th Ave, Hillcrest; 619/688-9210; map:O3), and Saint Cecilia's. The **DIVERSIONARY THEATER** (4545 Park Blvd, downtown; 619/220-0097; www.diversionary.org; map:P1) focuses on gay, lesbian, bisexual, and transgender issues. It's upstairs but is wheelchair accessible. Five productions are held annually. **SPRUCE STREET FORUM** (301 Spruce Street, downtown; 619/295-0301; www.sprucestreetforum.com; map: N4 &) is an art gallery exhibiting work by emerging and established artists that also features a warm and inviting space for live performances. The Fresh Sound Music Series focuses on jazz, improvised, and contemporary classical music, while the Rubble on Spruce series, offered in conjunction with the Trummerflora Collective, boasts electronic and experimental concerts.

# Classical Music and Opera

Classical music fans in San Diego find a diverse assortment of concerts and recitals to choose from—be it a full orchestra in an acoustically sophisticated hall or a small ensemble playing in the park to the backdrop of the Pacific's crashing waves. The San Diego Symphony is at home in Copley Symphony Hall, presenting a delightful series of concerts appealing to a broad range of listeners. The San Diego Chamber Orchestra, La Jolla Chamber Music Society, San Diego Early Music Society, and Athenaeum Music & Arts Library also fill the classical roster with concerts and festivals in a wide variety of venues that cater to every budget and lifestyle. Don your tux and pack a fat wallet for one of the highbrow performances, or slip into your best faded jeans and pack a picnic for an easygoing and affordable night out.

## Athenaeum Music & Arts Library

**1008 WALL ST, LA JOLLA; 858/454-5872** Amid thousands of art and music books both recent and ancient, and a 7-foot Steinway grand piano, the 103-year-old Athenaeum Library proudly presents classical and jazz concerts, chamber music recitals, and related lectures to sell-out audiences. Stacking chairs and a few upholstered seats hold fewer than 150 enraptured patrons, who cram in for the Chamber Music Series featuring nationally renowned musicians. If you don't make it in, try the free Mini-Concerts-at-Noon, held every other Monday from October through May. *Map:JJ7* &

## La Jolla Chamber Music Society

**7946 IVANHOE AVE #309, LA JOLLA; 858/459-3728** Established in 1968, the La Jolla Chamber Music Society is an offspring of the Musical Arts Society of La Jolla (founded in 1941 by Nikolai Sokoloff) and a major force in both California and San Diego County's classical music presentations. The society's esteemed Revelle Series has offered intimate performances to discriminating music lovers since its inception.

Other programs include the Celebrity Series, bringing world-famous artists, ensembles, and symphony orchestras to the San Diego Civic Theatre stage; the Discovery Series, an outreach program performing in city schools, hospitals, senior centers, and other nontraditional venues; and the Piano Series. The society's annual chamber music festival, SummerFest La Jolla, under artistic director Cho-Liang Lin, presents local and visiting musicians, as well as a composer-in-residence and workshops for younger musicians. *www.ljcms.org; map:JJ7* &

## Mainly Mozart Festival

**121 BROADWAY, STE 374, DOWNTOWN; 619/239-0100** The Mainly Mozart Festival, overseen by artistic director and conductor David Atherton, is one of the country's most acclaimed classical music festivals. The summer festival usually takes place in June, spilling across both sides of the U.S./Mexico border. It showcases some of North America's finest artists in orchestral, chamber, and choral music. Performances are held at an eclectic variety of sites including the historic Spreckels Theater; the California Center for the Arts, Escondido; La Jolla's Neurosciences Institute; Saint Paul's Cathedral; the Westgate Hotel; and the Centro Cultural in Tijuana. In addition to the summer festival, Mainly Mozart produces its Spotlight Series of chamber music concerts from January through April and the Seaside Series of jazz performances from August through October. *www.mainlymozart.org; map:N7* &

## San Diego Chamber Orchestra

**2210 ENCINITAS BLVD, STE M, ENCINITAS; 760/753-6402** Conductor Donald Barra and the San Diego Chamber Orchestra provide high-quality concerts with repertoire from baroque through contemporary, esteemed guest artists, and a choice of venues. Recent programs focused on "French Impressions," "The Royal Family of the Guitar," featuring the Romeros Guitar Quartet, and "Spain: New and Old." The 35-member ensemble performs October through April, and presents five performances each December of Handel's *Messiah,* a Christmas extravaganza accompanied by the 120-voice San Diego Master Chorale. Concerts are offered in the 500-seat Sherwood Auditorium at the Museum of Contemporary Art, San Diego; at Saint Joseph's Cathedral (downtown); and at the Fairbanks Ranch Country Club, with some performances during the season at the California Center for the Arts, Escondido. The organization also hosts the Carnival Concert Series for families at the Del Mar Fairgrounds, with themes such as "Castles and Kingdoms" and "Pirate Adventures" explored by full orchestras, local ensembles, and artists. *www.sdco.org; map:EE7* &

## San Diego Early Music Society

**3510 DOVE CT, HILLCREST; 619/291-8246** Top local and international performers and ensembles fill Saint James-by-the-Sea (743 Prospect St, La Jolla) with the joyous, playful, and haunting sounds of medieval, baroque, and Renaissance music. Recent concerts have boasted works from Italian convents in the 16th and 17th centuries performed by Cappella Artemisia, "Masters of the Baroque" by the King's Consort, and selections showcasing the viola da gamba by the Bottom Line. *www.sdems.org; map:M4* &

## CLOWNING AROUND

You don't have to be a kid to fall in love with **FERN STREET CIRCUS** (619/235-9756; www.fernstreetcircus.org), but a sense of humor is definitely required. Eclectic audiences spend many a sunny afternoon in Balboa Park enjoying a snow cone and a performance by this quirky and energetic group. The players create a new circus show each year with titles like the witty "The Fool's Parade," "World of Wonder" (based on a short story by Nigerian author Ben Okri), and "Hamar (The Big City)."

Led by a multilingual ringmaster, local professional circus and variety artists perform in a simple outdoor setting to live music, joined by teens and children taught in Fern Street's After-School Circus Skills Program. Audiences are treated to feats of strength and balance, tumbling, high-wire daring, and more. The performers have an infectious sense of adventure and pleasure in their skills, along with a finely honed sense of silliness. The audience is most appreciative.

Fern Street Circus was founded in 1990 to explore circus arts as a narrative form, to utilize circus arts performance and instruction as a means of "community-making," and to create a humane and collaborative atmosphere for practicing the many disciplines involved in the circus acts. The troupe provides entertainment throughout the year for a variety of community programs and corporate events, and members are often found at neighborhood street festivals across the county. The group's After-School Circus Skills Program convenes at the Golden Hill Recreation Center for lessons in trapeze, acrobatics, juggling, wire-walking, clowning, and stilt-walking. Many of these kids take part in the yearly productions. Fern Street Circus performances remind us that fun and play are important in our lives.

—*Leslie Venolia*

## San Diego Opera

**202 C ST, DOWNTOWN; 619/232-7636** San Diego Opera is Southern California's oldest opera company, offering productions of the highest quality. The company has been in existence 37 years, for the last 19 under the direction of Ian Campbell, formerly of the Metropolitan Opera in New York. The company produces five grand operas a year in San Diego's Civic Theatre (January to May), along with concerts and recitals in Sherwood Auditorium at the Museum of Contemporary Art, La Jolla. Through its participation in the North American Voices Project, initiated in 1994, the company has showcased contemporary operas by North American composers, including Carlisle Floyd's *Cold Sassy Tree* (2001) and *A Streetcar Named Desire* by Andre Previn (2000). It conducts the largest opera education and outreach programs in the country, aimed at all age levels. *www.sdopera.com; map:N7* &

## San Diego Symphony

**1245 7TH AVE, DOWNTOWN; 619/235-0804** The history of the San Diego Symphony has followed a boom-and-bust cycle that may finally have been broken, thanks to the creation of the bounteous New World Endowment by Joan and Irwin Jacobs in 2002. The symphony was nearly destroyed due to budgetary woes in 1996, but came back to life under the guidance of esteemed artistic director and principal conductor Jung-Ho Pak. Pak, who led the symphony back to prominence and confidence, has stepped down, and the company will continue with direction by staff conductor Matthew Garbutt and guest conductors until a new permanent artistic director is selected.

The symphony's series include the Jacobs' Masterworks Series, with grand-style, elegant orchestral presentations of Chopin, Rossini, et al.; the Light Bulb Concerts, with classical music presented in an interactive format; the Family Festival Series, offering introductions to classical music through playful programs; and the Winter Pops concerts. Most of the concerts are held at the symphony's own 2,225-seat Copley Symphony Hall (the beautifully restored 1929 Fox Theatre, located at 750 B St); several Thursday-evening performances are presented at the California Center for the Arts, Escondido. The Summer Pops concerts and special performances offered at Navy Pier are especially popular with locals, who enjoy the music while snacking from picnic hampers in an outdoor setting. *www.sandiegosymphony.com; map:O7* &

## Spreckels Organ Pavilion

**1549 EL PRADO, BALBOA PARK, DOWNTOWN; 619/702-8138** Civic organist Carol Williams and guest organists dazzle Balboa Park visitors with free, year-round concerts at 2pm each Sunday at the Spreckels Organ Pavilion. The magnificent outdoor organ, christened in 1915, features humongous lead alloy pipes (some stretching 32 feet long). The exquisitely ornate pavilion seats 2,400. In addition to the Sunday performances, the Spreckels Organ Society hosts its free International Summer Organ Festival on Monday nights from mid-June through August at 7:30pm. *www.serve.com/sosorgan; map:O5* &

# Dance

San Diego's dance scene, though small compared to the ones in New York, Los Angeles, and San Francisco, is nonetheless a vibrant force in this city of dancing fools. Resident companies, anchored by the prestigious and enduring California Ballet, include a toe-tapping, heel-stomping connoisseur's mix of classical, contemporary, and modern troupes overseen by prominent dancers such as John Malashock. Ensembles perform at various theaters and concert halls around town, including the Civic Theatre; California Center for the Arts, Escondido; Sushi Performance and Visual Art; Poway Center for the Performing Arts; East County Performing Arts Center; and stages at the campuses of University of California at San Diego and San Diego State University (led by artistic director Jean Isaacs). The universities and community colleges also present visiting dance troupes as well as festivals throughout the year. Big-name visitors such as Mikhail Baryshnikov's White Oak Dance Project, Alvin Ailey American Dance Theater, Tap Dogs, and Riverdance usually take the stage at **CALIFORNIA CENTER FOR THE ARTS, ESCONDIDO** (340 N Escondido Blvd, Escondido; 800/988-4253; www.artcenter.org; map:CC2), or the **CIVIC THEATRE** (202 C St, downtown; 619/570-1100; map:N7), while cutting-edge performers fit the bill at **SUSHI PERFORMANCE AND VISUAL ART** (310 11th St, downtown; 619/235-8469; map:O8).

## California Ballet Company

**4819 RONSON CT, CLAIREMONT; 858/560-6741** The class act California Ballet Company, now in its 34th year, performs under the artistic direction of Maxine Mahon. Four or five traditional and contemporary productions are presented annually at venues throughout the county. The company's flagship production, *Nutcracker,* runs from Thanksgiving through Christmas and is staged at downtown's Civic Theatre. Other recent productions include *A Midsummer Night's Dream* and a full-length *Sleeping Beauty. www.californiaballet.org; map:JJ4* &

## Eveoke Dance Theatre

**644 7TH AVE, DOWNTOWN; 619/238-1153** Eveoke Dance Theatre is not just about pretty dancing; the group seeks to "cultivate compassionate social action through arts education and evocative performance." Formed in 1994, Eveoke dancers have performed 250 shows in 24 full-length dance-theater productions and teach more than 30 classes each week. Their productions are always thought-provoking; *Fishtales* (summer 2001), described as "the tale of four fish out of water," was presented alfresco at the Broadway Street Pier downtown. Eveoke also produces the Celebrate Dance Festival every August in Balboa Park, with more than 35 dance companies performing and offering workshops on indoor and outdoor stages, for free. *www. eveoke.org; map:O8* &

## Malashock Dance

**3103 FALCON ST, STE J, MISSION HILLS; 619/260-1622** Heading into its 14th year as a fixture on the arts scene, Malashock Dance is known for its innovative and emotionally charged work. Founding artistic director John Malashock, a former principal dancer with Twyla Tharp, is also one of the best collaborators in town. In addition to an annual season at the Globe Theatres, Malashock Dance is a frequent partner to companies including the San Diego Opera and the La Jolla Chamber Music Society, and to individual artists including Steven Schick and Art Johnson. With more than 40 programs created in the last 13 years, Malashock productions combine repertory favorites and new offerings. *www.malashockdance.org; map:O5* &

## San Diego Ballet

**5304 METRO ST, STE B, BAY PARK; 619/294-7378** Don't be surprised if the San Diego Ballet becomes a regional dance company for the Southwest. At least that's the plan—no pipe dream when you see the push being made by this capable company under the direction of Robin Sherertz Morgan and Javier Velasco. The company performs both classical and contemporary ballets such as "Preludes and Poetry," set to music by composer David Burge, as well as "Valentine Specials for Lovers and Others," on stages across the city. *www.sandiegoballet.org; map:LL5* &

## AIRPORT ART

The San Diego Port Authority jumped on the public art bandwagon in 1996, designating three-eighths of 1 percent of yearly projected port revenues (or $160,000, whichever sum is greater) to go toward public art in the airport and marine areas. The program has generated some controversy, and has been criticized for lacking verve and for missing opportunities. The Port Authority spent several million dollars on art as part of the expansion at **SAN DIEGO INTERNATIONAL AIRPORT.** Some of the 21 significant, permanent pieces of art that have been installed are quite pleasing, including Christopher Lee's **WATER AND SUN,** a lovely aqua pyramidal fountain of flowing water, and **SEA RHYTHMS,** Terry Thornsley's circular fountain with bronze sea lions and fish cavorting in seaweed. The cheerful, colorful tile mosaics of Mary Lynn Dominguez, collectively called **SEESHELLS,** are interestingly placed at the entrance to 12 rest rooms.

But much of the art or its placement is dismissed by professional critics. Some of the pieces are indeed timid, and some are mispositioned. A case in point is Gary Hughes' statue of immobile, overladen passengers, **AT THE GATE.** Although whimsical, the white-resin and fiberglass piece looks temporary and lost at the west end of the baggage claim area. The monumental **LOS VOLADORES/THE SUN FLIERS,** by Julian Quintana and Mario Torero, also loses its impact because of poor location near Terminal 1's parking lot. Joan Irving's **PAPER VORTEX,** a panel of etched and painted glass that forms part of the Terminal 2 security checkpoint, might as well be invisible. People in transit hurry by, too worried about whether their belt buckles will set off the security alarm to even notice the glass panel. Tradition prevails with the bronze sculptures **IN SEARCH OF WILDERNESS,** by Les Perhacs, and **LINDBERGH: THE BOY AND THE MAN,** by Paul Granlund, both outside Terminal 2.

Several new installations were added in 2001. Carolyn Braaksma created a series of large concrete panels incised with images of marine life to line the pedestrian corridor connecting Terminals 1 and 2. More colorful is **TREELINES,** a composite piece by San Diego State professor Gail Roberts. When viewed together, the 34 paintings and two sculptures loosely resemble a tree; individually, each painting depicts a different type of tree found in the San Diego area. Look for this interesting piece in Terminal 2 East.

—Jane Onstott

# Film

Although San Diego movie theaters (and the films shown within) tend to be of the multiplex variety, foreign and artier films are shown regularly at the KEN CINEMA (4061 Adams Ave, Kensington; 619/283-5909; map:LL3), HILLCREST CINEMAS (3965 5th Ave, Hillcrest; 619/299-2100; map:N2), and THE COVE (7730 Girard Ave, La Jolla; 858/459-5404; map:JJ7). And though the city lost two of its historic cinemas (the Guild and the Park), North County's 1920s LA PALOMA (471 S Coast Hwy 101, Encinitas; 760/436-7469; map:EE7) is still showing a mix of art and commercial films and film series. Multiplex fiends should head for Mission Valley, where you can choose from the AMC FASHION VALLEY 18 (7037 Friars Rd; 858/558-2262; map:LL5) or AMC MISSION VALLEY 20 (1640 Camino del Rio N; 858/558-2262; map:LL4). In the Gaslamp Quarter is the PACIFIC GASLAMP 15 (701 5th Ave; 619/232-0400; map:O8).

Every now and then, a token non-mainstream film squeaks onto one of the screens at UNITED ARTISTS HORTON PLAZA 14 (475 Horton Plaza, downtown; 619/444-3456; map:N7), HAZARD CENTER (7510 Hazard Center Dr, Mission Valley; 619/291-7777; map:LL4), and LA JOLLA VILLAGE CINEMAS (8879 Villa La Jolla Dr; 858/453-7831; map:JJ7).

The University of California at San Diego hosts the SAN DIEGO INTERNATIONAL FILM FESTIVAL during April, boasting San Diego premieres of more than 20 international films, as well as short subjects (Price Center Theater, UCSD; 858/534-8497; map:II7). The San Diego Maritime Museum's MOVIES BEFORE THE MAST series runs April through September, with films projected on a special sail aboard the 1863 windjammer *Star of India* (moored at 1306 North Harbor Dr, downtown; 619/234-9153; www.sdmaritime.com; map:M7). Animated film aficionados head for Spike and Mike's annual FESTIVAL OF ANIMATION (in April, suitable for all ages) and the raunchy SICK AND TWISTED FESTIVAL (in the autumn, for those 21 and older), in Sherwood Auditorium at the Museum of Contemporary Art in La Jolla (700 Prospect St, La Jolla; 858/454-0267; www.spikeandmike.com; map:JJ7). The annual SAN DIEGO LATINO FILM FESTIVAL (619/230-1938; www. sdlatinofilm.com) takes place in March at the Mann Hazard Center 7. The 80 films and videos from throughout Latin America and the United States focus on the Latino experience. The MUSEUM OF PHOTOGRAPHIC ARTS (Balboa Park, downtown; 619/238-7559; www.mopa.org; map:O5) and the SAN DIEGO MUSEUM OF ART (Balboa Park, downtown; 619/696-1966; www.sdmart.org; map:O5) both present film screenings throughout the year. The IMAX screen at the REUBEN H. FLEET SCIENCE CENTER (1875 El Prado, Balboa Park, downtown; 619/238-1233; www. rhfleet.org; map:O5) offers everything from fantastic voyages inside *The Human Body* to upclose tours of Mount Everest and the International Space Station.

# Literature

The woeful state of San Diego's literary arts scene has been the subject of lamentation for years, but there are those who think the scene is growing quite nicely. The large bookstore chains such as Borders Books and Music and Barnes & Noble regularly host readings and signings by local and touring authors.

Refreshingly, it's the independent booksellers that seem willing and able to snag top literary figures, at least for one night. Wordsmiths Allen Ginsberg, Amy Tan, Jane Smiley, Paul Theroux, and Isabel Allende have all read their work at either **WARWICK'S** (7812 Girard Ave, La Jolla; 858/454-0347; www.warwicks.com; map:JJ7), **D. G. WILLS** (7461 Girard Ave, La Jolla; 858/456-1800; map:JJ7), **BOOK WORKS** (2670 Via de la Valle, Del Mar; 858/755-3735; www.book-works.com; map:), or **ESMERALDA BOOKS AND COFFEE** (1555 Camino del Mar, Del Mar; 858/755-2707; map:GG7). One of San Diego's crowning moments in literary history was the night that Ginsberg read at D. G. Wills. The bookstore was predictably packed and the crowd had overflowed onto chic Girard Avenue, so Ginsberg used a microphone. As the staid, wealthy La Jollans took their evening constitutionals, they were treated to Ginsberg's amplified meanderings about the rear ends of young boys.

During the academic year, a variety of resident and visiting intellectuals, philosophers, writers, and poets take the podiums at the University of California at San Diego (858/534-4090) and San Diego State University (619/594-5200); most of these events are open to the public.

The growth of "the scene" is perhaps best demonstrated in the growing popularity of poetry readings and poetry slams. Readings are held on a regular basis at **CLAIRE DE LUNE COFFEE LOUNGE** (2906 University Ave, North Park; 619/688-9845; www.clairedelune.com; map:MM3 ) and at **TWIGG'S TEA AND COFFEE** (4590 Park Blvd, University Heights; 619/296-0616; www.twiggs.org; map:P1). Local "certified Slam Master" Robt O'Sullivan Schleith describes poetry slams as poetry competitions where entertainment and audience participation are the primary focus, and no props, costumes, or accompaniment are allowed. Poetry slams are held at the **URBAN GRIND** (3793 Park Blvd, Hillcrest; 619/294-2920; http://poetryscenestealers.tripod.com; map:P3) on the last Sunday and the Friday closest to the 15th each month.

**ARTISTS ON THE CUTTING EDGE,** a "cross-fertilization" literary and music series under the artistic direction of author and UCSD professor Quincy Troupe, features such exciting and provocative novelists, poets, and musicians as Pulitzer Prize winner Robert Olen Butler, Kamau Braithwaite, Alan Cheuse, Lucille Clifton, Gary Bartz, Russell Banks, and Marge Piercy, with authors' book-signings following each program. The five-night series is held April through early May at the Museum of Contemporary Art, La Jolla (700 Prospect St, La Jolla; 858/454-3541; www.mcasandiego.org; map:JJ7 &).

# NIGHTLIFE

# Nightlife by Features

## ALTERNATIVE
Brick by Brick
'Canes
Casbah
Club Xanth
Java Joe's
Livewire
On Broadway
Plan B
Winston's Beach Club

## BLUES
Belly Up Tavern
Blind Melons
Buffalo Joe's
Humphrey's
Patrick's II

## CELTIC
The Field

## COCKTAIL LOUNGES
E Street Alley
Humphrey's
The Jewel Box
Kensington Club
Live Wire
MiXX
On Broadway
Onyx Room
Pacific Shores
Red Fox Room
Top of the Hyatt
Top of the Park
The Tower
The Waterfront

## COFFEE AND DESSERTS
Caffe Italia
Esmeralda Books &
    Coffee
Gelato Vero Caffe
Java Joe's

Karen Krasne's
    Extraordinary Desserts
The Living Room
    Coffeehouse
Miracles Cafe
Twiggs Tea & Coffee

## COMEDY
The Comedy Store
Flick's
4th & B

## COUNTRY
In Cahoots

## DANCING/DANCE FLOOR
Barefoot Bar & Grill
Belly Up Tavern
Brick by Brick
Club Montage
E Street Alley
4th & B
In Cahoots
Live Wire
On Broadway
Onyx Room
Plan B
Rich's
Sevilla

## DRINKS WITH A VIEW
Barefoot Bar & Grill
'Canes
Sunshine Company Saloon
    Limited
Top of the Hyatt
Top of the Park

## FOLK/ACOUSTIC
Belly Up Tavern
Java Joe's
Miracles Cafe
Plaza Bar
Sevilla

## GAY/LESBIAN
Club Montage
Rich's
Top of the Park

## JAZZ
Buffalo Joe's
Croce's Jazz Bar/Top Hat
E Street Alley
Humphrey's
Onyx Room

## OUTDOOR SEATING
Aero Club
Barefoot Bar & Grill
'Canes
Dick's Last Resort
Humphrey's
Sunshine Company Saloon
    Limited

## PIANO BARS
Mille Fleurs
MiXX
Plaza Bar
Red Fox Room

## POOL/BILLIARDS
Aero Club
Blind Melons
Brick by Brick
Casbah
E Street Alley
Flick's
Gaslamp Billiard Palace
In Cahoots
The Jewel Box
Kensington Club
Live Wire
On Broadway
Pacific Shores
Plan B
Society Billiard Cafe

Sunshine Company Saloon
  Limited
The Tower
The Waterfront

**PUBS/BREWERIES**
Aero Club
The Field
Gaslamp Billiard Palace
Karl Strauss Brewery &
  Grill
Princess Pub & Grille
South Beach Bar and Grill

**REGGAE/SKA/WORLD
BEAT**
Bar Dynamite
Belly Up Tavern

**ROCK**
Barefoot Bar & Grill
Belly Up Tavern
Casbah
E Street Alley
4th & B

**ROMANTIC**
Karen Krasne's
  Extraordinary Desserts
Mille Fleurs

The Onyx Room
Plaza Bar
Top of the Hyatt

**SPORTS BARS**
Sunshine Company Saloon
  Limited
Trophy's

**UNDERAGE/NO
ALCOHOL**
Dizzy's
Club Xanth
Mira Mesa Epicentre
The Scene

# Nightlife by Neighborhood

**CARDIFF-BY-THE-SEA**
Miracles Cafe

**CARLSBAD**
Karl Strauss Brewery & Grill
Sevilla

**COLLEGE AREA**
The Living Room Coffeehouse

**DEL MAR**
Esmeralda Coffee & Books
Pannikin Coffee and Tea

**DOWNTOWN**
Buffalo Joe's
Croce's Jazz Bar/Top Hat
Dick's Last Resort
E Street Alley
The Field
4th & B
Gaslamp Billiard Palace
The Jewel Box
On Broadway
Onyx Room
Pannikin Coffee and Tea
Patrick's II
Plaza Bar
Sevilla
Top of the Hyatt
Twiggs Tea & Coffee
The Waterfront

**ENCINITAS**
Pannikin Coffee and Tea

**HILLCREST**
Flick's
The Living Room Coffeehouse
MiXX
Rich's
Top of the Park

**KENSINGTON**
Kensington Club
The Tower

**LA JOLLA**
The Comedy Store
The Living Room Coffeehouse
Karl Strauss Brewery & Grill
Pannikin Coffee and Tea

**MIDDLETOWN**
Aero Club
Bar Dynamite
Caffe Italia
Casbah
Club Montage
Gelato Vero Caffe
Karen Krasne's Extraordinary Desserts
Princess Pub & Grille

**MISSION BAY**
Barefoot Bar & Grill

**MISSION BEACH**
'Canes

**MISSION VALLEY**
Brick by Brick
In Cahoots
Trophy's

**NORTH PARK**
Club Xanth
Red Fox Room

**OCEAN BEACH**
Java Joe's
Pacific Shores
South Beach Bar and Grill
Sunshine Company Saloon Limited
Winston's Beach Club

**OLD TOWN**
The Living Room Coffeehouse

**PACIFIC BEACH**
Blind Melons
Plan B
Society Billiard Cafe

**POINT LOMA**
The Living Room Coffeehouse
Pannikin Cafe

**RANCHO SANTA FE**
Mille Fleurs

**SHELTER ISLAND**
Humphrey's

**SOLANA BEACH**
Belly Up Tavern

**SORRENTO VALLEY**
Karl Strauss Brewery & Grill

**UNIVERSITY HEIGHTS**
Live Wire
Twiggs Tea & Coffee

# NIGHTLIFE

The sun rules in San Diego; only the young stay out past midnight. Hence, the nightlife scene ebbs and flows with current trends and clubs drift out of sight regularly. Fortunately, a handful of stalwart music venues, dive bars, clubs, and pubs withstand the vagaries of local tastes.

A 1998 state ban on smoking in bars created quite a furor among owners and barflies, and a few addicts still light up in their favorite dives (risking hefty fines). Some clubs have opened outdoor patios for those who need consistent nicotine fixes, and nonsmokers are delighted to be able to hear their favorite bands without going home smelling like an ashtray.

Listed below are the tried-and-true haunts, along with the latest hot spots. Phone numbers, opening hours, and other particulars change like the tides. Check the *San Diego Reader* (the largest free paper, which comes out on Thursdays), and the Night and Day section of the *San Diego Union Tribune* (also out on Thursdays) for updated information.

## Music and Clubs

### Bar Dynamite

**1808 W WASHINGTON ST, MIDDLETOWN; 619/295-8743** Located conveniently off I-5, at an intersection of roads that lead to downtown, Hillcrest, or Old Town, Bar Dynamite is often a preparty meeting spot that turns into an all-nighter. The DJs spin increasingly energetic rare groove, salsa, soul, trip-hop, break beats, house, techno, and trance throughout any given evening and hence are responsible for the bar's modish cred. A sleeper on the hipster circuit, tiny "Bar D" built a buzz the old-fashioned way: easy atmosphere, cool music, and word of mouth from the right lips. Local underground star DJ Greyboy has been the de facto resident jock. It's also an unpretentious kick to relax in this simple dive, where *everything* in the place is red—including the tint on the TV set. Bar Dynamite is a hit with the ladies, no doubt because the usual meat-market tactics are pleasantly absent. Expect to stand in line most nights—there's no cover. *AE, DIS, MC, V; no checks; Tues–Sun; full bar; map:K3* &

### Belly Up Tavern

**143 S CEDROS AVE, SOLANA BEACH; 858/481-8140** For 25 years the BUT, as it is locally known, has been considered one of the best live music venues in the county, with performances every night of the week. Bonnie Raitt played here frequently before she hit the Top 40; these days bands like Too Cynical to Cry and the Zydeco Bluez Patrol keep the crowds happy. With a great dance floor, an interesting blues photo collection, free sodas or juice for the designated driver (in a party of two or more), and a consistently safe environment, the BUT is one of our best faves. Come early for a great table and order dinner from the bar, or dine at the Wild Note Cafe, next door. The Wild Note also hosts live music on weekends, other nights during the week, and for a Sunday jazz brunch. Also at the Wild Note are "Wine Wednesdays," during which diners sample half a dozen vintages, each with a different appetizer. *AE, DIS, MC, V; no checks; every day; full bar; www.bellyup.com; map:FF7*

## Blind Melons

**710 GARNET AVE, PACIFIC BEACH; 858/483-7844** Just steps from the beach and pier, this classic blues bar hosts live bands every night, giving the occasional nod to jazz. Pool tables at the back add to the down-home ambiance, but it's the music that keeps the soul churning. There is a cover charge when groups are playing. *MC, V; no checks; every day; full bar; map:KK7*

## Brick by Brick

**1130 BUENOS AVE, MISSION VALLEY; 619/275-5483** This gritty mainstay of San Diego hard rock regularly hosts local metal and garage bands, plus an impressive roster of touring acts. Morphine, R.E.M., Rollins Band, and Sonic Youth have all played the Brick. Snuggled behind the I-5 and I-8 interchange, the club isn't as well known or crowded as hipster nemesis the Casbah. Here you can slap a high five with your underground hero onstage—and still have space to get a beer, relax on one of the couches, or shoot pool in the club's lounge. A roomy interior with good sight lines helps save the eardrums without missing the action. *AE, MC, V; no checks; every day; full bar; www.brickbybrick1.com; mhb1130@yahoo.com; map:LL6* &

## Buffalo Joe's

**600 5TH AVE, DOWNTOWN; 619/236-1616** Formerly a country bar, Buffalo Joe's has adapted to the times and become one of the leading-edge clubs in the Gaslamp Quarter. Alternately jazzy, funky, or down with the blues, visiting bands tease audiences with new combinations of retro styles and contemporary attitudes. Friday nights are usually '80s, Saturday nights belong to disco, and even the hip-hop sticks to the old-school style. Below the main club is the rap-friendly BK Lounge, open sporadically but worth the call ahead. Expect to stand in line. *AE, MC, V; no checks; every day; full bar; www.buffalojoes.com; info@buffalojoes.com; map:O8* &

## 'Canes

**3105 OCEAN FRONT WALK, MISSION BEACH; 858/488-1780** People-watching and sunbathing are sports at 'Canes, located right on the boardwalk in Mission Beach. Its two-block-long rooftop is a prime place to do both, or to get a burger, salad, or pasta. At night, the regulars fade away and 'Canes comes alive with young music fans: depending on the concert, kids as young as 16 may be admitted. DJs spin records at Saturday night's Club Pulse, when 18 and older are admitted in the main room, 21 and older in the back. If you don't have a California driver's license, bring two picture IDs (bouncers in Pacific and Mission Beaches are firm on this). *AE, DC, DIS, MC, V; no checks; every day; full bar; www.canesbarandgrill.com; map:LL7* &

## The Casbah

**2501 KETTNER BLVD, MIDDLETOWN; 619/232-4355** What appears to be a humble hodgepodge of rooms is actually the critical mass of San Diego's groovin' music scene. Local bands Three Mile Pilot, Rocket from the Crypt, and Drive Like Jehu open for touring acts; owner Tim Mays boasts that treating bands right has attracted such headliners as Nirvana, Smashing Pumpkins, and Alanis Morissette. The venue

## ALTERNATIVE VENUES

While San Diego has earned the rep of a party town populated by beer-soaked coeds and tequila shooters, a sober, all-ages nightlife has quietly grown up as an alternative in recent years. According to **SLAMM–SAN DIEGO'S MUSIC MAGAZINE** (3530 Camino del Rio N, Ste 105, Mission Valley; 619/281-7526; www.slammsd.com; slammsd@slammsd.com)—the biweekly authority on all things alternative, young, and music related in the city—San Diego now has more quality acts of varying styles and beliefs than ever before. Many, like Chula Vista's **P.O.D.** and local punkers **DOGWOOD,** live lifestyles that eschew the sex and drug clichés of rock and roll. Power pop, punk, and alternative hip-hop fans of any age can make **THE SCENE** (7514 Clairemont Mesa Blvd, Kearny Mesa; 858/505-9111; cash only; Thurs–Sat; no alcohol; www.thescenelive.com; contact@thescenelive.com). The converted print shop now offers a spacious stage and sound system for major touring acts like Le Tigre. The other punky teen venue is a non-profit, community outreach facility, **THE MIRA MESA EPICENTRE** (8450 Mira Mesa Blvd, Kearny Mesa; 858/271-4000; cash only; every day; no alcohol; www.epicentreconcerts.com; info@epicentreconcerts.com). The center books live music acts as part of a program to teach local youth entrepreneurial skills. Its **TWISTER CAFE** serves health-conscious snacks to fans of local bands and touring indie rockers alike, and like everything at the Epicentre, it's run by teens themselves, with volunteer adults as advisers. For a more mature adventure in age-unlimited musicianship, try **DIZZY'S** (344 7th Ave, downtown; 858/270-7467; checks OK; Wed–Sat; no alcohol; www.dizzyssandiego.com) in downtown's East Village. Run by local spoken-word and visual artist Chuck Perrin, Dizzy's evokes the Beat-era jazz clubs of its namesake neighborhood, New York City's East Village. Famous for hosting local horn hero **GILBERT CASTELLANO**'s all-night jam sessions, the club features an eclectic, artist-centered roster of acts—the most impressive of whom are often the big-band jazz ensembles. Finally, for those who need their music and sobriety in equally supportive surroundings, the Saturday night meetings of **ALCOHOLICS ANONYMOUS** at the **NORTH SHORES ALANO CLUB** (4861 Cass St, Pacific Beach; 619/483-4084; free; Sat; no alcohol; www.aasandiego.org) feature guest speakers and a blues jam session afterwards.

—*Will Shilling*

holds about 200, and there are a few seats—good luck getting one. MC, V; *no checks; every day; full bar; www.casbahmusic.com; map:M5*

## Club Montage

**2028 HANCOCK ST, MIDDLETOWN; 619/294-9590** Dazzling laser light shows and psychedelic video projections make this multistoried, fog-filled labyrinth of rooms, balconies, and dance pads all the more interesting. Montage is one of the few clubs open three hours after liquor sales cease. The majority of the crowd is straight, but gay clubbers are the real movers and shakers. Candy-striper drag queens and plenty of bare-chested young males strut their stuff on the rooftop patio. The crowd tops out at 1,500—naturally, the pickup action is lively. *Cash only; Thurs–Sat; full bar; www.clubmontage.com; party@clubmontage.com; map:J3*

## Club Xanth

**4225 30TH ST, NORTH PARK; 619/584-2720** One of the few 18-and-up nightclubs in town, the former Empire Club—which was an underage punk rock institution—has reinvented itself in an even less baby-boomer-friendly guise: goth. But don't be scared, Virginia, Club Xanth is fiercely devoted to a positive, drug-free environment for not just the under-21 crowd, but everybody who enjoys their music industrial, their eyeliner heavy, and their coffee strong. Friday splits the evening between an all-ages club until 10pm and a techno set for 18 and up later; Saturdays are the wildly popular, and wildly populated, gothic/industrial evenings. Live music and DJ sets are about fifty-fifty overall, but the weeknights offer the most eclectic styles, such as jungle, hip-hop, drum'n'bass, and break beats. *cash only; Tues–Sun; no alcohol; www.clubxanth.com; map:LL4* &

## The Comedy Store

**916 PEARL ST, LA JOLLA; 858/454-9176** This old-time venue attracts seasoned comics, including Pauly Shore and Tommy Davidson, local DJs and comics perfecting their shticks, and open-mike nights for the brave at heart. There's a two-drink minimum; the cover charge varies with the act. *AE, MC, V; no checks; Wed–Sun; full bar; map:JJ7*

## Croce's Restaurant & Jazz Bar

**802 5TH AVE, DOWNTOWN; 619/233-4355** Ingrid Croce, wife of the late Jim Croce, is the doyenne of two of the Gaslamp Quarter's most popular clubs. The Jazz Bar hosts live music every night of the week after 8:30, including well-known artists like Hollis Gentry. The adjacent Croce's Top Hat Bar & Grill (818 5th Ave; 619/233-6945; map:O7) is open Fridays and Saturdays only and invites specifically blues bands to play, including such local talent as Sue Palmer and Ruby and the Red Hots. *AE, DIS, MC, V; no checks; every day; full bar; www.croces.com; map:O7*

## E Street Alley

**919 4TH AVE, DOWNTOWN; 619/231-9200** An underground space with a maze of lounges and bars, E Street is a one-stop-fits-all club. Down-tempo jazz and trip-hop play in the comfy lounge, pool balls clink in the bar, and tanned tourists mingle with college students, dancing and flirting in the downtown Gaslamp Quarter's most consistently popular nightspot. With its classy atmosphere and crowd-pleasing DJs grooving on Top 40, hip-hop, house, and techno sounds—usually in that order—E Street is a ticket that draws hipsters and out-of-towners alike. Expect lines on weekend nights. *AE, DIS, MC, V; no checks; Thurs–Sat; full bar; www.estreetalley. com; map:N7*

## 4th & B

**345 B ST, DOWNTOWN; 619/231-2131** A clever developer has transformed a '70s-style bank into the top music venue in the city, with a capacity of 1,500 people. One of the eight bars is in the old vault; others are on the balcony and in the VIP lounge. The club books comedians as well as the best of the touring bands—everything from alternative and blues to hip-hop, rockabilly, and punk. On some nights the venue is rented to private parties, which might mean a corporate cigar-and-martini party or even a private birthday or anniversary celebration. The only real constant is Saturday club night, when DJs spin techno and house music. *AE, MC, V; no checks; every day; full bar; www.4thandb.com; map:N7* &

## Humphrey's

**2241 SHELTER ISLAND DR, SHELTER ISLAND; 619/224-3577** Best known for its summer series of outdoor concerts, Humphrey's also has live music most nights in the indoor lounge. Jazz, swing, and piano-bar musicians rotate through the schedule, which tends to change with the whims of the times; call ahead. The outdoor concert series attracts big-name bands (see Performing Arts chapter). *AE, DC, DIS, MC, V; no checks; call for schedule; full bar; map:F7* &

## In Cahoots

**5373 MISSION CENTER RD, MISSION VALLEY; 619/291-8635** As their slogan says, this is "the most fun you'll have with your boots on." The barn-like structure is perfect for long lines of dancers doing the Tush Push, Copperhead Row, or the Stomp. Novices mimic the moves in classes from 6:30 to 8pm (Wednesdays excepted) before joining the crowd. Cahoots offers more than dancing, including six pool tables and three bars. Pick up a beer at the bar, then search for seating—try for a stool at the wraparound upper deck with views of the dance floor and DJ. The crowd is amiable, though the occasional beer-hall battle keeps security guards on their toes. *AE, DIS, MC, V; no checks; Mon–Sat; full bar; www.incahoots.com/homepage.htm; in cahootssandiego@msn.com; map:LL4* &

## Livewire

**2501 KETTNER BLVD, MIDDLETOWN; 619/232-4355** An offshoot of the Jivewire in North Park, Livewire is not physically a bar or club, but a unique state of mind—think "indie-rock sock hop"—occurring either monthly or bimonthly, usually at the Casbah. Livewire is extremely popular for what it attempts: a playful, eclectic, usually retro-themed event with DJs. When it's held at the Casbah, two full bars and a beer jockey keep spirits high. Smokers have the luxury of an open-air patio between rooms. Often falling on the Sunday before a major holiday, Livewire is admission-free if you arrive by 9pm. Inevitably, long lines form later. *MC, V; no checks; schedule varies; full bar; www.casbahmusic.com; map:M5*

## Mille Fleurs

**6009 PASEO DELICIAS, RANCHO SANTA FE; 858/756-3085** Best known as one of the finest restaurants in the county (see Restaurants chapter), Mille Fleurs also draws a moneyed crowd to its classy piano bar. Pianist Randy Beecher has been at the keyboard since the early '90s, and he plays his fans like a finely tuned Steinway. Though the clientele is decidedly refined in dress and attitude, they don't mind belting out "Don't Cry for Me, Argentina" or the '70s classic "American Pie." There's no better place for the ultimate splurge in dining and entertainment. *AE, DC, MC, V; no checks; Thurs–Sat; full bar; www.millefleurs.com; map:EE5*

## On Broadway

**615 BROADWAY, DOWNTOWN; 619/231-0011** On Broadway aspires to another strata of nightclub from any other in town—and with several million dollars spent on remodeling a bank space in the once-tallest building in town, it succeeds. Jet-setters and twentysomethings alike enjoy the buzz of world-class sound and lighting systems, superstar DJs, and eight posh rooms of decadence. That is, once they get in: a très picky door crew favors VIPs over the hopefuls in line. Euro-trance and techno lovers groove upstairs, house and hip-hop heads bounce around the cavernous main room, and various A-list folk mingle in the down-tempo lounge. Other lavish features—a pink, mirrored ladies' "Barbie Room" being the gaudiest—add a top-shelf indulgence for the devoted, and moneyed, club-goer. *AE, DC, DIS, MC, V; no checks; Fri–Sat; full bar; info@obec.tv; www.onbroadway.signonsandiego.com; info@obec.tv; map:N7* &

## Patrick's II

**428 F ST, DOWNTOWN; 619/233-3077** This narrow bar is one of downtown's oldest and best places for drowning your sorrows to a guitar, zydeco, or swing beat. Patrick's has long been known for its support of local blues bands and is a favorite hideout for locals. *MC, V; no checks; every day; full bar; map:N7*

## Plan B

**945 GARNET AVE, PACIFIC BEACH; 619/483-9920** In Pacific Beach, every Saturday summer night seems like spring break, with Plan B at the epicenter. Pool tables near large windows beckon to passersby on Garnet Avenue, while party-goers, hidden by smoke and lights, shake it up just out of sight. A small black-lit dance floor pumps out alternative rock and hip-hop, accompanied by lights and lasers. Bring two picture IDs if you don't have a California driver's license. *Cash only; Wed–Sun; full bar; www.planbnightclub.com; map:KK7* &

## Plaza Bar (Westgate Hotel)

**1055 2ND AVE, DOWNTOWN; 619/238-1818** Classy and comfortable, the Plaza Bar is downtown's best spot for sipping Drambuie and humming a classic standard like "I Gotta Be Me" à la Sinatra. Enjoy piano music most nights, although Sundays and Mondays—featuring Latin guitar music—are a nice change. The Westgate's French Renaissance theme enhances the ambiance. Settle into an upholstered armchair or banquette and twirl a crystal brandy snifter in the candlelight. *AE, D, MC, V; no checks; every day; full bar; map:N7* &

## Rich's

**1051 UNIVERSITY AVE, HILLCREST; 619/497-4588** Club Hedonism, held at Rich's every Thursday night, is a blast of groove and tribal rhythms in an industrial-style pad. Hedonism is supposedly the only straight night at this otherwise gay club in the heart of Hillcrest, but that only results in a more eclectic, inclusive vibe—all types, styles, and tastes mix in a diverse glam-fest that has been running for more than a decade. On Fridays, women as well as men drool over multiple go-go boys. Beer is cheaper than chewing gum on Sundays from 7pm to 10pm. *Cash only; Thurs–Sun; full bar; www.richs-sandiego.com; map:O2*

## Sevilla

**555 4TH AVE, DOWNTOWN; 619/233-5979 / 3050 PIO PICO RD, CARLSBAD; 760/730-7558** Sevilla is an all-in-one night out. At street level, the lively Spanish restaurant (see Restaurants chapter) and tapas bar hosts dueling acoustic guitars that take advantage of the house's extraordinary sound system. In the evening, head to the cavelike basement for samba lessons or help with other difficult Latin rhythms, including merengue and salsa. On Fridays the club hosts Euro dance music. At both the original downtown location and the newer one in Carlsbad, you can also take in a flamenco or tango show with prix fixe dinner. *AE, DC, DIS, MC, V; no checks; every day; full bar; www.cafesevilla.com; map:O8 and CC8*

## Winston's Beach Club

**1921 BACON ST, OCEAN BEACH; 619/222-3802** A well-loved hole-in-the-wall with live music nightly, Winston's is an OB landmark. Local rock bands are often featured as well as nationally known bands any day of the week. *MC, V; no checks; every day; full bar; map:B2* &

# Bars, Pubs, and Taverns

## Aero Club

**3365 INDIA ST, MIDDLETOWN; 619/297-7211** Workers from nearby aerospace factories once claimed this seedy neighborhood bar as their own. Today the club has been transformed from a smoky dive into a welcoming, airy place serving two dozen draft beers along with the bottled imports. On sunny afternoons young revelers show off their smiles at the sidewalk counter. Lenny Kravitz, Iron Maiden, Lauryn Hill, B-Side Players, and local bands croon from the jukebox, adding a backdrop to pool games and lively conversation. *AE, MC, V; no checks; every day; beer and wine; map:L4*

## Barefoot Bar & Grill

**1404 W VACATION RD, MISSION BAY; 858/274-4630** Boogie your brains out on the sand at this open-air Mission Bay landmark in the massive Paradise Point Resort. It's quite a scene, where copper-toned locals pick up on vacationers on the big outdoor patio. The calypso beat takes over by midafternoon, and mai tais and frothy piña coladas introduce the cocktail hour. The Barefoot is good anytime, but extra special when the music, crowd, and weather are all in blissful sync. There's live music (mainly classic rock) most weekends during the summer. *AE, DC, DIS, MC, V; no checks; every day; full bar; map:LL6*

## LOVE, SAN DIEGO STYLE

San Diego may have a Gidget reputation as a wholesome surfside city, but its balmy Mediterranean climate, vivid sunsets, and natural beauty make it the perfect backdrop for any romance. Our picks for a great date—whether it's your first or your 50th—include:

Watch the sunset from a bench at **LA JOLLA COVE.**

Take a sunset stroll along Torrey Pines State Reserve's flat, cliff-top **GUY FLEMING TRAIL** for endless views of the Pacific.

Hike to the top of **COWLES MOUNTAIN** in Mission Trails Regional Park to watch the sun rise over the East County mountains.

Picnic by the fountain in Balboa Park's **ALCAZAR GARDEN**, then stroll through the cool **BOTANICAL BUILDING** and explore the shady Palm Canyon.

Sip champagne and cuddle in a gondola on the Coronado Cays with the **GONDOLA COMPANY** (619/429-6317; www.gondolacompany.com; $60 per couple); hour-long cruises depart from the marina at Loews Coronado Bay Resort.

Take to the sky on a balloon ride with **SKYSURFER BALLOON COMPANY** (858/481-6800; www.skysurferballoon.com; $135–$155 per person). Or soar over the coast in a vintage biplane with **AVIATION ADVENTURES** (760/438-7680; www.barnstorming.com; $98–$298 per couple).

Explore the 30-acre **QUAIL BOTANICAL GARDENS** (230 Quail Gardens Dr; 760/436-3036). Check out the lavender-scented Mediterranean garden and the lush jungle of the Tropical Rainforest Exhibit.

For a nostalgic thrill, ride the **BELMONT PARK GIANT DIPPER** (3190 Mission Blvd), an old-school roller coaster in Mission Beach.

Take a moonlit horse-drawn carriage ride along the downtown waterfront with **CINDERELLA CARRIAGE COMPANY** (619/239-8080; $50 for a half-hour for up to four adults).

—Alison Ashton

### Dick's Last Resort

**345 4TH AVE, DOWNTOWN; 619/231-9100** This giant old warehouse contains an all-American bar that draws crowds of college students and conventioneers. You'll find beer-hall seating, a large outdoor patio, buckets of good food (see Restaurants chapter), big-screen TVs, and the trademark irreverent rudeness. The service can be appalling and the clientele crude (it's part of the charm). Still, Dick's is a nonstop celebration, feting everything from Cinco de Mayo to St. Patrick's Day. Curiously, this is also a popular spot for children's birthday parties and tour groups during the day. There's live music every night except Monday. *AE, DC, DIS, MC, V; no checks; every day; full bar; www.dickslastresort.com; map:O8* &

## The Field

**544 5TH AVE, DOWNTOWN; 619/232-9840** The Field is arguably the best Irish pub in San Diego. It's packed from floor to rafters with real Irish rummage and collectibles. This bar offers fine whiskeys and all the traditional fare, along with cozy short stools near the faux fire and fiddlers on the small stage. Get there early, before the throngs of singles. Stop by to see the traditional Irish dancers on Sundays at 5pm, or come by a bit later to hear the musicians who gather 'round the fireplace. *AE, DIS, MC, V; no checks; every day; full bar; map:O8* &

## Flick's

**1017 UNIVERSITY AVE, HILLCREST; 619/297-2056** High-tech video jockeys play today's vogue flicks on four large screens. If you tire of the show, there's a pool table and, on the last Thursday of each month, live stand-up comedy with a gay theme. *Cash only; every day; full bar; map:O2*

## Gaslamp Billiard Palace

**379 4TH AVE, DOWNTOWN; 619/230-1968** An old-time feeling quickly settles over patrons at this pool hall and neighborhood bar. Don't be fooled by the airy, bright decor—if smoking were allowed in San Diego bars a fog bank would exude from the front door. On weeknights the Palace is a good place to unwind over a drink and shoot a game or two at the tables. Crowds take over on the weekend, when the second-story pool hall opens to handle the overflow. There are 35 tables in all; on weekend nights all could very well be claimed by 9pm. *AE, MC, V; no checks; every day; full bar; map:O8*

## The Jewel Box

**805 16TH ST, DOWNTOWN; 619/236-8685** Owner Alan Yorkman garnered a Downtown Partnership award for remodeling and reviving this watering hole in the warehouse district way beyond the trendy Gaslamp. Don't go looking for ferns and fine art; this is still a dive bar at its best, with free pool in the afternoons and all day Monday, a few tabletop shuffleboard games, two TVs, and a mixed clientele. Worker bees from downtown offices stop by to gossip; bikers proudly park their machines under the sign reading "Harley Parking Only—All Others Will Be Crushed." *Cash only; every day; full bar; map:P7*

## Karl Strauss Brewery & Grill

**1044 WALL ST, LA JOLLA (AND BRANCHES); 858/551-2739** San Diego's favorite home brew is now served at four friendly bars throughout the county. Regulars expound on the merits of amber versus light while downing burgers and salads (see Restaurants chapter). You can buy Karl Strauss beer at nearly every liquor store in the county; impress the locals by swearing it's the best you've ever quaffed. Branches include downtown, Sorrento Valley, and Carlsbad. *AE, MC, V; no checks; every day; full bar; map:JJ7*

## Kensington Club

**4079 ADAMS AVE, KENSINGTON; 619/284-2848** One of San Diego's best-kept secrets since it opened in 1933, the Ken leads a double life: it's a dark, loungelike dive by day and a trendy club by night. A back room was recently added to accommodate thirsty moviegoers from the Ken Cinema, next door. On weekends, bands thump in the red-lit, booth-strewn back room, rattling the nerves of old-timers accustomed to desultory discourse. Monday through Thursday nights, DJs play cha-cha, punk, or '80s music for the Gen-Xers. *Cash only; every day; full bar; map:LL3*

## Live Wire

**2103 EL CAJON BLVD, UNIVERSITY HEIGHTS; 619/291-7450** Live Wire could come off as cliquish, but the scenesters who frequent this popular dive bar are suspiciously friendly. Soon it's clear why: cheap drinks (even the imported beers), an even cheaper cover charge (none), and arguably the cream of San Diego's musicians, artists, and writers, who gather in a uniquely unpretentious, anti-meat-market setting. Most nights, DJs spin rare '70s funk, old-school rap, and hip-hop, punctuated by cartoons on the TV. Local heroes such as Mojo Nixon and Rocket from the Crypt have rocked this small bar in the past. Pool, pinball, and a stellar jukebox are also featured. *Cash only; every day; full bar; map:Q1*

## MiXX

**3671 5TH AVE, HILLCREST; 619/299-6499** Best known as one of the most exciting restaurants in town (see Restaurants chapter), MiXX is also a great place for a drink. The piano bar is one of the most popular in town, thanks to the see-and-be-seen attitude among the clientele. Well-dressed straights and gays gather in the lounge, where the walls are covered with contemporary art (good for a conversation starter). Sip a martini and take in the scene—as upscale hip as San Diego gets. *AE, CB, DC, DIS, MC, V; no checks; Thurs–Sat; full bar; map:N3* &

## Onyx Room

**852 5TH AVE, DOWNTOWN; 619/235-6699** Truly an underground joint— it's at the bottom of a street-level staircase, below Fifth Avenue—the Onyx Room boasts the rare juxtaposition of jazz sophistication and hip-hop flair. Ornate fixtures and retro design evoke '50s-era swing inside, and you're just as likely to catch rap poets rhyming as horn players soloing on the intimate stage. The club specialty is "old school," and the Onyx brings it back in a swanky way. A mellow down-easy dance floor surrounded by comfy seating makes the Onyx Room a favorite with the oh-so-fickle urban bohemian set—dressed to impress and to move. Funk, soul, hip-hop, house, rare groove, and live jazz are the musical modes. A Tuesday-night jam session, led by local Gilbert Castellanos, is a mainstay on the local jazz scene. On the weekends, DJs rule the dance floor. The cover is free, but the strict dress code—no sandals, shorts, T-shirts—is severely enforced. *MC, V; no checks; Tues–Sun; full bar; www.theonyxroom.com; map:O8*

## Pacific Shores

**4927 NEWPORT AVE, OCEAN BEACH; 619/223-7549** Pac Shores has a unique underwater atmosphere with black lights and no windows. Big, comfortable booths line the wall below neon portraits of sea creatures. College kids and old-timers meet around the long bar, the jukebox, and the small pool table in the tiny back room. *Cash only; every day; full bar; map:B3*

## Princess Pub & Grille

**1665 INDIA ST, MIDDLETOWN; 619/702-3021** Bartenders prepare perfect black and tans in this classic pub, where photos of Princess Di and other royals decorate the walls. Guinness, Bass, and all the best brews are on tap, and the accents among the drinkers are enough to transport you to the shores of the Thames. *DIS, MC, V; no checks; every day; full bar; map:M6*

## Red Fox Room

**2223 EL CAJON BLVD, NORTH PARK; 619/297-1313** There are old bars, and there are bars like the Fox with old things. Its wooden walls date from the 16th century, brought by a Brit who insisted on importing her favorite singing room (the acoustics are great). These days Shirley Allen and her backup band provide low-key entertainment; grab the mike if you know the song. The piano bar is a favorite among aficionados, and other local crooners take the stage when Shirley gets a day off. This is a good place to actually converse over a drink without having to shout over the music. *AE, DIS, MC; no checks; every day; full bar; map:Q1* &

## Society Billiard Cafe

**1051 GARNET AVE, PACIFIC BEACH; 858/272-7665** Huge street-side windows provide passersby with a full view of pool players in action. The 15 regulation tables provide plenty of action for pool sharks, and a good selection of salads and sandwiches keeps their energy from flagging. For those whose billiards game is embarrassingly rusty, there's a small upstairs room with just four tables. *MC, V; no checks; every day; full bar; map:KK7*

## South Beach Bar and Grill

**5059 NEWPORT AVE, OCEAN BEACH; 619/226-4577** At the end of Ocean Beach's Newport Avenue, ultracasual South Beach Bar and Grill hops with activity. The beach bar's open windows look out onto the Pacific and the Ocean Beach pier, but the real attraction is at the back of the bar where the stove is always cookin'. Sit here and watch as the short-order cooks conduct their own culinary symphony, preparing the tastiest seafood tacos around. A broad menu offers tacos (and burritos, salads, and nachos) stuffed with grilled or fried mahi mahi, wahoo, shrimp, lobster, and more. Our hands-down favorite: the succulent lobster tacos—an inexpensive treat filled with a generous helping of the sweet crustacean. Washed down with a microbrew, it's pure San Diego heaven. *Cash only; every day; full bar; map:B3* &

## Sunshine Company Saloon Limited

**5028 NEWPORT AVE, OCEAN BEACH; 619/222-0722** Smokers disgruntled with the 1998 smoking ban find solace on the open-air rooftop patio here, filled with scantily clad beach babes and surfer dudes. A palm tree juts up through a hole in the ceiling to shade the second-story covered patio and bar. Multiple TVs blast simultaneous sporting events, while shuffleboard, pool, and video games provide more involved alternatives. Sample the local microbrews—there are 12 in all. *Cash only; every day; full bar; map:B3*

### Top of the Hyatt

**1 MARKET PL, DOWNTOWN; 619/232-1234** This 40th-floor bar has the view from heaven, not to mention good spicy peanuts. On a clear night the million twinkling lights of Mexico add to the panoramic views of downtown, Coronado, and San Diego Bay. The hallway has an equally interesting photo collection of San Diego dating from the late 1800s. Since the Hyatt is close to the convention center, the bar is often packed with out-of-towners. But locals still brave the crowds on weekends, or take advantage of less-packed weekday evenings when they can loosen their ties, sip a frosty martini, and watch the sunset. *AE, DC, DIS, MC, V; no checks; every day; full bar; map:M8* &

### Top of the Park

**3167 5TH AVE, HILLCREST; 619/296-0057** Gay party men flock here for the looong Friday afternoon happy hour (5–10pm) to map out a weekend plan of attack over a superb view of San Diego. Although the bar is huge, standing room is at a premium by 8pm. It takes a bunch of bartenders to satisfy the troops; by 10pm the crowd is off to pillage the party scene. The dropped ceiling on the top floor adds a *Jetsons* look to this historic brick hotel, built in 1926. *AE, DC, DIS, MC, V; no checks; Fri only; full bar; www.parkmanorsuites.com; map:N3* &

### The Tower

**4757 UNIVERSITY AVE, KENSINGTON; 619/284-0158** Until recently, the king of San Diego dives was also a vibrant display of public art. In 1995, the city commissioned artists to paint the unusual geometric concrete tower atop this ovoid bar, creating a real eye-catcher and a source of neighborhood pride. The tower started leaning precariously in 1999 and was taken apart bit by bit. Cheap beer and complimentary peanuts flow freely during the bar's dart games and when the pool leagues play on Tuesdays and Thursdays. The jukebox plays nonstop; it's happy hour 2pm to 7pm, Monday through Friday. *AE, MC, V; no checks; every day; full bar; map:MM3*

### The Waterfront

**2044 KETTNER BLVD, MIDDLETOWN; 619/232-9656** Though set in the middle of a major redevelopment project that adds 45 lofts to the ever-more-trendy Little Italy district, the Waterfront is destined to remain one of San Diego's best neighborhood bars. Workers from the now-defunct Convair airplane factory on Pacific Highway began congregating at this dive bar in the 1930s. Neighborhood barflies and Waterfront fans from throughout the city still pack the small bar, which, by the way, is blocks away from the water and has no view. No matter: the pool table, hefty burgers, amiable crowd, and jukebox all keep patrons happy. *AE, MC, V; no checks; every day; full bar; map:M6*

# Desserts, Coffees, and Teas

## Caffe Italia

**1704 INDIA ST, MIDDLETOWN; 619/234-6767** There's a wonderful European air here, with classical music in the background and plenty of foreign and domestic mags and newspapers for sale. A local artist made the small brushed stainless steel tables; an Italian did the interior design. Out on India Street, dark green umbrellas provide shade for sipping a Vietnamese coffee or other specialty drinks. There are sandwiches and salads, tiramisu, gelato, and the popular Sam's Cheesecake. *Cash only; every day; no alcohol; map:M6*

## Esmeralda Books & Coffee

**1555 CAMINO DEL MAR (DEL MAR PLAZA), STE 307, DEL MAR; 858/755-2707** North County locals count on Esmeralda as much for great coffee and conversation as they do for its great selection of travel, art, and children's books. In the heart of Del Mar Plaza, this well-loved bookstore is open late on weekends and hosts poetry readings and book signings regularly. *AE, MC, V; local checks OK; every day; no alcohol; map:HH7*

## Gelato Vero Caffe

**3753 INDIA ST, MIDDLETOWN; 619/295-9269** This tiny venue at the foot of Washington Street has coffee and tea in addition to its namesake, a rich and creamy gelato. The space is cramped or cozy, depending on your frame of mind, with a few alfresco tables along India Street. Try the delicious gelato milk shakes. *Cash only; every day; no alcohol; map:K3*

## Java Joe's

**1956 BACON ST, OCEAN BEACH; 619/523-0356** Once a total dive, this coffee joint has moved to a newer, cleaner, and less funkified location in Ocean Beach. Live music commences most nights (Tuesdays excepted) at 8pm; Monday is open-mike night. *Cash only; every day; no alcohol; www.javajoes.org; map:B3*

## Karen Krasne's Extraordinary Desserts

**2929 5TH AVE, MIDDLETOWN; 619/294-7001** If you've always believed dessert is the main event, Extraordinary Desserts is a slice of heaven. Cordon Bleu–trained chef/owner Karen Krasne raises sweet treats to haute cuisine with tarts, tortes, and cakes that are bona fide works of art. This is no common bakery, but a Zenlike temple. Line up with the other blissed-out sugar junkies to peruse the fresh offerings. Splurge on an Extraordinary Brownie (flourless chocolate cake dressed up with shards of chocolate, edible gold dust, and flowers) or a White Chocolate Linzer Torte. Too much? Even smaller items, such as a slice of chocolate sour cream loaf or a cherry chocolate chip cookie, will satisfy a finicky sweet tooth. All of this is best accompanied by fresh-brewed Hawaiian Lion Coffee or imported Mariage Frères tea steeped in a heavy Japanese teapot. The surroundings are as delightful as the food. At night, blond-wood tables gleam by candlelight, but for privacy, scope out one of the taupe-upholstered booths or sit on the patio. Don't come if you're in a hurry; service is leisurely, even when it's quiet. *MC, V; local checks OK; every day; no alcohol; www.extraordinarydesserts.com; map:N4* &

**233**

### The Living Room Coffeehouse

**1417 UNIVERSITY AVE, HILLCREST (AND BRANCHES); 619/295-7911** Settle in with your journal or a good book at the most convenient of these casual, comfortable, homespun coffeehouses. Each has the same warm, homey feeling, with vintage couches, floor and table lamps, and framed prints on the walls. The coffee and tea list is long and varied. The San Diego State University branch (5900 El Cajon Blvd, College Area; 619/286-8434) is especially cozy, albeit not centrally located; the Rosecrans Street location (1018 Rosecrans St, Point Loma; 619/222-6852) buzzes late on weekend nights. Other branches are in La Jolla and Old Town. *MC, V; no checks; every day; no alcohol; map:O2*

### Miracles Cafe

**1953 SAN ELIJO BLVD, CARDIFF-BY-THE-SEA; 760/943-7924** North County residents love this cozy coffee shop across from San Elijo State Beach. You can get sandwiches and salads in addition to espresso, cappuccino, or a freshly brewed American coffee. For breakfast there are steamed scrambled eggs, bagels, and freshly made waffles. There's live music—most often acoustic guitar—for the laid-back Sunday brunch and on Friday and Saturday nights. Sit inside or on the outdoor patio. *No credit cards; local checks OK; every day; no alcohol; map:CC7*

### Pannikin Coffee and Tea

**3145 ROSECRANS ST, POINT LOMA (AND BRANCHES); 619/224-2891** Modern jazzy music drifts up toward the high ceiling at this popular cafe, where business execs, gangs of moms with toddlers, and loners tapping on laptops set out to drink some serious coffee. Pebble-gray Formica tables rest on a floor of distressed cement; seats from the legendary Loma Theater (now the Bookstar bookstore) line the walls, where large windows let in lots of natural light. They make a great cup of straight coffee here. For breakfast there are steamed scrambled eggs; for lunch or dinner order salads, soups, quiche, and yummy sandwiches. The store sells fresh-roasted beans and bulk and bag teas; the La Jolla store (7467 Girard Ave, La Jolla; 619/454-5453) and some of the others (Encinitas, Del Mar, and downtown) sell gift items and kitchen accessories as well. *AE, MC, V; no checks; every day; no alcohol; map:H3*

### Twiggs Tea & Coffee

**4590 PARK BLVD, UNIVERSITY HEIGHTS; 619/296-0616 / 702 ASH ST, DOWN-TOWN; 619/232-0436** Multipaned windows shed light on comfortable couches surrounded by coffee and end tables, fresh flowers, and potted plants. There are also tables for two or four inside and out along Park Boulevard. The staff is perky, friendly, and professional; ambient music tends toward the classical. Both the original Park Boulevard location and the new venue at the base of the old El Cortez Hotel, now converted to an apartment building, serve tasty homemade baked goods, sandwiches, and salads. Various genres of music, most often acoustic, are played live at the Park Boulevard location—if not nightly, then from Wednesday through Sunday. A block from Symphony Towers, the El Cortez location is open for pre- and post-concert dinners and serves microbrews and wine. *No credit cards (Park Blvd); DC, MC, V (El Cortez); local checks OK; every day; no alcohol (Park Blvd); beer and wine (El Cortez); http://twiggs.org; map:P1 and O7*

# ITINERARIES

# ITINERARIES

## Three-Day Tour

**DAY ONE**

**MORNING:** Walking the waterfront is an essential beginning to the day. Start early and walk along Harbor Drive past **SEAPORT VILLAGE** (849 W Harbor Dr; 619/235-4014). Stop to admire the yachts in the marina, the early-morning light on the water, and the seagulls announcing the morning like roosters. Continue north past fishing boats and sprinklers adding a sheen to green lawns until you reach the ticket office for **SAN DIEGO HARBOR EXCURSIONS** (1050 N Harbor Dr; 619/234-4111 or 800/442-7847). Board the first ferry (9am) to Coronado. After fueling your energies with a latte and croissant at **IL FORNAIO** (1333 First St, Coronado; 619/437-4911), rent a bike at **BIKES AND BEYOND** (at the Ferry Landing; 619/435-7180) or set out on foot. If you prefer sightseeing without exercise, board the **CORONADO SHUTTLE** (the Number 94 bus), which runs from the **FERRY LANDING** through downtown, along **ORANGE AVENUE,** and down the **SILVER STRAND**. Cruise down First Street to Orange Avenue, the most beautiful main drag in San Diego. Admire the trees, gazebos, and lawns at **SPRECKELS PARK** (601 Orange Ave; 619/522-7342) and the series of early-20th-century neoclassical buildings and Victorian houses on the side streets off the avenue. Stop by the **MUSEUM OF HISTORY AND ART** (1100 Orange Ave; 619/435-7242) and check out the displays on the island's early days as a seaside resort.

 **AFTERNOON:** For a taste of Hollywood glamour, have lunch at the **HOTEL DEL CORONADO** (1500 Orange Ave; 619/435-6611 or 800/HOTELDEL). Stretch your legs on the beach, then pedal, walk, or ride the shuttle back to the Ferry Landing and return downtown. Die-hard shoppers will find it hard to resist the shops at **SEAPORT VILLAGE**. If you're too tired to choose between kites, toys, T-shirts, and souvenirs, grab a snack from one of the takeout food stands and rest awhile on a bench with a water view.

 **EVENING:** Slip into your dining duds and head to the Gaslamp Quarter. Wander around Fourth and Fifth Avenues, stopping by **LE TRAVEL STORE** (745 4th Ave; 619/544-0005) for any forgotten necessities, and browse through the shops at **HORTON PLAZA** (entrances on Broadway, 4th Ave, G St, and 1st Ave; 619/238-1596), a fantasyland mall. Then choose a table amid the action at one of the many Gaslamp eateries, such as **SEVILLA** (see also the Top 150 Restaurants chapter). After a leisurely dinner, hail a horse-drawn **CINDERELLA CARRIAGE** (619/239-8080) for a romantic ride back to your hotel.

## KIDS' PLAY

Sea World, Legoland, Knott's Soak City U.S.A., the Wild Animal Park, the San Diego Zoo—what kid wouldn't be happy in San Diego? You might need a brand-new credit card before you're done—or, on the other hand, you could be creative and discover all the fun stuff to do that's free. The young ones get a kick out of building sand castles at Ocean Beach or the Silver Strand and sliding and swinging at Tecolote Park in Mission Bay. The 8-to-18 set all enjoy searching under rocks for starfish and sea anemones during low tide—the best hiding spots for the sea's clever creatures are at Bird Rock, La Jolla Cove, and the tide pools of Point Loma near Cabrillo Monument. There are endless bike and roller-skating trails in Mission Bay Park, and everyone enjoys watching the free fireworks show from Sea World while sitting at a bonfire at Ocean Beach, Fiesta Island, or Crown Point. One of the most fascinating adventures for kids of all ages is the Reuben H. Fleet Space Theater and Science Center in Balboa Park; they charge admission fees, but they're still far cheaper than the theme parks. A ride on Belmont Park's Giant Dipper roller coaster is a must, as is a burger in the Volkswagen booth at Hodad's in Ocean Beach. Fly a kite at Ellen Browning Scripps Park in La Jolla; take the ferry to Coronado; buy a Frisbee and carry it everywhere. The kids will have a great time.

*—Maribeth Mellin*

## DAY TWO

**MORNING:** Board the Old Town Trolley or a city bus to the incomparable **SAN DIEGO ZOO** (2920 Zoo Dr; 619/234-3153). Go ahead and pose for photos by the flamingo pond (everyone does), then board a double-decker bus for a 40-minute tour past elephants, brown bears, and tigers. After the ride, hoof it to the zoo's Gorilla Tropics and Polar Bear Plunge, then ride the Skyfari aerial tramway back to the entrance; keep an eye out for the tiled dome of Balboa Park's California Tower rising above the trees.

**AFTERNOON:** Grab a quick lunch at one of the zoo's food stands, get your hand stamped in case you want to return, and then walk past the carousel to **EL PRADO** and the park's museums. Stop by the **VISITORS CENTER** (619/239-0512) in the House of Hospitality and purchase a Passport to Balboa Park coupon book, valid for one week and good for admission to 13 park attractions. You won't be able to hit all the museums in one afternoon, but if you're in town for a few more days, you'll want to come back. On your first round, be sure to see the **MUSEUM OF MAN** (1350 El Prado; 619/239-2001) under the California Tower, the **SAN DIEGO MUSEUM OF ART** (1450 El Prado; 619/232-7931), and the **BOTANICAL BUILDING** (across from the House of Hospitality; no phone), where tree ferns stretch toward the sky under a lath roof. Take a break on the grass by the Lily Pond, then head to the **REUBEN H. FLEET SPACE THEATER AND SCIENCE CENTER** (1875 El Prado; 619/238-1233), beloved by children of all ages. Play with the gadgets in the Science

## MISTER HORTON BUILDS A CITY

Horton Plaza, downtown's mall-cum-amusement center, is named, fittingly enough, for downtown San Diego's founder. Alonzo Erastus Horton, the ultimate entrepreneur, came to town in 1867. He promptly decided that downtown San Diego should be located by San Diego Bay and bought 960 acres of waterfront property. Much of the Gaslamp District and critical modern buildings lie within Horton's original city plan. His dreams are honored at Horton Plaza, a "city square" with a fountain dedicated to his inspiration in 1910. Horton was also one of the masterminds who created Balboa Park and the surrounding neighborhoods; his name can be found on hotels, taverns, theaters, and businesses around downtown.

—*Maribeth Mellin*

Center, catch the latest spectacle at the Space Theater, and don't even try to resist the gizmos in the North Star Science Shop. When you're utterly exhausted, board the trolley or bus and ride back to your hotel.

**EVENING:** After such a strenuous day, you deserve to splurge on dinner at **STAR OF THE SEA** (1360 N Harbor Dr; 619/232-7408), the most elegant seafood restaurant downtown. End the night at the **TOP OF THE HYATT** (1 Market Pl; 619/232-1234), sipping a Cognac on the 40th floor of the hotel while gazing at the lights on Coronado.

### DAY THREE / FAMILY FUN DAY

**MORNING:** Time for some quality beach time. If you're traveling with the family, submit to your kids' pleas and head for **SEA WORLD** (500 Sea World Dr; 619/226-3901) at the edge of Mission Bay. Given the staggering admission fee, you may want to devote a full day to the aquatic park. Don't miss the Penguin Encounter, the sharks, and the trademark Shamu Show, with its awesome orca whales. There are plenty of places to eat at the park; try the **SHIPWRECK CAFE.**

**AFTERNOON:** When you're done with animal acts, pile in the car and cruise around **MISSION BAY PARK** (bordered by I-5, I-8, Grand Ave, and Mission Blvd; 619/221-8901). Check out the fishing boats at **SEAFORTH SPORTFISHING** (1717 Quivira Rd; 619/224-3383) and consider paddling about in a kayak or canoe at Santa Clara Point. Rentals are available at **MISSION BAY SPORTCENTER** (1010 Santa Clara Pl; 619/488-1004).

**EVENING:** Watch the sun settle into the sea as you dine on fresh fish and burgers at **QWIIGS BAR & GRILL** (5083 Santa Monica Ave, Ocean Beach; 619/222-1101); arrive early and claim a window table for a view of surfers riding the waves under rosy skies. After dinner, take a walk on the **OCEAN BEACH PIER** (at the foot of Niagara St). During the summer, fireworks explode from Sea World nightly at 9:30 pm. You can see the whole show from the pier as you listen to the surf pounding the pilings.

# La Jolla Day

**MORNING:** To truly appreciate La Jolla, you must stay in a view room at the **LA VALENCIA HOTEL,** or "La V" as the villagers say (1132 Prospect St; 858/454-0771 or 800/451-0772). The 1926 pink palace overlooking the water is an absolute charmer, from its domed roof to the gardens by the pool. Breakfast on fruit and French toast at the hotel's Mediterranean Room Patio, then keep the refined attitude going with a trip to Wisteria Cottage, aka **JOHN COLE'S BOOK SHOP** (780 Prospect St; 858/454-4766) and the **MUSEUM OF CONTEMPORARY ART SAN DIEGO** (700 Prospect St; 858/454-3541).

**AFTERNOON:** Have lunch on the rooftop terrace at **GEORGE'S AT THE COVE** (1250 Prospect St; 858/454-4244) and gaze at the palms lining the rocky coastline. Return to the hotel, don your swimsuits, pack up your beach toys, and walk down Girard Avenue to the expansive **ELLEN BROWNING SCRIPPS PARK** (1100 Coast Blvd; 858/221-8899). Toss a Frisbee on the lawns, then walk down the stairway to **LA JOLLA COVE** (1100 Coast Blvd; 619/221-8901), one of the prettiest beaches in all of San Diego.

**EVENING:** Stuff your wallet with cash and credit cards and tour the village's exclusive shops and boutiques. Then drive or take a cab to the **MARINE ROOM** (2000 Spindrift Dr; 858/459-7222), where waves splash against the elegant restaurant's windows.

# A Day at the Beach

**MORNING:** We're fond of all our beaches, but if you have only one day to pack in your ocean action, your best choice is **PACIFIC BEACH** (950 Grand Ave at Ocean Blvd). Cruise by the **MISSION BEACH CLUB** (704 Ventura Pl; 858/488-5050) to rent boogie boards, fins, and any other play equipment you desire. Submerge yourself in the surfer scene at **KONO'S CAFE** (704 Garnet Ave; 858/483-1669) for a hearty egg-and-pancake breakfast. Then arrange your towels, chairs, and gear on the beach near one of the lifeguard towers, toss a Frisbee around till you've worked up a sweat, and dive into the waves to cool off.

**AFTERNOON:** When you suddenly realize you've also worked up an appetite, claim a table at **NICK'S AT THE BEACH** (809 Thomas St; 858/270-1730) and scarf down crab cakes and chilled iced tea. Return to the sand for a nap or a few chapters of Tom Wolfe's *The Pump House Gang,* a classic surf novel set in San Diego. Stroll along the boardwalk for complete submersion into the local bikini scene.

**EVENING:** Return your rentals and walk over to **BELMONT PARK** (3146 Mission Blvd; 619/488-1549) for a sunset ride on the Giant Dipper roller coaster. Return to your hotel for a bracing shower, lather on moisturizer, and don your best sundress or polo shirt and shorts. Dine on frosty margaritas and chicken with spicy mole sauce at **EL AGAVE** (2304 San Diego Ave; 619/220-0692) in Old Town. Wander past the shops and cafes till you spot a group of mariachi. Go ahead and ask them to play "La Bamba"—it's the perfect song for a perfect play day.

# DAY TRIPS

# DAY TRIPS

## Carlsbad and Environs

*35 miles north of downtown (approximately 45 minutes). Drive north on Interstate 5 to the Carlsbad Village Drive exit and turn left. Turn right onto Carlsbad Boulevard.*

Situated along the coast, about 35 miles north of San Diego, this low-key coastal community was originally named for its mineral water, said to be like that of a 19th-century spa in Bohemia (now the Czech Republic). Today's **CARLSBAD MINERAL WATER SPA** (2802 Carlsbad Blvd; 760/434-1887; www.carlsbadmineralspa.com) is housed in the **ALT KARLSBAD HAUS**, site of the original well discovered by retired sea captain John Frazier as he was drilling away on his homestead in the 1880s. Frazier is also credited with naming the town (quite benevolently, since it had been known as "Frazier Station") and inspiring its Bavarian styling. German immigrant Gerhard Schutte took over the well and opened a seaside sanatorium in the late 1800s. It wasn't long before Carlsbad became a favorite stopover for the ailing public who came to "take the waters." Today, guests luxuriate in carbonated mineral-water baths said to soothe all sorts of ailments and smooth the skin. The water is also bottled and sold in local convenience stores and delivered to local homes.

**NEIMAN'S** (300 Carlsbad Village Dr; 760/729-4131), an 1887 Victorian mansion formerly owned by Gerhard Schutte (who bought the well from Frazier), is now a restaurant with a dining room, cafe, lunch buffets, nightly entertainment (that gets rather rowdy), and a renowned Sunday brunch. Carlsbad's "village" area—just a few blocks from the beach along Highway 101—is filled with shops, cafes, and restaurants. **STATE STREET** is a popular prowl for antique hunters. The nearby 1887 Santa Fe Depot is now home to the **CARLSBAD CONVENTION & VISITORS BUREAU** (400 Carlsbad Village Dr; 760/434-6093; www.carlsbadca.org), the perfect place to pick up maps and other tourist information. History and architecture buffs should visit **ST. MICHAEL'S EPISCOPAL CHURCH** (1896), **HERITAGE HALL** (1926), and **MAGEE HOUSE** (1887), all located near Garfield Street, between Beech and Cypress Avenues. The seawall near the village is a great spot for watching the ocean's ebb and flow, while three lagoons afford plenty of bird-watching, fishing, and nature-walk opportunities. **SNUG HARBOR MARINA** (Agua Hedionda Lagoon; 760/434-3089), on an inlet waterway, offers waterskiing, Jet Skis, kayak and canoe rentals, Waverunners, and water bikes, as well as a pro shop, equipment rentals, and instructions.

Serious shoppers won't want to miss **CARLSBAD COMPANY STORES** (on Paseo del Norte, off I-5 between Palomar Airport and Cannon Rds; 760/804-9000). Although this complex seems like an innocent Mediterranean village, it actually houses a credit-card-defying complex of outlet stores (including Donna Karan, Jones New York, Crate and Barrel, Gap, and Oshkosh B'Gosh), along with fine dining, art galleries, fast-food outlets, and—naturally—Starbucks. The mall's Tuscan-style **BELLEFLEUR WINERY AND RESTAURANT** (5610 Paseo del Norte; 760/603-1919; see Restaurants chapter) provides a delightful respite from arduous shopping.

# BEAUTIFUL VIEW

The second-largest city in San Diego County, **CHULA VISTA** is blessed with the pleasant climate of communities located on San Diego Bay. Just 7 miles from the Mexican border, this city is a good stopping point for travelers heading down the coast to visit our neighbors to the south. Chula Vista means "beautiful view" in Spanish, and anyone strolling near the 900-slip Chula Vista Marina enjoying an evening sunset would have to agree with the name choice.

There's much to keep you entertained in the South Bay's fastest-growing community. Visit the **CHULA VISTA NATURE CENTER** (1000 Gunpowder Point Dr; 619/409-5900), a fully accredited living museum, located on the Sweetwater Marsh National Wildlife Refuge. Bent on preserving California's diminishing coastal wetlands and its unique wildlife, the center seeks to educate its visitors with informative and interactive exhibits. Where else will the kids get a chance to pet a shark and a stingray? If you like your water without wildlife, take the family and head to **KNOTTS SOAK CITY** (2052 Entertainment Circle; 619/661-7373), an aquatic theme park just east of downtown Chula Vista. Open daily during the summer, weekends in the spring and fall, this fun water park features Balboa Bay, a half-million-gallon wave pool; Gremmie Lagoon for the wee ones; and speed slides for the more adventurous in the group. Next door to Knotts Soak City is the **COORS AMPHITHEATRE** (2050 Entertainment Circle; 619/671-3600), a newly constructed music venue that sits like a giant space station on the outskirts of town. This arena was constructed with music in mind and has the acoustics to prove it. John Mellencamp, Paul Simon, Dave Matthews Band, and San Diego's own Jewel have rocked the house, with 10,000 reserved seats and 10,000 more on the upper lawn area. Also in Chula Vista is the U.S. Olympic Committee's $65 million **ARCO TRAINING CENTER,** worth a visit for die-hard sports fans (see Organized Tours in the Exploring chapter).

When hunger strikes at the end of the day, check out the **BAJA LOBSTER RESTAURANT** (730 H St; 619/427-8690), specializing in Puerto Nuevo cuisine from Baja California. For $26.95 you can get a large lobster, just like they serve up in Mexico. If your stomach can't handle a whole crustacean, try the camarones rancheros, spicy shrimp best accompanied by a cold beer or soda. If there's still some pep in your step, stop by **BOB'S ON THE BAY** (570 Marina Pkwy; 619/476-0400) for an after-dinner drink or dessert and enjoy a wonderful view of the waterfront.

—Susan Humphrey

If you visit anytime from mid-March to early May, you'll be in sync with the blooms of the famous **FLOWER FIELDS AT CARLSBAD RANCH** (Paseo del Norte, off I-5 at Palomar Rd; 760/431-0352; www.theflowerfields.com), one of California's major commercial flower-growing centers. In March and April, you'll be knocked out by the thousands of vibrantly colored ranunculuses covering more than 50 acres of hillsides. For a fabulous overview of the flowers and the coastline, zoom above the scene with **AVIATION ADVENTURES** (2160 Palomar Airport Rd, 760/438-7680; www.barnstorming.com). During the December holiday season, Paul Ecke Ranch in nearby Encinitas sparks spirits with a virtual blaze of scarlet poinsettias arranged in the shape of a 166-foot star. Stock up on flowers (such as Carlsbad's official flower—the bird-of-paradise—first developed commercially here), bulbs, plants, and other unique products at the gift shop by the flower fields.

Long before the buzz of new development and remodeling, Carlsbad was home to renowned **LA COSTA HOTEL AND SPA** (2100 Costa del Mar Rd; 760/438-9111). The celebrity and tycoon hideaway has two PGA championship golf courses, a golf school, a large tennis center, a bevy of restaurants, and a world-famous full-service spa. The **FOUR SEASONS RESORT–AVIARA** (7100 Four Seasons Pt; 760/603-6800), overlooking Batiquitos Lagoon, is one of the county's most luxurious resorts, with opulent rooms, amenities galore, an outstanding spa, several restaurants (including the highly praised **VIVACE**), and the Arnold Palmer–designed **AVIARA GOLF COURSE**.

Carlsbad is also home to **LEGOLAND** (1 Lego Dr, off I-5 at Cannon Rd; 760/918-5346; www.legolandca.com; see Top 25 Attractions in the Exploring chapter). Nearby **CAMP PENDLETON** (in Oceanside, at the county's northwest border; 760/725-5727), established in 1942, is a Marine Corps amphibious training base. Visitors can take a self-guided driving tour unless the base is closed for security reasons. Call ahead for hours and restrictions. **MISSION SAN LUIS REY** (4050 Mission Ave; 760/757-3651), established in 1798, is the largest of the Franciscans' fabled 21 missions and includes a retreat, museum, and chapel.

Runners and bikers love the long stretches of road by the beach around Carlsbad. They show up by the thousands for January's **SAN DIEGO MARATHON** and March's **CARLSBAD 5000**, a premier 5K race with more than 10,000 competitors. The **CARLSBAD STREET FAIRES**—held the first Sundays in May and November—are huge street festivals, bringing hordes of people to the downtown area to browse hundreds of booths laden with arts and crafts. Throughout the summer, the city also hosts free **JAZZ CONCERTS** at city parks for a mellow picnic-and-blanket crowd.

# Escondido and Environs

*33 miles northeast of downtown (approximately 45 minutes). Drive north on Highway 163, which merges into Interstate 15 N. Take Interstate 15 to the Valley Parkway exit for downtown Escondido. Turn right onto West Valley Parkway, which becomes West Grand Avenue. To reach the Wild Animal Park take Interstate 15 to the Highway 78 E exit (San Pasqual Valley Road).*

The English translation of Escondido is "hidden valley," though this burgeoning city is anything but hidden these days. Situated about 30 miles northeast of downtown, the once-sleepy little community has become firmly entrenched in nouveau San Diego's space-sucking urban sprawl. Though Escondido has a prestigious arts center, some superb restaurants, and one of the largest shopping malls in the country (**NORTH COUNTY FAIR**, at I-15 and Via Rancho Pkwy; 760/489-2332), many San Diego residents and out-of-towners think of the city only in the vaguest terms— mainly as the turnoff to San Diego's famous **WILD ANIMAL PARK** (15500 San Pasqual Valley Rd; 760/747-8702; see Top 25 Attractions in the Exploring chapter). Nearby **SAN PASQUAL BATTLEFIELD STATE HISTORIC PARK AND MUSEUM** (15808 San Pasqual Valley Rd; 760/489-0076) commemorates soldiers, including Kit Carson, who in 1846 fought here during a high point of the Mexican-American War. Stop by the visitor center for a map of the self-guided nature trail, which encompasses native plants and a wide valley view.

One of the things that makes this mini-metropolis a cultural standout is the prominent **CALIFORNIA CENTER FOR THE ARTS, ESCONDIDO** (340 N Escondido Blvd; 760/839-4100 or 800/988-4253), which showcases plays, dance performances, and concerts. The **MINGEI MUSEUM** (see Museums chapter) has acquired a venue near the performing arts center to display some of its permanent collection; the plans for this annex museum are still evolving. Noteworthy restaurants within walking distance of the arts center include **SIRINO'S** (113 W Grand Ave; 760/745-3835) for excellent Italian specialties (try the signature veal prosciutto ravioli with Cognac) and **150 GRAND CAFE** (150 W Grand Ave; 760/738-6868; see Restaurants chapter), well regarded for its California-French cuisine and lovely setting.

Though bandleader Lawrence Welk has flown off to that big Champagne bubble in the sky, his 1,000-acre-plus, circa-1960s **WELK RESORT CENTER** (8860 Lawrence Welk Dr; 760/749-3000; www.welkresort.com) still flourishes. Aside from the plethora of hotel amenities and recreation options (including three golf courses), the resort boasts a museum laden with Welk memorabilia and a 339-seat dinner theater that presents first-rate musicals and variety shows. **DEER PARK** (29013 Champagne Blvd; 760/749-1666; open Thurs–Mon only) is an odd—but wonderful—combination car museum and winery. Drool over vintage convertibles, then mellow your envy at a wine tasting. Other Escondido-area wineries offering tours and tastings are **ORFILA WINERY** (13455 San Pasqual Valley Rd; 760/738-6500; open every day), near the Wild Animal Park, and **FERRARA WINERY** (1120 W 15th Ave, between Maple and Juniper Sts; 760/745-7632; open every day), a historic facility that began wine production in the early 1930s.

Though spa resorts are now common throughout the country, the **GOLDEN DOOR** (777 Deer Springs Rd, off I-15; 760/744-5777 or 800/424-0777; www. goldendoor.com) is a longtime classic. Established in the 1950s by mastermind Deborah Szekely, this operation is still a favorite get-fit getaway with the really, really rich and famous, who jet and limo in and pay thousands for a week of peace, privacy, and pampering.

The small community of **FALLBROOK**, about 20 miles northwest of Escondido, is the self-ordained "avocado capital of the world," with some 6,000 acres of the luscious fat-laden fruit, as well as macadamia nuts and other delights. **OLD MAIN STREET**, in the village center, is fun to explore on foot, with its antique and collectible shops and old-fashioned stores.

**RANCHO BERNARDO,** south of Escondido, an ever-growing bastion of early California-style suburbia and high-tech office parks, houses a golfer's paradise, the **RANCHO BERNARDO INN** (17550 Bernardo Oaks Dr; 858/675-8500). In keeping with the environment, the 287-room inn is a low-lying sprawl of adobe and Spanish flair, with a championship 18-hole golf course, driving range, putting green, 12 tennis courts, and the award-winning restaurant **EL BIZCOCHO** (see Restaurants chapter).

Heading back toward the coast from Escondido, take Via Rancho Parkway south for about 5 miles until **LAKE HODGES** appears below. Turn down toward the lake, where you'll find very non-suburban-type cottages and cabins tucked into the woodsy hillside. **HERNANDEZ HIDEAWAY** (19320 Lake Dr; 760/746-1444), at the bottom of the hill, has been an off-the-beaten-path favorite since 1972, serving up Mexican cuisine, Sunday brunch, cerveza, and margaritas in its lakefront setting.

# Palomar Mountain and Julian

*62 miles northwest of downtown (approximately 1½ hours). Drive north on Interstate 15 to Highway 76, then head east to County Road S6 (South Grade Road) and follow this twisting "Highway to the Stars" to the top of Palomar Mountain. From Palomar Mountain, drop back down County Road S6 to Highway 76 and continue southeast to Highway 79. Follow Highway 79 south to the crossroads town of Santa Ysabel, then take Highway 78/79 into Julian.*

Sandwiched between San Diego's golden beaches to the west and the vast Anza-Borrego Desert State Park to the east, pine-scented mountains offer an easy day escape from the hurly-burly of the city. Life in the mountain towns of Palomar, Santa Ysabel, and Julian moves at a slower pace—heck, you can't even find current magazines for sale in Julian. It's just too much trouble to haul them up to this Old West hamlet. You can combine Palomar Mountain and Julian into a one-day trip—if you hit the road early. But there's plenty to see and do in both places, so you may want to devote a day to each. Each is about an hour and a half from the heart of San Diego, but most of the driving is on scenic two-lane country roads.

The S6 road runs right into the parking lot of the **PALOMAR OBSERVATORY** (760/742-2119). Admission is free to this white-domed observatory that rises from the meadow like a nuclear mushroom cloud. The 200-inch **HALE TELESCOPE** remains one of the largest scientific instruments in the world. While visitors can't peer through it, they can admire this marvel of engineering from an observation deck. To learn more about some of the celestial discoveries astronomers have made through the telescope, as well as the tremendous efforts that went into building it on this remote mountaintop, stop at the **GREENWAY MUSEUM.** You'll pass it on the walk from the parking lot to the observatory.

As you wind back down S6, you can't miss the commercial hub of Palomar Mountain at the junction of S6 and S7. For a little down-home sustenance, maybe a cup of hot chocolate or a bowl of chili, stop at **MOTHER'S KITCHEN** (33120 Canfield Rd; 760/742-4233). Or pop into the **PALOMAR MOUNTAIN GENERAL STORE & TRADING CO.** (junction of Hwys S6 and S7; 760/742-3496) for groceries, camping supplies, and a fine selection of jewelry, small decorative objects, and books from around the world.

**PALOMAR MOUNTAIN STATE PARK** (1 mile west on S7 from the S6 junction; 760/742-3462) is a pristine, 1,897-acre paradise of hiking trails, campgrounds, and picnic sites. Check out the kid-friendly hiking trails, especially the easy **DOANE VALLEY NATURE TRAIL**. Little ones may spot mule deer among the ponderosa pines, cedar, and spruce. The park is most popular in winter, when it's blanketed in snow. Thanks to a 6,000-foot-plus elevation, Palomar Mountain gets plenty of snow and rain every year.

From Palomar Mountain, continue southeast to the roadside hamlet of Santa Ysabel at the intersection of Highways 78 and 79. It's a good place for a pit stop. Few San Diegans can drive past **DUDLEY'S BAKERY** (30218 Hwy 78, at the intersection with Hwy 79; 760/765-0488) without pausing for a loaf of date-nut-raisin bread or a few doughnuts. Just up the street, the **SANTA YSABEL ART GALLERY** (30352 Hwy 78; 760/765-1676) showcases first-rate work by local artists in a light-filled setting. Prices are pretty good too.

It's just a short haul up the hill into the mountain town of Julian, which looks like an Old West movie set. There really was a short-lived gold rush here in the 1870s, but 19th-century gold mines have given way to apple orchards that attract hordes of day-trippers on fall weekends. They come to sip cider and sample the apple pie sold in every cafe and bakery. Everyone claims to have the best pie, but we think it's a toss-up between **MOM'S PIES, ETC.** (2119 Main St; 760/765-2472), and the **JULIAN PIE CO.** (2225 Main St; 760/765-2449). For other grub, belly up to the marble counter at the Miner's Diner inside the **JULIAN DRUG STORE** (2134 Main St; 760/765-0332). Another good bet is the **JULIAN CAFE & BAKERY** (2112 Main St; 760/765-2712), which serves hearty vittles amid an impressive collection of cowboy memorabilia.

Walk off the pie by exploring Julian and its environs. The **JULIAN PIONEER MUSEUM** (2811 Washington St; 760/765-0227) is filled to the rafters with odds and ends donated by local residents. You'll find everything from vintage clothes to rusty mining tools and old photos. You also can hike up to the old **PIONEER CEMETERY** (at the top of A St off Main St) to check out the headstones of Julian's founding fathers.

The hike up the **VOLCAN MOUNTAIN WILDERNESS PRESERVE** (off Farmers Rd; no phone) is steep but short; views overlooking town, the surrounding meadows, and the Cuyamaca Mountains are ample reward. You can also explore Volcan Mountain on a trail ride with **JULIAN STABLES** (760/765-1598). Drop-in visits are discouraged; call ahead for reservations. If driving is your preferred mode of touring, head south on Highway 79 through the Cuyamaca Mountains and stretch your legs on any of the many marked trails (Green Valley Falls is especially nice). Then end the day with samples of locally made Chardonnay and Sauvignon Blanc at Julian's **MENGHINI WINERY** (1150 Julian Orchards Dr; 760/765-2072; open Mon–Thurs). Once you begin exploring, you may want to spend the night in pine-scented air. The **JULIAN BED & BREAKFAST GUILD** (760/765-1555; www.julianbnbguild.com) has more than a dozen member B&Bs that offer comfortable mountain lodgings.

# Anza-Borrego Desert and Borrego Springs

*78 miles northeast of San Diego (approximately 2 hours). Take Interstate 8 east to Highway 67 and go north to Ramona. Follow Highway 78 to Santa Ysabel. Go north on Highway 79 to Highway S2. Go east on Highway S2 and travel approximately 5 miles to S22, which takes you through the small town of Ranchita and into Anza-Borrego Desert State Park and Borrego Springs.*

Some teasingly call them desert rats—those people who love the hot, dry air and xeric habitat of the American Southwest. With daytime temperatures hovering over 105 degrees for weeks at a time (sometimes reaching 120 degrees), a stoic tolerance for heat is a boon to those 3,500 residents who call the community of Borrego Springs home. If you find that sort of heat unbearable, delay your drive to this part of the country until October through May, when the weather is downright perfect—warm and arid with clear blue skies. The town is also home to the headquarters for **ANZA-BORREGO DESERT STATE PARK** (760/767-5311), covering 600,000 acres (1,000 square miles) from Riverside County (north of San Diego) down to Mexico along the eastern border of San Diego County. The park is a wild wonderland where roadrunners dash across the asphalt dodging cars and trucks; golden eagles soar in the sky; kit foxes, mule deer, and bighorn sheep hide in isolated habitats; and desert iguanas and four species of rattlesnake slither about the desert floor.

Begin your desert experience at the park's **VISITORS CENTER** (200 Palm Canyon Dr; 760/767-4205, 760/767-4684 24-hour information line) in Borrego Springs. The facility is open every day from October through May, from 9am to 5pm, and weekends and holidays only from June through September. You'll find desert exhibits, a slide show, and an excellent gift shop with maps showing desert trails. Outside, the fascinating desert garden provides an overview of bizarre and beautiful cacti and wildflowers, all identified for the edification of novices. Pupfish, which survive in oases and small puddles of water, thrive in the garden's pond. Signs lead to the easy 1½-mile **PALM CANYON TRAIL** from the visitors center. The trail leads up a slight incline to palm groves, a seasonal stream, and a waterfall, which tumbles over boulders during the winter rainy season. Blooming cacti and wildflowers bring visitors by the thousands from January through March, creating traffic jams along the highways and in Borrego Springs. Try to visit during the week; weekend hordes detract from the wild, lonely feel of the desert.

There are several ways to explore the region without getting lost on hiking trails. In fact, unless you are an experienced hiker, you're best off sticking close to the road or joining a guided tour. One of the best options is a wild ride with **SAN DIEGO OUT-BACK TOURS** (619/980-3332, 760/767-0501, or 888/295-3377; www.desertjeep tours.com); call in advance for reservations. Tours in their air-conditioned four-wheel-drive Jeeps cover both the desert and the mountains and range from $60 to $90 per person; all include pickup and return to any location in Borrego Springs, a well-versed guide, and drinks and snacks. Find fossils in the badlands or visit an ancient Indian site. There are also specialized tours; if you're not claustrophobic you may want to explore some mud caves on the spelunking tour.

## GAMBLING GOES NATIVE

For thousands of years, Indians hunted small game and gathered acorns from California oaks in the rich coastal and inland areas of San Diego County. Today, three local bands, the Barona, Viejas, and Sycuan, are raking in the dough from Vegas-style casinos in the eastern part of the county, all just 30 minutes from downtown. The **BARONA CASINO** (1000 Wildcat Canyon Rd, Lakeside; 619/443-2300) is one of the largest Indian gaming facilities in California, with more than 1,500 video gaming machines and 20 tables for card playing. The **BARONA CREEK GOLF COURSE,** which debuted in 2001, is part of a $26 million expansion that will include a 400-room hotel and ranch-themed casino, both scheduled to open in 2003. Also on the premises is the **BARONA SPEEDWAY,** a dusty track where tiny cars and motorcycles race on the weekends. At the **SYCUAN CASINO** (5469 Casino Wy, El Cajon; 619/445-6002), those feeling lucky can gamble at poker, bingo, blackjack, or the video machines. Off-track satellite wagering on the ponies is available in the 450-seat Hall of Champions. And you can stuff yourself silly at the all-you-can-eat buffet for $12.95.

The only casino with a license to sell liquor, the **VIEJAS CASINO & TURF CLUB** (5000 Willows Rd, Alpine; 800/84-POKER) features Indian blackjack, poker tournaments, and 950 video terminals. There's live entertainment in the Dreamcatcher Showroom, sometimes with no cover charge, and lots of choices for dining. If you win a bundle in the poker room, make your way across the street to the stylish outlet center, home to more than 30 stores, including Liz Claiborne, Tommy Hilfiger, Linen Barn, and the Gap.

—*Susan Humphrey*

Self-guided driving tours are another sensible option; maps outlining routes and stops are available at the visitors center. The **SOUTHERN EMIGRANT TRAIL** runs 26 miles from Scissors Crossing at Highway 78 and County Road S2. The Emigrant Trail was one of the few year-round routes into California in the mid-1800s. Spanish explorers, Kit Carson, the Mormon Battalion, Sonoran gold seekers, and the Butterfield Overland Stage all passed along this historic route. The **EROSION ROAD TOUR** runs 18 miles from the visitors center on S22 and provides an overview of the desert's geology. It includes 10 stops that demonstrate the geologic forces that create mountains, canyons, alluvial fans, and earthquake faults; the best part is the overlook with endless vistas over the Borrego Badlands to the Salton Sea.

There are several restaurants and cafes in town; our favorite is the **KRAZY COYOTE SALOON AND GRILLE** (2220 Hoberg Rd, Borrego Springs; 760/767-7788), open every day for lunch and dinner. Homemade soups, gourmet pizzas, thick steaks, and great desserts make it a favorite hangout for locals; reservations are recommended. The restaurant is part of the Palms at Indian Head resort. Just outside the door is a 1½-mile self-guided nature trail with waterfalls, streams, and native fan palms around an oasis. Bighorn sheep can sometimes be spotted on cliffs around the resort. For desert memorabilia, check out **TUMBLEWEED TRADING COMPANY** (526 Palm Canyon Dr; 760/767-4244).

Don't miss seeing the desert at night. Stars and planets that are utterly invisible in the city shine bright in a midnight-blue sky. Critters scuttle about in the sand. Silver chollas seem to shimmer in moonlight. And the silence is nearly overwhelming. Our favorite desert hideaway is **LA CASA DEL ZORRO** (3845 Yaqui Pass Rd, Borrego Springs; 760/767-5323 or 800/824-1884). Though it's somewhat expensive, the resort's pools, restaurant, and rooms with fireplaces are worth the splurge. The **BORREGO VALLEY INN** (405 Palm Canyon Dr, Borrego Springs; 760/767-0311 or 800/333-5810) has 14 rooms with fireplaces, kitchenettes, and private patios; rates include a buffet breakfast, and there is a pool.

If camping is more your style, the park has two developed campgrounds, at Borrego Palm Canyon and Tamarisk Grove. Make reservations by calling Park Net (800/444-7275). There is also a small campground at Bow Willow and a horse camp located at the mouth of Coyote Canyon. Elsewhere in the park, backcountry camping is permitted with the purchase of a $5 daily park use permit; ask about the rules at the visitors center.

# Temecula

*60 miles northeast of downtown (approximately 70 minutes). Drive north on Highway 163, which merges into Interstate 15 N. Continue north to the Highway 79 S exit toward Temecula, and continue to the Front Street exit.*

Just over the county line in neighboring Riverside County, Temecula is a blend of the mundane and the marvelous. What began as a bedroom community of affordable housing is now coming into its own as a weekend escape for urban San Diegans. This metamorphosis is due in part to the area's nascent wine country. Temecula's Rainbow Gap, with its cool morning mists and sun-drenched afternoons, gives it the ideal climate for cultivating grapes. As yet, the wineries are no match in size or cachet to those in Northern California's Napa Valley, or even the Santa Ynez Valley of the central coast. Therein lies its charm, because Temecula doesn't put on airs. Spend the morning browsing antique shops, pass the afternoon sampling vintages at roadside tasting rooms, then kick up your heels line-dancing into the night.

In typical Southern California fashion, you'll need wheels to explore Temecula and its environs; it's about 60 minutes from downtown San Diego, driving north on Interstate 15. Call the **TEMECULA VALLEY WINEGROWERS ASSOCIATION** (800/801-WINE or 909/699-6586; www.temeculawines.org) for a free map of local vineyards.

With its tract-home subdivisions, Temecula seems like the epitome of a spanking-new Southern California planned community. In fact, its roots stretch back to 1858, when it was a stop on the Butterfield Overland Stagecoach route. The community indulges its nostalgia in Old Town Temecula, a six-block-long shopping district just west of Interstate 15 (exit west on Rancho California Rd and turn left on Front St). In 1998, the city spent $5.2 million on a lavish facelift to enhance the Old West theme with spiffy wooden sidewalks and old-timey benches and light fixtures.

There's plenty here to entice you to stay for a spell, including more than two dozen antique shops. Among the best are **NANA'S TOO** (28677 Front St; 909/699-3839), for vintage art-deco clothing and Victorian knickknacks, and the **CHAPARRAL ANTIQUE MALL** (28465 Front St; 909/676-0070), which houses 19th-century hardware alongside '60s kitsch. Up the street, you can two-step the night away at **TEMECULA STAMPEDE** (28721 Front St; 909/695-1761). The cover charge at this enormous country-western nightclub is $6 per person and includes live music and a chance to test your skill on the mechanical bull.

The nostalgia of Old Town Temecula isn't manufactured. Many of the district's buildings date back to the community's early days, and the **TEMECULA VALLEY MUSEUM** (28315 Mercedes St; 909/694-6452) houses an intriguing display of local historical tchotchkes. You also can peer in the window of the dinky **TEMECULA JAIL** (just off Main St), originally built as a wine cellar using granite mined from the Temecula Quarry, and glimpse a couple of mannequins posed as drunken Old West rascals. Old Town also has some of the best dining options for kids: casual **ROSA'S CANTINA** (28636 Front St; 909/695-2428) serves Mexican fare; for burgers and sandwiches, check out the very affordable **SWING INN CAFE** (28676 Front St; 909/676-2321). More adventurous young eaters may prefer the Greek dishes at the **SILVER SPOON CAFE** (28690 Front St; 909/699-1015).

For more nouveau California pleasures, spend the afternoon exploring the wineries that dot Rancho California Road just outside of town. Most have small tasting rooms open to the public (samples range from free to $6, depending on the winery). Once you drive past the new malls boasting every imaginable fast-food outlet, you're surrounded by bucolic vineyards carpeting the hillsides. **THORNTON WINERY** (32575 Rancho California Rd; 909/699-0099) is best-known for its méthode champenoise sparkling wines. Just across the street is **CALLAWAY COASTAL VINEYARD & WINERY** (32720 Rancho California Rd; 909/676-4001), Temecula's largest wine producer with more than 700 acres. Continuing northeast on Rancho California Road, you'll see signs for other wineries. The staff at **MAURICE CARRIE WINERY** (34225 Rancho California Rd; 909/676-1711) pours free samples in a charming farmhouse tasting room. Just off the main road, **TEMECULA CREST WINERY** (40620 Calle Contento; 909/676-8231) sits high on a hill with a commanding view of the valley. For the best picnic site, head to **MOUNT PALOMAR WINERY** (33820 Rancho California Rd; 909/676-5047), where you can sample vintages in the tasting room, pick up goodies from the gourmet deli, and then follow a short path from the parking lot to a hilltop picnic area. Magnificent views of the vineyards and citrus groves may have you asking: Is this Temecula or Tuscany?

Temecula also has some winning eateries to accompany its wine. Thornton Winery's **CAFE CHAMPAGNE** (32575 Rancho California Rd; 909/699-0088) serves a seasonally inspired menu in an elegant dining room or on a patio with vineyard views. The winery also hosts jazz concerts. You can practically reach out and snatch a grape from one of the alfresco tables at **CALLAWAY'S** restaurant (32720 Rancho California Rd; 909/694-0560). **BAILY WINE COUNTRY CAFE** (27644 Ynez Rd; 909/676-9567) offers a menu of fresh, California cuisine–style fish, chicken, and pastas accompanied by a wine list consisting entirely of local vintages.

No need to do any driving after all that wine tasting; Temecula has a couple of terrific places to spend the night. Fragrant vineyards surround you at the six-room **LOMA VISTA BED & BREAKFAST** (33350 La Serena Way; 909/676-7046). Rooms at the Mediterranean-style villa overlooking the valley run $105 to $195 a night, including breakfast. The 80-room **TEMECULA CREEK INN** (44501 Rainbow Canyon Rd; 877/517-1823 or 909/694-1000) boasts a 27-hole golf course, tennis courts, and spacious rooms for $120 to $195 per night.

# Disneyland

*94 miles north of downtown (approximately 2 hours). Drive north on Interstate 5 to the Katella Avenue exit. Turn left on East Katella Avenue, then left on West Freedman Way and proceed to Disneyland entrance.*

The "Happiest Place on Earth" has become—difficult as it may be to believe—even happier, thanks to recent renovations, spiffed-up attractions, and fresh entertainment. New on the scene is **CALIFORNIA ADVENTURE**, a paean to all the state's wonders. Roller coasters spin above a boardwalk reminiscent of a Southern California beach town, and the **GRIZZLY RIVER RUN** rushes down rivers in a pseudo redwood forest. Admission to this second park in Disney's ever-growing empire is a separate ticket from the original Disneyland—encouraging visitors to spend the night in a Disney hotel.

An entertainment and dining center, **DOWNTOWN DISNEY** (714/300-7800) sits between the parks, offering further enticements. Admission is free to this area filled with top-name chains, from **HOUSE OF BLUES** to **LEGO**. There's an **ESPN ZONE** filled with games, a surround-sound movie theater, and 10 restaurants (including a few for romantic evenings).

The best idea Disney has come up with so far is **FASTPASS**. It allows visitors to avoid long waits in line by giving tickets for a particular time your group can gain quick admission to popular rides. Check out your map when you first enter the park—FASTPASS rides are highlighted. Run to **SPACE MOUNTAIN** or the **INDIANA JONES ADVENTURE**, and slip your tickets into a machine that gives you another ticket with a specified time. Check out the area while others are standing in 45-minute long lines, then return at the appointed hour and get on the ride almost instantly. The service is available in both parks. Savvy visitors learn how to use the system efficiently.

The original **DISNEYLAND** is both familiar and surprising. Certain stalwarts—the Haunted House, Mister Toad's Wild Ride, the Matterhorn—are still there and remain fresh and exciting. Tomorrowland is appropriately high-technified. Don't let the techies in your group enter **INNOVENTIONS**, however, or you'll lose them for the day. Space Mountain and Star Tours, both with nerve-jangling thrills, are both on FASTPASS. Take a ride on the relaxing Monorail at night. You'll be able to see the lights of the new Disney mousetraps.

Like Tomorrowland, each of the theme areas has unique crowd pleasers, along with restaurants, fast-food takeouts, theme shops, and rest rooms. The action lasts long into the night as visitors claim seats on sidewalk curbs for the Parade of the

Stars. Try to get on the Matterhorn during the fireworks show—the flashes of light as you swoop down the mountain look like stars and planets gone wild.

The streets around the Disney development are filled with hotels and motels offering shuttle services to the parks. If you're visiting the park from a ground base in San Diego, you should consider spending the night. It's hard to fully appreciate the experience if you're facing a long freeway drive. Naturally, kids of all ages prefer to stay at one of the **DISNEYLAND RESORT HOTELS**—a complex comprising the Disneyland Hotel, Disney's Grand Californian Hotel (which looks like a mountain lodge), and Disney's Paradise Pier Hotel. All have good restaurants, great pool areas, and links to the parks via the Monorail.

For more information about Disneyland, phone 714/781-4565 for recorded information; 714/781-7290 to consult with a live person between 8am and 7pm daily; or log on at www.disneyland.com. If you're looking for general area visitor information, the Anaheim/Orange County Visitor and Convention Board (800 W Katella Ave; 714/765-8888; www.anaheimoc.org) can fill you in.

# BAJA

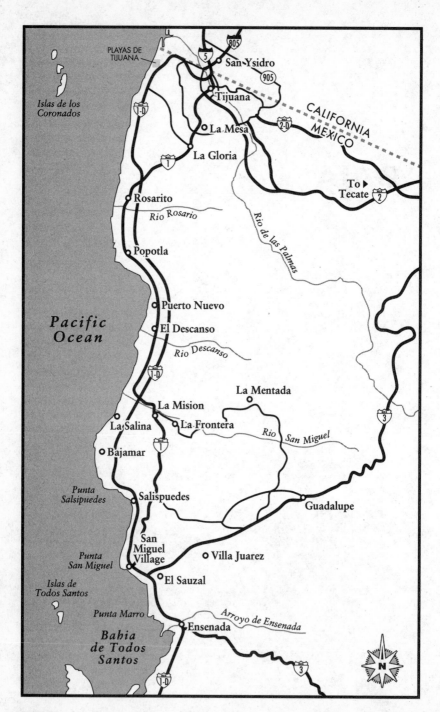

Islas de los Coronados

PLAYAS DE TIJUANA

San Ysidro

Tijuana

La Mesa

La Gloria

Rosarito

Rio Rosario

Popotla

Pacific Ocean

Puerto Nuevo

El Descanso

Rio Descanso

La Mentada

La Mision

La Salina

La Frontera

Bajamar

Rio San Miguel

Punta Salsipuedes

Salispuedes

Guadalupe

San Miguel Village

Villa Juarez

Punta San Miguel

El Sauzal

Islas de Todos Santos

Punta Marro

Arroyo de Ensenada

Bahia de Todos Santos

Ensenada

CALIFORNIA

MEXICO

To Tecate

Rio de las Palmas

N

# BAJA

## Baja, California, Mexico

The busiest border crossing in the world lies just 18 miles south of downtown San Diego, where San Ysidro, California, meets Tijuana, Mexico. Locals from both sides of the border cross frequently to visit family and friends, attend concerts and sporting events, shop for groceries and gifts, and dine in favorite restaurants. Travelers to Tijuana and San Diego can't resist visiting another country for at least one day; once inducted, they almost always want more.

Tijuana is just the beginning of a fascinating journey into Mexico's Baja California Peninsula. The nearly 1,000-mile-long strip of stark desert and mountains is firmly anchored between the Pacific Ocean and the Mar de Cortés. The peninsula was divided into two states—Baja California and Baja California Sur—in 1974. The northern portion is one of the fastest-growing parts of Mexico. Tijuana, in fact, is that nation's fourth-largest city. Development has spread south from Tijuana to the coastal community of Rosarito and on to the port city of Ensenada. Hundreds of U.S. citizens live in this portion of Mexico; hundreds more have vacation homes in private communities.

The Baja side of San Diego is an attraction few cities can claim, and one well worth exploring. Go over the options described in each section below, and choose the cities that best fit your time frame and interests. See "Border Sense" in this chapter for information on transportation, money, health, and safety. *Feliz viaje*— have a happy trip.

## Tijuana

*18 miles south of San Diego, off US Interstate 5.*

Tijuana's influence over San Diego is evident for miles before you reach the border. Signs on roadways and storefronts combine Spanish and English instructions and descriptions. Soon the spoken language slips into Spanglish, a combination of the two languages with its own special slang. The border itself assaults the senses with congested traffic, a significant police presence, and entirely foreign sights and smells. The aromas of meat, onions, and chiles sizzling on grills at taco stands immediately set the stomach growling. Shops and souvenir arcades get fingers twitching. And the eyes are constantly challenged by fascinating distractions. Beyond the obvious tourist attractions, Tijuana has a busy international airport, a thriving arts and culture scene, and hotels and restaurants befitting business travelers and wealthy Mexican families. It also is gaining a reputation as a major hub for drug cartels from both sides of the border. So unless you're a seasoned and highly savvy foreign traveler, stick with the tourist zones described below and keep a close hold on your possessions at all times.

**AVENIDA REVOLUCIÓN,** the traditional tourist zone, is lined with shopping arcades, franchise restaurants, and a few truly Mexican restaurants. Its bars have always catered to a rowdy crowd. These days, sleazy topless clubs (usually down a dark stairway) compete with rock-and-roll bars (usually up a stairway to a rooftop terrace).

The real reason Revolución is often crowded to the max is its shopping opportunities. The avenue, from Calle 1 to Calle 8, is lined with shops selling trinkets, mementos, and crafts from cheap and tacky to elegant and expensive, including silver jewelry, serapes (cotton blankets), embroidered dresses and blouses, carved figures of onyx or wood, huaraches (leather sandals), and more. Bargaining is expected on the streets and in less formal shops, but not in the nicer stores. Shopkeepers throughout Tijuana generally speak excellent English and accept dollars.

Some shoppers find the hawkers, shills, and touts who loudly beckon and proclaim from outside the storefronts a little disconcerting. These folks may feel more comfortable in the mini-malls and modern arcades. **BAZÁR DE MEXICO** (Av Revolución at Calle 7; 664/638-4737) is clean (it even has decent public rest rooms) and packed with vendors. **SANBORN'S** (Av Revolución at Calle 8; 664/688-1462), a classy coffee shop/restaurant popular with middle- and upper-class Mexicans, also has folk art from throughout the country, excellent books and CDs, and a delectable assortment of chocolates, cakes, and pastries. **TOLÁN** (Av Revolución 1471 between Calles 7 and 8; 664/688-3637) is a high-end arts and antiques boutique with the latest designs by artist Sergio Bustamante, beautiful Christmas ornaments and decorations, Talavera pottery from the state of Puebla, and lots of other elegant and rustic items from throughout Mexico. Artisans' stands line Calle 2 between the border and Revolución. For gifts and housewares, including lots of large lighting fixtures of wrought iron, visit **MALLORCA** (Calle 4a 8224 between Revolución and Madero; 664/688-3502).

More orderly shopping is available at **PLAZA RÍO TIJUANA** (Av Paseo de los Héroes between Avs Cuauhtémoc and Independencia; 664/684-0402), a full-scale mall with department stores, boutiques, a Sanborn's coffee shop, and a multiplex theater. Closer to the border, **PUEBLO AMIGO** (Vía Oriente 9211; no phone) is home to a few bars, taco stands, and restaurants as well as Ley, a grocery that sells real Mexican delicacies such as candied papaya and fresh spicy sauces for seafood and meat. If you'd like to see a real Mexican market (where you can practice your Spanish), head for the **MERCADO HIDALGO** (Avs Independencia and Sánchez Taboada, 5 blocks east of Revolución). The souvenirs here are of a practical bent—sandals, piñatas, soaps and potions with intriguing labels—and the market is a great place to people-watch or take discreet photos and see life outside the tourist zone.

To reward the kids for putting up with your shopping spree, take them to **MUNDO DIVERTIDO** (Calle José María Velasco 2578 at Av Paseo de los Héroes; 664/634-3213; weekdays noon–8:30pm, weekends 11am–9:30pm), with its miniature golf course, batting cages, roller coaster, and enormous video-game hall. Rides are inexpensive and there are stands selling fast food.

The amusement park and several of the city's finer restaurants are located in the **ZONA RÍO** (between Blvd Agua Caliente and the border) on Avenida Paseo de los Héroes. The avenue runs parallel to the dry Tijuana River and is a main thoroughfare with large statues of historical figures, including one of Abraham Lincoln, in the center of the *glorietas* (traffic circles). The heart of the Zona Río is the **TIJUANA CULTURAL CENTER** (Centro Cultural, Av Paseo de los Héroes at Av Independencia; 664/687-9600). The **CALIFORNIA MUSEUM** ($2, closed Mon) gives an overview of the peninsula's history, and the **OMNIMAX THEATER** ($3.50, closed Mon), with its 180-degree screen, shows a variety of interesting films—with at least one daily in English. These often complement the center's rotating art and culture exhibits. The bookstore has a good selection of books in both Spanish and English, and the coffee shop is a nice place to take a break.

Although many find the spectacle of man (and occasionally, woman) fighting raging bull to be barbaric, bullfighting still has its aficionados, especially in Mexico. Many visitors also are curious to witness a legendary *corrida de toros*. These are held at **EL TOREO DE TIJUANA** (Av Agua Caliente at Av Diego Rivera; no phone) May through October, generally on Sundays around 4pm. During summer months you can often see these fights at the Plaza de Toros Monumental (Playas de Tijuana, near the U.S. border, Ensenada Hwy; 664/685-2210). Admission cost depends on seat location and the matador's fame. For less bloodthirsty entertainment, take a tour of the **L. A. CETTO WINERY** (Cañón Johnson 2108, at Av Constitución Sur; 664/685-3031; closed Sun). Cost is $1 per person, $2 including generous tastings. Pick up souvenirs and vintages at the winery gift shop.

Even if you spend only a few hours in Tijuana, you must have an authentic Mexican meal. If you prefer an elegant and (by Mexican standards) expensive meal, **CIEN AÑOS** (Av José María Velasco 1407 in the Zona Río; 664/634-3039) offers exotic cuisine from mainland Mexico. Traditional ingredients such as *huitlacoche* (a fungus grown on corn), nopal cactus, papaya, and tamarind are combined just so to produce interesting and delicious dishes. A more modest but equally delicious spot for Mexican classics is **EL POTRERO** (Blvd Salinas 4700; 664/681-8082), across from the country club. This longtime Tijuana favorite was for years nicknamed "el Sombrero," and from outside the round restaurant does look like an outrageously large Mexican hat. Inside it is more subtle, and the comprehensive menu tempts the palate with cold and hot appetizers, soups—try the mushroom soup in chicken broth or the Sonora-style *sopa de carne seca,* (dried meat soup)—as well as a wide range of meats and seafood, and a few pastas. Within Pueblo Amigo, **SEÑOR FROG'S** (Vía Oriente 60 at Paseo de Tijuana; 664/682-4962), of the Carlos Andersen chain, serves tasty if predictable Mexican food, barbecued chicken, and ribs. Upstairs is a raucous bar and discotheque where roving bands of hyperactive, bilingual waiters dispense lots of cerveza, shots of tequila, and overpriced munchies.

Avenida Revolución is packed with restaurants. Our favorite for inexpensive, authentic Mexican cooking and ambiance is **LA ESPECIAL** (Av Revolución 718; 664/685-6654), which opened in 1952. The enchiladas, carne asada, and puerco adobado are excellent; few meals cost more than $7. Another old-timer, **CHICKI JAI** (Av Revolución at Calle 7; 664/685-4955), opened in 1947 in a tiny tiled building. The cuisine is centered around old-world Basque—try the calamari *en su tinto* or the savory paella, rice cooked in chicken broth with shrimp, pork, chicken, and seasonings.

## BORDER SENSE

Many leaders and citizens on both sides of the border speak of San Diego and Tijuana as an enormous binational metropolis. A cross-border language, cuisine, and culture has emerged over the last century, and the two cities will forever be entwined. As a result, traveling to northern Baja is almost as easy as heading north to Los Angeles. But there are some differences. Here are some tips you should heed to be sure of a comfortable and rewarding journey.

**GETTING THERE:** The San Diego Trolley line ends in San Ysidro at the border. Pedestrians either walk over the border on a seemingly endless bridge, or board a Mexican bus or cab and ride through the border (a 10-minute trip across Interstate 5 to the Mexican entry). Drivers park in lots at the end of Interstate 5 near Mexican customs and walk through a few gates, or follow the often long lines of vehicles feeding past the border guards.

**GETTING BACK:** Pedestrians and drivers pass through customs booths, where they must declare their citizenship and describe what they're bringing back into the United States. Both walking and driving through the border take considerable time and patience, especially when world events cause heightened security measures. Adults are allowed to bring back 1 liter of alcohol and 1 carton of cigarettes—don't load up on tequila for souvenirs. Cuban cigars are also forbidden. Anyone can be pulled aside for secondary inspection, which can last minutes or hours.

**MONEY:** The peso is the official currency in Mexico, but dollars and U.S. credit cards and traveler's checks are readily accepted.

**PAPERWORK:** Everyone crossing the border must have proof of citizenship. A U.S. driver's license usually suffices; travelers from countries other than the States must have

Well-off Mexicans frequent the fancy **FOUQUET'S DE PARIS** restaurant in the elegant Camino Real Hotel (Av Paseo de los Héroes 10305; 664/633-4000). Ideally situated close to shopping and the cultural center, this five-star hotel has amenities such as direct-dial phones and fax service, but no pool or hot tub. Also within the Camino Real, **AZULEJOS** restaurant offers less formal dining and excellent, extensive breakfast and lunch buffets Monday through Saturday as well as a lavish Sunday brunch. If you want to treat yourself to an overnight in Tijuana, consider the **FIESTA INN VITA SPA** (Av Paseo de los Héroes 18818, Zona Río; 664/634-6901 or 800/343-7821). Although sandwiched between two busy thoroughfares, the building straddles an underground thermal spring—the same ones that fed the glamorous Agua Caliente Spa (now a school) in the 1920s. The rooms at this former Holiday Inn property have been redecorated since it was purchased by the Fiesta Inn their passports. Mexican tourist cards are not required for Baja visits unless you plan to stay in the country more than 72 hours. If you need a tourist card, stop by the immigration office just inside the border crossing area. U.S. car insurance does not cover travel in Mexico. Stop at one of the many Mexican auto-insurance booths on the San Ysidro side of the border and purchase a policy covering your vehicle during your stay. Most U.S. rental companies do not allow their cars to be taken into Mexico or limit their policies to cover only Tijuana to Ensenada; always ask agents about their company's regulations.

**TELEPHONES:** To call Mexico from the United States dial 011-52 before the numbers in this chapter. Within Mexico, phoning is always a challenge. The area codes for all numbers in the country changed in November 2001 (for the third time in as many years). Phone numbers in the towns in this chapter now look exactly like U.S. numbers, with a 3-digit area code and a 7-digit number. Within a city, dial only the 7-digit local phone number; between cities first dial 01. The area codes for the cities in this chapter are Tijuana 664; Rosarito 661; Puerto Nuevo 661; Ensenada 646; and Bajamar 646.

**TOURS AND RESERVATIONS:** Without a doubt, the easiest way to visit Mexico is to join a tour. Several excellent options are available in San Diego. **BAJA CALIFORNIA TOURS** (7734 Herschel Ave, La Jolla; 858/454-7166; 800/336-5454; www.baja-tours.signonsandiego.com) offers a fascinating array of day and overnight trips, some featuring cultural and recreational themes. **MEXICOACH** (Av Revolución between Calles 6 and 7, Tijuana; 664/685-1470; 619/428-9517; www.mexicoach.com) offers several organized tours and shuttle buses to Tijuana and Rosarito. **BAJA INFORMATION** (6855 Friars Rd, Mission Valley; 619/298-4105, 800/522-1516 in CA, NV, and AZ, 800/225-2786 from the rest of the U.S. and Canada; impamexicoinfo@juno.com) is a great overall source of information and can arrange hotel reservations.

—*Maribeth Mellin*

chain, but for most guests the draw is the treatments at the spa, where private tubs are fed directly from the mineral springs. You can sign up for a facial, massage, or mud wrap as well.

Tijuana still merits its reputation as a serious party town, and several discos carry on long and hard, especially on Saturday nights. The best known is **BABY ROCK** (Calle Diego Rivera 1482, Zona Río; 664/634-1313), the original Acapulco disco's trendy baby sister, which has a hip, well-heeled, and generally youngish following. Thursday is ladies' night; Saturday it's no-holds-barred dancing to cumbia, rock, salsa, and "dance" music. Casual dressers beware: Tijuana's discos usually have strict dress codes—no T-shirts, jeans, or beach sandals allowed.

# Rosarito

*24 km (15 miles) south of Tijuana on the Tijuana-Ensenada Toll Road.*

Rosarito Beach, as it's most commonly called, is northern Baja's newest boomtown. Its population, now nearly 100,000, continues to grow steadily. So does its reputation as party central among die-hard young fans of dancing, drinking, and general rabble-rousing. MTV touted Rosarito as a perfect spot for the spring-break party scene, and college kids raced down to test the waters—and the fire waters. Since then, government-sponsored advertising blitzes have warned young revelers of the consequences of too many tequila shooters, but the party rages nonetheless during school holidays and on hot summer weekends.

The young and the restless aren't the only ones attracted to Rosarito, whose 5-mile-long beach stretches without interruption from the power plant at the town's northern border all the way to the Hotel Rosarito Beach. Surfers have their favorite breaks, and snowbirds flock to private residences, trailer parks, condos, and hotels in search of respite from Canadian and Midwestern winters. Twentieth Century Fox built a studio south of town in 1995, using it as a base for filming the megahit *Titanic* in 1996 and 1997, which increased Rosarito's prestige and growth. Scenes for other films, including *Pearl Harbor,* have also been shot at the studio.

Despite the recent hobnobbing with Hollywood glamour-pusses, Rosarito isn't synonymous with sophistication or culture. It's about sun and sea, relaxing and boogying. The town careens haphazardly along both sides of the Old Ensenada Highway, now more commonly known as **BOULEVARD BENITO JUÁREZ**. The street is strewn with restaurants, bars, and shops in an alarming mix of building styles and degrees of completion. Although you can visit Rosarito on a day trip from San Diego, many adopt the Mexican mañana attitude and delay their return home for one or more days. It's certainly worth considering, since there's enough shopping, outdoor activities, and good restaurants to keep you busy throughout the day and on into the night.

The traditional holiday headquarters is the **ROSARITO BEACH HOTEL** (Blvd Juárez 31, south end of town; 661/612-0144, 800/343-8582 in the U.S. and Mexico; www.rosaritobeachhotel.com). Built in the 1920s as an elegant hotel and gambling palace, the hotel is still the nicest in town. The sum of its parts makes for a more impressive package than the individual guest rooms would imply. Although these are acceptable, it's the long beach, happening bar, and two good restaurants (one French, the other Mexican and Continental) that make this old icon a standout. Also receiving high marks is the hotel's **CASA PLAYA SPA**, which offers massage and beauty treatments and has saunas, steam rooms, and hot tubs. One of Rosarito's few other beachfront hotels is **LOS PELÍCANOS** (Calle Ebano 113 at Calle Cedros; 661/612-0445). Ask for a room with a balcony overlooking the beach. Although there's no pool, rooms are pleasant and airy, and the second-story restaurant and bar are a great place to watch the sun set. Golfers should check out the secluded, all-suites **MARRIOTT REAL DEL MAR RESIDENCE INN** (km 19.5, Tijuana-Ensenada toll road; 664/631-3670, 800/662-6180 in the U.S.; www.realdelmar.com.mx), overlooking the sea 10 kilometers (6 miles) north of Rosarito Beach. Many units have both fireplaces and kitchens, and the hotel's **PEDRÍN'S** restaurant has reliable seafood dishes and Mexican favorites. Vacation packages include green fees at the 18-hole golf course. Before your game you can stretch out in the exercise room, or take a post-play dip in the property's pool.

If golf's not your bag, there are other recreational possibilities. The best surfing beaches near San Diego are south of Rosarito on the Old Ensenada Highway, which runs parallel to Mexico Highway 1. Beaches are usually designated by kilometer signs. Locals and Southern Californians habitually check the waves at **POPOTLA** (km 32.5), **CALAFIA** (km 35.5), and just beyond at **COSTA BAJA** (km 36). For horseback riding on the beach, look for signs along Boulevard Juárez or clumps of horses standing in the shade on the beach. Cost is about $8 to $10 per hour.

If the thought of all this exercise has made you hungry, take heart: there are lots of good restaurants in Rosarito, some serving traditional Mexican favorites. At **LA FLOR DE MICHOACÁN** (Blvd Juárez 291; 661/612-1858), grilled meats rule the day, served in the style of Michoacán state—on the grill with a side of guacamole, lots of fresh salsa, and stacks of homemade tortillas. Tacos and tostadas round out the menu of this casual eatery (closed Wed). The busy **FESTIVAL PLAZA** (Av Juárez at Calle Nogal; 661/612-2950 or 800/453.8606; www.festivalbaja.com) has several bars and good restaurants in addition to its hotel rooms, villas, and penthouse suites. Among the best of the restaurants here is **EL PATIO** (661/612-2950), another great spot to relax over a bona fide Mexican meal. Rather than the typical tacos and tostadas, look for spicy chiles rellenos (batter-fried chiles stuffed with cheese or ground meat), grilled quail, and savory crepes, as well as bar drinks and beer.

Across the street and a few blocks north, **LE COUSTEAU** (Blvd Juárez 184; 661/612-2655) is a pretty and moderately priced bistro serving French and Mediterranean food, including some interesting pasta dishes along with daily Continental specials. Both owner Philippe Chauvin and his chef are Parisians who married local women and immigrated to rustic Rosarito Beach.

After a large midday meal, many will opt for a relaxing nap in a hammock or air-conditioned hotel room. The stalwart, however, will opt to shop. Consumer opportunities have multiplied like unglazed ceramic rabbits over the last 10 years, and Rosarito now has a respectable number of stores selling indoor and outdoor furniture, pottery, and other decorative items. Small souvenir shops are sprinkled all along Boulevard Juárez, and the larger hotels have shopping arcades and crafts stores. Before Rosarito's many restaurants and Johnny-come-lately hotels sprang up, Rosarito was known for the pottery stands that lined the Old Ensenada Highway. You can still find shops (generally at the north and south extremes of town) selling huge ceramic planters and pots as well as furniture and accessories. Among the most interesting of these are **APISA** (Blvd Juárez 2400; 661/612-0125), which sells fancy furnishings and iron sculpture from Guadalajara, and **FELIX FURNITURE** (Blvd Juárez 316; 661/612-0091), where rustic-looking furniture is made to order. At the south end of town, you can watch carvers create lovely rustic wooden furniture right on the premises at **CASA LA CARRETA** (km 29, Old Ensenada Hwy; 661/612-0502).

For entertainment, Rosarito has boisterous bars, piano lounges, and more sedate restaurant/bars. Drinking-and-driving laws are strictly enforced—take a cab or assign a designated driver if you plan to imbibe. Within Festival Plaza (see above),

**EL MUSEO CANTINA TEQUILA** (661/612-0842) is a bar-cum-tequila-museum where you can literally choose your poison; there are more than 125 brands of the agave-based liquor at this fun bar frequented by party-hungry locals and tourists. You can get both food and drink at **ROCK & ROLL TACO,** also within the plaza. Two blocks toward the beach, the enormous indoor/outdoor installation of **PAPAS&BEER** (Av Eucalipto at Av Mar Adriático; 661/612-0444) generally attracts a rowdy younger crowd. You'll find a mixed crowd of old and young revelers at the **ROSARITO BEACH HOTEL** (see above), which has live music on weekend nights. For a sunset cocktail, nothing beats **CALAFIA** (km 35.5, Old Ensenada Hwy; 661/612-1580, 877/700-2093 in the U.S.), where the small tables are set down the cliff—each overlooks the ocean on its own miniature terrace. Live music is sometimes performed near the base of the cliffs. It's a 10-minute ride south of Rosarito by car or cab.

# Puerto Nuevo (Newport)

*12 km (7½ miles) south of Rosarito, at km 44 on the Old Ensenada Highway.*
Twenty years ago this collection of restaurants was a tiny outpost of local gastronomy along the road to Ensenada. The menu was—and still is—simple: lobster, boiled and then grilled; refried beans; mountains of Spanish rice; and all of the homemade tortillas and salsa you can eat. Over the years these seafood shacks became legendary, then mainstream. The once-rutted entry road has been partially paved, and souvenir shops mark the entrance to dozens of restaurants. Most aficionados have their favorite haunts among the dozens of lobster houses, which are almost identical in menu and price if not in character and service. Poke your head into several restaurants, check out the vibe (and the bar, if you're a drinker; some have beer and wine only). Then pull up a chair—painted, varnished, plastic, or otherwise. Of all the restaurants in this enclave, **COSTA BRAVA** is among the fanciest, with tablecloths and a window opening onto the sea below. Also recommended is **LA CASA DE LA LANGOSTA.** Lobsters are almost universally priced by size, with a medium-size specimen with all the trimmings running about $17. Lobster season in these parts is October through March; the crustacean is imported year-round, however, as the supply cannot keep up with the demand. Most places are open for lunch and dinner.

Entrepreneurs have finally noticed a marketing niche and established a few hotels at Puerto Nuevo, solving the drinking-and-driving dilemma. Devotees of **LAS ROCAS HOTEL** (km 38.5, Old Ensenada Hwy; 661/612-2140, 888/527-7622 in the U.S. and Canada; www.lasrocas.com) have more than lobster and beer in mind; they're more interested in the seaside hotel's fabulous spa. Treatments are less expensive than in the United States, but are administered by excellent technicians, and the whirlpool tubs look out to the crashing surf. The hotel has standard rooms and suites with fireplaces; the pool sits right above the ocean and the grounds are a popular wedding venue. **NEW PORT BEACH HOTEL** (km 45, Old Ensenada Hwy; 661/614-1180, 800/582-1018 in the U.S. and Canada; www.newportbeachhotel.com) is situated just south of the lobster shanties. Heaters warm the 147 guest rooms on cool evenings, and many rooms have a small balcony overlooking the surf. The hotel has its own restaurant and bar, as well as a hot tub and heated swimming pool, two tennis courts, and an exercise room. Substantial discounts are available midweek. About 9 miles south of Newport, **LA FONDA** (km 59, Old Ensenada Hwy; 661/155-1307; lafonda@telnor.net) has been luring Southern Californians for decades. The 26-room inn is decorated with what looks like castoffs from a less-kind, less-genteel era; sofas, lamps, and paintings can only be described as extremely funky. Many rooms have an excellent view of the sea from both their wide front windows and furnished decks, however, and in a rare reprieve from technology, there is no television or telephone. If you get lonely in your seaside room, head for the lively and friendly bar, quite the happening place on weekend nights. The weekend brunch is definitely worth investigating, and the rest of the week you can enjoy succulent steaks on the restaurant's outdoor patio overlooking the beach.

# Ensenada

*75 km (47 miles) south of Rosarito, 104 km (65 miles) south of Tijuana.*
The toll road (called Ensenada Cuota) from Tijuana, completed in 1973, is a faster ride than the old Mexico Highway 1 to Ensenada. The latter (also called the Old Road to Ensenada) is nonetheless a perfectly acceptable two-lane road that heads inland about halfway to Ensenada, returning to the coast to become Boulevard Costero at the northern entrance to town.

One of Mexico's largest seaports, Ensenada (Spanish for "cove" or "inlet") has grown slowly but steadily since the bay on which it lies, Bahía de Todos Santos (All Saints' Bay), was first seen by Portuguese explorer Juan Rodríguez Cabrillo. Since then the town has supported ranchers, gold miners, wineries, and a prosperous fishing fleet and fish-processing industry. Along the boulevard fronting Ensenada's perfect, fishhook-shaped harbor you'll find boat repair docks, fishing vessels, and commercial shipping warehouses.

There are no beaches in Ensenada itself, and the burgeoning beach facilities and accommodations to the north at Rosarito over the last 15 years have siphoned off a substantial amount of the town's tourist trade. Most of those who choose Ensenada over Rosarito or other beach destinations are seeking a glimpse of the "real Mexico" as close to the U.S. border as possible. Others feel the need to experience the legendary **HUSSONG'S CANTINA** (Av Ruíz 113; 646/178-3210). The large, long saloon opened more than a century ago and is apparently in no danger of closing—ever! Although during morning and early afternoons you might find just a handful of locals sitting at the bar, by eventide things are heating up. Roving mariachi and ranchera musicians add to the cacophony produced by party animals from north of the border. Believe it or not, there are some who make Hussong's the point and focus of their trip. More traditional pilgrims may find succor at the city's cathedral, **NUESTRA SEÑORA DE GUADALUPE** (Av Floresta at Av Juárez), which honors Mexico's patron saint, Our Lady of Guadalupe.

Although Ensenada can be visited as a day trip, many choose to spend one or more nights in this bayside city. If you're looking for a luxurious property with loads of amenities, check out the **HOTEL CORAL & MARINA** (km 102, Tijuana-Ensenada toll road; 646/175-0000; 877/233-5839 in the U.S.; www.hotelcoral.com), built in 1995. With a marina that can accommodate 600 boats, the resort is frequent host

## THE WHOLE ENCHILADA

Please don't eat at Burger King or McDonald's when you're in Mexico; you'll miss half the reason for being there! All the restaurants described in this chapter take extra precautions with food preparation and use purified water for cooking. If you're really wary, take a swig of Pepto-Bismol or another stomach-coating salve before you eat, and stick with cooked foods. And remember: never drink water from the tap. Some of the most popular south-of-the-border treats include:

**BURRITOS:** Flour tortillas wrapped around a wide range of fillings, from refried beans and cheese to grilled meats with guacamole.

**CARNE ASADA:** Marinated and grilled strips of beef served in tacos and burritos or as part of a combo plate with beans, rice, guacamole, and tortillas.

**CARNITAS:** Marinated pork served as above.

**CHILES RELLENOS:** A large semispicy green chile stuffed with cheese, coated with batter, fried, and covered with sauce.

**ENCHILADAS:** Corn tortillas wrapped around cheese, chicken, or beef and baked in a semispicy sauce.

**FLAN:** This custardlike dish with a caramel flavor is quite possibly the most popular dessert in Mexico. Some chefs prepare it with tropical fruits or fancy sauces.

**GUACAMOLE:** Some novices call it "that green stuff"; few retain their aversion. Mashed avocados are mixed with lime, onions, tomatoes, cilantro, and all manner of ingredients following family recipes. Usually served with corn chips or in a dollop with entrees.

to fishing tournaments and boat races. Its 147 suites are found in three eight-story towers; all have balconies with ocean view, cable TV, and direct-dial phones. For recreation, there are several tennis courts, an exercise room, three pools (one indoor), and two hot tubs. Diving and fishing tours can be organized on-site. The more intimate **LAS ROSAS** (Mexico Hwy 1, 2 miles north of Ensenada; 646/174-4320; 800/522-1516 in Arizona, California, and Nevada, 800/225-2786 elsewhere in U.S. and Canada; www.lasrosas.com) is true to its name: "the Roses" hotel is delicate and pink. Elegant touches are found throughout the lobby: marble floors, windows overlooking the sea, a green glass ceiling above the atrium. All 32 well-appointed rooms overlook either the pool and hot tub or the ocean; some have fireplaces. **PUNTA MORRO** (Mexico Hwy 1, 2 miles north of town; 646/178-3507, 800/526-6676 in the U.S.; www.punta-morro.com) is a secluded hideaway as recommended for its charming restaurant overlooking the ocean as for its 30 suites, all with kitchenettes and terraces facing the bay. Although this isn't an ideal swimming beach (the surf is rough), the setting is cozy and romantic (some rooms have fireplaces) with great views of the bay. The property also has a bar, pool, and hot tub. Golfers gravitate toward **BAJAMAR** (km 77.5, Old Ensenada Hwy; 646/155-0151, 800/342-2644 in the U.S.; 888/311-6076 for tee times), which lies between Ense-

**HUEVOS RANCHEROS:** Fried eggs on corn tortillas topped with a spicy, tomato-based sauce.

**HUITLACOCHE:** It's a black fungus grown on corn, but don't let that scare you. The taste is like an earthy mushroom, especially good in quesadillas and crepas (crepes).

**MOLE:** This blend of spices used for sauces on chicken, pork, and enchiladas comes in several varieties. Black mole often includes bitter chocolate and chiles; yellow mole is seasoned with pumpkin seeds. Mole is an acquired taste but worth sampling.

**PAN DULCE:** Sweet breads sold in bakeries, or *panaderias*. Cookies, muffins, Danish pastries, and fruit breads all taste different in Mexico; in the bakeries, preservatives are shunned and lard and butter are the favored fats. Stop by a bakery, grab a metal platter and a pair of tongs, and stockpile your snacks for the day.

**SOPA DE TORTILLA:** Tortilla soup is wonderful when made properly. The best ones have a spicy chicken broth and are served with a platter of crumbled cheese, chopped avocado, cilantro, and crisp tortilla strips.

**TACOS:** Fried or soft corn tortillas stuffed with every imaginable ingredient. Baja specialties include fish tacos and tacos *al pastor*, made with thin slices of rotisserie pork.

**TAMALES:** Beef, chicken, or fruit fillings mixed with cornmeal and wrapped in corn husks.

**TORTA:** A sandwich made on a thick, crusty roll called a *bolillo*.

—*Maribeth Mellin*

nada and Rosarito. Revamped in late 1993, this challenging 18-hole course is set high on the cliffs overlooking the ocean (there's a nine-hole course near the beach). On-site, the **HACIENDA BAJAMAR** hotel (646/155-0152, 800/342-2644 in the U.S.) has a restaurant, bar, and pool along with a few tennis courts. Rooms overlook either the sea or the links.

South of Ensenada you'll find the moderately priced **ESTERO BEACH RESORT** (Mexico Hwy 1 between Ensenada and Maneadero; 646/176-6235 or 646/176-6230; www.hotelesterobeach.com), a comfortable place favored by families. It's located right on a calm estuary and beach about 6 miles south of Ensenada. Some rooms have kitchenettes, perfect for keeping soft drinks cold and cooking simple meals. Ask for a room right on the sand, and inquire about midweek discounts. There are tennis courts, pool, horseback riding, volleyball, and a children's playground. Nonguests can use the hotel's facilities for a small fee.

Whether spending the night or just the day, start your tour of Ensenada's waterfront at the **FISH MARKET** (north end of Blvd Costero). Here you'll find stands selling Ensenada's legendary fish tacos (spawned in this region and copied at fast-food Mexican restaurants throughout San Diego and beyond). These original Baja beauties are made of fresh, piping-hot corn tortillas, fresh deep-fried fish, chopped cabbage, a squeeze of lime, and salsa. Of course, you might actually be here to haggle for the tuna, dorado, marlin, snapper, and other local species for sale at the ocean-front market. Continue south along the coast road to the **SPORTFISHING PIER** (Malecón at Av Alvarado), whence fishing and whale-watching boats depart regularly. Tried-and-true **GORDO'S SPORTFISHING** (Blvd Costero at Av Alvarado; 646/178-3515 or 646/178-2377; www.gordos.8m.com) has charter boats, group boats ($45 for a half day or $100 for overnight), and whale watching in season. If you want to book before arriving, contact **BAJA CALIFORNIA TOURS** (858/454-7166). The best fishing is generally April through November.

South of the sportfishing pier, admire the sculptures of Mexican heroes Benito Juárez, Miguel Hidalgo, and Venustiano Carranza at the bare-bones **PLAZA CÍVICA** (Blvd Costero at Av Riveroll). Continue on to the **CENTRO ARTESANAL DE ENSE-NADA** (Blvd Costero 1094), where trade ebbs and flows as the cruise ships dock and decamp. Some tenants have fled as traffic has been diverted from the area in recent years; others, such as **GALERÍA DE PÉREZ MEILLÓN** (646/174-0394), stick it out. In business for 13 years, this small store carries museum-quality folk art, including rustic but elegant pottery from Mata Ortiz, Chihuahua; pit-fired pottery made by the Paipai Indians; and willow baskets made by the Kumeyaay.

For a taste of Prohibition-era luxury and style, continue south to **RIVIERA DEL PACÍFICO** (Blvd Costero and Av Riviera; 646/176-4310). Although this former gambling palace, hotel, restaurant, and bar closed shortly after its inauguration when gambling was outlawed, it's now a cultural center and a glamorous reminder of Ensenada's past. Tour the mansion's ballrooms, visit the flower gardens, and stop in at the **MUSEO DE HISTORIA DE ENSENADA.**

If you're ready to relax over a cerveza and regional barbecue, head for **EL CHARRO** (Av López Mateos 454; 646/178-3881), where locals and visitors chow down on rotisserie chicken, beans, rice, and tortillas. Patrons sniff the air hungrily as they watch the chicken rotate slowly above the open wood fire. If you prefer seafood, the **CASAMAR** (Blvd Lázaro Cárdenas 987; 646/174-0417) is an old favorite known for its lobster or shrimp prepared al mojo de ajo (sautéed in butter and garlic). For an elegant dinner visit **EL REY SOL** (Av López Mateos 1000; 646/178-1733). This enduring favorite, with heavy drapes, subdued lighting, and stained-glass panels, has delighted visitors as well as locals since the 1950s. French and Mexican dishes feature vegetables grown in the Santo Tomás Valley, and the patisserie turns out excellent baked goods. All three are open every day.

If you want souvenirs of your trip, Ensenada's shopping zone is found just one block east of the Boulevard Costero. It runs for about eight blocks along **AVENIDA LÓPEZ MATEOS** (also called **CALLE 1A** along this stretch) between Avenidas Castillo and Obregón. Here restaurants and bars share the sidewalk with shops selling silver and shell jewelry, blankets, knitted shawls, ceramic piggy banks, and more sophisticated objects. Among the nicest shops are **BAZÁR CASA RAMÍREZ** (Calle López Mateos 496; 646/178-8209), where traditional techniques and materials are used in the creation of innovative objets d'art. **LOS CASTILLO** (Av López Mateos 815; 646/176-1187), which has franchises throughout Mexico, sells a nice selection of silver jewelry at this and several other locations along López Mateos.

**LAS BODEGAS DE SANTO TOMÁS** (Av Miramar 666; 646/178-2509) in downtown Ensenada is Baja California's oldest winery. **LA ESQUINA DE BODEGAS** (646/678-2509), across the street from the winery, is one of the few cafe/galleries in the city. In addition to coffee and tiramisu, the small restaurant serves a fixed-price lunch menu, soups, salads, and sandwiches.

If you prefer to escape the city, take the afternoon to explore the coast south of Ensenada. Drive or take a cab to **LA BUFADORA** (Hwy 23 west of Maneadero, 22 miles south of Ensenada), an impressive blowhole at the point known as Punta Banda, where the mountains come crouching down over the sea. The blowhole shoots up nearly 80 feet in the air every few minutes, spraying excited children and their parents as they stand behind a protective fence. Just before you reach the point, you can buy a variety of cooked foods and souvenirs, and sometimes locally grown olives or garlic, at roadside stands. There is a small fee to park near the blowhole.

# RECREATION

# RECREATION

## Outdoor Activities

Forget your shopping, your wining and dining, and all your other indoor pursuits. When it comes to the number-one favorite local pastime, outdoor recreation is where it's at. San Diegans practically live outdoors, and resent rain and chilly fog for impeding fun in the sun. We bike to work; skate, run, and walk at lunch; surf at dusk and dawn. Mental-health days (aka sick days) are spent in the fresh air; after all, there's nothing like a boat ride on the sea to clear the brain. The county's varied terrain offers unlimited opportunities, from surfing to desert hiking. Activities are overseen by an amalgamation of volunteer and governmental organizations as outlined in the categories below. And please remember, if you lack skills or experience, don't participate in any of these sports without getting training or guidance first.

### BICYCLING

San Diego is a perfect cycling region, thanks to its enviable dry, mild climate and wide range of scenery and terrain. An essential tool for serious cyclists is the San Diego Region Bike Map (Ridelink Bicycle Information; 619/231-BIKE). The map clearly illustrates bike lanes, paths, trails, and routes, highlighted in different colors. Follow the red lines if you're interested in casual rides, teal if you want to cover vast distances. You can also get information on renting bike lockers (favored by cycling commuters) when ordering the map. There are bike racks on some city buses, including those stopping at major tourist sites; for specifics call or stop by the **TRANSIT STORE** (102 Broadway, Downtown; 619/234-1060; map:N7).

Several cycling organizations lead casual bike rides and organized tours. The **SAN DIEGO COUNTY BICYCLE COALITION** (619/685-7742 or 858/487-6063; www.sdcbc.org) is a good source of overall biking information and can direct you to contacts for cycling clubs, along with bike etiquette and safety classes. Seasoned roadies gravitate toward **CYCLO VETS** (619/584-0087; www.cyclo-vets.org), a robust clan of more than 300 cyclists nationwide, including more than 100 national and international champions. Others who favor long, challenging backcountry road rides join the **SAN DIEGO BICYCLING TOURING SOCIETY** (619/332-6215; www.members.home.net/patveth/sdbts/rides.htm). Recreational cyclists enjoy the cultured **KNICKERBIKERS** (858/450-0373; www.znetwork.net/knickerbikers), which schedules rides about the city on Tuesday evenings and weekend days and also arranges national and international tours. The **RAINBOW CYCLISTS OF SAN DIEGO** (760/729-9491; www.rainbowcyclists.org) is a gay and lesbian organization promoting biking for riders of all ages and abilities. The **SAN DIEGO TANDEM CLUB** (858/509-9808; www.sunnyside.ws/sdtc) hosts weekend rides and monthly events for tandem enthusiasts. The **SAN DIEGO MOUNTAIN BIKING ASSOCIATION** (619/258-9140; www.sdmba.com) is a nonprofit organization dedicated to protecting the rights of off-road cyclists and maintaining and developing bike trails. **HIKE BIKE KAYAK SAN DIEGO** (858/551-9510; www.hbksandiego.com) offers guided bike tours for all levels. Tours include rental bikes, helmets, and hotel pickup and drop-off. The tour of the Temecula wine country includes a bike ride, then a van tour for wine tastings and lunch.

San Diego is the site of several annual racing events, most of which have a festive party spirit. A case in point is the **MIDNIGHT MADNESS** fund-raising ride, during which thousands of cyclists dressed in their pajamas and fancy lingerie race around the streets of downtown. The 20-mile ride is held each August in the wee hours; prizes are given for most interesting nighttime attire. Another party-on-wheels is the twice-yearly **ROSARITO TO ENSENADA FUN BICYCLE RIDE**, sponsored by Bicycling West Inc. (619/583-3001), which draws 8,000 to 10,000 fun-minded people (all with different levels of expertise) to career 50-some miles from Rosarito to Ensenada. The coast highway (aka Mexico Highway 1, or the "free road") is closed to vehicular traffic; riders speed by tossing candy to children running alongside. Rides take place each April and September, when temperatures are pleasant. The scenery is superb, but gravel on the downhills, along with the occasional drunken cyclist, can make the ride hazardous.

Some of the area's other standout rides are listed below.

## Coronado

**END OF 10TH ST NEAR THE HOTEL DEL CORONADO, CORONADO; NO PHONE** Many Sunday biking enthusiasts bring their wheels aboard the San Diego–Coronado ferry to cruise around Coronado's classy neighborhoods, past historic mansions and modernistic condos. Pedaling along the streets past flower gardens and beaches is great fun. Take the ferry from downtown and rent a cruiser, tandem, or baby-seat bike from **BIKES AND BEYOND** (619/435-7180) at the Ferry Landing, and pedal along paths beside Tidelands Park, under the San Diego–Coronado Bay Bridge, and along the golf course and waterfront to Glorietta Bay. *Map:NN5*

## Fiesta Island

**FIESTA ISLAND RD BETWEEN E MISSION BAY AND SEA WORLD DRS, MISSION BAY; 619/276-8200** Fiesta Island is a fun, flat, albeit dusty place to ride with the family while speedboats, Jet Skis, Wave Runners, and water-skiers zip around in the bay. Traffic is light, and although the paved road must be shared with vehicular traffic, the 25mph speed limit makes for a comfortable ride. *Map:LL6*

## Mission Bay Park

**BOUNDED BY MISSION BAY AND SEA WORLD DRS, MISSION BAY; 619/221-8901** Large chunks of this 4,600-acre park are accessible to bikers, with concrete paths running over grassy slopes and along the beach and the bay. Expect to share the path, however, with walkers, runners, in-line skaters, and babies in strollers. Start at De Anza Cove, near the end of East Mission Bay Drive, where there is plenty of free parking, and ride the paths south past the Hilton Hotel and Tecolote Shores Park. From this path you can access Fiesta Island (see above), Sea World Drive, and bike paths along the San Diego River flood-control channel. From Crown Point Shores Park (Corona Oriente Dr at La Playa Ave) you can ride on pavement all the way around Sail Bay and down to the southern tip of West Mission Bay. *Map:LL6*

## Mission Trails Regional Park

**I FATHER JUNIPERO SERRA TRAIL, TIERRASANTA; 619/668-3275** About 10 miles northeast of downtown, this urban park offers everything from gut-wrenching mountain-bike climbs to a pleasant roll around Lake Murray. Moms pushing baby-jogger carriages, dedicated bladers, runners, walkers, and bikers share the wide cement path that nearly circumvents the lake. It's a flat 7 miles in and out (3.5 miles each way). For a more challenging ride, stop in at the recreation center on the north side of the lake for maps and information. Free parking and rest rooms. *Map:JJ2*

## Mission and Pacific Beaches

**NORTH AND SOUTH OF BELMONT PARK, MISSION BEACH; 619/221-8901** For more of a cruise than a bike ride, head for the boardwalk at Belmont Park. Bike rentals are abundant (check out **MISSION BEACH CLUB**, 704 Ventura Pl; 858/488-5050; map:LL7) and it's reasonably uncrowded—midweek in the dead of winter or when it's pouring rain, that is. Most other times, the boardwalk is as clogged as a freeway during rush hour. You can escape the crowds by riding south along the boardwalk to the Mission Bay Channel (separating Mission Beach from Ocean Beach) or jump into the melee by heading north along the boardwalk to Crystal Pier. *Map:LL7–KK7*

## North Torrey Pines

**N TORREY PINES RD FROM GENESEE AVE TO DEL MAR HEIGHTS AVE, DEL MAR; NO PHONE** Thrills await those with hardy thighs and calves along one of the county's most scenic routes. A heart-pounding steep hill descends from the Torrey Pines Mesa (next to Torrey Pines State Reserve) to sea level at Torrey Pines State Beach. The road then climbs again toward Del Mar. True devotees continue on up the coast along paths, frontage roads, and Highway 101 through North County beach communities. *Map:II7–GG7*

## Point Loma

**VOLTAIRE ST IN OCEAN BEACH TO THE CABRILLO NATIONAL MONUMENT, POINT LOMA; NO PHONE** The drudgery and traffic at the beginning of this ride quickly give way to some of the coast's most spectacular scenery as you pedal the Point Loma Peninsula past Navy facilities, Fort Rosecrans National Cemetery (a good spot to stop and take in the awesome views), and on to Cabrillo Monument. *Map:LL6–OO6*

## San Diego Bay

**W HARBOR DR AT THE FOOT OF BROADWAY, DOWNTOWN; 619/686-6200** This is a relaxing, flat, 4.5-mile ride along the picturesque bay, where sailboats moored offshore provide a painterly foreground and downtown's skyscrapers loom large behind them. The route follows bike paths and sidewalks, passing the historic clipper ship *Star of India*, now part of a floating maritime museum. This ride is best in early morning or late evening, when pedestrian traffic is light. There are metered parking lots in the area, and bike racks are near the tourist attractions. *Map:NN4–NN6*

## San Diego Velodrome

**2221 MORLEY FIELD DR, BALBOA PARK, DOWNTOWN; 619/296-3345** This regulation outdoor velodrome, or bicycle-racing track, is open to the public daily, except when track or training events are scheduled; spectators are welcome. *www.velo dromes.org; map:P3*

## Silver Strand

**STRAND WY TO SILVER STRAND BLVD TO IMPERIAL BEACH, CORONADO** Cyclists let loose on a 7-mile straightaway along lagoons and the Coronado Cays with views of the Pacific across the road. A wide path runs the length of the ride; cyclists, skaters, and pedestrians have room to share the road—though those moving slowly should stay to the right and listen for speed freaks headed their way. Beware: The ride back can take twice as long, as you battle ocean winds all the way. *Map:QQ4*

## Soledad Mountain

**NAUTILUS ST AND SOLEDAD MOUNTAIN RD, PACIFIC BEACH** This challenging 5.8-mile hilly ride provides a million-dollar view of practically all of San Diego and La Jolla. *Map:KK6*

# MOUNTAIN BIKING

The rough, hilly trails are there for cyclists seeking a dusty, hard ride; although most of these are outside the city limits, you can find decent thrills even in Balboa Park. **TEAM SPOKEY DOKES** (858/530-0760; www.members.home.net/nccc/tsd.html) of the North County Cycle Club organizes rides along the numerous mountain bike paths in remote parks. The **R&B BICYCLE CLUB** (760/765-2200; www.julian active.com) sponsors several annual races and festivals in the Julian area. Special events include the **JULIAN BICYCLE FESTIVAL** one weekend in May, including your choice of a 22-mile off-road or 56-mile road ride ending with apple pie à la mode and camping out under the stars. In September, the club sponsors the **TOUR DE JULIAN,** which includes several road-racing events in addition to a 22-mile mountain-bike event beginning at Jess Martin Park and following pavement, single-track paths, and dirt roads to Banner, returning to Julian in a 1,300-foot climb.

In search of a gnarly ride? Try these off-road trails:

## Florida Canyon

**1700 MORLEY FIELD DR, EAST SIDE OF BALBOA PARK, DOWNTOWN; 619/235-1100** The east side of Florida Canyon is largely undeveloped, and the trails are tough going because of rocks and brush. This 2-mile, moderately difficult ride takes you through some of Florida Canyon's eucalyptus and pepper tree groves. Turn right into Morley Field's tennis complex, make an immediate right, and start down the trail off the lower parking lot south of the tennis courts. *Map:P3*

## Lake Hodges

**20102 LAKE DR, AT VIA RANCHO PKWY, ESCONDIDO; 619/668-2050** An 8-mile tour of this canyon lake winds through the off-road trails on the northern shores near a small stream, and usually takes about an hour round-trip. On Fridays, Saturdays, or Sundays, start from the boat launch parking lot, which is only open those days. On other days, park on Lake Drive and bike around a gate at the park entrance. The stretch along Lake Drive from Del Dios Highway to Via Rancho Parkway is scenic as well. *www.lakehodges.net; map:CC2*

## BOATING

The mouth of **SAN DIEGO BAY** separates Coronado Island and the tip of Point Loma at Cabrillo Monument. The bay curves south from Point Loma past Shelter and Harbor Islands to the downtown Embarcadero, where antique sailing vessels join Navy freighters and cruise ships at dock. This banana-shaped bay flows under the San Diego–Coronado Bay Bridge to Coronado's tiny **GLORIETTA BAY** (map: NN4), located near the storybook Hotel del Coronado. Surrounded by green parks and the municipal golf course, this bay has a good public boat launch.

**SHELTER ISLAND** (map:F8) also has a 24-hour boat ramp; anglers wait in line to launch when the fishing's good offshore. Boaters touring the bay can take in the shores of Point Loma and Coronado and various Navy installations, the airport, the cruise ship terminal, and the South Bay all the way to the Chula Vista Nature Center.

**MISSION BAY PARK**'s boating areas include Sail Bay, Fiesta Bay, and Mariners and Quivira Basins. An excellent map of Mission Bay Park, showing bike paths, launch sites, water recreation areas, and the like can be obtained free at the **MAIN LIFEGUARD STATION** (2581 Quivira Ct, Mission Bay; 619/221-8899; map:C1).

Following are some good places to launch your craft or board someone else's boat:

### Dana Landing Marina

**2590 INGRAHAM ST, MISSION BAY; 619/224-2513** One of Mission Bay's major boat launches also has a fuel dock and a kayak launch site. Boat slips are rented by the day or month. Within the marina you'll find The Market, where you can get a fishing license, a bag of ice, and a cheese sandwich before climbing aboard your rented electric or motor boat, Jet Ski, catamaran, or other sailing vessel for a tour of the bays or the open ocean. Free parking lot and launch ramp. *Map:LL6*

### De Anza Cove

**NORTHERN END OF N MISSION BAY DR, MISSION BAY; 619/221-8900** This public boat launch at the northwestern point of the bay provides access to Fiesta Island, Ski Island, and Crown Point. As throughout the park, there are free public parking lots and rest rooms. *Map:LL6*

### Lake Hodges

**20102 LAKE DR, AT VIA RANCHO PKWY, ESCONDIDO; 619/465-3474** The lake is open Friday, Saturday, and Sunday only (sunrise to sunset) March through October, and it gets crowded with fishermen angling for bass when the season first opens. You can rent a motorboat or a rowboat for the day (or a canoe or pedal boat by the hour). The store here has food and drink as well as bait and tackle. Free parking. *www.lake hodges.net; map:EE3*

### Lake Murray Community Park

**7051 LAKE MURRAY BLVD, LA MESA; 619/465-3474** This 78-square-mile urban lake allows swimming as well as sailing, waterskiing, fishing, and canoeing. Water activities are allowed Wednesdays, Saturdays, and Sundays, although the park is open for picnicking and hiking daily; free parking. *Map:LL2*

## Quivira Basin

**QUIVIRA RD AT W MISSION BAY DR, MISSION BAY; NO PHONE** Though it lacks a public boat ramp, Quivira Basin is a great spot for admiring private yachts in the marina and boarding fishing boats. *Map:LL6*

## Santa Clara Point

**SANTA CLARA PL OFF MISSION BLVD, MISSION BAY; 619/221-8900** This tiny point juts into the aptly named Sail Bay, where windsurfers and sailors practice their skills. The Mission Bay Aquatic Center (1001 Santa Clara Pl, Mission Bay; 858/488-1036) offers rentals and lessons for nearly any water sport. *Map:LL7*

## Seaforth Boat Rental

**1641 QUIVIRA RD, MISSION BAY; 619/223-1681, 888/834-2628** Seaforth rents powerboats up to 20 feet, sailboats up to 36 feet, Jet Skis, and ocean kayaks by the hour, half day, and full day. Good meals are available at the adjacent Landing (1729 Quivira Rd; 619/222-3317) and Sportsmen's Seafoods (1617 Quivira Rd; 619/224-3551). *www.seaforthboatrental.com; map:LL6*

## Ski Beach

**BETWEEN NORTH AND SOUTH INGRAHAM ST BRIDGES, MISSION BAY; 619/221-8900** On the northeast side of Vacation Isle is a long, sandy takeoff and landing area for water-skiers, north of the boat launch and near rest-room facilities. This area gets heavy use on weekends (the parking lot fills up fast) and gives good access to all of Mission Bay. *Map:LL6*

## South Shores

**SOUTH SHORES DR AT SEA WORLD DR, MISSION BAY** The newest part of Mission Bay Park, South Shores opened in 1998. It has a wide boat ramp with plenty of parking and rest rooms, all open 24 hours. *Map:LL6*

## DIVING/SNORKELING

The underwater realm off San Diego holds wonders well worth exploring for both snorkelers and scuba divers. Wet suits are a must in winter and essential year-round for deep divers, though you can snorkel in swimsuits when the water's warm, especially in August and September. Local divers celebrate the first Wednesday in October with particular glee—it marks the opening of lobster season. The season lasts until March; sport divers capturing the crustaceans must have a fishing license and follow set limits regarding size and catch. Contact the **CALIFORNIA DEPARTMENT OF FISH AND GAME** (4949 Viewridge Ave, Mission Valley; 619/467-4201; map:KK4) or any dive shop for a license and list of regulations. For gear rentals and sales, lessons, and offshore dive trips, try **OCEAN ENTERPRISES** (7710 Balboa Ave, Kearny Mesa; 858/565-6054; www.oceanenterprises.com; map:JJ5), **OE EXPRESS** (2158 Ave de la Playa, La Jolla; 858/454-6195; www.oeexpress.com; map:JJ7), and **THE DIVING LOCKER** (1020 Grand Ave, Pacific Beach; 858/272-1120; www.diving

locker.com; map:KK7). Some of the best underwater spots accessible from shore or on a short boat ride are listed below.

## La Jolla Cove

**1100 COAST BLVD, LA JOLLA; 858/221-8900** Snorkelers need only submerge their faces to spot golden garibaldi, blue neons, and angelfish in this sheltered cove, part of 6,000-acre San Diego–La Jolla Underwater Park. Divers swim beyond the cove to find bass, lobsters, moray eels, bat rays, smelt, and other creatures along rocky points. There are no rentals at the cove; the nearest shop is OE Express (see above). *Map:JJ7*

## La Jolla Shores

**8200 CAMINO DEL ORO, LA JOLLA; 858/221-8900** Scuba classes are often held at this ideal spot, where divers can enter the water from shore and quickly access the underwater park. *Map:JJ6*

## Mission Bay Park Artificial Reefs

**OFF SOUTH MISSION BEACH, MISSION BAY** Several sunken ships and concrete rubble form a chain of artificial reefs from North County to the border. The Mission Bay reef is the easiest to reach from central San Diego, though you still need to arrive by boat. The *Yukon,* a worn-out Navy vessel, was sunk in the area in 2000. On artificial reefs such as these, mussels, clams, barnacles, and baby abalone cling to the hull, in turn attracting larger species and, at the top of the food chain, scuba divers. *Map:LL6*

# SALTWATER FISHING

Anglers think they've died and gone to a watery heaven when they begin to explore San Diego's fishing options. They cast lines from the beach or shores of freshwater lakes, dangle hooks from ocean piers, and chase their quarry on everything from rubber rafts to massive yachts.

Saltwater anglers follow the sea's calendar, chasing tuna in spring and summer, dorado in autumn, halibut and cod in winter. Several fishing companies offer half-day, full-day, and overnight trips, along with long-range expeditions lasting a few nights or many weeks. Most shops sell fishing licenses, and staff are well acquainted with the laws. For other information, contact the **CALIFORNIA DEPARTMENT OF FISH AND GAME** (4949 Viewridge Ave, Mission Valley; 858/467-4201; map:KK4). For reputable operators, try **FISHERMAN'S LANDING** (2838 Garrison St, Point Loma; 619/221-8500; www.fishermanslanding.com; map:E6); **POINT LOMA SPORTFISHING** (1403 Scott St, Point Loma; 619/223-1627; www.pointlomasport fishing.com; map:E7); **H&M LANDING** (2803 Emerson St, Point Loma; 619/222-1144; www.hmlanding.com; map:E6); **SEAFORTH SPORTFISHING** (1717 Quivira Rd, Mission Bay; 619/224-3383; map:D1), and **ISLANDIA SPORTFISHING** (1551 W Mission Bay Dr, Mission Bay; 619/222-1164; www.islandiasport.com; map:D1).

Mission Bay offers various opportunities for fisher folk. The west side of **VACATION ISLE** (between N and S Ingraham St Bridges) is a good site for shore fishing. There are decent parking and rest-room facilities here, and it's one of the better picnicking areas on the bay. Many people fish from the rocky shores of **SHELTER**

## WEIRD SPORTS

Given the local passion for recreation, San Diegans tend to go a bit over the line with their enthusiasm. Case in point—the annual **OVER THE LINE (OTL) TOURNAMENT** held in July at Fiesta Island. A beach version of back-lot softball, OTL consists of three-player teams batting and catching the ball before it flies over a line in the sand. Teams from Southern California beach towns take this annual competition quite seriously (despite the general revelry). They can be spotted practicing on Fiesta Island for weeks before the event.

Frisbees are essential San Diego play gear. The pros carry half a dozen discs of various weights and sizes when playing **DISC GOLF** at Balboa Park's Morley Field Sports Complex (corner of Pershing Dr and Redwood St, Downtown; 619/692-3607; map:Q5). Playing the 18-hole course is a hoot as long as you're not teamed up with hotshots. Wire baskets serve as the golf holes; players must loft their discs over canyons and above trees to reach their targets. The course is open daily from sunrise to sunset; cost is $1 per person on weekdays, $1.50 on weekends. Discs can be rented at the pro shop.

Also in Balboa Park, older gents in dapper attire queue up against rivals both young and old at the **PETANQUE COURTS**, while archers test their strength and precision at the **ARCHERY RANGE.**

In less traditional sports, corporate types work out their tensions and kids run amok at **ULTRAZONE** (3146 Sports Arena Blvd, Loma Portal; 619/221-0100; map:G2). This indoor laser-tag playground is a dark, foggy underground city with ramps, mazes, and secret passageways; teams chase each other about, zapping the competition.

Naturally, the ocean harbors all sorts of strange happenings. Scuba divers **CARVE PUMPKINS UNDERWATER** in an annual Halloween spectacle (858/565-6054); they also brave the chilly water to watch squid spawn in January. Master swimmers stroke through waves during the **LA JOLLA ROUGH WATER COMPETITION** (the largest such competition in the United States) at La Jolla Cove in September. And above it all, hang gliders lift off from the **TORREY PINES GLIDER PORT** (2800 Torrey Pines Scenic Dr, La Jolla; 858/452-9858; map:II8) and soar above the ocean while strapped to what look like enormous kites—talk about ultimate thrills.

*—Maribeth Mellin*

**ISLAND** (Shelter Island Dr off Rosecrans Ave; map:F7), **HARBOR ISLAND** (Harbor Island Dr, across from the airport; map:J6), and **QUIVIRA BASIN** (Quivira Wy and Quivira Rd, South Mission Bay; map:D1).

Fishing is allowed from **PIERS** at Ocean Beach, Pacific Beach, and Imperial Beach. Catches include halibut, croaker, bonito, surf perch, sand bass, jacksmelt, shark, and rays. Pay attention to warnings of water pollution broadcast on local news and in the papers (see "Contamination Blues" in this chapter).

## FRESHWATER FISHING

Inland lakes provide fly casters and anglers with excellent opportunities for snagging catfish, bass, and trout. The following lakes permit fishing; info on licenses is available at the rental offices at the lakes.

### Lake Henshaw

**26439 HWY 76, SANTA YSABEL; 760/782-3501** This arid spot about 60 miles northeast of San Diego is rather desolate, but the fishing is good. The on-site Lake Henshaw Resort rents inexpensive cabins with kitchens (stove, fridge, sink, and necessary utensils, pans, and dishes) and linens. There are RV hookups and tent camping. A nofrills cafe is open daily. Open year-round exclusively for fishing, the reservoir tempts anglers with crappie, bluegill, bass, bullheads, and channel catfish. Free parking.

### Lake Hodges

**20102 LAKE DR, AT VIA RANCHO PKWY, ESCONDIDO; 619/465-3474 OR 619/668-2050** The main draw at this pleasant lake is bass fishing, and bad boys weighing up to 20 pounds have been snagged by crafty anglers. Nestled in a chaparral-covered canyon just 30 miles north of San Diego, the lake tends to be most crowded at the beginning of the season, which runs March through October; it's open Friday, Saturday, and Sunday only (sunrise to sunset) during those months. The bait shop sells some food and drink as well, and there's a small picnic area. There are motorboats, rowboats, and canoes for rent. Free parking. *www.lakehodges.net; map:EE3*

### Lake Jennings County Park

**10108 BASS RD, LAKESIDE; 619/466-0585** About a half-hour's drive from downtown San Diego, Lake Jennings offers a respite from city stresses and some excellent views of the San Diego River Valley and surrounding mountains. Trout are stocked October to May, blue and channel catfish from June to September. You'll also find largemouth bass and sunfish. Tent camping and RV hookups permit overnighting for first-thing-in-the-morning fishing. (Make your reservations several weeks in advance; 858/565-3600.) The lake is open for fishing on Saturdays, Sundays, and Mondays (although shore fishing is permitted daily). There's a fee for fishing and a boat-launch charge; motorboats and rowboats are for rent. Free parking.

### Lake Miramar

**10710 SCRIPPS LAKE DR, AT SCRIPPS RANCH BLVD, MIRAMAR; 619/668-2050 OR 619/465-3474** This small lake, in the foothills near Scripps Ranch about 20 miles northeast of downtown San Diego, has a fantastic view of Mount Soledad and the Pacific Ocean. Fishing and boating are allowed Saturday through Tuesday (closed in October), but no swimming. Although bass skulk about, most often caught are trout, which you can fish for both winter and summer. Free parking. *Map:HH3*

### Lake Morena County Park

**2550 LAKE MORENA DR, CAMPO; 858/694-3049** Like Lake Jennings, this countyadministered lake and park offers fishing—go for trout in fall and bass in the spring. Nestled in the skirts of the Laguna Mountains at around 3,000 feet above sea level, the reservoir is open daily for sailboarding as well as fishing. Bring your own boat or rent one here. Serious anglers can spend the night, at RV or tent sites or in one of a handful of wilderness cabins, and be on the lake by daybreak. (Make camping reservations in advance if possible; 858/565-3600.) Free parking. *www.co.san-diego.ca.us*

### Lake Murray Community Park

**7051 LAKE MURRAY BLVD, LA MESA; 619/465-3474** Set among rolling grass hills and hillside homes not far from downtown La Mesa, this urban lake has bass, catfish, and crappie in the summer and trout from November to May. Motorboats are available for rent, or you can fish from shore year-round on Wednesdays, Saturdays, and Sundays. The bait store sells permits and fishing licenses. Fee for boat launch and fishing; free parking. *Map:LL2*

### Lake Poway Recreation Area

**14644 LAKE POWAY RD, POWAY; 858/679-5466** Situated in the foothills of Poway, this is the place for trout fishing—especially from November through mid-May, when 1,200 pounds of rainbow trout are stocked weekly. Fishing and boating are permitted Wednesday to Sunday, with night fishing during the summer (Friday and Saturday only), when channel catfish abound. The Trout Derby (held February or March) is free for kids, and the largest catfish wins a prize, too. Large bass have been caught here, as well as bluegill and sunfish. Rowboats, motorboats, sailboats, and pedal boats are rented; with the exception of float tubes, private vessels are not permitted (there's also no swimming, waterskiing, or windsurfing). Near the dam, the Lake Poway Wilderness Campground has barbecues, picnic tables, and rest rooms, but no showers (it's a hike in of about 1 mile; contact 858/679-4342 for reservations). Pay parking. *www.ci.poway.ca.us/lake poway.html; map:FF2*

## GOLFING

San Diego has 92 championship golf courses, most of them open to the public. Some overlook the sea; others are found in Mission Valley, along the San Diego River, or in the East County near Escondido, Temecula, Jamul, and El Cajon. The San Diego Convention and Visitors Bureau (401 B St, Ste 1400, downtown; 619/232-3101; www.sandiego.org; map:N7) publishes an annual San Diego golf guide and a San Diego golf map. Many San Diego companies are available to arrange golf tournaments for groups as well as individual and group tee times. Check with **AMERICAN GOLF CORPORATION** (619/297-4431), **SAN DIEGO GOLF EVENTS** (619/232-4707), and **SPECTRUM GOLF** (858/509-8558). Golf equipment rentals are available at **POLAR GOLF** (3877 Pacific Hwy, Downtown; 619/291-3186; map: M7).

### Balboa Park Golf Course

**2600 GOLF COURSE DR, DOWNTOWN; 619/239-1632 OR 619/570-1234 FOR COMPUTERIZED RESERVATIONS** Designed for the 1915–1916 Panama-California Exposition, this municipal course tends to be uneven. It's short, with plenty of opportunities to get into trouble—great for the straight hitter. It's well located near downtown and the airport, and getting a tee time is fairly easy. There's an 18-hole championship course and a nine-hole executive course. Twenty-seven holes, 8,442 yards, course rating 69.8. *Map:Q6*

## Carlton Oaks Country Club

**9200 INWOOD DR, SANTEE; 619/448-4242 OR 619/448-8500 FOR TEE TIMES**
Despite the name, this country club traversed by the San Diego River has more sycamore and cottonwood trees than oaks. It's a challenging course, with five sets of tees and an undulating green. Facilities include a driving range and two practice chipping and putting greens; packages can be arranged for stays at the attached lodge. The club hosts free youth clinics on weekends as well as inexpensive two-hour lessons for adults. Eighteen holes, 7,088 yards, course rating 74.6. *www.carltonoaks golf.com; map:JJ1*

## Coronado Golf Course

 **2000 VISALIA ROW, CORONADO; 619/435-3121** This wonderful course is inexpensive for both residents and out-of-towners—it's one price for all. A flat course favored by walkers, it's known to be a fun and easy par 72 (former President Clinton claimed it was the first time he broke 80). It's a great location with several holes right on the water and views of the Coronado Bridge and Glorietta Bay. The clubhouse is open to the public and is a nice secret spot for lunch with views of the bay. Eighteen holes, 6,633 yards, course rating 71.8. *Map:NN5*

## Four Seasons Resort–Aviara

**7447 BATIQUITOS DR, CARLSBAD; 760/603-6900** Despite the high green fees, it can be a challenge to get a tee time at this lovely course overlooking Batiquitos Lagoon and the Pacific. Arnold Palmer designed the course and its fast, true greens. Many golfers stay at the luxurious resort to attend the golf academy or take private lessons. Eighteen holes, 7,007 yards, course rating 74.2. *Map:CC7*

## La Costa Resort

**COSTA DEL MAR RD, CARLSBAD; 760/438-9111** Golfers of all abilities appreciate the traditional design of this course, site of the World Golf and Accenture Match Play Championships. Three-day or three-afternoon instruction packages are available, and green fees at the two PGA championship courses of this luxury resort are high. Thirty-six holes. North course 6,987 yards, rating 74.8; south course 6,894 yards, rating 74.4. *www.lacosta.com; map:CC7*

## Mount Woodson Country Club

**16422 N WOODSON DR, RAMONA; 760/788-3555** This is a fine, short, target-oriented golf course with extreme changes in elevation, bunkers strategically placed within fairways, and plenty of water. It's a challenging one, favoring skill over strength. Walking is not permitted; cart rental cost included in green fees. Eighteen holes, 6,113 yards, course rating 68.3.

## Rancho Bernardo Inn & Golf Course

**17550 BERNARDO OAKS DR, RANCHO BERNARDO; 858/675-8470** Designed by Ted Robinson, this championship course has a signature 18th: a par-5 with a three-tiered green, a creek, and a lake. Eighteen holes, 6,631 yards, course rating 72.3. *Map:FF3*

## Riverwalk Golf Course

**1150 FASHION VALLEY RD, MISSION VALLEY; 619/298-0511** Set in the middle of Mission Valley's shopping center district, this 27-hole course provides a pleasant greenbelt for freeway drivers and accessible golf for guests in the neighborhood's many hotels. There are water features (including a man-made lake, on 13 holes). The driving range is lit at night, and there's a full-service pro shop. Twenty-seven holes, 6,550 yards, course rating 72. *Map: KK4*

## Singing Hills Golf Resort

**3007 DEHESA RD, EL CAJON; 619/442-3425 OR 800/457-5568** This reasonably priced course is part of a 450-acre resort that's rated "women friendly" by *Golf for Women* magazine and offers golf and tennis packages. The Pine Glen course is an easy, par-3 layout; the regulation courses are a lot of fun, with a double green, a few neat water holes, and at least one blind tee shot. Willow Glen Course, 18 holes, 6,605 yards, course rating 72.3; Oak Glen Course, 18 holes, 6,597 yards, course rating 71.1. *www.singinghills.com; map:KK1*

## Steele Canyon Golf & Country Club

**3199 STONEFIELD DR, JAMUL; 619/441-6900** This challenging, hilly, Gary Player Signature Course has three championship nine-hole courses, one of which received a four-star rating from *Golf Digest*. Each has a different feel. Twenty-seven holes, 6,741 yards, course rating 72.5. *www.steelcanyon.com*

## Torrey Pines Municipal Golf Course

**11480 NORTH TORREY PINES RD, LA JOLLA; 800/985-4653** Rated among the 50 "must-play" courses in the nation by *Links Digest* magazine, this course is home to the Buick Invitational in February. The views from atop the cliff overlooking the ocean are fantastic. There are two 18-hole courses; the south course was completely remodeled in 2001 to rave reviews. "You have a golf course now that is a U.S. Open–style course," the world's number-two-ranked golfer, Phil Mickelson, declared when touring it. The owners are trying to book a major championship tournament in the near future. Tee times are hard to come by, but green fees are reduced for locals. Thirty-six holes; south course 7,055 yards, course rating 74.6; north course 6,647 yards, course rating 72.1. *www.torreypinesgolfcourse.com; map:HH7*

# HIKING

Outdoor lovers in San Diego County have plenty of hiking opportunities, what with all the mountains, deserts, coastal canyons, bays, and beaches to explore. You'll find urban hikes suitable for the casual hiker, as well as challenging rural assaults for the zealot intent on pushing his or her personal envelope. See the calendar section of the **SAN DIEGO WEEKLY READER** (www.sdreader.com) for information about current physical phenomena worth investigating, such as grunion runs and desert flower blooms, along with listings of group hikes led by area organizations. In the same publication, Jerry Schad's "Roam-A-Rama" column recommends a different outdoor destination each week. Schad's softcover tome *Afoot & Afield in San Diego County* is an invaluable guide to outdoor adventures, from coastal San Diego to the mountains and deserts. The local chapter of the **SIERRA CLUB** (3820 Ray St, North

Park; 619/299-1744; www.sierraclub.org/chapters/sandiego/; map:MM4) offers wilderness training courses as well as hiking and backpacking outings, as do outdoor gear suppliers **ADVENTURE 16** (4620 Alvarado Canyon Rd, San Diego; 619/283-2362, ext. 139; www.adventure16.com; map:KK3) and **REI** (5556 Copley Dr, Kearny Mesa; 858/279-4400; www.rei.com; map:JJ4). **WALKABOUT INTERNATIONAL** (835 5th Ave, Downtown; 619/231-7463; map:O7) offers free urban outings of varying degrees of difficulty throughout the county. Patty Fares, a diehard explorer, conducts walks of San Diego's neighborhoods with **URBAN SAFARIS** (619/944-9295; www.walkingtoursofsandiego.com). Those wanting informative, easy to moderately paced guided hikes of San Diego's canyons can join the **SAN DIEGO NATURAL HISTORY MUSEUM** (619/232-3821; www.sdnhm.org) outings on weekend mornings.

San Diego's city dwellers appreciate the proximity of **MISSION TRAILS REGIONAL PARK** (1 Father Junipero Serra Trail, Tierrasanta; 619/668-3275; www.mtrp.org; map:JJ2) for the accessibility of hiking trails and Cowles Mountain, which at 1,592 feet above sea level offers a 360-degree view of the city. This moderately challenging hike has an elevation gain of almost 1,000 feet; the trailhead is approximately 75 yards down Barker Way (on the left) off Boulder Lake Avenue. (There are several other routes to scale Cowles Mountain, should you tire of this approach.) Also within the park, the historic Old Mission Dam is a starting point for hikes into Oak Canyon; the East, North, and South Fortuna Mountain regions; the Father Junipero Serra Trail; and the San Diego River. All these are good for bird-watching, and the San Diego River walk is wheelchair accessible.

San Diego's vast desert is a world unto itself. **ANZA-BORREGO DESERT STATE PARK** comprises more than 600,000 acres of desert scrub and badlands punctuated with surprising palm-studded oases. As the summer heat is scorching, the best time to visit the desert is from October through May; remember to bring a hat and drinking water for even the shortest hike. For an overview of the desert flora and fauna and suggested hikes, visit the **VISITORS CENTER** (200 Palm Canyon Dr, Borrego Springs; 760/767-5311; www.anzaborrego.statepark.org). It's open daily October to May, but only on weekends and holidays during the summer months. Don't go wandering about in the desert without checking in at the Visitors Center and getting a map of marked trails.

### Cuyamaca Rancho State Park

**12551 HWY 79, DESCANSO; 760/765-0755** Once the summer home of California Indians, and later the property of Mexicans granted the land in 1845, this 25,000-acre park now attracts picnickers, hikers, equestrians, and, to a lesser extent, backpackers. The park extends from chaparral-covered lowlands through open mesas interspersed with groves of sycamore, alder, and willow. In the highest elevations, black and live oak thrive, as do white fir and ponderosa pines. Because the state park lies just about 40 miles from the coast and is split by well-trafficked Highway 79, it receives lots of visitors anxious to flee city life, if only for the day. Trailheads line Highway 79, leading hikers into the wilderness on treks of varying difficulty.

### Laguna Mountain Recreation Area

**SUNRISE HWY, MILE 23.5, MOUNT LAGUNA; 619/445-6235** Between the Cuyamaca Mountains and the desert lie the Laguna Mountains, drier than the former but not nearly as dry as the latter. At around 6,000 feet, Laguna Crest is the highest point in San Diego County accessible by road. There are more than 70 miles of hiking trails in the Laguna Mountains, including part of the Pacific Crest Trail. On summer weekend nights, visitors can view the heavens through the Mount Laguna Observatory's 21-inch telescope. Also in the summer, rangers and volunteers offer interpretive walks and special events. For information on these events, or to obtain maps of the area hiking trails, contact the Visitor Information Office (619/473-8547).

## KAYAKING/CANOEING

Mission Bay has excellent opportunities for kayaking. During the summer, music fans launch canoes and kayaks along the bayside shores of Shelter Island. After rounding the point past the harbor police station, tie up near **HUMPHREY'S CONCERTS BY THE BAY** (2241 Shelter Island Dr, Downtown; 619/224-3577; www.humphreysbythebay.com; map:F7) to enjoy a night's outdoor entertainment for free. **HIKE BIKE KAYAK SAN DIEGO** (858/551-9510; www.hbksandiego.com) offers guided kayaking tours and classes for all levels. Tours range from calm paddles in Mission Bay to open-sea whale-watching excursions.

### Dana Landing Marina

**2590 INGRAHAM ST, MISSION BAY; 619/224-2513** The marina has a kayak launch site and free parking lot. There's also a market selling snacks and bait. *Map:LL6*

### Lake Miramar

**10710 SCRIPPS LAKE DR, AT SCRIPPS RANCH BLVD, MIRAMAR; 619/668-2050** Although there's no swimming here, this pretty little lake is open Saturday through Tuesday for canoeing and fishing (and you can hike or picnic here daily). Located near the foothills of Scripps Ranch, it's convenient to central San Diego. Waterskiing and jet-boating are not permitted, meaning canoe enthusiasts can explore the lake's small bays and coves in relative tranquillity. Canoes, pedal boats, and motor- and rowboats can be rented. Free parking. *Map:HH3*

### Mission Bay Aquatic Center

**1001 SANTA CLARA PL, MISSION BAY; 858/488-1036** Kayaking, water-skiing, sailing, surfing, and rowing are taught at a summer camp for kids ages 6 to 17 and in year-round classes for adults. Closed Mondays. Rental equipment is available but restrictions apply; call ahead for information. *www.mbac.nu; map:LL6*

### Mission Bay Sportcenter

**1010 SANTA CLARA POINT, MISSION BAY; 858/488-1005** The center rents sea kayaks and canoes, and teaches kids a variety of sea sports at a summer camp; adult classes are held year-round on weekends. *www.missionbaysportcenter.com; map:LL6*

## ABOVE IT ALL

When the traffic jams are in full swing, it's a perfect time to take to the skies. Colorful **HOT-AIR BALLOONS** lift off from Del Mar for dusk and dawn panoramas of the rising or setting sun, the Pacific Ocean, the backcountry, and the far-away-from-it-all freeway congestion below. Floats last about an hour and are followed by champagne or other celebratory refreshments. Balloon companies include California Dreamin' (760/438-9550, www.californiadreamin.com) and Skysurfer Balloon Company (858/481-6800). **TORREY PINES GLIDER PORT** (2800 Torrey Pines Scenic Dr, La Jolla; map:II8), poised on the cliffs 300 feet above the Pacific, affords hang gliders one of the most exquisite jumping-off-the-edge spots in the world. Lessons as well as tandem rides are available from the on-site Hang Gliding Center (858/452-9858). Live out wartime or *Out of Africa* fantasies in vintage aircraft with open cockpits—where the term "backseat driver" takes on new meaning—with **BARNSTORM BIPLANE ADVENTURES** (760/438-7680). Planes take off from Carlsbad's McClellan-Palomar Airport for 20-minute to one hour scenic or mock combat flights. For a **WHIRLYBIRD TOUR** of the coast, sign on with Corporate Helicopters of San Diego (619/291-4356).

—*Marael Johnson*

### Lake Hodges Aquatic Center

**20102 LAKE DR, ESCONDIDO; 760/735-8088** Lake Hodges Aquatic Center rents canoes and kayaks—tandem, touring, and recreational—by the hour or day. Group kayaking lessons (beginner and intermediate) are given at summer camps for kids ages 6 to 16 by the day or week; lessons are also available for adults. The lake is open March through October, Friday through Sunday from sunrise to sunset. *www. lakehodges.net; map:DD4*

## ROLLER-SKATING/IN-LINE SKATING

Follow the running/biking paths in Mission Bay and Mission and Pacific Beaches (see Running) for nearly unlimited, relatively flat skating. You can rent equipment (including ever-important kneepads) at **MISSION BEACH CLUB** (704 Ventura Pl, Mission Beach; 858/488-5050; map:LL7). Other excellent flat, scenic venues are found along **SPANISH LANDING** (N Harbor Dr near the Sheraton Hotel on Harbor Island; map:I6) and in **CORONADO**, where trails lead through Tidelands Park on the west side facing downtown, and along Strand Way and Silver Strand Boulevard to Imperial Beach. Young skateboarders in helmets and pads (required) can be seen flying through the air at **ROBB FIELD SKATE PARK** (Sunset Cliffs Blvd at W Point Loma Dr, Ocean Beach; 619/525-8486; map:D2)—not always with the greatest of ease, but with much bravado. Kids as young as 6 can practice at this cement skate park by purchasing daily or annual passes.

## ROWING

### Mission Bay Aquatic Center

**1001 SANTA CLARA PL, MISSION BAY; 858/488-1036** The center teaches classes in basic sweep rowing—crew teams of eight to 30 people—and individual sculling. Rentals are available but restrictions apply; call ahead for details. The **MISSION BAY ROWING ASSOCIATION** (619/969-2901) uses this aquatic center as its base; novice rowers are encouraged to take classes here before joining the coed club. The **SAN DIEGO ROWING CLUB** (1220 El Carmel Pl, Mission Beach; 858/488-1893; sdrc-row.org; map:LL6) emphasizes both recreation and competition and hosts weekend classes and summer training camps.

## RUNNING

San Diego's weather provides little in the way of excuses for not keeping in shape, and plenty of scenic places to occupy your eyes as your feet pound the dirt or pavement. There are neighborhood parks for those who prefer a flat, grassy surface; state parks offering a change of elevation for runners who want more of a challenge; concrete footpaths along the bay; and wide beaches perfect for running year-round. The **SAN DIEGO TRACK** (www.sdtc.com) is a membership club that stages road races and track meets and publishes the *San Diego Running* newsletter. Their web site lists a calendar of race events, a message board, and other helpful info. **CLUB SURF** (858/456-5725), aka San Diego Ultra Running Friends, is a group of long-distance runners that holds social functions and 50-mile races, most on scenic backcountry trails.

City races are beginning to get noticed around the country, and the **AMERICA'S FINEST CITY HALF MARATHON** (858/792-2900; www.afchalf.org), initiated in 1977, was rated one of the best races in the country by *Runner's World* magazine. Every August up to 6,000 runners take to the San Diego streets, beginning at scenic Cabrillo Monument in Point Loma and winding their way along Harbor Island and the Embarcadero to end in historic Balboa Park; there's a 5K walk/run as well. The **SUZUKI ROCK 'N' ROLL MARATHON** (858/450-6510; www.rnrmarathon.com), held in June, draws more than 20,000 runners. Participants are encouraged in their endeavors by live music on 26 stages along the way, with everything from world beat to country rock, alternative to oldies. Equally important yet less strenuous is the annual *Union-Tribune* **DR. SEUSS RACE FOR LITERACY,** whose "magic mile" race for kids and 8K races benefit the San Diego Council on Literacy (888/850-7323).

Here are several other running opportunities:

### Lake Miramar

**10710 SCRIPPS LAKE DR, MIRAMAR; 619/668-2050** A flat, paved loop of just under 5 miles circles this reservoir. Along part of the route there's a trail parallel to the road, but if you run there, keep an eye out for rattlesnakes. From the west end of the loop, near the top of the dam, you can watch planes take off and land at nearby Miramar Air Station. *Map:HH3*

## Mission Bay Park

**BORDERED BY I-5, I-8, GRAND AVE, AND MISSION BLVD; 619/221-8900**
Many activities are popular at this large, loopy aquatic park, and jogging is one of them. From De Anza Cove (where there's plenty of parking) you can follow the path south past the Hilton and Fiesta Island to the flood-control channel; return the same way. Another popular path connects Crown Point to the Mission Bay Channel, skirting Sail Bay and Riviera Drive—smooth sailing and great bay views all the way. Park at either end and go as far as you like before returning along the same path. *Map:LL6*

## Mission Beach and Pacific Beach

**BETWEEN S MISSION BEACH AND CRYSTAL PIER, PACIFIC BEACH; NO PHONE** Along this stretch of boardwalk joining South Mission Beach and Pacific Beach, you'll have the ocean on your left as you run north, sharing the path with bladers, strollers, skaters, and cyclists. If you get thirsty, this strip is fronted by bars, restaurants, and burger shacks, most of which have outdoor patios for observing the scene. *Map:LL6–KK6*

## Mission Trails Regional Park

**1 FATHER JUNIPERO SERRA TRAIL, TIERRASANTA; 619/668-3275** This 5,760-acre park has many trails with small-to-moderate hills suitable for short or lengthy runs. Stop in at the visitor center to select your trail; maps there show trails' lengths and degree of difficulty. Within the park, **LAKE MURRAY** (619/668-3275) is popular with joggers, although since the concrete path doesn't form a loop all the way around the lake, you must return the way you came. The trail is 3.5 miles start to finish, or 7 miles total. You can watch the boats, the people fishing, and the water-fowl on weekends, although with all of the wheeled and foot traffic, you'd best keep your eyes on the wide path. Also within the park, **COWLES MOUNTAIN** proves a challenging run, with a change in elevation of nearly 1,000 feet. A fire road down the mountain's backside starts just to the left of the monument at the summit; either way it's 1.5 miles between the trailhead and the top. The trailhead is off Navajo Road, about half a mile to the east of Jackson Road near the rest rooms. Wear a hat and bring water, especially in summer months when temperatures climb. Various running clubs train here on weekend mornings. *Map:JJ2*

## Silver Strand State Beach

**5000 HWY 75, CORONADO; 619/435-5184** If you like to run on the beach, this wide, white sand beach stretches for 2.5 miles. There's a large pay parking lot. *Map:NN5*

## Torrey Pines State Park

**12600 N TORREY PINES RD, LA JOLLA; 858/755-2063** Great single tracks here have views of the Pacific Ocean and the tall pines for which the park was named. The 8 miles of hilly trails are a mixture of sand and clay, which can get slippery when it rains. The Broken Hill Trail is a popular loop heading down to the beach, then north along the beach for about a mile, and finally uphill on the park road. *www.torreypine.org; map:HH7*

## SAILING

San Diego Bay is the main harbor for both the city of San Diego and North Island's military machine. It's interesting to sail among the behemoth aircraft carriers and other floating war machines and to explore the coast south to the **CHULA VISTA NATURE CENTER** (1000 Gunpowder Point Dr, Chula Vista; 619/409-5900; www.chulavistanaturecenter.org; map:OO3). Coronado's Glorietta Bay, located across from the landmark Hotel del Coronado, is a small bay within San Diego Bay, surrounded by lush parks and the municipal golf course. **CORONADO BOAT RENTALS** (1715 Strand Wy, Coronado; 619/437-1514; map:N9) rents sailboats and canoes on the bay.

Rent a 14- to 36-foot sailboat by the hour, half day, or full day at **SEAFORTH BOAT RENTALS** (www.seaforthboatrental.com) and venture into San Diego Bay. There are two locations: in Mission Bay Park (1641 Quivira Rd, Mission Bay; 619/223-1681, 888/834-2628; map:E6), and downtown (333 W Harbor Dr; 619/239-2628; map:M8). There's a public boat launch and limited free parking at both Glorietta Bay and Shelter Island. If you need instruction before setting sail, **HARBOR SAILBOATS** (2040 Harbor Island Dr, Ste 104, Point Loma; 619/291-9568; www.harborsailboats.com; map:G6) offers sailing and navigation classes for land-lubbers (beginners) as well as for more advanced sailors; they also rent boats.

On Mission Bay, Santa Clara Point and Sail Bay are alive with sailboat activity. Both **MISSION BAY AQUATIC CENTER** (1001 Santa Clara Pl; 858/488-1036; map:LL6) and **MISSION BAY SPORTCENTER** (1010 Santa Clara Pt; 858/488-1005; map:LL6) rent sailboats and offer classes for children and adults. Some knowledge of sailing is required; call ahead for information. Guests at the bayside resort **HYATT ISLANDIA** (1441 Quivira Rd; 858/224-1234; map:C1) can rent 14- to 30-foot sailboats, as well as powerboats, kayaks, canoes, and pedal boats. The **SAN DIEGO HILTON** (1775 E Mission Bay Dr; 619/275-8945; map:LL5) rents catamarans, Hobie Cats, and 16-foot monohulls as well as kayaks, Wave Runners, Jet-Skis, sailboards, and powerboats. Basic and advanced sailing and sailboard lessons are also available. **DANA LANDING MARINA** (2590 Ingraham St; 619/224-2513; map:LL6) rents boat slips by the day or month. Within this marina, **THE MARKET** (619/226-2929) rents lots of different sailboats (and motorboats) for a tour of the bays or the open ocean. **LAKE HODGES AQUATIC CENTER** (20102 Lake Dr, Escondido; 760/735-8088; www.lakehodges.net; map:DD4) rents 14-foot monohull sail craft for up to four adults and gives group and private lessons for beginning sailors. Those seeking professional-level instruction should check out the **SAN DIEGO SAILING ACADEMY** (1500 Quivira Wy, Mission Bay; 619/223-6253, www.sdsa.com; map:D1), where graduates receive American Sailing Association certification. **SOUTH SHORES** (South Shores Dr at Sea World Dr; map:LL6) is a 24-hour boat ramp with a large parking lot and new rest rooms.

## SURFING

San Diego surfers take their art seriously, and cool ocean temperatures tend to discourage dabblers. The best surfing beaches often have riptides that could and should discourage weak swimmers. Not that tourists and first-timers can't enjoy the surf—but a modicum of caution can help avoid a catastrophe. **TOURMALINE SURF PARK**

(Tourmaline St and La Jolla Blvd, Pacific Beach; 619/221-8900; map:KK7) is where beginners go to learn and where older surfers go to enjoy themselves and avoid cutthroat competition. **SAN DIEGO SURFING ACADEMY** (PO Box 99938, San Diego, CA 92169; 858/565-6892 or 800/447-7873; www.surfsdsa.com) offers year-round group or private longboard lessons, surfing camp, and wave-seeking excursions. Cost of lessons includes surfboard and wet-suit rental. **SURF DIVA** (2160 Avenida de la Playa, La Jolla; 858/454-8273; www.surfdiva.com; map:KK8) offers weekend workshops and individual lessons taught by—you guessed it—female surfers. Billed as a "Surf School for Women and Girls (with Guys on the Side)," Surf Diva has its own line of boards built for women, along with clothing and skateboards. **MISSION BAY AQUATIC CENTER** (1001 Santa Clara Pl, Mission Bay; 858/488-1036; map:LL6) has summer surf camp for ages 6 to 17 and year-round classes and clinics for adults. Less demanding than a short or long fiberglass board, body boards (such as the Morey Boogie Board) can be used at many San Diego beaches for easier, entertaining rides on San Diego's swells (but remember, you can get crunched on a body board as well). Body boards can be rented daily at **PLAY IT AGAIN SPORTS** (1401 Garnet Ave, Pacific Beach; 858/490-0222; map:KK7), and **MISSION BEACH CLUB** (704 Ventura Pl, Mission Beach; 858/488-5050; map:LL7) rents body boards and surfboards by the day or the hour. If you want to watch pro bodysurfers make the sport look easy, check out the annual **WORLD BODYSURFING CHAMPIONSHIP** each August at the Oceanside Pier.

Here's a survey of prime surfing spots:

### Bird Rock

**BIRD ROCK AVE AND DOLPHIN PL, SOUTH LA JOLLA; 619/221-8900** This uncrowded beach, with a rocky shore, tide pools, lots of little coves, and very little sand at high tide, is accessed by a stairway at the foot of Bird Rock Avenue. South Bird has an inconsistent swell that's fast and fun when it works. It's best at low to medium tide, although often ruffled by onshore winds. North Bird breaks less frequently, usually on a south or southwest swell. No rest rooms or lifeguards; parking on adjacent streets. *Map:KK7*

### Black's Beach

**2800 TORREY PINES SCENIC DR, AT N TORREY PINES RD, LA JOLLA; 858/221-8900** Swells abruptly hitting La Jolla's submarine canyon make Black's the best beach break in San Diego, surfable year-round. It's not recommended for the novice, as there are strong riptides and big, powerful waves. Black's is at its finest when fall or winter Santa Ana winds combine with a northwest swell. There are no regular lifeguards or rest rooms, although there are portable toilets and a shower at the top of the cliffs. Parking is usually plentiful; there is also limited parking on nearby streets. *Map:II7*

### Cardiff State Beach

**OLD HWY 101 AT MANCHESTER AVE, CARDIFF-BY-THE-SEA; 858/221-8900** Almost any swell brings longboarders to Cardiff Reef at the north end of this beach. There are rest rooms here, and lifeguards are on duty during the summer months.

## CONTAMINATION BLUES

Sad to say, water pollution is an ever-increasing unnatural phenomenon in San Diego. Leaks from aged sewage pipes and facilities sometimes make parts of the ocean off Point Loma very unhealthy for surfers and swimmers. Runoff from the San Diego River and sewage lines sometimes shuts down parts of Ocean Beach. Wise locals don't eat fish from San Diego or Mission Bays. And Imperial Beach and much of South Bay are off-limits nearly year-round, thanks to flooding from the Tijuana River and a lack of cooperation on the issue between Mexico and the United States. Die-hard surfers ignore contamination warnings and pick up all sorts of nasty infections, from ear diseases to hepatitis.

San Diegans try to protect the ocean by participating in beach and ocean cleanup days, keeping oil and toxins out of sewage lines, and painting warnings on street curbs by storm drains. But regular contamination warnings are inevitable. Obey the signs posted at beaches and bays, and when recommended, stay out of the water.

*—Maribeth Mellin*

Limited parking along Highway 101 tends to fill up quickly; there's also a pay lot. *Map:EE7*

### Garbage Beach

**SUNSET CLIFFS DR AT LADERA ST, OCEAN BEACH; 619/221-8900** Both North and South Garbage have reliable reef waves that work best on a medium to low tide. Relatively easy access makes the breaks popular with longboarders. As at many Sunset Cliffs surf spots, the locals dominate the scene and tend to intimidate outsiders. There's on-street parking, or park in the lot at the top of the hill. Stairs at the bottom of Ladera Street lead to the beach, although they are inaccessible at high tide. There are no rest rooms or lifeguards, but there's a shower across the street from the top of the stairs. *Map:A7*

### Marine Street

**300 MARINE ST, LA JOLLA; 858/221-8900** This wide, clean beach tends to fill up during the summer, although body-boarders and bodysurfers come year-round for the easily accessed waves. The lack of rest rooms and parking lots (look for a spot on Marine Street or Sea Lane) keeps some beachcombers away. There is lifeguard service during the peak summer months. *Map:JJ7*

### Newbreak

**SUNSET CLIFFS DR AT CORNISH DR, OCEAN BEACH; 619/221-8900** This reliable spot, largely protected from winds, is just as fiercely protected by local surfers, who don't appreciate sharing their realm with novices. Although it breaks with all tides and swells, it's best at medium to low tide, though the latter can be dangerous for all but advanced surfers. Parking is available at the Sunset Cliffs Natural Park lot at the end of Cornish Drive. Walk toward Point Loma College, turn right after the softball field, and watch to see where others descend the cliffs; Newbreak is to the south. No lifeguards or rest rooms. *Map:A7*

## Swami's

**1298 OLD HWY 101, ENCINITAS; 760/633-2880** Tucked below the gold and white Self-Realization Fellowship church, this beach break is always fun and therefore always crowded. It's most rewarding at low or medium tide; swell size is no object. Free parking and nearby rest rooms. *Map:EE7*

## SWIMMING

The ocean is fine for some swimmers, but others prefer warm, fresh water for their laps. Most San Diegans rely on backyard pools and fitness clubs for aquatic work-outs, but there are a few fine public pools in the area. Call ahead for schedules and fees, as they vary with the season.

The **MISSION BEACH PLUNGE** (3115 Ocean Front Walk, Mission Beach; 858/488-3110; map:LL6), is a 175-foot-long enclosed swimming pool that has entranced water lovers since 1925. Swimmers have dozens of lanes to choose from; other areas are sectioned off for kids and classes. The **KEARNS MEMORIAL POOL** (2229 Morley Field Dr, Balboa Park, Downtown; 619/692-4920; map:P3) offers year-round recreational and lap swimming, youth polo, and swim classes. The indoor pool at the **DOWNTOWN YMCA** (500 W Broadway; 619/232-7451; map:M7) is also open to the public. For information on neighborhood pools operated by the San Diego City Parks and Recreation Department, call 619/685-1322.

## TENNIS

The pros often make their way to San Diego for major tennis tournaments at private courts affiliated with resorts, including La Costa and the Rancho Bernardo Inn. But there are plenty of amateurs whacking at balls in public courts throughout the county. The **BARNES TENNIS CENTER** (4490 W Point Loma Blvd, Ocean Beach; 619/221-9000; www.tennissandiego.com; map:D2) is a great tennis venue, especially for kids under 18, who always play free (no membership dues). In addition to 20 hard and four clay lighted courts, there are full-size basketball courts, a sand volleyball pit, and banquet and meeting rooms. The center is open daily 8am to 9pm.

The **BALBOA TENNIS CLUB** (Morley Field Tennis Complex, Balboa Park, Downtown; 619/295-9278; www.balboatennis.com; map:Q3), one of the most popular venues in the city, was formed in 1939 and is open to members as well as nonmembers; the latter pay a daily fee. The club maintains the Morley Field Tennis Complex, with 25 courts, 18 of which are lighted. Reservations accepted for members only.

Other public courts include:

**LAKE MURRAY TENNIS CLUB**: 7003 Murray Park Dr, Kensington; 619/469-3232; www.lakemurraytennis.com; map:LL2

**PACIFIC BEACH TENNIS CLUB**: 2639 Grand Ave, Pacific Beach; 619/273-9177; www.pbtennis.com; map:KK7

**PENINSULA TENNIS CLUB**: 2525 Bacon St, Ocean Beach; 619/226-3407; map:C2

## WINDSURFING

A board, a sail, strong arms, and a great sense of balance are all you need to skim across the water while windsurfing. Sounds easy, right? Don't count on it. Try pulling a sail upright while treading water, then climbing on your board without turning the contraption upside down. Still want to windsurf? Take a few classes at one of the centers described below.

### Lake Hodges Aquatic Center

**SOUTHWEST END OF LAKE HODGES NEAR RANCHO AND LAKE DRS, ESCONDIDO; 619/668-2050** The Aquatic Center runs a school for windsurfing and kayaking at Windsurf Beach on Lake Hodges. Summer youth camps teach the skills to kids ages 6 to 16; adults can take individual or group lessons April through October. The lake is open Friday through Sunday only (sunrise to sunset), March through October, although sailboarding rentals and lessons don't begin until mid-April at the earliest. *Map:EE4*

### Mission Bay Aquatic Center

**1001 SANTA CLARA PL, MISSION BAY; 858/488-1036** Classes in windsurfing are available at this full-service water sports center on a quiet section of the bay. *Map:LL6*

### San Diego Hilton

**1775 E MISSION BAY DR, MISSION BAY; 619/275-8945** Well situated on East Mission Bay's tranquil Pacific Passage, the Hilton boat yard rents sailboards and offers windsurfing instruction as well. *Map:LL5*

# Spectator Sports

Although reasonably dedicated to their major-league baseball and football teams, San Diego's support of other major sports has been lackluster. Despite a winning record, the San Diego Sockers disbanded in 1996 (to be reborn in 2001 in another indoor league), and the Clippers basketball team moved to Los Angeles after the 1983–1984 season, even though that city already had an NBA team, the Lakers. With so much sunshine and so many outdoor opportunities, San Diegans seem to prefer participating in sports to watching them live or on TV. Die-hard sports fans get their kicks from hockey's San Diego Gulls: the team has won the Taylor Cup Championship more often than not.

### Del Mar Racetrack

**HWY 5 AT VIA DE LA VALLE ON THE DEL MAR FAIRGROUNDS, DEL MAR; 858/755-1141** This lovely racetrack "where the turf meets the surf," in operation since 1939, has seen many a thoroughbred speed by during the annual 43-day summer meeting, which begins mid-July and ends in early September. Opening day is a must-do event for many San Diegans, when normally bareheaded women stage an informal competition for the finest hat. Among the major stakes races, the track's signature event is the $1 million, 1.25-mile Pacific Classic, usually held near the end of the season. Two years of physical improvements in the early '90s, costing about $80 million, replaced the 50-year-old grandstand with a modern six-story structure;

**293**

that overhaul may have helped boost lagging attendance. Special post-race events—including the Jazz at Del Mar concerts (now in its 10th season), Family Fun Days, and the Sports and Fitness Festival—also draw crowds. These events are free with track entrance and occur after the last race, usually on the track's grassy infield. *www.dmtc.com*; *map:GG7*

## San Diego Chargers

**QUALCOMM STADIUM, 9449 FRIARS RD, MISSION VALLEY; 858/874-4500** San Diego football fans have had a rough time since 1995, when the team made its first (and only) Super Bowl appearance. Despite the inspiration of veterans like quarterback Doug Flutie, signed in 2000, and Junior Seau—a fine defensive linebacker who systematically fires up his teammates—the blue-and-gold Bolts have had a string of dismal seasons. Ineffectual head coach Mike Riley was fired after a 5–11 season in 2001; fans hope the new coach, Marty Schottenheimer, will significantly improve on Riley's three-season win/loss record of 14–34. During his first year with the Chargers, Flutie gained the most passing yards since the good old days of quarterback Dan Fouts (now a *Monday Night Football* announcer) under stern-faced but highly successful coach Don Coryell. But despite Flutie's impressive passing yardage in 2000 and 2001, and 1,000-yard season stats by rookie running back LaDainian Tomlinson and wide receiver Curtis Conway in 2001, Chargers games have more often than not been pronounced "missed opportunities." Fans have become accustomed to the agony of games lost in the final minutes of play. Although discouraged by the Bolts' ongoing losing streak, San Diegans are even more distressed by the specter of the team's possible defection to Los Angeles, which has no NFL team of its own. Acrimony over the city's ticket-guarantee fiasco (which costs taxpayers millions of dollars a year) and the Chargers' dissatisfaction (despite $4.5 million of Super Bowl–related improvements) with aging Qualcomm Stadium have led many to wonder if the Bolts will remain in San Diego after the 2002–2003 season. *www.chargers.com*; *map:LL4*

## San Diego Gulls

**SAN DIEGO SPORTS ARENA, 3500 SPORTS ARENA BLVD, MIDWAY; 619/224-4625** San Diego's very impressive ice hockey team belongs to the seven-year-old West Coast Hockey League. The minor-league team won the Taylor Cup Championship for the first three years of the league's existence, beginning in the 1995–1996 season, and again in 2001, making it the WCHL's winningest team. The regular season runs from October to mid-April. *www.sandiegogulls.com*; *map:G2*

## San Diego Padres

**QUALCOMM STADIUM, 9449 FRIARS RD, MISSION VALLEY; 619/280-4636** Although they were National League champions in 1984 and 1998, the Pads have never conquered the World Series. They lost 0–4 in 1998 to the unstoppable New York Yankees, but so besotted the San Diego fans by their brush with greatness that the voters conceded to their demand for their very own multimillion-dollar stadium, to be located in downtown San Diego. Since then the erection of the new ballpark has been continuously delayed by controversy, multiple lawsuits, and political scandals. In the years since their brush with greatness, the Padres have lost many of their best players to free agency. These include slugger Ken Caminiti to the Houston Astros; Steve Finley to the Arizona Diamondbacks; and Greg Vaughn, the outfielder who hit 50 home runs in the 1998 season, to the Cincinnati Reds. And San Diego's hero, Tony Gwynn—who played with the Padres his entire 20-year career—has finally retired. In addition to being the best hitter of his generation, Gwynn holds a .338 lifetime batting average and made more than a dozen (16 to be exact) All-Star appearances. San Diego will not lose him, however; he'll coach baseball at his alma mater, San Diego State University, where his son, Tony Gwynn Jr, plays center field. *www.padres.com; map:LL4*

## San Diego Sockers

**SAN DIEGO SPORTS ARENA, 3500 SPORTS ARENA BLVD, MIDWAY; 858/836-4625** The darling of indoor soccer in the 1980s, the San Diego Sockers returned (after a five-year hiatus) in 2001 to win the regular season of the neophyte, five-team World Indoor Soccer League (WISL). The team lost the championship to the Dallas Side-kicks in sudden-death overtime. Beginning in 2002, the WISL will join the Major Indoor Soccer League (MISL) to form a stronger, larger league of 10 to 12 teams. A winter playing season (most likely October through April), salary caps of around $250,000 per player, and the fusion of the country's two indoor leagues should allow the MISL to thrive. The 10-time world champion San Diego Sockers hope to remain in the black and slowly build their fan base. *www.sockers.com; map:G2*

## San Diego Spirit

**UNIVERSITY OF SAN DIEGO'S TORERO STADIUM, 5998 ALCALA PARK, LINDA VISTA; 619/692-9872** The year 2001 saw the formation of the WUSA (Women's United Soccer Association) and San Diego's first professional women's soccer team. In addition to star defensive players from China (Fan Yunjie and Wen Lirong) and offensive angel Mercy Akide, of Nigeria, the spirited San Diego team has benefited from savvy, high-profile players from the U.S. National Team, including captain Julie Foudy. Other U.S. National Team transplants (and WUSA founding players) include forward Shannon MacMillan and defender Joy Fawcett. The team, which ended its first season 7-7-7, enjoyed 93 percent capacity at USD's 7,000-seat Torero stadium. *www.sandiegospirit.com; map: KK6*

# Index

## A

A La Française, 140, 177
AAA Southern California, 15
Abbey, The, 188
"Above it All," 286
Access Shuttle, 3
Accessible San Diego, 8
Adams Avenue, 142, 172
Adam's Steak & Eggs, 37
Adelaide's Flowers and Gifts, 144, 185
Adventure 16, 176, 193, 284
Aero Club, 227
Africa and Beyond, 156
Airplanes
  Barnstorm Biplane Adventures, 286
  charter, 3
  private, 3
  tours, 168
  See also Helicopters
"Airport Art," 213
Airports
  art at, 213
  Gillespie Field, 3
  lodgings near, 101
  McClellan-Palomar Airport, 3
  Montgomery Field, 3
  parking, 2
  San Diego International Airport at
    Lindbergh Field, 2
  transportation to, 2–3
Aladdin Mediterranean Cafe, 37
Alcala Gallery, 156
Alcazar Garden, 118, 228
Alfonso's, 37
Alt Karlsbad Haus, 242
"Alternative Venues," 223
AMC Fashion Valley 18, 214
AMC Mission Valley 20, 214
American Golf Corporation, 281
Americana, 38
America's Finest City Half Marathon, 287
Amtrak, 3
Anatomic Rag, 196
Andres Latin American Market, 184
Antique(s), 173–75
  See also Furniture
Antique Radio Store, The, 173
Antique Warehouse, The, 176
Anza-Borrego Desert State Park, 248–50
Apache Trading Post, 186
Apisa, 263
Apparel, 175–77
  See also Clothing

Aquariums
  Birch Aquarium at Scripps, 130, 144
  Sea World, 127
Architectural Salvage of San Diego, 173
ARCO Training Center, 168, 243
Ariana, 175
Art, 154–55
  See also Galleries; Museum(s)
Art museums. See Museums
Art Tours, 170
Artesia Day Spa and Salon, 109
Artists Gallery, The, 156
Artists' Loft, The, 116
Artists on the Cutting Edge, 215
Art-Te Company, 191
Ascot Shop, The, 175
Assenti's Pasta Company, 184
Athenaeum Music & Arts Library, 156, 208
Athens Market Taverna, 38
ATMs, 17
Atomic Trading Company, 175
Attractions, 118–38
Automobile. See Car
Aveda Lifestyle Store, 179
Avenida López Mateos, 268
Avenida Revolución, 257–58
Aviara Golf Course, 244
Aviation Adventures, 168, 228, 244
Avo Playhouse, 202
Azul La Jolla, 38
Azulejos, 260
Azzura Point, 39, 138

## B

B. Dalton, 21
Babcok & Story Bar, 124
Babette Schwartz, 140, 186
Baby Rock, 261
Bahia Sternwheelers, 168
Bai Yook Thai Cuisine, 39
Baily Wine Country Cafe, 251
Baja
  description of, 257
  Ensenada, 265–69
  map of, 256
  Puerto Nuevo, 264–65
  Rosarito, 262–64
  Tijuana, 14, 257–61
  See also Mexico
Baja California Tours, 261, 268
Baja Lobster Restaurant, 243
Bajamar, 266
Baked by Etta, 178

Bakeries, 177–79, 247
  See also Desserts
Balboa Park
  attractions, 118
  Mingei International Museum, 150, 245
  Museum of Contemporary Art San Diego, 144, 151, 239
  Museum of History and Art, 138, 236
  Museum of Photographic Arts, 151, 214
  Reuben H. Fleet Space Theater & Science Center, 128, 214, 237
  San Diego Aerospace Museum, 152
  San Diego Automotive Museum, 152
  San Diego Hall of Champions Sports Museum, 152
  San Diego Model Railroad Museum, 153
  San Diego Museum of Art, 134, 214, 237
  San Diego Museum of Man, 136, 237
  San Diego Natural History Museum, 153, 167
  Timken Museum of Art, 153
Balboa Park Golf Course, 281
Balboa Park Inn, 98
Balboa Tennis Club, 292
Bank of America, 17
Banks, 17
Bar Dynamite, 221
Barefoot Bar & Grill, 227
Barnes & Noble Booksellers, 180
Barnes Tennis Center, 292
Barnstorm Biplane Adventures, 286
Barona Casino, 249
Barona Creek Golf Course, 249
Barons, 198
Bars, 227–32
  See also Breweries; Beer; Wineries
Baseball
  San Diego Padres, 294
Bay Books, 180
Bay Club, The, 103
Bay Park, 141
Bayou Bar and Grill, 39
Bayside Trail, 122
Bazaar del Mundo, 129, 172
Bazár Casa Ramírez, 268
Bazár de Mexico, 258
Beach(es), 160–67
  Black's Beach, 161, 290
  Cardiff State Beach, 290
  Children's Pool Beach, 161
  City Beach, 9
  Coronado Municipal Beach, 161
  Dog Beach, 9
  Embarcadero Marina Park, 163
  Fiesta Island, 9, 123, 163, 273
  Garbage Beach, 291
  Imperial Beach, 163
  itinerary for, 239
  La Jolla Shores, 144, 164, 278

  Mission Beach. See Mission Beach
  Newbreak, 291
  Ocean Beach. See Ocean Beach
  Pacific Beach.Ssee Pacific Beach
  San Elijo State Beach, 131
  Swami's, 131, 292
  Torrey Pines State Beach, 166
  Windansea Beach, 167
Beach Terrace Inn, 113
"Beautiful View," 243
Beauty Kliniek Day Spa and Wellness Center, 20, 109
Bed & Breakfast Inn of La Jolla, The, 107
Beer, 198–99
  See also Bars; Breweries; Taverns; Pubs
Beer King, 198
Bella Luna, 40
Bellefleur Winery & Restaurant, 41, 242
Belly Up Tavern, 176, 221
Belmont Park, 133, 228, 239
  Giant Dipper, 133, 228
Bertrand at Mr. A's, 41
Best Western Hacienda Suites, 104
Bicycle(s), 16
  Performance Bicycle Shop, 194
  Rusty Spokes Vintage Bicycles, 175
  tours, 16
  Bicycling, 272–76
  See also Mountain biking
Big Kitchen, The, 41
Bike Tours of San Diego, 16
Bikes and Beyond, 16, 236
Billiards, 218–19
Birch Aquarium at Scripps, 130, 144
Bird Rock, 290
Birdcage, 176
Bit by Bit Computer Rentals, 20
Black, The, 186
Black's Beach, 161, 290
Blind Melons, 222
Blue Meannie Records, 192
Blue Planet Theater, 130
Blue Point Coastal Cuisine, 42
Blues, 218
Blumberg's at Samson's La Jolla, 42
Bo Danica, 187
Boardwalk and Belmont Park, 133
Boat tours, 168
Boating, 276–77
Bob's on the Bay, 243
Body care, 179–80
Bombay, 43, 142
Book Works, 215
Bookstar, 180
Bookstores, 21, 180–82, 215
  Barnes & Noble Booksellers, 180
  Bay Books, 180
  Book Works, 215
  Bookstar, 180

Borders Books & Music, 180
Casa del Libro, 181
Controversial Bookstore, 181
D.G. Wills, 215
Earth Song Bookstore, 147
Esmeralda Books & Coffee, 215, 233
F Street Bookstore, 187
Hillcrest Newsstand, 140, 181
John Cole's Book Shop, 144, 181, 239
Newport News, 181
Obelish Books, 10
Upstart Crow Bookstore & Coffeehouse,
    The, 21, 182
Wahrenbrock's Book House, 182
Warwick's, 144, 182, 215
White Rabbit, The, 144, 182
Boomerang for Modern, 197
Border crossing, 260–61
"Border Sense," 260
Borders Books & Music, 180
Borrego Springs
    lodgings, 116
    tour of, 248–50
Borrego Valley Inn, 250
Brad Burt's Magic Shop, 196
Bread & Cie, 140, 178
Breakfast, 32
Breweries, 219
    See also Bars; Beer; Taverns
Brick by Brick, 222
Brigantine, The, 43
Buffalo Joe's, 222
Bully's, 43
Bus, 2–3, 15
Business services, 19

C

Cabrillo, Juan Rodríguez, 8
Cabrillo National Monument, 122
Cafe 222, 45
Cafe 1134, 138
Cafe Athena, 44
Cafe Champagne, 251
Cafe Japengo, 44
Cafe Pacifica, 45
Cafe W, 45
Cafe Zinc, 46, 176
Cafe Zucchero, 46
Caffe Italia, 233
Cal Stores, 193
Calafia, 264
Cal-A-Vie, 108
California Ballet Company, 212
California Center for the Arts, Escondido, 202,
    245
California Cuisine, 46, 141
California Department of Fish and Game, 277,
    278
California Museum, 259

California Surf Museum, 149
California Tower, 118, 136
Callaway Coastal Vineyard & Winery, 251
Camp Pendleton, 167, 244
Campanario, 137
Candelas, 47
Candy, 182–83
'Canes, 222
Canoeing, 285–86
Car
    parking of, 15–16
    rental of, 15
    transportation by, 3–4, 15–16
Caravan Market, 184
Cardiff State Beach, 290
Cardiff-by-the-Sea
    history of, 131
    lodgings, 113
    nightlife, 220
    restaurants, 30
Cardiff-by-the-Sea Lodge, 113
Carlsbad, 132
    lodgings, 113–14
    nightlife, 220
    restaurants, 30
    tour of, 242–44
Carlsbad 5000, 244
Carlsbad Company Stores, 242
Carlsbad Convention & Visitors Bureau, 242
Carlsbad Inn Beach Resort, 114
Carlsbad Mineral Water Spa, 242
Carlsbad Street Faires, 244
Carlton Oaks Country Club, 282
Carve Pumpkins Underwater, 279
Casa de Bandini, 129
Casa de Pico, 130
Casa del Libro, 181
Casa la Carreta, 263
Casa Playa Spa, 262
Casamar, 268
Casbah, The, 222
Casino, 249
Cass Street Bar & Grill, 47
Cassidy West, 176
Catamaran Resort Hotel, The, 106
Cathedral, 140
Cathedral Church of Saint Paul, 18
Cecil's Cafe & Fish Market, 48
Cedros Design District, 131, 176
Cedros Gardens, 176
Centro Artesanal de Ensenada, 268
Chaparral Antique Mall, 251
Chart House, 48
Charter airplanes, 3
Cheese Shop, The, 48
Chez Loma, 49, 138
Chicano Park, 155
Chicki Jai, 259
Chilango's Mexico City Grill, 49

Children
    attractions for, 237
        Children's Zoo, 120
        tips for, 7
Children's Healthcare Referral Service, 7
Children's Museum/Museo de los Niños, 149
Children's Pool Beach, 161
Chino's Vegetable Shop, 149
Chocolates, 182–83
Chopra Center, 108
Chrome Photo Labs & Digital, 19
Chula Vista, 243
Chula Vista Nature Center, 243, 289
Church of Jesus Christ of Latter-Day Saints, 18
Churches, 18, 242
Cien Años, 259
Cinderella Carriage Company, 228, 236
Circa a.d., 189
City Beach, 9
City Delicatessen & Bakery, 140
Civic Helicopters, 168
Claire de Lune Coffee Lounge, 215
Clairemont
    description of, 141
    restaurants, 30
Classic Sailing Adventures, 169
Classical music, 208–11
Claudia's Cinnamon Rolls, 128
Clayton's Coffee Shop, 138
Clean Touch, 19
Climate, 4–5
Clothing, 196–98
Cloud 9 Shuttle, 3
"Clowing Around," 210
Club Montage, 223
Club Xanth, 224
Clubs, 221–27
CMX, 19
Coastline Shuttle, 3
Cocktail lounges, 218
Coffee Bean & Tea Leaf, The, 183
Coffeehouses, 147, 183–84, 215, 218, 233–34
Cold Stone Creamery, 132
Collector, The, 187
College Area, 220
Column One, 140, 190
Comedy clubs, 218
Comedy Store, The, 24
Comfort Inn and Suites, 104
Committee of 100, 167
Computer Care, 20
Computer Clinic, 20
Computer Museum of America, 150
Computer repairs and rental, 20
Congregation Beth El, 18
Congregation Beth Israel, 18
"Contamination Blues," 291
Controversial Bookstore, 181
Coors Amphitheatre, 243

Copy services, 19
Corner Stone, The, 174
Coronado
    attractions, 138
    bicycling in, 273
    lodgings, 102–03
    map of, 139
    restaurants, 30
    shopping, 172
    skating in, 286
    tours of, 138
Coronado Bay Bridge, 3, 14
Coronado Boat Rentals, 289
Coronado Golf Course, 282
Coronado Municipal Beach, 161
Coronado Playhouse, 138, 202
Coronado Shuttle, 236
Coronado Walking Tour, 170
Coronado/San Diego Ferry, 125
Cortez Hill, 23
Cost of living, 6–7
Costa Brava, 264
Country clubs, 218
Country Friends Shop, 148
Courtyard by Marriott, 99
Cove Theatre, 144
Cow, 192
Cowles Mountain, 228
Cream of the Crop, 177, 197
Crest Cafe, 49
Crest Liquor, 198
Croce's Restaurant & Jazz Bar, 224
Crown Point, 123
Crown Room, 124
Cruise ships, 125
Cruises, 169
Crystal Pier, 134
Crystal Pier Hotel & Cottages, 107, 134
Currency exchange, 10
Cuyamaca Rancho State Park, 284
Cyber Café, 24
Cycling. See Bicycles
Cyclo Vets, 272

**D**

D. D. Allen Antiques, 174
D. Z. Akin's, 52
Dana Inn, 105
Dana Landing Marina, 276, 285, 289
Dancing, 218
Datel, 20
Dave & Buster's, 50
David Zapf Gallery, 156
Day trips
    Anza-Borrego Desert, 248–50
    Borrego Springs, 248–50
    Carlsbad, 242–44
    Disneyland, 252–53
    Escondido, 244–46

Julian, 246–47
  Palomar Mountain, 246–47
  Temecula, 250–52
De Anza Cove, 276
Debra Owen Gallery, 156
Deer Park, 245
Del Mar
  attractions, 145–47
  description of, 9, 14
  lodgings, 111–12
  map of, 146
  nightlife, 220
  restaurants, 30
Del Mar Fairgrounds, 147
Del Mar Pizza, 51
Del Mar Plaza, 147, 173
Del Mar Racetrack, 293
Del Mar Regional Chamber of Commerce, 147
Del Mar Thoroughbred Club, 147
Delicatessens, 140, 185
Delicias, 50, 148
Dental services, 17–18
"Designer Shopping," 176
Desserts, 32, 178–79, 218, 233–34
  See also Bakeries
D.G. Wills, 215
Dick's Last Resort, 228
Disabled people
  services for, 8
  Tecolote Playground, 123
Disc Golf, 279
Discount Hobby Warehouse, 196
Disneyland, 252–53
Disneyland Resort Hotels, 253
Diversionary Theatre, 208
Diving, 277–78
Diving Locker, The, 193, 277
Dizzy's, 223
Doane Valley Nature Trail, 247
Dobson's Bar & Restaurants, 51
Dog Beach, 9
  See also Pets
"Doggie Dining," 40
Doubletree San Diego Mission Valley, 104
Downtown
  lodgings, 98–101
  nightlife, 220
  restaurants, 30
Downtown Hostel, 101
Downtown Information Center, 23
Downtown Johnny Brown's, 51
Downtown Waterfront, 124
Downtown YMCA, 292
Dr. Seuss Race for Literacy, 287
Dry cleaners, 19
Dudley's Bakery, 247

E

E Street Alley, 224
Earth Song Bookstore, 147
East County Performing Arts Center, 203
East San Diego, 141
East Village, 22
1890 Graham Memorial Presbyterian Church,
  18
El Agave, 52, 239
El Bizcocho, 52, 246
El Campo Cemetery, 129
El Charro, 268
El Cordova Hotel, 102
El Indio Shop, 53
El Museo Cantina Tequila, 264
El Patio, 263
El Potrero, 259
El Prado, 237
El Rey Sol, 268
El Toreo de Tijuana, 259
Electro Rent, 20
Ellen Browning Scripps Park, 121, 144, 162, 239
Embarcadero, 12, 125
Embarcadero Marina Park, 163
Embassy Suites San Diego Bay, 99
Empire Enterprise, 175
Encinitas
  attractions, 131
  nightlife, 220
  restaurants, 30
Encore of La Jolla, 177
Epazote, 53
Escondido
  description of, 141
  restaurants, 30
  tour of, 244–46
Esmeralda Books & Coffee, 215, 233
Espresso Mío, 140
Estero Beach Resort, 267
Ethnic markets, 184–85
European Cake Gallery, 178
Eveoke Dance Theatre, 212
Everett Stunz Company Ltd., 190

F

F Street Bookstore, 187
Fairouz Restaurant & Gallery, 54
Fallbrook, 245–46
Family activities and services, 7, 238
Fashion Valley, 173
Father Luis Jayme Museum, 137
Felix Furniture, 263
Fern Street Circus, 210
Ferrara Winery, 245
Ferry, 16–17, 125
Ferry Landing Marketplace, 138
Festival of Animation, 214

Festival Plaza, 263
Fidel's, 54
Field, The, 229
Fiesta Inn Vita Spa, 260
Fiesta Island, 9, 123, 163, 273
Fifth Avenue, 121
Filippi's Pizza Grotto, 54, 184
Film, 214
    *See also* Theaters
Film festivals, 214
Fingerhut Gallery, 157
Fio's Cucina Italiana, 55
Fish. *See* Seafood
Fish Market Restaurant, 55, 267
Fisherman's Landing, 278
Fishing
    freshwater, 280–81
    Gordo's Sportfishing, 268
    Islandia Sportfishing, 278
    Point Loma Sportfishing, 278
    saltwater, 278–79
    Seaforth Sportfishing, 123, 195, 238, 278
Flashbacks Recycled Fashions, 197
Fletcher Cove Beach Park, 131
Flick's, 229
Floral Fantasia, 185
Florida Canyon, 275
Florists, 185–86
Flower Fields at Carlsbad Ranch, The, 160, 244
Folk Arts Rare Records, 192
Food
    costs of, 7
    healthy, 189
    in Mexico, 266–67
    restaurants by, 32–36
    *See also* Restaurants; Grocery stores;
        Bakeries; Desserts
Football
    San Diego Chargers, 294
    San Diego State University, 10, 24
Foreign visitors, services for, 10
Fort Rosecrans National Cemetery, 123
Fouquet's de Paris, 260
Four Seasons Resort-Aviara, 109, 114, 244, 282
Fourth Avenue, 121
4th & B, 225
"Freeway Frenzy," 4
French Accent, 184
French Garden Shoppe, 140, 187
French Pastry Shop, 56
"Fresh From the Sea," 89
Fritz Theatre, 208

**G**

Gaia Day Spa, 20, 109
Galería de Pérez Meillón, 268
Galileo Cafe, 119
Galleries, 156–59
Gallery Alexander, 157

Gallery Eight, 157
"Gambling Goes Native," 249
Garbage Beach, 291
Garden(s), 159–60
    Alcazar Garden, 118
    Inez Grant Parker Memorial Rose Garden,
        118
    Zoro Garden, 118
    *See also* Parks
Gaslamp Billiard Palace, 229
Gaslamp Photo, 19–20
Gaslamp Quarter, 12, 22, 120, 172
Gaslamp Quarter Historical Foundation, 121,
    170
Gaslamp Stadium 15, 121
Gateway Computers, 6
Gay and Lesbian Times, 10
Gays/Lesbians
    nightlife, 218
    services for, 10
Gelato Vero Caffe, 233
Genghis Khan, 190
George White and Anna Gunn Marston House,
    150
George's at the Cove, 56, 239
Gepetto's, 196
GI Joe's Army-Navy Surplus, 193
Giant Dipper (Belmont Park), 133, 228
Gifts, 186–88
Gillespie Field, 3
Gliding, 279
Globe Theatres, The, 167, 203
Glorietta Bay, 276
Glorietta Bay Inn, 102, 138
Glorious Antiques, 174
Golden Door, 108, 245
Golden Hill
    description of, 141
    restaurants, 30
Golden Triangle, 141
Golf courses, 134, 244, 249
Gondola Company, 228
Gordo's Sportfishing, 268
Grant Grill, The, 56
Grape Street Park, 9
Gray Line San Diego, 3
Great News Cooking Supplies, 187
Greater San Diego Business Association, 10
Greek Islands Cafe, 57
Green Flash, The, 134
Greenway Museum, 246
Greyhound Bus Lines, 3
Grocery stores, 19
Grove Pastry Shop, 178
"Growth and Dreams," 195
Grunion, 133
Gulf Coast Grill, 57
Guy Fleming Trail, 228

# H

Hacienda Bajamar, 267
Hale Telescope, 246
Hamburger Mary's, 57
Harbor Island, 279
Harbor Sailboats, 289
Hardware, 188–89
Hash House a Go Go, 58
Hazard Center, 214
Healthy Back Store, The, 187
Healthy food, 189
Helen Woodward Animal Center, 149
Helicopters, 168
Henry's Market Place, 189
Heritage Hall, 242
Heritage Park Inn, 105
Heritage Park Victorian Village, 129
Hernandez Hideaway, 246
Hesco, 19
Highlights, 190
Highway 101, 131
Hike Bike Kayak San Diego, 272, 285
Hiking, 153, 283–85
Hillcrest
    attractions, 140
    nightlife, 220
    restaurants, 30
    shopping, 172
Hillcrest Ace Hardware, 188
Hillcrest Cinemas, 188, 214
Hillcrest Newsstand, 140, 181
Hilton San Diego Gaslamp Quarter, 99, 109
Hilton San Diego Resort, 106, 123
Historic Highway 101, 131
H&M Landing, 278
Hoa Hing, 185
Hob Nob Hill, 58
Hockey
    San Diego Gulls, 294
Hodad's, 59
"Holes in the Ground," 22
Home Accents of La Jolla, 190
Home furnishings, 189–91
Homie's Cinnamon Rolls, 178
Hook, Line & Sinker, 193
Hornblower Cruises & Events, 169
Horton Grand Hotel, 99
Horton Grand Theatre, 204
Horton Plaza, 12, 22, 127, 172–73, 236, 238
Hospitals, 17–18
Hostels, 101
Hot Topic, 197
Hot-air balloons, 286
Hotel(s). See Lodgings; specific hotel
Hotel Coral & Marina, 265
Hotel del Coronado, 102, 109, 124, 138, 236
Hotel Parisi, 109
House of Hospitality, 118
House of Pacific Relations, 118

"How to Pass for a Local," 13
Humphrey's, 225, 285
Hussong's Cantina, 265
Hyatt Islandia, 289

# I

Ichiban, 59
Il Fornaio, 59, 138, 236
IMAX, 128
Imperial Beach, 163
In Cahoots, 225
In Harmony, 189
"In the Beginning," 8
Indigo Grill, 60
Indigo Way, 197
Inez Grant Parker Memorial Rose Garden, 118
In-line skating, 286
Inn at Rancho Santa Fe, The, 112, 148
International Groceries of San Diego, 185
International Information Center, 14
Internet access, 24
Islandia Sportfishing, 278
Itineraries
    Beach, 239
    La Jolla, 239
    three-day tour, 236–38

# J

Jake's Del Mar, 60
Jasmine, 61
Java Joe's, 233
Jewel Box, The, 229
Jimmy Carter's Cafe, 61
Joe's Crab Shack, 61
John Cole's Book Shop, 144, 181, 239
JP and Company, 174
Julian
    lodgings, 116
    tour of, 246–47
Julian Bed & Breakfast Guild, 247
Julian Cafe & Bakery, 247
Julian Drug Store, 247
Julian Pie Co., 247
Julian Pioneer Museum, 247
Julian Stables, 247
Junipero Serra Museum, 129
Jyoti Bihanga, 62, 142

# K

Kaiser Permanente, 17–18
Kaiserhof, 62
Karen Krasne's Extraordinary Desserts, 178, 233
Karen's Consignment Gallery, 197
Karl Strauss Brewery & Grill, 62, 229
Kate Sessions Memorial Park, 164
Kayaking, 285–86
Kazumi Sushi, 140
Kearns Memorial Pool, 292

Kearny Mesa
    description of, 141
    restaurants, 30
Kemo Sabe, 63, 142
Ken Cinema, 214
Ken Theater, 143
Kensington Club, 230
Kensington Grill, 63, 142
Kensington Video, 143
Kensington/Adams Avenue
    attractions, 142
    map of, 143
    nightlife, 220
    restaurants, 30
Kern & Co., 176
Kids. See Children
"Kids' Play," 237
King and Company, 174
King's Fish House, 63
Kinko's, 19, 24
Ki's, 64
Knickerbikers, 272
Knotts Soak City, 243
Kono's Cafe, 64, 134, 239
Korea House, 65
Krazy Coyote Saloon and Grille, 249
Kumeyaay Indians, 8
Kurt's Camera Repair, 20

**L**

L. A. Cetto Winery, 259
La Bufadora, 269
La Casa de Estudillo, 129
La Casa del Zorro, 116, 250
La Case de la Langosta, 264
La Compagnie de Provence, 179
La Costa Resort & Spa, 108, 244, 282
La Especial, 259
La Esquina de Bodegas, 269
La Flor de Michoacán, 263
La Fonda, 265
La Fresqueria, 65
La Jolla
    attractions, 144
    lodgings, 107–11
    map of, 145
    nightlife, 220
    restaurants, 30–31
    shopping, 172
    tours, 239
La Jolla Chamber Music Society, 208
La Jolla Cove, 121, 144, 228, 239, 278
La Jolla Cove Suites, 110
La Jolla Fiber Arts, 157
La Jolla Indians, 8
La Jolla Light, 21
La Jolla Playhouse, 204
La Jolla Rough Water Competition, 279

La Jolla Shores, 144, 164, 278
La Jolla Shuffleboard Club, 122
La Jolla Union Square, 173
La Jolla Village Cinemas, 214
La Mesa
    description of, 141
    restaurants, 31
La Paloma, 131, 214
La Panaderia, 130
La Pensione Hotel, 100
La Taverna, 65
La Valencia Hotel, 110, 144, 239
Laguna Mountain(s), 12
Laguna Mountain Recreation Area, 285
Lake Henshaw, 280
Lake Hodges, 246, 275–76, 280
Lake Hodges Aquatic Center, 286, 289, 293
Lake Jennings County Park, 280
Lake Miramar, 280, 285, 287
Lake Morena County Park, 280
Lake Murray Community Park, 276, 281
Lake Murray Tennis Club, 292
Lake Poway Recreation Area, 281
Lamb's Players Theatre, 205
Lamp Shades Unlimited, 190
Landing, The, 123
Las Bodegas de Santo Tomás, 269
Las Rocas Hotel, 264
Las Rosas, 266
L'Auberge Del Mar, 109, 111, 147
Laundromats, 19
Laurel Restaurant & Bar, 66
Lawyer Referral & Information Service, 19
Le Cousteau, 263
Le Fontainebleau, 66
Le Travel Store, 21, 187, 236
Legal services, 19
Legoland California, 137, 244
Lemon Grove, 141
Les Artistes, 112
Lesbian(s)
    nightlife, 218
    services for, 10
Lesbian and Gay Men's Community Center, 10
Lestat's, 142
Leucadia, 131
Libraries, 21
Libros, 181
Lighthouses
    Old Point Loma Lighthouse, 122
Lindbergh Field, 2
Liquor, 198–99
Literature, 215
Little Italy, 23, 141
Live Wire, 230
Livewire, 225
Living Room Coffeehouse, The, 234
Locals, 13
Lodge at Torrey Pines, The, 110

Lodgings, 98–116
    Airport Area, 101
    Borrego Springs, 116
    Cardiff-by-the-Sea, 113
    Carlsbad, 113–14
    children, 7
    Coronado, 102–03
    costs of, 7
    Del Mar, 111–12
    Downtown, 98–101
    Julian, 116
    La Jolla, 107–11
    Mission Bay, 105–06
    Mission Valley, 104–05
    Oceanside, 115
    Old Town, 104–05
    Pacific Beach, 106–07
    Point Loma, 103–04
    Rancho Bernardo, 115
    Rancho Santa Fe, 112–13
    Shelter Island, 103–04
    See also specific lodging
Loews Coronado Bay Resort, 103
Logan Heights, 31
Loma Vista Bed & Breakfast, 252
Longs, 19
Los Angeles Times, 21
Los Castillo, 268
Los Pelícanos, 262
"Love, San Diego Style," 228
Lyceum Theater, 128

# M

Mac Rentals, 20
Macy's, 128
Magee House, 242
Maidhof Brothers, 190
Mail Boxes Etc., 19
Mainly Mozart Festival, 209
Maison en Provence, 140, 191
Make Mine Sweet, 182
Malashock Dance, 212
Malcolm X Library, 154
Mallorca, 258
Malls, 173, 251
Manchester Grand Hyatt, 22, 125
Maps
    Adams Avenue, 143
    Baja, 256
    Coronado, 139
    Del Mar, 146
    Kensington, 143
    La Jolla, 145
Marathons
    America's Finest City Half Marathon, 287
    San Diego Marathon, 244
    Suzuki Rock 'N' Roll Marathon, 287
    See also Running
Marina District, 22

Marine Room, The, 67, 144, 239
Marine Street, 291
Maritime Museum, 125
Market, The, 289
Market Cafe, 67
Marriott Hotel and Marina, 125
Marriott Real Del Mar Residence Inn, 262
Martin Luther King Promenade, 126
Mary Star of the Sea, 18
Maurice Carrie Winery, 251
"Maze of Neighborhoods, A," 141
McClellan-Palomar Airport, 3
Meats, 191
Medical services, 17–18
Menghini Winery, 247
Mercado Hidalgo, 258
Mervyn's, 128
Messenger Express, 19
Messenger services, 19
Metro Info Line, 8
Mexico
    Ensenada, 265–69
    food in, 266–67
    Puerto Nuevo, 264–65
    Rosarito, 262–64
    Tijuana, 14, 257–61
    See also Baja
Mexicoach, 261
Michele Coulon Dessertier, 179
Middletown
    nightlife, 220
    restaurants, 31
Midway, 31
Miguel's Cocina, 138
Military tours, 167–68
Mille Fleurs, 68, 148, 225
Mills Manor, 136
Mimmo's Italian Village, 68
Mingei International Museum, 150, 245
Mira Mesa Epicentre, The, 223
Miracles Cafe, 234
Mission Basilica San Diego de Alcalá, 8, 18, 134, 137
Mission Bay
    fishing, 278
    lodgings, 105–06
    nightlife, 220
Mission Bay Aquatic Center, 285, 287, 289–90, 293
Mission Bay Park, 123, 238, 273, 276, 288
Mission Bay Park Artificial Reefs, 278
Mission Bay Park Headquarters, 124
Mission Bay Rowing Association, 287
Mission Bay Sportcenter, 123, 238, 285, 289
Mission Beach
    attractions, 14, 164
    bicycling, 274
    nightlife, 220
    restaurants, 31

running, 288
shopping, 173
Mission Beach and Pacific Beach, 288
Mission Beach Club, 16, 133, 194, 239, 286, 290
Mission Beach Plunge, 133, 292
Mission Cafe & Coffee Shop, 68
Mission Hills
    attractions, 139
    restaurants, 31
    shopping, 172
Mission Hills Cafe, 69, 140
Mission Hills Nursery, 140, 186
Mission San Luis Rey, 137, 244
Mission Trails Golf Course, 134
Mission Trails Regional Park, 134, 274, 284, 288
Mission Valley
    description of, 141
    lodgings, 104–05
    nightlife, 220
    restaurants, 31
Mistral la Compagnie de Provence, 176
MiXX, 69, 230
Mom's Pies, Etc., 247
Mona Lisa Italian Delicatessen, 185
Montanas, 70
Montgomery Field, 3
Moonlight Amphitheater, 205
Morton's of Chicago, 70
Mother's Kitchen, 246
Mount Palomar Winery, 251
Mount Soledad Natural Park, 165
Mount Woodson Country Club, 282
Mountain biking, 272, 275–76
Movie theaters. See Theaters; specific theater
Movies Before the Mast, 214
"Mr. Horton Builds a City," 238
Mundo Divertido, 258
Museo de Historia de Ensenada, 268
Museum(s), 149–54
    California Museum, 259
    California Surf Museum, 149
    Computer Museum of America, 150
    Father Luis Jayme Museum, 137
    Greenway Museum, 246
    Julian Pioneer Museum, 247
    Junipero Serra Museum, 129
    Maritime Museum, 125
    Mingei International Museum, 150, 245
    Museum of Contemporary Art San Diego, 144, 151, 239
    Museum of History and Art, 138, 236
    Museum of Photographic Arts, 151, 214
    Museum of the San Diego Historical Society, 151
    San Diego Aerospace Museum, 152
    San Diego Automotive Museum, 152
    San Diego Hall of Champions Sports Museum, 152
    San Diego Model Railroad Museum, 153
    San Diego Museum of Art, 134, 214, 237
    San Diego Museum of Man, 136, 237
    San Diego Natural History Museum, 153, 167
    San Pasqual Battlefield State Historic Park and Museum, 245
    Temecula Valley Museum, 251
    Timken Museum of Art, 153
Music
    nightlife, 221–27
    shopping, 191–93
Mystery Cafe Dinner Theatre, 205

N

Nana's Too, 251
National University, 24
Naval Air Station at North Island, 122, 138
Neighborhoods
    nightlife, 220
    restaurants, 30–31
    shopping, 172–73
    See also individual neighborhood
Neiman's, 242
Nelson Photo Supplies, 19
New Port Beach Hotel, 264
Newbreak, 291
Newport Avenue, 135
Newport News, 181
Newspapers, 20–21
Nickelodeon Records, 192
Nick's at the Beach, 70, 239
Nicole Miller, 177
Nightlife, 218–34
    alternative, 223
    bars, 227–32
    clubs, 221–27
    coffeehouses, 147, 183–84, 215, 218, 233–34
    desserts, 233–34
    music, 221–27
    pubs, 227–32
    taverns, 227–32
    tea, 233–34
    types of, 218–19
Nine Ten, 71
99 Ranch, 185
Nofufi Garden Gallery, 157
Nordstrom, 128
Normal Heights, 31, 141
Norpine Mountain Sports, 194
North Coast Repertory Theatre, 205
North County Fair, 245
North County Times, 21
North Island Naval Air Station, 122, 138
North Park, 141, 220
North Shores Alano Club, 223
North Torrey Pines, 274
Nuestra Señora de Guadalupe, 265
Nurseries, 184–85

# O

OB People's Natural Foods, 136
Obelish Books, 10
Ocean Beach
    attractions, 165
    description of, 14
    exploring of, 135
    nightlife, 220
    restaurants, 31
    shopping, 173
Ocean Beach Antiques Mall/Empire Enterprise, 174
Ocean Beach International Hostel, 101
Ocean Beach Paint and Hardware, 188
Ocean Beach Pier, 135, 238
Ocean Beach Pier Cafe, 135
Ocean Enterprises, 277
Ocean Song Music of Del Mar, 147
Oceanside, 115
Oceanside Marina Inn, 115
OE Express, 277
Off the Record, 192
Old Mission Dam, 134
Old Point Loma Lighthouse, 122
Old Town
    lodgings, 104–05
    nightlife, 220
    restaurants, 31
    shopping, 172
Old Town Mexican Cafe, 71
Old Town San Diego State Historic Park, 9, 129
Old Town Trolley Tours of San Diego, 169
Old Venice Italian Restaurant Caffe & Bar, 71
Olé Madrid, 72
Omnimax Theater, 259
On Broadway, 226
150 Grand Cafe, 72, 245
One Stop Laundry in Pacific Beach, 19
Ono Sushi, 73
Onyx Room, 230
Opera, 210
Orange Cab, 16
Orchestra, 209
Orfila Winery, 245
Ortega's, 73
Outdoor activities. See Recreation
Outdoor gear, 193–96
Over the Line Tournament, 279

# P

Pacific Beach
    attractions, 14, 165
    bicycling, 274
    itineraries, 239
    lodgings, 106–07
    nightlife, 220
    restaurants, 31
    running, 288
    shopping, 173
Pacific Beach Tennis Club, 292
Pacific Coast Grill, 74
Pacific Gaslamp 15, 214
Pacific Shores, 230
Pacifica Del Mar, 73
Palisades Park, 134
Palm Canyon Trail, 248
Palomar Mountain, 246–47
Palomar Mountain General Store & Trading Co., 246
Palomar Mountain State Park, 247
Palomar Observatory, 246
Pamplemousse Grille, 74
Panache, 188
Panda Inn Chinese Restaurant, 74
Pannikin Coffee and Tea, 183, 234
Papas&Beer, 264
Paradise Point Resort, 106, 109
Parallel 33, 75
Paras Newsstand, 181
Parisi Gallery and Sculpture Garden, 158
Park(s)
    Anza-Borrego Desert State Park, 248–50
    Chicano Park, 155
    Cuyamaca Rancho State Park, 284
    Deer Park, 245
    Ellen Browning Scripps Park, 121, 144, 162, 239
    Fletcher Cove Beach Park, 131
    Grape Street Park, 9
    Kate Sessions Memorial Park, 164
    Mission Bay Park, 123, 238, 273, 288
    Mission Trails Regional Park, 134, 274, 284, 288
    Mount Soledad Natural Park, 165
    Palisades Park, 134
    Palomar Mountain State Park, 247
    Pioneer Park, 140
    Presidio Park, 129
    Robb Field State Park, 286
    San Diego–La Jolla Underwater Park, 122
    Seagrove Park, 145
    Spreckels Park, 166, 236
    Tidelands Park, 166
    Tourmaline Surf Park, 289–90
Park Boulevard Pharmacy, 19
Parking
    airport, 2
    car, 15–16
Patina, 188
Patrick's II, 226
Pearl of the Pacific, 155
Pedríns, 262–63
Peet's Coffee & Tea, 183
Peninsula Tennis Club, 292

Peohe's, 138
People's Organic Foods Market, 189
Performance Bicycle Shop, 194
Performing arts
    classical music, 208–11
    dance, 211–13
    film, 214
    literature, 215
    opera, 208–11
    theater, 202–07
Periodicals, 180–82
Pets
    Dog Beach, 9
    Helen Woodward Animal Center, 149
    services for, 9, 20, 40
Pharmacies, 19
Photography
    equipment and services, 19–20
    Museum of Photographic Arts, 151, 214
Piano bars, 218
Piatti, 75
Pied-à-Terre, 175
Pilar's Beachwear, 177
Pioneer Cemetery, 247
Pioneer Park, 140
Pizza, 34
Pizza Nova, 76
Pizza Port, 76
"Places of Worship," 18
Plan B, 226
Play It Again Sports, 16, 194, 290
Plays. See Theater (performing arts)
Plaza Bar (Westgate Hotel), 226
Plaza Cívica, 268
Plaza Río Tijuana, 258
Plunge, 133, 292
Point Loma
    bicycling, 274
    description of, 14, 141, 274
    lodgings, 103–04
    nightlife, 220
    restaurants, 31
Point Loma Hostel, 101
Point Loma Seafoods, 76, 191
Point Loma Sportfishing, 278
Poisoning, 7
Polar Golf, 281
Police, 16–17
Pool tables, 218–19
Porkyland, 77
Post office, 18
Postal Annex, 19
Poway Center for the Performing Arts, 206
Prado Restaurant at Balboa Park, The, 77, 119
Pratt Gallery, 158
Presidio Park, 129
Primo, 20
Prince and the Pauper, 142
Prince of Wales, The, 77

Princess Pub & Grille, 231
Private airplanes, 3
Professional Photographic Repair, 20
Prospect Street, 144
Public art, 154–55
Public libraries. See Libraries
Public rest rooms, 17
Public transportation. See Transportation
Pubs, 219, 227–32
Pueblo Amigo, 258
Puerto Nuevo, 264–65
Punta Morro, 266

**Q**

Quail Botanical Gardens, 137, 228
Quicksilver Stained Glass & Antiques, 142
Quint Contemporary Art, 158
Quivira Basin, 277, 279
Qwiigs Bar & Grill, 78, 238

**R**

Radio stations, 21, 23–24
Rainbow Cyclists of San Diego, 272
Rainfall, 5
Ralph's, 19
Rancho Bernardo
    description of, 141
    lodgings, 115
    restaurants, 31
    tour of, 246
Rancho Bernardo Inn & Golf Course, 109, 115,
    246, 282
Rancho La Puerta, 108
Rancho Santa Fe
    attractions, 147–49
    lodgings, 112–13
    nightlife, 220
    restaurants, 31
Rancho Santa Fe Polo Field, 149
Rancho Valencia Resort, 112, 149
Rancho Valencia Restaurant, 78
Rand McNally Map & Travel Store, 182
Reader, The, 7, 10, 21, 283
Recreation
    bicycling, 272–76
    boating, 276–77
    canoeing, 285–86
    diving, 277–78
    golfing, 281–83
    in-line skating, 286
    kayaking, 285–86
    outdoor activities, 272–76
    roller skating, 286
    rowing, 287
    running, 287–88
    sailing, 289
    snorkeling, 277–78
    surfing, 289–92

swimming, 292
tennis, 292
windsurfing, 293
Recreational Equipment, Incorporated (REI), 194
Red Bus Shuttle, 2
Red Fox Room, 231
Red Lion Hanalei Hotel, 105
Red Sails Inn, 79
Reed's Hobby Shop, 196
Reggae, 219
Rei, 284
Religion, 18
Rentals
    canoe, 285–86
    car, 15
    computer, 20
    kayak, 285–86
Rest rooms, 17
Restaurants, 37–95
    Cardiff-By-The Sea, 30
    Carlsbad, 30
    Clairemont, 30
    Coronado, 30
    Del Mar, 30
    Downtown, 30
    Encinitas, 30
    Escondido, 30
    by food, 32–36
    Golden Hill, 30
    Hillcrest, 30
    Kearny Mesa, 30
    Kensington, 30
    La Jolla, 30–31
    La Mesa, 31
    Logan Heights, 31
    Middletown, 31
    Midway, 31
    Mission Beach, 31
    Mission Hills, 31
    Mission Valley, 31
    by neighborhood, 30–31
    Normal Heights, 31
    Ocean Beach, 31
    Old Town, 31
    Pacific Beach, 31
    Point Loma, 31
    Rancho Bernardo, 31
    Rancho Sante Fe, 31
    Solana Beach, 31
    Sorrento Valley, 31
    star ratings of, 28–29
    University Heights, 31
    with views, 36
    See also specific restaurant
Retro clothing, 196–98
Reuben H. Fleet Space Theater & Science
    Center, 128, 214, 237
Revivals, 198
Rich's, 226

Ridelink, 16
Rite Aid, 19
Riverwalk Golf Course, 283
Riviera del Pacífico, 268
Robb Field State Park, 286
Robson Gallery, 158
Rock & Roll Taco, 264
Roller skating, 286
Romantic sites, 228
Ron Stuart Men's Clothing, 177
Roppongi Restaurant, Bar, and Cafe, 79
Rosarito, 262–64
Rosarito Beach Hotel, 262, 264
Rosarito to Ensenada Fun Bicycle Ride, 273
Rosa's Cantina, 251
Rowing, 287
Royal Touch Cleaners, 19
Royale Brasserie, 79
Roy's, 80
Rubio's, 80
Ruby's Diner, 81
Running, 287–88
    See also Marathons
Rusty Spokes Vintage Bicycles, 175

S
Safety, 17
Saffron Noodles and Saté, 81
Sail Bay, 123
Sailing, 289
Sally's, 81
Salons, 20, 108–09
    See also Body care; Spas
Sammy's California Woodfired Pizza, 82
San Diego
    costs of, 6–7
    growth of, 195
    orientation of, 12–14
    time zone, 5
    weather, 4–5
    what to bring, 5–6
San Diego Aerospace Museum, 152
San Diego Animal Control, 20
San Diego Art Institute, 158
San Diego Automotive Museum, 152
San Diego Ballet, 212
San Diego Bay, 12, 274
San Diego Bicycling Touring Society, 272
San Diego Business Journal, 21
San Diego Cab, 16
San Diego Chamber Orchestra, 209
San Diego Chargers, 294
San Diego Civic Theatre, 206
San Diego Convention and Visitors Bureau, 6,
    14, 281
San Diego Convention Center, 22, 126
San Diego County Administration Center, 125
San Diego County Bar Association, 19
San Diego County Bicycle Coalition, 272

San Diego Daily Transcript, 21
San Diego Early Music Society, 209
San Diego Gulls, 294
San Diego Hall of Champions Sports Museum,
    152
San Diego Harbor Excursion, 125, 169, 236
San Diego Hardware, 189
San Diego Harley-Davidson, 188
San Diego Hilton, 289, 293
San Diego House, 184
San Diego Humane Society, 20
San Diego International Airport at Lindbergh
    Field, 2
San Diego International Film Festival, 214
San Diego Latino Film Festival, 214
San Diego Main Public Library, 24
San Diego Marathon, 244
San Diego Metropolitan Uptown Examiner, 21
San Diego Model Railroad Museum, 153
San Diego Mountain Biking Association, 272
San Diego Museum of Art, 134, 214, 237
San Diego Museum of Man, 136, 237
San Diego Natural History Museum, 153, 167,
    284
San Diego North Convention & Visitors Bureau,
    132
San Diego Opera, 210
San Diego Outback Tours, 248
San Diego Padres, 294
San Diego Police Department, 16
San Diego Repertory Theatre, 206
San Diego Rowing Club, 287
San Diego Sailing Academy, 289
San Diego Sockers, 295
San Diego Spirit, 295
San Diego State University, 10, 24
San Diego Surfing Academy, 290
San Diego Symphony, 211
San Diego Tandem Club, 272
San Diego Track, 287
San Diego Transit Company, 15
San Diego Trolley, 15
San Diego Union-Tribune, 20–21
San Diego Velodrome, 275
San Diego Visitor Information Center, 14
San Diego Watercolor Society Showcase Gallery,
    159
San Diego Weekly Reader, 7, 10, 21, 283
San Diego Wine Company, 199
San Diego Zoo, 119, 237
San Diego–Coronado Bay Ferry, 16–17
San Diego–Coronado Bridge, 14
San Diego–La Jolla Underwater Park, 122
San Elijo Lagoon, 131
San Elijo State Beach, 131
San Pasqual Battlefield State Historic Park and
    Museum, 245
Sanborn's, 258

Santa Clara Point, 123, 277
Santa Ysabel Art Gallery, 247
Santé Ristorante, 82
Sav-On, 19
Scene, The, 223
Scripps Inn, 111
Scripps Memorial Hospital, 17
Sea Lodge, 111
Sea World, 123, 127, 238
Seafood, 34, 89, 191
    See also Sushi
Seaforth Boat Rentals, 277, 289
Seaforth Sportfishing, 123, 195, 238, 278
Seagrove Park, 145
Seal Tours, 169
Seaport Village, 125, 172, 236
Seaside Market, 131
See's Candies, 183
Self-Realization Fellowship, 18, 131, 160
Seniors, services for, 8
Señor Frog's, 259
Sephora, 179
Sevilla, 82, 227, 236
Shake Rag-Epicenter, 198
Shakespeare Pub and Grille, 83
Shamu, 127
Sharp Memorial Hospital, 17
Shelter Island
    boating, 276
    description of, 141
    fishing, 278–79
    lodgings, 103–04
    nightlife, 220
Shelter Pointe Hotel and Marina, 103
Sheraton San Diego Hotel and Marina, 101
Sherwood Auditorium, 151
Shopping, 172–99
    antiques, 173–75
    apparel, 175–77
    bakeries, 177–79
    beer, 198–99
    body care, 179–80
    books, 180–82
    candy, 182–83
    chocolates, 182–83
    coffee, 183–84
    ethnic markets, 184–85
    fish, 191
    florists, 185–86
    gifts, 186–88
    hardware, 188–89
    healthy food, 189
    home furnishings, 189–91
    liquor, 198–99
    malls, 173
    meats, 191
    music, 191–93
    by neighborhood, 172–73

nurseries, 184–85
outdoor gear, 193–96
periodicals, 180–82
tea, 183–84
toys, 196
vintage/retro, 196–98
wine, 198–99
Shuttles, 3, 236
Sick and Twisted Festival, 214
Sierra Club, 283–84
Siesel's Old-Fashioned Meats, 191
Silver Skillet, The, 188
Silver Spoon Cafe, 251
Silver Strand State Beach, 133, 236, 275, 288
Singing Hills Golf Resort, 283
Sirino's, 245
Sixth Avenue, 121
Skating, 286
Ski Beach, 277
Sky Room, The, 83
Skysurfer Balloon Company, 228
Slamm–San Diego's Music Magazine, 223
Sledgehammer Theatre, 206
"Sleeping on a Shoestring," 101
Snorkeling, 277–78
Snug Harbor Marina, 242
Soccer
San Diego Sockers, 295
San Diego Spirit, 295
Society Billiard Cafe, 231
Solana Beach, 131
nightlife, 220
restaurants, 31
Soledad Mountain, 275
Solo, 176
Solunto Baking Company, 179
Sorrento Mesa, 141
Sorrento Valley
description of, 141
nightlife, 220
restaurants, 31
Souplantation, 84
South Beach Bar and Grill, 231
South Coast Surf Shop, 195
South Shores, 277, 289
Southern Emigrant Trail, 249
Spanish Landing, 286
Spas, 20, 108–09, 242, 260, 262
See also Salons; Body care
"Spas and Salons," 108
Spectator sports, 293–95
Spectrum Golf, 281
Spices Thai Cafe, 84
Spirits of St. Germain Liquors, 199
Sportfishing
Gordo's Sportfishing, 268
Islandia Sportfishing, 278
Point Loma Sportfishing, 278
Seaforth Sportfishing, 123, 195, 238, 278

Sportfishing Pier, 268
Sports, 279, 293–95
Sports bars, 219
Sportsmen's Seafoods, 123, 191
Spreckels Organ Pavilion, 119, 211
Spreckels Park, 166, 236
Spruce Street Forum, 208
St. Michael's Episcopal Church, 242
Stacey Himmel Stationery, 188
Star of the Sea, 85, 238
Starlight Theatre, 207
State Street, 242
Steele Canyon Golf & Country Club, 283
Strand Theatre, 136
Sunset Cliffs, 136
Sunshine Company Saloon Limited, 231
Supreme Shuttle, 3
Surf Diva, 290
Surfing, 195, 289–92
Susan Street Fine Art Gallery, 159
Sushi, 34, 140
Sushi Deli One, 85
Sushi Deli Too, 85
Sushi on the Rock, 86
Suzuki Rock 'N' Roll Marathon, 287
Swami's, 131, 292
Sweet & Sugar Free, 183
Swimming, 292
Swing Inn Cafe, 251
Sycuan Casino, 249
Symphony, 211

T
Tasende Gallery, 144, 159
Taste of Thai, 86
Taverns, 227–32
Taxis, 3, 16
Tea, 183–84, 233–34
Tea Pavilion, 119
Tecolote Playground, 123
Telephone numbers, 24–25
Television stations, 24
Temecula, 250–52
Temecula Creek Inn, 253
Temecula Crest Winery, 251
Temecula Stampede, 251
Temecula Valley Museum, 251
Temecula Valley Winegrowers Association, 250
Tennis, 292
Theater(s)
AMC Fashion Valley 18, 214
AMC Mission Valley 20, 214
Blue Planet Theater, 130
Cove Theatre, 144
Hazard Center, 214
Hillcrest Cinemas, 188, 214
Ken Cinema, 214
Ken Theater, 143
La Jolla Village Cinemas, 214

La Paloma, 214
Lyceum Theater, 128
Omnimax Theater, 259
Pacific Gaslamp 15, 214
Strand Theatre, 136
United Artists Horton Plaza, 214
United Artists Theatre, 128
See also specific theater
Theater (performing arts), 167, 202–07
Theatre in Old Town, 207
Thee Bungalow, 86
Thinker Things, 196
3rd Corner, The, 87
Thomas Cook Foreign Exchange, 10, 17
Thornton Winery, 251
"Ticket Alert," 203
Ticketmaster, 203
"Tide Pool Tango," 162
Tidelands Park, 166
Tijuana, 14, 257–61
Tijuana Cultural Center, 259
Time zone, 5
Timken Museum of Art, 153
Tip Top Meats, 87, 191
Tolán, 258
Tony's Jacal, 88
Top o' the Cove, 88
Top of the Hyatt, 232, 238
Top of the Market, 55
Top of the Park, 232
"Top 25 Attractions," 119
Tori Tori New Japanese Cuisine, 88
Torrey Pines Glider Port, 279, 286
Torrey Pines Lodge, 132
Torrey Pines Municipal Golf Course, 283
Torrey Pines State Beach, 166
Torrey Pines State Park, 288
Torrey Pines State Reserve, 132, 147
Tourmaline Surf Park, 289–90
Tours, 167–70
    air, 168
    Baja California, 261
    bicycling, 16
    boat, 168
    Mexico, 261
    military, 167–68
    motor, 169
    walking, 170
Tower, The, 232
Town & Country Salon and Day Spa, 109
Toys, 196
Trade Roots Reggae, 193
Train, 3
Transit Store, 15, 272
Transportation
    airport. See Airports
    bicycle, 16
    border, 260
    bus, 3, 15

car, 3–4, 15–16
charter airplane, 3
for disabled people, 8
ferry, 16–17
information resources, 8
taxi, 3, 16
train, 3
trolley, 15
Trattoria Acqua, 89
Travelex America, 10
Trios Gallery, 176
Trolley, 15
Trophy's, 90
T's Cafe, 90
Tumbleweed Trading Company, 250
Tunaman's Memorial, 155
Turf Supper Club, 90
Tutto Mare Ristorante, 91
TV stations. See Television stations
Tweet Street, 23
Twigg's Tea and Coffee, 215, 234
Twister Cafe, 223

**U**

UCSD Medical Center, 7, 17
Ultrazone, 279
Underage clubs, 219
Union Bank, 17
Union-Tribune Publishing, 10
United Artists Horton Plaza, 214
United Artists Theatre, 128
United Methodist Church, 18
University Avenue, 172
University City, 141
University Heights
    description of, 141
    nightlife, 220
    restaurants, 31
University of California at San Diego, 10, 24, 155
University of California at San Diego Theatre, 207
University of Phoenix, 24
University of San Diego, 24
University Towne Center, 173
Upstart Crow Bookstore & Coffeehouse, The, 21, 182
Uptown District, 173
Urban Grind, 215
Urban Safaris, 170, 284
U.S. House Apothecary and Soap Shop, 180
USS Midway, 125
UTC, 173

**V**

VCA Emergency Animal Hospital and Referral Service, 20
Vegetarian, 35
Vegetarian Zone, 91, 189

Venetian, The, 91
Vermont Street Pedestrian Bridge, 154
Via Italia Trattoria, 92
Viejas Casino & Turf Club, 249
Vigilucci's, 92
Village Hillcrest, 173
Vintage Wines Limited, 199
Visitor information
    International Information Center, 14
    San Diego Visitor Information Center, 14
Visitors Center, 237
Vivace, 93
Volcan Mountain Wilderness Preserve, 247

## W

Wahrenbrock's Book House, 182
Walden Ashe, 20, 109
Walkabout International, 170, 284
Walking tours, 170
Walter Andersen Nursery, 186
Warwick's, 144, 182, 215
Washington Mutual, 17
Waterfront, The, 93, 232
Wear It Again Sam, 198
Weather, 4–5
Websites, 10
Weidner's Gardens, 186
"Weird Sports," 279
Welk Resort Center, 245
Welk Resort Theatre, 207
Wells Fargo, 17
Westfield Shoppingtown Horton Plaza, 12, 22, 127, 172–73, 236, 238

Westfield Shoppingtown Mission Valley, 173
Westfield Shoppingtown UTC, 173
Westgate Hotel, The, 100
Whaley House, 129
Whaling Bar, The, 93
When in Rome, 94
Whirlybird Tour, 286
White Rabbit, The, 144, 182
"Whole Enchilada, The," 266
Wild Animal Park, 126, 245
William Heath Davis House, 121
Windansea Beach, 167
Windsor Lawn, 124
Windsurfing, 293
Wine, 198–99
Wine Bank, 199
Wine Connection, The, 199
Wine Lover, 142
Wineries, 245, 247, 251, 259
WineSellar & Brasserie, 94, 199
Winston's Beach Club, 227
Women, services for, 9
World Bodysurfing Championship, 290
World Curry, 94
Wyndham U. S. Grant Hotel, 100

## X–Y–Z

Yellow Cab, 16
Yokohama Friendship Bell, 155
Yoshino, 95
    Zona Río, 258–59
Zoo. See Children, San Diego Zoo
Zoro Garden, 118

# We Stand By Our Reviews

Sasquatch Books is proud of *Best Places San Diego*. Our editors and contributors go to great lengths and expense to see that all of the restaurant and lodging reviews are as accurate, up-to-date, and honest as possible. If we have disappointed you, please accept our apologies; however, if a recommendation in this 2nd edition of *Best Places San Diego* has seriously misled you, Sasquatch Books would like to refund your purchase price. To receive your refund:

1. Tell us where and when you purchased your book and return the book and the book-purchase receipt to the address below.
2. Enclose the original restaurant or lodging receipt from the establishment in question, including date of visit.
3. Write a full explanation of your stay or meal and how *San Diego Best Places* misled you.
4. Include your name, address, and phone number.

Refund is valid only while this 2nd edition of *Best Places San Diego* is in print. If the ownership, management, or chef has changed since publication, Sasquatch Books cannot be held responsible. Tax and postage on the returned book is your responsibility. Please allow six to eight weeks for processing.

Please address to Satisfaction Guaranteed, *Best Places San Diego*, and send to:
Sasquatch Books
615 Second Avenue, Suite 260
Seattle, WA 98104

# Best Places San Diego Report Form

Based on my personal experience, I wish to nominate the following restaurant, place of lodging, shop, nightclub, sight, or other as a "Best Place"; or confirm/correct/disagree with the current review.

_____

_____

_____

(Please include address and telephone number of establishment, if convenient.)

# REPORT

Please describe food, service, style, comfort, value, date of visit, and other aspects of your experience; continue on another piece of paper if necessary.

_____

_____

_____

_____

_____

_____

I am not concerned, directly or indirectly, with the management or ownership of this establishment.

_____
**SIGNED**

_____
**ADDRESS**

_____

_____
**PHONE**                                    **DATE**

Please address to *Best Places San Diego* and send to:
**SASQUATCH BOOKS**
**615 SECOND AVENUE, SUITE 260**
**SEATTLE, WA 98104**
Feel free to email feedback as well: **BESTPLACES@SASQUATCHBOOKS.COM**

# Best Places San Diego Report Form

Based on my personal experience, I wish to nominate the following restaurant, place of lodging, shop, nightclub, sight, or other as a "Best Place"; or confirm/correct/disagree with the current review.

_____

_____

_____

_____

(Please include address and telephone number of establishment, if convenient.)

## REPORT

Please describe food, service, style, comfort, value, date of visit, and other aspects of your experience; continue on another piece of paper if necessary.

_____

_____

_____

_____

_____

_____

_____

I am not concerned, directly or indirectly, with the management or ownership of this establishment.

_____

**SIGNED**

_____

**ADDRESS**

_____

_____

**PHONE**                                    **DATE**

Please address to *Best Places San Diego* and send to:
**SASQUATCH BOOKS**
**615 SECOND AVENUE, SUITE 260**
**SEATTLE, WA 98104**
Feel free to email feedback as well: **BESTPLACES@SASQUATCHBOOKS.COM**

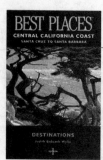